AMNESTY INTERNATIONAL REPORT 2014/15

THE STATE OF THE WORLD'S HUMAN RIGHTS

CONTENTS
ANNUAL REPORT 2014/15

AMNESTY INTERNATIONAL

Amnesty International is a global movement of more than 7 million people who campaign for a world where human rights are enjoyed by all. Our vision is for every person to enjoy all the rights enshrined in the Universal Declaration of Human Rights and other international human rights standards.

Amnesty International's mission is to conduct research and take action to prevent and end grave abuses of all human rights – civil, political, social, cultural and economic. From freedom of expression and association to physical and mental integrity, from protection from discrimination to the right to housing – these rights are indivisible.

Amnesty International is funded mainly by its membership and public donations. No funds are sought or accepted from governments for investigating and campaigning against human rights abuses. Amnesty International is independent of any government, political ideology, economic interest or religion. Amnesty International is a democratic movement whose major policy decisions are taken by representatives from all national sections at International Council Meetings held every two years. Check online for current details.

First published in 2015 by
Amnesty International Ltd
Peter Benenson House
1 Easton Street
London WC1X 0DW
United Kingdom

© Amnesty International 2015
Index: POL 10/001/2015

ISBN: 978-0-86210-488-7

A catalogue record for this book is available from the British Library.

Original language: English

This report documents Amnesty International's work and concerns through 2014. The absence of an entry in this report on a particular country or territory does not imply that no human rights violations of concern to Amnesty International have taken place there during the year. Nor is the length of a country entry any basis for a comparison of the extent and depth of Amnesty International's concerns in a country.

Kazakhstan 209
Kenya 212
Korea (Democratic People's Republic of) 216
Korea (Republic of) 218
Kuwait 220
Kyrgyzstan 222
Laos 224
Latvia 225
Lebanon 227
Libya 229
Lithuania 235
Macedonia 236
Malawi 237
Malaysia 238
Maldives 241
Mali 242
Malta 244
Mauritania 245
Mexico 247
Moldova 251
Mongolia 253
Montenegro 254
Morocco/Western Sahara 255
Mozambique 259
Myanmar 261
Namibia 265
Nauru 266
Nepal 267
Netherlands 269
New Zealand 270
Nicaragua 271
Niger 272
Nigeria 274
Norway 279
Oman 280
Pakistan 281
Palestine (State of) 285
Panama 288
Papua New Guinea 289
Paraguay 291
Peru 292
Philippines 294
Poland 296
Portugal 298
Puerto Rico 299
Qatar 300
Romania 303
Russian Federation 305

Rwanda 310
Saudi Arabia 313
Senegal 317
Serbia 319
Sierra Leone 322
Singapore 325
Slovakia 326
Slovenia 327
Somalia 328
South Africa 332
South Sudan 336
Spain 340
Sri Lanka 342
Sudan 345
Suriname 349
Swaziland 349
Sweden 351
Switzerland 352
Syria 353
Taiwan 358
Tajikistan 360
Tanzania 362
Thailand 363
Timor-Leste 366
Togo 367
Trinidad and Tobago 369
Tunisia 370
Turkey 373
Turkmenistan 377
Uganda 379
Ukraine 382
United Arab Emirates 387
United Kingdom 389
United States of America 393
Uruguay 398
Uzbekistan 399
Venezuela 401
Viet Nam 404
Yemen 406
Zambia 410
Zimbabwe 411

ABBREVIATIONS

ASEAN
Association of Southeast Asian Nations

AU
African Union

CEDAW
UN Convention on the Elimination of All
Forms of Discrimination against Women

CEDAW Committee
UN Committee on the Elimination of
Discrimination against Women

CERD
International Convention on the Elimination of
All Forms of Racial Discrimination

CERD Committee
UN Committee on the Elimination of Racial
Discrimination

CIA
US Central Intelligence Agency

ECOWAS
Economic Community of West African States

EU
European Union

**European Committee for the Prevention of
Torture**
European Committee for the Prevention of
Torture and Inhuman or Degrading Treatment
or Punishment

European Convention on Human Rights
(European) Convention for the Protection of
Human Rights and Fundamental Freedoms

ICC
International Criminal Court

ICCPR
International Covenant on Civil and Political
Rights

ICESCR
International Covenant on Economic, Social
and Cultural Rights

ICRC
International Committee of the Red Cross

ILO
International Labour Organization

**International Convention against enforced
disappearance**
International Convention for the Protection of
All Persons from Enforced Disappearance

LGBTI
Lesbian, gay, bisexual, transgender and
intersex

NATO
North Atlantic Treaty Organization

NGO
Non-governmental organization

OAS
Organization of American States

OSCE
Organization for Security and Co-operation in
Europe

UK
United Kingdom

UN
United Nations

UN Convention against Torture
UN Convention against Torture and Other
Cruel, Inhuman or Degrading Treatment or
Punishment

UN Refugee Convention
UN Convention relating to the Status of
Refugees

**UN Special Rapporteur on freedom of
expression**
UN Special Rapporteur on the promotion and
protection of the right to freedom of opinion
and expression

UN Special Rapporteur on racism
UN Special Rapporteur on contemporary
forms of racism, racial discrimination,
xenophobia and related intolerance

UN Special Rapporteur on torture
UN Special Rapporteur on torture and other
cruel, inhuman or degrading treatment or
punishment

**UN Special Rapporteur on violence against
women**
UN Special rapporteur on violence against
women, its causes and consequences

UNHCR, the UN refugee agency
Office of the United Nations High
Commissioner for Refugees

UNICEF
United Nations Children's Fund

UPR
UN Human Rights Council Universal Periodic
Review

USA
United States of America

WHO
World Health Organization

PREFACE

The *Amnesty International Report 2014/15* documents the state of the world's human rights during 2014. Some key events from 2013 are also reported.

The foreword, five regional overviews and survey of 160 countries and territories bear witness to the suffering endured by many, whether it be through conflict, displacement, discrimination or repression. The Report also highlights the strength of the human rights movement, and shows that, in some areas, significant progress has been made in the safeguarding and securing of human rights.

While every attempt is made to ensure accuracy of information, information may be subject to change without notice.

AMNESTY INTERNATIONAL REPORT 2014/15

FOREWORD AND REGIONAL OVERVIEWS

FOREWORD

"Clashes between the government forces and armed groups turned my neighbourhood of Yarmouk, in Damascus, into a beehive. It was so busy. Yarmouk became a shelter for people fleeing from other neighbourhoods.

"I worked in humanitarian assistance and as a media activist, but the masked men didn't differentiate between humanitarian workers and armed opposition fighters. I hid as more and more of my friends were arrested.

"I decided it was time to get out, and packed my bags. But where could I go? Palestinian refugees from Syria are not allowed to enter any country without a visa.

"I thought maybe Lebanon would be the least difficult option, but I heard that Palestinian refugees in Lebanon are exposed to racism and deprived of many of their rights."

A Palestinian refugee from Syria, who eventually fled to Europe via Egypt, Turkey, and a dangerous sea crossing to Italy.

This has been a devastating year for those seeking to stand up for human rights and for those caught up in the suffering of war zones.

Governments pay lip service to the importance of protecting civilians. And yet the world's politicians have miserably failed to protect those in greatest need. Amnesty International believes that this can and must finally change.

International humanitarian law - the law that governs the conduct of armed conflict - could not be clearer. Attacks must never be directed against civilians. The principle of distinguishing between civilians and combatants is a fundamental safeguard for people caught up in the horrors of war.

And yet, time and again, civilians bore the brunt in conflict. In the year marking the 20th anniversary of the Rwandan genocide, politicians repeatedly trampled on the rules protecting civilians - or looked away from the deadly violations of these rules committed by others.

The UN Security Council had repeatedly failed to address the crisis in Syria in earlier years, when countless lives could still have been saved. That failure continued in 2014. In the past four years, more than 200,000 people have died - overwhelmingly civilians - and mostly in attacks by government forces. Around 4 million people from Syria are now refugees in other countries. More than 7.6 million are displaced inside Syria.

The Syria crisis is intertwined with that of its neighbour Iraq. The armed group calling itself Islamic State (IS, formerly ISIS), which has been responsible for war crimes in Syria, has carried out abductions, execution-style killings, and ethnic cleansing on a massive scale in northern Iraq. In parallel, Iraq's Shi'a militias abducted and killed scores of Sunni civilians, with the tacit support of the Iraqi government.

The July assault on Gaza by Israeli forces caused the loss of 2,000 Palestinian lives. Yet again, the great majority of those - at least 1,500 - were civilians. The policy was, as Amnesty International argued in a detailed analysis, marked by callous indifference and involved war crimes. Hamas also committed war crimes by firing indiscriminate rockets into Israel causing six deaths.

In Nigeria, the conflict in the north between government forces and the armed group Boko Haram burst onto the world's front pages with the abduction, by Boko Haram, of 276 schoolgirls in the town of Chibok, one of countless crimes committed by the group. Less noticed were horrific crimes committed by Nigerian security forces and those working with them against people believed to be members or supporters of Boko Haram, some of which were recorded on video, revealed by Amnesty International in August; bodies of the murdered victims were tossed into a mass grave.

In the Central African Republic, more than 5,000 died in sectarian violence despite the presence of international forces. The torture, rape and mass murder barely made a showing on the world's front pages. Yet again, the majority of those who died were civilians.

And in South Sudan - the world's newest state - tens of thousands of civilians were killed and 2 million fled their homes in the armed conflict between government and opposition forces. War crimes and crimes against humanity were committed on both sides.

The above list - as this latest annual report on the state of human rights in 160 countries clearly shows - barely begins to scratch the surface. Some might argue that nothing can be done, that war has always been at the expense of the civilian population, and that nothing can ever change.

This is wrong. It is essential to confront violations against civilians, and to bring to justice those responsible. One obvious and practical step is waiting to be taken: Amnesty International has welcomed the proposal, now backed by around 40 governments, for the UN Security Council to adopt a code of conduct agreeing to voluntarily refrain from using the veto in a way which would block Security Council action in situations of genocide, war crimes and crimes against humanity.

That would be an important first step, and could save many lives.

The failures, however, have not just been in terms of preventing mass atrocities. Direct assistance has also been denied to the millions who have fled the violence that has engulfed their villages and towns.

Those governments who have been most eager to speak out loudly on the failures of other governments have shown themselves reluctant to step forward and provide the essential assistance that those refugees require - both in terms of financial assistance, and providing resettlement. Approximately 2% of refugees from Syria had been resettled by the end of 2014 - a figure which must at least triple in 2015.

Meanwhile, large numbers of refugees and migrants are losing their lives in the Mediterranean Sea as they try desperately to reach European shores. A lack of support by some EU Member States for search and rescue operations has contributed to the shocking death toll.

One step that could be taken to protect civilians in conflict would be to further restrict the use of explosive weapons in populated areas. This would have saved many lives in Ukraine, where Russian-backed separatists (despite unconvincing denials by Moscow of its involvement) and pro-Kyiv forces both targeted civilian neighbourhoods.

The importance of the rules on protection of civilians means that there must be true accountability and justice when these rules are violated. In that context, Amnesty International welcomes the decision by the UN Human Rights Council in Geneva to initiate an international inquiry into allegations of violations and abuses of human rights during the conflict in Sri Lanka, where in the last few months of the conflict in 2009, tens of thousands of civilians were killed. Amnesty International has campaigned for such an inquiry for the past five years. Without such accountability, we can never move forward.

Other areas of human rights continued to require improvement. In Mexico, the enforced disappearance of 43 students in September was a recent tragic addition to the more than 22,000 people who have disappeared or gone missing in Mexico since 2006; most are believed to have been abducted by criminal gangs, but many are reported to have been subjected to enforced disappearance by police and military, sometimes acting in collusion with those gangs. The few victims whose remains have been found show signs of torture and other ill-treatment. The federal and state authorities have failed to investigate these crimes to establish the possible involvement of state agents and to ensure effective legal recourse for the victims, including their relatives. In addition to the lack of response, the government has attempted to cover up the human rights crisis and there have been high levels of impunity, corruption and further militarization.

In 2014, governments in many parts of the world continued to crack down on NGOs and civil society - partly a perverse compliment to the importance of civil society's role. Russia increased its stranglehold with the chilling "foreign agents law", language resonant of the Cold War. In Egypt, NGOs saw a severe crackdown, with use of the Mubarak-era Law on Associations to send a strong message that the government will not tolerate any dissent. Leading human rights organizations had to withdraw from the UN Human Rights Council's Universal Periodic Review of Egypt's human rights record because of fears of reprisals against them.

As has happened on many previous occasions, protesters showed courage despite threats and violence directed against them. In Hong Kong, tens of thousands defied official threats and faced down excessive and arbitrary use of force by police, in what became known as the "umbrella movement", exercising their basic rights to freedoms of expression and assembly.

Human rights organizations are sometimes accused of being too ambitious in our dreams of creating change. But we must remember that extraordinary things are achievable. On 24 December, the international Arms Trade Treaty came into force, after the threshold of 50 ratifications was crossed three months earlier.

Amnesty International and others had campaigned for the treaty for 20 years. We were repeatedly told that such a treaty was unachievable. The treaty now exists, and will prohibit the sale of weapons to those who may use them to commit atrocities. It can thus play a crucial role in the years to come - when the question of implementation will be key.

2014 marked 30 years since the adoption of the UN Convention against Torture - another Convention for which Amnesty International campaigned for many years, and one reason why the organization was awarded the Nobel Peace Prize in 1977.

This anniversary was in one respect a moment to celebrate - but also a moment to note that torture remains rife around the world, a reason why Amnesty International launched its global Stop Torture campaign this year.

This anti-torture message gained special resonance following the publication of a US Senate report in December, which demonstrated a readiness to condone torture in the years after the 11 September 2001 attacks on the USA. It was striking that some of those responsible for the criminal acts of torture seemed still to believe that they had nothing to be ashamed of.

From Washington to Damascus, from Abuja to Colombo, government leaders have justified horrific human rights violations by talking of the need to keep the country "safe". In reality, the opposite is the case. Such violations are one important reason why we live in such a dangerous world today. There can be no security without human rights.

We have repeatedly seen that, even at times that seem bleak for human rights - and perhaps especially at such times - it is possible to create remarkable change.

We must hope that, looking backward to 2014 in the years to come, what we lived through in 2014 will be seen as a nadir - an ultimate low point - from which we rose up and created a better future.

Salil Shetty, Secretary General

AFRICA REGIONAL OVERVIEW

As Africa remembers the 20th anniversary of the Rwandan genocide, violent conflicts dogged much of the continent throughout 2014 – unfolding or escalating in a particularly bloody way in the Central African Republic (CAR), South Sudan and Nigeria, and continuing unresolved in the Democratic Republic of the Congo (DRC), Sudan and Somalia.

These conflicts were enmeshed with persistent patterns of gross violations of international human rights and humanitarian law. Armed conflicts bred the worst crimes imaginable, injustice and repression. Marginalization, discrimination and persistent denial of other fundamental freedoms and basic socioeconomic rights have in turn created fertile grounds for further conflict and instability.

In many ways, Africa continued to be viewed as a region on the rise. The development context and landscape in many countries is changing. Throughout 2014, rapid social, environmental and economic change continued to sweep across the continent. A fast growing population, rapid economic growth and urbanization combined to alter people's lives and livelihoods at a remarkable pace. Many African states have made remarkable progress towards achieving the UN Millennium Development Goals (MDGs) despite steep challenges. The Africa MDG Report 2014 reveals that eight of the world's top 10 best performers in accelerating rapidly towards the goals are in Africa.

However, many indicators left bitter reminders that rapid economic growth has failed to improve living conditions for many. While the overall poverty rate in Africa has dropped in the past decade, the total number of Africans living below the poverty line (US$1.25 per day) has increased. Two of the conflict-plagued nations, Nigeria (25.89%) and DRC (13.6%), account for almost 40% of the continent's poor. Africa has one of the highest youth unemployment rates in the world and it remains the second most unequal region in the world, after Latin America. All these point towards the nexus between conflicts and fragility on the one hand, and the denial of basic socioeconomic rights, social exclusion, inequality and deepening poverty on the other.

The impacts of repression and persistent denial of fundamental human rights in contributing to instability and violent conflicts were vivid in 2014, as demonstrated in Burkina Faso, CAR, South Sudan and Sudan. A trend of repression and shrinking of political space continued in many African countries during the year. In several, security forces responded to peaceful demonstrations and protests with excessive force. In far too many places, freedoms of expression, association and peaceful assembly continued to be severely curtailed. The trend was not only visible in countries ruled by authoritarian governments but also in those which are less authoritarian and in the process of or preparing for political transition.

Many African countries, including Kenya, Somalia, Nigeria, Mali, and countries in the Sahel region, faced serious security challenges in 2014, as a direct result of increased violence by radical armed groups, including al-Shabab and Boko Haram. Tens of thousands of civilians have lost their lives, hundreds have been abducted and countless others continue to live in a state of fear and insecurity. But the response of many governments has been equally brutal and indiscriminate, leading to mass arbitrary arrests and detentions, and extrajudicial executions. The year ended with Kenya enacting the Security Laws (Amendment) Act 2014, which amended 22 laws and which has far-reaching human rights implications.

Another common element in conflict situations across the Africa region has been impunity for crimes under international law committed by security forces and armed groups. 2014 not only saw a cycle of impunity continuing unabated, including in CAR, DRC, Nigeria, Somalia, South Sudan and Sudan, but it was also a year marked with a serious political backlash against the International Criminal Court (ICC). There was also an unprecedented political momentum in Africa championing immunity from prosecution for serving heads of state and officials for crimes against humanity and other international crimes. This culminated in a retrogressive amendment to the Protocol on the Statute of the African Court of Justice and Human Rights, granting immunity to serving heads of state or other senior officials before the Court.

2014 marked the 10th anniversary of the establishment of the AU Peace and Security Council (PSC), the AU's "standing decision-making organ for the prevention, management and resolution of conflicts" in Africa. The AU and its PSC have taken some remarkable steps in response to the emerging conflicts in Africa, including the deployment of the International Support Mission to the Central African Republic (MISCA), the establishment of a Commission of Inquiry on South Sudan, the Special Envoy for Women, Peace and Security, and several political statements condemning violence and attacks on civilians. But in many cases, these efforts appeared too little and too late, pointing to capacity challenges of the AU in responding to conflicts. In some instances, complicity by AU peacekeeping missions in serious human rights violations was also alleged, as with MISCA and specifically its Chadian contingent which withdrew from the mission in CAR following such allegations.

Nonetheless, failure to address conflict challenges in Africa goes beyond the level of the AU. In CAR, for example, the UN dragged its heels before eventually sending in a peacekeeping force that, although saving many lives, did not have the full resources needed to stem the continued wave of human rights violations and abuses. At other times there was silence. The UN Human Rights Council failed to respond effectively to the conflicts in Sudan, for example, despite a critical need for independent human rights monitoring, reporting and accountability. In Darfur, a review of investigations into the UN Mission in Darfur (UNAMID) was announced by the UN Secretary-General in July, in response to allegations that UNAMID staff had covered up human rights abuses.

Addressing the mounting challenges of conflicts in Africa calls for an urgent and fundamental shift in political will among African leaders, as well as concerted efforts at national, regional and international levels to end the cycle of impunity and address the underlying causes of insecurity and conflicts. Otherwise the region's vision of "silencing the guns by 2020" will remain a disingenuous and unachievable dream.

CONFLICT – COSTS AND VULNERABILITY

Conflict and insecurity blighted the lives of countless people in Africa, and – with varying degrees of intensity – affected almost all countries. These conflicts were characterized by persistent abuses and atrocities committed by both government forces and armed groups.

CAR was plagued by a cycle of sectarian violence and mass atrocities, including killings, torture, rape, mutilation of bodies, abductions, forced displacement and the recruitment and use of child soldiers. Despite a ceasefire signed in July and the deployment of a UN peacekeeping mission in September, the last months of 2014 were scarred by an escalating wave of attacks in the country's central regions. Civilians were subjected to a range of human rights abuses during a surge in conflict between different armed groups. Fresh violence rocked the capital, Bangui, in October. All sides – Séléka, anti-Balaka and armed members of the Peulh ethnic group – systematically and with impunity – targeted civilians. The deployment of the UN Multidimensional Integrated Stabilization Mission (MINUSCA) in September raised hopes of change – yet just a month later there was a significant upsurge in violence across the country. This demonstrated the clear need to strengthen the capacity and reactivity of the international forces on the ground.

In neighbouring South Sudan tens of thousands of people – many of them civilians – were killed and 1.8 million forced to flee their homes in the conflict that erupted in December 2013. Government and opposition forces demonstrated a total disregard for international humanitarian and human rights law, committing war crimes and crimes against humanity. All parties to the conflict targeted and killed civilians on the basis of ethnicity, including those seeking safety in places of worship and hospitals. Sexual violence was widespread, as was rampant looting and destruction of property. Despite the scale of the abuses – and even though millions remained at risk of famine and disease – both sides ignored several ceasefire deals. The year ended with no meaningful signs of addressing impunity, including the findings of the AU's Commission of Inquiry on South Sudan, which remained unknown.

Following a deepening campaign of violence by the Islamist armed group Boko Haram during 2013, the armed conflict in Nigeria's northeast intensified in scope and casualties, powerfully illustrating the threats to the stability of Africa's most populous nation and to regional peace and security. The conflict intensified in smaller towns and villages in 2014 with more than 4,000 civilians killed since 2009. The abduction in April of 276 schoolgirls by Boko Haram was one emblematic case of the group's campaign of terror against civilians, which continued unabated. On the other hand, communities already terrorized for years by Boko Haram became increasingly vulnerable to violations by the state security forces, which regularly responded with heavy-handed and indiscriminate attacks and with mass arbitrary arrests, beatings and torture. Gruesome video footage, images and eyewitness accounts gathered by Amnesty International provided fresh evidence of probable war crimes, crimes against humanity and other serious human

rights violations and abuses committed by all sides.

Torture and other ill-treatment was routinely and systematically practised by Nigeria's security services throughout the country, including in the context of the conflict in the northeast. Security officials were rarely held accountable. A pattern of mass arbitrary arrests and detentions carried out by the military in the northeast visibly escalated after the declaration of a state of emergency in May 2013, and there were ongoing reports of extrajudicial executions by the military and police by the end of the year.

Meanwhile, there was no apparent resolution in sight for already protracted conflicts.

Sudan's conflicts in Darfur, Southern Kordofan and Blue Nile continued unabated, and spread to Northern Kordofan. Violations of international human rights and humanitarian law were committed by all sides. In Darfur, widespread abuses and violence between warring communities and attacks by government-allied militias and armed opposition groups triggered a significant increase in displacement and civilian deaths.

An upsurge in violence by armed groups in eastern DRC, within the context of Operation Sokola 1, cost thousands of lives and forced more than a million people to flee their homes. The increased violence was also marked by killings and mass rapes by both government security forces and armed groups.

In southern and central Somalia, over 100,000 civilians were killed, injured or displaced in the ongoing armed conflict between pro-government forces, the African Union Mission in Somalia (AMISOM) and the Islamist armed group al-Shabaab. All parties to the conflict violated international human rights and humanitarian law. Armed groups forcibly recruited people, including children, and abducted, tortured and unlawfully killed others. Rape and other forms of sexual violence were widespread. The humanitarian situation deteriorated rapidly due to the conflict, drought and reduced humanitarian access. More than one million people were in humanitarian crisis and another 2.1 million in need of assistance at the end of 2014.

Warning signs of future conflicts were also visible. The Sahel region remained especially volatile, due to combined effects of political insecurity, surge of radical armed groups and organized crime, extreme poverty as well as social exclusion. This was illustrated in Mali, where internal armed conflict left the country in a state of persistent insecurity – particularly in the north where some areas remained outside the control of the authorities. Despite a peace agreement signed between the government and armed groups in 2013, armed groups committed abuses including abductions and killings, and outbreaks of violence persisted in 2014 even as peace discussions between the government and armed groups continued.

Violence and insecurity were heightened by a surge in acts of terrorism – as in Somalia, Kenya, Nigeria, and across the Sahel region – which were often met by serious human rights violations by government forces. Abuses by armed groups included unlawful killings, abductions, torture and indiscriminate attacks. In Somalia, al-Shabaab factions tortured and unlawfully killed people they accused of spying or not conforming to their strict interpretation of Islamic law. They killed people in public – including by stoning – and carried out amputations and floggings. In Cameroon as well, Nigerian Islamist groups including Boko Haram killed civilians, carried out hostage-taking and abductions, and attacked human rights defenders.

SHRINKING POLITICAL SPACE AND PERSISTENT DENIAL OF FUNDAMENTAL RIGHTS

In far too many countries in Africa, a trend of repression and shrinking of political space continued during the year.

In Eritrea, no political opposition parties, independent media or civil society organizations were allowed to operate, and thousands of prisoners of conscience and political prisoners continued to be held in arbitrary detention. In Ethiopia, there was renewed targeting of independent media including bloggers and journalists, arrests of opposition party members and peaceful protesters. Space for criticism of government's policy towards human rights by civil society was almost non-existent in Rwanda . In Burundi, critical voices, including opposition members, civil society activists, lawyers and journalists, were restricted as the 2015 elections approached. Freedom of assembly and association was curtailed, with meetings and marches regularly prohibited.

In Gambia, President Yahya Jammeh marked his 20th anniversary in power – two decades characterized by severe intolerance of dissent in which journalists, political opponents and human rights defenders continue to be intimidated and tortured. The year ended with an attempted coup on the night of 30 December, leading to dozens of arrests and widespread crackdowns on media outlets. In Burkina Faso, a transitional government was installed in November to steer the country towards legislative and presidential elections in 2015. This followed the ousting of former President Blaise Compaoré after widespread popular protests against a bill to modify the Constitution.

Security forces responded to demonstrations and protests with excessive force in Angola, Burkina Faso, Chad, Guinea, Senegal and Togo, among other countries. In most cases, the authorities failed to investigate excessive use of force and no one was held accountable.

In many countries, journalists, human rights defenders and political opponents faced widespread patterns of threats, arbitrary arrest and detention, beatings, torture, enforced disappearances and even death at the hands of government operatives or armed groups. Crackdowns or restrictions on rights to freedom of expression, association and peaceful assembly took place in Angola,

Burkina Faso, Cameroon, Chad, Eritrea, Ethiopia, Gambia, Guinea, Mauritania, Rwanda, Somalia, Swaziland, Togo, Uganda, Zambia and Zimbabwe.

In Angola, Burundi and Gambia new legislation and other forms of regulations further restricted the work of the media and civil society.

In Sudan, freedoms of expression, association and peaceful assembly continued to be severely curtailed despite the government's expressed commitments to begin a national dialogue to achieve peace in Sudan and protect constitutional rights. The government continued to use the National Intelligence and Security Services (NISS) and other security forces to arbitrarily detain perceived opponents of the ruling National Congress Party, to censor media and to shut down public forums and protests.

South Sudan's National Security Service (NSS) seized and shut down newspapers, and harassed, intimidated and unlawfully detained journalists, in a clampdown that restricted freedom of expression and curtailed public debate about how to end the armed conflict. A National Security Service Bill granting the NSS broad powers, including to arrest and detain without adequate provisions for independent oversight or safeguards against abuse, was passed by parliament and was awaiting presidential assent.

IMPUNITY – FAILURES TO ENSURE JUSTICE

Impunity was a common denominator in Africa's armed conflicts, with those suspected of criminal responsibility for crimes under international law rarely held to account.

In CAR, there were some arrests of lower-level members of armed groups, while the Prosecutor of the ICC announced the opening of a new preliminary examination into the violence. Such signs of hope were however the exception; impunity continues to fuel conflict in CAR. Almost all leaders of armed groups suspected of crimes under

international law in the country remained at large at the end of the year.

In DRC, efforts to ensure accountability for crimes under international law committed by the Congolese army and armed groups achieved few visible results. The trial before a military court of Congolese soldiers for the mass rape of more than 130 women and girls, as well as murder and looting in Minova, concluded with only two convictions for rape out of the 39 soldiers on trial. Others accused were convicted of murder, looting and military offences.

A failure to ensure accountability was a systemic problem outside conflict zones also, with perpetrators of human rights violations largely able to operate freely. Torture and other ill-treatment persisted in countries such as Equatorial Guinea, Eritrea, Ethiopia, Gambia, Mauritania, Nigeria and Togo, largely because of failures to ensure accountability for these crimes.

Efforts to ensure accountability for international crimes, including crimes against humanity, committed during the 2007/2008 post-election violence in Kenya remained inadequate. At the ICC, the trial of Deputy President Samoei Ruto and Joshua Arap Sang continued, although undermined by allegations of witness intimidation and bribery. Charges against President Uhuru Kenyatta were withdrawn following the rejection of a petition filed by the ICC Prosecutor for a finding of non-co-operation by the Kenyan government. At the national level, there was no progress in ensuring accountability for serious human rights violations committed during the post-election violence.

On the other hand, in 2014 the ICC confirmed the verdict and sentence in the Thomas Lubanga Dyilo case – he had been found guilty in 2012 of the war crimes of enlisting and conscripting children under the age of 15 and using them to participate actively in hostilities in DRC. In addition, Germain Katanga, commander of the Force de Résistance Patriotique en Ituri, was found guilty of crimes against humanity and war crimes and sentenced to a total of 12 years' imprisonment. Charges against Bosco Ntaganda for crimes against humanity and war crimes, including crimes of sexual violence, allegedly committed in 2002-2003 in Ituri, DRC, were confirmed by the ICC. The trial is scheduled for June 2015. The charges against former President of Côte d'Ivoire Laurent Gbagbo, accused of crimes against humanity, were confirmed by the ICC in June. The trial is currently set for July 2015.

Emerging national attempts to combat impunity for crimes under international law included the launch of an investigation in Mali into cases of enforced disappearance. Former Chadian President Hissène Habré remained in custody in Senegal awaiting trial before the Extraordinary African Chambers created by the AU following his July 2013 arrest on charges of crimes against humanity and war crimes committed in Chad between 1982 and 1990.

In March, Côte d'Ivoire surrendered Charles Blé Goudé to the ICC, who is accused of crimes against humanity committed during the post-election violence in 2010. In December, the Pre-Trial Chamber of the ICC confirmed four charges of crimes against humanity and committed him to trial before a Trial Chamber. In December, the Pre-Trial Chamber rejected Côte d'Ivoire's challenge to the admissibility of the case against Simone Gbagbo, who is suspected of commission of crimes against humanity.

Encouragingly, a landmark decision on universal jurisdiction was passed in October by the Constitutional Court of South Africa (CCSA) in the National Commissioner of the South African Police Service v. Southern African Human Rights Litigation Centre and Another case. In that judgment the CCSA ruled that allegations of torture committed in Zimbabwe by and against Zimbabwean nationals must be investigated by the South African Police Service – based on the principle of universal jurisdiction.

Yet on the international and regional stage, there was serious backsliding on previous advances on international justice in Africa. Although the Rome Statute of the ICC has 34 state parties from Africa – more than any other region – politically expedient manoeuvring during 2014 undermined such bold progress by Africa towards ensuring accountability. Kenya proposed five amendments to the Rome Statute, including that Article 27 be amended to preclude the ICC from prosecuting heads of state and government while they hold office.

In May, AU ministers considering amendments to the Protocol on the Statute of the African Court of Justice and Human Rights agreed to extend the range of categories of people who could enjoy immunity from the court's newly established criminal jurisdiction. The AU Assembly at its 23rd Ordinary Session subsequently approved this amendment which aims to grant sitting African leaders and other senior state officials immunity from prosecution for genocide, war crimes and crimes against humanity – a backward step and a betrayal of victims of serious violations of human rights. Heads of state and government chose to shield themselves and future leaders from prosecution for serious human rights violations, rather than ensuring justice for victims of crimes under international law.

Irrespectively, the ICC will retain the power to investigate serving African heads of state and government of any state party to the Rome Statute for such crimes – but 2014 will be remembered as a year where some African states and the AU actively mobilized political efforts to undermine the ICC's work.

POVERTY AND DEPRIVATION
Despite the continued rapid economic growth during the year, living conditions for many Africans have yet to improve. Many states have made remarkable progress towards achieving the Millennium Development Goals but Africa still lags behind most other developing regions in achieving many of the targets by 2015. Poverty in Africa is continuing to decline, but the pace is not

sufficient for the region to achieve the target of halving poverty by 2015. In fact, indications are that the total number of Africans living below the poverty line (US$1.25 per day) has increased. Other targets including reducing numbers of underweight children and maternal mortality are also unlikely to be met.

As African cities expanded at an unprecedented pace, rapid urbanization was accompanied by insecurity and inequality. Urban poverty left many without adequate housing and basic facilities, particularly those living in informal settlements or slums. Forced evictions left people without their livelihoods and possessions, and drove them deeper into poverty. In Angola, at least 4,000 families were forcibly evicted in Luanda province. In Kenya, courts continued to confirm the right to adequate housing and the prohibition on forced evictions. The High Court ordered the government to pay compensation of 33.6 million shillings (approximately US$390,000) to the residents of City Carton informal settlement in the capital, Nairobi, who were forcefully evicted from their homes in 2013.

The outbreak of the Ebola Virus Disease epidemic in some countries in West Africa in March led to what the World Health Organization (WHO) described as the largest and most complex Ebola outbreak since the virus was discovered in 1976. By late 2014, Ebola had claimed the lives of over 8,000 people across Guinea, Liberia, Mali, Nigeria and Sierra Leone. More than 20,000 people were infected (suspected, probable and confirmed cases), and there were fears that a major food crisis could unfold in early 2015. Communities and health services were shattered or pushed to breaking point.

The most severely affected countries – Guinea, Liberia and Sierra Leone – already had very weak health systems, having only recently emerged from long periods of conflict and instability. In Guinea – where hundreds of people died, including at least 70 health workers – the government's delayed response, and a lack of resources,

contributed to the epidemic's rapid and fatal spread.

All these not only point to failures by governments to respect, protect and fulfil the right to the highest attainable standard of health of their citizens but also the failures of the international community to respond to this crisis. By late 2014, leading aid agencies were calling for greater support from the international community. The UN said that it needed US$1.5 billion to stop Ebola from spreading for the period October 2014 - March 2015; as of December only US$1.2 billion had been donated. If the outbreak continues at its present rate, the UN estimates a further US$1.5 billion will be needed for the period April to September 2015.

DISCRIMINATION AND MARGINALIZATION

Hundreds of thousands of people were – or continued to be – displaced by armed conflicts, political persecution, or in search of better livelihood. Most were forced to flee their homes and livelihoods in arduous and dangerous attempts to find safety within their own countries or across international borders. Vast numbers of refugees and migrants languished on the frontline of further violations and abuses, many in camps with limited access to health, water, sanitation, food and education.

Their numbers were swelled monthly by thousands of people who fled Eritrea, most of them due to the system of indefinite conscription into national service. Many were at risk from human trafficking networks, including in Sudan and Egypt. In Cameroon, thousands of refugees from CAR and Nigeria were living in dire conditions in crowded camps in border areas after fleeing from armed groups. Many displaced by Sudan's conflict – more than a million people – remained in the country, with at least 600,000 living in refugee camps in Chad, South Sudan or Ethiopia. The plight of thousands of Somali refugees in Kenya was exacerbated by a policy of forced encampment, which forced them from their homes in the towns and into squalid and overcrowded camps. Refugees and asylum-seekers in South Africa continued to be subjected to xenophobic attacks with little or no protection from the authorities.

Many other groups were also excluded from human rights protection or denied the means to get redress for abuses. Women can play an essential role in strengthening the resilience of conflict-affected societies, but were frequently marginalized from national peace-building processes. In many countries suffering conflict or hosting large populations of refugees or displaced people, women and girls were subjected to rape and other forms of sexual violence, for example in South Sudan and Somalia. Violence against women was pernicious outside countries in conflict too, sometimes because of cultural traditions and norms, but also because in some countries gender-based discrimination was institutionalized by legislation.

For lesbian, gay, bisexual, transgender and intersex (LGBTI) people there was hope in 2014 when the African Commission on Human and Peoples' Rights adopted a landmark resolution condemning acts of violence, discrimination and other human rights violations against people on the basis of their sexual orientation or gender identity. Other signs of hope for equality and justice included expressed commitments by Malawi to decriminalize consensual same-sex sexual activity.

Nevertheless, people continued to be persecuted or criminalized for their perceived or real sexual orientation in many countries, including Cameroon, Gambia, Senegal, Uganda and Zambia.

In a retrograde trend, several countries strove to increase criminalization of people due to their sexual identity, either by entrenching already unjust laws or introducing new ones. Nigeria's President signed the oppressive Same Sex Marriage (Prohibition) Act into law, allowing discrimination based on real or perceived sexual orientation and gender identity. Uganda's introduction of an Anti-Homosexuality Act – although overturned by the country's Constitutional Court because Parliament had passed it without quorum – left many LGBTI people, and those perceived as being so, continuing to face arbitrary arrests and beatings, evictions from homes, loss of jobs and mob attacks. Gambia's President assented to a bill passed by parliament, the Criminal Code (Amendment) Act 2014, creating the offence of "aggravated homosexuality" – a vague definition open to wide-ranging abuse and carrying a life sentence. A homophobic bill was also before Chad's parliament, threatening to impose sentences of up to 20 years' imprisonment and heavy fines for people "found guilty" of same-sex activity.

LOOKING AHEAD

Throughout 2014, individuals and communities across the region built and strengthened understanding of, and respect for, human rights. By speaking out and taking action – sometimes at risk to their own lives and safety – this growing human rights movement provided a vision of justice, dignity and hope.

Nevertheless, the year was a potent reminder of the scale of Africa's human rights challenges, and of the need for deeper and faster progress towards realizing all such rights.

Events sharply illustrated the urgent need for concerted and consistent action to defuse and resolve violent conflicts in Africa. Looking ahead, the AU Commission's efforts in establishing a roadmap towards silencing all guns in Africa must be embraced and driven forwards. A far more robust, consistent and coherent approach to addressing conflict, based on international human rights law – by both international and regional institutions – is desperately needed.

Another essential prerequisite for peace, security and justice is for African states to withdraw their collective attack

on international justice – including the
work of the ICC – and instead stand firm
on confronting impunity, both regionally
and internationally, and work towards
effective accountability for gross human
rights violations and other crimes under
international law.

The coming years are almost certainly
going to be marked by profound change. Not
least, the post-2015 framework that follows
the Millennium Development Goals will be
a historic opportunity for AU member states
to agree on a human rights framework that
could transform countless lives for the better.
Accountability should be embedded in the
post-2015 framework through robust targets
and indicators on access to justice, and
this must be combined with strengthening
rights around participation, equality, non-
discrimination, the rule of law, and other
fundamental freedoms.

AMERICAS REGIONAL OVERVIEW

Across the Americas, deepening inequality, discrimination, environmental degradation, historical impunity, increasing insecurity and conflict continued to deny people the full enjoyment of their human rights. Indeed, those at the forefront of promoting and defending those rights faced intense levels of violence.

2014 saw mass public responses to these human rights violations the length and breadth of the continent, from Brazil to the USA and from Mexico to Venezuela. In country after country, people took to the streets to protest against repressive state practices. The demonstrations were a very public challenge to high levels of impunity and corruption and to economic policies that privilege the few. Hundreds of thousands of people joined these spontaneous mobilizations using new technologies and social media to rapidly bring people together, share information and expose human rights abuses.

These outpourings of dissatisfaction and demands that human rights be respected took place against the backdrop of an erosion of democratic space and continuing criminalization of dissent. Violence by both state and non-state actors against the general population, and in particular against social movements and activists, was on the rise. Attacks on human rights defenders increased significantly in most countries in the region, both in terms of sheer numbers and in the severity of the violence inflicted.

This growing violence was indicative of an increasingly militarized response to social and political challenges in recent years. In many countries in the region, it has become commonplace for the authorities to resort to the use of state force to respond to criminal networks and social tension, even where there is no formal acknowledgement that conflict exists. In some areas, the increasing power of criminal networks and other non-state actors, such as paramilitaries and transnational corporations, posed a sustained challenge to the power of the state, the rule of law and human rights.

Grave human rights violations continued to blight the lives of tens of thousands of people throughout the region. Far from making further advances in the promotion and protection of human rights for all, without discrimination, the region appeared to be going backwards during 2013 and 2014.

The UN High Commissioner for Human Rights recorded 40 killings of human rights defenders in Colombia during the first nine months of 2014.

In October, the Dominican Republic publicly snubbed the Inter-American Court of Human Rights after the Court condemned the authorities for their discriminatory treatment of Dominicans of Haitian descent and Haitian migrants.

In September, 43 students from the Ayotzinapa teacher training college were subjected to enforced disappearance in Mexico. The students were detained in the town of Iguala, Guerrero state, by local police acting in collusion with organized criminal networks. On 7 December, the Federal Attorney General announced that the remains of one of the students had been identified by independent forensic experts. By the end of the year, the whereabouts of the other 42 remained undisclosed.

In August, Michael Brown, an 18-year-old unarmed African American man, was fatally shot by a police officer, Darren Wilson, in Ferguson, Missouri, USA. People took to the streets following the shooting and in November to protest against a grand jury decision not to indict the officer. The protests spread to other major cities in the country, including New York in December, after a grand jury declined to indict a police officer for the death of Eric Garner in July.

Also in August, prominent *campesino* (peasant farmer) leader Margarita Murillo was shot dead in the community of El Planón, northwestern Honduras. She had reported being under surveillance and receiving threats in the days immediately prior to the attack.

In February, 43 people died, including members of the security forces, and scores more were injured in Venezuela during clashes between anti-government protesters, the security forces and pro-government supporters.

In El Salvador in 2013, a young woman known as Beatriz was refused an abortion despite the imminent risk to her life and the fact that the foetus, which lacked part of its brain and skull, could not survive outside the womb. Beatriz' situation provoked a national and international outcry and weeks of sustained pressure on the authorities. She was finally given a caesarean in her 23rd week of pregnancy. The total ban on abortion in El Salvador continues to criminalize girls' and women's sexual and reproductive choices, putting them at risk of losing their lives or freedom. In 2014, 17 women sentenced to up to 40 years' imprisonment for pregnancy-related issues requested pardons; a decision on their cases was pending at the end of the year.

In May 2013, former Guatemalan President General Efrain Rios Montt was convicted of genocide and crimes against humanity. However, the conviction was quashed just 10 days later on a technicality, a devastating outcome for victims and their relatives who had waited for more than three decades for justice. Rios Montt was the President and Commander-in-Chief of the Army in 1982-1983 when 1,771 Mayan-Ixil Indigenous people were killed, tortured, subjected to sexual violence or displaced, during the internal armed conflict.

This long list of grave human rights abuses shows how, despite the fact that states in the region have ratified and actively promoted most regional and international human rights standards and treaties, respect for human rights remains elusive for many throughout the region.

PUBLIC SECURITY AND HUMAN RIGHTS

Time and again, protests against government policies met with excessive use of force by the security forces. In Brazil, Canada, Chile, Ecuador, Guatemala, Haiti, Mexico, Peru, the USA and Venezuela, the security forces flouted international standards on the use of force in the name of protecting public order. Instead of sending a clear message that excessive force would not be tolerated, governments failed even to question or raise concerns about the violence meted out.

Early in 2014, Venezuela was shaken by mass protests for and against the government in various parts of the country. The protests and the response of the authorities reflected the growing polarization that has gripped the country for more than a decade. This wave of social discontent and violent clashes between demonstrators and the security forces were the setting for widespread human rights violations, including killings, arbitrary detentions, torture and other cruel, inhuman or degrading treatment. Thousands of protesters were detained, many arbitrarily, and there were reports of torture or other ill-treatment. At least 43 people were killed and 870 injured, including members of the security forces, in the context of the protests and the security forces' response to them.

Thousands of people in Brazil took to the streets to protest as the country prepared to host the 2014 World Cup. Demonstrators sought to express their discontent at increases in the cost of public transport and at the level of spending on the World Cup in contrast with the lack of sufficient investment in public services. The scale of the protests was unprecedented, with hundreds of thousands of people participating in mass demonstrations in dozens of cities. In many instances, the police response to the wave of protests in 2013 and 2014, including during the World Cup, was violent and abusive. Military police units used tear gas on protesters indiscriminately – in one case even inside a hospital – fired rubber bullets at people who posed no threat and beat people with batons. Hundreds were injured, including Sérgio Silva, a photographer who lost his left eye after being hit by a rubber bullet. Hundreds more were indiscriminately rounded up and detained, some under laws targeting organized crime, despite the absence of any evidence that the individual had been involved in criminal activity.

In the USA, the shooting of Michael Brown and the decision of the grand jury not to indict the police officer responsible sparked months of protests in and around Ferguson. The use of heavy-duty riot gear and military-grade weapons and equipment to police the demonstrations served to intimidate protesters exercising their right to peaceful assembly. Protesters and journalists were injured by the security forces who used rubber bullets, tear gas and other aggressive dispersal tactics in situations where such action was not warranted.

TORTURE AND OTHER ILL-TREATMENT

The Americas has some of the most robust anti-torture laws and mechanisms at the national and regional level. And yet throughout the region, torture and other ill-treatment remain widespread and those responsible are rarely brought to justice.

In a report, *Out of control: Torture and other ill-treatment in Mexico*, Amnesty International documented a worrying increase in torture and other ill-treatment in the country. It also highlighted a prevailing culture of tolerance and impunity for torture in Mexico during the past decade; only seven torturers have been convicted in federal courts and even fewer have been prosecuted at state level.

The incomplete and limited investigations into human rights violations committed in the case of the 43 disappeared student teachers in Mexico highlighted serious failures on the part of the Mexican government in investigating widespread and entrenched

corruption and collusion between state officials and organized crime, as well as shocking levels of impunity.

Torture and other ill-treatment were frequently used against criminal suspects to obtain information, extract confessions or inflict punishment. Daniel Quintero, a 23-year-old student, was kicked and punched in the face and ribs and threatened with rape when he was detained for allegedly participating in an anti-government demonstration in Venezuela in February 2014. In the Dominican Republic, Ana Patricia Fermín received death threats in April 2014 after she reported that two of her relatives had been tortured while in police custody in the capital Santo Domingo. Her husband and one of the tortured men were shot dead by police in September.

ACCESS TO JUSTICE AND THE FIGHT TO END IMPUNITY

Meaningful access to justice remained out of reach for many people, especially those from the most deprived communities. Obstacles to justice included inefficient judicial systems, a lack of independence in the judiciary, and a willingness among some sectors to resort to extreme measures to avoid accountability and to protect vested political, criminal and economic interests.

Difficulties in getting access to justice were exacerbated by attacks against human rights defenders, witnesses, lawyers, prosecutors and judges. Journalists trying to expose abuses of power, human rights violations and corruption were also frequently targeted. In addition, the use of military courts to try members of the security forces who commit human rights violations persisted in a number of countries, including in Chile, Ecuador and the USA, amid concerns about the independence and impartiality of these processes.

There was some progress in the investigation and prosecution of human rights violations committed by military regimes in the last century, including in Argentina and

Chile. However, impunity for thousands of enforced disappearances and extrajudicial executions in the region during the second half of the 20th century remained entrenched, largely owing to the lack of political will to bring those responsible to justice. Thousands of victims and their relatives continued to demand truth and justice in various countries including Brazil, Bolivia, El Salvador, Guatemala, Haiti, Mexico, Paraguay, Peru and Uruguay.

PRISON CONDITIONS

As incarceration rates have soared across the region over the past two decades, human rights groups have documented how Latin American jails have become nightmarish places where serving time is a battle to survive. Tens of thousands of people were held in pre-trial detention for long periods because of delays in criminal justice systems.

In most countries in Latin America and the Caribbean, prisons were grossly overcrowded, violent and sometimes lacked even the most basic services. Lack of food and clean drinking water, unhygienic conditions, lack of medical care and the failure to provide transport for prisoners to attend their hearings so that their cases could progress through the courts were reported in many countries in the Americas region, as were attacks, including killings between inmates. Despite the fact that several of the region's current leaders themselves spent time behind bars, prison conditions failed to move up the political agenda to any significant degree.

Across the USA, tens of thousands of prisoners remained in isolation in state and federal prisons, confined to their cells for between 22 and 24 hours a day in conditions of stark social and environmental deprivation.

Governments failed to take steps to address the urgent need for fully resourced plans to tackle these serious concerns. Very little progress was made in ensuring that prison facilities complied with international human rights standards and that prisoners'

rights to life, physical integrity and dignity were protected.

RIGHTS OF MIGRANTS AND THEIR DESCENDANTS

Insecurity and social deprivation in their home countries drove increasing numbers of Central American migrants, particularly unaccompanied children, to cross Mexico en route for the USA. Migrants travelling through Mexico continued to face killings, abduction and extortion by criminal gangs, often operating in collusion with public officials, as well as ill-treatment by the Mexican authorities. Women and children were at particular risk of sexual violence and people trafficking. The vast majority of these violations are never investigated and the perpetrators remain at large. Deportations increased and administrative detention pending deportation continued to be the norm.

Between October 2013 and July 2014, 52,193 unaccompanied migrant children were apprehended in the USA, nearly twice as many as during the previous 12-month period. The US government estimated that the total number of apprehended unaccompanied children could exceed 90,000 by the end of November 2014 in border states such as Texas, Arizona and California. Many of these children were fleeing insecurity and poverty in their home countries. In addition, the unprecedented levels of gang-related violence and organized crime in countries such as El Salvador, Guatemala, Honduras and Nicaragua spurred thousands of unaccompanied minors to migrate to the USA.

Discrimination against migrants and their descendants was pervasive, with states showing little political willingness to address the causes of such entrenched exclusion. In September 2013, the Dominican Republic's Constitutional Court issued a widely criticized judgment which had the effect of retroactively and arbitrarily depriving Dominicans of foreign descent born between 1929 and 2010 of their Dominican nationality; the vast majority of those affected were of Haitian descent. This sparked an outcry at the national and international levels, including from the Haitian authorities.

Ángel Colón, a member of the Afro-descendant Garífuna community in Honduras, was released unconditionally in October 2014 after spending five years in a Mexican prison. He had been arrested in 2009 by police in Tijuana as he was travelling between Honduras and the USA. Police beat him, forced him to walk on his knees, kicked and punched him in the stomach and put a plastic bag over his head to provoke near asphyxiation. He was stripped and forced to lick clean the shoes of other detainees and perform humiliating acts. Amnesty International considered him to be a prisoner of conscience detained, tortured and prosecuted because of discrimination based on his ethnic origin and his status as an undocumented migrant.

INDIGENOUS PEOPLES' RIGHTS

After more than 20 years of fighting for their traditional land, in June an expropriation law was passed to return land to the Sawhoyamaxa Indigenous community in Paraguay. However, Indigenous Peoples in the region continued to encounter social, political and economic threats to their collective well-being and their very existence. Their cultural heritage, ancestral lands and right to self-determination were under constant attack. Both state and non-state actors, such as businesses and powerful landowners, continued to forcibly remove them from their lands in the name of social and economic development. Development programmes often resulted in environmental and cultural destruction and community displacement. Those living in voluntary isolation were at even greater risk, particularly in the Amazon Basin.

The right of Indigenous Peoples to meaningful consultation and free, prior and informed consent over development projects affecting them, including extractive industry projects, continued to be undermined, despite the fact that all states in the region have endorsed the 2007 UN Declaration on the Rights of Indigenous Peoples.

The failure to respect the rights of Indigenous Peoples had a negative impact on their livelihoods and also resulted in communities being threatened, harassed, forcibly evicted or displaced, attacked or killed as the drive to exploit resources intensified in the areas where they live. Their rights to oppose and demand their free prior and informed consent continued to be met with intimidation, attacks, excessive use of force, arbitrary detention and the discriminatory use of judicial systems. For example, in July, the Inter-American Court of Human Rights ruled that the convictions of eight Mapuche in Chile were based on discriminatory stereotypes and prejudice.

Indigenous women continued to experience disproportionate levels of violence and discrimination. In May, the Royal Canadian Mounted Police admitted that 1,017 Indigenous women and girls had been murdered between 1980 and 2012, a homicide rate at least four times higher than that faced by women in the rest of the population. In January 2014, the Public Prosecutor's Office in Lima, Peru, closed the cases of over 2,000 Indigenous and *campesino* women who were sterilized in the 1990s without their full and informed consent. The 2,000 cases represented only a small proportion of a total of more than 200,000 women who were sterilized in the 1990s. None of the government officials responsible for implementing the programme that resulted in these forced sterilizations has been brought to justice.

HUMAN RIGHTS DEFENDERS AT RISK

Human rights defenders continued to face attacks and abuses in reprisal for their legitimate human rights work in many countries including Brazil, Colombia, Cuba, the Dominican Republic, Ecuador,

Guatemala, Haiti, Honduras, Mexico, Peru and Venezuela. Defenders faced a range of abuses including attacks on their life and physical integrity and on their rights to freedom of expression, association and assembly. They were also vilified in the press and by government officials and were victims of the misuse of the justice system in an effort to criminalize those who defend human rights. Very worryingly, in some countries, such as Colombia and Guatemala, local human rights organizations reported an increase in attacks against defenders. The perpetrators of these abuses were almost never brought to justice.

Defenders fighting against impunity, those working on women's rights and those focusing on human rights issues related to land, territory and natural resources remained at particular risk.

Even in countries where mechanisms to protect human rights defenders at risk have been established, such as Brazil, Colombia and Mexico, in many cases protection measures were not granted or were not granted effectively and promptly. This was due in particular to a lack of political will and of resources to ensure effective implementation. In addition, there were concerns that a differentiated approach to protection measures that included a gender perspective had not been put in place.

With courage, dignity and tenacity human rights defenders throughout the region continued to fight for the realization of human rights for all, despite the very unsafe and hostile environment they faced.

RIGHTS OF WOMEN AND GIRLS

States in the region failed to put protecting women and girls from rape, threats and killings at the forefront of their political agendas. Slow and patchy implementation of legislation to combat gender-based violence remained a serious concern and the lack of resources available to investigate and prosecute these crimes raised questions about official willingness to address the issue. The failure to bring to justice those responsible for these crimes further entrenched impunity for gender-based violence and helped foster a climate where violence against women and girls was tolerated.

In August 2013, states in the region appeared to be moving forward when they reached a historic agreement in Montevideo, Uruguay, acknowledging that the criminalization of abortion causes increased maternal mortality and morbidity and does not reduce the number of abortions. In December, abortion was decriminalized in the Dominican Republic.

However, at the end of 2014, women's and girls' sexual and reproductive rights continued to be violated with appalling consequences for their lives and health. In Chile, El Salvador, Haiti, Honduras, Nicaragua and Suriname, a total ban on abortion in all circumstances, including for girls and women pregnant as a result of rape or who experience life-threatening complications in their pregnancies, remained in place. Those seeking or providing an abortion risked lengthy imprisonment.

On taking office in March 2014, President Michele Bachelet promised that one of her priorities would be to reverse the total ban on abortion in Chile. In El Salvador, the future continued to look still bleak. At least 129 women have been incarcerated on pregnancy-related grounds in the past decade. Seventeen of these women were awaiting the outcome of a request for a state pardon at the end of the year. They were serving prison sentences of up to 40 years for aggravated homicide, having initially been charged with having an abortion.

In most countries where access to abortion services was granted in law in certain circumstances, protracted judicial procedures made access to safe abortion almost impossible, especially for those who could not afford to pay for private abortion services. Restricted access to contraception and information on sexual and reproductive issues remained a concern, particularly for the most marginalized women and girls in the region.

In some countries, the decriminalization of abortion in cases of rape was gradually becoming a reality. In Bolivia, the Constitutional Court ruled in February that the request for judicial authorization for an abortion that is the result of rape was unconstitutional. And in Peru Congress was discussing a draft bill to decriminalize abortion if the pregnancy is the result of rape at the end of the year. However, in Ecuador a similar attempt was blocked by President Rafael Correa in 2013.

Most countries in the region have passed laws to combat violence against women and girls in the private and public sphere. However, effective and fully resourced mechanisms to protect women and girls from violence were largely absent, especially in marginalized and poor communities.

Increasing rates of violence against women have been reported across the region. The Inter-American Court of Human Rights and the Inter-American Commission on Human Rights expressed concern at the levels of violence against women and impunity, concluding that underlying societal beliefs about the inferiority of women have created a culture of discrimination within law enforcement and judicial institutions, resulting in negligent investigations and a lack of sanctions against perpetrators.

ARMED CONFLICT

The failure to stem the human rights consequences of the Colombian armed conflict, coupled with the failure to bring to justice the majority of those suspected of criminal responsibility in such crimes, threatened to undermine the long-term viability of any eventual peace agreement.

Peace talks held in Cuba between the Colombian government and the Revolutionary Armed Forces of Colombia (Fuerzas Armadas Revolucionarias de Colombia, FARC) made progress. The negotiations offered the best chance in over a decade to put a definitive

end to the region's longest-running internal armed conflict. But all sides continued to commit human rights violations and abuses and violations of international humanitarian law, principally against Indigenous, Afro-descendant and *campesino* communities, human rights defenders and trade unionists.

The government continued to promote legislation to broaden the scope of military jurisdiction and make it easier for military courts to be assigned cases in which members of the security forces are implicated in human rights violations. This threatened to reverse the little progress that civilian courts had made to uphold the right of victims to truth and justice.

COUNTER-TERROR AND SECURITY

President Barack Obama acknowledged that the USA used torture in its response to the 11 September 2001 terrorist attacks on the USA (9/11), but he remained silent on accountability and redress. By the end of 2014, 127 men were held at the US detention facility at Guantánamo, Cuba. The majority were held without charge or trial, while six were still facing trial by military commission and a government seeking the death penalty under a system falling short of international fair trial standards.

In late 2012, the US Senate Select Committee on Intelligence (SSCI) completed a review it had begun in 2009 into the secret detention and interrogation programme operated by the Central Intelligence Agency (CIA) after 9/11. On 3 April 2014, the SSCI voted 11 to three to submit for declassification the summary of the report and its 20 findings and conclusions. The summary was finally released on 9 December, providing more damning detail of the human rights violations that were carried out in the programme, operated under presidential authority. The full report remained classified and out of public view, held, according to SSCI Chairperson Senator Dianne Feinstein, "for declassification at a later time". Although there has for years been much information in the public domain about the CIA programme, no one has yet been brought to justice for the human rights violations, including the crimes under international law of torture and enforced disappearance, carried out under that programme.

DEATH PENALTY
The USA was the only country in the region that carried out executions. However, here too momentum against the application of the death penalty continued to grow with the announcement in February that the Governor of Washington State would not allow executions there while he held that office. This followed Maryland's abolition of the death penalty in 2013, bringing to 18 the number of abolitionist states. There were also strong indications that no executions would occur in Colorado under its current governor.

In the Caribbean several Greater Caribbean states reported empty death rows for the first time since 1980.

ASIA-PACIFIC REGIONAL OVERVIEW

The Asia-Pacific region covers half the globe and contains more than half its population, much of it young. For years, the region has grown in political and economic strength and is rapidly changing the orientation of global power and wealth. China and the USA tussle for influence. Dynamics among large powers in the region, such as between India and China and the Association of Southeast Asian Nations (ASEAN), were also significant. Trends in human rights must be read against this background.

Despite some positive developments in 2014, including elections of some governments that have promised improvements in human rights, the overall trend was regressive due to impunity, continuing unequal treatment of and violence against women, ongoing torture and further use of the death penalty, crackdowns on freedom of expression and assembly, pressure on civil society and threats against human rights defenders and media workers. There were worrying signs of rising religious and ethnic intolerance and discrimination with authorities either being complicit or failing to take action to combat it. Armed conflict in parts of the region continued, particularly in Afghanistan, the Federally Administered Tribal Areas (FATA) in Pakistan, and in Myanmar and Thailand.

The UN released a comprehensive report on the human rights situation in the Democratic People's Republic of Korea (North Korea), which gave details on the systematic violation of almost the entire range of human rights. Hundreds of thousands of people continued to be detained in prison camps and other detention facilities, many of them without being charged or tried for any internationally recognizable criminal offence.

At the end of the year these concerns were recognized in the UN General Assembly and discussed in the Security Council.

Refugees and asylum-seekers continued to face significant hardship. Several countries, such as Malaysia and Australia, violated the international prohibition of *refoulement* by forcibly returning refugees and asylum-seekers to countries where they faced serious human rights violations.

The death penalty continued to be imposed in several countries in the region. In December, the Pakistani Taliban-led attack on Army Public School in Peshawar resulted in 149 deaths, including 132 children, making it the deadliest terrorist attack in Pakistan's history. In response, the government lifted a moratorium and swiftly executed seven men previously convicted for other terror-related offences. The Prime Minister announced plans for military courts to try terror suspects, adding to concerns over fair trials.

Homosexuality remained criminalized in several countries in the region. In India, the Supreme Court granted legal recognition to transgender people and in Malaysia the Court of Appeal ruled that a law making cross-dressing illegal was inconsistent with the Constitution. However, cases of harassment and violence against transgender people continued to be reported.

An increase in activism by younger populations, connected by more affordable communications technologies, was positive. However, in the face of this group claiming their rights, authorities in many countries resorted to putting restrictions on freedom of expression, association and peaceful assembly and attempted to undermine civil society.

INCREASE IN ACTIVISM

Younger populations, connected by affordable communication technologies and utilizing social media, claimed their rights as 2014 saw an increase in activism in the region, with women often at the forefront.

Elections provided the space for people to air their grievances and demand changes. In Indonesia's July elections, Joko Widodo was swept into power after making campaign promises to improve human rights. In Fiji, peaceful elections in September – the first since the 2006 military coup – saw vigorous debate by society and the media, despite ongoing restrictions on freedom of expression. By the end of 2014, a year after elections and mass demonstrations in Cambodia, peaceful protests in the capital, Phnom Penh, had become an almost daily occurrence.

Activists and human rights defenders increasingly came together to hold governments to account. In Myanmar in February members of the Michaungkan community resumed a sit-in protest close to Yangon's City Hall after the authorities failed to resolve their land dispute case.

More human rights activists looked to the international arena for support. Vietnamese authorities allowed Amnesty International to visit the country for the first time in more than 20 years. Although several new groups were formed and activists increasingly exercised their right to freedom of expression, they continued to face harsh censorship and punishments. Despite the early release of six dissidents in April and June, at least 60 prisoners of conscience remained imprisoned.

In Hong Kong, thousands of protesters, predominantly led by students, took to the streets from September to call for universal suffrage. More than 100 activists were subsequently detained in mainland China for their support of the Hong Kong protesters, and at the end of the year 31 remained in detention.

REPRESSION OF DISSENT

In the face of increasing activism, authorities in many countries resorted to putting restrictions on freedoms of expression and peaceful assembly. The crackdown on rights activism intensified during the year in China. Individuals associated with a loose network of activists called the New Citizens' Movement were sentenced to between two and six and a half years' imprisonment. Human rights defender Cao Shunli died in a hospital in March after being denied adequate medical treatment in detention.

In North Korea, there appeared to be no independent civil society organizations, newspapers or political parties. North Koreans were liable to be searched by the authorities and could be punished for reading, watching or listening to foreign media materials.

Military and security forces used excessive force to further repress dissent. In response to peaceful protests in Cambodia, security forces used excessive force including live ammunition against protesters, shooting dead protesting garment workers in January. Housing rights activists were jailed for peacefully protesting. The May coup in Thailand and imposition of martial law saw many people detained arbitrarily, political gatherings of more than five people banned and the trial of civilians in military courts with no right of appeal. Legislation was also used to restrict freedom of expression.

In Malaysia the authorities began using colonial-era sedition legislation to investigate, charge and imprison human rights defenders, opposition politicians, a journalist, academics and students. Media outlets and publishing houses faced sweeping restrictions under legislation requiring that licences be obtained for print publications, which could be arbitrarily revoked by the Minister of Home Affairs. Independent media outlets faced difficulty in obtaining licences.

In Indonesia, cases continued to be documented of the arrest and detention of peaceful political activists, particularly in areas with a history of pro-independence movements such as Papua and Maluku. Freedoms of expression and peaceful assembly remained severely restricted in Myanmar, with scores of human rights defenders, journalists, political activists and farmers arrested or imprisoned solely for the peaceful exercise of their rights.

Human rights defenders have consistently faced heavy pressure from some governments. In Sri Lanka, a memorandum issued by the Ministry of Defence warned all NGOs to stop holding media events and not to disseminate press releases. This contributed to the already prevalent climate of fear and repression, with journalists and human rights defenders continuing to face physical attacks, death threats and politically motivated charges.

Trade unions are also facing increasing restrictions. In the Republic of Korea (South Korea), Kim Jung-woo, a trade union leader, was sentenced to imprisonment after he tried to prevent municipal government officials from dismantling sit-in tents and a memorial altar at a protest. He is at risk of being given a heavier sentence at the High Court after an appeal by the prosecution. There have also been attempts by the authorities to deregister some of the major unions, and lawsuits have been filed against them.

Politically motivated attacks against journalists were a worrying trend. In Pakistan, at least eight journalists were killed in direct response to their work, making the country one of the most dangerous for the media profession. In Afghanistan, there was an increasing number of journalists killed – those covering the election were particularly at risk. In Maldives, several journalists came under attack from non-state actors who have gone unpunished.

There has also been evidence of narrowing down media space. In Sri Lanka, intimidation continued, including temporarily closing down *Uthayan* newspaper. In Bangladesh, bloggers and human rights defenders were arrested and faced trial and imprisonment. Pakistan has seen suspensions of TV channels. Chinese state censors attempted to ban photos and block any positive mentions online of the pro-democracy protests, while allowing TV and newspapers to run only government-approved news.

TORTURE AND OTHER ILL-TREATMENT

Torture and other ill-treatment continued to be committed by governments in several countries.

Torture by police was seldom investigated or punished in the Philippines. Despite the ratification of the two key international treaties against torture, severe beatings as well as methods such as electric shocks and waterboarding continued to be employed by officers who torture mostly for extortion and to extract confessions. In December, Amnesty International reported in *Above the Law: Police Torture in the Philippines* that a pervasive culture of impunity is allowing torture by police to go unchecked.

China consolidated its position as a major manufacturer and exporter of a growing range of law enforcement equipment, including items with no legitimate policing function such as electric shock stun batons and weighted leg cuffs, as well as equipment that could be used legitimately in law enforcement but is easy to abuse, such as tear gas. Torture and other ill-treatment remained widespread in China. In March, four lawyers who were investigating torture reports in a Legal Education Centre in Jiansanjiang, Heilongjiang Province, were themselves then arbitrarily detained and tortured. One lawyer reported he was hooded, handcuffed behind his back and suspended by his wrists, while police beat him.

In North Korea, hundreds of thousands of people remained detained in political prison camps and other detention facilities, where they were subject to gross human rights violations such as extrajudicial executions and torture and other ill-treatment.

Accountability mechanisms remained inadequate to deal with allegations of torture, often leaving victims and their families without access to justice and other effective remedies. In Afghanistan, allegations of human rights violations by National Directorate of Security (NDS) personnel continued, including torture and enforced disappearances. In Sri Lanka, torture and other ill-treatment of detainees remained widespread.

Prolonged pre-trial detention and overcrowding in prisons remained a serious concern in India. Indiscriminate arrests, slow investigations and prosecutions, weak legal aid systems and inadequate safeguards contributed to the problem. The Supreme Court directed district judges to immediately identify and release all pre-trial detainees who had been in prison for over half of the term they would have faced if convicted.

In Japan, the *daiyo kangoku* system, which allows police to detain suspects for up to 23 days prior to charge, continued to facilitate torture and other ill-treatment in order to extract confessions during interrogation. No steps were taken to abolish or reform the system to bring it into line with international standards. Torture and other ill-treatment of prisoners while in military detention, as well as by police, were reported in Thailand.

ARMED CONFLICT

In Afghanistan, the 13-year NATO mission reached its conclusion although a continued presence of international forces was agreed. Abuses by armed groups continued on a significant scale, with attacks at an all-time high in the first half of 2014. Pakistan also continued to see internal armed conflict in FATA, with the army launching a major operation in North Waziristan in June. US drone strikes resumed. The most devastating attack in the country's history occurred in December when several militants from the Pakistani Taliban attacked Army Public School in Peshawar where 149 people were killed, including 132 children, and dozens injured in firing which targeted children and teachers and in suicide bombings.

The armed conflict in Myanmar's Kachin and Northern Shan states continued into its fourth year, with violations of international humanitarian and human rights law reported on both sides, including unlawful killings and torture and other ill-treatment, including rape and other crimes of sexual violence. In Thailand, armed violence continued in the three southern provinces of Pattani, Yala, Narathiwat and parts of Songkhla. Security forces were implicated in unlawful killings and torture and other ill-treatment, while attacks targeting civilians were believed to have been carried out by armed groups through the year, including the bombing of public places.

IMPUNITY

A common theme was ongoing impunity for past and recent human rights violations including in the context of armed conflict. In India, state authorities often failed to prevent and also committed crimes against Indian nationals. Arbitrary arrest and detention, torture and extrajudicial executions often went unpunished. The overburdened criminal justice system contributed to justice being denied to those who suffered abuses, and to violations of the right to a fair trial. Violence by armed groups put civilians at risk.

There have been some convictions and arrests for past crimes. The Extraordinary Chambers in the Courts of Cambodia (the Khmer Rouge Tribunal) convicted Nuon Chea, the former second in command of the Khmer Rouge regime, and Khieu Samphan, the regime's former head of state, of crimes against humanity and sentenced them to life imprisonment. In the Philippines, retired Major General Jovito Palparan was arrested in August. He faced charges of abduction and illegal detention of university students.

Victims of past human rights violations and abuses continued to demand justice, truth and reparation for crimes under international law which occurred under the rule of former President Suharto (1965-1998) and during the subsequent *reformasi* period in Indonesia. No progress was reported on numerous cases of alleged gross violations of human rights that were submitted by the National Human Rights Commission (Komnas HAM) to the Attorney General's Office after a preliminary pro-justicia inquiry was conducted.

In Sri Lanka, the UN Human Rights Council established an international inquiry into reports of war crimes committed during the civil war. Government officials and supporters threatened human rights defenders not to have contact with the investigators or to contribute to the inquiry. In April in Nepal, the parliament passed the Truth and Reconciliation Commission (TRC) Act, establishing two commissions, a TRC and a Commission on Enforced Disappearances, with the power to recommend amnesties, including for serious human rights violations. This was despite a Supreme Court ruling in January that a similar 2013 TRC ordinance with the power to recommend amnesties contravened international human rights law and the spirit of the 2007 Interim Constitution.

PEOPLE ON THE MOVE

Several countries violated the international prohibition of refoulement by forcibly returning refugees and asylum-seekers to countries where they faced serious human rights violations. In Malaysia in May, the authorities forcibly returned two refugees and one asylum-seeker who were under the protection of UNHCR, the UN refugee agency, to Sri Lanka where they were at risk of torture. Sri Lanka detained and forcefully deported asylum-seekers without adequately assessing their asylum claims.

Afghans continued to account for a very high number of refugees according to UNHCR. Neighbouring Iran and Pakistan hosted 2.7 million registered Afghan refugees. In March, UNHCR documented 659,961 Afghans who were internally displaced due to armed conflict, deterioration of security and natural disasters. There were concerns that displacement could increase following the security transition scheduled for the end of 2014 as local insurgents fought to occupy territory previously under the control of international forces.

Internal migrants also faced discrimination. In China, changes to the household registration system known as *hukou* made it easier for rural residents to move to small

or mid-size cities. Access to benefits and services, including education and health care, continued to be linked to *hukou* status, which remained a basis for discrimination. The *hukou* system forced many internal migrants to leave their children behind in the countryside.

Migrant workers continued to face abuse and discrimination. In Hong Kong a high-profile trial began involving three women Indonesian migrant domestic workers. Their former employer faced 21 charges including causing grievous bodily harm with intent and failure to pay wages. In October, Amnesty International published a report based on interviews with migrant agricultural workers across South Korea, who under the Employment Permit System (EPS) endured excessive working hours, underpayment, denial of their weekly paid rest day and annual leave, illegal subcontracting and poor living conditions. Many were also discriminated against at work due to their nationality.

Australia's hard-line approach to asylum-seekers continued, with those arriving by boat either sent back to their country of departure, transferred to offshore immigration detention centres on Papua New Guinea's Manus Island or Nauru, or detained in Australia.

RISING RELIGIOUS AND ETHNIC INTOLERANCE

There were signs in 2014 of rising religious and ethnic intolerance and discrimination and authorities either being complicit or failing to take action to combat it. In Pakistan blasphemy laws continued to be linked to vigilante violence. Police were warned of some impending attacks on "blasphemy" suspects but failed to take adequate measures to protect them. Blasphemy laws also contributed to an atmosphere of intolerance in Indonesia. In November Amnesty International recommended repeal of Indonesia's blasphemy law and called for all those imprisoned under it to be released immediately.

Violent attacks on grounds of religious and ethnic identity continued on a significant scale. The failure of governments to address rising religious and ethnic intolerance was evident. The Myanmar and Sri Lankan governments failed to address ongoing incitement to violence based on national, racial and religious hatred by Buddhist nationalist groups despite violent incidents. The government of Myanmar also failed to allow equal access to full citizenship to Rohingyas. In Pakistan, Shi'a Muslims were killed in attacks by armed groups; Ahmadis and Christians were also targeted. Sri Lanka also saw violence against Muslims and Christians carried out by armed groups, and police failed to protect them or to investigate incidents.

Ethnic Tibetans continued to face discrimination and restrictions on their rights to freedoms of thought, conscience and religion, expression, association and peaceful assembly in China. Tibetan demonstrators were reportedly shot by police and security forces in Kardze (Chinese: Ganzi), Sichuan Province, where a crowd had gathered to protest against the detention of a village leader. Uighurs faced widespread discrimination in employment, education and housing, and faced curtailed religious freedom, as well as political marginalization.

Some government authorities used religion as a justification for ongoing discrimination. In Malaysia the Federal Court rejected an appeal seeking to overturn a ban preventing a Christian newspaper from using the word "Allah" in its publications. The authorities claimed that the use of the word in non-Muslim literature was confusing and could cause Muslims to convert. The ban led to intimidation and harassment of Christians.

India marked the 30th anniversary of the massacre of Sikhs in 1984 amid ongoing impunity for this and other large-scale attacks against religious minorities.

DISCRIMINATION

People in many countries continued to face discrimination, particularly where authorities failed to take adequate measures to protect them and their communities.

Discrimination, including on the basis of gender, caste, class, ethnic origin and religion, persisted in Nepal. Victims were subject to exclusion, torture and other ill-treatment, including sexual violence. Women from marginalized groups, including Dalits and impoverished women, continued to face particular hardship because of multiple forms of discrimination. In India, Dalit women and girls continued to face multiple levels of caste-based discrimination and violence. Self-appointed village councils issued illegal decrees ordering punishments against women for perceived social transgressions.

The Japanese government failed to speak out against discriminatory rhetoric, or curb the use of racially pejorative terms and harassment against ethnic Koreans and their descendants, who are commonly referred to as *Zainichi* (literally "residing in Japan"). In December the Supreme Court ruled to ban the group Zainichi Tokken wo Yurusanai Shimin no Kai from using racially pejorative terms against Koreans, while holding public demonstrations near an ethnic Korean elementary school.

Discrimination against ethnic, linguistic and religious minorities, including members of Tamil, Muslim and Christian communities, continued in Sri Lanka. Minorities were singled out for arbitrary restrictions on freedom of expression and association.

SEXUAL AND REPRODUCTIVE RIGHTS

Progress towards respect, protection and fulfilment of sexual and reproductive rights is still needed in many countries of the region.

In April, the Philippine Supreme Court upheld the Reproductive Health Law, which paves the way for government funding for modern contraceptive methods and seeks to introduce reproductive health and sexuality education in schools. However, the

Philippines still has one of the most restrictive abortion laws in the world, criminalizing abortion on all grounds with no exceptions. In Indonesia, legislation was passed in July restricting to 40 days the time period for rape survivors to access legal abortion. It was feared that this shortened timeframe would prevent many rape survivors from being able to access safe abortion provisions.

Government efforts to eradicate gender discrimination against women and girls continued to be ineffective in reducing women's risk of uterine prolapse in Nepal, where Amnesty International Secretary General Salil Shetty launched the "My Body My Rights" campaign among women affected by the issue in rural communities.

VIOLENCE AGAINST WOMEN

Women across the region continued to face violence, including when seeking to exercise their rights. In Pakistan, for example, a *jirga* (traditional decision-making body) of Uthmanzai tribal chiefs from North Waziristan tribal agency threatened women with violence for seeking access to humanitarian assistance in displaced persons camps.

In India, the authorities did not effectively implement new laws on crimes against women that were enacted in 2013, or undertake meaningful reforms to ensure that they were enforced. Rape within marriage was still not recognized as a crime if the wife was over 15 years of age.

Children were forced to marry in several countries in the region. So-called "honour" killings were reported in both Afghanistan and Pakistan. In Afghanistan, the number of cases reported under the law on the Elimination of Violence against Women increased – although it was not clear whether this was due to an increase in crimes or in reporting. Crimes related to violence against women remained some of the most underreported crimes. The Afghanistan Independent Human Rights Commission registered 4,154 cases of violence against women for the first half of 2014 alone. Authorities approved or amended

several laws which barred family members of both victims and perpetrators of crimes from testifying. Since most gender-based violence was reported as happening within the family, this made successful prosecutions in cases of forced and child marriage and domestic violence nearly impossible.

In Japan the results were made public of a government-appointed study which re-examined the drafting process of the Kono Statement (a government apology made two decades earlier to the survivors of the military sexual slavery system before and during World War II). Several high-profile public figures made statements to deny or justify the system. The government continued to refuse to officially use the term "sexual slavery", and to deny effective reparation to its survivors.

There were further reports of women and children being subjected to violence, sometimes resulting in death, following accusations of sorcery in Papua New Guinea. The UN Special Rapporteur on extrajudicial, summary or arbitrary executions highlighted sorcery-related killings as a major concern.

DEATH PENALTY

The death penalty was retained by several countries in the region; China continued its extensive use of the death penalty.

Executions continued in Japan. In March a court ordered a retrial and the immediate release of Hakamada Iwao. Hakamada Iwao had been sentenced to death in 1968 after an unfair trial on the basis of a forced confession, and was the longest-serving death row inmate in the world.

In Viet Nam, executions continued and several individuals were sentenced to death for economic offences.

National and international criticism had some impact. In Malaysia, the executions of Chandran Paskaran and Osariakhi Ernest Obayangbon were postponed. However, death sentences continued to be imposed and reports indicated that executions were carried out in secret.

In January, the Indian Supreme Court ruled that undue delay in the carrying out of death sentences amounted to torture, and that the execution of people suffering from mental illness would be unconstitutional. It also laid down guidelines for safeguarding the rights of people under sentence of death.

In December, in the wake of the Pakistani Taliban attack on a school in Peshawar, Pakistan lifted a moratorium on executions and began executing prisoners convicted of terrorism-related charges. It was reported that more than 500 people are at risk of being executed.

Afghanistan continued to apply the death penalty, often after unfair trials. In October, six men were executed in Kabul's Pul-e-Charkhi prison. The trial proceedings of at least five of the men in connection with a gang rape were considered unfair, marred by public and political pressure on the courts to hand down a tough sentence while the accused claimed to have confessed following torture by police in detention.

CORPORATE ACCOUNTABILITY

Companies have a responsibility to respect human rights. However, in several countries in the Asia-Pacific region that respect was not evident. Thousands of people remained at risk of being forcibly evicted from their homes and lands for large infrastructure and commercial projects in India. Particularly vulnerable were Adivasi (Indigenous) communities living near new and expanding mines and dams. In Papua New Guinea, tensions escalated at the site of Porgera gold mine between the mining company and local residents. In June, around 200 homes were burned to the ground by police enforcing an eviction. Reports were received of physical and sexual violence by police during the forced eviction.

December marked the 30th anniversary of the 1984 Bhopal gas leak disaster in India. Survivors continued to experience serious health problems linked to the leak and to continuing pollution from the factory site. Dow Chemical Company and Union Carbide failed to respond to a criminal summons issued by a Bhopal court. The Indian government is yet to clean up the contaminated factory site.

In Cambodia, conflicts over land and forced evictions continued. This led to increased protests and confrontations, often involving local authorities and private companies. In October a group of international law experts provided information to the ICC alleging on behalf of 10 victims that "widespread and systematic" land grabbing by the Cambodian government was a crime against humanity.

RIGHTS OF LESBIAN, GAY, BISEXUAL, TRANSGENDER AND INTERSEX PEOPLE

Homosexuality remained criminalized in several countries in the region. On a positive note, in April in India, the Supreme Court granted legal recognition to transgender people in a landmark judgment. It directed authorities to recognize transgender persons' self-identification as male, female or a "third gender" and put in place social welfare policies and quotas in education and employment. However, cases of harassment and violence against transgender people continued to be reported.

In a landmark decision in Malaysia in November, the Court of Appeal ruled that a Negri Sembilan Shari'a law making cross-dressing illegal was inconsistent with the Constitution. However, Amnesty International received reports about the arrest and imprisonment of LGBTI people purely on the basis of their sexuality, and they continued to face discrimination.

In October, Singapore's Supreme Court upheld section 377A of the Penal Code which criminalizes consensual same-sex relations between men. In Brunei, the new Penal Code imposed death by stoning as a possible punishment for conduct that should not be criminal, such as extramarital sexual relations and consensual sex between people of the same gender, as well as for offences such as theft and rape.

In conclusion, the seismic geopolitical and economic shifts that are taking place in the Asia-Pacific region render it even more urgent that human rights safeguards are strengthened and lapses are redressed so that all people in the region can claim genuine citizenship without risk of sanction.

EUROPE AND CENTRAL ASIA REGIONAL OVERVIEW

9 November 2014 marked the 25th anniversary of the fall of the Berlin Wall, the end of the Cold War and, according to one commentator, "the end of history". Celebrating the anniversary in Berlin, German Chancellor Angela Merkel declared "the fall of the Wall has shown us that dreams can come true" – and, for many in communist Europe, indeed they did. But a quarter of a century later, the dream of greater freedom remained as distant as ever for millions more in the former Soviet Union, as the opportunity for change has been ripped from people's hands by the new elites that emerged, seamlessly, from the old.

2014 was not another year of stalled progress. It was a year of regression. If the fall of the Berlin War marked the end of history, the conflict in eastern Ukraine and the Russian annexation of Crimea clearly signalled its resumption. Speaking on the same day as Angela Merkel, former leader of the Soviet Union Mikhail Gorbachev put it bluntly: "The world is on the brink of a new Cold War. Some are even saying that it's already begun."

The dramatic events in Ukraine exposed the dangers and difficulty of dreaming. Over 100 people were killed as the EuroMaydan protest reached its bloody conclusion in February. By the end of the year, over 4,000 more had died in the course of the fighting in eastern Ukraine, many of them civilians. Despite the signing of a ceasefire in September, localized fighting continued and there was little prospect of a rapid resolution by the end of the year. Russia continued to deny that it was supporting the rebel forces with both troops and equipment, in the face of mounting evidence to the contrary. Both sides were responsible for a range of international human rights and humanitarian law violations including indiscriminate shelling, which resulted in hundreds of civilian casualties. As law and order progressively broke down along the lines of conflict and in rebel-held areas, abductions, executions and reports of torture and ill-treatment proliferated, both by rebel forces and pro-Kyiv volunteer battalions. Neither side showed much inclination to investigate and rein in such abuses.

The situation in Crimea deteriorated along predictable lines. With its absorption into the Russian Federation, Russian laws and practices were employed to restrict freedoms of expression, assembly and association of those opposed to the change. Pro-Ukrainian activists and Crimean Tatars were harassed, detained and, in some cases, disappeared. In Kyiv, the huge task of introducing the reforms needed to strengthen the rule of law, eliminate abuses in the criminal justice system and combat endemic corruption was delayed by Presidential and Parliamentary elections and the inevitable distractions of the conflict still raging in the east. Little progress had been made in investigating the killings of EuroMaydan protesters by the end of the year.

The rupturing of the geopolitical fault line in Ukraine had numerous consequences in Russia, simultaneously boosting President Putin's popularity and rendering the Kremlin more wary of dissent. The breakdown in east-west relations was reflected in the aggressive promotion of anti-western and anti-Ukrainian propaganda in the mainstream media. At the same time, the space to express and communicate dissenting views shrunk markedly, as the Kremlin strengthened its grip on the media and the internet, clamped down on protest and harassed and demonized independent NGOs.

Elsewhere in the former Soviet Union, the hopes and ambitions unleashed by the fall of the Berlin Wall receded further. In Central Asia, authoritarian governments remained entrenched in Kazakhstan, and even more so in Turkmenistan. Where they appeared to wobble slightly, as in Uzbekistan, it was more the result of in-fighting among the ruling elite than in response to wider discontent, which continued to be suppressed.

Azerbaijan proved particularly aggressive in its repression of dissent; by the end of the year Amnesty International recognized a total of 23 prisoners of conscience in Azerbaijan, including bloggers, political activists, civil society leaders and human rights lawyers. Azerbaijan's presidency of the Council of Europe in the first half of the year failed to induce restraint. Indeed, more broadly in Azerbaijan, but also elsewhere in Central Asia, strategic interests consistently prevailed over principled international criticism and engagement on widespread human rights violations. Even for Russia, international criticism of the growing clampdown on civil and political rights remained strangely muted.

If Russia remained the market leader in popular, "democratic" authoritarianism, the trend was also observable elsewhere in the region. In Turkey, Recep Erdoğan demonstrated his vote-winning powers once again by comfortably winning the Presidential elections in August, despite a series of high-profile corruption scandals implicating him and his family directly. His response to these, as it had been to the Gezi protests the year before, was unflinching: hundreds of prosecutors, police officers and judges suspected of being loyal to one-time ally Fetullah Gülen were transferred to other posts. The blurring of the separation of powers in Hungary continued after the re-election of the ruling Fidesz party in April and, in moves that echoed developments further east, critical NGOs were attacked for supposedly acting in the interests of foreign governments. By the end of the year, a number of NGOs faced the threat of criminal prosecution for alleged financial irregularities.

Across the European Union (EU), entrenched economic difficulties and the dwindling confidence in mainstream political parties prompted a rise in populist parties at both ends of the political spectrum. The influence of nationalist, thinly-veiled xenophobic attitudes was particularly evident in increasingly restrictive migration policies, but it was also reflected in the growing distrust of supra-national authority. The EU itself was a particular target, but so too was the European Convention on Human Rights. The UK and Switzerland led the charge, with ruling parties in both countries openly attacking the European Court of Human Rights and discussing withdrawal from the Convention system.

In short, at no time since the fall of the Berlin Wall had the integrity of, and support for, the international human rights framework in the Europe and Central Asia region appeared quite so brittle.

FREEDOMS OF EXPRESSION, ASSOCIATION AND ASSEMBLY

Throughout the former Soviet Union, autocratic governments maintained or strengthened their grip on power. The deterioration in the respect for the rights to freedoms of expression, assembly and association in Russia since the return of Vladimir Putin to the presidency accelerated. Penalties, including greater criminal liability for violations of the law on demonstrations, were increased. Small-scale spontaneous protests were routinely dispersed, however peaceful, with hundreds arrested and fined or sentenced to short periods of detention, during the course of the year. A few larger planned protests, such as the anti-war protests in March and September, were allowed to proceed. Independent critical NGOs were consistently portrayed in the media and by leading politicians as a fifth column acting in the pay and interests of nefarious foreign powers. Discredited by media smear campaigns, dozens of NGOs were also distracted by judicial proceedings, challenging the requirement to register themselves under the politically toxic label "foreign agents"; five dissolved themselves as a result.

In Belarus, the highly restrictive law on demonstrations continued to be applied in a way that effectively prohibited public protest. The few who attempted it endured brief periods of detention for their pains. In the lead-up to the Ice Hockey World Championship in May, 16 civil society activists were arrested and sentenced to between five and 25 days' administrative detention. Eight were arbitrarily arrested in connection with a peaceful march commemorating the Chernobyl nuclear disaster. They were charged with "petty hooliganism" and "disobeying police orders". Eight others, all known for their political activism, were detained in the days before the march under similar charges.

Civil society and political activists were particularly targeted in Azerbaijan. Ten leading human rights organizations were forced to shut down or cease their activities and at least six prominent human rights defenders were imprisoned on spurious charges related to their work. Bloggers and opposition youth leaders were typically charged with drug-related offences. Independent journalists continued to face harassment, violence and trumped-up criminal charges.

The situation in Central Asia showed no signs of improvement. There were still no genuinely independent media outlets, NGOs or political parties in Turkmenistan despite nominal legislative reforms in recent years supposedly designed to facilitate their emergence. Internet access and freedom of expression online continued to be severely restricted. In Uzbekistan, a few hardy human rights activists continued to operate, but were forced to do so under the radar and at considerable personal risk. In both countries, protest remained virtually impossible. In Kyrgyzstan civil society activists operated in a far freer environment, but continued to report harassment. Even here, however, the government proposed legislation that would abolish the right to establish unregistered associations and noises were made in Parliament about the introduction of a "foreign agents" law akin to that in Russia.

In Kazakhstan, the new Criminal Code introduced a number of offences that could be used to restrict the legitimate activities of NGOs, and the government likewise began to consider tighter restrictions on the foreign funding of NGOs. Public protests took place, but participants risked fines and detention. The freedom of the media shrank and the internet was subjected to ever greater restrictions; social networks and blogs were often restricted and internet-based resources blocked by court decisions taken in closed proceedings.

In Turkey, the ruling AK Party strengthened its influence over the media, mostly through the exploitation of public – and private – business ties. Critical independent journalists continued to be fired by nervous editors or displeased owners and self-censorship remained rife. Freedom of peaceful assembly, brutally supressed in 2013 during the Gezi protests, continued to be violated by restrictive legislation on demonstrations and the violent dispersal of peaceful protesters, whenever they threatened to congregate in large numbers or on particularly sensitive topics. In December, several journalists were detained under sweeping anti-terror laws for reporting on corruption allegations.

REFUGEES' AND MIGRANTS' RIGHTS

The number of displaced people across the globe topped 50 million for the first time since the end of the Second World War. The response of the EU and its member states was, with few exceptions, driven above all by the desire to keep them out. This was shockingly obvious in the EU's response to the Syrian refugee crisis. By the end of the year, only around 150,000 of the approximately 4 million Syrian refugees were living in the EU – roughly the same number as arrived in Turkey in a single week following the advance of the Islamic State on Kobani.

EU countries pledged to take in only 36,300 of the approximately 380,000 Syrian refugees identified by UNHCR, the UN refugee agency, as in need of resettlement. Germany offered 20,000 resettlement places. The UK, France, Italy, Spain and Poland, with a combined population of 275 million people, offered just over 2,000 places, amounting to 0.001% of their populations.

In the absence of safe legal routes for refugees and migrants to reach to Europe, and in the face of the EU's determination to seal its land borders, record numbers attempted to reach Europe by sea – and record numbers drowned. By the end of the year UNHCR estimated that 3,400 refugees and migrants had lost their lives in the Mediterranean, making it the most dangerous sea route for migrants in the world.

For the first 10 months of the year, greater casualty numbers at sea were avoided thanks to Italy's unilateral and impressive search and rescue operation, Mare Nostrum, which rescued over 100,000 people – over half of them refugees from countries including Syria, Eritrea and Somalia. In the face of significant pressure from fellow EU member states, however, the operation was terminated on 31 October. In its place, the EU offered a collective substitute, Operation Triton, co-ordinated by its border agency, Frontex, which was significantly reduced in scale, scope and mandate.

Those who managed to scale or circumvent the ever-higher, ever-longer fences along the EU's external land borders risked being illegally pushed back by Spain, Greece and Bulgaria to Turkey and Morocco. At the end of the year, the ruling party in Spain tabled an amendment to the draft Law on Public Security that would legalize summary expulsions to Morocco from Ceuta and Melilla. Push-backs were increasingly supplemented by pull-backs, as the EU sought to strengthen its border control management with these countries.

Immigration detention centres – the dungeons of Fortress Europe – remained full, often to bursting. Irregular migrants and asylum-seekers, including families and children, continued to be detained in large numbers, often for lengthy periods and occasionally in appalling conditions.

TORTURE AND OTHER ILL-TREATMENT

The publication in December of the US Senate Select Committee on Intelligence's report on the Central Intelligence Agency (CIA) detention programme exposed not just the shocking details of the abuses involved, but also the full extent of the complicity of European countries. Several hosted secret detention sites (Poland, Lithuania and Romania) or otherwise assisted the US government in the illegal transfer, enforced disappearance, and torture and other ill-treatment of dozens of detainees, including in particular the UK, Sweden, Macedonia and Italy. In none of these countries was there any significant progress in holding those responsible to account. While there were some positive developments in respect of individual complaints brought by victims in Poland, Lithuania and the UK (the European Court of Human Rights found in July that the Polish government colluded with the CIA to establish a secret prison in the country between 2002 and 2005), accountability continued to be undermined by evasion, denial and delays.

In June, the Irish TV channel RTÉ broadcast previously undisclosed evidence in the possession of the UK government relating to five torture techniques used by British security forces in Northern Ireland under internment powers in 1971 and 1972. The techniques closely resembled those used by the CIA 30 years later. The European Court of Human Rights had previously ruled that the techniques amounted to ill-treatment, not torture, in an inter-state case brought by the Irish government. In December, the Irish Government announced that it would seek a revision of the European Court of Human Rights' ruling.

Torture and other ill-treatment remained pervasive throughout the former Soviet Union. Those accused of terror-related offences or suspected of belonging to Islamist groups were particularly susceptible to torture at the hands of national security forces in Russia and Central Asia, but throughout the region corrupt and poorly supervised law enforcement officials frequently resorted to torture or other ill-treatment to extract confessions and bribes. In the absence of effective, independent investigations, impunity for such abuses was, overwhelmingly, the norm.

In Turkey the routine use of excessive force by police in the course of demonstrations remained very much in evidence, even if torture in places of detention continued its downward trend. Justice continued to be denied or delayed for the handful of deaths and hundreds of seriously injured as a result of police abuses during the 2013 Gezi Park protests. Law enforcement officers in Greece and, occasionally, Spain continued to use excessive force to disperse demonstrations – encouraged here too by the prevailing impunity for such abuses.

The most dramatic protest-related abuses occurred in Ukraine, during and at the bloody conclusion of the EuroMaydan demonstration in Kyiv. At least 85 demonstrators, as well as 18 police officers, died as a direct result of the violence; there were no exact figures for the number of wounded. Following the first use of force by riot police on peaceful protesters on 30 November 2013, recurring incidents of abusive use of force, as well as arbitrary arrests and attempts to initiate criminal proceedings against demonstrators, took place in the early months of the year. At the end of February, firearms with live ammunition, including sniper rifles, were deployed, though it remained unclear which forces had used them and under whose orders they had acted. On the margins of the protest, several dozen EuroMaydan activists went missing. Some resurfaced later having been abducted and tortured; the fate of

over 20 remained undisclosed at the end of the year.

After the downfall of Ukraine's President Viktor Yanukovych, the new authorities publicly committed to effectively investigating and prosecuting those responsible for the killings and other abuses committed in the course of EuroMaydan. However, apart from indicting the former senior political leadership, few if any concrete steps were taken in this direction. By the end of the year only a handful of low-ranking law enforcement officers had been convicted for EuroMaydan-related abuses.

DEATH PENALTY

At least three men were executed in Belarus, which remained the only country in the region to retain the death penalty in practice. All three executions took place despite requests by the UN Human Rights Committee for a stay so it could consider the three men's cases.

TRANSITIONAL JUSTICE

The trials of former Bosnian Serb leader Radovan Karadžić and former General Ratko Mladić continued at the International Criminal Tribunal for the former Yugoslavia (ICTY), as it slowly worked its way through the few remaining cases pending before it. At the national level, progress in ensuring accountability for war crimes and crimes against humanity committed during the various conflicts in the former Yugoslavia remained painfully slow. The number of new indictments remained low, trials dragged on and political attacks on national war crimes courts continued. War crimes courts, prosecutors and investigative units remained understaffed and under-resourced as the lack of political will to deliver justice increasingly hid behind the expressed desire to move on.

Across the region, civilian victims of war, including victims of sexual violence, continued to be denied access to reparations due to the failure to adopt comprehensive legislation regulating their status and guaranteeing their rights. In September, Croatia, Serbia and Bosnia and Herzegovina signed a regional co-operation agreement with a view to accelerating the to-date slow progress in resolving the fate and returning the bodies of the many thousands of people still missing since the conflict. The rights and livelihoods of relatives in all three countries continued to be undermined by the lack of legislation on missing persons.

In Northern Ireland, the mechanisms and institutions set up or mandated to address conflict-related human rights violations continued to operate in a fragmented and often unsatisfactory manner. The Historical Enquiries Team, set up in 2006 to re-examine all deaths attributed to the conflict, was closed following widespread criticism. Some of its work was planned to be transferred to a new unit within the Police Service of Northern Ireland, prompting concerns over the independence of future case reviews. The major Northern Ireland parties agreed in principle in December 2014 to take forward proposals set out a year earlier by US diplomat Richard Haass for two new mechanisms: a Historical Investigation Unit and an Independent Commission for Information Retrieval. Details of finance, resourcing, timeframes and legislation, however, were not completely resolved.

COUNTER-TERROR AND SECURITY

Across the region, governments remained tight-lipped about the extent of their surveillance of internet-based communications, despite the protestations of many in the wake of the revelations of the extent of the US surveillance programme by Edward Snowden in 2013. In the UK, Amnesty International and other NGO litigants sought unsuccessfully to challenge the human rights compatibility of the UK's surveillance system through the courts and will now seek review in Strasbourg.

EU countries continued to use unreliable diplomatic assurances to return individuals considered a risk to national security to countries where they faced a risk of torture or other ill-treatment. The practice gained increasing currency in Russia as it sought to circumvent repeated European Court of Human Rights rulings staying the extradition of wanted individuals to Central Asian countries. Across the former Soviet Union, co-operating states frequently returned – both legally and clandestinely – terror suspects wanted in other countries in which they faced the very strong likelihood of torture.

The security situation in the North Caucasus remained volatile and security operations were routinely marred by serious human rights violations. In a particularly vivid illustration of law enforcement abuses, forces loyal to Chechen leader Ramzan Kadyrov made good on his threat to seek reprisals against the families of perpetrators of a large-scale attack on Grozny in December, by burning down several houses.

In Turkey, broadly framed anti-terrorism legislation continued to be used to prosecute the legitimate exercise of freedom of expression, though new limits set on the maximum length of pre-trial detention resulted in the release of many.

DISCRIMINATION

Discrimination continued to affect the lives of millions across the region. Long-standing victims of prejudice, including Roma, Muslims and migrants bore much of the brunt, but anti-Semitism also remained widespread and sporadically manifested itself in violent attacks. There were both advances and setbacks in the respect for the rights of lesbian, gay, bisexual, transgender and intersex (LGBTI) people.

Political declarations, action plans and national strategies continued to have minimal impact on the lives of millions of marginalized Roma – invariably because they were not accompanied by the necessary political will to implement them and because they consistently failed to identify and tackle the main reason behind the social exclusion of Roma, namely prejudice and racism.

As a result, the discrimination of Roma in housing, education and employment remained widespread. Hundreds of thousands of Roma living in informal settlements continued to struggle to access social housing or were excluded by criteria that failed to recognize, let alone prioritize, their manifest need. Legislative initiatives designed to tackle the insecurity of tenure of those in informal settlements were mooted in a number of countries, but nowhere adopted. As a result, people living in informal settlements across Europe remained vulnerable to forced evictions.

The segregation of Roma in education remained widespread throughout central and eastern Europe, particularly in Slovakia and the Czech Republic, despite repeated promises by national authorities to address a long-identified problem. In a positive development, the EU initiated infringement proceedings against the Czech Republic for breach of EU anti-discrimination legislation (the Race Equality Directive) for the discrimination of Roma in education. Italy and a number of other undisclosed EU states were also being examined by the EU Commission for other possible breaches of the Race Equality Directive for discrimination against Roma in a range of areas – signalling at last, perhaps, a willingness on the part of the EU to enforce legislation adopted a decade ago.

In July, the European Court of Human Rights ruled that the French ban on the complete covering of the face in public did not violate any of the rights set out in the European Convention of Human Rights, despite its obvious targeting of full face veils and the restrictions entailed on the rights to freedoms of expression, religious belief and non-discrimination of Muslim women choosing to wear them. In a perverse ruling with worrying implications for freedom of expression, the European Court justified the restrictions by reference to the nebulous requirements of "living together".

Violent hate crimes – targeting in particular Roma, Muslims, Jews, migrants and LGBTI individuals – continued across the continent. Several countries, including a number of EU member states, still failed to include sexual orientation and gender identity as prohibited grounds in hate crime legislation. Across the region, hate crimes remained under-reported and poorly investigated. Stand-alone hate crime offences and penal code provisions allowing discriminatory motives to be punished as an aggravating circumstance were frequently unused, as investigators failed to investigate possible discriminatory motives and prosecutors failed to charge perpetrators appropriately, or present relevant evidence in court.

A growing number of countries granted equal rights to same-sex partnerships (though rarely in respect of adoption) and successful, safe Pride marches were held for the first time in Serbia and Montenegro, under the watchful eye of the EU. Homophobia remained widespread, however, and growing tolerance in the west was often matched – indeed pointed to as a reason for – greater restrictions on the freedom of expression of LGBTI individuals further east. In Russia, LGBTI activists were routinely prevented from organizing public events, with local authorities often invoking legislation prohibiting the promotion of homosexuality among minors. Similar legislation was used to ban a book of fairy tales, including stories of same-sex relationships, in Lithuania. In Kyrgyzstan legislation banning the "promotion of non-traditional sexual relations" was considered by Parliament. Attacks on LGBTI individuals, organizations and events were common occurrences throughout much of eastern Europe and the Balkans, and were rarely responded to appropriately by indifferent criminal justice systems.

VIOLENCE AGAINST WOMEN AND GIRLS

Gender-based and domestic violence remained pervasive across the region. According to a report published by the EU Fundamental Rights Agency in March, one in three women in the EU had suffered physical

and/or sexual abuse since the age of 15.
The entry into force of the Council of Europe
Convention on preventing and combating
violence against women and domestic
violence was therefore timely, but by the end
of the year still only 15 countries had ratified
the treaty.

Despite this positive development, victims
of domestic and sexual violence continued
to be poorly served by criminal justice and
protection systems across the continent.
A lack of shelters for victims of domestic
violence and high attrition rates in the
investigation and prosecution of allegations of
sexual violence remained common problems
throughout the region.

SEXUAL AND REPRODUCTIVE RIGHTS
Access to abortion remained prohibited
under all circumstances in Malta. Ireland
and Poland both failed to fully implement
European Court of Human Rights rulings,
in 2010 and 2012 respectively, requiring
that women be guaranteed effective access
to abortion under certain circumstances.
Despite this, the Committee of Ministers
decided to close its monitoring of the
execution of the judgment in the Irish case.

MIDDLE EAST AND NORTH AFRICA REGIONAL OVERVIEW

As 2014 drew to a close, the world reflected on a year that was catastrophic for millions of people across the Middle East and North Africa; a year that saw unceasing armed conflict and horrendous abuses in Syria and Iraq, civilians in Gaza bearing the brunt of the deadliest round of fighting so far between Israel and Hamas, and Libya come increasingly to resemble a failed state caught up in incipient civil war. Yemen too remained a deeply divided society whose central authorities faced a Shi'a insurgency in the north, a vocal movement for secession in the south, and continuing insurgency in the southwest.

With the year in view, the heady hopes for change that drove the popular uprisings that shook the Arab-speaking world in 2011 and saw longstanding rulers ousted in Tunisia, Egypt, Libya and Yemen appeared a distant memory. The exception was Tunisia, where new parliamentary elections passed off smoothly in November and the authorities took at least some steps to pursue those responsible for the legacy of gross violations of human rights. Egypt, by contrast, gave far less cause for optimism. There, the military general who led the ousting of the country's first post-uprising president in 2013 assumed the presidency after elections and maintained a wave of repression that targeted not only the Muslim Brotherhood and its allies, but political activists of many other stripes as well as media workers and human rights activists, with thousands imprisoned and hundreds sentenced to death. In the Gulf, authorities in Bahrain, Saudi Arabia and the United Arab Emirates (UAE) were unrelenting in their efforts to stifle dissent and stamp out any sign of opposition to those holding power, confident that their main allies among the western democracies were unlikely to demur.

2014 also saw human savagery meted out by armed groups engaged in the armed conflicts in Syria and Iraq, notably the group calling itself Islamic State (IS, formerly ISIS). In Syria, fighters of IS and other armed groups controlled large areas of the country, including much of the region containing Aleppo, Syria's largest city, and imposed "punishments" including public killings, amputations and floggings for what it considered transgressions of its version of Islamic law. IS also gained ascendancy in the Sunni heartlands of Iraq, conducting a reign of terror in which the group summarily executed hundreds of captured government soldiers, members of minorities, Shi'a Muslims and others, including Sunni tribesmen who opposed them. IS also targeted religious and ethnic minorities, driving out Christians and forcing thousands of Yezidis and other minority groups from their homes and lands. IS forces gunned down Yezidi men and boys in execution-style killings, and abducted hundreds of Yezidi women and girls into slavery, forcing many to become "wives" of IS fighters, who included thousands of foreign volunteers from Europe, North America, Australia, North Africa, the Gulf and elsewhere.

Unlike many of those who perpetrate unlawful killings but seek to commit their crimes in secret, IS was brutally brazen about its actions. It ensured that its own cameramen were on hand to film some of its most egregious acts, including the beheadings of journalists, aid workers, and captured Lebanese and Iraqi soldiers. It then publicized the slaughter in polished but grimly macabre videos that were uploaded onto the internet as propaganda, hostage-bargaining and recruitment tools.

The rapid military advances achieved by IS in Syria and Iraq, combined with its summary killings of western hostages and others, led the USA to forge an anti-IS alliance in

September that came to number more than 60 states, including Bahrain, Jordan, Saudi Arabia and the UAE, which then launched air strikes against IS positions and other non-state armed groups, causing civilian deaths and injuries. Elsewhere, US forces continued to mount drone and other attacks against al-Qa'ida affiliates in Yemen, as the struggle between governments and non-state armed groups took on an increasingly supranational aspect. Meanwhile, Russia continued to shield the Syrian government at the UN while transferring arms and munitions to feed its war effort without regard to the war crimes and other serious violations that the Syrian authorities committed.

IS abuses, and the publicity and sense of political crisis that they evoked, threatened for a time to obscure the unremitting and large-scale brutality of Syrian government forces as they fought to retain control of areas they held and to recapture areas from armed groups with seemingly total disregard for the lives of civilians and their obligations under international humanitarian law. Government forces carried out indiscriminate attacks on areas in which civilians were sheltering using an array of heavy weapons, including barrel bombs, and tank and artillery fire; maintained indefinite sieges that denied civilians access to food, water and medical supplies; and attacked hospitals and medical workers. They also continued to detain large numbers of critics and suspected opponents, subjecting many to torture and appalling conditions, and committed unlawful killings. In Iraq, the government's response to IS's advance was to stiffen the security forces with pro-government Shi'a militias and let them loose on Sunni communities seen as anti-government or sympathetic to IS, while mounting indiscriminate air attacks on Mosul and other centres held by IS forces.

As in most modern-day conflicts, civilians again paid the heaviest price in the fighting, as warring forces ignored their obligations to spare civilians. In the 50-day conflict between Israel and Hamas and Palestinian armed groups in Gaza, the scale of destruction, damage, death and injury to Palestinian civilians, homes and infrastructure was appalling. Israeli forces carried out attacks on inhabited homes, in some cases killing entire families, and on medical facilities and schools. Homes and civilian infrastructure were deliberately destroyed. In Gaza more than 2,000 Palestinians were killed, some 1,500 of whom were identified as civilians, including over 500 children. Hamas and Palestinian armed groups fired thousands of indiscriminate rockets and mortar rounds into civilian areas of Israel, killing six civilians, including one child. Hamas gunmen also summarily executed at least 23 Palestinians they accused of collaborating with Israel, including untried detainees, after removing them from prison. Both sides committed war crimes and other serious rights abuses with impunity during the conflict, repeating an all too familiar pattern from earlier years. Israel's air, sea and land blockade of Gaza, in force continuously since 2007, exacerbated the devastating impact of the 50-day conflict, severely hindered reconstruction efforts, and amounted to collective punishment – a crime under international law – of Gaza's 1.8 million inhabitants.

The political and other tensions at play across the Middle East and North Africa in 2014 reached their most extreme form in the countries torn by armed conflict, but throughout the region as a whole there were institutional and other weaknesses that both helped fuel those tensions and prevented their ready alleviation. These included a general lack of tolerance by governments and some non-state armed groups to criticism or dissent; weak or non-existent legislative bodies that could act as a check on or counterweight to abuses by executive authorities; an absence of judicial independence and the subordination of criminal justice systems to the will of the executive; and a failure of accountability, including with respect to states' obligations under international law.

REPRESSION OF DISSENT

Governments throughout the region continued to crack down on dissent, curtailing rights to free speech and other expression, including through social media. Laws criminalizing expression deemed offensive to the head of state, government or judicial officials, or even foreign government leaders, were used to imprison critics in Bahrain – where a court sentenced one prominent woman activist to three years in prison for tearing up a photograph of the King – as well as in Egypt, Jordan, Kuwait, Morocco, Oman and Saudi Arabia. In Iran, critics faced trial on charges including *moharebeh* ("enmity against God"), a capital offence. In the UAE, the authorities continued to sentence pro-reform advocates to long prison terms after unfair trials and introduced new anti-terrorism legislation so sweeping as to equate peaceful protests with terrorism, punishable by possible death sentences.

The UAE and some other Gulf states, including Bahrain, Kuwait and Oman, created or used powers to penalize peaceful critics by stripping them of their nationality, and thus their rights as citizens, potentially rendering them stateless. Bahrain, Kuwait and the UAE exercised these powers during the year.

Freedom of association was widely curtailed. Many governments did not permit independent trade unions; some governments, including those of Algeria and Morocco/Western Sahara, required independent associations, including human rights organizations, to obtain official registration in order to operate legally but prevented their registration or harassed those that had registered previously. In Egypt, the authorities threatened the very existence of independent NGOs.

The right to peaceful assembly, so evident during the protests that shook the region in 2011, was greatly curtailed by many governments in 2014. Algerian authorities snuffed out protests by blocking access to venues and arresting activists. In Kuwait, the authorities continued to prohibit protests by members of the Bidun community, many of whom continue to be denied Kuwaiti nationality. Bahraini, Egyptian and Yemeni security forces used excessive force, including unnecessary lethal force, against demonstrators, causing deaths and injuries. Israeli soldiers and border police in the West Bank shot Palestinian stone throwers and others at protests against settlements, the wall/fence and other aspects of Israel's longstanding military occupation.

Elsewhere, unidentified gunmen committed unlawful killings with impunity, sometimes targeting those who spoke up for human rights and the rule of law. In Libya, Salwa Bughaighis, a human rights lawyer who had been one of the leading voices in the 2011 uprising, was shot dead by gunmen who entered her Benghazi home shortly after she had criticized the country's powerful but lawless armed groups in a media interview.

JUSTICE SYSTEM

Arbitrary arrests and detentions, prolonged detention without trial, enforced disappearances and unfair trials were common throughout the region, constant reminders of the corruption of criminal justice systems as tools of repression for the authorities. Thousands were held in Syria, Egypt, Iraq and Saudi Arabia, with some detained without charge or trial and others jailed after unfair trials. Smaller numbers of detainees were also held in Bahrain, Iran, the UAE and elsewhere; some were subject to enforced disappearance. Israeli authorities held some 500 Palestinians in administrative detention without trial; thousands of other Palestinians were serving prison terms in Israel. Palestinian authorities in both the West Bank and Gaza continued to detain political opponents; in Gaza, military and other courts sentenced alleged "collaborators" with Israel to death.

In Libya, rival militia forces held thousands of detainees, some since the fall of Mu'ammar al-Gaddafi in 2011, subjecting many of them to harsh and degrading conditions with no prospect of early release.

Across much of the region, courts tried and sentenced defendants with little regard for due process, often imposing long prison terms and sometimes death sentences on the basis of torture-tainted "confessions" and charges so broadly and vaguely framed as to virtually guarantee conviction. In Egypt, one judge issued preliminary death sentences against hundreds accused of taking part in deadly attacks on police stations after two fundamentally flawed trials; another judge sentenced three prominent media workers to lengthy prison terms without substantive evidence; and the new head of state decreed increased powers for notoriously unfair military courts to try civilians on terrorism and other charges. In both Bahrain and the UAE, courts did the government's bidding when trying those accused on security-related charges or for causing offence to those in power; in both countries, courts imposed prison terms on family members campaigning for the release of their wrongly imprisoned relatives. Iran's revolutionary courts continued to convict defendants on scarcely definable charges and handed down harsh sentences, including death. In Saudi Arabia, those targeted and sentenced to prison terms included lawyers who had acted as defence counsel in security-related trials and criticized the unfairness of the courts.

Saudi Arabia, Iran and Iraq remained the region's principal state executioners; in all three, authorities carried out scores of executions of defendants, many of whom had been sentenced after unfair trials. Those executed in Saudi Arabia, where many victims – 26 in August alone – were publicly beheaded, included a man convicted of sorcery and others convicted of non-violent drugs offences. Egypt resumed executions in June after a break of more than 30 months, perhaps presaging a large-scale increase in executions once hundreds of Muslim Brotherhood supporters and others sentenced to death during the year have

exhausted all appeals. Jordan also resumed executions in December after an eight-year hiatus. In Lebanon, courts continued to impose death sentences, but the authorities refrained from executing people, as did the authorities in Algeria, Morocco and Tunisia, who maintained longstanding de facto moratoriums on executions.

TORTURE AND OTHER ILL-TREATMENT

Throughout the region, security forces tortured and otherwise ill-treated detainees in their custody, sometimes on an industrial scale. In Syria, children were among the victims and large numbers of deaths of detainees from torture or other ill-treatment were reported but often difficult to verify. In January, photographic evidence emerged of thousands of deaths of detainees, many apparently due to beatings or other torture or starvation in Syrian government detention. Torture was endemic in Egypt, where the victims ranged from minor criminal suspects to Muslim Brotherhood activists swept up in the government's crackdown. Commonly reported torture methods in these and other countries included beatings on the soles of the feet, beatings while suspended by the limbs, prolonged standing or squatting in stress positions, electric shocks to the genitals and other sensitive areas, threats against the detainee and their family and, in some cases, rape and other sexual abuse. Often, torture was used to gather information leading to the detention of other suspects or to obtain "confessions" that could be used by courts to sentence government critics or opponents to prison terms, but it was also used to degrade, humiliate and mentally and physically scar the victims. Generally, the perpetrators used torture with impunity: governments frequently flouted their international legal obligation to independently investigate torture allegations, rarely prosecuted alleged torturers, and seldom if ever secured convictions when they did so.

IMPUNITY

It was not only torturers who benefited from impunity. So too did the political and military leaders who were the architects of, or who ordered, the war crimes and other violations of international law committed by government forces during the conflicts in Syria, Iraq, Libya and Yemen, by Israeli forces and Palestinian armed groups in Gaza and Israel, and those who presided over the large-scale human rights violations committed in Egypt, Iran, Saudi Arabia, the UAE and elsewhere. In Bahrain, the government committed to holding an independent investigation into torture in 2011 in response to the findings of an independent inquiry conducted by international experts, but it had not done so by the end of the year. In Algeria, the authorities maintained their long refusal to allow investigations into unlawful killings and other historical violations; in Yemen, the country's former President and his close associates continued to benefit from immunity agreed when he relinquished office following protests in 2011 in which his forces killed many protesters. In Tunisia, the new authorities did prosecute some former senior officials and members of the security forces for unlawfully killing protesters during the uprising there, only for a military appeals court to reduce the charges and sentences to such an extent that most of those convicted walked free.

Amid the failure or incapability of national justice systems to address impunity in Syria, human rights groups including Amnesty International made repeated calls to the UN Security Council to refer the situations in Syria and in Israel and the Occupied Palestinian Territories to the jurisdiction of the International Criminal Court (ICC), but these fell on deaf ears. Meanwhile, Libya remained under ICC jurisdiction following a UN Security Council referral in 2011, but the ICC prosecutor failed to open new investigations despite a rash of new war crimes as the country returned to civil war.

DISCRIMINATION – ETHNIC AND RELIGIOUS MINORITIES

Amid the political turmoil, religious and ethnic divisiveness and sectarianism that gripped the region, governments and non-state armed groups viewed minorities with increased suspicion and intolerance. This was most brutally reflected in the conflicts in Iraq and Syria, where many people were arrested, abducted, "ethnically cleansed" from their homes, or killed on account of their place of origin or their religion, but it was evident too in Libya, where killings on ethnic or tribal grounds were common and on the rise.

In the Gulf, the Iranian government continued to imprison Baha'is and bar them from higher education, and to restrict the rights of other religious minorities as well as those of Azeris, Kurds and other ethnic minorities, and were reported to have secretly executed Ahwazi Arab rights activists. In Saudi Arabia, the authorities maintained a crackdown on Shi'a critics of the government in the country's oil-rich Eastern Province, sentencing rights activists to long prison terms and, in at least one case, the death penalty after unfair trials. In Kuwait, the government continued to withhold citizenship and its associated entitlements to tens of thousands of Bidun residents.

REFUGEES AND INTERNALLY DISPLACED PEOPLE

In 2014, the Syrian crisis surpassed other such crises to become the world's worst in terms of refugee flows and internally displaced people. By the end of the year, approximately 4 million refugees had fled the conflict in Syria. The vast majority – about 95% – were being hosted in neighbouring countries: at least 1.1 million in Lebanon, more than 1.6 million in Turkey, more than 600,000 in Jordan, more than 220,000 in Iraq and more than 130,000 in Egypt, according to UNHCR, the UN refugee agency. International relief efforts received insufficient funding to meet the needs of those displaced. In December, the UN's annual Syria Regional Refugee Response plan for 2014 remained only 54% funded, and the World Food Programme was forced to temporarily suspend a food aid scheme to 1.7 million Syrians due to a lack of funding. In many places, the rapid influx of so many refugees placed huge burdens on the resources of the main host countries, sparking tension between refugee populations and host communities. Authorities in both Jordan and Lebanon took steps to bar the entry of Palestinian refugees from Syria and, increasingly, of anyone seeking refuge from Syria; the Egyptian authorities forcibly returned some refugees to Syria.

Within Syria, a further 7.6 million people were internally displaced, with many forced from their homes by fighting or sectarian attacks. Some had been repeatedly displaced; many were in locations beyond the reach of international humanitarian agencies or were trapped in areas besieged by government forces or non-state armed groups. Their situation was perilous in the extreme, with faint prospect of alleviation.

While nothing else matched the Syrian crisis for scale, its overflow into Iraq also saw thousands internally displaced there, due partly to IS violence and abuses but also to attacks and abuses committed by pro-government Shi'a militias. In Libya, thousands of people forced from the town of Tawargha in 2011 by Misrata armed militia continued to be prevented from returning to their homes and faced further displacement when the capital, Tripoli, and other areas plunged into armed conflict mid-year. In Gaza, Israeli bombing and other attacks destroyed thousands of homes, displacing thousands, during the 50-day armed conflict that began on 8 July. In Israel itself, the government detained newly arrived asylum-seekers from Sudan, Eritrea and other countries at a facility in the Naqab/Negev desert and returned others to their home countries under an ostensibly "voluntary" procedure that contained no guarantees of their safety and entailed a high risk of refoulement.

MIGRANTS' RIGHTS

Migrant workers fuelled the economies of many states across the region, not least in the oil and gas-rich states of the Gulf, where they performed vital roles in construction and other industries and in the service sector. Despite their importance to local economies, in most states migrant workers remained inadequately protected under local labour laws and were subject to exploitation and abuse. Qatar's selection to host the football World Cup in 2022 ensured that its official policies and practices in relation to the workers it hired to build new stadiums and other facilities remained under scrutiny, and the government made promises of reform in response to pressure. Nevertheless, in Qatar as in other Gulf states, the sponsorship, or kafala, system used to recruit migrant workers and regulate their employment facilitated rights abuses that were exacerbated by a common absence of official enforcement measures to uphold migrants' rights. Many migrant workers in the region were required by employers to work excessive hours without rest or days off, and were prevented by threat of arrest and deportation from leaving abusive employers.

Perhaps most vulnerable of all were the many thousands of women from Asia, in particular, who were employed as domestic workers, and could be subjected to physical or other abuse, including sexual abuse as well as other forms of labour abuse without any or adequate means of remedy. The Saudi Arabian authorities engaged in mass expulsions of "surplus" migrant workers to Yemen and other countries, often after first detaining them in harsh conditions. Elsewhere, in countries such as Libya where lawlessness prevailed, migrant workers faced discrimination and other abuses, including violence and armed robbery at checkpoints, roadblocks and on the streets.

Thousands of people, many of them prey to human traffickers and people smugglers, sought to escape and make new lives for themselves by boarding often overcrowded and unseaworthy vessels to cross the

Mediterranean Sea. Some made it to Europe; others were pulled from the sea by the Italian navy, and at least 3,000 were reported to have drowned.

FORCED EVICTIONS

In Egypt, the authorities continued to evict residents of "informal settlements" in Cairo and elsewhere without providing adequate notice or alternative accommodation or compensation. Those affected included residents who had made their homes in areas that the authorities deemed "unsafe", and whose removal they required to facilitate new commercial developments. The army also forcibly evicted at least 1,000 families living alongside the border with Gaza as part of efforts to create a "buffer" zone. The Israeli authorities also carried out forced evictions. In the West Bank, including East Jerusalem, they punitively destroyed the family homes of Palestinians who mounted attacks on Israeli civilians, and demolished dozens of homes of Palestinians which they said had been constructed illegally. In Israel, the authorities forcibly evicted Bedouin living in officially "unrecognized villages" in the Naqab/Negev region.

WOMEN'S RIGHTS

Across the region, women and girls faced discrimination under the law and as a result of official policies, and were inadequately protected against sexual and other violence. Such discrimination was deeply entrenched and few improvements were apparent in 2014. Three years on since women demonstrated with unprecedented visibility during the popular uprisings that swept the region in 2011, they appeared to be among the main losers of the political changes that ensued. In Egypt, groups of men attacked and sexually assaulted women protesters in the streets around Cairo's Tahrir Square. Tunisia was the notable exception. There, two police officers convicted of rape received lengthy prison terms, the government lifted Tunisia's reservations to CEDAW and appointed an

expert committee to draft a framework law to combat violence against women and girls. Algerian and Moroccan authorities also took some positive, albeit limited, legal measures, the former finally recognizing the right to compensation for women raped during the internal armed conflict of the 1990s, and the latter abolishing a Penal Code provision that allowed rapists to escape prosecution if they married their victim.

In the Gulf, despite their implacable mutual hostility on political and religious issues, the governments of Iran and Saudi Arabia both had appalling records on women's rights. In Iran, where many women's rights activists have been detained or imprisoned in recent years, the authorities detained girls and women who protested about an official ban on their attending certain sporting events as spectators. In Saudi Arabia, the authorities arrested or threatened women who dared defy an official ban on driving. In both countries, authorities also enforced strict dress and behavioural codes for women, and retained laws that punish adultery with death. In Yemen, women and girls continued to face early and forced marriage and, in some provinces, high rates of female genital mutilation.

Amid a general failure by governments to afford women and girls adequate protection against sexual violence and violence within the family, the excesses of IS forces in Iraq, where possibly thousands of ethnic or religious minority women and girls were forcibly abducted and sold as "wives" or slaves to members of armed groups including IS, represented a new nadir, yet one that elicited only muted condemnation from religious leaders.

2014 was a year of appalling suffering throughout much of the Middle East and North Africa, one that saw some of the worst excesses in recent history and that, at its close, held few signs of early improvement. And yet, amidst the horrors, local actors and activists of many different political hues continued through various means to speak truth to power, to express defiance in the face of tyranny, to assist the wounded and the powerless, and to stand up not only for their own rights but for the rights of others, often at huge personal cost. It was the dauntless courage of such individuals, many of them aptly termed human rights defenders, that was perhaps the most remarkable, and enduring, feature of 2014, and that which holds the most hope for the future of human rights in the region.

AMNESTY INTERNATIONAL REPORT 2014/15
COUNTRY ENTRIES

AFGHANISTAN

Islamic Republic of Afghanistan
Head of state and government: **Muhammad Ashraf Ghani Ahmadzai (replaced Hamid Karzai in September)**

There was growing insecurity throughout the country in expectation of the planned withdrawal of 86,000 foreign troops in December, as the mandate of NATO's International Security Assistance Force (ISAF) ended. The USA committed its troops to remain engaged in combat until the end of 2015. The UN Assistance Mission in Afghanistan (UNAMA) reported that casualties among civilians not involved in hostilities in Afghanistan were at an all-time high. The Taliban and other armed insurgent groups were responsible for more than 74% of civilian casualties, with 9% attributed to pro-government forces. A further 12% of casualties occurred during ground engagement between pro-Afghan government and Taliban insurgents and could not be attributed to any group. The remaining were as a result of the conflict. A lack of accountability in cases where civilians were killed or otherwise harmed unlawfully left many victims and their families without access to justice and reparation. During the year, the Parliament and the Ministry of Justice approved or amended a number of laws, including the Criminal Procedure Code, which barred family members of both victims and perpetrators of crimes from testifying. Since most gender-based violence was reported as happening within the family, this would have made successful prosecutions in such cases nearly impossible. The law was approved by both houses of parliament but was not signed and was rejected by then President Karzai following an outcry from national and international human rights organizations.

BACKGROUND

With no clear winner in the April presidential election and a June run-off marred by accusations of massive and systematic fraud against both candidates, electoral deadlock ensued for five months. Following long negotiations and interventions by US Secretary of State John Kerry and UN Special Representative in Afghanistan Jan Kubis, the two front runners agreed to form the country's first unity government as election results were announced on 22 September. Ashraf Ghani was sworn in as President on 29 September, with rival candidate Abdullah Abdullah serving as chief executive, a role similar to that of a prime minister. By the end of 2014, the new cabinet had yet to be announced, three months after President Ghani was sworn into office.

In June, in response to international pressure to curb the financing of terrorism within Afghanistan's jurisdiction, a bill against money laundering was approved by both houses of the Afghan Parliament and signed into law by then President Karzai.

On 30 September, President Ghani signed the Bilateral Security Agreement (BSA) with the USA and the Status of Forces Agreement (SOFA) with NATO, allowing 9,800 US and 2,000 additional NATO troops to remain in Afghanistan beyond the end of formal combat operations in December. Their role will largely be to provide training and mentoring to Afghan government forces.

ABUSES BY ARMED GROUPS

Between 1 January and 30 June, the number of casualties among civilians not involved in hostilities reached 4,853, of which more than 70% were caused by the Taliban and other armed insurgent groups. This figure marked a doubling since 2009 and an increase of 24% on the same period in 2013. Of these, 1,564 deaths were recorded and 3,289 people injured.

UNAMA said that improvised explosive devices and suicide attacks claimed the highest number of casualties. Ground engagements caused two out of every five civilian casualties, with 474 killed and 1,427 injured. This represented 39% of all civilian casualties, an increase of 89% from 2013.

The Taliban and other armed insurgent groups frequently attacked targets within easy reach, causing large numbers of civilian casualties. Child casualties and women casualties both increased by 24% from 2013, accounting for 29% of all recorded casualties in the first half of 2014.

Between January and August 2014 the NGO Safety Organization in Afghanistan recorded 153 attacks on aid workers, resulting in 34 people killed and 33 injured. The government attributed the majority of these attacks to gunmen belonging to insurgent groups, including the Taliban.

VIOLATIONS BY INTERNATIONAL AND AFGHAN GOVERNMENT FORCES

ISAF and NATO forces continued to launch night raids and aerial and ground attacks, claiming dozens of civilian lives, despite completing the handover of responsibility for security to the Afghan National Security Forces (ANSF) in June 2013. UNAMA said that 9% of the total civilian casualties were caused by pro-government forces (8% to ANSF and 1% to ISAF/NATO forces) with ground combat and crossfire accounting for the majority of deaths. The total number of civilians killed by pro-government forces during the first six months of 2014 fell from 302 to 158, mostly due to reduced aerial military operations. The ANSF were responsible for greater civilian casualties due to their full involvement in military operations and ground engagement.

There were significant failures of accountability for civilian deaths, including a lack of transparent investigations and a lack of justice for the victims and their families.[1]

In May, the English High Court ruled as unlawful the detention policy adopted by UK forces in Afghanistan after reviewing the case of Serdar Mohammed, held since 2010. The Court found that his detention beyond

the 96 hours permitted had been arbitrary, in violation of the European Convention on Human Rights. Following the ruling, the Afghan government ordered the UK to hand over 23 detainees held in two UK-run facilities in Helmand.

VIOLENCE AGAINST WOMEN AND GIRLS

The Afghanistan Independent Human Rights Commission (AIHRC) registered 4,154 cases of violence against women in the first half of the year alone, a 25% increase on the same period in 2013. There was an increase in reported crimes against women and girls, but it was not clear whether this was due to an increase in violence or in awareness and access to complaint mechanisms for women. A 2013 UN report found that the Law on the Elimination of Violence Against Women was applied in only 17% of all reported cases of violence against women in Afghanistan.

In a move seen as positive by women's and human rights groups, former President Karzai refused to sign into law the Criminal Procedure Code passed by the Afghan Parliament, which would have prohibited relatives of the accused from testifying in criminal cases. Since most gender-based violence was reported as happening within the family, this would have made successful prosecutions much more difficult to achieve and would have denied justice to victims of rape and domestic violence, as well as those subjected to underage and forced marriages. On the other hand, the reduction in the quota of women's seats in provincial councils, and the absence of women in the peace negotiation process with the Taliban, constituted backward steps for women's rights.

According to the Afghan Ministry of Public Health, there were 4,466 cases of self-poisoning and 2,301 cases of self-immolation by women during the year, resulting in the deaths of 166 women. Gender-based violence was reported as the primary cause of these acts of self-harm, followed by conflict-related trauma and displacement.

On 30 April a cleric was arrested for tying up and raping one of his Qur'an pupils, a 10-year-old girl, in Kunduz province.[2]

ARBITRARY ARRESTS AND DETENTIONS, AND TORTURE AND OTHER ILL-TREATMENT

Arbitrary arrests and detentions, including some incommunicado detention, continued under the intelligence service, the National Directorate of Security (NDS) and the police. Suspects were routinely denied due process, including being denied access to a lawyer or to their families. Allegations continued of violations by NDS personnel, including torture and other ill-treatment and enforced disappearances.

At least 50 non-Afghan prisoners remained in US custody in Parwan detention facility (formerly known as Bagram) at the end of the year. Some were believed to have been held since 2002. Their identities and any possible charges against them remained undisclosed, as did details of their legal representation and access to medical care.

FREEDOM OF EXPRESSION – JOURNALISTS

The government failed to investigate adequately and prosecute perpetrators of attacks on journalists and other media workers who were peacefully exercising their right to freedom of expression.

There was a reported 50% rise in the number of journalists killed in 2014 and a 60% increase in the number of attacks in the first half of the year, compared with 2013 figures.

Journalists were arrested, threatened, beaten or killed in apparently politically motivated attacks by government workers, international forces, insurgent groups and supporters of election candidates. According to Afghan media watchdog Nai, 20 journalists were attacked and seven killed. Journalists covering the presidential election were particularly at risk.

REFUGEES AND INTERNALLY DISPLACED PEOPLE

UNHCR, the UN refugee agency, estimated that Afghans continued to account for the highest number of refugees in the world. Neighbouring Iran and Pakistan hosted 2.7 million registered Afghan refugees. In March, UNHCR documented 659,961 Afghans who were internally displaced due to armed conflict, deterioration of security and natural disasters.

Afghanistan's Ministry of Refugees and Repatriation launched the landmark National Internally Displaced People (IDP) Policy on 11 February 2014, providing a legal definition for displaced people and establishing the government's primary responsibilities in providing emergency assistance, long-term support and protection. There were concerns that displacement could increase, however, following the security transition scheduled for the end of 2014 as local insurgents fought to occupy territory previously under the control of international forces.

Displaced people continued to migrate to larger cities such as Kabul, Herat and Mazar-e-Sharif. Inadequate makeshift shelters, overcrowding and poor hygiene, combined with harsh weather conditions, led to an increase in communicable and chronic diseases such as malaria and hepatitis. Efforts to eradicate the polio virus through vaccination programmes were impeded by opposition armed groups, including the Taliban, and cases continued to be reported.

DEATH PENALTY

Afghanistan continued to apply the death penalty, often after unfair trials.

On 8 October, six men were executed in Kabul Pul-e-Charkhi prison, less than two weeks after President Ghani's inauguration. Five had been convicted in connection with the gang-rape of four women in Paghman district. A sixth man had been convicted in a separate case of a series of kidnappings, murders and armed robberies. On 28 September, then President Karzai signed the death warrants for the six men. The trial proceedings of five men were considered unfair and controversial, marred by public and political pressure on the courts to hand down a tough sentence while the accused claimed to have confessed following torture by police in detention.

President Ghani ordered a review of nearly 400 death row cases.

1. Left in the dark: Failures of accountability for civilian casualties caused by international military operations in Afghanistan (ASA 11/006/2014)
www.amnesty.org/en/documents/asa11/006/2014/en/
2. Afghanistan: Ten-year-old rape survivor faces "honour" killing (ASA 11/013/2014)
www.amnesty.org/en/documents/asa11/013/2014/en/

ALBANIA

Republic of Albania
Head of state: **Bujar Nishani**
Head of government: **Edi Rama**

Domestic violence remained widespread and survivors rarely received justice. Impunity for cases of torture and other ill-treatment continued. Access to habitable and affordable housing for people living in poverty, including Roma, remained very limited, despite government pledges. A former barracks designated as temporary accommodation for victims of forced eviction did not meet international standards.

BACKGROUND

In June, the EU Council of Ministers approved EU candidate status for Albania, conditional on further judicial reform, combating corruption and organized crime and ensuring the protection of human rights, including the rights of Roma, anti-discrimination policies, and the implementation of property rights.

Albania's first Pride march took place in May.

ENFORCED DISAPPEARANCES

The whereabouts of the body of Remzi Hoxha, an ethnic Albanian from Macedonia who was forcibly disappeared in 1995 by state security agents, was not revealed to his son, despite assurances by the Prime Minister in 2013 that the location of his grave would be identified.

UNLAWFUL KILLINGS

Prosecutors reviewed the case of Aleks Nika, a demonstrator who died after being shot during anti-government demonstrations in January 2011 in the capital Tirana. In May, police officers who allegedly ill-treated some demonstrators during and after the protests were questioned. In July, the state prosecutor filed charges against the former General Director of Police and his deputy for failing to arrest six Republican Guard officers suspected of shooting at the demonstrators.

HOUSING RIGHTS

The Ministry of Urban Development and Tourism and the National Housing Authority proposed to increase the stock of social housing and access for those in inadequate housing. In February, the Ministry announced a new housing strategy to include Roma and Egyptians, to promote the legalization of informal settlements, and to improve access to water and sanitation. However, little progress was made.

In March 2014, a former barracks in the Shishtufinë area of Tirana was formally designated as the National Emergency Transition Centre for victims of forced evictions. Over 50 Roma families evicted from Rruga e Kavajes in Tirana had been resettled in Shishtufinë in October 2013. Conditions at the centre – which was located far from sources of employment and basic services – were inadequate and did not meet international standards for adequate housing.

On International Roma Day in April, some of the 100 Roma families at risk of eviction from Selita in Tirana demonstrated to demand alternative housing. The government rejected a proposed amendment to the law on the legalization of illegal construction in May, requested in a petition signed by 6,000 Roma and Egyptians which called for procedural protections against forced eviction and adequate alternative accommodation.

In July the UN Human Rights Committee issued an interim protection measure suspending the demolition of seven Roma families' houses in Elbasan pending the hearing of their complaint and compensation claim.

The government failed to guarantee the legal right of homeless registered orphans up to the age of 30 to priority access to social housing. In May, on national Orphans Day, orphans demonstrated calling for education and housing, and describing the financial assistance provided by the state as derisory.

TORTURE AND OTHER ILL-TREATMENT

Impunity generally persisted for allegations of ill-treatment by law enforcement officers. In May, Parliament introduced a new Internal Issues and Complaints Service to combat police corruption and human rights violations. In August the Head of the Public Order sector of the State Police in Kukës was charged with abuse of office and unlawful deprivation of liberty, for the ill-treatment of a detainee.

Former political prisoners organized hunger strikes in protest against the government's failure to fairly distribute compensation for their imprisonment by the communist government between 1944 and 1991, when thousands were imprisoned or sent to labour camps and subjected to torture and other ill-treatment.

VIOLENCE AGAINST WOMEN

In June the High Council of Justice published a review of domestic violence cases in 38 courts, and recommended changes to the law and court practice. They found that criminal proceedings were slow and that courts violated procedural deadlines for reviewing protection orders and issuing decisions.

Some 3,094 incidents of domestic violence were reported to the police by the end of September, with women accounting for the majority of the victims. Just over a third (1,292) of these reports resulted in criminal proceedings.

By the end of September, 1,882 women had sought protection orders in civil proceedings; however, in the Tirana District Court, for example, more than two-thirds of applications for protection orders were withdrawn or discontinued. Where protection orders were issued they were often not enforced.

REFUGEES AND ASYLUM-SEEKERS

In response to EU pressure, Albania developed a new border management strategy. Over 500 undocumented migrants and refugees, including Syrians, were detained between January and June. Others were returned to Greece without access to an asylum process. By the end of September, over 12,000 Albanians had applied for asylum in EU member states, on grounds including domestic violence and discrimination against LGBTI people and Roma.

ALGERIA

People's Democratic Republic of Algeria
Head of state: **Abdelaziz Bouteflika**
Head of government: **Abdelmalek Sellal**

The authorities restricted freedoms of expression, association and peaceful assembly, particularly in the run-up to April's presidential election, dispersing demonstrations and harassing activists.

Women faced discrimination in law and practice and remained inadequately protected against violence, despite proposed legislative reforms. Impunity prevailed for perpetrators of gross human rights abuses during the 1990s and acts of torture committed in subsequent years. Irregular migrants faced discrimination, abuse and arbitrary expulsion. Armed groups carried out lethal attacks. Death sentences were imposed; no executions were carried out.

BACKGROUND

2014 saw continued social unrest caused by tensions between the Mozabite and Arab communities in the city of Ghardaia. There were demonstrations against unemployment, poverty and corruption in the oil and gas-rich south, as well as protests focused on President Bouteflika's decision to run for re-election in April.

Following the election, the government opened consultations on proposed revisions to the Constitution but some political parties boycotted these consultations and most independent civil society organizations were excluded. At the end of the year the process appeared to have stalled.

There were new clashes between the security forces and armed groups, notably Al Qa'ida in the Islamic Maghreb (AQIM), mostly in southern and eastern Algeria. Foreign governments increased their security co-operation with Algeria following the attack in January 2013 by an armed group at the In Amenas gas extraction complex, in which dozens were killed and hundreds taken hostage, including foreign civilian workers. In September, an armed group calling itself Jund al-Khalifa (Soldiers of the Caliphate) abducted a French national in the Tizi-Ouzou region, an area where people had previously been kidnapped for ransom, and published a video on the internet showing him beheaded. His killing was in apparent reprisal for France's participation in a US-led alliance fighting the Islamic State armed group in Iraq. In December, the government said its forces had killed the leader of Jund al-Khalifa and two of his associates.

Algeria became a member of the UN Human Rights Council in January but the government continued to fail to agree to long-requested visits by key UN bodies and experts, including those concerned with torture, counter-terrorism, enforced disappearances and the right to freedom of association. The authorities did not grant visas to Amnesty International staff to visit Algeria.[1]

FREEDOM OF EXPRESSION

Journalists and government critics faced restrictions and judicial harassment by the authorities. On 12 March, the security forces closed down Al-Atlas TV, a private television station that had reported on anti-government protests and given airtime to a number of government critics. The authorities accused Al-Atlas TV of broadcasting without a licence.[2]

On 10 June, a court sentenced Youcef Ouled Dada to two years' imprisonment and a fine for posting a video on the internet showing police officers stealing from a shop during clashes in Ghardaia. The court convicted him of publishing photos and videos against the national interest and insulting a state institution. His sentence was confirmed on appeal.

FREEDOM OF ASSEMBLY

The authorities maintained a ban on all demonstrations in the capital Algiers although the security forces allowed some to go ahead without interference. In other cases, the police forcibly dispersed demonstrators, especially those from the Barakat (Enough) movement protesting against the President's decision to stand for re-election for a fourth term of office in April, and arrested some demonstrators, often releasing them after a few hours in custody.[3] Police also forcibly dispersed protests in other cities.

On 20 April, police used excessive force to disperse demonstrators in Tizi-Ouzou city who were commemorating the violent repression of protesters in 2001 in the Kabylia region.

Witnesses reported that police beat unarmed protesters and fired plastic bullets, one of which hit Lounis Aliouat, blinding him in one eye. The authorities said they had suspended five police officers pending an investigation into the beatings but they did not disclose the outcome of the investigation.

In May, a court imposed suspended six-month sentences on Mohand Kadi, a student, and Tunisian national Moez Benncir on charges of "participating in a non-armed gathering that may disturb public order". Police had arrested both men on 16 April near a Barakat movement demonstration in Algiers, although both denied participating in it.[4] Mohand Kadi's sentence was confirmed on appeal.

FREEDOM OF ASSOCIATION

In January, the deadline for registering existing associations under Law 12-06 expired. The law imposed wide-ranging and arbitrary restrictions on associations, including NGOs and civil society organizations, and penalties of imprisonment for up to six months plus a fine for membership of unregistered, suspended or dissolved associations. While some associations were able to register, others remained in legal limbo as they waited for the authorities' response to their registration application.

Amnesty International Algeria was one of a number of independent NGOs to file its registration application in accordance with the procedures set out in Law 12-06 but received no acknowledgement or other response from the authorities, despite repeated requests.

WOMEN'S RIGHTS

The authorities took some steps to improve women's rights. On 1 February, the adoption of Decree 14-26 provided for the first time for financial compensation to be paid by state authorities to women raped by members of armed groups during the internal conflict of the 1990s. At the end of the year it was unclear how many women had received compensation under Decree 14-26.

In June, the government proposed new legislation to criminalize physical violence against a spouse and indecent assaults on women when they are carried out in public. The proposed legislation would also make it a punishable offence to abandon a spouse or to use coercion or intimidation to obtain a spouse's financial resources. The proposed law establishing a state fund to assist divorced women with custody of their children whose former husbands failed to pay them alimony was adopted by Parliament on 26 November. At the end of the year, the other proposed amendments were still awaiting enactment.

Despite these advances, women remained inadequately protected from violence, including sexual violence, under the law. For example, a provision under which men who rape girls under the age of 18 are granted immunity from criminal prosecution if they marry their victim remained in force. Women's rights groups continued their long campaign for a comprehensive law to combat violence against women. Women also continued to face discrimination under the Family Code in relation to marriage, divorce, child custody and inheritance.[5]

IMPUNITY

The authorities took no steps to investigate thousands of enforced disappearances and other human rights abuses committed during the internal conflict of the 1990s and in subsequent years. Families of those forcibly disappeared continued to demand information about the fate of their relatives, including on the anniversary of the vote for the Charter for Peace and National Reconciliation, which gave immunity to the security forces and criminalized public criticism of their conduct.

The UN Human Rights Committee ruled on five cases of enforced disappearance and urged the authorities to investigate them thoroughly, bring the perpetrators to justice and provide effective remedies to the relatives of the disappeared.

The authorities took no steps to implement the UN Committee against Torture's recommendations, issued in November 2013, on the death of Mounir Hammouche, who died in the custody of the Department for Information and Security (DRS) in December 2006. The Committee called for an impartial investigation into his death, with a view to ensuring the prosecution of those responsible for his torture, and for his relatives to be afforded full redress.

COUNTER-TERROR AND SECURITY

Armed groups carried out a series of attacks targeting members of the security forces. In September, the Jund al-Khalifa armed group abducted and killed French national Hervé Gourdel, and posted a video on the internet showing him beheaded.

The authorities and the media reported scores of killings of members of armed groups by the security forces but disclosed few details of the circumstances in which these killings occurred, prompting fears that some may have been extrajudicial executions.

The DRS, despite reports of infighting among decision-makers over its role, continued to wield wide powers of arrest and detention, including incommunicado detention of terrorism suspects, facilitating torture and other ill-treatment. In June, the President issued Decree 14-183. This established a judicial investigation service within the DRS charged with preventing and suppressing acts of terrorism, acts that undermine state security and the activities of international criminal organizations deemed to threaten Algeria's national security.

In March, the US authorities returned Ahmed Belbacha to Algeria from Guantánamo Bay, Cuba, where they had imprisoned him without trial for over 12 years. In 2009 an Algerian court sentenced him after a trial held *in absentia* to 20 years' imprisonment. In December, he was acquitted of terrorism charges by the Algiers criminal court.

REFUGEES' AND MIGRANTS' RIGHTS

Migrants continued to face abuses including discrimination and arbitrary deportation. The government did not disclose how many migrants it expelled but they were reported to number several hundred, with many expelled without due process and safeguards.

Irregular or undocumented migrants remained vulnerable to violence, xenophobia and expulsion. In January, a woman from Cameroon was detained for illegally residing in Algeria when she went to the police in the city of Oran to report being raped.

Thousands of Algerian would-be migrants known as "harragas", and foreign nationals, mostly from sub-Saharan Africa, continued to attempt the hazardous sea crossing from Algeria to Europe, despite a 2009 law that criminalized "illicit" exit from Algeria using forged documents or through locations other than official border exit ports.

DEATH PENALTY

Death sentences were imposed; no executions have been carried out since 1993.

In November, Algeria voted in support of a UN General Assembly resolution calling for a worldwide moratorium on the death penalty.

---

1. Algeria: Allow rights groups to visit: No response from Algiers to requests from UN Bodies : Joint statement (MDE 28/001/2014) www.amnesty.org/en/library/info/MDE28/001/2014/en
2. Algeria: Authorities shut down TV channel (MDE 28/003/2014) www.amnesty.org/en/documents/MDE28/003/2014/en/
3. Algeria: Crackdown on peaceful assembly ahead of presidential elections (MDE 28/002/2014) www.amnesty.org/en/documents/MDE28/002/2014/en/ Algeria: Key human rights concerns ahead of presidential elections (MDE 28/004/2014) www.amnesty.org/en/documents/MDE28/004/2014/en/
4. Algeria: Two young men arbitrarily detained and prosecuted (MDE 28/006/2014) www.amnesty.org/en/documents/MDE28/006/2014/en/
5. Algeria: Comprehensive reforms needed to end sexual and gender-based violence against women and girls (MDE 28/010/2014) www.amnesty.org/en/documents/mde28/010/2014/en/

ANGOLA

Republic of Angola
Head of state and government: **José Eduardo dos Santos**

Freedom of association and assembly continued to be suppressed. Thousands of families were forcibly evicted. A youth was tried and acquitted for criminal defamation against the President and the trial of another man for criminal defamation against state officials commenced. The trial of state agents in connection with the disappearance of two men in 2012 started, was suspended and then restarted.

BACKGROUND

In January, President José Eduardo dos Santos became chair of the International Conference on the Great Lakes Region.

There were reports of sporadic political violence between members of the ruling People's Movement for the Liberation of Angola (*Movimento Popular de Libertação de Angola*, MPLA) and the National Union for the Total Independence of Angola (*União Nacional para a Independência Total de Angola*, UNITA).

From 28 April to 12 May, Angola hosted the 55th Ordinary Session of the African Commission on Human and Peoples' Rights in the capital, Luanda.

Between 16 and 31 May, Angola conducted a general population and housing census. The census was the first since 1970, prior to independence. The preliminary results, which were released in October, set the population at above 24.3 million with 52% being women.

Angola's human rights record was assessed under the Universal Periodic Review (UPR) in October.[1] Angola accepted 192 out of a total of 226 recommendations made. It also took the remaining 34 recommendations under further consideration, including those related to freedom of expression, association and assembly.

HOUSING RIGHTS – FORCED EVICTIONS

Authorities carried out forced evictions on a larger scale than in the past couple of years. At least 4,000 families had their homes demolished and were forcibly evicted in Luanda province. At least 700 of these families were left without adequate housing. There were also reports of evictions in other provinces, including Cabinda.

From 20 January a reported 2,000 families were forcibly evicted from their homes in the Chicala neighbourhood of Luanda. The houses had been earmarked for demolition for two years. Some of those forcibly evicted were rehoused in Zango in Luanda, while others were given tents in an undeveloped area in Kissama, about 100km from the city. It was only in September that they received land and iron sheets to construct houses.

From 28 May to 6 June a reported 600 families had their homes demolished and were forcibly evicted from the Areia Branca neighbourhood of Luanda. It is believed they were evicted to make way for construction of a hotel. Armed police, including riot police and a canine brigade, reportedly beat those being evicted. Most of the residents had lived in the area for six to 10 years and some reported that they had legal title to the land. The families were moved to a location in the Samba district of Luanda and reportedly remained there at the end of the year in makeshift cardboard houses.

FREEDOM OF ASSEMBLY

Police and security forces used force or the threat of force, as well as arbitrary detentions, to suppress peaceful demonstrations in Angola.[2] On a number of occasions police detained demonstrators and beat them before leaving them hundreds of kilometres away from where they were detained. In July, young demonstrators began demonstrating in the informal settlements as part of what they call the project "Movement for Demonstrations in the Musseques" (o projecto Movimento das Manifestações nos Musseques, MMM). Musseques is the colloquial word for informal settlements in Angola. According to the youth organizers, the movement aimed to peacefully demonstrate for better living conditions in the informal settlements.

Police reportedly beat and arrested young people peacefully demonstrating on the anniversary of the 27 May 1977 killings. About 100 people reportedly met at Independence Square in Luanda to demonstrate and call for commissions of inquiry into the 1977 killings, as well as those of three activists in 2012 and 2013. Police detained 20 young people for several hours and reportedly beat them before leaving them in Catete, some 60km outside Luanda.

On 21 June, riot police used teargas and violently dispersed a peaceful protest of the Teachers' Union, Sindicato Nacional de Professores (SINPROF), in Lubango and arrested 20 teachers. The teachers were demonstrating to demand overdue payment of their salaries. They were released on 23 June after acquittal in a summary trial.

UNLAWFUL KILLINGS

Police and security forces continued to enjoy impunity for some cases of unlawful killings. Police and security forces were responsible for unlawful killings in various provinces including Luanda, Malanje, Lunda Sul and Lunda Norte.

In May, plain-clothed police officers identified as belonging to the 32nd Police Station of Kilamba Kiaxi district in Luanda reportedly shot and killed Manuel Samuel Tiago, Damião Zua Neto "Dani" and Gosmo Pascoal Muhongo Quicassa "Smith". Witnesses stated that the youths had been in a vehicle parked outside a canteen in the 28 de Agosto neighbourhood of Kilamba Kiaxi. The police stopped beside the vehicle and reportedly fired shots at it. Manuel Samuel Tiago's brother, who witnessed the scene, reported that his brother had got out of the car and pleaded with the police

to stop shooting, but had been shot by the police officer. An investigation into the case was instituted. No further information was available by the end of the year.

In July a private security guard shot and killed Lucas Tiago in Cuango, Lunda Norte. Police and private security guards were reportedly in the area carrying out an operation against illegal diamond mining and in the process Lucas Tiago was shot in the back. This resulted in a confrontation between the other diamond miners and the police and security guards. Police and security guards reportedly arrested 22 miners. An investigation was instituted into Lucas Tiago's death. No further information was available by the end of the year.

FREEDOM OF EXPRESSION

Authorities continued to subject individuals to criminal defamation charges. The appeals of two journalists, Armando Chicoca and William Tonet, against their individual convictions for criminal defamation in 2011, had still not been heard.

On 14 August, Manuel Nito Alves was tried and acquitted of criminal defamation against the President of Angola due to lack of sufficient evidence. The charges were brought against him in connection with commissioning T-shirts with words deemed to be offensive to the President. He had been arrested by police officers and State security agents on 12 September 2013, when he was 17 years old, as he was collecting the T-shirts in the store where the printing had been commissioned.

On 19 August, journalist and human rights activist Rafael Marques de Morais was arraigned before the Luanda Provincial Court on charges of criminal libel brought against him by the head of the Intelligence Bureau at the Presidency, six other generals and the mining company Sociedade Mineira do Cuango (SMC). The charges related to a book, Diamantes de Sangue: Tortura e Corrupção em Angola (Blood Diamonds: Torture and Corruption in Angola) that had been published in Portugal. The book implicates the head of the Intelligence Bureau and the six generals in human rights violations in the diamond mines of the Lunda Norte and Lunda Sul provinces. Rafael Marques de Morais is reportedly being sued for US$1.2 million and could face a prison sentence. No trial date had been set at the time of writing.

Police beat and arrested journalists reporting on human rights violations. At least two journalists were detained for reporting on police activities.

On 2 February, police detained Queirós Anastácio Chiluvia, a journalist of the UNITA radio station, Rádio Despertar, as he attempted to report on shouts for help of detainees for a fellow detainee in the Municipal Police Command of Cacuaco. Queirós Anastácio Chiluvia was reportedly held for five days without charge before being tried and convicted on 7 February for insulting the police, defamation and working illegally as a journalist. He was sentenced to six months' imprisonment which was suspended for two years.

ENFORCED DISAPPEARANCES

The whereabouts of journalist Milocas Pereira (who disappeared in 2012), Cláudio António "Ndela" and Adilson Panela Gregório "Belucho" (who both disappeared in 2013) were still unknown. A trial opened into the disappearance of two men in the Luanda Provincial Court.

On 18 November the trial of eight state agents for the abduction in May 2012 and subsequent murder of Silva Alves Kamulingue and Isaías Sebastião Cassule was restarted in the Luanda Provincial Court. It initially started on 1 September and was suspended on 4 September as one of the accused, the Head of the State Security and Intelligence Service at the time of the abduction, was promoted to the position of General reportedly by President Eduardo dos Santos. The trial had to be suspended as the Luanda Provincial Court does not have the jurisdiction to try a General. On 22 September, the President

revoked the promotion and ordered an investigation into the process of promotion. No further information regarding the trial was available at the end of the year.

---

1. Angola: Amnesty International submission for the UN Universal Periodic Review September 2014 (AFR 12/005/2014) www.amnesty.org/en/library/info/AFR12/005/2014/en

2. Punishing Dissent: Suppression of freedom of association, assembly and expression in Angola (AFR 12/004/2014) www.amnesty.org/en/library/info/AFR12/004/2014/en

ARGENTINA

Argentine Republic
Head of state and government: **Cristina Fernández de Kirchner**

Women continued to face obstacles to accessing legal abortions. Discrimination against Indigenous Peoples remained a concern. Courts held trials for crimes committed during the military dictatorship. Reports of torture were not investigated.

BACKGROUND

In December 2013, the police went on strike over pay sparking violence and looting around the country. At least 18 people were killed. The violence spread across many of the 23 provinces; hundreds of people were injured and thousands of businesses damaged.

Under the Universal Jurisdiction Principle, the justice system also investigated crimes against humanity committed during the Spanish Civil War and the Franco era (1936 to 1975). In April, the Spanish Court of Justice rejected petitions to extradite two former security agents to Argentina.

Also in April, in Tucumán Province, 10 defendants accused of the kidnapping and forced prostitution of Marita Verón in

2002 had their acquittals revoked and were sentenced to prison terms.

WOMEN'S RIGHTS

More than half of jurisdictions did not have protocols in place for hospitals to guarantee access to abortions, which were legal if the pregnancy resulted from sexual abuse or put the woman's life or health at risk. In March, the Supreme Court rejected the motion for a public hearing to evaluate the necessary measures to effectively enforce its March 2012 sentence, which dispelled any doubts about the legality of abortions.

In April, the authorities of a hospital in Moreno, Buenos Aires Province, denied a 13-year-old girl an abortion whose pregnancy was the result of rape, due to her gestation of 23 weeks and health, despite neither the World Health Organization nor international norms specifying terms for access to this right. The abortion was finally carried out in a private facility.[1]

INDIGENOUS PEOPLES' RIGHTS

Although the National Constitution recognized Indigenous Peoples' rights to ancestral land and to participation in natural resource management, these rights were rarely fulfilled. In April, the La Primavera community (Potae Napocna Navogoh) in the Formosa Province rejected the land demarcation process, claiming that the provincial and national government had not respected their rights to consultation and free, prior and informed consent. At the same time, authorities were using the judicial system to prosecute individuals fighting for their rights. The leader of La Primavera, Félix Díaz, was tried in May for the theft of two police weapons during a 2010 community protest; he denied the allegations. Indigenous communities also faced violence at the hand of civilians; perpetrators were not brought to justice.

In March, the Comunidad India Quilmes, an Indigenous community in the northwest of the country, was attacked with firearms, bats and chains. Armed intruders assaulted and shot at the villagers and took over the community's holy site called "ciudad sagrada". Seven residents were injured. The community was trying to reclaim their sacred land through the national judicial system. At the end of the year, no one had been prosecuted for the usurpation. Investigations into the attacks were under way.

TRANSITIONAL JUSTICE

Throughout the country, courts conducted public trials for crimes against humanity committed under the military rule from 1976 to 1983. In Buenos Aires, 22 accused were prosecuted for their alleged involvement in the Plan Condor, an agreement between the military governments of Argentina, Bolivia, Brazil, Chile, Paraguay and Uruguay to eliminate their political opponents.

Also, trials were held for more than 100 defendants accused of crimes committed in the clandestine detention and torture centres in the School of Navy Mechanics in Buenos Aires, and La Perla in Córdoba, among others.

IMPUNITY

18 July marked the 20th anniversary of the attack against the building of the Argentine Israelite Mutual Association in Buenos Aires, which left 85 people dead. The government failed to provide justice and reparation to the victims. Iran refused to comply with an Argentine court order which called for the capture of five suspects. In 2013, the Argentine and Iranian governments signed an agreement to interrogate these suspects in Tehran, but the accord did not take effect. In Argentina, high-ranking officials, including former president Carlos Menem, were tried for diverting the investigation. The public trial was pending at the end of the year.

TORTURE AND OTHER ILL-TREATMENT

In April, the government regulated the National System for the Prevention of Torture but failed to create a National Committee, which should have been integrated with legislators, government officials and civil society organization representatives. The Committee's functions would include visiting detention centres and establishing criteria for the use of force, control of overpopulation and transfer regulations.

Allegations of torture and other ill-treatment were not investigated, as in the cases of prisoners Marcelo Tello and Iván Bressan, imprisoned in the province of Santiago del Estero.[2]

In Mendoza, there were recurring reports of torture but no one was brought to justice. A number of jails were overcrowded and some prisoners were kept in isolation for more than 20 hours a day.[3]

---

1. Argentina: Deben investigarse denuncias de tortura en Santiago del Estero
   www.amnistia.org.ar/noticias-y-documentos/archivo-de-noticias/argentina-99
2. Argentina: La provincia de Mendoza tiene la obligación de investigar las denuncia de tortura en las cárceles
   www.amnistia.org.ar/noticias-y-documentos/archivo-de-noticias/argentina-103
3. Argentina: El acceso al aborto no punible debe ser garantizado en la provincia de Buenos Aires y entodo el país
   www.amnistia.org.ar/noticias-y-documentos/archivo-de-noticias/argentina-91

ARMENIA

Republic of Armenia
Head of state: **Serzh Sargsyan**
Head of government: **Hovik Abrahamyan**

Peaceful protesters were dispersed by police using excessive force in several instances. Activists working on controversial issues were threatened and attacked.

BACKGROUND

Between July and August, skirmishes in the disputed region of Nagorno-Karabakh along the Armenia-Azerbaijan border turned into heavy fighting resulting in the reported death of 13 Azerbaijani soldiers and five Armenians, including two civilians.

On 17 July, the Armenian government announced its plans to sign an agreement joining the Russia-led Eurasian Economic Union by the end of the year, after it had opted out of signing the EU Association Agreement in 2013.

FREEDOM OF ASSEMBLY

Police broke up peaceful protests using excessive force on a number of occasions throughout the year. On 7 March, hundreds gathered outside the Ministry of Finance to protest against a controversial pension reform proposal. Police dispersed the peaceful protesters using excessive force. Three persons were arrested, fined and released the next day; two were allegedly ill-treated while in detention. On 23 June, police violently dispersed around 50 demonstrators in Yerevan protesting against electricity price increases, arresting 27. Later the same day, police officers physically assaulted three journalists waiting for the release of protesters outside the Kentron police station.

WOMEN'S RIGHTS

On 5 November, staff of the NGO Women's Resource Centre and other women's rights activists were threatened and verbally assaulted as they were leaving a court room where they had been assisting a victim of domestic violence. In 2013, the Women's Resource Centre had received anonymous death threats following its calls for gender equality legislation. No effective investigations into either of these incidents had been conducted by the end of the year.

RIGHTS OF LESBIAN, GAY, BISEXUAL, TRANSGENDER AND INTERSEX PEOPLE

The adoption of a draft bill prohibiting all forms of discrimination was put on hold, while provisions expressly prohibiting discrimination on the basis of sexual orientation were removed. The anti-discrimination bill was drafted as part of the requirements for Armenia's EU Association membership, but was abandoned after the government opted instead to join the Russia-led Eurasian Economic Union.

On 25 July 2013, a court in Yerevan sentenced two young men who threw Molotov cocktails into a lesbian, gay, bisexual, transgender and intersex people friendly bar to two-year suspended sentences. Despite admitting the homophobic motives behind their attack, both men were amnestied in October 2013.

CONSCIENTIOUS OBJECTORS

By the end of the year, all 33 Jehovah's Witnesses who had been detained for refusing to perform alternative service in previous years were released and required to perform alternative service.

TORTURE AND OTHER ILL-TREATMENT

Local human rights defenders continued to raise concern over high numbers of reported beatings and ill-treatment in police custody.

Authorities still had to effectively investigate the allegations of ill-treatment in custody of the opposition leader Shatn Harutyunyan. Shatn Harutyunyan and 13 other activists were arrested following clashes with the police on 5 November 2013, when they were attempting to march to the presidential building. Allegations of ill-treatment by two activists detained during protests on 7 March also remained without effective investigation.

AUSTRALIA

Australia
Head of state: **Queen Elizabeth II, represented by Sir Peter Cosgrove (replaced Quentin Bryce in March)**
Head of government: **Tony Abbott**

Australia's hard-line approach to asylum-seekers continued, with those arriving by boat either sent back to their country of departure, transferred to offshore immigration detention centres, or detained in Australia. Indigenous Peoples continued to be heavily over-represented in prisons despite comprising only a fraction of the population, with Indigenous youth being imprisoned at 25 times the rate of non-Indigenous youth. Regressive new legislation, introduced in the name of counter-terrorism and security, failed to protect the rights to privacy and freedoms of expression and movement.

REFUGEES AND ASYLUM-SEEKERS

Australia maintained its offshore processing policy, transferring anyone who arrived by boat after 19 July 2013 to Australian-run immigration detention centres on Papua New Guinea's Manus Island or Nauru. By 1 December 2014, approximately 2,040 asylum-seekers were detained in these centres, including 155 children on Nauru. Violence and possibly inadequate medical treatment resulted in the deaths of two asylum-seekers at the Australian-run immigration detention centre on Manus Island (see Papua New Guinea entry).

Australia continued to turn away boats containing asylum-seekers. By September, 12 boats with 383 people on board had been turned back at sea. An additional two boats were returned directly to Sri Lanka.

In October, the government introduced legislation to "fast track" the processing of over 24,000 asylum applications that had been suspended. The legislation removed a number of important safeguards and will allow people to be returned to other countries regardless of Australia's *non-refoulement* obligations under international law.

Australia also maintained its mandatory detention policy for those arriving without valid visas. By 1 December, there were 3,176 individuals in detention centres in mainland Australia and on Christmas Island, including 556 children. In August, the government announced it would transfer the majority of children and their families from onshore detention centres to the community on bridging visas.

INDIGENOUS PEOPLES' RIGHTS

Due to the failure of successive governments to effectively address Indigenous disadvantage, Indigenous Peoples continued to be over-represented in prisons. They comprised 27.4% of adults and 57.2% of juveniles in prisons, despite accounting for just 2.3% of all adults and 5.5% of youth in the general population.

In August, a young Aboriginal woman died in police detention in Western Australia when she was returned to custody twice by the local hospital with serious internal injuries. She had been detained to pay a fine, a policy that disproportionately affects Indigenous Peoples.

Between September and December, the Western Australian government demolished the majority of buildings in the remote Aboriginal community of Oombulgurri following a 2011 forced eviction. Many remote communities across Australia were at risk following the Federal government's decision in September to discontinue funding essential and municipal services.

COUNTER-TERROR AND SECURITY

National laws were introduced broadening intelligence agency powers, monitoring online activity and preventing the reporting of unlawful conduct by members of those agencies. New laws criminalized travel to areas abroad designated by the government as places where a listed terrorist organization was engaged in "hostile activity", while shifting the evidentiary burden on to the accused. The operation of controversial preventative detention and control orders were extended and an ill-defined offence of "advocating" terrorism introduced.

TORTURE AND OTHER ILL-TREATMENT

Australia had its fifth periodic review before the UN Committee against Torture in November. The Committee criticized Australia for continuing with its policies of mandatory detention and offshore processing of asylum-seekers. It also raised concerns about overcrowding in prisons and the disproportionately high rates of Indigenous incarceration. The Committee called on Australia to swiftly ratify the Optional Protocol to the Convention against Torture.

AUSTRIA

Republic of Austria
Head of state: **Heinz Fischer**
Head of government: **Werner Faymann**

Chronic neglect of detainees in preventive detention was exposed. Inquiries were ongoing into allegations of excessive use of force by police during demonstrations. Second-partner adoption was made legal for same-sex partners. Protection gaps remained in anti-discrimination legislation. A new humanitarian programme to grant refugee status to 1,000 Syrian nationals was launched. Asylum procedures remained long and the provision of independent legal advice to asylum-seekers was inadequate. Austria ratified the Council of Europe Convention on preventing and combating violence against women and domestic violence and the Arms Trade Treaty.

PRISON CONDITIONS

Media investigations exposed structural shortcomings in the juvenile prison and preventive detention systems. In May, reports of the neglect of detainees prompted the Minister of Justice to accelerate the planned reform of the preventive detention system for dangerous offenders. Recommendations issued in October 2013 by a taskforce on the detention of juveniles, established by the Ministry of Justice, were gradually being implemented. Also in May, media reports revealed that in Stein prison a 74-year-old man held in preventive detention since 2008 had been gravely neglected for several months, including being left without medical care. Criminal investigations were opened against prison officials and guards.

POLICE AND SECURITY FORCES

In January and May, clashes between police and protesters prompted allegations that police used excessive force to contain demonstrators. An inquiry by the Ombudsman Board was ongoing. In May, the Minister of the Interior told media that police officers could be equipped with body cameras. A group of experts was instructed to look into their use. The Minister reiterated the government's rejection of a compulsory identification system for police officers.

DISCRIMINATION

Legal amendments were introduced to allow same-sex couples to adopt each other's biological children, following a European Court of Human Rights judgment in February 2013. In all other circumstances, adoption continued to be denied to same-sex couples.

Despite the government's commitment in the UN Universal Periodic Review follow-up process to fill protection gaps, the Anti-Discrimination Law did not ensure equal protection against all forms of discrimination. Gaps remained in particular as to protection against discrimination on the basis of religion and belief, age and sexual orientation in the access to goods and services.

REFUGEES, ASYLUM-SEEKERS AND MIGRANTS

In April, Austria launched a new humanitarian admission programme for 1,000 Syrian refugees from countries neighbouring Syria and committed to granting refugee status to all upon arrival.

The asylum procedure remained long, often lasting several years. The authorities failed to ensure effective and adequate access for all asylum-seekers to independent legal advice throughout the procedure.

Asylum-seekers' access to adequate housing, social benefits and health care remained inadequate. Conditions in some reception centres were reportedly poor and unhygienic and in some cases amounted to degrading treatment.

AZERBAIJAN

Republic of Azerbaijan
Head of state: Ilham Aliyev
Head of government: Artur Rasizade

At least six prominent human rights defenders were imprisoned and leading human rights organizations forced to shut down or cease their activities. Independent journalists continued to face harassment, violence and trumped-up criminal charges. Freedom of assembly remained restricted. There were frequent reports of torture and other ill-treatment.

FREEDOM OF ASSOCIATION

NGO leaders continued to face threats and harassment from the authorities, including raids by security forces, the confiscation of equipment and imposition of travel bans. At least 10 leading human rights NGOs were prevented from operating as their bank accounts were frozen under a high-profile criminal investigation from May onwards.

Additional restrictions concerning NGO registration and activities were introduced in the law and used arbitrarily to open criminal proceedings against several NGO leaders. On 13 May, the Prosecutor General's Office launched an investigation into a number of foreign and local NGOs leading to the arrest of six prominent human rights defenders in connection with their organizations' activities.

PRISONERS OF CONSCIENCE

The authorities continued to imprison government critics, political activists and journalists. At the end of the year, there were at least 20 prisoners of conscience.

Journalist Hilal Mammadov, sentenced in earlier years under charges of drug possession and treason, remained in prison.

Khadija Ismayilova, an outspoken investigative journalist who had published extensively on corruption and human rights violations, was arrested on 5 December on charges of "inciting someone to attempt suicide". She also faced separate charges of criminal libel. Khadija Ismayilova had been previously targeted and harassed by the authorities, including with the imposition of a travel ban prior to her arrest.

Online and social media activities critical to the authorities continued to be prosecuted on fabricated charges, typically drugs-related. Among these cases were Abdul Abilov and Rashad Ramazanov, both arrested and sentenced in 2013, to five and a half and nine years in prison respectively. Political activist Faraj Karimov, who co-ordinated popular Facebook groups calling for the resignation of the President, and his brother Siraj Karimov, were arrested in July on spurious drugs charges.

Nine activists from the pro-democracy youth organization NIDA were arrested between March and May 2013 and in January 2014 on trumped-up charges ranging from illegal drugs and weapon possession to organizing public disorder. They were sentenced to imprisonment ranging from six to eight years in May. All claimed innocence at the time of detention, although some later made confessions, allegedly under duress. Shahin Novruzlu and Bakhtiyar Guliyev were released on 18 October under a presidential pardon after they had sent clemency appeals to the President, thereby "recognizing" their crimes. Activists Zaur Gurbanli and Uzeyir Mammadli were released on 29 December following a presidential pardon. Mammad Azizov, Rashad Hasanov, Rashadat Akhundov, Ilkin Rustamzade and Omar Mammadov remained imprisoned.

Opposition activists Ilgar Mammadov, Tofig Yagublu and Yadigar Sadigov, arrested in 2013 on charges of inciting public disorder and hooliganism, were given prison sentences of seven, five and six (reduced to four on appeal) years respectively. On 22 May, the European Court of Human Rights ruled that the actual purpose of Ilgar Mammadov's arrest was to "silence or punish" him for criticizing the government.

In a major crackdown on human rights activists, six prominent NGO leaders were remanded on charges of fraud, illegal entrepreneurship and "abuse of power".

On 26 May, Anar Mammadli, chairman, and Bashir Suleymanli, executive director, of the Election Monitoring and Democracy Studies Centre (EMDS) were sentenced to five years and six months' and three years and six months' imprisonment respectively. EMDS had exposed electoral violations during the presidential election in October 2013.

Prominent human rights defender Leyla Yunus, director of the Peace and Democracy Institute, was arrested on 30 July, followed by her husband Arif Yunus' arrest on 5 August. They were charged with "crimes" relating to their NGO work, including treason in connection with activities to promote peace and reconciliation with Armenia over the disputed Nagorno-Karabakh region.

Rasul Jafarov, founder of the NGO Human Rights Club (HRC), was arrested on 2 August. HRC had been denied registration since its establishment in 2010. Intigam Aliyev, a human rights lawyer renowned for helping in dozens of cases reaching the European Court of Human Rights (ECtHR), was arrested on 8 August 2014.

Former prisoners of conscience, human rights defenders Bakhtiyar Mammadov and Ihlam Amiraslanov, were released on 9 December 2013 and 26 May 2014 respectively under presidential pardon. Youth activist Dashgin Melikov was released on parole on 8 May 2014, and journalist Sardar Alibeyli was released on 29 December 2014.

FREEDOM OF EXPRESSION

Independent journalists continued to face threats, violence and harassment. On 26 December, the offices of Radio Free Europe/Radio Liberty's Azerbaijani service were raided and sealed off by members of the Prosecutor's Office without official explanation after confiscating documents and equipment. Twelve radio employees were detained and questioned, and released after signing a document on non-disclosure.

On 21 August, journalist and NGO activist Ilgar Nasibov was severely beaten by several men who stormed the office of the Democracy and NGO Development Resource Centre in Nakhichevan, an autonomous exclave of Azerbaijan. He suffered severe head injuries, including broken facial bones. The authorities opened an investigation against one alleged assailant. Charges were also brought against Ilgar Nasibov for allegedly stepping on the assailant's foot first.

FREEDOM OF ASSEMBLY

Demonstrations remained effectively prohibited outside officially designated, and typically remote, areas. In central Baku, the capital, law enforcement authorities used violence and excessive force to prevent and break up "unauthorized", peaceful assemblies throughout the year.

On 1 May, around 25 youth activists peacefully gathered in Sabir Garden, in Baku, to commemorate May Day. Within minutes, dozens of plain-clothed and uniformed police officers violently broke up their assembly.

Protesters were beaten and dragged into police cars. Six were arrested, including two minors who were released the same day. The remaining four were sentenced to administrative detention ranging from 10 to 15 days.

On 6 May, some 150 people gathered peacefully outside the court building in Baku where NIDA activists were standing trial but were forcefully dispersed by plain-clothed and uniformed police officers. At least 26 protesters, including one journalist, were dragged into a bus and taken to a police station. Five were sentenced to administrative detention ranging from 15 to 30 days, and 12 protesters received fines of 300-600 manats (US$380-760) for participating in an "unauthorized demonstration".

TORTURE AND OTHER ILL-TREATMENT

Torture and other ill-treatment was frequently reported, but allegations were not effectively investigated.

Kemale Benenyarli, an activist of the opposition party Azerbaijani Popular Front Party, was arrested on 6 May during the NIDA trial. She complained of beating and other ill-treatment inside Nasimi District Police Station after she refused to sign a "confession" written by the police. She was punched, dragged and locked in a cell, where she was kept without food or water until her trial the following morning. Another arrested protester, Orkhan Eyyubzade, reported being stripped naked, dragged by the hair, punched, kicked and threatened with rape after he engaged in an argument with police officers during his detention on 15 May.

Three of the arrested NIDA activists, Mahammad Azizov, Bakhtiyar Guliyev and Shahin Novruzlu, appeared on national television on 9 March 2013, "confessing" their plans to use violence and cause disorder during a forthcoming "unauthorized" street protest. Mahammad Azizov told his lawyer that he had been forced to "confess" under threats of prosecution against members of his family. Shahin Novruzlu, who was 17 at the time, was questioned without the presence of his legal guardian. Four of his front teeth were missing as a result of beating when he subsequently appeared in court. No investigation was launched into his ill-treatment.

BAHAMAS

Commonwealth of the Bahamas
Head of state: **Queen Elizabeth II, represented by Dame Marguerite Pindling (replaced Sir Arthur Alexander Foulkes in July 2014)**
Head of government: **Perry Gladstone Christie**

There were calls for resumptions in executions. Excessive use of force was reported and sentences had yet to be handed down in cases of torture or other ill-treatment in detention.

BACKGROUND

A referendum on amendments to the Constitution on gender equality was postponed until 2015. The referendum followed recommendations made in a 2013 report by the Constitutional Commission, and had originally been scheduled for November 2014. There was opposition to these amendments, including from local churches, due to concern that they would allow same-sex marriage.

Violent crime continued to rise. In 2013, police reported the second highest homicide rate since 2000, with 120 murders. No further statistics on homicide rates were published in 2014.

DEATH PENALTY

There had been no executions in the Bahamas since 2000. Hundreds demonstrated in 2014 for the resumption of executions in order to reduce crime.

In March, the Bahamas rejected a call for abolition of the death penalty and reiterated its retentionist position at the OAS.

EXCESSIVE USE OF FORCE

Torture or other ill-treatment and excessive use of force by police officers continued to be reported.

In April, Leslie Louis required medical treatment after police attempted to arrest him. He was allegedly beaten, but was not charged with any criminal offence. When his sister asked the police why he was being interrogated, she was pushed and grabbed by the throat.

DEATHS IN CUSTODY

By the end of the year, no judicial sentence had been handed down in the case of Aaron Rolle who died in police custody in February 2013. In May 2013, the coroner's inquest found the death to be an "unlawful killing".

REFUGEES' AND MIGRANTS' RIGHTS

The sentencing of five marines before a military court in November 2013 was still pending at the end of the year. They were charged following allegations of ill-treatment of Cuban asylum-seekers at the Carmichael Road Detention Centre in May 2013.

A new migration policy put in place on 1 November resulted in dozens of arbitrary detentions of migrants, disproportionately targeting Haitians and Bahamian-Haitian communities with the risk of deportation without due process.

RIGHTS OF LESBIAN, GAY, BISEXUAL, TRANSGENDER AND INTERSEX PEOPLE

In February, the Minister of Foreign Affairs and Immigration publicly advocated for greater tolerance in member states of the Caribbean Community (CARICOM) towards LGBTI people. In August, the Bahamas' first ever Pride event was cancelled due to threats and intimidation against the organizers.

WOMEN'S RIGHTS

Despite promises made during the Bahamas' 2013 UN Universal Periodic Review (UPR) to criminalize marital rape, no legislation had been approved by the end of the year.

BAHRAIN

Kingdom of Bahrain
Head of state: **King Hamad bin 'Issa Al Khalifa**
Head of government: **Shaikh Khalifa bin Salman Al Khalifa**

The government continued to stifle and punish dissent and to curtail freedoms of expression, association and assembly. Security forces used excessive force to disperse protests, killing at least two people. Opposition activists sentenced after unfair trials in previous years continued to be held, including prisoners of conscience. Torture of detainees continued and a climate of impunity prevailed. Twenty-one Bahrainis convicted on terrorism charges were stripped of their nationality. The courts sentenced five people to death; there were no executions.

BACKGROUND

Tension between the Sunni-dominated government and main opposition political associations remained high throughout the year following the suspension in January of the National Dialogue initiative. There were new protests by activists from the Shi'a majority population demanding political reform, including some violent protests, to which the security forces frequently responded with excessive force, including shotgun fire. In March, a bomb explosion at al-Daih village killed three police officers. In December, bomb attacks in the villages of Karzakan and Demistan killed a police officer and another person. The government banned the "14 February Coalition", a youth movement, and two other organizations declaring them terrorist groups.

Bahrain's first parliamentary elections since unrest broke out in 2011 were held on 22 November but were boycotted by the main opposition, led by al-Wefaq National Islamic Society, the largest Shi'a political association.

Amendments to anti-terrorism legislation adopted in December increased police powers, allowing them to detain terrorism suspects incommunicado for up to 28 days.

Representatives of the UN High Commissioner for Human Rights visited Bahrain from February to May to assess human rights training needs. In September, the government issued a mid-term review of its progress in implementing recommendations it had accepted at the UN Universal Periodic Review of Bahrain in 2012.

FREEDOM OF EXPRESSION

The authorities continued to clamp down on dissent. In February, shortly before the third anniversary of the outbreak of public protests in 2011, the government increased the penalty for publicly insulting the King, the Bahraini flag or the national emblem to between one and seven years in prison and a heavy fine.

Dr Sa'eed Mothaher Habib al-Samahiji, an ophthalmologist, was arrested on 1 July to serve a one-year prison term imposed on him in December 2013 on a charge of "publicly insulting the King" in a speech at the funeral of a protester killed by a police car. He was held at Jaw Prison, south of Manama, at the end of the year.

Other prisoners of conscience held at Jaw Prison included opposition leaders and human rights activists sentenced after unfair trials in previous years. Human rights defender Nabeel Rajab was released in May after completing a two-year prison term for "illegal gathering" but was rearrested in October on charges of insulting public institutions. He was released on bail in November but banned from travel, pending a court verdict on his case in January 2015. Activist Zainab Al-Khawaja was arrested in October and sentenced in November and December to prison terms totalling four years and four months, including three years on a charge of "insulting the King". She was at liberty at the end of the year awaiting the outcome of an appeal. Women's rights activist Ghada Jamsheer, arrested in September, faced trial on various charges, including assaulting a police officer. She was released on bail in December.

FREEDOM OF ASSEMBLY

All public gatherings in the capital Manama remained indefinitely banned under government decrees issued in 2013. However, sporadic protests were held in other places. The security forces arrested scores of people for participating in protests; some received prison sentences.

Ahmad Mshaima' stood trial in May, five months after his arrest, charged with "illegal gathering with an intent to commit crimes and disturb public security". He alleged that security officials tortured him in the days following his arrest, but the authorities did not investigate his allegations. He was released on bail in June but rearrested in November and sentenced in December to one year's imprisonment on a charge of "insulting the King".

In December, human rights defender Mohammad al Maskati and 10 other defendants were sentenced to six-month prison terms on charges of "illegal gathering".

FREEDOM OF ASSOCIATION

The government restricted freedom of association using new powers that allowed the Minister of Justice to suspend or dissolve political associations on vague grounds. The Minister filed suspension cases against two main political opposition associations, Wa'ad and al-Wefaq, for alleged irregularities during their activities. The Ministry of Justice dropped its case against Wa'ad in November. In October a court ordered the suspension of

al-Wefaq for three months. The court action began shortly after the Public Prosecution charged al-Wefaq's leader, Sheikh Ali Salman, and his deputy with "meeting foreign officials without notifying" the government, after they met with the visiting US Assistant Secretary of State for Democracy, Human Rights and Labor, Tom Malinowski. In late December, the authorities arrested Sheikh Ali Salman on charges including incitement to promote the change of the political system by force, threats and other illegal means.

DEPRIVATION OF NATIONALITY

In July, the King decreed amendments to the 1963 Nationality Law giving the courts new powers to strip Bahrainis of their nationality, including if they are convicted of terrorism offences. The law also allowed the authorities to revoke the nationality of people who live abroad continuously for more than five years without informing the Ministry of the Interior. Twenty-one people had their nationalities revoked by the courts in 2014. In August, the High Criminal Court revoked the citizenship of nine Bahraini men after it convicted them on terrorism-related charges. They also received prison sentences of up to 15 years after the court convicted them partly on the basis of "confessions" that some defendants alleged had been obtained through torture. In October, a court sentenced to deportation several people whose Bahraini nationality was arbitrarily revoked in 2012. The court considered that they had remained in the country illegally after their nationality was revoked. Their appeal was set for April 2015.

TORTURE AND OTHER ILL-TREATMENT

Torture continued to be reported despite the establishment of a number of official bodies to investigate allegations of torture and other ill-treatment in custody. In some instances, detainees complained that police or other security officials violently assaulted them during arrests and house searches, or while they were being transported to police stations or prisons in police vehicles, and during interrogation by Criminal Investigations Directorate officers, when they were held without access to their lawyers and families for several days. Methods of torture reported included severe beating, punching, electric shocks, suspension by the limbs, rape and threats of rape, and deliberate exposure to extreme cold.

Mohamed 'Ali al-'Oraibi alleged that security officials tortured him over five days following his arrest on 2 February at Manama International Airport when he arrived from abroad. He said officials kept him naked while they interrogated him, subjected him to electric shocks on his genitals, suspended him by his limbs and beat him with a stick, and sexually assaulted him. He was released on 17 April, pending further investigations. He complained to the authorities but no investigation into his alleged torture was known to have been conducted.

EXCESSIVE USE OF FORCE

In March a royal decree (Decree 24 of 2014) was issued regulating the use of force and firearms.

The security forces regularly used excessive force to disperse opposition protests. Among other methods, they fired shotguns and tear gas at protesters, causing injuries and at least two deaths.

Sayed Mahmoud Sayed Mohsen, aged 14, died on 21 May after security forces fired tear gas and shotguns at protesters participating in a funeral procession on the island of Sitra. His family said he had shotgun pellets in his chest suggesting that he had been shot at close range. The Ministry of the Interior announced an investigation but had not disclosed its outcome by the end of the year.

IMPUNITY

The number of investigations into torture and other ill-treatment of detainees remained low and the authorities continued to detain some of those that the Bahrain Independent Commission of Inquiry said had been tortured in 2011. In practice, despite a few

prosecutions of low-ranking officers, the security forces operated with a large degree of impunity amid continuing reports of torture of detainees and the use of excessive force against protesters. The authorities prosecuted eight police officers in connection with the killing of one person and the death in custody of another. One officer, charged with assault, was acquitted; the others remained on trial at the end of the year. In the two years since trials of members of the security forces began, a total of 15 security officers were acquitted of torturing or killing protesters and six were sentenced to between six months' and three years' imprisonment in relation to deaths in custody and killings of protesters.

Two officers accused of causing the death of 16-year-old Hussein al-Jazairi at a protest on 14 February 2013 in al-Daih reportedly remained at liberty and did not stand trial in 2014. They faced charges of assault resulting in death, but were released on bail in May 2013 by the High Criminal Court. Hussain al-Jazairi died after he was hit in the chest by shotgun pellets fired at close range.

In September, the High Court of Justice in England quashed a ruling by the United Kingdom (UK) Crown Prosecution Service that the King of Bahrain's son, Prince Nasser bin Hamad Al Khalifa, had diplomatic immunity in the UK. The High Court ruled that he could face prosecution in the UK for alleged complicity in torturing detainees in 2011 if he entered the UK.

DEATH PENALTY

The death penalty remained in force for murder and other crimes. The courts passed five death sentences during the year, one of which was annulled by the Court of Appeal in December. There were no executions.

Mahir Abbas al-Khabaz was sentenced to death on 19 February after he was convicted of killing a police officer in 2013. The court accepted a "confession" allegedly obtained through torture as evidence against him. An appeal court confirmed his death sentence and he was awaiting a final decision by the Court of Cassation at the end of the year.

BANGLADESH

People's Republic of Bangladesh
Head of state: **Abdul Hamid**
Head of government: **Sheikh Hasina**

Dozens of people were forcibly disappeared. Journalists and human rights defenders continued to be attacked and harassed. Violence against women was a major human rights concern. Police and other security forces committed torture with impunity. Factory workers continued to be at risk owing to hazardous safety standards in the workplace. At least one person was executed with no right to appeal against his death sentence.

BACKGROUND

The government of Prime Minister Sheikh Hasina continued in office after her party, the Awami League, was declared the winner in the January elections. The elections were boycotted by the opposition party, the Bangladesh Nationalist Party, and its allies. More than 100 people were killed during opposition protests against elections, some after police opened fire on demonstrators who were often violent. None of these deaths were believed to have been investigated. Supporters of opposition parties reportedly attacked bus commuters with petrol bombs, killing at least nine people and injuring many others.

Verdicts by the International Crimes Tribunal, a Bangladeshi court set up in 2009 to try crimes committed during the 1971 Bangladesh independence war, were delivered amid a highly polarized political atmosphere. Supporters of these trials demanded death sentences for those on trial

regardless of the strength of the evidence presented against them.

ENFORCED DISAPPEARANCES

The exact number of people who were forcibly disappeared was not known; some estimates suggested over 80. Of the documented cases of 20 people subjected to enforced disappearance between 2012 and 2014, nine people were subsequently found dead. Six had returned to their families after periods of captivity lasting from weeks to months, with no news of their whereabouts until their release. There was no news about the circumstances of the other five.

Following the enforced disappearance and subsequent killing of seven people in Narayanganj in April, three officers of the Rapid Action Battalion (RAB) were detained and investigated for their alleged involvement in abductions and killings; this rose to at least 17 RAB officers by the end of the year. This was the first such action since the formation of the battalion in 2004. Amnesty International welcomed the investigation as a move towards holding law enforcement officials accountable for alleged human rights violations. However, concerns continued that the government might drop the cases if public pressure to bring them to justice lessened. Apart from this case, there were no clear indications of a thorough investigation into other incidents such as the unexplained abduction and killing of Abraham Linkon in February.[1]

FREEDOM OF EXPRESSION

The government's use of Section 57 of the Information and Communication Technology (ICT) Act severely restricted the right to freedom of expression. Under this section, those convicted of violating the Act could be sentenced to a maximum of 10 years in prison if the charges were brought against them before 6 October 2013; at that time, an amendment not only increased the maximum punishment to 14 years in prison but also imposed a minimum punishment of seven years.

Section 57 of the ICT Act criminalized a wide array of peaceful actions such as criticizing Islamic religious views in a newspaper article or reporting on human rights violations. At least four bloggers, two Facebook users and two officials of a human rights organization were charged under Section 57 of the ICT Act during 2013-2014. They included bloggers Asif Mohiuddin, Subrata Adhikari Shuvo, Mashiur Rahman Biplob and Rasel Parvez; and human rights defenders Adilur Rahman Khan and Nasiruddin Elan.

More than a dozen media workers, including journalists, said that they had been threatened by security agencies for criticizing the authorities. The threats were usually in phone calls directly to the journalists, or via messages to their editors. Many journalists and talk show participants said they exercised self-censorship as a result.

Freedom of expression was also threatened by religious groups. In at least 10 instances, these groups were reported to have spread rumours that a certain individual had used social media to insult Islam, or had engaged in allegedly anti-Islamic activity in the workplace. At least five people were subsequently attacked; two were killed and others sustained serious injuries. The two killed were Ahmed Rajib[2] and a Rajshahi University teacher, AKM Shafiul Islam, who died of stab wounds in November 2014, allegedly perpetrated by members of a group who denounced his opposition to female students wearing *burqa* in his class as "un-Islamic".

VIOLENCE AGAINST WOMEN AND GIRLS

Violence against women remained a major human rights concern. A women's rights organization, Bangladesh Mahila Parishad, said its analysis of media reports showed that at least 423 women and girls were subjected to various forms of violence in October 2014 alone. The organization said that more than 100 of those women were raped, of whom 11 were then killed. More than 40 were subjected to physical violence because their families could not provide the dowry demanded by the husband or his family, 16 of whom died from their injuries. Women and girls were also subjected to domestic violence, acid attacks and trafficking.

TORTURE AND OTHER ILL-TREATMENT

Torture and other ill-treatment was widespread and committed with impunity. Police routinely tortured detainees in their custody. Methods included beating, suspension from the ceiling, electric shocks to the genitals and, in some cases, shooting detainees' legs. At least nine people died in police custody between January and July 2014, allegedly as a result of torture.

WORKERS' RIGHTS

Safety standards in factories and other workplaces were dangerously low. At least 1,130 garment workers were killed and at least 2,000 more injured when Rana Plaza, a nine-storey building that housed five garment factories, collapsed on 24 April 2013. It later emerged that managers had ordered workers to go into the building that day despite it having been closed on the previous day after cracks had appeared in the walls. A similar incident had occurred in 2012, when at least 112 workers died in a fire at the Tazreen Fashions factory in Dhaka after managers stopped them from escaping, saying it was a false alarm.

Initiatives to provide compensation to the victims of workplace disasters involving the government, global brands and the ILO proved insufficient, and survivors continued to struggle to support themselves and their families.

DEATH PENALTY

Courts continued to impose death sentences. Eleven were imposed by the International Crimes Tribunal. One death sentence was imposed directly by the Supreme Court after the government appealed against the defendant's life sentence by the Tribunal. He was executed in December 2013. Prisoners whose death sentences were upheld on appeal were at imminent risk of execution.

1. Bangladesh: Stop them, now! Enforced disappearances, torture and restrictions on freedom of expression (ASA 13/005/2014)
www.amnesty.org/en/documents/asa13/005/2014/en/
2. Bangladesh: Attacks on journalists rise with tension around war crimes tribunal (PRE 01/085/2013)
www.amnesty.org/en/articles/news/2013/02/bangladesh/

BELARUS

Republic of Belarus
Head of state: **Alyaksandr Lukashenka**
Head of government: **Mikhail Myasnikovich**

Belarus remained the only country in Europe to carry out executions. Opposition politicians and human rights activists were detained for legitimate activities. The right to freedom of expression was severely restricted and journalists faced harassment. Severe restrictions on freedom of assembly remained in place. NGOs continued to be arbitrarily denied registration.

DEATH PENALTY

Following 24 months in which there were no executions, at least three men were executed in secrecy. Pavel Selyun and Ryhor Yuzepchuk, both sentenced to death in 2013, were executed in April and Alyaksandr Haryunou was executed in November. Judicial appeals and appeals sent to the President asking for clemency were rejected. In all cases, the UN Human Rights Committee requested that the sentences not be carried out until it had considered the respective communications; the Belarusian authorities proceeded with the executions regardless, in violation of their obligations under the International Covenant on Civil and Political Rights (ICCPR). One other man, Eduard Lykau, was a death row prisoner at the end of the year.

In October, the UN Human Rights Committee ruled that the execution of Vasily Yuzepchuk in 2010 constituted a violation of his right to life under Article 6 of the ICCPR. It was the third such ruling by the Committee against Belarus. The Committee also found that he had been subjected to torture in order to extract a confession, that his right to a fair trial had been violated and that his trial had failed to meet the necessary criteria for independence and impartiality.

FREEDOM OF EXPRESSION – MEDIA

Freedom of expression was severely restricted. The media remained largely under state control and was used to smear political opponents. Independent media outlets were harassed, and bloggers, online activists and journalists were subjected to administrative and criminal prosecution. State-run distribution outlets refused to disseminate independent periodicals and internet activity remained closely monitored and controlled.

In April, the authorities started using Article 22.9 of the Administrative Code ("unlawful creation and dissemination of mass media produce") to prosecute freelance journalists writing for media outlets based outside Belarus, claiming that they required formal accreditation as foreign journalists with the Ministry of Foreign Affairs.

On 25 September, Maryna Malchanava was fined 4,800,000 roubles (US$450) by a court in Babruisk after an interview she had recorded locally was broadcast by Poland-based satellite TV channel, Belsat. At least three other Belarusian journalists were fined similar amounts under Article 22.9 and several others received police warnings or had administrative proceedings opened against them.

FREEDOM OF ASSEMBLY

The Law on Mass Events remained unchanged, effectively prohibiting street protests including by a single individual despite continuing calls from UN human rights mechanisms for Belarus to review its restrictive legislation on public assemblies and to decriminalize the organization of public events without official permission. Peaceful protesters were repeatedly arrested and sentenced to short periods of detention.

The annual rally to mark the anniversary of the Chernobyl disaster took place in April. According to civil society representatives, 16 participants were arbitrarily detained in connection with the event. They included Yury Rubtsou, an activist from Homel, who was detained for wearing a T-shirt with the slogan "Lukashenka, leave!" and accused of "failing to obey police orders" and "swearing". He was sentenced to 25 days' administrative detention in a trial in which he appeared topless after police had confiscated his T-shirt. In August a criminal case was opened against him, purportedly for insulting the judge during his earlier court appearance, and in October he was sentenced in a closed court hearing to two years and six months' imprisonment in an open regime prison (reduced by a year under an amnesty law). His appeal was pending at the end of the year.

In October a local activist and newspaper distributor, Andrei Kasheuski, was sentenced to 15 days' administrative detention on charges which included holding an "unauthorized mass event" and wearing a T-shirt with the slogan "Freedom to Political Prisoners" with a list of names on the back.

PRISONERS OF CONSCIENCE

In the lead-up to the Ice Hockey World Championship on 9-25 May, 16 civil society activists were arrested and sentenced to between five and 25 days' administrative detention. Eight were arbitrarily arrested during or immediately after they attended a peaceful march commemorating the Chernobyl nuclear disaster. They were charged with "petty hooliganism" and "disobeying police orders". Eight others, all known for their political activism, were detained in the days before the march under similar charges. They included former prisoner of conscience Zmitser Dashkevich, who had ended a three-year prison term in August 2013. Arrested outside his home on 24 April, Dashkevich was sentenced to 25 days' administrative detention for "disobeying police orders" and "violating restrictions imposed on him following his release from prison". His detention lasted almost the entire period of the championship.

Long-term prisoner of conscience and former presidential candidate Mikalai Statkevich was awaiting transfer to a penal colony, scheduled for January 2015, to complete his six-year sentence for participating in post-election demonstrations. Originally sentenced in 2011, he was transferred to a strict regime prison in January 2012.

Eduard Lobau, an activist and member of youth organization Malady Front, was released in December having completed a four-year sentence for alleged random attacks on pedestrians.

On 21 June, the Chair of the Belarusian Human Rights Centre "Vyasna" and Vice-President of the International Federation for Human Rights, Ales Bialiatski, was released under a prison amnesty. He had served almost three years of a four-and-a-half-year sentence on charges of tax evasion.

FREEDOM OF ASSOCIATION

The authorities continued to restrict arbitrarily the right to freedom of association.

Article 193.1 of the Criminal Code, which criminalizes activities by unregistered organizations, continued to be used to obstruct the legitimate activities of civil society organizations in Belarus.

In February, Minsk Central District Court rejected the complaint by Valyantsin Stefanovich, Deputy Chairman of the NGO

Human Rights Centre "Vyasna", against the blocking of the NGO's website, with no right of appeal. The NGO's registration applications had been repeatedly rejected. In 2011 the Prosecutor General's Office restricted access to the website under Article 193.1.

In November, the authorities nullified the residence permit of Russian citizen and human rights defender Elena Tonkacheva who was given one month to leave the country. Her appeal was pending at the end the year. The permit was due to expire in 2017. Elena Tonkacheva is head of the human rights organization Centre for Legal Transformation and has been living in Belarus for 30 years. The authorities claimed that the decision was linked to her violating public traffic regulations by driving over the speed limit. It was widely believed that she had been targeted for her legitimate human rights activities.

BELGIUM

Kingdom of Belgium
Head of state: **King Philippe**
Head of government: **Charles Michel (replaced Elio Di Rupo in October)**

Detention conditions remained poor and offenders with mental health issues continued to be detained in inadequate structures with limited access to appropriate health services. In October, the newly appointed government committed to creating a National Human Rights Institution. Transgender people could not obtain legal gender recognition without complying with compulsory medical treatment such as sterilization.

PRISON CONDITIONS

Overcrowding continued to have a detrimental impact on detention conditions. In March, according to official statistics, the inmate population exceeded the prisons' maximum capacity by more than 22%. In January, the UN Committee against Torture raised concerns about poor prison conditions and recommended greater use of non-custodial measures.

The Committee also highlighted that offenders with mental health issues continued to be detained in psychiatric wards within regular prisons with very limited access to adequate health care. In January, the European Court of Human Rights found in *Lankester v. Belgium* that the detention of an offender in the psychiatric ward of a regular prison constituted degrading treatment.

DEATHS IN CUSTODY

In 2013, an investigation was launched into the death of Jonathan Jacob, who died in 2010 after being physically assaulted by police while in custody. The results of the investigation and the decision regarding its follow-up, due in October 2014, were still pending at the end of the year.

DISCRIMINATION

In March, the UN Committee on the Elimination of Racial Discrimination raised concerns about allegations of racially motivated violence and ill-treatment by police against migrants, and recommended the strengthening of police complaints mechanisms.

In February, the European Committee against Racism and Intolerance highlighted that Muslims, and especially Muslim women wearing headscarves, continued to be discriminated against in access to employment and goods and services.

In 2013, the Board of Education of the Flemish Community (GO!) confirmed the general ban on religious symbols and dress in all its schools in the Flemish-speaking part of the country. On 14 October 2014, the Council of State found that the general ban violated the right to freedom of religion of a Sikh pupil who was forbidden to wear the turban in a secondary school.

RIGHTS OF LESBIAN, GAY, BISEXUAL, TRANSGENDER AND INTERSEX PEOPLE

In January 2013, the government adopted a comprehensive roadmap to combat discrimination on grounds of sexual orientation and gender identity. In May, a new law prohibiting discrimination on grounds of gender identity and expression was introduced.

While the roadmap included the commitment to amend the 2007 law on legal recognition of gender, plans regarding its amendments remained unclear at the end of the year. Transgender people were required to comply with criteria that violated their human rights in order to obtain legal recognition of their gender. These included psychiatric diagnosis and sterilization, as well as other compulsory medical treatments.

TORTURE AND OTHER ILL-TREATMENT

In January the Committee against Torture expressed concerns about the planned extradition and *refoulement* of third-country nationals to countries that provided diplomatic assurances. The Committee reiterated that such assurances did not mitigate the risk of torture or other ill-treatment.

In September, the European Court of Human Rights found that the extradition of Nizar Trabelsi, a Tunisian national, to the USA in October 2013 amounted to a violation of Articles 3 and 34 of the European Convention on Human Rights. Belgian authorities had ignored the interim measure issued by the Court on the extradition.

VIOLENCE AGAINST WOMEN AND GIRLS

In February 2014, a country-wide survey undertaken by Amnesty International found that a quarter of women in Belgium had allegedly experienced sexual violence at the hands of their partners and that 13% had been raped by someone other than their partners. A coordinated and comprehensive approach to combat these forms of violence was still lacking at the end of the year.

BENIN

Republic of Benin
Head of state and government: **Thomas Boni Yayi**

Municipal elections initially planned for April 2013 had not been held by the end of 2014. In June 2013, the government resubmitted a bill for the revision of the Constitution. In November 2014 the Constitutional Court ruled against any revision of the Constitution that could prolong the term of office of the President. The Constitutional Court had previously ruled in 2011 that parts of the Constitution relating to the Presidential term could not be submitted to referendum.

POLITICAL PRISONERS

In May, President Boni Yayi pardoned Patrice Talon and his associate Olivier Bocco, both living in France, as well as six other people, including one woman, who had been detained in Benin since 2012 and 2013. In the first case, Patrice Talon, Olivier Bocco and four others were accused of attempting to poison the President in October 2012. In the second case, two men were accused of crimes against the security of the state following a suspected coup attempt in May 2013.

FREEDOMS OF EXPRESSION AND ASSEMBLY

A demonstration against police violence was held in March in Cotonou in response to the break-up by security forces of a peaceful demonstration by union members in December 2013, in which over 20 people, including six women, were injured.

In June, the Court of First Instance in Cotonou sentenced John Akintola, publishing director of *L'Indépendant* newspaper, to a three-year suspended prison term and a fine for "insulting the Head of State" following the publication of an article concerning possible illicit financing of trips abroad. The author of the article, Prudence Tessi, was sentenced to two months' imprisonment and the newspaper was suspended for three months.

DEATH PENALTY

Thirteen people remained under sentence of death despite Benin's ratification in 2012 of the Second Optional Protocol to the International Covenant on Civil and Political Rights, aiming at the abolition of the death penalty.

BOLIVIA

Plurinational State of Bolivia
Head of state and government: **Evo Morales Ayma**

Victims of human rights violations committed during past military regimes continued to be denied truth, justice and full reparation. Indigenous Peoples' rights to consultation and to free, prior and informed consent and equal access to sexual and reproductive rights remained unfulfilled.

BACKGROUND

In October, President Evo Morales was re-elected for a third term. More than 50% of parliamentary candidates were women. This was the result of the first time implementation of the 2010 Electoral Law gender equality clause.

In October, Bolivia accepted most of the recommendations of the UN Universal Periodic Review process, including to investigate past human rights violations and ensure a full and effective reparation,

to review legislation that criminalizes abortion and to improve prison conditions. Concerns around these same issues had been highlighted by the UN Human Rights Committee in October 2013[1] and the UN Committee against Torture in May 2013.

IMPUNITY AND THE JUSTICE SYSTEM

Five decades after the military and authoritarian regime (1964–1982), no progress in providing justice to victims of political violence or measures to implement a mechanism to unveil the truth of the human rights violations committed during that period was made.[2] The authorities ignored national and international bodies' concerns about the lack of transparency and unfairness of the reparation process that ended in 2012 and in which just over a quarter of applicants qualified as beneficiaries.

In February 2014, a campsite of the victims' organization, Platform of Social Activists against Impunity, for Justice and Historical Memory of the Bolivian People, outside the Ministry of Justice was set on fire[3] and files and documents were destroyed. Preliminary investigations indicated that the fire was caused by an electrical fault. However, the organization complained that it was an intentional attack. Criminal investigations were ongoing at the end of the year. Investigations into an attack against a member of the same victims' group in February 2013 were reported[4] as being delayed.

In July, Bolivia's second request to extradite former President Gonzalo Sánchez de Lozada to Bolivia was filed in the USA. He faced charges in connection with the "Black October" case, when 67 people were killed and more than 400 injured during protests in El Alto, near La Paz, in late 2003. A previous extradition request was rejected in 2012. In May 2014, a Federal Judge in the USA had allowed a civil lawsuit against the former President and his Minister of Defence for their responsibility in the events.

Trial proceedings connected to the 2008 Pando massacre in which 19 people, mostly peasant farmers, were killed and 53 others injured, continued but were subject to delays.

Hearings in the case of 39 people accused of involvement in an alleged plot in 2009 to kill President Evo Morales continued. By the end of the year, there had been no investigations into allegations of lack of due process or into the killings of three men in 2009 in connection with the case. In March, the Prosecutor who resigned after denouncing political interference in the case and who was subsequently charged with involvement in extortion, requested political asylum in Brazil. In August, the UN Working Group on Arbitrary Detention stated that the detention of one of the suspects in the case was arbitrary and recommended his immediate release and reparation.

In June, criminal proceedings against three judges of the Constitutional Court were initiated for breach of duty, among other crimes, before the Congress. The judges were suspended.

VIOLENCE AGAINST WOMEN AND GIRLS

According to a 2014 study by the Panamerican Health Organization, Bolivia has the highest rate of violence against women by an intimate partner and the second highest rate of sexual violence in the region. In October, a norm that regulates the budget and implementation of the 2013 Law 348 to guarantee women's rights to a life free of violence was promulgated.

SEXUAL AND REPRODUCTIVE RIGHTS

Although in February the Plurinational Constitutional Court decided that the request for judicial authorization for an abortion, as requested by article 266 of the Criminal Code, was unconstitutional, the implementation of the decision was still pending.

A 2012 bill on sexual and reproductive rights guaranteeing the right to receive information about sexual and reproductive health services to prevent unplanned or unwanted pregnancies, and the right to sexual education in schools, among other provisions, was still under discussion in the Congress.

INDIGENOUS PEOPLES' RIGHTS

In November, 14 police officials were charged in connection with the excessive use of force in 2011 during a peaceful march against the construction of a road in the Isiboro-Sécure Indigenous Territory and National Park. The Prosecutor's office dismissed the involvement of high rank civil authorities, as claimed by victims. Plans to build the road remained on hold following a controversial consultation with the affected Indigenous communities in 2012.

A new Mining Law passed in May excluded consultation with Indigenous Peoples for prospecting and exploration of mining activities and did not recognize the principle of free, prior and informed consent in relation to projects that are going to have an impact on them. A draft law on Free, Prior and Informed Consultation was finalized.

HUMAN RIGHTS DEFENDERS

Concerns remained over the requirements specified by the 2013 law to grant legal identity to NGOs. Under this regulation, organizations have to specify their "contribution to the economic and social development" of the state. In 2013 the UN Human Rights Committee recommended that Bolivia eliminate these requirements because they placed restrictions on the organizations' ability to operate freely, independently and effectively.

In January, members of the Consejo Nacional de Ayllus y Markas del Qullasuyu (CONAMAQ), who were holding a vigil outside the organization's office in La Paz, were violently evicted by other Indigenous Peoples' groups who adjudicated themselves the leadership of CONAMAQ. There were complaints that the police did not intervene to stop the violent eviction.

In March, the Danish NGO IBIS Dinamarca closed most of its projects in Bolivia after the government announced its expulsion from the country in December 2013, arguing that they were interfering in political issues and had contributed to divisions within the Indigenous movement.

PRISON CONDITIONS

A lack of security and poor prison conditions remained a concern. Delays in concluding trials within a reasonable time, the excessive use of pre-trial detention and the limited use of alternatives to detention, all contributed to prison overcrowding. Presidential decrees enacted in 2013 and 2014 granting pardons and amnesties, intended to deal with over-population in prisons, were not having the expected outcome.

In August, the Ombudsman reported little progress in the investigation into the deaths of more than 30 inmates in Palmasola prison, Santa Cruz, in August 2013.[5]

In September, four inmates died and a dozen were injured in clashes between inmates in El Abra prison, Cochabamba. Investigations were ongoing at the end of the year.

1. Bolivia: Submission to the United Nations Human Rights Committee (AMR 18/005/2013)
   www.amnesty.org/en/library/info/AMR18/005/2013/en
2. Bolivia: "No me borren de la historia": Verdad, justicia y reparación en Bolivia (1964-1982) (AMR 18/002/2014)
   www.amnesty.org/es/library/info/AMR18/002/2014/es
3. Bolivia: Victims of military regimes' campsite burnt (AMR 18/001/2014)
   www.amnesty.org/en/library/info/AMR18/001/2014/en
4. Bolivia: Protester attacked, police take no notice (AMR 18/001/2013)
   www.amnesty.org/en/library/info/AMR18/001/2013/en
5. Bolivia: Las autoridades bolivianas deben investigar completamente la tragedia en la cárcel de Palmasola (AMR 18/004/2013)
   www.amnesty.org/es/library/info/AMR18/004/2013/es

BOSNIA AND HERZEGOVINA

Bosnia and Herzegovina
Head of state: **Rotating presidency - Bakir Izetbegović, Dragan Čović, Mladen Ivanić**
Head of government: **Vjekoslav Bevanda (Incumbent)**

High levels of unemployment and dissatisfaction with government institutions prompted popular protests that spread throughout Bosnia and Herzegovina (BiH) and were accompanied by clashes between demonstrators and the police. The prosecution of crimes under international law continued before domestic courts, but progress remained slow and impunity persisted. Many civilian victims of war were still denied access to justice and reparation.

TORTURE AND OTHER ILL-TREATMENT

In February, popular protests, initially fuelled by the large-scale dismissal of the workforce of industrial companies in the Tuzla Canton, spread across the country, resulting in clashes between demonstrators and the police. Law enforcement officials subjected at least 12 detainees, some of them minors, to ill-treatment while in detention.

FREEDOM OF EXPRESSION – JOURNALISTS

At least one journalist was beaten by police officers while recording the February protests. Intimidation of journalists by state officials persisted throughout the year, including beatings, death threats and a police raid on a newsroom. The authorities frequently failed to open investigations into complaints.

DISCRIMINATION

The 2009 judgment of the European Court of Human Rights in the case of *Sejdić-Finci v. BiH,* which found the power-sharing arrangements set out in the Constitution to be discriminatory, remained unimplemented. Under the arrangements, citizens such as Jews and Roma who do not declare themselves as belonging to one of the three constituent peoples of the country (Bosniaks, Serbs and Croats) are excluded from running for legislative and executive office. The discriminatory nature of these arrangements was confirmed again in July when the European Court ruled in favour of the plaintiff in the *Zornić v. BiH* case.

A number of schools in the Federation continued to operate under the so-called "two schools under one roof" arrangement, resulting in discrimination and segregation based on ethnicity. Bosniak and Croat pupils attended classes in the same building while being physically separated and studying different curricula.

Roma continued to face widespread and systematic discrimination in accessing their basic rights, including to education, work and health care, entrenching the cycle of poverty and marginalization. Many Roma were particularly affected by the poor response of the authorities to the severe flooding in May.

The number of people at risk of statelessness, the majority of whom were Roma, reached a peak of 792 by April but had significantly decreased by the end of the year. However, a state-level law on free legal aid that would, among other provisions, have assisted Roma with registering in the national public registry and accessing public services, was still lacking.

Lesbian, gay, bisexual, transgender and intersex (LGBTI) people continued to face widespread discrimination. In February, three people were injured as a group of 12-14 masked men interrupted the LGBTI festival "Merlinka" staged at a cinema in Sarajevo. The men stormed the premises, shouted homophobic threats and physically attacked and injured the three festival participants. Following their participation in the Belgrade Pride in September, members of an LGBTI NGO based in Banja Luka received death threats. Although the Criminal Code of Republika Srpska contained provisions on hate crime, there was no investigation into the threats against the activists.

CRIMES UNDER INTERNATIONAL LAW

Proceedings continued at the International Criminal Tribunal for the former Yugoslavia against former Bosnian Serb leader Radovan Karadžić and former General Ratko Mladić, for genocide, crimes against humanity and violations of the laws or customs of war, including at Srebrenica. In October, the hearing in the Karadžić case ended.

The War Crimes Chamber of the State Court of BiH made slow progress in the prosecution of crimes under international law, and was undermined by repeated criticism by high-ranking politicians.

The Criminal Code continued to fall short of international standards relating to the prosecution of war crimes of sexual violence. Entity courts continued to apply the Criminal Code of the Socialist Federal Republic of Yugoslavia; impunity prevailed in the absence of a definition of crimes against humanity, command responsibility, and crimes of sexual violence. Impunity for war crimes of sexual violence remained rampant; between 2005 and the end of 2014 less than 100 cases had come to court. The estimated number of victims of rape during the war ranged between 20,000 and 50,000.

In April a Law on Witness Protection was adopted, but it applied only to witnesses testifying before the State Court of BiH. Adequate witness support and protection measures were absent at entity courts, despite the fact that half of all pending war crimes cases were due to be heard at this level.

Legislation that would enable effective reparation, including a comprehensive programme for victims of crimes under international law, and free legal aid services to victims of torture and civilian victims of war, had yet to be put in place. The harmonization of the entity laws regulating the rights of civilian victims of war was still not completed.

By the end of the year, the remains of 435 people had been exhumed at a mass grave in Tomašica village. The victims had disappeared and were subsequently killed by Bosnian Serb forces in the Prijedor area in 1992. In August, BiH signed a regional declaration on missing persons, and committed to establishing the fate and whereabouts of those 7,800 still missing. The Law on Missing Persons had not been implemented at the end of the year, leaving the families of the missing with no access to reparation.

BRAZIL

Federative Republic of Brazil
Head of state and government: **President Dilma Rousseff**

Serious human rights violations continued to be reported, including killings by police and the torture and other ill-treatment of detainees. Young and Black residents of *favelas* (shanty towns), rural workers and Indigenous Peoples were at particular risk of human rights violations. Protests that swept the country, particularly around the football World Cup, were often suppressed using excessive and unnecessary force by the security forces. Arbitrary detentions and attempts to criminalize peaceful protesters were reported in various parts of the country. Although legislation allowing same-sex marriage was approved, lesbian, gay, bisexual, transgender and intersex (LGBTI) people continued to face discrimination and attacks. Brazil continued to play a significant role on the international stage on issues such as privacy, the internet and discrimination based on sexual orientation and gender identity. Some progress was made in addressing impunity for past grave human rights violations under the dictatorship (1964-1985).

BACKGROUND

Brazil continued serving its third mandate in the UN Human Rights Council, where it was a key supporter of resolutions against discrimination based on sexual orientation and gender identity. At the General Assembly, the Brazilian and German governments presented a resolution on privacy in the internet age, which was approved in December 2013. In April 2014, Brazil approved its Civil Framework for the Internet, ensuring the neutrality of the web and setting out rules to protect freedom of expression and privacy.

HUMAN RIGHTS VIOLATIONS IN THE CONTEXT OF SOCIAL PROTESTS

In 2014, thousands of protesters took to the streets in the run-up to and during the football World Cup in June and July. The protests echoed huge demonstrations that had taken place the previous year to express discontent over a number of issues including increased public transport costs, high spending on major international sports events and insufficient investment in public services. The police frequently responded to protests with violence. Hundreds of people were rounded up and arbitrarily detained, some under laws targeting organized crime, even though there was no indication that those detained were involved in criminal activity.[1]

In April, ahead of the World Cup, soldiers from the Army and Marines were deployed to the Maré complex in Rio de Janeiro. Initially, it was stated that they would remain until the end of July, but the authorities subsequently declared that the troops would remain there indefinitely. This raised serious concerns given the weak accountability mechanisms for human rights abuses during military operations.

By the end of the year, the only person convicted of offences related to violence during the protests was Rafael Braga Vieira, a Black homeless man. Although he was not taking part in a demonstration, he was arrested for "carrying explosives without authorization" and sentenced to five years in prison. The forensic report concluded that the chemicals in his possession – cleaning fluids – could not have been used to create explosives, but the court disregarded the finding.

Excessive use of force

Military Police often used excessive and unnecessary force to disperse protesters.[2]

In Rio de Janeiro, military police used tear gas to disperse peaceful protesters on many occasions, including in confined spaces such as the Pinheiro Machado Health Centre in July 2013 and subway stations in June and September 2013 and June 2014.

Freedom of expression and association – journalists

According to the Brazilian Association of Investigative Journalism, at least 18 journalists were assaulted while working during the World Cup in cities including São Paulo, Porto Alegre, Rio de Janeiro, Belo Horizonte and Fortaleza. In Rio de Janeiro, on 13 July, the day of the World Cup final, at least 15 journalists were assaulted by police officers while covering a demonstration. Some had their equipment broken. In February, Santiago (Ilídio) Andrade, a cameraman, died after being hit by fireworks being used by protesters. The police arrested two men in connection with the killing. They were charged with intentional homicide and were awaiting trial at the end of the year.

PUBLIC SECURITY

Public security remained the context for widespread human rights violations.

According to official statistics, 424 people were killed by police in the state of Rio de Janeiro during security operations in 2013. The first six months of 2014 showed an increase in the number of such deaths, with 285 people being killed by police, 37% more than during the same period in 2013.

Claudia Silva Ferreira was shot and wounded by police officers in a shoot-out in the Morro da Congonha favela in March. While she was being taken to the hospital by police in the boot of their car, she fell out and was dragged along the ground for 350m. The incident was recorded and broadcast in the Brazilian media. At the end of the year, six police officers were under investigation, but remained at liberty.

Douglas Rafael da Silva Pereira, a dancer, was found dead in April 2014 following a police operation in the Pavão-Pavãozinho *favela*. The death sparked protests during which Edilson Silva dos Santos was shot dead by police. By the end of the year, no one had been charged in connection with the deaths.

In November, at least 10 people were killed, allegedly by off-duty military police officers, in the city of Belém in the state of Pará. Residents of the neighbourhood told Amnesty International that military police vehicles closed off streets prior to the killings and that people in unidentified cars and on motorcycles threatened and attacked residents.[3] There were indications that the killings may have been a reprisal for the killing of a policeman.

Ten police officers, including the former commander of a battalion, were tried between December 2012 and April 2014 and convicted in connection with the murder of Judge Patrícia Acioli in August 2011. She had been responsible for sentencing 60 officers convicted of involvement in organized crime.

PRISON CONDITIONS

Severe overcrowding, degrading conditions, torture and violence remained endemic in Brazil's prisons. Several cases regarding prison conditions were submitted to the Inter-American Commission on Human Rights and Inter-American Court of Human Rights in recent years and conditions remained a serious concern.

In 2013, 60 detainees were murdered in the prison of Pedrinhas, in the state of Maranhão. More than 18 were killed in the prison between January and October 2014. Videos of beheadings were broadcast in the media. An investigation into the incident was continuing at the end of the year.

From April 2013 to April 2014 the courts sentenced 75 police officers for the killing of 111 prisoners in the 1992 Carandiru prison riots. The officers lodged appeals and remained on active service at the end of the year. The commander of the police operation had been convicted in 2001, although this was overturned; he was murdered by his girlfriend in 2006. The prison governor and the Minister of Public Security at the time of the riots were not charged in connection with the case.

TORTURE AND OTHER ILL-TREATMENT

There were several reports of torture and other ill-treatment at the time of arrest and during interrogation and detention in police stations.

In July 2013, Amarildo de Souza, a bricklayer, was detained by the police as he was returning home in Rocinha, Rio de Janeiro. He died under torture in the custody of the local Pacification Police Unit. The police denied that Amarildo de Souza was ever in custody despite video footage showing that he had been detained. Twenty-five police officers were charged in connection with the case, including the commander of the unit, and six of them were detained awaiting trial at the end of 2014.

The National System to Fight and Prevent Torture, created by law in 2013, had yet to be fully established by the end of 2014. Although the System did not fully meet international standards in terms of its independence, it represented an important step forward in fulfilling the country's obligations under the Optional Protocol to the UN Convention against Torture, which Brazil had ratified in 2007.

IMPUNITY

The establishment of the National Truth Commission generated widespread public interest in the human rights violations committed under the 1964-1985 dictatorship. This led to the creation of more than 100 truth commissions in states, cities, universities and trade unions. These engaged in investigations into cases such as the enforced disappearance of former congressman Rubens Paiva in 1971. They also highlighted less well-known violations against Indigenous Peoples and rural workers, such as the military attacks (1968-1975) against the Waimiri-Atroari in the Amazon and the torture of peasant farmers during the Araguaia guerrilla conflict (1967-1974).

The Truth Commission published its final report on 10 December recommending that the 1979 Amnesty Law should not be an obstacle to criminal charges being brought against the perpetrators of serious human rights violations. The report also recommended several public security reforms such as the demilitarization of the police. Federal prosecutors trying to bring the perpetrators of these crimes to justice condemned the Amnesty Law as incompatible with international human rights treaties. To date, judges have rejected these arguments. However, at the end of the year, three bills were before Congress which proposed changes to the interpretation of the Amnesty Law so that it would no longer apply to agents of the state charged with crimes against humanity.

HUMAN RIGHTS DEFENDERS

The National Programme for the Protection of Human Rights Defenders continued to face numerous difficulties in fulfilling its mandate, including lack of resources, judicial insecurity, lack of coordination with state officials, and disputes about the scope of the programme and who should benefit from it. The authorities refused to include a woman sex worker known as "Isabel" in the programme. She had lodged a complaint about police violence against herself and her colleagues during their eviction in May 2014 from the building where they lived in Niterói, in the state of Rio de Janeiro. After lodging the complaint, Isabel was kidnapped and beaten by men who showed her photos of her son. Fearing for her safety, she left the area and was still in hiding at the end of the year.

In April 2013, two men were convicted of the murder in 2011 of José Cláudio Ribeiro and Maria do Espírito Santo, rural workers' leaders in the state of Pará who had reported illegal logging. In August 2014, a retrial was ordered of a landowner accused of ordering their assassination; he had been acquitted of involvement in the killings in 2013. However, he evaded arrest and remained at liberty at the end of the year. Maria do Espírito Santo's sister, Laísa Santos Sampaio received death threats because of her human rights work and was part of the National Programme for the Protection of Human Rights Defenders. Although she received some protection, including a police escort, concerns for her safety persisted.

In the state of Rio de Janeiro, the government's failure to guarantee the safety of the Fishermen's Association of Guanabara Bay resulted in the closure of its headquarters. Its president and his wife have not been able to return to their home since November 2012 because of threats to their lives. Other fishermen from AHOMAR, such as Maicon Alexandre, also received death threats.

LAND DISPUTES AND INDIGENOUS PEOPLES' RIGHTS

Indigenous Peoples and *Quilombola* communities (descendants of former slaves) continued to face grave threats to their human rights.

In September 2013, the Guarani-Kaiowá community of Apika'y, in the state of Mato Grosso do Sul, occupied a sugarcane plantation that they claim as their traditional land. A local court ordered them to leave, but they refused to comply. At the end of the year they remained on the land but at risk of eviction. In 2007, the federal government had signed an agreement with public prosecutors to demarcate the community's land until 2010, but the process was never completed.

At the end of the year, a bill was pending in Congress which, if passed, would transfer responsibility for demarcating Indigenous land from the Executive to the Legislature, where the agribusiness lobby was very strong. The new Mining Code proposal also puts traditional communities at risk of having corporate activity on their land without their permission, in breach of international law.

Quilombola communities continued to fight for recognition of their right to land. The slow process of resolving land entitlement claims resulted in conflict and left communities at risk of threats and violence from gunmen and local ranchers. The community of São José de Bruno in the state of Maranhão was under direct threat in October 2014 after a landowner invaded part of their land.

Thirty-four people were killed as a result of conflict over land in 2013, three of them in the state of Maranhão. Between January and October 2014, five people were killed due to conflict over land in the state. Impunity for these crimes continued to feed a cycle of violence.

Those responsible for the killing of *Quilombola* leader Flaviano Pinto Neto in October 2010 had not been brought to justice, despite the fact that a police investigation had identified four suspects.[4]

RIGHTS OF LESBIAN, GAY, BISEXUAL, TRANSGENDER AND INTERSEX PEOPLE

In May 2013 the National Council of Justice approved a resolution authorizing same-sex marriage, following a 2011 ruling by the Supreme Court. However, frequent homophobic statements by political and religious leaders continued. Conservative politicians vetoed attempts by the federal government to distribute human rights education materials in schools to curb discrimination on the grounds of sexual orientation. Homophobic hate crimes were frequent. According to the NGO Bahia Gay Group (Grupo Gay da Bahia), 312 people were killed as a result of homophobic or transphobic hate crimes in 2013.

SEXUAL AND REPRODUCTIVE RIGHTS

Religious groups continued to put pressure on the authorities to criminalize abortion in all circumstances – Brazilian law allows abortion in cases of rape, threat to the life of the woman and anencephalic foetuses. This limited range of possibilities results in many women resorting to clandestine, unsafe abortions. In September 2014, the cases of Jandira dos Santos Cruz and Elisângela Barbosa caused a national outcry. The two women died in Rio de Janeiro following clandestine abortions in clinics. The body of Jandira dos Santos Cruz was hidden from her family and burned by clinic employees.

ARMS TRADE

Brazil signed the Arms Trade Treaty on 4 June 2013, the first day it was open for signature. By the end of 2014, it had yet to ratify the treaty. The Brazilian government did not publish data on arms exports and refused requests under the Freedom of Information Act from researchers and journalists for details of the country's involvement in the arms trade, such as, for example, whether weapons had been exported to countries where mass human rights violations were being committed.

---

1. Brazil: Protests during the World Cup 2014: Final overview: No Foul Play, Brazil! Campaign (AMR 19/008/2014)
   www.amnesty.org/en/library/info/AMR19/008/2014/en
2. Brazil: They use a strategy of fear: Protecting the right to protest in Brazil (AMR 19/005/2014)
   www.amnesty.org/en/library/info/AMR19/005/2014/en
3. Brazil: At least nine killed overnight in north Brazil (AMR 19/013/2014)
   www.amnesty.org/en/library/info/AMR19/013/2014/en
4. Brazil: Killers of community leader must be brought to justice (News story)
   www.amnesty.org/en/news/brazil-killers-community-leader-must-be-brought-justice-2014-10-30

BRUNEI DARUSSALAM

Brunei Darussalam
Head of state and government: **Sultan Hassanal Bolkiah**

Lack of transparency and scarcity of information made independent monitoring of the human rights situation difficult. Amid strong international criticism, the amended Penal Code came into force on 1 May, although it was announced that its implementation would be phased. The new Code, purporting to impose Shari'a law, contained a number of provisions that violate human rights, widening the scope of offences punishable by the death penalty, expanding the imposition of torture and cruel, inhuman or degrading punishment, restricting the rights to freedom of expression and religion or belief, and discriminating against women. Also in May, the country's human rights record was assessed under the UN Universal Periodic Review (UPR) mechanism.

DEATH PENALTY

The new Penal Code[1] imposed death by stoning as a possible punishment for conduct that should not be criminal, such as extramarital sexual relations and consensual sex between people of the same gender, as well as for offences such as theft and rape. It also allowed for the imposition of the death penalty for child offenders and for offences such as mocking the Prophet Muhammad. However, while Brunei Darussalam retained the death penalty in law, it remained abolitionist in practice.

TORTURE AND OTHER ILL-TREATMENT

Brunei Darussalam has not ratified the UN Convention against Torture. The country's new Penal Code significantly expanded the scope of corporal punishments that amount or could amount to torture (including death by stoning – see above).

A wide range of offences including theft were punishable by whipping or amputation. Judicial caning remained a common punishment for crimes including possession of drugs and immigration offences. At least three caning sentences were known to have been carried out in 2014. Under existing law, children could be sentenced to whipping; under the revised Penal Code children could also be sentenced to amputations. The Penal Code also introduced laws discriminating against women, including punishing abortion with public flogging.

FREEDOM OF EXPRESSION

Journalists continued to be censored. In February, the Sultan ordered a halt to criticism of the new Penal Code.

FREEDOM OF RELIGION

The Constitution protects non-Muslims' right to practise their religion, but laws and policies restricted this right for Muslims and non-Muslims alike. The revised Penal Code criminalized exposing Muslim children to the beliefs and practices of any religion other than Islam.

COUNTER-TERROR AND SECURITY

The Internal Security Act (ISA) permitted detention without trial for indefinitely renewable two-year periods, and was used to detain anti-government activists. An Indonesian detained without trial under the ISA since February was initially refused visits by his embassy for two months.

---

1. Brunei Darussalam: Authorities must immediately revoke new Penal Code (ASA 15/001/2014)

   www.amnesty.org/en/library/info/ASA15/001/2014/en

BULGARIA

Republic of Bulgaria
Head of state: **Rosen Plevneliev**
Head of government: **Boyko Borisov (replaced Georgi Bliznashki in November)**

The reception conditions for asylum-seekers entering Bulgaria partially improved but concerns remained over access to Bulgarian territory and the integration of refugees. Prevention and investigation of hate crimes by the authorities was inadequate.

BACKGROUND

In July, the government coalition headed by the Bulgarian Socialist Party resigned following heavy losses in the European Parliament elections. Its year in power had been plagued by protests against government corruption and backroom dealing sparked by the controversial appointment of Delyan Peevski, a prominent media mogul and MP, as head of the Bulgarian Security Agency. New parliamentary elections were set for October 2014, less than 18 months after the previous round, which was also prompted by the resignation of the government. Following the elections, a new government under Prime Minister Boyko Borisov from the GERB party was appointed in November.

REFUGEES AND ASYLUM-SEEKERS

In August 2013, Bulgaria experienced a large increase in the number of refugees, asylum-seekers and migrants entering the country irregularly. By the end of 2013 over 11,000 people, many of them refugees from Syria, had crossed the border, compared to a total of 1,700 in 2012.

The Bulgarian authorities initially struggled to respond adequately. Hundreds of people in need of international protection ended up living for months in substandard conditions without access to asylum procedures. In January 2014, UNHCR, the UN refugee agency, stated that asylum-seekers in Bulgaria faced a real risk of inhuman and degrading treatment due to systemic deficiencies in the Bulgarian asylum and reception system. It called on the EU Member States to suspend transfers of asylum-seekers back to Bulgaria.[1] The reception conditions for new arrivals improved, thanks in large measure to EU and bilateral assistance. In April, UNHCR reviewed the situation in Bulgaria and found that despite progress made by the authorities, serious shortcomings remained. It lifted its call for the general suspension of transfers with the exception of certain groups, especially those with special needs.

The number of refugees and migrants dropped dramatically in 2014, to 3,966 by October as a result of a government policy adopted in November 2013 that aimed to decrease the number of people irregularly entering Bulgaria. A number of NGOs, including Amnesty International, documented violations including unlawful expulsions of people back to Turkey (push-backs) without giving them a chance to seek asylum, which the authorities strenuously denied. An official investigation was initiated only in one such case.

Integration of refugees

Recognized refugees faced problems in accessing education, housing, health care and other public services. In August, the government rejected a plan prepared by the State Agency for Refugees and the Ministry of Labour for the implementation of the National Integration Strategy adopted earlier in the year.

According to the State Agency for Refugees, in September only 98 out of 520 registered refugee children were enrolled in school. This was due to the Schools Act which requires any new pupil to pass an exam in the Bulgarian language and in other subjects. A draft Law on Asylum and Refugees, which was intended to ensure unhindered access to primary education for refugee children, was not adopted due to the fall of the government.

HUMAN RIGHTS DEFENDERS

A prominent human rights NGO, the Bulgarian Helsinki Committee (BHC), faced a tax inspection as well as harassment by far right groups. These were seen as intimidatory since the BHC is known for its criticism of the government's human rights record, in particular the treatment of asylum-seekers and the failure to prevent and address hate crimes. In January, prompted by a request by VMRO-BND, an ultra-nationalist political party, the National Revenue Agency carried out a large-scale audit of the BHC's finances for the period 2007-2012. The audit did not establish any breach.

On 12 September, a far right political party, the Bulgarian National Union, organized a rally under the slogan "Let's ban BHC!" The rally concluded outside the offices of the BHC, where participants verbally abused staff and visitors. They reportedly also called for the banning of all NGOs in Bulgaria. The police officers present at the rally did not intervene to prevent or stop the harassment and verbal assaults. In November, in communication with Amnesty International, the Ministry of Interior denied any harassment or intimidation of BHC staff or visitors during the protest.

TORTURE AND OTHER ILL-TREATMENT

Concerns remained regarding the effectiveness and independence of investigations into allegations of police ill-treatment. Investigations into several allegations of the excessive use of force by police during the protests in the capital, Sofia, in June 2013 were still ongoing by the end of 2014.[2]

HATE CRIMES AGAINST ETHNIC MINORITIES AND MIGRANTS

In the second half of 2013, many violent attacks targeting ethnic and religious minorities, including migrants, refugees and asylum-seekers, were reported by the media and NGOs, exposing shortcomings in the prevention and investigation of such hate crimes.[3] In March, the European Court of Human Rights found in *Abdu v. Bulgaria* that authorities had failed to thoroughly investigate the racist motive associated with the physical assault of a Sudanese national in 2003.

Between July and September, Amnesty International researched 16 cases of alleged hate crimes against individuals and properties. The hate motive was investigated only in one of them.

Legislative gaps regarding hate crimes on other protected grounds, such as sexual orientation, gender identity or disability, persisted. In January, the government proposed a draft new Criminal Code closing some of these gaps, but it had not been adopted by the end of the year.

---

1. Bulgaria: Refugees continue to endure bad conditions (EUR 15/001/2014)
    www.amnesty.org/en/library/info/EUR15/001/2014/en
2. Bulgaria: Investigations into alleged excessive use of force during Sofia protests must be prompt and thorough (EUR 15/001/2013)
    www.amnesty.org/en/library/info/EUR15/001/2013/en
3. Because of who I am: Homophobia, transphobia and hate crimes in Europe (EUR 01/014/2013)
    www.amnesty.org/en/library/info/EUR01/014/2013/en

BURKINA FASO

Burkina Faso
Head of state: **Michel Kafando (replaced Blaise Compaoré in November)**
Head of government: **Yacouba Isaac Zida (replaced Luc Adolphe Tiao in November)**

Concerns remained over the use of torture and other ill-treatment and excessive force by police and other security personnel. High levels of maternal mortality persisted.

BACKGROUND

President Compaoré resigned at the end of October following widespread protests against a bill proposing constitutional amendments that would allow him to run for re-election in 2015. Following the bill's withdrawal, a transitional government led by interim President Michel Kafando was sworn in in November to steer the country towards legislative and presidential elections.

TORTURE AND OTHER ILL-TREATMENT

In October, following a riot at MACO prison in Ouagadougou, at least 11 prisoners were repeatedly beaten and otherwise ill-treated by prison guards and accused of organizing an escape attempt. Two prisoners died following the riot, reportedly as a result of dehydration and lack of ventilation in their cell during a lockdown.

More than 30 prisoners alleged that they had been tortured and otherwise ill-treated at the time of arrest, and while being held in gendarmerie (military police) detention centres and police stations around the country in 2013 and 2014. One detainee described being tortured for a period of 17 days at the central Ouagadougou police station; his hands were handcuffed to his ankles, an iron bar was put underneath his knees and he was suspended in a squatting position between two tables. Other detainees also said they were beaten and forced to sign statements without knowledge of their content.

EXCESSIVE USE OF FORCE

During protests in October and November, security forces used excessive, sometimes lethal, force against peaceful protesters, resulting in at least 10 deaths with hundreds more injured.

On 30 and 31 October, prison guards and gendarmes used excessive and lethal force to repress a prison riot and attempted escape at the MACO prison in Ouagadougou. Three prisoners were shot dead.

RIGHT TO HEALTH – MATERNAL MORTALITY

Concerns about high levels of maternal deaths remained. The World Health Organization (WHO) estimated that 2,800 women died during or following childbirth in 2013. WHO also reported a persistently high unmet need for contraception information, services and goods.

The Ministry of Health, working with the UN Population Fund (UNFPA) and other agencies, launched the first National Family Planning Week in 2013 aimed at raising awareness about contraception and challenging persistent negative stereotypes about women and girls who take contraception.

FREEDOM OF EXPRESSION

In a ruling in March, the African Court on Human and Peoples' Rights held that the Burkinabé state – in its failure to diligently investigate and bring to justice those responsible for the assassination of journalist Norbert Zongo and three of his companions, found burned to death in a car in 1998 – had violated the right to freedom of expression by causing "fear and worry in media circles".

In another ruling in December, in the case of *Konaté v. Burkina Faso*, the Court ruled that imprisonment for defamation violated the right to freedom of expression while criminal defamation laws should be used only in limited circumstances. The Court ordered Burkina Faso to change its criminal defamation laws.

BURUNDI

Republic of Burundi
Head of state and government: **Pierre Nkurunziza**

Government repression of critical voices intensified during the year. Violations of the rights to freedom of expression, association and peaceful assembly increased. Members of the opposition, civil society activists, lawyers and journalists were among those who faced heightened restrictions as the 2015 elections approached. Meetings and marches were not allowed to take place. Allegations of harassment and violence committed by members of the ruling party's youth wing, Imbonerakure, were not effectively investigated.

BACKGROUND

Political tensions ran high as President Nkurunziza looked set to stand for a third term, a move perceived by many as a violation of Burundi's Constitution. In March, the National Assembly narrowly rejected a bill proposing constitutional amendments that would have allowed the President to stand for a further term. Official statements indicated that the Constitutional Court would rule on the issue at a later date. Critics accused the ruling National Council for the Defense of Democracy-Forces for the Defense of Democracy (CNDD-FDD) of jeopardizing ethnic power-sharing principles agreed in Burundi's post-conflict Arusha Accord.

The United Nations Office in Burundi (BNUB), established in January 2011, closed at the end of 2014.

Strong criticism of the civil and political rights situation in Burundi was made by UN Secretary-General Ban Ki-moon, the UN High Commissioner for Human Rights, the African Union (AU) and some donor countries, including France and the USA.

FREEDOMS OF ASSOCIATION AND EXPRESSION

The authorities refused to grant opposition groups, the press, the Burundian Bar Association and civil society organizations authorization to hold legitimate meetings and peaceful demonstrations.[1]

For example, in February, the Mayor of Bujumbura prevented the Burundian Bar Association from holding its General Assembly and another planned training workshop. In March, youth members of the Movement for Solidarity and Democracy (MSD) were denied permission to hold a meeting at a local centre in the commune of Gihosha, Bujumbura, to discuss the proposed amendments to the Constitution. The authorities gave no explanation for their decision.

Political figures and opposition parties were subject to official interference, harassment and arbitrary arrest. For example, irregular arrest and trial proceedings in relation to corruption allegations against Frédéric Bamvuginyumvira limited his political activities. He was released from detention in March on health grounds.

Repressive legislation

The Press Law, promulgated in June 2013, provided for official restriction of press activities and freedom of expression. The law stipulates that journalists can be required to reveal their sources on a number of issues from public order to state security.

The Law on Public Gatherings was used to arbitrarily deny opposition groups and civil society permission to meet publicly or hold demonstrations.

HUMAN RIGHTS DEFENDERS

Members of civil society organizations and the media, especially those working on potentially sensitive subjects relating to human rights or state accountability, were subject to harassment.

Leading human rights defender and prisoner of conscience Pierre Claver Mbonimpa was detained in May and charged with threatening state security and using false documents. He was arrested shortly after his comment that young men were receiving arms and uniforms and travelling to the neighbouring Democratic Republic of the Congo for military training was broadcast on the radio. He was provisionally released on medical grounds in September. His imprisonment sent a chilling signal to the rest of civil society that individuals reporting on

sensitive subjects would be at risk of arbitrary arrest.[2]

In April, a march organized by civil society organizations to commemorate the fifth anniversary of the killing of Ernest Manirumva, Vice-President of the Anti-corruption and Economic Malpractice Observatory (OLUCOME), was prevented from going ahead. At the time when the march should have taken place, the Prosecutor General issued a statement claiming that the prosecution had incriminating evidence linking Gabriel Rufyiri, President of OLUCOME, to the death of Ernest Manirumva. No investigation had been initiated into the alleged involvement of several high-ranking members of the security services in the killing.

IMPUNITY

Human rights abuses by Imbonerakure

Members of Imbonerakure, the youth wing of the CNDD-FDD, committed human rights abuses on the pretext of maintaining security. They prevented opposition party meetings and intimidated, attacked and even killed members of the opposition with impunity.

On 14 March, Ananias Nsabaganwa, a member of the Front for Democracy in Burundi, was visited at his home in the Commune of Busoni, Kirundo Province, by two local administrative officials, three members of Imbonerakure (including the head of Nyagisozi zone) and two soldiers. He was reportedly shot dead by one of the soldiers on the orders of one of the local officials and an Imbonerakure member.

In April, a leaked internal cable sent by the BNUB reported that in one province two members of the military had supplied Imbonerakure and demobilized soldiers with weapons and military and police uniforms. The government denied these allegations but took no steps to investigate them.

Extrajudicial executions

Most allegations of politically motivated killings carried out between 2010 and 2012 were not investigated. Victims and witnesses remained at risk because of the lack of effective protection mechanisms.

The African Commission on Human and Peoples' Rights agreed in June to consider a complaint from civil society groups and Track Impunity Always (TRIAL) in relation to four cases of extrajudicial executions.

JUSTICE SYSTEM

The justice system lacked material, financial and logistical resources. Generalized problems were regularly cited in relation to the judiciary including a heavy backlog of cases, a lack of transport to transfer suspects from detention facilities to court and cases not being opened or prepared for court by prosecutors. There were also reports of corruption within the judiciary and the authorities continued to fail to effectively investigate politically sensitive cases.

TRUTH AND RECONCILIATION COMMISSION

On 15 May, a law establishing a Truth and Reconciliation Commission (TRC) was passed. The law failed to include clear language on the setting up of a special tribunal to prosecute individuals responsible for crimes under international law, including war crimes and crimes against humanity. The TRC officially began on 10 December 2014 as 11 Commissioners were sworn into office.

1. Burundi: Locked down: A shrinking of political space (AFR 16/002/2014)
   www.amnesty.org/en/library/info/AFR16/002/2014/en
2. Pierre Claver Mbonimpa is a prisoner of conscience (AFR 16/003/2014)
   www.amnesty.org/en/library/info/AFR16/003/2014/en

CAMBODIA

Kingdom of Cambodia
Head of state: **King Norodom Sihamoni**
Head of government:**Hun Sen**

Respect for the right to freedoms of expression, association and assembly deteriorated with a seven months' ban on public gatherings. The authorities used excessive force against peaceful protesters, resulting in deaths and injuries. Human rights defenders and political activists faced threats, harassment, prosecution and sometimes violence. Impunity for perpetrators of human rights abuses persisted, with no thorough, impartial and independent investigations into killings and beatings. Two further convictions at the Extraordinary Chambers in the Courts of Cambodia for crimes against humanity during the Khmer Rouge period resulted in life sentences; a second trial against the same defendants was ongoing. Thousands of people affected by land grabbing by private companies for development and agro-industry faced forced eviction and loss of land, housing and livelihood.

BACKGROUND

In July the opposition Cambodian National Rescue Party (CNRP) ended its year-long boycott of the National Assembly following an agreement with Prime Minister Hun Sen and his ruling Cambodian People's Party (CPP) over electoral reform. The opposition, which won 55 out of 123 seats in the July 2013 national elections, had alleged electoral fraud favouring the CPP.

Two new laws – the Law on the Organization of the Courts and the Law on the Status of Judges and Prosecutors – were enacted in July, along with an amended Law on the Organization and Functioning of the Supreme Council of Magistracy. The laws gave excessive powers over judges and prosecutors to the Ministry of Justice and the Supreme Council of Magistracy, contrary to international standards.

Amid widespread criticism from human rights and refugee organizations, including UNHCR, the UN refugee agency, Cambodia signed a controversial Memorandum of Understanding with Australia in September to accept an unknown number of recognized refugees relocated from the Pacific island of Nauru. Australia undertook to fund the costs of relocation and services for the refugees for one year in Cambodia and to provide additional aid worth US$40 million over a four-year period.

EXCESSIVE USE OF FORCE

Security forces used excessive force to respond to peaceful assemblies, leading to deaths and injuries. On 2 January, 10 men, including four human rights defenders, were beaten with wooden sticks and metal bars and then arrested during a violent operation by soldiers in response to mostly peaceful protests by striking garment factory workers.

The following day, four men were shot dead and 21 others injured when security forces fired live ammunition during violent clashes with striking garment workers and others in the Pur Senchey district of the capital, Phnom Penh. Although some protesters threw rocks, no threat was posed to the lives of security forces or others. The use of live ammunition appeared to be an unnecessary response and was therefore in violation of international standards. Dozens of people were hospitalized, including many with bullet wounds. Teenagers were among the casualties; Khem Saphath, a 16-year-old youth, was last seen with a gunshot wound and was presumed to have died.[1]

District security guards and plain-clothed men were deployed to break up peaceful demonstrations in Phnom Penh throughout the year. They used weapons including sticks, wooden batons, metal bars, electroshock weapons and slingshots. Human rights

monitors and journalists were among those specifically targeted and beaten.

In June Cambodia rejected recommendations by states participating in the review of the government's human rights record under the UN Human Rights Council's Universal Periodic Review to investigate the use of excessive force against protesters and killings during demonstrations and to end impunity for such abuses. No one was held accountable for any of the deaths or injuries sustained.[2]

FREEDOM OF ASSEMBLY

On 5 January, the Ministry of Interior announced that demonstrations "must be provisionally suspended" following a three-day crackdown on protests that resulted in at least four deaths and 23 arrests. Official requests from individuals and groups for permission to hold gatherings in Phnom Penh were repeatedly rejected. In April, Phnom Penh's Freedom Park – an area designated for peaceful assembly under the Law on Peaceful Demonstrations – was barricaded with barbed wire. Those who tried to gather despite the ban were violently dispersed by security forces. Restrictions on peaceful assembly were loosened and Freedom Park reopened in August following a political agreement reached between the government and opposition party.

In addition to the 10 men arrested on 2 January, another 13 workers were arrested on 3 January during the lethal clashes in Phnom Penh's Pur Senchey district. Some of the 23 arrested were severely beaten by security forces and denied access to medical care. All were charged with intentional violence and other crimes and detained. They were convicted in May following trials regarded by local observers as unfair; their sentences were suspended and all were released.

Eight officials of the opposition CNRP were arrested and charged with leading an "insurrection" following a violent clash between some CNRP supporters and district security guards at an attempted peaceful gathering at Freedom Park in July. They were all released a week later as the political agreement was reached. However, 10 youth activists and one CNRP official, five of whom were in pre-trial detention, were subsequently summoned for trial on 25 December on charges of "insurrection"; the trial was adjourned until January 2015. Legal action was initiated in September against six trade union leaders for "incitement". Although they were not detained, the court issued supervision orders, meaning they could not take part in or organize protests.

In November, seven women housing rights defenders from the Boeung Kak community were imprisoned for a year after a summary trial for taking part in a peaceful street protest. Three other women and a Buddhist monk were also imprisoned for calling for their release outside the court.[3]

Meetings and forums elsewhere in the country were also prevented by local authorities. In March and June the Cambodian Youth Network attempted to hold training sessions in Kampong Thom province on human rights issues, including illegal logging, but the sessions were disrupted by armed police. In June a planned public forum on illegal logging in Preah Vihear province was also banned.

LAND DISPUTES
Conflicts over land continued, with disputes over land grabbing, forced evictions, Economic Land Concessions and environmental concerns. This led to increased protests and confrontations, often involving local authorities and private companies. In April, local rights group the Cambodian League for the Promotion and Defense of Human Rights (LICADHO) estimated that the total number of people affected since 2000 by land grabbing and forced evictions in 13 provinces monitored – about half the country – had passed half a million.

Land disputes remained unresolved, leaving thousands either without adequate housing and land, and therefore unable to

make a living, or at risk of forced eviction. In March, the Cambodian Human Rights and Development Association (ADHOC) re-submitted complaints to the relevant authorities on behalf of around 11,000 families involved in protracted disputes, some lasting more than 10 years. The families came from 105 communities in 17 of Cambodia's 25 provinces.

Despite numerous promises from the authorities to find a solution, more than 100 out of 300 families forcibly evicted from Borei Keila in Phnom Penh in January 2012 remained homeless and living in harsh conditions.

In October a group of international law experts provided information to the ICC on behalf of 10 victims alleging that "widespread and systematic" land grabbing by the Cambodian government was a crime against humanity.

INTERNATIONAL JUSTICE
In August, Nuon Chea, 88, the former second-in-command of the Khmer Rouge regime, and Khieu Samphan, 83, the former head of state, were sentenced to life imprisonment by the Extraordinary Chambers in the Courts of Cambodia (ECCC, Khmer Rouge tribunal). They were convicted of the forced movement of the population from Phnom Penh and elsewhere, and the execution of soldiers from the Khmer Republic, the regime toppled by the Khmer Rouge. Both appealed the sentences. Eleven reparation projects designed by victims with external funding were also endorsed by the ECCC.

Case 002/02 against the two men began in October focusing on alleged crimes against humanity at agricultural co-operatives and a security centre in Takeo province.

---

1. Cambodia: Open letter urging an immediate investigation into the disappearance of Khem Saphath (ASA 23/002/2014)
   www.amnesty.org/en/library/info/ASA23/002/2014/en

2. Cambodia rejects recommendations to investigate killings of protesters: Human Rights Council adopts Universal Periodic Review outcome on Cambodia (ASA 23/005/2014)
www.amnesty.org/en/library/info/ASA23/005/2014/en
3. Women defenders and Buddhist monk sentenced (ASA 23/007/2014)
www.amnesty.org/en/library/info/ASA23/007/2014/en

CAMEROON

Republic of Cameroon
Head of state: **Paul Biya**
Head of government: **Philémon Yang**

Freedoms of association and assembly continued to be restricted. Human rights defenders were frequently intimidated and harassed by government security agents. Lesbian, gay, bisexual, transgender and intersex people continued to face discrimination, intimidation, harassment and other forms of attacks. The Nigerian Islamist armed group Boko Haram stepped up attacks in the northeastern region of Cameroon, including killings, burning villages and hostage-taking. Arbitrary arrests, detentions and extrajudicial executions of people suspected of being members of Boko Haram were reportedly carried out by security agents. Hundreds of thousands of refugees from Nigeria and the Central African Republic were living in crowded refugee camps in dire conditions.

BACKGROUND

There were signs of instability across the country as a result of internal political tensions and external developments, including ongoing cross-border attacks by Boko Haram, and violence in neighbouring Central African Republic (CAR). Security forces including the Rapid Intervention Brigade (BIR) were responsible for human rights violations including killings, extrajudicial executions, enforced disappearances,

arbitrary arrests and illegal detentions. Most of these violations were committed in the context of the fight against Boko Haram.

EXTRAJUDICIAL EXECUTIONS

A number of people suspected of being linked to Boko Haram were allegedly killed by security forces, including by members of the BIR, in northern Cameroon. On 1 June, nurse Nzouane Clair René was shot dead near the town of Mora, following arrest by security forces. On the same day, Ousmane Djibrine and Gréma Abakar, traders travelling to a village market in Zigagué, were reportedly killed by BIR members in the village of Dabanga. On 15 June Malloum Abba was killed by BIR members in the village of Tolkomari. On 20 June Oumaté Kola was reportedly found shot dead in the Mozogo forest following his arrest by BIR members a few days earlier. The same day, Boukar Madjo was shot dead, allegedly by BIR members, in the town of Nguetchewé.

ENFORCED DISAPPEARANCES

Several cases of enforced disappearance were reported, especially in the extreme north of the country where security forces were fighting Boko Haram. Most of the reported cases were allegedly committed by members of the BIR.

On 2 June, Abakar Kamsouloum was reportedly arrested by security forces at his home in Kousseri and transferred to a military camp. His fate and whereabouts remained unknown to his family and local civil society organizations at the end of the year, despite several requests for information to the local authorities.

ABUSES BY ARMED GROUPS

Boko Haram was responsible for human rights abuses, especially in the northeastern region. Houses were burned and a number of people were killed during raids on villages, often in punitive attacks for real or perceived co-operation with Cameroonian security forces.

Boko Haram fighters conducted several abductions in Cameroon during the year. Some of those abducted were released, reportedly often after payment of a ransom by the government. The authorities continued to refute this allegation. On 27 July, the residence of Cameroonian Vice-Prime Minister Amadou Ali was attacked by Boko Haram members in the village of Kolofata, close to the Nigerian border. Seventeen people were abducted including the Vice-Prime Minister's wife. Several others including police officers were killed during the attack. All those abducted were released in October together with 10 Chinese workers who were abducted in May.

REFUGEES' AND MIGRANTS' RIGHTS

Thousands of refugees were living in dire conditions in crowded camps in border areas after fleeing violence in the CAR and Nigeria. At the end of the year there were around 40,000 refugees from Nigeria and some 238,517 from the CAR in the country. At least 130,000 refugees from the CAR crossed into Cameroon following violence that erupted in the CAR between the Séléka and Anti-balaka armed groups in December 2013. Conditions were difficult in the camps and attacks on camps by unidentified armed groups were reported. These attacks led UNHCR, the UN refugee agency, to move refugees from border areas to more secure places within Cameroon.

RIGHTS OF LESBIAN, GAY, BISEXUAL, TRANSGENDER AND INTERSEX PEOPLE

Discrimination, intimidation, harassment and violence directed towards LGBTI people remained of serious concern. LGBTI individuals, mostly men but also women, were arrested for alleged same-sex sexual activity. Some of those arrested were sentenced to prison terms of up to five years. Others were arbitrarily detained and later released.

On 1 October, five people, including one transgendered person, were arrested after police raided a home in the capital Yaoundé.

They were later detained at a nearby police station and a sixth person was also detained when he visited those already in detention. Two of those arrested were released the same day. The other four were charged with prostitution and "disturbance" and remained in detention until 7 October, when they were released pending an investigation.

HUMAN RIGHTS DEFENDERS

Human rights defenders and groups were frequently intimidated, harassed and threatened. Offices of some human rights organizations were placed under surveillance and at times attacked, allegedly by security agents.

On the night of 12 June, the premises of the Central Africa Human Rights Defenders' Network (REDHAC) were burgled by a group of eight unidentified armed men. They threatened to kill the guard before forcing their way into the offices, searching through documents and reportedly taking two television sets, three laptops, an iPad and some money. The incident was the fourth time REDHAC's offices had been attacked, but despite the organization lodging complaints with the police, no concrete measure was taken by the authorities to effectively and fully investigate the incidents.

ARBITRARY ARRESTS AND DETENTIONS

People continued to be arrested and detained without charge by security forces including by members of the BIR in the context of its operation against Boko Haram in the northern regions. There were several cases of people being detained incommunicado. In most cases, detainees were prevented from receiving visits from family members, doctors or lawyers. There were also several reported cases of people being arbitrarily arrested and detained by the police and gendarmerie for civil matters, contrary to provisions of the Constitution and domestic legislation.

FREEDOMS OF ASSOCIATION AND ASSEMBLY

Perceived or actual opponents of the government continued to be denied the right to organize peaceful activities and demonstrations.

On 3 October, reggae singer Joe de Vinci Kameni, known as Joe La Conscience, was arrested by police outside the French consulate in Douala as he was preparing to start a peaceful demonstration. A local journalist was arrested alongside him and later released. Joe de Vinci Kameni was released on 9 October without charge.

CANADA

Canada
Head of state: **Queen Elizabeth II, represented by Governor General David Johnston**
Head of government: **Stephen Harper**

There were systematic violations of the rights of Indigenous Peoples. Attacks against two Canadian soldiers provoked a debate about terrorism and national security laws.

INDIGENOUS PEOPLES' RIGHTS

In February, the government rejected a proposed mine in the traditional territory of the Tsilhqot'in people in the province of British Columbia, which an environmental assessment concluded would cause irreversible and profound harm to Tsilhqot'in culture and society.[1] However, the federal government gave resource development precedence over Indigenous rights in a series of other large-scale projects, including the Northern Gateway oil sands pipeline, approved in June, and the Site C dam megaproject, approved in October.

In May, the UN Special Rapporteur on the rights of Indigenous Peoples reported that the situation of Indigenous Peoples in Canada had reached "crisis proportions in many respects", including "distressing socio-economic conditions" and a disproportionately high number of Indigenous people in prison.

In June, the Supreme Court for the first time recognized an Indigenous nation's pre-colonial land title, upholding the right of the Tsilhqot'in to own and manage a large part of their traditional territories.

In September, Canada was the only state to take issue with part of the UN World Conference on Indigenous Peoples' outcome document.

In October, the Canadian Human Rights Tribunal heard concluding arguments in a case alleging discriminatory federal under-funding of child protection in First Nation Indigenous communities.

WOMEN'S RIGHTS

In May, the Royal Canadian Mounted Police reported that at least 1,017 Indigenous women and girls were murdered between 1980 and 2012, four and a half times the homicide rate for all other women. Despite mounting demands, including by provincial and territorial governments, the federal government refused to initiate a national action plan or public inquiry.

In November, separate allegations of sexual assault and/or harassment against a radio host and two Members of Parliament sparked a national debate about violence against women.

COUNTER-TERROR AND SECURITY

In January, it was revealed that a national security agency, Communications Security Establishment Canada, had monitored thousands of travellers' electronic devices at a major airport and for days after they left the airport.

In May, the Supreme Court ruled that using Special Advocates in "immigration security certificate" hearings provided a fair process even though they were generally barred from communicating with the individuals concerned after accessing secret evidence.

In June, the Citizenship Act was reformed, allowing dual nationals convicted of terrorism and some other offences to be stripped of Canadian citizenship. There were concerns about dual tiers of citizenship and unfairness in the revocation procedure.

In July, the Alberta Court of Appeal ruled that Omar Khadr should be treated as a juvenile offender. He was apprehended by US forces in Afghanistan when he was 15 years old and held for 10 years at the US detention centre at Guantánamo Bay in Cuba until his transfer to Canada in 2012 to complete his prison sentence.

In October, two Canadian soldiers were killed in separate attacks; Patrice Vincent in St-Jean-Sur-Richelieu and Nathan Cirillo in Ottawa. The gunman who killed Nathan Cirillo then entered the Canadian Parliament and was killed by security officers. The government subsequently proposed law reforms to increase the powers of the Canadian Security Intelligence Service. The bill did not address concerns about inadequate national security oversight.

REFUGEES AND ASYLUM-SEEKERS

In July, the Federal Court ruled that cuts to the Interim Federal Health Program for refugees were unconstitutional.

In October, the government proposed legislation allowing for provincial and territorial governments to deny social assistance to refugee claimants.

Also in October, a coroner's inquest into the 2013 death by hanging of Mexican national Lucía Vega Jiménez in a Vancouver airport holding cell recommended changes to immigration detention.

There were concerns about the low numbers of Syrian refugees given resettlement places in Canada.

FREEDOM OF EXPRESSION

In May, the Special Commission on the events of Spring 2012 (Commission

spéciale d'examen des événements du printemps 2012) criticized the Quebec provincial government's handling of student protests in 2012, including policing tactics. The Quebec government rejected the Commission's recommendations.

Numerous civil society organizations that criticized government policies were targeted for audits related to their charitable tax status and the permissibility of their advocacy work.

There were concerning disclosures about police surveillance of Indigenous land rights activists, including sharing the information with corporations.

JUSTICE SYSTEM

In October, the Supreme Court upheld the State Immunity Act, barring the family of Zahra Kazemi, a Canadian/Iranian national who was tortured and died in Iranian custody in 2003, from bringing a lawsuit against Iran in Canada.

CORPORATE ACCOUNTABILITY

In May, the third annual report assessing the human rights impact of the Canada-Colombia Free Trade Agreement was released. It failed to consider significant human rights concerns facing Indigenous Peoples in Colombia.

Lawsuits alleging human rights abuses were filed against Canadian mining companies Tahoe Resources in June and Nevsun Resources in November, in connection with their operations in Colombia and Eritrea respectively.

In November, changes to the Office of the Extractives Sector Corporate Social Responsibility (CSR) Counsellor fell short of calls for an Ombudsperson with power to investigate companies and recommend sanctions and remedies for non-compliance. Corporate participation in the complaints process remained voluntary, although companies faced withdrawals of certain government services if they did not respect Canada's CSR strategy.

LEGAL, CONSTITUTIONAL OR INSTITUTIONAL DEVELOPMENTS

A bill which would add gender identity to the Canadian Human Rights Act and Criminal Code hate crime provisions was stalled in the Senate at the end of the year.

Despite repeated calls, the government did not ratify the Arms Trade Treaty or the Optional Protocol to the UN Convention against Torture.

---

1. Canada: Submission to the United Nations Human Rights Committee, 112th Session (AMR 20/001/2014)

CENTRAL AFRICAN REPUBLIC

Central African Republic
Head of state: **Catherine Samba-Panza**
Head of government: **Mahamat Kamoun**

Crimes under international law such as war crimes and crimes against humanity were regularly committed, including killings, mutilation of bodies, abductions, recruitment and use of child soldiers and forced displacement of populations. In December 2013 a coalition of the mainly Christian and animist anti-Balaka armed groups attacked the capital Bangui and the mostly Muslim Séléka forces retaliated, killing dozens of civilians. The United Nations Multidimensional Integrated Stabilization Mission in the Central African Republic (MINUSCA) – which replaced the African-led International Support Mission to the Central African Republic (MISCA) in September 2014 – has not stopped or prevented abuses in the region. Many of those suspected of criminal responsibility, including commanders of the Séléka, anti-Balaka, and their allies, have not been investigated or arrested and no action has been taken to bring them to justice.

BACKGROUND

Violence continued in the Central African Republic (CAR) despite the deployment of MINUSCA, in September 2014, and the presence of French forces (known as Sangaris) and European Union forces (EUFOR). Deadly attacks against civilians, including on those in sites for internally displaced persons (IDP), by the anti-Balaka, Séléka and armed Peulh fighters (members of the Peulh ethnic group) continued. According to the UN, in mid-November, 7,451 military and 1,083 police personnel had been deployed to MINUSCA.

On 10 January, Séléka leader and CAR President Michel Djotodia resigned following pressure from the international community and CAR civil society organizations. Catherine Samba-Panza was sworn in as the new Transitional President on 23 January.

On 7 February 2014 the Prosecutor of the International Criminal Court (ICC) announced a new preliminary examination into crimes allegedly committed in the CAR since September 2012. In September, the Office of the Prosecutor announced its conclusion that there was a reasonable basis for investigating crimes defined under the Rome Statute committed in CAR since September 2012.

On 11 July, a Séléka congress designated former President Djotodia and former commander and Minister Nourredine Adam as the group's president and vice-president respectively. Those two individuals are under UN and US sanctions for their alleged involvement in human rights violations and abuses.

Prime Minister André Nzapayéké and his entire cabinet resigned following the ceasefire agreement signed in July 2014 in Brazzaville, Republic of Congo, by armed groups' representatives, political parties, churches and civil society organizations. On 22 August, Transitional President Samba-

Panza appointed the new Prime Minister Mahamat Kamoun.

On 7 August, a memorandum of understanding was signed between MINUSCA and the government to "establish a Special Jurisdiction created by national legislation, in which international judicial and prosecutorial executive functions would be attached to a national judicial body". However, legislation for the "Special Criminal Court" has yet to be passed and no funding has been provided.

Fresh violence erupted in the capital Bangui in mid-October. A series of violent incidents occurred in Bangui, with MINUSCA forces facing protests and attacks. At least a dozen people were killed and thousands were forced to flee and live in camps for IDPs. Escalating violence by the Séléka, armed Peulh fighters and anti-Balaka was observed in the central region, especially around the city of Bambari. On 9 October 2014, a MINUSCA convoy was attacked leaving one peacekeeper dead, another severely wounded, and seven others injured. Sporadic clashes between anti-Balaka fighters and international forces, including EUFOR, continued. According to UNHCR, the October violence displaced some 6,500 people in Bangui, but that number could be higher. As of October 2014 there were 410,000 IDPs and some 420,000 people had fled to neighbouring countries.

On 29 October, the UN Panel of Experts on CAR released its final report which highlighted credible evidence of crimes under international law committed by armed groups. It also referred to the exploitation of natural resources by armed groups; the illicit transfer of arms and ammunition; arms proliferation; and violations of international humanitarian law, including attacks on schools and hospitals, sexual violence and the use of child soldiers.

By the end of 2014, anti-Balaka and Séléka groups lacked co-ordination, leading to the creation of various other groups among them. The mostly Muslim Séléka forces clashed with the mainly Christian and animist anti-Balaka militia. All sides systematically targeted civilians believed to support the other side's fighters.

On 10 December, MINUSCA announced that it had arrested Abdel Kader "Baba Ladde", leader of the Chadian armed group Popular Front for Recovery near Kabo at the border with Chad. Baba Ladde and members of his armed group had been accused of attacking civilians in northern CAR and recruiting child soldiers.

ABUSES BY ARMED GROUPS
Abuses by Séléka
Séléka forces were allegedly responsible for serious human rights abuses, including killings, burning houses and villages mostly belonging to Christians, forced displacement of the populations and enforced disappearances. Christian communities frequently attributed responsibility for Séléka's abuses to the country's Muslim minority; acts of retaliation were reported and the already serious sectarian divisions deepened. No effective investigations were conducted into most incidents.

On 22 January, more than 100 Christian civilians including children were allegedly killed by Séléka fighters and armed Muslim civilians in Baoro. On 17 April, Father Wilibona was allegedly killed by Séléka and armed Peulh fighters after being ambushed at Tale village. On 26 April, 16 people, including 13 local leaders and three aid workers from Médecins Sans Frontières (MSF), were killed by a Séléka group, prompting MSF to reduce its CAR activities. On 7 July, 26 people were killed and 35 seriously wounded during an attack at a church and IDP site in Bambari. More than 10,000 people fled. On 1 October, Séléka fighters attacked an IDP camp next to the MINUSCA base in Bambari (which accommodated Christian and animist IDPs). Several people were killed. On 10 October, Séléka fighters attacked an IDP site in the Catholic Church compound in Dekoa. Nine civilians including a pregnant woman were killed and several wounded.

Abductions by Séléka

In April, the Séléka in Batangafo abducted a bishop and three priests. They were later released following negotiation between the authorities, the Catholic Church and Séléka commanders. Those allegedly responsible for the abduction were identifiable but no investigation was opened.

Abuses by the anti-Balaka

Anti-Balaka armed group members were responsible for war crimes and crimes against humanity. They were the main perpetrators of abuses committed against Muslims in Bangui and in western CAR, especially following the former President's resignation in January 2014, and the retreat of most Séléka forces to the northeastern region.

Since 8 January 2014, a series of deadly attacks on Muslims were carried out across western CAR. Some attacks were allegedly carried out in revenge for the previous killing of Christians by Séléka forces and armed Muslims. On 16 January, 20 civilians were killed and dozens injured outside the town of Bouar, when their vehicle was attacked by anti-Balaka militias. Some victims were hacked to death with machetes, others were shot. Among the victims was an 11-year-old girl. On 14 January, after stopping a truck in Boyali and demanding the Muslims get off, anti-Balaka fighters killed six members of a family: three women and three small children, aged one, three, and five. On 18 January, at least 100 Muslims were killed in the town of Bossemptele. Two days later, anti-Balaka fighters killed four Muslim women who had hidden in a Christian family's house. On 29 September, Abdou Salam Zaiko, a Muslim from Bambari, was killed when the vehicle he was travelling in was attacked. According to witnesses, the anti-Balaka allowed the Christian driver and passengers to leave the vehicle, but killed Zaiko and other Muslim passengers. On 8 October, seven Muslim passengers in a car owned by Saidu Daouda were killed after the car was ambushed. On

14 October, in the Bangui neighbourhood of Nguingo, anti-Balaka members killed three civilians, seriously injured at least 20 more, and burned down 28 houses and a church. The attack was revenge for an earlier assault on some of their members by the local population following a previous attack by the armed group. Over 1,000 people fled to the Democratic Republic of Congo (DRC)'s Equator province, while 100 took refuge at a Catholic Church compound. In September, Djimbété encampment for the Peulh ethnic group was attacked. Several people were killed including a six-year old boy.

Abuses committed by armed Peulh fighters

Armed Muslim Peulh fighters who were often allies of the Séléka conducted attacks killing and injuring mainly Christians, pillaging and burning villages and houses. In October, armed Muslim Peulh fighters allegedly carried out several attacks on villages around Bambari and in central and northern CAR. At least 30 people were killed.

VIOLATIONS COMMITTED BY AFRICAN UNION PEACEKEEPERS

Chadian national army (ANT) members and those of the Chadian contingent of MISCA were allegedly involved in serious human rights violations. In some instances MISCA forces failed to protect civilians, while in others members of its contingents allegedly committed serious human rights violations with impunity.

On 4 February, members of the ANT allegedly shot dead three people in the town of Boali, while they were repatriating Chadians and Muslims to Chad. On 18 February, Chadian troops were responsible for killing at least eight people including children, when they indiscriminately opened fire on a crowd in Damara and at the PK12 neighbourhood of Bangui. On 29 March, troops opened fire on a market crowd in Bangui killing and injuring several civilians. Following criticism from the international community, the Chadian authorities withdrew their 850 soldiers from MISCA in April. On 24 March

MISCA's Congolese (Brazzaville) contingent were allegedly implicated in the enforced disappearance of at least 11 people, including four women, from the home of a local militia leader in Boali.

No MISCA peacekeepers had been investigated for human rights violations by the end of the year.

PRISON CONDITIONS

The conditions and security at Bangui's Ngaragba prison remained of concern. On 3 November, 584 prisoners were registered, including 26 minors. The prison's capacity was 500 adults. In late November more than 650 inmates were held in cramped cells. There was a lack of adequate sanitation and protection against malaria. Prisoners defecated in plastic bags which they threw outside, jeopardizing their own health and that of people living nearby.

Anti-Balaka militia attacked the prison in January 2014 and killed at least four suspected Séléka members detained there. That led to the escape of all prisoners. CAR officials told Amnesty International that the anti-Balaka members who led the attack were well known to them. However, by the end of the year, no action had been taken to bring the perpetrators to justice.

On 24 November, a riot erupted at Ngaragba prison. Some prisoners, suspected of being anti-Balaka members, armed with at least three Kalashnikov rifles and hand grenades, attacked the prison guards and the UN contingent guarding the prison. According to witnesses, at least one UN peacekeeper and 13 inmates were wounded. The riot followed the death of a detainee allegedly for lack of medical treatment and harsh detention conditions. The detainees also demanded that their cases be heard in reasonable time, with some complaining of having been in detention for 10 months without trial.

FREEDOM OF EXPRESSION

The few journalists who remained operational were often victims of harassment and intimidation by armed groups and the transitional authorities. Several journalists were reportedly killed because of their work. No effective investigations were known to have been carried out into these incidents. On 29 April, two journalists were attacked in Bangui. Désiré Luc Sayenga, a *Démocrate* newspaper journalist, died after being knifed and shot by a group of young men. René Padou, who worked with the protestant church Radio La Voix de la Grâce, died after an armed group threw grenades and shot him. Both journalists had previously denounced crimes committed across the CAR.

IMPUNITY

The transitional authorities and the UN failed to effectively investigate crimes under international law, including war crimes and crimes against humanity committed in CAR, therefore perpetuating the cycle of violence and fear. In July, Amnesty International published a dossier naming 20 individuals, including anti-Balaka and Séléka commanders, against whom it had credible evidence to suspect that they could be responsible for war crimes, crimes against humanity and other serious human rights abuses committed since December 2013. In December the organization revealed that some of these men were allegedly implicated in interference with the administration of justice and further crimes under international law between September and October 2014.

CHAD

Republic of Chad
Head of state: **Idriss Déby Itno**
Head of government: **Kalzeubé Payimi Deubet**

Serious human rights violations continued to take place with almost total impunity.

The rights to freedom of expression and to peaceful assembly were frequently violated. Human rights defenders, journalists and trade unionists were victims of harassment, intimidation, arbitrary arrest and detention. People, including protesters, were killed by members of the security services during demonstrations.

BACKGROUND

Issues related to economic, social and cultural rights were of great concern throughout the year. Across the country, people, including civil servants, organized demonstrations demanding pay increases and denouncing the high cost of living. Chad was hosting more and more refugees from the Central African Republic (CAR), Sudan and recently Nigeria, putting pressure on the already scarce resources and creating tensions within the communities, especially in south, east and northwestern parts of the country. Individuals responsible for committing human rights violations, including members of the police, the gendarmerie and the National Intelligence Agency (ANS), continued to do so with almost total impunity.

IMPUNITY

Members of the army and the Chadian component of the then African Union mission to the Central African Republic (MISCA), who were involved in killing civilians and other serious human rights violations in the CAR, had impunity after they withdrew from MISCA on 3 April. On 29 March, Chadian troops opened fire at a crowd in a market in the PK12 district of Bangui, the capital of the CAR, killing and wounding dozens of people. Chadian troops were involved in other incidents including killings of civilians in the towns of Boali, Damara and in PK12 in February. On 19 July, President Idriss Déby appointed the Chadian rebel leader Abdel Kader "Baba Ladde" as préfet of Grande Sido prefecture at the border with the CAR. He was appointed despite the fact that he and members of his armed group Popular

Front for Recovery (Front Populaire pour le Redressement, FPR) had been accused of serious human rights abuses including the recruitment and use of child soldiers in northern CAR. They had also been accused of setting fire to villages in northern CAR between January and July. He later fled Chad and on 10 December, he was arrested by UN peacekeepers near the town of Kabo in northern CAR, at the border with Chad. He was arrested on an arrest warrant issued by judicial authorities in Bangui in May and remained detained in the prison in Bangui at the end of the year.

ARBITRARY ARRESTS AND DETENTIONS

According to the UN Panel of Experts on CAR, three civil servants from the CAR, namely the *sous-préfet* of Markounda, the secretary-general of the *sous-préfecture* and the director of a public school, were arrested by Chadian security forces in the CAR on 17 May and taken to N'Djamena, the capital of Chad. The three were not released despite several requests from the CAR authorities.

On 23 June, two members of the UN Panel of Experts on CAR were arrested by Chadian defence and security forces at a border post in the CAR while conducting investigations. The UN Panel reported that its experts had identified themselves, explained their mandate, privileges and immunities but that they were forcibly driven from the border post to the town of Goré in Chad where they were detained for four hours, before being escorted back to the border and released.

PRISON CONDITIONS

Conditions remained harsh in most of the country's prisons. According to witnesses, conditions were worse in detention facilities where visits were not allowed. These were run by the police, the gendarmerie and the national security services. N'Djamena remained without a prison after the demolition of the city's prison in December 2011. Detainees were held in a former gendarmerie barrack compound in Amsinéné on the outskirts of the city.

Harsh conditions in prisons frequently led to prison escapes and revolts. On 4 November, a revolt erupted in Amsinéné prison after the prison authorities had not allowed some prisoners to stay in the prison courtyard and forced them to stay in cells instead. In solidarity with the punished inmates, other prisoners gathered in the main courtyard. The gendarmes guarding the prison started shooting at the prisoners. According to various sources, at least one prisoner was killed and several others wounded.

FREEDOM OF EXPRESSION

Human rights defenders, journalists and trade unionists regularly faced violations of their right to freedom of expression. They were frequently intimidated, harassed or arbitrarily arrested by security service officers and administrative authorities.

On 8 October, community Radio FM Liberté was suspended for seven days following a decision by the High Council for Communication. The station had broadcast a statement signed by 12 human rights NGOs criticizing the absence of fuel on the market.

FREEDOM OF ASSEMBLY

Trade unions and political and human rights groups were frequently denied the right to peaceful activities or protests. Most demonstrations were violently disrupted by security forces.

On 11 November, protesters, including teachers, demonstrating against the high cost of living in N'Djamena and the towns of Moundou and Sarh, were attacked by security forces. According to various sources, at least one person was killed and several were wounded after being shot.

RIGHTS OF LESBIAN, GAY, BISEXUAL, TRANSGENDER AND INTERSEX PEOPLE

The government proposed a draft bill amending the penal code to criminalize same-sex conduct between consenting adults with jail sentences of between 15 and 20 years, and a fine of 50,000 to 500,000 CFA francs (US$100 to 1,000). The bill was not passed into law at the end of the year.

INTERNATIONAL JUSTICE

At the end of the year, the Extraordinary African Chambers (the Chambers) in Dakar, Senegal, was finalizing its investigation into alleged crimes by the former Chadian President Hissène Habré. The Chambers indicted him in July 2013 and, if the investigating judges decided that there was sufficient evidence, his trial would be scheduled to start in May 2015. Habré's reign from 1982-1990 was marked by serious human rights violations, including torture and other ill-treatment, arbitrary arrests and illegal detentions.

On 14 November, the trial of 26 former state security agents connected to the Habré era commenced in Chad. International and local human rights organizations expressed concern that the trial could undermine the upcoming trial of Hissène Habré in Dakar, Senegal. In October, the Chambers requested Chad to send these suspects to Dakar but Chad declined to transfer them and refused another request by the Chambers to travel to Chad to interview them. There were also concerns from the victims and human rights organizations that the trial may not meet international fair trial standards.

REFUGEES' AND MIGRANTS' RIGHTS

Despite efforts by the international community and the authorities to assist the tens of thousands of people who recently fled into the country from the CAR and Nigeria, their living conditions remained dire. Shelter, food and medical facilities were needed by more than 150,000 refugees and Chadian returnees. Most of them were living in camps in southern Chad near the border with CAR. Throughout the year, violence caused by the armed group Boko Haram in Nigeria also forced thousands to flee to Chad, mostly to the area near Lake Chad; 368,000 refugees from Darfur were living in refugee camps in eastern Chad. Some 97,000 refugees from CAR who fled their country stayed in camps in southern Chad.

On 8 August, the authorities of Logone Oriental province in southern Chad forcibly and without prior notice relocated people from the Doba transit site to another site in the village of Kobitey.

CHILE

Republic of Chile
Head of state and government: **Michelle Bachelet Jeria (replaced Sebastián Piñera Echenique in March)**

Cases of police violence continued to be dealt with by military courts. Legal proceedings against those responsible for past human rights violations continued.

BACKGROUND

In March, Michelle Bachelet Jeria took office promising to decriminalize abortion in certain circumstances. She also pledged to bring the anti-terrorism law and the military justice system into line with international standards.

Chile accepted most of the recommendations made under the UN Universal Periodic Review. These included a call for the 1978 Amnesty Law to be repealed and for reform to legislation regulating sexual and reproductive rights. In June, the UN Human Rights Committee made similar recommendations.[1]

POLICE AND SECURITY FORCES

In August, the police made public the security protocols used during demonstrations. This followed repeated complaints about the lack of transparency of the methods used by the police to respond to protests. There had been repeated allegations of excessive use of force by police during protests since 2011.

MILITARY JUSTICE SYSTEM

Cases of human rights violations involving members of the security forces continued to be dealt with by military courts.[2] Decisions by the Supreme Court and the Constitutional Court, upholding the right to due process and international human rights obligations, transferred some cases to ordinary courts.[3]

In May, a former police officer was sentenced to three years and 61 days' imprisonment for fatally shooting 16-year-old Manuel Gutierrez Reinoso and injuring Carlos Burgos Toledo during a protest in 2011. However, as the sentence imposed was for less than five years, the officer was conditionally released. The family's appeal against the sentence was pending before a higher military court at the end of the year.[4]

In 2013, a police officer was found responsible by a military court for inflicting serious injuries on journalist Víctor Salas Araneda and sentenced to 300 days' conditional release and suspended from work. However, Víctor Salas Araneda, who lost the sight in his right eye while he was reporting on a protest in 2008, was not granted reparation.

Death in custody

In May, Iván Vásquez Vásquez died in custody in Chile Chico, Aysén region. The family's lawyers argued that he was beaten to death and that more than one police officer was involved in the crime. A first autopsy indicated that suicide was not the cause of death, as initially indicated by the police. A police officer was charged by a military court with using unnecessary violence resulting in death. However, the charges were dropped in October after a second autopsy requested by the defence stated that the cause of death was suicide. Concerns remained around the impartiality of this autopsy. Full results of the autopsy were pending at the end of the year.

IMPUNITY

Some progress was made in bringing to justice those responsible for human rights violations committed under General Pinochet's regime. According to the President of the Supreme Court, by March there were 1,022 active cases, of which 72 related to allegations of torture. Official data from the Ministry of the Interior Human Rights Programme indicated that, by October, 279 people had been convicted in connection with these crimes; these convictions were not subject to appeal. At the end of 2014, 75 people were serving prison sentences in connection with these crimes.

In May, 75 former agents of the secret police (Dirección de Inteligencia Nacional, DINA) were convicted in connection with the enforced disappearance of Jorge Grez Aburto in 1974.[5] In October the Supreme Court convicted former DINA members, including its former head Manuel Contreras Sepúlveda, of the enforced disappearance of Carlos Guerrero Gutiérrez and Claudio Guerrero Hernández, in 1974 and 1975 respectively.

Investigations into the torture of Leopoldo García Lucero were continuing at the end of the year. In August 2013, in its first ruling on a case of a Chilean torture survivor, the Inter-American Court of Human Rights condemned the excessive delays in initiating the investigations into this crime.[6]

In June, the authorities announced legal reforms that would, if implemented, make torture a specific offence in the Criminal Code.

In September, the government announced its intention to speed up the discussion of a 2006 bill to overturn the 1978 Amnesty Law. The debate around the amnesty law was ongoing before the Congress at the end of the year.[7]

INDIGENOUS PEOPLES' RIGHTS

There were renewed allegations of excessive use of force and arbitrary detention during police operations against Mapuche Indigenous communities. There were particular concerns about abuses against minors in the context of the conflict.

In May, the Supreme Court confirmed the 18-year prison sentence of Celestino Córdova, a Mapuche *machi* (traditional healer), in connection with the deaths in January 2013 of Werner Luchsinger and Vivianne Mackay. The couple died following an arson attack on their house in the Vilcún community, Araucanía region. The Oral Criminal Court of Temuco, which ruled in the first instance, dismissed the prosecution's allegation that this was a terrorist attack. The defence alleged that Celestino Córdova's trial was politically motivated and had fallen short of international fair trial standards, and was another example of how the authorities dealt with the issue by criminalizing Mapuche land claims rather than seeking to resolve underlying issues.

In October, José Mauricio Quintriqueo Huaiquimil died after being run over by a tractor while he and other Mapuche were entering a farm in the Araucanía region. According to reports, they had gone to the farm in connection with a proposal they were preparing for the authorities about what part of the land could be given to them. The community had been occupying part of the farm with the owner's agreement. A man suspected of responsibility for the death was detained and the investigation was continuing at the end of the year.

In April, the UN Special Rapporteur on the promotion and protection of human rights and fundamental freedoms while countering terrorism published a report on his 2013 visit to Chile highlighting discrepancies between the national anti-terrorism law and the principle of legality and due process in the context of Mapuche proceedings. A bill to reform the anti-terrorism law was under discussion in Congress at the end of the year.

In May, the Inter-American Court of Human Rights condemned Chile for human rights violations in its application of the anti-terrorism law against eight Mapuche sentenced in 2003. The Inter-American Court also ordered the state to adopt all necessary measures to ensure that court decisions in these cases were not enforced. The Inter-American Court argued that the stereotyping of the accused in these cases violated the principles of equality, and non-discrimination and equal protection before the law.

SEXUAL AND REPRODUCTIVE RIGHTS

Abortion remained a criminal offence in all circumstances. A bill to decriminalize abortion in cases of rape, incest, threats to the life of the woman and foetal malformation was announced by the government but not submitted to the Congress.

DISCRIMINATION

In October, legislation on civil partnerships, including for same-sex couples, was passed by the Senate. At the end of the year, it was under discussion by the Deputies Chamber .

A bill on the right to gender identity that would allow people to change their name and gender on official documents was before the Senate at the end of the year.

1. Chile: Submission to the United Nations Human Rights Committee: 111th session of the Human Rights Committee (7-25th July 2014) (AMR 22/003/2014)
   www.amnesty.org/en/library/info/AMR22/003/2014/en
2. Chile: Urge reformar la justicia militar (AMR 22/007/2014)
   www.amnesty.org/es/library/info/AMR22/007/2014/es
3. Chile: Importante decisión del Tribunal Constitucional sobre la aplicación de la jurisdicción militar en un caso de tortura (AMR 22/005/2014)
   www.amnesty.org/en/library/info/AMR22/005/2014/es
   Chile: Corte Suprema resuelve a favor de una aplicación restrictiva de la justicia militar (AMR 22/006/2014)
   www.amnesty.org/en/library/info/AMR22/006/2014/es
4. Chile: "No sabía que existían dos tipos de justicia hasta que nos ocurrió esto" (22 August 2014)
   www.amnesty.org/es/news/chile-no-sab-que-exist-dos-tipos-de-justicia-hasta-que-nos-ocurri-esto-2014-08-22
5. Chile: Important conviction against 75 former agents of Pinochet in a case of enforced disappearance (AMR 22/001/2014)
   www.amnesty.org/en/library/info/AMR22/001/2014/en
6. Chile: 40 years on, Chile torture victim finally finds justice
   www.amnesty.org/en/articles/news/2013/11/years-chile-torture-victim-finally-finds-justice/
7. Chile: Pinochet victims see justice within their grasp, 6 October 2014 (Press release)
   www.amnesty.org.au/news/comments/35724/

CHINA

People's Republic of China
Head of state: **Xi Jinping**
Head of government: **Li Keqiang**

The authorities continued to severely restrict the right to freedom of expression. Activists and human rights defenders risked harassment and arbitrary detention. Torture and other ill-treatment remained widespread and access to justice was elusive for many. Ethnic minorities including Tibetans, Uighurs and Mongolians faced discrimination and increased security crackdown. Record numbers of workers went on strike demanding better pay and conditions. In November 2013, the Central Committee of the Chinese Communist Party in its Third Plenum issued a blueprint for deepening economic and social reforms, paving the way for modifications to family planning policies and China's household registration system. The abolition of the Re-education Through Labour system was also announced in 2013. The Fourth Plenum in October 2014 focused on the rule of law.

BACKGROUND

Throughout 2014, President Xi Jinping continued to pursue a high-profile anti-corruption campaign, targeting both low- and high-ranking officials. In July, state media announced that Zhou Yongkang, a former Minister of Public Security and Communist Party Politburo Standing Committee member, had been under investigation for alleged corruption since late 2013. He was the most senior official targeted in the campaign, in which, thus far according to official sources, more than 100,000 officials had been investigated and punished.

The UN Committees on Economic, Social and Cultural Rights and on the Elimination of Discrimination against Women, reviewed China's implementation of the ICESCR and CEDAW[1] in May and October respectively. In December 2013 the UN Human Rights Council adopted the outcome document of China's second Universal Periodic Review.

ARBITRARY DETENTION

The National People's Congress officially abolished China's notorious Re-education Through Labour system in December 2013. Following its abolition, the authorities made extensive use of other forms of arbitrary detention, including Legal Education Centres, various forms of administrative detention, "black jails", and illegal house arrest. In addition, police frequently used vague charges of "picking quarrels and provoking trouble" and "disturbing order in a public place" to arbitrarily detain activists for up to 37 days. Members of the Chinese Communist Party suspected of corruption were held under the secretive system of *shuanggui* (or "double-designation") without access to legal assistance or their families.

TORTURE AND OTHER ILL-TREATMENT

Torture and other ill-treatment remained widespread. In March, four lawyers who were investigating a Legal Education Centre in Jiansanjiang, Heilongjiang Province, were arbitrarily detained and tortured. One of them, Tang Jitian, said that he was strapped to an iron chair, slapped in the face, kicked, and hit so hard over the head with a plastic bottle filled with water that he passed out. He said he was later hooded and handcuffed behind his back and suspended by his wrists, while police continued to beat him.[2]

In a rare case, an appeal court in Harbin, Heilongjiang Province, in August upheld the convictions of four people charged with torture. They and three others had been found guilty by the court of first instance of torturing several criminal suspects in March 2013, and were sentenced to between one and two and a half years in prison. Only three of the seven were police officers; the other four were "special informants" – ordinary citizens allegedly "helping" the police to investigate crimes. One of their victims died in custody after being tortured with electric shocks and beaten with a shoe.

TRADE IN TORTURE INSTRUMENTS AND MISUSE OF LAW ENFORCEMENT EQUIPMENT

China consolidated its position as a major manufacturer and exporter of a growing range of law enforcement equipment, including items with no legitimate policing function such as electric shock stun batons and weighted leg cuffs. In addition, equipment that could be used legitimately in law enforcement but was easy to abuse, such as tear gas or riot control vehicles, has been exported from China without adequate controls even when there was a substantial risk of serious human rights violations by the receiving law enforcement agencies.[3]

DEATH PENALTY

In May, the Supreme People's Court in a landmark ruling overturned the death sentence of Li Yan, a victim of domestic violence, and ordered a retrial. This was still pending at the end of the year. The Ziyang City Intermediate People's Court had sentenced Li Yan to death in 2011 for the murder of her husband, ignoring evidence of sustained abuse.

In a rare case of acquittal, the High Court in Fujian Province in August overturned the death sentence of food stall owner Nian Bin for allegedly poisoning neighbours with rat poison. Nian Bin had originally been sentenced to death in 2008, despite his claim that he had confessed under torture.[4] The High Court cited insufficient evidence but did not address the allegations of torture.

Similarly, in the case of Hugjiltu, a man from Inner Mongolia who was executed for rape and murder in 1996, in December the Inner Mongolia People's Court declared his innocence and rescinded its original verdict. His family was awarded over 2 million yuan in compensation.

HUMAN RIGHTS DEFENDERS

Human rights defenders continued to risk harassment, arbitrary detention, imprisonment, and torture and other ill-treatment for their legitimate human rights work. Cao Shunli died from organ failure in a hospital in March after being denied adequate medical care in detention for an existing condition.[5] She had been detained at a Beijing airport in September 2013 when on her way to a human rights training in Switzerland.

The crackdown on rights activism intensified during the year. Individuals associated with a loose network of activists called the New Citizens' Movement were sentenced to between two and six and a half years' imprisonment. The movement campaigned for equal education rights for children of migrant workers, abolition of the household registration system, greater government transparency and against corruption.[6] More than 60 activists were arbitrarily detained or put under illegal house arrest in the run-up to the 25th anniversary in June of the violent crackdown in 1989 of pro-democracy protests in and around Tiananmen Square in Beijing. Several remained in detention awaiting trial, including prominent human rights lawyer Pu Zhiqiang.[7] In late September and early October, approximately 100 activists across China were detained for their support of pro-democracy protests in Hong Kong. Thirty-one remained in detention at the end of the year.[8]

FREEDOM OF EXPRESSION

The Chinese leadership increased its efforts to systematically restrict freedom of information. In late 2013, the Communist Party set up a group to "coordinate internet security". However, a group member reportedly described the task as engaging in a battle "against ideological penetration" from "foreign hostile forces".

In June, the All China Lawyers Association released draft regulations that would prohibit lawyers from discussing ongoing cases or writing open letters, or from criticizing the legal system, government policies and the Communist Party. Also in June, the State Administration of Press, Publication, Radio, Film and Television banned journalists from reporting on issues or areas outside their current field of reporting and from posting critical articles that had not been approved by their work unit.

The authorities continued to use criminal law to suppress freedom of expression, including by detaining and imprisoning activists whose internet postings were viewed more than 5,000 times or re-posted more than 500 times.

Criminal charges were brought against journalists. Gao Yu, a prominent journalist, was taken away in April and later detained on suspicion of "illegally disseminating state secrets internationally". Xiang Nanfu, a contributor to Boxun, one of the largest independent Chinese language news sources, was detained in May. Both were shown on national TV "confessing" to their alleged crimes even before their trials began.

Ilham Tohti, a Uighur scholar and founder of the website Uighur Online, was sentenced to life imprisonment in September after being convicted of "separatism". Articles from the website were the main evidence cited by the authorities. Ilham Tohti was denied access to legal counsel for five months after being detained, and was tortured and denied food in pre-trial detention.[9]

FREEDOM OF RELIGION

People practising religions banned by the state, or without state permission, risked harassment, arbitrary detention, imprisonment, and torture and other ill-treatment. In the Xinjiang Uighur Autonomous Region (XUAR), the authorities stepped up already onerous restrictions on Islam with the stated aim of fighting "violent terrorism and religious extremism". Numerous counties posted notices on their websites stating that students should not be permitted to observe Ramadan, and many teachers gave food and sweets to children to ensure that they did not observe the fast. Prohibitions on government employees and Communist Party cadres adhering to a religion were reinforced and several Uighur cadres were punished for downloading religious materials from the internet or "worshipping openly". Outward signs of adherence to Islam such as beards or veils were often banned.

In Zhejiang province, a large-scale campaign against churches was carried out under the pretext of rectifying structures with building code violations. The authorities demolished churches and removed crosses and crucifixes. In May, a building of the Xiaying Holy Love Church in Ningbo was reportedly demolished because it was "eye-catching". People practising banned religions, such as those worshipping Christianity in "house churches" or Falun Gong practitioners, continued to face persecution.

REPRODUCTIVE RIGHTS

The changes to China's family planning policies enabled married couples to apply to have two children if either parent is an only child. The Standing Committee of China's National People's Congress formalized the changes in December 2013, and provinces began to implement them in 2014. Many restrictions on reproductive rights remained in place.

MIGRANT WORKERS' RIGHTS

Changes to the household registration system known as *hukou* made it easier for rural residents to move to small or mid-size cities. Access to benefits and services, including education, health care and pensions, continued to be linked to *hukou* status, which remained a basis for discrimination. The *hukou* system forced many internal migrants to leave their children behind in the countryside.

XINJIANG UIGHUR AUTONOMOUS REGION (XUAR)

Authorities ascribed numerous violent incidents which occurred in the XUAR or other regions to Uighur individuals, and used these to justify a heavy-handed response. In May, a "strike hard" campaign was launched to target "violent terrorism and religious extremism", raising concerns that accused individuals would not receive fair trials. Top officials prioritized speed in making arrests and convening trials, while calling for greater "co-operation" between prosecuting authorities and courts. By 26 May, XUAR officials had announced the detention of over 200 suspected members of "terrorist and extremist groups" and the breaking up of 23 "terror rings". On 29 May, at one of the several "sentencing rallies" since the launch of the campaign, 55 people, all believed to be Uighurs, were sentenced for crimes including terrorism in front of nearly 7,000 spectators in a stadium.[10]

On 28 July, state media reported that 37 civilians were killed when a "knife-wielding mob" stormed government offices in Yarkand County (in Chinese: Shache) and that security forces had shot dead 59 attackers. Uighur groups disputed this account, putting the death toll much higher and saying rather that police opened fire on hundreds of people who were protesting against the severe restrictions placed on Muslims during Ramadan. Uighurs faced widespread discrimination in employment, education, housing and curtailed religious freedom, as well as political marginalization.

TIBET AUTONOMOUS REGION AND TIBETAN POPULATED AREAS IN OTHER PROVINCES

Ethnic Tibetans continued to face discrimination and restrictions on their rights to freedoms of religious belief, expression, association and assembly. Several Tibetan monastic leaders, writers, protesters and activists were detained.

In August, Tibetan demonstrators were reportedly shot by police and security forces in Kardze (in Chinese: Ganzi), Sichuan Province, where a crowd had gathered to protest against the detention of a village leader. At least four demonstrators died from their wounds and one protester committed suicide in detention.

Seven people set themselves on fire in Tibetan populated areas in 2014 in protest against repressive policies by the authorities; at least two died as a result. The number of known self-immolations since March 2011 rose to 131. The authorities targeted some relatives and friends of those who self-immolated for allegedly "inciting" or "abetting" such acts.

In some counties, family members of self-immolators, or those who have attended the Dalai Lama's teachings, were sympathetic towards the "Dalai Clique" or had "connections overseas", were barred from senior positions or from standing as candidates in village elections.

HONG KONG SPECIAL ADMINISTRATIVE REGION

Freedom of assembly

Large-scale protests took place in Hong Kong in 2014. On 1 July, organizers estimated that more than 500,000 people took part in a pro-democracy march, followed by a sit-in in the business district. More than 500 protesters were arrested the following night.[11] Some reported they were not allowed access to lawyers and were not provided with food and water for several hours before being released without charge. In late September, thousands of students staged a week-long class boycott that culminated in a sit-in in front of the Civic Square, near the headquarters of the Hong Kong government. Later that night some of the protesters entered the fenced-off portion of the Civic Square. Police responded with pepper spray and contained 70 of the protesters in the Square, 20 of whom were arrested the following day.[12]

This led to calls for the start of a civil disobedience campaign – "Occupy Central" – to occupy streets in central Hong Kong. On 28 September, the police used tear gas and pepper spray in an attempt to disperse thousands of peaceful protesters who had gathered in streets near the administrative headquarters. On 3 October, counter-demonstrators attacked protesters, including sexually assaulting, harassing and intimidating women and girls, while the police failed to intervene for several hours.[13] Journalists covering the protests complained that police prevented them from doing their job. On 15 October, six police officers were filmed beating up a protester in a dark corner in the Admiralty protest zone.[14] During the clearance of the Mongkok protest zone[15] and outside the government complex in Admiralty, in late November police used arbitrary force against protesters, journalists and bystanders. The largely peaceful protests ended in mid-December and, according to Hong Kong Police Commissioner Andy Tsang, 955 people were arrested in relation to the Occupy protests and more arrests would be made later.

Freedom of expression

Fears for the right to freedom of the press were raised when Kevin Lau Chun-to, the former chief editor of *Ming Pao* newspaper, was removed from his post in January. Under Lau, *Ming Pao* had reported on alleged human rights violations and wrongdoings of high-ranking officials in Hong Kong and China.

In October, over 20 journalists from Television Broadcasts Limited, a local television station, issued an open letter criticizing perceived self-censorship by the broadcaster in its reporting of the police beating of "Occupy Central" protester Ken Tsang Kin-Chiu.

Migrant domestic workers

Thousands of the approximately 300,000 migrant domestic workers in Hong Kong, nearly all women, were trafficked for exploitation and forced labour, and heavily indebted with illegal and excessive agency fees. The "Two-Week Rule", which stipulates that after an employment contract ends migrant domestic workers must find new employment or leave Hong Kong within two weeks, and the requirement that migrant domestic workers must live with their employers, increased their risk of suffering human and labour rights abuses. Employers often subjected them to physical or verbal abuse; restricted their freedom of movement; prohibited them from practising their faith; paid them less than the statutory Minimum Allowable Wage; denied them adequate rest periods; and arbitrarily terminated their contracts, often in collusion with employment agencies. The Hong Kong authorities failed to properly monitor employment agencies and punish those who violated the law.

In December, the District Court began a high-profile trial involving three female Indonesian migrant domestic workers: Erwiana Sulistyaningsih, Nurhasanah and Tutik Lestari Ningsih. Their former employer, Law Wan-tung, faced 21 charges including causing grievous bodily harm with intent, assault, criminal intimidation and failure to pay wages.[16]

MACAU SPECIAL ADMINISTRATIVE REGION

Pro-democracy academics reported being targeted for their political participation and criticism of the government. Bill Chou Kwok-ping, an academic at the University of Macau and vice-president of Macau's largest pro-democracy group, said he was suspended for "imposing political beliefs" on his students; after an inquiry, the university did not renew his contract. Another academic, Eric Sautede, a lecturer at the University of St. Joseph, lost his post in July; the university rector told a local Portuguese language newspaper it was due to Eric Sautede's political commentary.

---

1. China: Hong Kong SAR: Submission to the United Nations Committee on the Elimination of Discrimination Against Women: 59th session, 20 October – 7 November 2014 (ASA 17/052/2014)
    www.amnesty.org/en/library/info/ASA17/052/2014/en

2. China: Amnesty International calls for an investigation in to the allegations of torture of four lawyers in China (ASA 17/020/2014)
    www.amnesty.org/en/library/info/ASA17/020/2014/en

3. China's trade in tools of torture and repression (ASA 17/042/2014)
    www.amnesty.org/en/library/info/ASA17/042/2014/en

4. China: Death row inmate freed after six years of trials and appeals (Press release)
    www.amnesty.org/en/articles/news/2014/08/china-death-row-inmate-freed-after-six-years-trials-and-appeals/

5. China: Fear of cover-up as Cao Shunli's body goes missing (Press release)
    www.amnesty.org/en/articles/news/2014/03/china-fear-cover-cao-shunli-s-body-goes-missing/

6. China: Xu Zhiyong four year jail sentence shameful (Press release)
    www.amnesty.org/en/articles/news/2014/01/china-xu-zhiyong-four-year-jail-sentence-shameful/
    China: Three anti-corruption activists jailed on 'preposterous' charges (Press Release)
    www.amnesty.org/en/news/china-three-anti-corruption-activists-jailed-preposterous-charges-2014-06-19

7. Tiananmen crackdown: Repression intensifies on eve of 25 anniversary (Press release)
    www.amnestyusa.org/news/news-item/tiananmen-crackdown-repression-intensifies-on-eve-of-25th-anniversary

8. China: Release supporters of Hong Kong protests (Press release)
    www.amnesty.org/en/china-release-supporters-hong-kong-protests-2014-10-01

9. China: Deplorable life sentence for Uighur academic (Press release)
    www.amnesty.org/en/articles/news/2014/09/china-deplorable-x-year-jail-sentence-uighur-scholar/

10. China: Shameful stadium 'show trial' is not justice (Press release)
    www.amnesty.org/en/news/china-shameful-stadium-show-trial-not-justice-2014-05-29

11. Hong Kong: Mass arrests a disturbing sign for peaceful protest (Press release)
www.amnesty.org/en/news/hong-kong-mass-arrests-disturbing-sign-peaceful-protest-2014-07-02

12. Hong Kong: Police response to student pro-democracy protest an alarming sign (Press release)
www.amnesty.org/en/news/hong-kong-police-response-student-pro-democracy-protest-alarming-sign-2014-09-27

13. Hong Kong: Women and girls attacked as police fail to protect peaceful protesters (Press release)
www.amnesty.org/en/news/hong-kong-women-and-girls-attacked-police-fail-protect-peaceful-protesters-2014-10-04

14. Hong Kong: Police officers must face justice for attack on protester (Press release)
www.amnesty.org/en/news/hong-kong-police-officers-must-face-justice-attack-protester-2014-10-15

15. Hong Kong: Heavy-handed policing will only inflame protests (Press release)
www.amnesty.org/en/articles/news/2014/11/hong-kong-heavy-handed-policing-will-only-inflame-protests/

16. Hong Kong: The government has to put an end to the exploitation of migrant domestic workers (Press release)
www.amnesty.ca/news/news-releases/hong-kong-the-government-has-to-put-an-end-to-the-exploitation-of-migrant

COLOMBIA

Republic of Colombia
Head of state and government: **Juan Manuel Santos Calderón**

The peace talks between the government and the guerrilla group, the Revolutionary Armed Forces of Colombia (Fuerzas Armadas Revolucionarias de Colombia, FARC) continued to make progress, despite a three-week suspension of negotiations towards the end of the year. The two sides reached partial agreements on several key issues. The peace process emerged as a key theme in the May presidential election, which was won by the incumbent Juan Manuel Santos following a second round in June.[1] The election campaign was marred by a scandal involving the wiretapping of government and FARC negotiators by elements within the security forces and intelligence services in an attempt to derail the peace process. Despite the ongoing peace talks, human rights violations and violations of international humanitarian law (IHL) continued to be committed by both sides, as well as by paramilitary groups operating alone or in collusion with or with the acquiescence of sectors of the security forces. Indigenous People, Afro-descendant and peasant farmer communities, women and girls, human rights defenders, community activists and trade unionists bore the brunt of the human rights consequences of the 50-year-long armed conflict. Such abuses included forced displacements, unlawful killings, hostage taking and abductions, death threats, enforced disappearances, torture and sexual violence. The government promoted legislation that threatened to exacerbate impunity and undermine the little progress made in recent years to bring to justice some of those suspected of crimes under international law and other human rights abuses and violations.

INTERNAL ARMED CONFLICT

The civilian population, especially Indigenous, Afro-descendant and peasant farmer communities, as well as human rights defenders continued to be the most affected by the armed conflict. According to the latest figures available from the NGO CODHES (Consultoría para los Derechos Humanos y el Desplazamiento), almost 220,000 people were forcibly displaced in 2013.

According to the National Indigenous Organization of Colombia (Organización Nacional Indígena de Colombia, ONIC), 10 Indigenous people were killed for conflict-related reasons and at least 2,819 forcibly displaced in the first nine months of 2014.[2] In 2013, 30 killings and 3,185 victims of forced displacement were recorded.

On 12 September, two Embera Dovida Indigenous leaders were killed in Alto Baudó Municipality, Chocó Department, reportedly by the guerrilla group, National Liberation Army (Ejército de Liberación Nacional, ELN).

Afro-descendant communities in the south western port city of Buenaventura were the target of a growing wave of violence, including killings and enforced disappearances, carried out mostly by paramilitaries and criminal gangs. Some of the victims were dismembered. The violence was concentrated in poor areas of the city earmarked for the development of port infrastructure and other economic projects.[3]

The sheer scale of human rights abuses was underscored by a report published by the state's National Centre of Historic Memory in 2013. It concluded that between 1985 and 2012, almost 220,000 people were killed, 80% of them civilians. At least 25,000 people were the victims of enforced disappearances, carried out mostly by paramilitaries and the security forces. Some 27,000 people were kidnapped between 1970 and 2010, mostly by guerrilla groups, and more than 5 million people were forcibly displaced between 1985 and 2012. By November, the government had registered more than 7 million victims.

PEACE PROCESS

The peace negotiations, held in Havana, Cuba, between the government and the FARC continued to offer the best chance in over a decade to put an end to hostilities. However, on 17 November, the government suspended talks in protest at the capture of an army general by the FARC in Chocó Department. He was released on 30 November and talks resumed on 10 December. On 17 December, the FARC declared a unilateral ceasefire that began on 20 December.

At the end of the year, the two sides had reached partial agreements on three of the six agenda items. A framework agreement on a fourth, on victims' rights, was made public in June.

The framework agreement marked a significant step forward as both sides acknowledged their responsibility for human rights abuses, that victims' rights lay at the heart of the peace process and that these rights were non-negotiable. The framework agreement did not, however, make an explicit commitment to guarantee justice for all victims. There were fears this could undermine the long-term viability of an eventual peace agreement.[4]

SOCIAL PROTEST

Senior state officials claimed that a national strike by peasant farmers in April had been infiltrated by guerrilla groups. This placed demonstrators at risk of revenge attacks by paramilitaries. In May, paramilitaries sent a death threat to human rights defenders accusing them of organizing the strike, which they claimed was supported by guerrilla groups.[5]

Similar accusations by the authorities were made during protests by Indigenous communities in October 2013, a national peasant farmer strike in August 2013, and peasant farmer demonstrations in Catatumbo in June 2013. There were allegations that the security forces used excessive and disproportionate force during the protests. The UN High Commissioner for Human Rights stated that nine protesters, five bystanders and one police officer were killed with firearms during the protests in 2013.

SECURITY FORCES

Extrajudicial executions by the security forces continued to be reported, albeit in fewer numbers than during the administration of President Álvaro Uribe (2002-2010). However, the Office of the Attorney General failed to make progress in bringing to justice most of those responsible for these crimes, especially senior officers. Many cases continued to be referred to military courts. These courts, which are neither independent nor impartial, failed to deliver justice. According to the report on the situation of human rights in Colombia published by the UN High Commissioner for Human Rights in January, 48 cases of extrajudicial executions attributed to the security forces were transferred to the military justice system and "numerous other cases were transferred directly by civilian prosecutors" in the first eight months of 2013.

PARAMILITARIES

The Justice and Peace Law (Law 975 of 2005), through which thousands of paramilitaries who laid down their arms in a government-sponsored process were to benefit from a maximum of eight years in prison in return for confessions about human rights violations, failed to respect the right of victims to truth, justice and reparation. The process began in 2005, but by September 2014, only 63 paramilitaries had been convicted of human rights violations under Law 975. Most of the 30,000 paramilitaries who reportedly laid down their arms failed to submit themselves to the limited scrutiny of Law 975.

These groups, which the government referred to as criminal gangs (*bandas criminales*, Bacrim), continued to operate and to commit serious human rights violations, either alone or in collusion with or with the acquiescence of sectors of the security forces. Such groups targeted human rights defenders, community leaders and trade unionists, as well as Indigenous, Afro-descendant and peasant farmer communities.[6]

Around 160 paramilitaries who submitted themselves to Law 975 were eligible for release in 2014. Some were high-ranking leaders who had been in prison on remand but had served the maximum eight years stipulated in Law 975. Many were expected to return to their original areas of operation, raising concerns about the impact on the safety of victims and human rights defenders in these areas.

GUERRILLA GROUPS

Guerrilla groups committed serious human rights abuses and violations of international humanitarian law, especially against communities in rural areas. Despite the FARC's public commitment to end kidnappings, cases continued to be reported. The NGO País Libre reported 233 kidnappings in the first nine months of 2014, compared to 299 in the whole of 2013. Most kidnappings were attributed to common criminals, with guerrilla groups responsible for 21% and paramilitaries for 3% of the total.

Landmines, mostly laid by the FARC, continued to kill and maim civilians and members of the security forces. Guerrilla groups, as well as paramilitary groups, continued to conscript children, mostly in rural areas, forcing many families to flee their homes to protect their children. The FARC also carried out indiscriminate attacks that placed civilians at risk.

IMPUNITY

Impunity remained a hallmark of the conflict, with very few perpetrators of human rights abuses held to account. The government's support of legislation that threatened to boost impunity called into question its commitment to the right of victims to truth and justice.

In October, the government presented two bills to Congress. The first sought to expand the crimes that could be considered acts of service under the remit of the military justice system. The second could ensure that human rights violations committed by the security forces would not be investigated as criminal actions, but rather in a manner to determine whether or not they constitute breaches of international humanitarian law. This could result in those responsible escaping criminal prosecution by presenting the crime as a proportionate action in the course of armed conflict.

In September, 12 UN human rights experts warned that Senate Bill No. 85, which was under discussion in Congress at the time of writing, would be a step backwards for human rights: "[I]f adopted, Bill No.85 could seriously weaken the independence and impartiality of the judiciary … Its adoption would also … represent a major setback in the Colombian state's long-standing fight against impunity for cases of violations of international humanitarian law and international human rights law." The bill listed a number of crimes that would be dealt with exclusively by the military justice system, including homicide and breaches of international humanitarian law . Since extrajudicial executions are not a separate crime in the Criminal Code, they could be defined as homicide and thus investigated by military prosecutors.

In August 2013, the Constitutional Court had upheld the constitutionality of the Legal Framework for Peace, approved by Congress in June 2012. This could enable alleged human rights abusers to evade justice by giving Congress the power to limit criminal trials to those "most responsible" for human rights abuses, and to suspend prison sentences handed down to paramilitary, guerrilla and security force combatants convicted of such crimes. But the Court ruled that the sentences of those "most responsible" could not be suspended if they were responsible for crimes against humanity, genocide or war crimes. However, there was no clear definition of, or criteria to determine, "most responsible".

LAND RESTITUTION

The Victims and Land Restitution Law, which came into force in 2012, sought to provide full reparation, including land restitution, to some of the victims of the conflict. The legislation was an important step forward in efforts to acknowledge some victims' right to reparation, but it remained flawed and its implementation progressed slowly. By August 2014, only some 30,000 hectares of land had been adjudicated to peasant farmers and only one 50,000-hectare territory to Indigenous communities. Official figures suggested that in the course of the conflict an estimated 8

million hectares of land had been subject to abandonment or dispossession.

Land claimants and those representing them, including human rights defenders and state officials, were threatened or killed, mostly by paramilitary groups.[7] By August 2014, the Office of the Attorney General was investigating the killing of at least 35 individuals who had a suspected association with land restitution. On 8 July, Robinson Álvarez Quemba, a topographer working with the government's Land Restitution Unit, was shot by an unidentified assailant while working in the municipality of San Roque, Antioquia Department. He died of his injuries three days later.

HUMAN RIGHTS DEFENDERS

Human rights defenders faced grave dangers. The Office in Colombia of the UN High Commissioner for Human Rights recorded 40 killings of human rights defenders between January and September. This compared to more than 70 human rights defenders killed in 2013, according to the NGO Somos Defensores. Indigenous and Afro-descendant leaders, land activists and community leaders were among the victims. According to the NGO, National Trade Union School (*Escuela Nacional Sindical*), 20 members of trade unions were killed by 11 December; at least 27 were killed in 2013.

These attacks, as well as the theft of sensitive information, ongoing death threats and the misuse of the legal system to bring bogus charges against human rights defenders, undermined the work of human rights organizations and fostered a climate of fear. There was an increase in the number of death threats towards the end of 2014. In September and October, more than 100 human rights defenders, community leaders, peace activists, land restitution leaders, politicians and journalists, received a series of mass email death threats from several paramilitary groups.[8] Only a few of those responsible for threats against and killings of human rights defenders were identified, let alone brought to justice.

The state's protection programmes, coordinated by the National Protection Unit (Unidad Nacional de Protección, UNP), continued to provide security to thousands of individuals at risk, including human rights defenders. But these programmes suffered from serious weaknesses, including severe delays in implementing security measures.

In September, the UNP was rocked by a corruption scandal in which senior UNP officials, including the administrative director and secretary general, were accused of taking kickbacks from private contractors to whom the UNP subcontracts most of its protection work. The UNP also acknowledged in September that because of a budget shortfall it would have to withdraw the protection schemes of some beneficiaries.

VIOLENCE AGAINST WOMEN AND GIRLS

All the parties to the conflict carried out rapes and other forms of sexual violence, primarily against women and girls. The authorities continued to fail to implement Constitutional Court Judicial Ruling 092 of 2008. This ordered the authorities to put an end to such crimes and to bring to justice those responsible.

In June, President Santos signed into law legislation on conflict-related sexual violence (Law 1719).[9] The law defined such violence as a war crime and a crime against humanity. It addressed a number of specific practices that continued to be carried out in the conflict, including sexual slavery and sexual exploitation, and enforced sterilization, prostitution, abortion, pregnancy and nudity. Under the law, no statute of limitations is applicable in cases of genocide, crimes against humanity and war crimes.

US ASSISTANCE

US assistance to Colombia continued to fall. In 2014, the USA allocated some US$214.5 million in military and around US$164.9 million in non-military assistance to Colombia, compared to some US$228.6 million and around US$195.9 million, respectively, in 2013. In September 2014, 25% of the total military assistance for the year was released after the US Secretary of State determined that the Colombian government had made progress in improving human rights.

INTERNATIONAL SCRUTINY

In her report on the human rights situation in Colombia, published in January, the UN High Commissioner for Human Rights congratulated the Colombian government on "its determined pursuit of a negotiated end to the internal armed conflict", but noted that all parties to the conflict were still responsible for human rights abuses and violations. The report also stated that the unwillingness of state institutions "to accept responsibility for human rights violations undermines further advances in human rights".

In August, the Inter-American Commission on Human Rights (IACHR) published its report on the human rights situation in Colombia. The report welcomed progress in the peace talks but noted that the armed conflict continued to have a serious impact on human rights. It warned that the human rights situation could not be resolved without also addressing the problem of impunity.

In March, the IACHR requested that the Colombian government adopt precautionary measures for Bogotá Mayor Gustavo Petro and that his removal from office, ordered by the Office of the Procurator General in January, be suspended until the IACHR could rule on the case. The government initially refused to comply with the request and only reversed its decision after it was ordered to do so by Colombia's Constitutional Court in April.

The UN Human Rights Council adopted the outcome of the September 2013 Universal Periodic Review of Colombia. Amnesty International welcomed Colombia's support of recommendations to fight impunity, but reiterated its concerns that legislation to broaden the scope of military jurisdiction and the Legal Framework for

Peace would seriously undermine efforts to combat impunity.

1. Colombia: Open letter to Presidential candidates. Putting human rights at the heart of the election campaign (AMR 23/014/2014)
www.amnesty.org/en/library/info/AMR23/014/2014/en

2. Colombia: Two Indigenous leaders killed, third at risk (AMR/23/001/2014)
www.amnesty.org/en/library/info/AMR23/001/2014/en

3. Colombia: Death threats received in "humanitarian zone" (AMR 23/016/2014)
www.amnesty.org/en/library/info/AMR23/016/2014/en

4. Historic Colombia-FARC declaration fails to guarantee victims' right to justice
www.amnesty.org/en/articles/news/2014/06/historic-colombia-farc-declaration-fails-guarantee-victims-right-justice/

5. Colombia: Paramilitaries threaten human rights activists (AMR 23/017/2014)
www.amnesty.org/en/library/info/AMR23/017/2014/en

6. Colombia: Election candidates receive death threats (AMR 23/005/2014)
www.amnesty.org/en/library/info/AMR23/005/2014/en

7. Colombia: Land rights activists threatened in Colombia (AMR 23/019/2014)
www.amnesty.org/en/library/info/AMR23/019/2014/en

8. Colombia: Mass death threats to human rights defenders (AMR 23/030/2014)
www.amnesty.org/en/library/info/AMR23/030/2014/en

9. Colombia: New law aims to address impunity for conflict-related crimes of sexual violence (AMR 23/24/2014)
www.amnesty.org/en/library/info/AMR23/024/2014/en

CONGO (REPUBLIC OF)

Republic of Congo
Head of state and government: **Denis Sassou Nguesso**

Serious human rights violations including cases of rape and other sexual violence, arbitrary arrests and detention, excessive use of force, and torture and other ill-treatment were committed, including during the mass forced expulsion of people from the Democratic Republic of the Congo (DRC). Freedoms of expression, assembly and association were restricted.

REFUGEES' AND MIGRANTS' RIGHTS

More than 179,000 foreign nationals from the DRC, including refugees and asylum-seekers, were forcibly returned during police operation "Mbata ya Mokolo". Some DRC nationals who remained were in hiding, fearing deportation. The operation was carried out by police in cities nationwide, ostensibly to reduce irregular immigration and criminality, and targeted people from the DRC in particular.

FREEDOM OF EXPRESSION

Freedom of expression including press freedom was seriously limited including in relation to proposed constitutional amendments to allow President Nguesso a third term in office. Journalists were subject to harassment and intimidation by the police and local authorities. Human rights defenders feared for their security and were consequently reluctant to denounce violations involving high-profile officers.

On 26 September, Cameroonian journalist Elie Smith was expelled following a statement by the Ministry of the Interior accusing him of "seditious and subversive acts" and "intelligence with foreign powers working against the interests of the Republic of Congo". Local human rights organizations claimed that the decision was politically motivated.

On 23 September, freelance journalist Sadio Kanté was forced to leave the country, accused of illegal residence among other charges. She denied all the allegations.

FREEDOM OF ASSEMBLY

Freedom of peaceful assembly, especially for trade unions and perceived or actual political opponents of the government, was severely restricted during the year.

On 4 November, police burst into the Brazzaville residence of Clément Mierassa, opposition leader and president of the Congolese Democratic Social Party, and disbanded a political meeting. According to witnesses, the police beat some of the participants. Around 30 arrests were made.

ARBITRARY ARRESTS AND DETENTIONS

Several cases of arbitrary arrests and detentions were reported during operation Mbata ya Mokolo targeting DRC nationals, including refugees and asylum-seekers legally living in Congo. Opposition party members, trade unionists and their family members were also frequently subject to arbitrary arrest and detention by the police.

On 4 January, police arrested Tamba Kenge Sandrine and her four children. They were released the same day without charge. The arresting officer had come to arrest her husband, Kouka Fidele, because of his trade union activities, and arrested his wife and children instead. Kouka Fidele spent several months in hiding, fearing arrest.

Jean-Bernard Bossomba "Saio", a refugee from the DRC was arrested by the police on 22 May and detained in a national police cell in Brazzaville until 22 July. No formal charges were made. A former army officer in the DRC, he said that he feared for his security if returned there.

VIOLENCE AGAINST WOMEN AND GIRLS

Reports were received in September alleging that Congolese police officers were raping women, including within refugee and asylum-seeker communities. At the end of the year, no action was known to have been taken by the authorities to investigate the allegations.

A five-year-old girl was raped, allegedly by police who, according to relatives, took her and other family members from their home in Brazzaville during the night. Officers separated the girl from the group before forcing them all to board a ferry to Kinshasa, DRC. The child was taken to hospital on arrival in Kinshasa, where it

was confirmed that she had been raped. In September, Amnesty International researchers referred the girl to a specialized medical centre for additional treatment and psychological support.

IMPUNITY

Police officers suspected of committing serious human rights violations continued to enjoy impunity. Congolese soldiers accused of serious human rights violations, including enforced disappearances, while serving in regional peacekeeping forces in the Central African Republic were not investigated.

In May the authorities announced that 18 police officers involved in human rights violations during the Mbata ya Mokolo operation had been suspended from their duties. It was not clear if the suspension remained in force at the end of year or if the authorities had conducted any investigations to establish whether police officers had been responsible for violations.

In June the African Union announced that it would open investigations into allegations of Congolese members of the African-led International Support Mission to the Central African Republic (MISCA) being implicated in the enforced disappearance on 24 March of at least 11 people in the Central African Republic. However, by the end of the year, no such investigations were known to have been initiated by the authorities.

CÔTE D'IVOIRE

Republic of Côte d'Ivoire
Head of state: **Alassane Ouattara**
Head of government: **Daniel Kablan Duncan**

Côte d'Ivoire was examined by the UN Universal Periodic Review mechanism which raised concerns about the adequacy of the government's action on several issues including on women's rights and the lack of (or selective) accountability for crimes committed during the post-electoral violence in 2010-2011. Hundreds of detainees awaited trial in connection with post-electoral violence. Côte d'Ivoire refused entry to more than 400 Ivorian refugees who had fled to Liberia during the post-electoral crisis. Lesbian, gay, bisexual, transgender and intersex (LGBTI) people continued to face discrimination.

BACKGROUND

In December 2013, the government renewed the mandate of the Special Investigation Commission tasked with investigating crimes committed during the 2010-2011 post-electoral violence as well as the mandate of the Commission for Dialogue, Truth and Reconciliation (CDVR). The CDVR published its findings in December 2014 and expressed concern about selective justice.

In April 2014, Côte d'Ivoire was examined by the UN Universal Periodic Review mechanism, which raised concerns about the adequacy of the government's action on several issues including: action to ensure accountability for crimes committed during the post-electoral violence in 2010-2011; measures taken to implement the national reconciliation process; efforts to ensure an open and free election campaign before the 2015 presidential elections; steps to ensure a safe and enabling environment for civil society; and women's rights, including measures to prevent sexual violence.

In July 2014, Côte d'Ivoire refused entry to over 400 Ivorian refugees who had fled to Liberia during the post-electoral violence. Côte d'Ivoire claimed it was to prevent the spread of the Ebola Virus Disease, which was present in Liberia, but UNHCR, the UN refugee agency, had ensured that every refugee had had a medical screening. Despite the screenings more than 35,000 Ivorian refugees were waiting in Liberia for the Ivorian authorities to reopen the border.

In November, the government agreed to pay the outstanding wages and bonuses claimed by soldiers who had protested over two years of back pay and housing benefits. Also in November, the opposition party, Ivorian Popular Front (FPI), confirmed Laurent Gbagbo's candidacy for the 2015 Presidential elections, despite the fact that he is awaiting trial at the International Criminal Court (ICC). In December, the Abidjan Tribunal declared Laurent Gbagbo's candidacy inadmissible.

JUSTICE SYSTEM

In January and May, more than 180 political prisoners held in relation to post-electoral violence of 2010-2011 were released, some on a provisional basis in view of an upcoming trial in 2015. More than 600 detainees were awaiting trial in connection with the violence. Some political prisoners held in the Maison d'Arrêt et de Correction (MACA) Abidjan prison staged a hunger strike to protest against detention conditions and the slow judicial process. Three political detainees died in custody in the MACA in unclarified circumstances.

In July, the Minister of Justice announced that the investigation into the disappearance of journalist Guy André Kieffer would be reopened, as would the investigation into the death of Yves Lambelin, head of the Société immobilière et financière de la côte africaine (SIFCA) who was killed during the post-electoral crisis.

The trial of 83 people, including Simone Gbagbo and Michel Gbagbo, wife and son respectively of the former President Laurent Gbagbo, and former senior officials of the Gbagbo administration, began in late December 2014. The accused face charges including threatening state security and the creation of armed groups.

INTERNATIONAL JUSTICE

Former President Gbagbo remained in ICC custody. In June, the ICC confirmed the charges against him and committed his case to trial. He will be tried for crimes against humanity. The trial is currently set for July 2015.

In March, Côte d'Ivoire surrendered Charles Blé Goudé, accused of crimes against humanity committed during post-electoral violence, to the ICC. In December, the ICC confirmed four charges of crimes against humanity against him and committed him to trial.

In December, the Pre-Trial Chamber of the ICC rejected Côte d'Ivoire's challenge to the admissibility of the case against Simone Gbagbo, who was charged by the ICC in February 2012 with murder, sexual violence, persecution and other inhuman acts, allegedly committed during the post-electoral crisis. Côte d'Ivoire has filed an appeal against the decision.

RIGHTS OF LESBIAN, GAY, BISEXUAL, TRANSGENDER AND INTERSEX PEOPLE

Lesbian, gay, bisexual, transgender and intersex (LGBTI) people faced increasing discrimination. In January, the office of Alternative Côte d'Ivoire, an organization working for the rights of LGBTI people living with HIV, was ransacked by a large mob. Computers were stolen, walls were daubed with homophobic slogans and a staff member was badly beaten. Police refused to respond or investigate the incident. The Director of Alternative Côte d'Ivoire's house was also later attacked. A security forces member was reportedly among the attackers. Several staff members subsequently went into hiding.

CORPORATE ACCOUNTABILITY

Eight years after the dumping of toxic waste in Abidjan no medical study had been conducted to assess the long-term health implications of exposure to the waste. The company that made and sent the waste to Abidjan – oil trader Trafigura – has never disclosed the full information about the waste content and its potential impact; nor has it been properly held to account for its role in the dumping. In October 2014, the UN Environment Programme (UNEP) confirmed that it will carry out an environmental audit of the dump sites in 2015.

ABUSES BY ARMED GROUPS

In December 2013, the UN Operation in Côte d'Ivoire (UNOCI) released a report on the Dozo, a group of traditional hunters who fought on behalf of Alassane Ouattara during the post-electoral crisis. The report documented serious human rights violations allegedly committed by members of the Dozo between March 2009 and May 2013, including unlawful killings, illegal arrest and detentions, looting and extortions. At least 228 people were killed, 164 others injured by bullets, machetes and knives, and 162 arbitrarily arrested and illegally detained. In addition, 274 cases of looting, arson and extortion were verified and confirmed, including in the regions of Gbôklé, Haut-Sassandra, Gôh, Cavally, Guemon, Tonkpi, Marahoué, Nawa, Indenie-Djuablin, Poro and Moronou.[1]

---

1. Côte d'Ivoire: The Victors' Law – the human rights situation two years after the post-electoral crisis (AFR 31/001/2013)
   www.amnesty.org/en/library/info/AFR31/001/2013/en

CROATIA

Republic of Croatia
Head of state: **Ivo Josipovic** Head of government: **Zoran Milanovic**

Discrimination against Croatian Serbs and Roma continued. Same-sex partnerships were legally recognized. The rate of investigation and prosecution of war crimes remained at a low level.

DISCRIMINATION

Croatian Serbs

Croatian Serbs continued to face discrimination in public sector employment and the restitution of tenancy rights to social housing vacated during the 1991-1995 war.

In July, the Constitutional Court ruled unconstitutional a referendum petition seeking to restrict the use of minority language rights to local self-government units where at least half of the population is from an ethnic minority. Although the referendum petition applied to the whole country, the referendum petitioners, a Croat veteran group, specifically sought to ban the use of bilingual public signs in the Cyrillic (Serb) alphabet in Vukovar. The current law on minority rights sets the threshold at one third of the population.

Roma

Many Roma continued to live in segregated settlements without security of tenure and with limited access to basic services such as water, electricity, sanitation and transport facilities. Four years after the 2010 judgment of the European Court of Human Rights in the case of *Oršuš and Others v. Croatia*, many Roma children were still attending segregated classes. Discrimination in the labour market contributed to significantly higher rates of unemployment among Roma compared with other ethnic groups. Those living in rural areas and young women were particularly disadvantaged.

Rights of lesbian, gay, bisexual, transgender and intersex people

A Law on Life Partnership was adopted in July that granted equal rights to same-sex partnerships in all matters except adoption. The law introduced the institution of "partner-guardianship" to allow parents in same-sex partnerships to extend the full range of parental rights and obligations in relation to their children to their partners. The first same-sex partnership was registered in September. Three safe and successful Pride marches were held in Split, Zagreb and Osijek. In March, Croatia granted asylum to a gay man from Uganda who had sought protection following the criminalization of homosexuality in the country.

INTERNATIONAL JUSTICE

In November, an indictment was issued against a former member of the Croatian armed forces for crimes committed during Operation Storm in 1995. In March, Croat Army Officer Božo Bačelić became the first person to be convicted in national courts for war crimes committed during the same Operation Storm. Two further trials relating to war crimes committed during Operation Storm were ongoing by the end of the year. In total, eight members of Croatian military formations and 15 members of Serb formations stood trial for war crimes during the course of the year.

The European Court of Human Rights initiated communication with the government on 17 cases submitted by civilian victims of war alleging violations of the right to life due to the failure of the state to carry out effective investigations into the killing or disappearance of their relatives.

Croatia continued to stall on the adoption of a comprehensive legislative framework that would regulate the status of, and access to reparation for, all civilian victims of war. In a positive development in March, the Ministry of Veterans' Affairs presented a draft Act on the Rights of Victims of Sexual Violence in the Homeland War, which would grant victims access to psychosocial and medical support, free legal aid, and monetary compensation. However, the draft law failed to specify the level of financial compensation that would be made available.

In August, Croatia signed a regional declaration on missing persons, and committed to pursuing measures to establish the fate and whereabouts of the 2,200 still missing in Croatia. Croatia had yet to ratify the International Convention for the Protection of All Persons from Enforced Disappearance. The rights of relatives of missing persons continued to be undermined by the absence of a law on missing persons.

CUBA

Republic of Cuba
Head of state and government: **Raúl Castro Ruz**

Freedoms of expression, association and assembly continued to be repressed. The number of short-term arrests increased sharply and politically motivated criminal prosecutions continued.

BACKGROUND

Amendments to the Migration Law which became effective in January 2013 facilitated travel abroad for all Cubans. Although government critics were allowed to travel abroad without hindrance, there were reports of documents and other materials being confiscated on their return to Cuba.

By the end of the year Cuba had still failed to ratify the International Covenants on Civil and Political Rights and on Economic, Social and Cultural Rights, both of which it had signed in February 2008. The government did not respond to requests to visit Cuba from the UN Special Rapporteur on the rights to freedom of peaceful assembly and of association, sent in October 2013, or from the Special Rapporteur on torture and other cruel, inhuman or degrading treatment or punishment, sent in March 2014. The authorities have not granted Amnesty International access to the country since 1990.

An exchange of prisoners between the USA and Cuba in December, and the announcement of the further release of over 50 political prisoners, raised hopes for significant human rights change amid efforts to normalize relations between the two countries, which decided to renew their diplomatic relations.

FREEDOM OF EXPRESSION, ASSOCIATION, ASSEMBLY AND MOVEMENT

Criticism of the government continued to be repressed and was routinely punished by various means, including arbitrary and short-term detentions, "acts of repudiation" (demonstrations led by government supporters with the participation of state security officials), intimidation, harassment and politically motivated criminal prosecutions. The judicial system remained firmly under political control, gravely undermining the right to trial by an independent and impartial tribunal.

Government critics, independent journalists and human rights activists were frequently detained for exercising their rights to freedom of expression, association, assembly and movement. Activists were detained as a preventive measure to stop them from attending public demonstrations or private meetings.

There were increasing reports of government critics being threatened and also physically assaulted by state actors or individuals in their pay.

In June 2014, Roberto de Jesús Guerra Pérez, director of the independent news agency Hablemos Press, received threatening telephone calls and was assaulted on the streets of the capital, Havana, by an unidentified individual, in what he believed was an attempt by the authorities to dissuade him from continuing his journalist activities.[1]

The government continued to exert control over all media, while access to information on the internet remained challenging due to technical limitations and restrictions on content. Independent journalists were systematically subjected to harassment, intimidation and detention for reporting information that was not sanctioned by the state apparatus.

In May, blogger Yoani Sánchez and her husband launched an online news website called 14 y medio. Shortly after it went live, the website was hacked and anyone accessing it from Cuba was redirected to a webpage which carried propaganda against Yoani Sánchez.

PRISONERS OF CONSCIENCE

At the end of the year, five prisoners of conscience detained solely for peacefully exercising their right to freedom of expression, remained imprisoned. Three of them, brothers Alexeis, Vianco and Django Vargas Martín, were sentenced in November on charges of "public disorder of a continuous nature" after having spent more than a year and a half in pre-trial detention. Alexeis was sentenced to four years' imprisonment, and Vianco and Django to two and a half years.[2]

Articles 72-90 of the Criminal Code which criminalize "dangerousness" and punish those deemed to be likely to commit a crime in the future, were increasingly used as a means to incarcerate government critics. Prisoners of conscience Emilio Planas Robert and Iván Fernández Depestre were sentenced to three and a half and three years' imprisonment in October 2012 and August 2013 respectively for "dangerousness". Emilio Planas Robert was accused of putting up posters in Guantánamo City with "anti-government" slogans.

Despite the relaxation of travel restrictions, 12 former prisoners of conscience arrested as part of the mass crackdown in 2003 and released in 2011 were not allowed to travel abroad as they were deemed to be serving their sentence outside prison.

ARBITRARY ARRESTS AND DETENTIONS

Short-term arbitrary detentions as a tactic to silence dissent increased sharply. The Cuban Commission on Human Rights and National Reconciliation reported 8,899 politically motivated short-term detentions during 2014, an increase of more than 27% compared with 2013.

Members of the independent civil society organization Ladies in White faced constant harassment and every Sunday dozens were detained for several hours to prevent them from travelling to attend mass and carry out peaceful marches. The organization reported that 1,810 of its members had been arrested during 2013.

Dozens of government critics were arbitrarily detained or pressurized not to travel to Havana during the second summit of the Community of Latin American and Caribbean States on 28 and 29 January. As a result of the arrests and the wave of intimidation, various meetings that were due to be held in parallel to the summit had to be cancelled.[3]

On 9 December, Ladies in White member Sonia Garro Alfonso, her husband Ramón Alejandro Muñoz González, and dissident Eugenio Hernández Hernández, were released and put under house arrest after having spent more than two and a half years in prison without trial. They were detained in March 2012 during the visit of Pope Benedict XVI, accused of assault, public disorder and attempted murder.[4]

US EMBARGO AGAINST CUBA

In September, the USA renewed the Trading with the Enemy Act, which imposes financial and economic sanctions on Cuba and prohibits US citizens from travelling to and engaging in economic activities with the island. In October 2014, the UN General Assembly adopted, for the 23rd consecutive year, a resolution calling on the USA to lift the unilateral embargo. US President Obama announced in December that he will engage in discussions with the US Congress in order to lift the embargo on Cuba.

---

1. Cuba: Journalist threatened and attacked (AMR 25/001/2014)
   www.amnesty.org/en/library/info/AMR25/001/2014/en
2. Cuba: Sentencing of three brothers postponed (AMR 25/003/2014)
   www.amnesty.org/en/library/info/AMR25/003/2014/en

3. Cuba steps up repression on the eve of the CELAC summit (Press release)
   www.amnesty.org/press-releases/2014/01/cuba-steps-repression-eve-celac-summit/
4. Cuba: Further information – Government critics under house arrest (AMR 25/005/2014)
   www.amnesty.org/en/library/info/AMR25/005/2014/en

CYPRUS

Republic of Cyprus
Head of state and government: **Nicos Anastasiades**

Immigration authorities continued to routinely detain hundreds of migrants and certain categories of asylum-seekers in prison-like conditions for extended periods while awaiting deportation. Those detained included Syrian refugees. Some women detainees were separated from their young children.

BACKGROUND

In February, the Greek Cypriot and Turkish Cypriot leaders resumed negotiations regarding the reunification of the island after an 18-month break, but no progress had been made by the end of the year.

REFUGEES' AND MIGRANTS' RIGHTS

Irregular migrants, rejected asylum-seekers and certain categories of asylum-seekers were routinely detained for prolonged periods at the country's main immigration detention facility in the village of Menoyia, while awaiting deportation. Syrian refugees were also detained despite Cyprus' formal policy not to deport Syrian nationals.

People held at Menoyia were detained in cramped, prison-like conditions. Detainees complained about the limited time allowed to exercise outside, the quality of the food and the fact that their cells were locked between 10.30pm and 7.30am. A small number of migrant women were held in police stations pending deportation. In at least two cases, detained women were forcibly separated from their young children.[1]

In May, the UN Committee against Torture raised concerns about the routine and prolonged detention of irregular migrants and asylum-seekers; the detention conditions in Menoyia; and the reports that asylum-seekers were deported to their countries of origin despite facing a serious risk of torture or religious persecution. The Committee also criticized the fact that asylum-seekers were not protected from *refoulement* during the judicial review process and that there was no effective judicial remedy to challenge deportation decisions and halt deportations pending the outcome of appeals.

TRAFFICKING IN HUMAN BEINGS

In April, a law was adopted with the aim of bringing national legislation on combating trafficking in line with EU and other international standards. However, the law did not provide for appeals against decisions by the Office of the Police for Combating Trafficking in Human Beings not to recognize an individual as a victim of trafficking. Concerns were also raised that police employed a definition of a victim of trafficking that fell short of international standards.

ENFORCED DISAPPEARANCES

Between January and August, the Committee of Missing Persons in Cyprus exhumed the remains of 65 people, bringing the total number of exhumations since 2006 to 948. Between August 2006 and August 2014, the remains of 564 missing individuals (430 Greek Cypriots and 134 Turkish Cypriots) had been identified and restored to their families. However, no perpetrators were identified or prosecuted for the disappearances and killings in either Cyprus or Turkey at the end of the year. The graves date from the inter-communal fighting which took place between 1963 and 1964, and during the Turkish invasion in 1974.

TORTURE AND OTHER ILL-TREATMENT

A report published in December by the European Committee for the Prevention of Torture highlighted a number of allegations of ill-treatment by police officers that were received by the Committee's delegates during their visit to Cyprus in September and October 2013. The allegations mainly concerned ill-treatment of foreign nationals during their transportation or interviews at police stations. The European Committee for the Prevention of Torture also received a number of allegations concerning physical ill-treatment, verbal abuse and inappropriate use of tear gas by police guards against migrants held at the Menoyia immigration detention facility. Similar allegations were received by the UN Committee against Torture.

---

1. Cyprus: Abusive detention of migrants and asylum-seekers flouts EU law (Press release)
   www.amnesty.org/en/news/cyprus-abusive-detention-migrants-and-asylum-seekers-flouts-eu-law-2014-03-18

CZECH REPUBLIC

Czech Republic
Head of state: **Miloš Zeman**
Head of government: **Bohuslav Sobotka**

Roma continued to face widespread discrimination. The European Commission initiated infringement proceedings against the Czech Republic for the discrimination against Roma pupils in education. The ill-treatment of persons with mental disabilities in state institutions was exposed. Muslims faced growing public hostility.

BACKGROUND

In October, the police announced an investigation into allegations of the manipulation and buying of votes of Roma citizens in the local elections held the same month. According to NGOs monitoring the elections, the practice of vote-buying was used by a number of political parties in several regions.

DISCRIMINATION
Roma

In June, the UN Committee on Economic, Social and Cultural Rights criticized the authorities for the large number of Roma pupils in so-called "practical schools" (former special schools), designed for pupils with mild mental disabilities. The Committee called on the government to abolish practices that lead to the segregation of Roma pupils and to phase out practical schools. It recommended that mainstream schools should provide inclusive education to children from socially disadvantaged backgrounds and Roma pupils.

In September, the European Commission initiated infringement proceedings against the authorities for breaching the prohibition of discrimination in education set out in the EU Race Equality Directive.

In August, over four years after the government's apology for the enforced sterilization of Roma women, the Human Rights Minister announced a draft law offering financial compensation of between 3,500 and 5,000 euros to individual victims. According to the NGO Czech Helsinki Committee, almost 1,000 women were forcibly sterilized between 1972 and 1991 and should be entitled to financial remedy.

In November, the government acknowledged that Roma continued to face discrimination regarding access to housing, education, health care and labour market. The government-commissioned report on the situation of the Roma minority highlighted obstacles in accessing affordable housing, including discrimination by private landlords. The report also highlighted the over-representation of Roma children in practical schools.

Hate crimes

In October, the Constitutional Court rejected an appeal by two perpetrators against the length of their sentences for an arson attack against a Roma family in April 2009. The attack had left a two-year-old Roma girl with burns to 80% of her body.

Muslims

The media reported occasional acts of vandalism on the Prague mosque, including daubing of islamophobic messages. The police were still investigating these incidents at the end of the year.

In September, over 25,000 people signed a petition calling on the authorities not to grant "enhanced rights" to the registered Association of Muslim Communities. The Law on Churches allowed religious organizations, which had been registered for 10 years, to apply for enhanced rights, including the right to teach religion in state schools and the recognition of religious wedding ceremonies. The petition called on the government not to permit the opening of Muslim schools and not to allow the teaching of Islam in state schools or Muslim worship in prisons. By the end of the year, the Association of Muslim Communities had not applied for "enhanced rights".

In September, the Public Defender of Rights (Ombudswoman) held that a secondary school for nurses had discriminated against two women, a refugee from Somalia and an asylum-seeker from Afghanistan, by prohibiting them from wearing headscarves. The Public Defender clarified that the law did not restrict the use of religious symbols in schools and that the seemingly neutral prohibition of any covering of the head was indirectly discriminatory. A complaint by the Somali student to the Czech School Inspectorate was rejected.

TORTURE AND OTHER ILL-TREATMENT

Patients with mental disabilities continued to be ill-treated in mental health institutions. In June, the Mental Disability Advocacy Center and the League of Human Rights called on the government to immediately prohibit the use of net beds and other inhumane restraint techniques. In a report which assessed the situation in eight psychiatric hospitals, the NGOs provided evidence of the continuous use of restraint techniques, such as net beds, bed straps as well as the unregulated use of excessive medication. In response to the NGO report, the Public Defender of Rights visited six hospitals in August and also found evidence of the use of restraint techniques. She criticized the lack of effective monitoring of their use and called for legislative changes introducing greater safeguards.

HUMAN RIGHTS DEFENDERS

In October, during a "week against anti-racism and xenophilia", the websites of the NGOs Czech Helsinki Committee and Life Together (Vzájemné soužití) were attacked by far-right hackers. The personal email of the co-ordinator of an Amnesty International group in the city of Brno was also attacked by the hackers, who published the members' internal communication on their websites. The Czech Helsinki Committee announced that it would submit a criminal complaint against the hackers.

REFUGEES AND ASYLUM-SEEKERS

Despite initial plans to start a small resettlement programme for Syrian refugees, the government decided in October to restrict its support to the provision of humanitarian assistance to Syrian refugees with acute medical needs in Jordan.

DEMOCRATIC REPUBLIC OF THE CONGO

Democratic Republic of the Congo
Head of state: **Joseph Kabila**
Head of government: **Augustin Matata Ponyo Mapon**

The security situation in eastern Democratic Republic of the Congo (DRC) remained dire and an upsurge in violence by armed groups claimed the lives of thousands of civilians and forced more than a million people to leave their homes. Human rights abuses, including killings and mass rapes, were committed by both government security forces and armed groups. Violence against women and girls was prevalent throughout the country. Plans to amend the Constitution to allow President Kabila to stay in office beyond 2016 prompted protests. Human rights defenders, journalists and members of the political opposition were threatened, harassed and arbitrarily arrested by armed groups and by government security forces.

BACKGROUND

The Congolese army, with the support of the UN peacekeeping force MONUSCO (UN Organization Stabilization Mission in the DRC), succeeded in defeating and disbanding the armed group March 23 (M23) in 2013. However, the conflict in eastern DRC did not end and other armed groups expanded their areas of operation and continued to target civilians.

In January, the government launched a military operation against the armed group Allied Democratic Forces (ADF) in Beni territory, North Kivu province. While "Operation Sokola 1" ("Operation Clean-up" in Lingala) forced the ADF rebels from their forest base, they regrouped and in October launched a series of attacks, killing and kidnapping civilians.[1]

Other armed groups remained active in North Kivu, Katanga, South Kivu and Ituri, committing serious human rights abuses against civilians.

Some fighters from the Forces Démocratiques de Libération du Rwanda (FDLR) participated in a demobilization programme run by MONUSCO and a few were confined in government camps. However, others carried on armed activities in the east of the country. The MONUSCO Demobilization, Disarmament, Repatriation, Resettlement and Reintegration programme included former FDLR child soldiers.

In July, President Kabila appointed Jeannine Mabunda as his special envoy on sexual violence and recruitment of child soldiers.

In November, several hundred magistrates went on strike over pay.

ABUSES BY ARMED GROUPS

Armed groups committed atrocities against civilians in eastern DRC, especially in northern Katanga, Ituri, North Kivu and South Kivu. Abuses included unlawful killings, summary executions, forced recruitment of children, rape and sexual violence, large-scale looting, burning of homes and destruction of property. Attacks were characterized by extreme violence, sometimes ethnically motivated. Some of the fighting was for control over natural resources and trade. The violence was facilitated by easy access to weapons and ammunition.

Armed groups that committed abuses against civilians included: the FDLR; the ADF; Nyatura; the Lord's Resistance Army (LRA); the Nduma Defence of Congo (NDC) known as Mai Mai Sheka; and various other Mai Mai groups including Mai Mai Lafontaine, Mai Mai Simba and Mai Mai Bakata Katanga.

In June, attacks by Nyatura in Rutshuru territory, North Kivu, left at least four civilians dead and dozens of houses burned to the ground.

On the night of 6 June, in Mutarule, Uvira territory, South Kivu, at least 30 civilians were killed in an attack by an unidentified armed group. Most of the victims were from the Bafulero ethnic group. The attack took place just a few kilometres from a MONUSCO base.

Between early October and late December, the ADF allegedly carried out a spate of attacks on civilians in several towns and villages in Beni territory, North Kivu, and Ituri district, Province Orientale, killing at least 270 civilians and abducting others. The assailants also looted civilians' property.

Between 3 and 5 November, FDLR fighters killed 13 people in Misau and Misoke villages, Walikale territory, North Kivu.

VIOLENCE AGAINST WOMEN AND GIRLS

Rape and other forms of sexual violence against women and girls remained endemic, not only in areas of conflict, but also in parts of the country not affected by armed hostilities. Acts of sexual violence were committed by armed groups, by members of the security forces and by unarmed civilians. The perpetrators of rape and other sexual violence enjoyed virtually total impunity.

Mass rapes, in which dozens of women and girls were sexually assaulted with extreme brutality, were committed by armed groups and by members of the security forces during attacks on villages in remote areas, particularly in North Kivu and Katanga. Such attacks often also involved other forms of torture, killings and looting.

Between 4 and 17 July, Mai Mai Simba combatants reportedly raped at least 23 women and girls in Mangurejipa village and mining sites located in surrounding areas in Lubero territory, North Kivu.

In October, dozens of women and girls were raped in Kansowe village, Mitwaba territory, Katanga province by special commando soldiers of the Congolese army deployed there to fight the Mai Mai Bakata Katanga armed group.

Between 3 and 5 November, at least 10 women were raped, allegedly by FDLR

fighters, in Misau and Misoke villages, Walikale territory, North Kivu province.

CHILD SOLDIERS

Armed groups recruited children. Many were subjected to sexual violence and cruel and inhuman treatment while being used as fighters, carriers, cooks, guides, spies and messengers.

INTERNALLY DISPLACED PEOPLE

The demise of the M23 armed group in 2013 facilitated the progressive closure of camps for internally displaced people (IDPs) around the city of Goma. However, due to the upsurge of armed group violence against civilians, new IDP camps had to be set up for people fleeing human rights abuses. By 17 December, about 2.7 million people were internally displaced within DRC. Most of the displacement took place in connection with the armed conflicts in North Katanga, North Kivu, South Kivu and Ituri districts.

TORTURE AND OTHER ILL-TREATMENT

Torture and other ill-treatment were endemic throughout the country, and often took place during unlawful arrests and detention by state security services. Some cases of death under torture were reported. Police, intelligence officers and members of the presidential guard were all accused of responsibility for torture and other ill-treatment.

COMMUNAL VIOLENCE

In Tanganyika district, Katanga, tensions between the Batwa and Luba intensified and led to a violent confrontation between the two communities. This added to the insecurity already caused by the activities of the armed group Mai Mai Bakata Katanga. The violence was marked by a deliberate targeting of civilians and serious human rights abuses. Members of both communities committed killings, abductions and acts of sexual violence. They used children in the violence and burned down and looted houses.

In June and July, more than 26 Batwa women and girls were captured and raped in Longa village, Kabalo territory, Katanga. Another 37 women from the same village were kidnapped and kept for sexual purposes by alleged Luba militias in Luala. At least 36 more women were raped when they were trying to flee to Nyunzu.

IMPUNITY

Impunity continued to fuel further human rights violations and abuses. Efforts by judicial authorities to increase the capacity of the courts to deal with cases, including cases involving human rights abuses, had only limited success. Efforts to ensure accountability for crimes under international law committed by the Congolese army and armed groups also achieved few visible results.

The verdict in the trial for the mass rape of more than 130 women and girls, murder and looting committed in and around the eastern town of Minova by Congolese soldiers fleeing the advance of M23 rebels in November and December 2012 was handed down on 5 May 2014. Despite overwhelming evidence of mass rape in Minova, including victim and witness testimonies, only two soldiers of the 39 on trial were convicted of rape. Other accused were convicted of murder, looting and military offences.

The M23 leader, General Bosco Ntaganda, had turned himself in at the US embassy in Kigali in 2013 and asked to be transferred to the International Criminal Court (ICC), which had issued a warrant for his arrest in 2006. Other M23 leaders in exile in Uganda and Rwanda continued to enjoy impunity for the crimes they had reportedly committed in Rutshuru and Nyiragongo territories.

In May, parliament rejected a legislative proposal on the domestication of the Rome Statute of the ICC, along with a proposal to create specialized criminal chambers to deal with crimes under international law committed before the entry into force of the Rome Statute.

UNFAIR TRIALS

The judicial system was weak and suffered from a lack of resources. The courts were often not independent of outside influence and corruption was widespread. Legal aid was not available, so that many defendants did not have a lawyer, and the rights of defendants were frequently violated.

PRISON CONDITIONS

The prison system continued to be under-funded. Prisoners and detainees were held in decaying facilities, with overcrowding and unhygienic conditions. Dozens died as a result of malnutrition and lack of appropriate medical care.

Insecurity for inmates was increased by the failure to separate women from men, pre-trial detainees from convicted prisoners and members of the military from civilians.

HUMAN RIGHTS DEFENDERS

The demise of the M23 armed group contributed to some improvement in the situation for human rights defenders in Rutshuru and Nyiragongo territories. However, human rights defenders and trade unionists across the country continued to face threats, intimidation and arrest by state security services and armed groups. Some were forced to flee after they received repeated death threats through text messages, anonymous phone calls, and visits at night by armed men.

ARBITRARY ARRESTS AND DETENTIONS

Arbitrary arrests and detentions continued to be routine throughout the country. Security services, in particular the national police, the intelligence services and the national army, carried out arbitrary arrests. They also frequently extorted money and items of value from civilians during law enforcement operations or at checkpoints.

A number of political opposition supporters who attended demonstrations calling for political dialogue and protesting against attempts to amend the Constitution were arbitrarily arrested and ill-treated.

FREEDOM OF EXPRESSION

Freedom of expression was significantly curtailed. In particular, opposition to the prospective amendment of the Constitution was severely repressed. Peaceful meetings and demonstrations were routinely banned or violently disrupted by the security services.

The main targets of repression were political opponents, members of civil society organizations and journalists. Some were arrested and ill-treated, some imprisoned after unfair trials on trumped-up charges. For example, one political opponent of the government – Jean Bertrand Ewanga of the opposition party Union pour la Nation Congolaise (UNC) – was imprisoned on charges of insulting the President. The Canal Futur television station, reportedly owned by opposition leader Vital Kamerhe, remained closed by the authorities throughout the year.

On 16 October, following the release by the UN Joint Human Rights Office (UNJHRO) of a report on extrajudicial executions and enforced disappearances during a police operation in Kinshasa, Scott Campbell, Head of the UNJHRO, was declared *persona non grata* by the Minister of the Interior and expelled from the DRC.[2] Other UNJHRO officials also reported receiving threats after the report's publication.

REFUGEES AND ASYLUM-SEEKERS

More than 170,000 DRC nationals were expelled from the Republic of Congo to the DRC between 4 April and early September. Among them were refugees and asylum-seekers. Some of the expelled were allegedly arrested and detained incommunicado in Kinshasa.

Little assistance was provided by the DRC government, and as of September, more than 100 families were living on the streets of Kinshasa without tents, health care, food or any assistance.

INTERNATIONAL JUSTICE

On 7 March, the ICC convicted Germain Katanga, commander of the Force de Résistance Patriotique en Ituri (FRPI), of crimes against humanity and war crimes. The crimes were committed on 24 February 2003 during an attack on the village of Bogoro, in Ituri district. On 23 May, he was sentenced to 12 years' imprisonment.

On 9 June, the International Criminal Court (ICC) Pre-Trial Chamber II confirmed charges of war crimes and crimes against humanity against Bosco Ntaganda allegedly committed in 2002 and 2003 in Ituri district.

Sylvestre Mudacumura, alleged commander of the armed branch of the FDLR, remained at large despite the issuance by the ICC of an arrest warrant for war crimes on 13 July 2012.

---

1. DRC: Civilian death toll rises as rebels embark on campaign of sporadic slaughter
   www. amnesty.org/en/news/drc-civilian-death-toll-rises-rebels-embark-campaign-sporadic-slaughter-2014-10-31
2. DRC: Rescind expulsion of UN official and investigate extra-judicial killings and disappearances (AFR 62/002/2014)
   www.amnesty.org/download/Documents/4000/afr620022014en.pdf

DENMARK

Kingdom of Denmark
Head of state: **Queen Margrethe II**
Head of government: **Helle Thorning-Schmidt**

The government refused to investigate allegations of unlawful surveillance practices following revelations by US whistleblower Edward Snowden. Legislation was amended to criminalize sexual abuse by a spouse. Asylum determination practices for lesbian, gay and bisexual asylum-seekers improved. Vulnerable asylum-seekers were held in detention.

COUNTER-TERROR AND SECURITY

In June 2013, following revelations by whistleblower Edward Snowden about the US National Security Agency's mass surveillance of data traffic in European countries in co-operation with European intelligence agencies, Danish MPs and the public called on the Danish government to disclose whether foreign intelligence agencies had carried out or were carrying out surveillance activities in Denmark and, if so, whether this included surveillance of Danish citizens. The government announced in response that it did "not find reason to believe" that US intelligence agencies were carrying out "illegal surveillance activities targeting Denmark or Danish interests". The government refused to investigate whether any such agencies had operated or were operating on Danish territory and to present an overview of the applicable laws clarifying the distinction between lawful and unlawful surveillance activities.

POLICE AND SECURITY FORCES

In October, a joint working group of the National Police and the Police Trade Union presented a report on the introduction of identification numbers on police uniforms. The proposals lacked clarity on the visibility required of any such identification numbers.

VIOLENCE AGAINST WOMEN AND GIRLS

In June 2013, Parliament amended the criminal code to criminalize sexual abuse by a spouse where the victim was in a "helpless state" and to annul the possibility of reduced or rescinded criminal punishment if the perpetrator and the victim marry each other or remain married after a rape.

The government did not take steps to establish a national plan to improve the rights of and support to rape victims. Nor did it move to investigate the reason for the disproportionately high rate of attrition in investigating and prosecuting reported rapes.

REFUGEES AND ASYLUM-SEEKERS

The Refugee Appeals Board amended its previous practice of refusing protection to asylum-seekers who were at risk of persecution at home due to their sexual orientation on the basis that they should "hide" their sexual identity. Since 2013, lesbian, gay and bisexual asylum-seekers at risk of persecution on grounds of the overall homophobic practices of their country of origin have been granted refugee status.

Since September 2013, asylum-seekers from areas in Syria affected by the ongoing armed conflict have been granted refugee status without any further individual assessment. In October 2014, the government presented a bill to introduce a temporary protection permit for all Syrian asylum-seekers. The bill proposed that family reunification procedures not be initiated during the first 12 months of the asylum-seekers' stay in Denmark.

Vulnerable people – including victims of torture, unaccompanied minors and persons with mental illness – continued to be detained for immigration control purposes. The government maintained that the present practice of screening by a nurse of all asylum-seekers was sufficient to identify people who are unfit to be placed in detention.

In October, the Eastern High Court found that the "tolerated stay" of Elias Karkavandi, an Iranian citizen, had over time become "disproportionate". Elias Karkavandi's refugee status had been revoked in 2007 following the completion of a custodial sentence for drugs offences; he had spent seven years under the so-called "tolerated stay" regime, which barred him indefinitely from working, studying, marrying and living outside a designated reception centre.

DOMINICAN REPUBLIC

Dominican Republic
Head of state and government: **Danilo Medina Sánchez**

The number of killings by police rose again. Most people of Haitian descent remained stateless following a September 2013 judgement by the Constitutional Court. Violence against women and girls remained widespread. Parliament failed to adopt legislation that could have advanced the protection of the rights of women and girls.

BACKGROUND

In September 2013, the Constitutional Court issued a widely criticized judgement (TC 0168-13) which had the effect of retroactively and arbitrarily depriving Dominicans of foreign descent born between 1929 and 2010 of their Dominican nationality; the vast majority of those affected were of Haitian descent. This sparked an outcry at national and international levels, including by the Haitian authorities. As a consequence, the Dominican Republic and Haiti held a number of high-level bi-national meetings to discuss several issues of common interest, including migration and nationality.

The first Human Rights Ombudsman was appointed in May 2013, 12 years after the institution was established by law. However, a number of human rights organizations filed an appeal with the Constitutional Court challenging the constitutionality of the appointment. A ruling was pending at the end of 2014. The Ombudsman dealt with a number of cases, but failed to carry out a public information campaign about her Office's role.

In June, the UN Human Rights Council examined the Dominican Republic's human rights record under the Universal Periodic Review.

POLICE AND SECURITY FORCES

The police continued to kill large numbers of people, often in circumstances suggesting that the killings may have been unlawful. Between January and June, the number of killings increased by 13% compared with the same period in 2013.[1] Allegations of torture and other ill-treatment by the police continued to be reported.

Although the Dominican Republic adopted the UPR recommendations aimed at expediting a comprehensive reform of the police, the adoption of a law reforming the police was not finalized. The National Security Plan, which was formally launched in March 2013, was not made public and there were no progress reports on its implementation.

IMPUNITY

Many police officers alleged to have committed abuses were not brought to justice despite compelling evidence. The authorities failed to investigate the disappearance of three men – Gabriel Sandi Alistar, Juan Almonte Herrera and Randy Vizcaíno González – who were last seen in police custody in July 2009, September 2009 and December 2013 respectively.

The Office of the Prosecutor General reopened the investigation into the disappearance of Narciso González following a 2012 ruling by the Inter-American Court of Human Rights establishing the responsibility of the state. However, no significant progress had been made by the end of 2014.

DISCRIMINATION – DOMINICO-HAITIANS

A law introduced into Parliament by the President in response to the debate sparked by Constitutional judgement TC 0168-13 was adopted in May 2014 (Law 169/14). However, the law failed to provide for Dominican nationality to be automatically restored to those who had it under the domestic legal system in force between 1929 and 2010.[2]

In particular, the law established that those who had been registered at some point in the Dominican civil registry (group A) could access Dominican nationality after undergoing a process of regularization by the Central Electoral Board. However, the law obliges those who were never registered (group B) to undergo a lengthy process that requires them to register as foreigners, participate in the National Regularization Plan for Foreigners with Irregular Migration Status and then apply for naturalization two years later. Poor implementation of the law meant that only a minority of those belonging to group A were able to have their Dominican nationality recognized and only a few of those in group B were able to be registered. As a consequence, thousands of Dominicans of Haitian descent remained stateless and continued to be prevented from exercising their human rights. In October, the Inter-American Court of Human Rights found that judgement TC 0168-13 and part of Law 169-14 violated the American Convention on Human Rights.[3]

In November, the Constitutional Court issued a judgement declaring the state's acceptance of the jurisdiction of the Inter-American Court of Human Rights invalid.[4]

The Dominican authorities rejected all the recommendations to guarantee the right to a nationality and to adopt measures to identify, prevent and reduce statelessness.

MIGRANTS' RIGHTS

In December 2013, the government launched the National Regularization Plan for Foreigners with Irregular Migration Status. Following a first preparatory phase, the second phase of the plan started on 1 June 2014, giving migrants 12 months to apply for regularization. By 30 September only 200 out of the 68,814 people who applied had been regularized. According to migrants' rights organizations, the small number was due to migrants facing difficulties in gathering the required, and costly, documentation and to the inadequate processing of applications by public officials, especially in the initial stages of the process.

The decree launching the National Regularization Plan banned the deportation of migrants who had applied for regularization. However, despite this, Dominican human rights organizations continued to report arbitrary mass repatriations throughout the year.

VIOLENCE AGAINST WOMEN AND GIRLS

In the first six months of 2014, the number of gender-based killings increased by 53% compared with the same period in 2013. The Office of the Prosecutor General reported a substantive increase in the number of convictions in cases of gender-based violence and in July adopted a protocol for the investigation of gender-based killings. Women's rights groups continued to criticize the lack of coordination among relevant national institutions, the inadequacy of the budget allocated to preventing and punishing gender-based violence, and the failure to implement the agreed protocols for the provision of care to victims of gender-based violence. Parliament had yet to adopt a comprehensive law to prevent and address violence against women which had been approved by the Senate in 2012.

SEXUAL AND REPRODUCTIVE RIGHTS

In September, the Lower Chamber started considering a draft law on sexual and reproductive health, which had been drafted with the participation of women's rights groups.

Following a veto by the President of the Republic on the proposed reform of the Criminal Code, which maintained full criminalization of abortion, on 16 December the Congress adopted amendments decriminalizing abortions where pregnancy posed a risk to the life of a pregnant woman or girl, in cases where the foetus would be unable to survive outside the womb, and in cases where the pregnancy was the result of rape or incest. The reform of the Criminal

Code was enacted on 19 December and is supposed to enter into force within a year.[5]

HOUSING RIGHTS – FORCED EVICTIONS

Local NGOs continued to report cases of forced evictions and excessive use of force by police in some instances.

The latest version of the proposed amendments to the Penal Code criminalized the occupation of private property, sparking concerns that, if adopted, these provisions could be used to legitimize forced evictions.

1. Dominican Republic: Killings at the hands of the police rise while reforms stall (Press release)
   www.amnesty.org/en/articles/news/2014/08/dominican-republic-killings-hands-police-rise-while-reforms-stall/

2. Dominican Republic: Open letter to President Danilo Medina regarding Law 169/14 "establishing a special regime for people who were born in the national territory and irregularly registered in the Dominican Civil Registry and on naturalization" (AMR 27/008/2014)
   www.amnesty.org/en/library/info/amr27/008/2014/en

3. Dominican Republic: Reaction to Court ruling shows shocking disregard for international law (Press release)
   www.amnesty.org/en/articles/news/2014/10/dominican-republic-reaction-court-ruling-shows-shocking-disregard-international-law/

4. Dominican Republic: Withdrawal from top regional human rights court would put rights of hundreds of thousands at risk (Press release)
   www.amnesty.org/en/articles/news/2014/11/dominican-republic-withdrawal-top-regional-human-rights-court-would-put-rights-risk/

5. Dominican Republic: Proposed reform puts women and girls at risk (AMR 27/016/2014)
   www.amnesty.org/en/library/info/AMR27/016/2014/en
   Dominican Republic: Further information: President vetoes full ban on abortion (AMR 27/018/2014)
   www.amnesty.org/en/library/info/AMR27/018/2014/en
   Dominican Republic decriminalizes abortion (AMR 27/020/2014)
   www.amnesty.org/en/library/info/AMR27/020/2014/en

ECUADOR

Republic of Ecuador
Head of state and government: **Rafael Vicente Correa Delgado**

Human rights defenders and government critics continued to be attacked and discredited. The right of Indigenous Peoples to consultation and to free, prior and informed consent was not fulfilled.

BACKGROUND

Mass protests in opposition to government policies remained common. In July, Indigenous groups marched to the capital Quito to protest against the approval of a new law regulating water resources, which they claimed did not address all of their concerns.

In November 2013, the National Court upheld a ruling against US oil company Chevron for environmental damage. The court ruled that Chevron was liable to pay over US$9.5 billion to the Amazon Indigenous communities affected. In March, following a lawsuit filed by Chevron in the USA, a federal court blocked US courts from being used to collect the amount granted for rainforest damage, stating that the Ecuadorean court judgment was obtained by corrupt means. In October, victims of Chevron's environmental damage sued the company's directors before the International Criminal Court.

Sixty people, including six police officers accused of attempting to kill the President, were convicted of involvement in police protests over pay cuts in 2010, which were regarded by the government as an attempted coup. Another 36 were acquitted.

HUMAN RIGHTS DEFENDERS

Human rights defenders continued to be attacked and discredited.

The Indigenous and environmental rights organization Fundación Pachamama remained closed, having been shut down by the authorities in December 2013 using an executive decree granting the authorities wide powers to monitor and dissolve NGOs. Days before the closure, members of Fundación Pachamama had participated in a demonstration outside the Ministry of Energy.

INDIGENOUS PEOPLES' RIGHTS

In October the government apologized to the Kichwa People of Sarayaku, accepting that the state had put their lives and livelihoods at risk when in 2002 and 2003 it allowed an oil company to conduct exploration work in their territory. The Kichwa People of Sarayaku had won a legal battle before the Inter-American Court of Human Rights in 2012. However, at the end of 2014 Ecuador had not yet finalized the removal of 1.4 tons of explosives left in the Indigenous community's territory and had not regulated the right to consultation and free, prior and informed consent for all Indigenous Peoples as ordered by the Inter-American Court in 2012.

Government plans to exploit oil resources in Yasuni National Park, home to the Tagaeri and Taromenane Indigenous communities, continued to provoke public protests. In May, the Confederacion Kichwa del Ecuador (Ecuarunari), one of the country's main Indigenous organizations, presented a legal action before the Constitutional Court arguing that the government was not complying with precautionary measures granted by the Inter-American Commission on Human Rights in 2006 in favour of the Tagaeri and Taromenane Indigenous communities. At the end of 2014 the Constitutional Court had not ruled on the legal action.

REPRESSION OF DISSENT

The authorities continued to clamp down on anti-government protests, in what appeared to be attempts to deter opposition.

In September over 100 protesters were detained for up to 15 days for taking part in anti-government demonstrations, amid reports of clashes between protesters and the police. Dozens of detainees complained of ill-treatment during arrest and while in police custody. Medical reports stated that scores of those detained had bruising and other injuries caused by blunt instruments. At the end of the year no investigation into these allegations had begun and the President publicly rejected the allegations.

FREEDOM OF EXPRESSION

In January, El Universo newspaper and caricaturist Javier Bonilla (known as Bonil) were fined and forced to retract the content of a caricature, under a 2013 Communications Law. The caricature portrayed police officers abruptly raiding the house of journalist Fernando Villavicencio, an outspoken critic of the government. Fernando Villavicencio was one of three men convicted in 2013 for slander against the President and given prison sentences of between 18 months and six years, later reduced to between six and 12 months. At the end of 2014 Villavicencio and one of the other men remained at large.

IMPUNITY

In December 2013, the National Assembly passed a law guaranteeing the right to reparation to relatives and victims of human rights violations between 1983 and 2008 documented by the Truth Commission established in 2007.

In January 2014, former Police Chief Edgar Vaca was arrested in the USA pending his extradition. Edgar Vaca was one of 10 former police and military officers accused of torture and enforced disappearances during Febres Cordero's presidency (1984 to 1988). This was the first case of members of the security forces being tried for crimes against humanity.

SEXUAL AND REPRODUCTIVE RIGHTS

The New Penal Code enacted in January maintained the criminalization of abortion in case of rape unless the victim has a mental disability. Attempts to decriminalize abortion for all rape victims met with strong opposition from the President, who threatened to resign if such a proposal was even discussed in the National Assembly. The proposal was withdrawn and three Congress members of the ruling party were sanctioned.

EGYPT

Arab Republic of Egypt
Head of state: **Abdel Fattah al-Sisi (replaced Adly Mansour in June)**
Head of government: **Ibrahim Mahlab (replaced Hazem Beblawi in March)**

The year saw a continued dramatic deterioration in human rights following the ousting of President Mohamed Morsi in July 2013. The government severely restricted freedoms of expression, association and assembly. Thousands were arrested and detained as part of a sweeping crackdown on dissent, with some detainees subjected to enforced disappearance. The Muslim Brotherhood remained banned and its leaders were detained and jailed. Torture and other ill-treatment of detainees remained routine and was committed with impunity. Hundreds were sentenced to prison terms or to death after grossly unfair trials. Security forces used excessive force against protesters and committed unlawful killings with impunity. Women faced discrimination and violence. Some refugees were forcibly returned. Forced evictions continued. Dozens of people faced arrest and prosecution for their sexual orientation or identity. Courts imposed hundreds of death sentences; the first executions since 2011 were carried out in June.

BACKGROUND

Presidential elections in May saw former army chief Abdel Fattah al-Sisi elected as President. He took office in June, and in September pledged to uphold freedom of expression, judicial independence and the rule of law in a speech to the UN General Assembly. In practice, his government clamped down on free expression, widened the jurisdiction of military courts to try civilians, and allowed security forces to use torture and excessive force with impunity.

Over 1,400 people were killed in protests between July 2013, when Mohamed Morsi was ousted as President, and the end of 2014. The vast majority were killed by security forces dispersing sit-ins by Morsi supporters at Rabaa al-Adawiya and al-Nahda Squares in Greater Cairo on 14 August 2013. The crackdown also saw the arrest and detention or imprisonment of at least 16,000 people, according to official estimates published by the Associated Press news agency, with the activist group Wikithawra later estimating that over 40,000 people had been detained, charged or indicted. Most of those detained were Muslim Brotherhood supporters but they also included left-wing and secular activists and other government critics.

An upsurge in lethal attacks on the security forces by armed groups led to the deaths of at least 445 soldiers and security officers, according to official statements. Most attacks took place in Sinai, where at least 238 security forces officers were killed. After renewed attacks in October, the government declared a state of emergency in North Sinai, imposed a curfew, closed Egypt's border with Gaza, and began constructing a "buffer" zone along it. Military reinforcements launched a "combing" operation to identify what they called "militants" within the area's population, posing a risk of further human rights violations.[1]

INTERNATIONAL SCRUTINY

Members of the UN Human Rights Council examined Egypt's human rights record under the UN Universal Periodic Review (UPR) mechanism in November, recommending that the authorities combat torture, investigate excessive use of force by security forces, and lift restrictions on civil society. With the exception of the UPR, Egypt largely evaded international scrutiny in spite of the deteriorating human rights situation in the country.

FREEDOM OF EXPRESSION

The authorities targeted those who criticized the government or expressed dissent. Media workers who documented rights violations or questioned the authorities' political narrative faced arrest and prosecution. Journalists who reported on army activities faced unfair trials before military courts.[2]

In June, a court in Cairo sentenced three staff members of the Al Jazeera English television station to between seven and 10 years' imprisonment after a grossly unfair trial. The court convicted Mohamed Fahmy, a Canadian-Egyptian dual national; Peter Greste, an Australian; and Baher Mohamed, an Egyptian, on charges that included aiding the Muslim Brotherhood and reporting "false" news. The prosecution failed to produce any substantive evidence against them, or against other media workers who were tried in their absence.

Some individuals faced prosecution and imprisonment on charges such as "inciting sectarian strife" and/or "defamation of religion". The authorities also increased monitoring of social media.

FREEDOM OF ASSOCIATION

The authorities shut down groups linked to the banned Muslim Brotherhood group and other centres of opposition, and imposed onerous new restrictions on human rights organizations.

In April, the 6 April Youth Movement, one of the activist groups that led the 2011 uprising, was banned by a court which ruled that some of its members had committed offences that would "disturb peace and public order".

In August, a court dissolved the Freedom and Justice Party, which was founded by the Muslim Brotherhood and won the largest number of seats in Egypt's 2012 parliamentary elections.

Human rights organizations faced threats of closure and criminal prosecution, forcing many activists to scale down their work or leave the country. In July, the Ministry of Social Solidarity gave NGOs a 45-day deadline, later extended to November, to register under the repressive Law on Associations (Law 84 of 2002), warning that it would hold groups that failed to register "accountable". The Ministry later announced that it would deal with NGOs on a case-by-case basis, following criticism from other states during Egypt's UPR.

The authorities disrupted peaceful NGO activities, raiding the Alexandria offices of the Egyptian Center for Economic and Social Rights in May when it held a conference to support detained human rights activists.

In September, the government amended the Penal Code to prohibit the funding of acts harmful to Egypt's national interest, territorial integrity or public peace. The government also proposed a new Law on Associations that, if enacted, would give the authorities additional powers to deny NGOs legal registration and curtail their activities and funding.

In November, Egypt's Cabinet approved draft legislation which, if passed, would give the authorities sweeping powers to classify organizations as terrorist entities.

FREEDOM OF ASSEMBLY

Security forces ruthlessly suppressed protests, and courts jailed scores of people for protesting without authorization, among them supporters of Mohamed Morsi, prominent opposition activists, and left-wing and human rights activists.[3] The authorities continued to enforce Law 107 of 2013 on protests, which required demonstrations to have prior authorization; security forces used excessive force against peaceful protesters.

Women university students Abrar Al-Anany and Menatalla Moustafa, and a woman teacher, Yousra Elkhateeb, were jailed in May for between two and six years for protesting peacefully at Mansoura University.

In November, a court in Alexandria sentenced 78 children to prison terms of between two and five years after convicting them of participating in an unauthorized protest in support of Mohamed Morsi.

ARBITRARY ARRESTS AND DETENTIONS

Thousands of actual and suspected government opponents were arrested during protests, at their homes or on the street. Many were not informed of the reason for their arrest and were arbitrarily detained and held in pre-trial detention for periods that in some cases exceeded one year, or else were brought before the courts and sentenced to lengthy prison terms after unfair trials. Many were also beaten or ill-treated during arrest or in detention. In some instances, security forces seized family members or friends if the wanted person was not present.

ENFORCED DISAPPEARANCES

Some detainees were subjected to enforced disappearance and held in secret detention at Al Azouly Prison within the Al Galaa military camp in Ismailia, 130km northeast of Cairo. Detainees were held at Al Galaa without official acknowledgement and were denied access to lawyers and their families. Detainees, who included alleged protest leaders and people accused of terrorism-related offences, were held at the camp for up to 90 days without judicial oversight and faced torture and other ill-treatment by military intelligence and National Security Agency (NSA) officers to extract "confessions". Public prosecutors told families of the disappeared that they had no jurisdiction over military prisons.

TORTURE AND OTHER ILL-TREATMENT

Torture and other ill-treatment of criminal suspects was routinely used to extract confessions and punish and humiliate suspects. It reportedly led to several deaths of detainees. NSA officials particularly targeted members and alleged supporters of the Muslim Brotherhood, some of whom they held and reportedly tortured in unofficial detention facilities, including NSA offices across the country.

Commonly reported methods of torture included electric shocks to the genitals and other sensitive areas, beating, suspension by the limbs while handcuffed from behind, stress positions, beatings and rape.

Al Azhar university student Omar Gamal El Shewiekh said that security officials arrested and tortured him after he participated in a protest in Cairo in March. He said that NSA officials subjected him to electric shocks and repeatedly inserted objects into his anus until he "confessed" to crimes on video. In May a court sentenced him to five years in prison on the basis of the forced "confession".

Deaths in detention were reported, with some apparently attributable to torture or other ill-treatment or inadequate conditions in police stations.[4]

Ezzat Abdel Fattah died in Cairo's Mattareya Police Station in May. A post-mortem report issued by the forensic authority found that he had injuries that included nine broken ribs, cuts and concussion.

The authorities failed to conduct genuine investigations into allegations of torture. When prosecutors did investigate, they generally closed cases citing lack of evidence. In some cases, victims and their families said that police threatened them to make them withdraw torture allegations.

IMPUNITY

The criminal justice system failed to hold any members of the security forces accountable for gross human rights violations committed during the 2013 unrest, including the mass killings of pro-Morsi protesters at Rabaa al-Adawiya and al-Nahda Squares on 14 August 2013. On 7 June, an appeals court quashed the verdicts against four police officers convicted of killing 37 detainees in August 2013.

A court retrying former President Hosni Mubarak on charges of killing protesters during the 2011 uprising dismissed the case against him in November on a legal technicality. His Interior Minister and several security officials were also acquitted of the same charges.

A government-appointed fact-finding committee, established after security forces killed hundreds of protesters on 14 August 2013, announced its findings in November. Ignoring disparities between security forces casualties and protesters, it concluded that protesters had started the violence. The committee downplayed human rights violations by security forces, merely calling for them to receive training in policing demonstrations.

UNFAIR TRIALS

Courts throughout Egypt sentenced hundreds of Muslim Brotherhood and other opposition activists to long prison terms or to death after grossly unfair trials, often on trumped-up charges. Courts also sentenced children to death in contravention of international and Egyptian law.

Former President Mohamed Morsi faced four trials, including for capital offences. Other senior members of the Muslim Brotherhood were imprisoned and sentenced to death.

Trials before the criminal courts were riddled with due process violations. Some trials proceeded in the absence of the defendants and their lawyers . In others, judges prevented defendants or their lawyers from presenting evidence in their own defence or cross-examining prosecution witnesses. In many cases, courts convicted defendants despite an absence of substantive evidence against them.

Many trials were conducted within the Tora Police Institute, adjacent to the Tora Prison Complex, with families and independent media unable to attend. Defendants were also unable to communicate with their lawyers during court sessions because they were confined behind a dark glass screen.

The Public Prosecution increasingly did not seek to determine individual criminal responsibility, instead bringing identical charges against groups of accused, and relied heavily on reports and testimonies by police and security forces. The impartiality and independence of the investigations were thus brought into question.

In October, President al-Sisi decreed that military courts could try civilians for offences against "vital public facilities". It was feared that the decision would see a return to mass unfair trials of civilians before military courts, including peaceful protesters and university students.

WOMEN'S RIGHTS

Women continued to face discrimination in law and in practice, including high levels of gender-based violence.

In June, outgoing President Adly Mansour approved a law to combat sexual harassment. Renewed sexual assaults by mobs of men against women in Cairo's Tahrir Square during President al-Sisi's inauguration spurred the new administration to promise action. The authorities announced measures to combat violence against women, including improved policing and public awareness-raising campaigns; however, such measures had not materialized by the end of the year.

RIGHTS OF LESBIAN, GAY, BISEXUAL, TRANSGENDER AND INTERSEX PEOPLE

Men suspected of having consensual sex with other men, as well as transgender people, faced arrest and prosecution on prostitution and public morality charges under the Law on Debauchery (Law 10 of 1961). The authorities subjected some to forcible anal examinations, which violate the prohibition on torture and other ill-treatment.

Security forces arrested over 30 men in a raid on a Cairo bathhouse in November, and the trial of 26 of the men on charges of "debauchery" began in December.

In a separate case, eight men received three-year prison terms in November for attending an alleged same-sex wedding on a Nile riverboat. An appeals court reduced their prison sentences to one year in December.

DISCRIMINATION – RELIGIOUS MINORITIES

The authorities failed to tackle discrimination against religious minorities, including Coptic Christians, Shi'a Muslims and Baha'is. Coptic Christian communities, in particular, reported new sectarian attacks and faced restrictions on building and maintaining their places of worship.

HOUSING RIGHTS – FORCED EVICTIONS

Security forces forcibly evicted thousands of people from their homes in Cairo and Rafah, without informing them in advance or providing them with alternative housing or adequate compensation.[5]

REFUGEES' AND MIGRANTS' RIGHTS

The authorities failed to respect the rights of refugees, asylum-seekers and migrants. In August, they forcibly returned 13 Palestinian refugees to Syria and 180 Syrians to Syria, Lebanon and Turkey. At least six were returned to Gaza in December. Other refugees from Syria faced arbitrary arrest and were unlawfully detained.

Security forces arrested refugees, asylum-seekers and migrants who sought to enter or leave Egypt irregularly, sometimes using excessive force. Criminal groups operating in Sinai also reportedly held refugees, asylum-seekers and migrants captive.

DEATH PENALTY

The death penalty was used on an unprecedented scale. The courts imposed death sentences, many in the defendant's absence, after grossly unfair trials. Most of those sentenced were convicted of taking part in violence during political unrest in 2013. They included many members and supporters of the Muslim Brotherhood. The

first executions since 2011 were carried out in June.

A court in El-Minya, Upper Egypt, sentenced 37 defendants to death in April, including at least two children, and a further 183 defendants to death in June after grossly unfair trials arising from attacks on police stations in 2013.[6] The court had recommended the death penalty for over 1,200 defendants but reversed its decisions after consulting the Grand Mufti, a legal process that must take place under Egyptian law before a court formally hands down its sentence.

1. Egypt: End wave of home demolitions, forced evictions in Sinai amid media blackout (News story)
www.amnesty.org/en/news/egypt-end-wave-home-demolitions-forced-evictions-sinai-amid-media-blackout-2014-11-27

2. Egypt: End military trial of journalists (News story)
www.amnesty.org/en/news/egypt-end-military-trial-journalists-2014-02-25

3. 'The walls of the cell were smeared with blood' – third anniversary of Egypt's uprising marred by police brutality (News story)
www.amnestyusa.org/news/news-item/%E2%80%98the-walls-of-the-cell-were-smeared-with-blood-third-anniversary-of-egypt-s-uprising-marred-by-polic

4. Egypt: Rampant torture, arbitrary arrests and detentions signal catastrophic decline in human rights one year after ousting of Morsi (NWS 11/125/2014)
www.amnesty.org/en/news/egypt-anniversary-morsi-ousting-2014-07-02

5. Egypt: Further information: Evicted families attacked by security forces (MDE 12/011/2014)
www.amnesty.org/en/library/info/MDE12/011/2014/en

6. Egypt sentences a further 183 people to death in new purge of political opposition (NWS 11/117/2014)
www.amnesty.org/en/articles/news/2014/06/egypt-sentences-further-people-death-new-purge-political-opposition/

EL SALVADOR

Republic of El Salvador
Head of state and government: Salvador Sánchez Cerén (replaced Carlos Mauricio Funes Cartagena in June)

The total abortion ban remained in place and the implementation of legislation to combat violence against women was still weak. Impunity for human rights violations committed during the 1980-1992 armed conflict persisted, despite some steps to combat it.

BACKGROUND

President Sánchez Cerén of the Farabundo Martí National Liberation Front took office.

Violent crime rose sharply. Official sources recorded 1,857 homicides in the first six months of 2014; the figure for the same period in 2013 was 1,048. The rise was thought to be due to the reported collapse of a truce between rival criminal gangs.

In June, the Legislative Assembly ratified amendments to the Constitution formally recognizing Indigenous Peoples' rights and the state's obligations to uphold them.

The ratifications of key international agreements, including ILO Convention No. 169 on Indigenous and Tribal Peoples, the Rome Statute of the International Criminal Court, the Optional Protocol to the Convention against Torture, the International Convention against enforced disappearance and the Inter-American Convention on Forced Disappearance of Persons, were still pending at the end of the year.

During consideration of El Salvador's human rights record under the UN Universal Periodic Review in October 2014, states called on El Salvador to ratify these international agreements. Several states also recommended that El Salvador decriminalize abortion and make safe abortion available, particularly in cases where the life or health

of the woman was at risk or when the pregnancy was the result of incest or rape. Two states also recommended that women incarcerated for undergoing abortion or having a miscarriage be released. El Salvador responded that it would examine these recommendations and provide a response at the next session of the Human Rights Council in 2015.

WOMEN'S RIGHTS

Between January and September, the police reported 216 killings of women, compared with 215 for the whole of 2013.[1] This indicated that violence against women was once more on the increase following a period of sustained decrease since 2011. Despite some welcome progress in the implementation of the 2012 Special Comprehensive Law for a Life Free from Violence for Women, few cases of killings were prosecuted as the gender-based crime of femicide.

A unified database recording violence against women, provided for in the 2012 Special Law, was still not operational and only one state shelter for women fleeing violent partners was in place at the end of 2014.

In its 2014 report to the UN on the progress of the Millennium Development Goals, the government acknowledged that the total abortion ban was hampering efforts to reduce maternal mortality. Despite this, the total ban on abortion remained in place at the end of 2014. The state also acknowledged that "socio-cultural" and economic factors, lack of access to contraceptives and the prevalence of violence against women and girls were all impeding the achievement of the Goals.

In December 2013, human rights organizations presented a petition to the Inter-American Commission on Human Rights against the state for the grave human rights violations suffered by a 22-year-old woman known as "Beatriz". Beatriz, who suffers from lupus, had been refused an abortion despite the imminent risk to her life and the knowledge that the fetus, which lacked part of its brain and skull, could not survive outside the womb. Two months after she first requested the medical treatment she needed, and after 23 weeks of pregnancy, Beatriz was given a caesarean. The fetus survived just a few hours.

In April, after exhausting other legal avenues, the Citizens Group for the Decriminalization of Therapeutic, Ethical and Eugenic Abortion presented a petition for a state pardon on behalf of 17 women, who were incarcerated on pregnancy-related grounds. They were serving sentences of up to 40 years in prison for aggravated homicide, having been initially charged with having had an abortion. Their cases raised serious concerns regarding the right to non-discrimination, as well as the rights to due process and fair trial, including the right to effective legal defence. The cases remained pending at the end of 2014; Congress was awaiting recommendations from the Supreme Court of Justice before issuing its decision.

IMPUNITY

The 1993 Amnesty Law, which for over two decades has ensured impunity for those responsible for human rights violations during the 1980-1992 conflict, remained in place.

Tutela Legal, the Catholic Archbishopric's human rights office, was shut down without warning in September 2013. There were serious concerns that its extensive archive of evidence relating to unresolved human rights cases dating back to the internal armed conflict might not be preserved. Survivors and relatives of the victims submitted a habeas corpus challenge to get access to the files; the case was pending before the Supreme Court at the end of 2014.

The office of the human rights organization Pro-Búsqueda, which works to find children who were the victims of enforced disappearance during the conflict years, was raided by three armed men in November 2013. During the raid, three staff members were held captive while information was set

on fire and computers containing sensitive information on cases were stolen. The stolen computers contained information on three cases of enforced disappearance that were before the Supreme Court. Days before the attack, military officials accused of involvement in the disappearances failed to attend a hearing in one of the cases.[2]

At end of 2013, the Attorney General's Office reopened the investigation into the 1981 El Mozote massacre in which more than 700 civilians, including children and elderly people, were tortured and killed by the military in the village of El Mozote and nearby hamlets over a three-day period. The investigation was continuing at the end of 2014.

In October 2013, the authorities issued a decree establishing a reparations programme for survivors who suffered human rights violations during the conflict.

In February 2014, the Supreme Court ordered that an investigation be reopened into the San Francisco Angulo massacre in which 45 people, mostly women and children, were killed, allegedly by members of the army, in 1981. The investigation was continuing at the end of the year.

In August, 32 years after the events, the state finally acknowledged the 1982 El Calabozo massacre, in which more than 200 people were killed by the army. However, no one had been brought to justice for the crime by the end of 2014.

In October, in its ruling in the case of *Rochac Hernandez et al. v. El Salvador*, the Inter-American Court of Human Rights found the state responsible for failing to investigate the enforced disappearance of five children between 1980 and 1982 in the context of military counter-insurgency operations during the conflict .

---

1. On the brink of death: Violence against women and the abortion ban in El Salvador (AMR 29/003/2014)

    www.amnesty.org/en/library/info/AMR29/003/2014/en

2. El Salvador: Human rights organization's office attacked (AMR 29/011/2013)

    www.amnesty.org/en/library/info/AMR29/011/2013/en

EQUATORIAL GUINEA

Republic of Equatorial Guinea
Head of state and government: **Teodoro Obiang Nguema Mbasogo**

Nine prisoners were executed in January shortly before a temporary moratorium on the death penalty was declared. Detainees and prisoners were routinely tortured. Several political opponents were arbitrarily arrested and held incommunicado for long periods without charge, including one man abducted from a neighbouring country by Equatorial Guinea security forces in December 2013. Military courts were used to try civilians.

BACKGROUND

In February President Obiang signed a decree establishing a temporary moratorium on the death penalty, apparently to secure full membership of the Community of Portuguese-speaking Countries. Equatorial Guinea was granted full membership in July at the organization's summit in Dili, East Timor.

In May, the UN Human Rights Council, under its Universal Periodic Review process, examined the human rights situation in Equatorial Guinea and made a number of recommendations. The government accepted most recommendations in principle, but rejected those urging ratification of the Rome Statute of the International Criminal Court.

In October, President Obiang decreed a general amnesty for all those convicted or indicted for political crimes. This was one of the demands made by opposition political parties for their participation in a national dialogue in November. However, no prisoners were released and President Obiang stated that all convicted prisoners had been convicted of common crimes. In November, three independent opposition parties withdrew from the national dialogue on the basis that their demands, including the release of prisoners, had not been met.

DEATH PENALTY

Nine men convicted of murder were executed in late January, 13 days before the establishment of a temporary moratorium on the death penalty. This was the highest number of people known to have been executed in any one year over the past two decades, and the first known executions since 2010.[1]

TORTURE AND OTHER ILL-TREATMENT

Torture by the security forces continued with impunity. Detainees and prisoners were also subjected to other forms of cruel, inhuman or degrading treatment. Many were held incommunicado for long periods without charge or trial and denied adequate medical treatment.

Cipriano Nguema Mba, a refugee in Belgium since 2012, was abducted by Equatorial Guinea security personnel in December 2013 while visiting relatives in Nigeria. He was taken clandestinely to the National Security Headquarters in Malabo, where he was tortured. His ankles and elbows were tied together behind his back and he was then suspended from a metal bar and his whole body was beaten with batons. He was held incommunicado throughout the year.

Roberto Berardi, an Italian businessman in partnership with President Obiang's eldest son Teodoro "Teodorín" Nguema Obiang in a civil construction company, was beaten and tortured on several occasions since his arrest in January 2013, first in Bata police station and subsequently in Bata prison. On one occasion, in January 2014, he was held down by prison guards and flogged. Throughout the year he was held in solitary confinement for long periods and was denied medical treatment for typhoid fever and emphysema. He was taken to hospital after he became very ill in June, but was returned to prison the following day against medical advice. According to his lawyer, the purpose of Roberto Berardi's arrest was to prevent him testifying before the US Justice Department and other foreign jurisdictions about Teodorín Nguema Obiang's alleged corruption. He remained in prison at the end of the year.

ARBITRARY ARRESTS AND DETENTIONS

Following Cipriano Nguema Mba's abduction (see above), in January, 11 people suspected of having had contact with him, including two women, were arrested without warrants in Malabo, Mongomo and Ebebiyín, and held incommunicado. Five of the male detainees were released without charge in June. Four of the remaining six people were still detained incommunicado at the end of 2014. In July, the military judicial authorities charged Cipriano Nguema, Ticiano Obama Nkogo, Timoteo Asumu, Antonio Nconi Sima, Leoncio Abeso Meye (charged in his absence) and the two women, Mercedes Obono Nconi and Emilia Abeme Nzo, with "threatening state security and the physical integrity of the head of state". According to their lawyers, they were interrogated without their lawyers present and were not informed of the charges against them.

On 27 September they were tried by a military court, again without their lawyers present. Instead, they were allocated military officers with no judicial training as their legal counsel. Three days later they were convicted as charged. Mercedes Obono and Timoteo Asumu received 15-year custodial sentences, while the other defendants were each sentenced to 27 years' imprisonment.

PRISONERS OF CONSCIENCE

Agustín Esono Nsogo was released from prison in February 2014, after being held for 16 months without charge. He had been arbitrarily arrested and detained in Bata in October 2012 after exchanging money with a foreign national and accused of attempting to destabilize the country. His arrest and detention were politically motivated and unjustified.[2]

---

1. Equatorial Guinea: Executions just weeks before announcement of a "temporary moratorium" on the death penalty raises serious questions (AFR 24/001/2014)
   www.amnesty.org/en/library/info/AFR24/001/2014/en

2. See Equatorial Guinea: Free Agustin Esono Nsogo (AFR 24/015/2013)
   www.amnesty.org/en/documents/AFR24/015/2013/en/

ERITREA

State of Eritrea
Head of state and government: **Isaias Afewerki**

No political opposition parties, independent media, civil society organizations or unregistered faith groups were permitted to operate. There were severe restrictions on freedom of expression and association. Military conscription was compulsory, and frequently extended indefinitely. Thousands of prisoners of conscience and political prisoners continued to be held in arbitrary detention, in harsh conditions. Torture and other cruel, inhuman or degrading treatment was common. Eritreans continued to flee the country in large numbers.

BACKGROUND

On 21 January 2013, around 200 soldiers took control of the Ministry of Information in the capital, Asmara, in an apparent coup attempt. The director of Eritrean state television was forced to read a statement on air containing the soldiers' demands, including freeing all political prisoners, implementing the 1997 Constitution, and putting in place a transitional government. The broadcast was cut off mid-transmission.

In July 2013, the UN Monitoring Group on Somalia and Eritrea observed "emerging fissures within the political and military leadership" in Eritrea. In October 2014, they also reported the continued use of coercive measures to collect the "diaspora tax" (a 2% levy on income imposed on Eritrean nationals living abroad) in a number of countries.

After hundreds of Eritreans drowned while trying to reach the Italian island of Lampedusa in October 2013, four Eritrean Catholic bishops issued a letter in May 2014. In a rare public expression of dissent, they criticized the situation that led so many people to continue to leave the country.

PRISONERS OF CONSCIENCE
Thousands of people were arbitrarily detained and held in incommunicado detention without charge or trial for various reasons, including: criticizing government policy or practice; for their work as journalists; for suspected opposition to the government; practising a religion not recognized by the state; evading or deserting national service conscription; or for trying to flee the country, or in the place of family members who had fled. In most cases relatives were not aware of the detainee's whereabouts. Some prisoners of conscience had been in prison without charge or trial for two decades.

The government continued to refuse to confirm reports that nine of the 11 so-called G15 prisoners – a group of high-profile politicians detained since 2001 – had died in detention from a range of illnesses, as well as a number of the journalists arrested alongside them. There were unconfirmed reports that eight detainees held since 2005/2006, including government officials and medical doctors, were released in April 2014.

FREEDOM OF RELIGION
Only four faith groups were permitted to operate – the Eritrean Orthodox, Roman Catholic and Lutheran Churches, and Islam.

Members of other banned groups, including Pentecostal and Evangelical Christian denominations, continued to be subject to arbitrary detention and torture and other ill-treatment for practising their religion.

MILITARY CONSCRIPTION
National service continued to be mandatory for all men and women aged between 18 and 50, with no provision for conscientious objection. All school pupils were required to complete their final school year at Sawa military camp, effectively conscripting children into the military. The initial 18-month period of service continued to be frequently extended indefinitely, with minimal salaries and no choice over the nature of work assigned – a system that amounted to forced labour. Conscripts faced harsh penalties for evasion, including arbitrary detention and torture and other ill-treatment. Children at Sawa were kept in poor conditions and received harsh punishments for infractions.

TORTURE AND OTHER ILL-TREATMENT
Torture and other ill-treatment was reported to be widely used as punishment, interrogation, and as coercion. Common methods included tying prisoners in painful positions for long periods and prolonged solitary confinement.

Appalling prison conditions amounted to cruel, inhuman or degrading treatment or punishment. Many detainees were held in overcrowded underground cells or metal shipping containers, often in desert locations, suffering extremes of heat and cold. Food, water and sanitation were inadequate.

REFUGEES AND ASYLUM-SEEKERS
As of January 2014 UNHCR, the UN refugee agency, reported 338,129 persons of concern originating from Eritrea, including 308,022 refugees and 30,038 asylum-seekers. Around 3,000 people fled the country each month.

Human trafficking networks continued to prey upon Eritreans fleeing the country, including in Sudan and Egypt. Victims were held hostage, sometimes for a year or longer, and subjected to violence by criminal groups attempting to extract ransom payments from their families. The UN Monitoring Group reported that it had identified a Swiss bank account that had been used to collect such payments.

In April 2014, 266 Eritrean refugees and asylum-seekers were released from detention in neighbouring Djibouti and transferred to a refugee camp in the south of the country.

INTERNATIONAL SCRUTINY

Eritrea faced increased international scrutiny. Appointed to the newly created role of UN Special Rapporteur on the human rights situation in Eritrea in October 2012, Sheila Keetharuth presented wide-ranging concerns and recommendations in reports to the UN Human Rights Council in June 2013 and June 2014, and to the UN General Assembly in October 2013 and October 2014. The Special Rapporteur's requests for access to the country have not been granted since her appointment in 2012.

In June 2014, a three-member UN Commission of Inquiry was established for one year to investigate all alleged violations of human rights in Eritrea outlined in the reports of the Special Rapporteur.

ESTONIA

Republic of Estonia
Head of state: **Toomas Hendrik Ilves**
Head of government: **Taavi Rõivas (replaced Andrus Ansip in March)**

Legislation allowing unmarried, including same-sex, couples to register their cohabitation was passed. About 91,000 people remained stateless. Few asylum-seekers were granted protection and the number of asylum applications remained low. The government accepted the transfer of a Guantánamo detainee.

RIGHTS OF LESBIAN, GAY, BISEXUAL, TRANSGENDER AND INTERSEX PEOPLE

On 9 October, parliament passed a gender-neutral Cohabitation Act, due to enter into force on 1 January 2016. The Act allows unmarried, including same-sex, couples to register their cohabitation. It also extends to them many of the rights of married couples, for example regarding benefits. Couples in a registered cohabitation agreement will be allowed to adopt the partner's biological children.

DISCRIMINATION – ETHNIC MINORITIES

UNHCR, the UN refugee agency, stated that about 91,000 people (approximately 6.8% of the population) remained stateless; the vast majority were Russian speakers. Stateless people enjoyed limited political rights.

Efforts by the authorities to facilitate the naturalization of children born of stateless parents fell short of granting them automatic citizenship at birth, leaving Estonia in breach of its obligations under the International Covenant on Civil and Political Rights and the Convention on the Rights of the Child.

Ethnic minorities continued to be disproportionately affected by unemployment and poverty, leading to concerns that ethnic and linguistic discrimination could be a contributing factor. Language requirements for employment were reportedly placing ethnic minorities at a disadvantage.

REFUGEES AND ASYLUM-SEEKERS

The number of asylum applications remained low. Approximately 120 were made in the first 10 months of the year, of which some 35 were from Ukrainian nationals. At least 20 people had been granted asylum as of the end of November. There was concern that asylum-seekers could be denied access to asylum at borders and refused entry.

Reports indicated that the provision of legal aid and interpretation to asylum-seekers had improved.

COUNTER-TERROR AND SECURITY

In October, following a request from the USA, the government agreed to accept for resettlement a former Guantánamo detainee. Neither his identity nor the date of transfer were disclosed.

ETHIOPIA

Federal Democratic Republic of Ethiopia
Head of state: **Mulatu Teshome Wirtu**
Head of government: **Hailemariam Desalegn**

Freedom of expression continued to be subject to serious restrictions. The government was hostile to suggestions of dissent, and often made pre-emptive arrests to prevent dissent from manifesting. Independent media publications were subject to further attack. Peaceful protesters, journalists, and members of opposition political parties were arbitrarily arrested. The Charities and Societies Proclamation continued to obstruct the work of human rights organizations. Arbitrary detention and torture and other ill-treatment were widespread, often used as part of a system for silencing actual or suspected dissent.

BACKGROUND

Economic growth continued apace, along with significant foreign investment including in the agriculture, construction and manufacturing sectors, large-scale development projects such as hydroelectric dam building and plantations, and widespread land-leasing, often to foreign companies.

The government used multiple channels and methods to enforce political control on

the population, including politicizing access to job and education opportunities and development assistance, and high levels of physical and technological surveillance.

The politicization of the investigative branch of the police and of the judiciary meant that it was not possible to receive a fair hearing in politically motivated trials.

Federal and regional security services were responsible for violations throughout the country, including arbitrary arrests, the use of excessive force, torture and extrajudicial executions. They operated with near-total impunity.

Armed opposition groups remained in several parts of the country or in neighbouring countries, although in most cases with small numbers of fighters and low levels of activity.

Access to some parts of the Somali region continued to be severely restricted. There were continuing reports of serious violations of human rights, including arbitrary arrests and extrajudicial executions. There were also multiple allegations of the rape of women and girls by members of the security services.

EXCESSIVE USE OF FORCE – EXTRAJUDICIAL EXECUTIONS

In April and May, protests took place across Oromia region against a proposed "Integrated Master Plan" to expand the capital Addis Ababa into Oromia regional territory. The government said the plan would bring services to remote areas, but many Oromo people feared it would damage the interests of Oromo farmers and lead to large-scale displacement.

Security services, comprising federal police and military special forces, responded with excessive force, firing live ammunition at protesters in Ambo and Guder towns and Wallega and Madawalabu universities, resulting in the deaths of at least 30 people, including children. Hundreds of people were beaten by security service agents during and after the protests, including protesters, bystanders, and parents of protesters for failing to "control" their children, resulting in scores of injuries.

Thousands of people were arbitrarily arrested. Large numbers were detained without charge for several months, and some were held incommunicado. Hundreds were held in unofficial places of detention, including Senkele police training camp. Some detainees were transferred to Maikelawi federal police detention centre in Addis Ababa. Over 100 people continued to be detained in Kelem Wallega, Jimma and Ambo by security service agents after courts ordered their release on bail or unconditionally.

Many of those arrested were released after varying detention periods, between May and October, but others were denied bail, or remained in detention without charge. Others, including students and members of the Oromo Federalist Congress (OFC) opposition political party, were prosecuted and convicted in rapid trials on various charges relating to the protests.

FREEDOM OF EXPRESSION, ARBITRARY ARRESTS AND DETENTIONS

2014 saw another onslaught on freedom of expression and suggestions of dissent, including further targeting of the independent media and arrests of opposition political party members and peaceful protesters. Several attempts by opposition political parties to stage demonstrations were obstructed by the authorities. The Anti-Terrorism Proclamation continued to be used to silence dissidents. Opposition party members were increasingly targeted ahead of the 2015 general election.

In late April, six bloggers of the Zone 9 collective and three independent journalists associated with the group were arrested in Addis Ababa, two days after the group announced the resumption of activities, which had been suspended due to significant harassment. For nearly three months, all nine were held in the underground section of Maikelawi, denied access to family members and other visitors, and with severely restricted access to lawyers.

In July, they were charged with terrorism offences, along with another Zone 9 member charged in their absence. The charge sheet cited among their alleged crimes the use of "Security in a Box" – a selection of open-source software and materials created to assist human rights defenders, particularly those working in repressive environments.

Six of the group said they were forced to sign confessions. Three complained in remand hearings that they had been tortured, but the court did not investigate their complaints. The trial continued at the end of 2014.

Early in 2014, a "study" conducted by the national Press Agency and Ethiopian News Agency and published in the government-run *Addis Zemen* newspaper targeted seven independent publications, alleging that they had printed several articles which "promoted terrorism", denied economic growth, belittled the legacy of former Prime Minister Meles Zenawi, and committed other "transgressions". In August, the government announced that it was bringing charges against several of the publications, causing over 20 journalists to flee the country. In October, the owners of three of the publications were sentenced in their absence to over three years' imprisonment each for allegedly inciting the public to overthrow the government and publishing unfounded rumours.

The OFC opposition party reported that between 350 and 500 of its members were arrested between May and July, including party leadership. The arrests started in the context of the "Master Plan" protests, but continued for several months. Many of those arrested were detained arbitrarily and incommunicado. OFC members were among over 200 people arrested in Oromia in mid-September, and further party members were arrested in October.

On 8 July, Habtamu Ayalew and Daniel Shebeshi, of the Unity for Democracy and Justice (UDJ) Party, and Yeshewas Asefa of the Semayawi Party were arrested in Addis

Ababa. Abraha Desta of the Arena Tigray Party, and a lecturer at Mekele University, was arrested in Tigray, and was transferred to Addis Ababa. They were detained in Maikelawi and initially denied access to lawyers and family. In late October, they were charged under the Anti-Terrorism Proclamation. Yeshewas Asefa complained in court that he had been tortured in detention.

The Semayawi Party reported numerous arrests of its members, including seven women arrested in March during a run to mark International Women's Day in Addis Ababa, along with three men, also members of the party. They had been chanting slogans including "We need freedom! Free political prisoners!" They were released without charge after 10 days. In late April, 20 members of the party were arrested while promoting a demonstration in Addis Ababa. They were released after 11 days.

In early September, Befekadu Abebe and Getahun Beyene, party officials in Arba Minch city, were arrested along with three party members. Befekadu Abebe and Getahun Beyene were transferred to Maikelawi detention centre in Addis Ababa. In the initial stages of detention, they were reportedly denied access to lawyers and family members. In late October, party member Agbaw Setegn, was arrested in Gondar, and was also transferred to Maikelawi, and held incommunicado without access to lawyers or family.

On 27 October, editor Temesgen Desalegn was sentenced to three years' imprisonment for "defamation" and "inciting the public through false rumours", in the now-defunct publication *Feteh*, after a trial that had lasted more than two years. The publisher of *Feteh* was also convicted in their absence.

People were detained arbitrarily without charge for long periods in the initial stages, or throughout the duration, of their detention including numerous people arrested for peaceful opposition to the government or their imputed political opinion. Arbitrary detention took place in official and unofficial detention centres, including Maikelawi. Many detainees were held incommunicado, and many were denied access to lawyers and family members.

Numerous prisoners of conscience, imprisoned in previous years based solely on their peaceful exercise of their freedom of expression and opinion, including journalists and opposition political party members, remained in detention. These included some convicted in unfair trials, some whose trials continued, and some who continued to be detained without charge.

Access to detention centres for monitoring and documenting the treatment of detainees continued to be severely restricted.

TORTURE AND OTHER ILL-TREATMENT

Torture took place in local police stations, Maikelawi federal police station, federal and regional prisons and military camps.

Torture methods reported included: beating with sticks, rubber batons, gun butts and other objects; burning; tying in stress positions; electric shocks; and forced prolonged physical exercise. Some detention conditions amounted to torture, including detaining people underground without light, shackled and in prolonged solitary confinement.

Torture typically took place in the early stages of detention, in conjunction with the interrogation of the detainee. Torture was used to force detainees to confess, to sign incriminating evidence and to incriminate others. Those subjected to torture included prisoners of conscience, who were arrested for their perceived or actual expression of dissent.

Defendants in several trials complained in court that they were tortured or otherwise ill-treated in detention. The courts failed to order investigations into the complaints.

In several cases, prisoners of conscience were denied access to adequate medical care.

OROMIA REGION

Ethnic Oromos continued to suffer many violations of human rights in efforts to suppress potential dissent in the region.

Large numbers of Oromo people continued to be arrested or remained in detention after arrests in previous years, based on their peaceful expression of dissent, or in numerous cases, based only on their suspected opposition to the government. Arrests were arbitrary, often made pre-emptively and without evidence of a crime. Many were detained without charge or trial, and large numbers were detained in unofficial places of detention, particularly in military camps throughout the region. There was no accountability for enforced disappearances or extrajudicial executions during 2014 or in previous years.

In the aftermath of the "Master Plan" protests, increased levels of arrests of actual or suspected dissenters continued. Large numbers of arrests were reported, including several hundred in early October in Hurumu and Yayu Woredas districts in Illubabor province, of high-school students, farmers and other residents.

There were further reports of arrests of students asking about the fate of their classmates arrested during the "Master Plan" protests, demanding their release and justice for those killed, including 27 reported to have been arrested in Wallega University in late November.

REFUGEES AND ASYLUM-SEEKERS
Forcible returns

Ethiopian government agents were active in many countries, some of which cooperated with the Ethiopian authorities in forcibly returning people wanted by the government.

In January, two representatives of the rebel Ogaden National Liberation Front were abducted and forcibly returned to Ethiopia from Nairobi, Kenya. They were in Nairobi to participate in further peace talks between the group and the government.

On 23 June, UK national Andargachew Tsige, Secretary General of the outlawed Ginbot 7 movement, was rendered from Yemen to Ethiopia. On 8 July, a broadcast was aired on state-run ETV showing Tsige looking haggard and exhausted. By the end of the year, he was still detained incommunicado at an undisclosed location, with no access to lawyers or family. The UK government continued to be denied consular access, except for two meetings with the Ambassador, to one of which Andargachew Tsige was brought hooded, and they were not permitted to talk privately.

In March, former Gambella regional governor Okello Akway, who has Norwegian citizenship, was forcibly returned to Ethiopia from South Sudan. In June, he was charged with terrorism offences along with several other people, in connection with Gambella opposition movements in exile.

FIJI

Republic of Fiji
Head of state: **Ratu Epeli Nailatikau**
Head of government: **Josaia Voreqe Bainimarama**

Laws, policies and practices failed to adequately protect human rights, placing sweeping restrictions on freedoms of expression, peaceful assembly and association. Victims of serious human rights violations, including torture and other ill-treatment, were unable to seek redress in the courts due to widespread immunities for government officials and security forces.

BACKGROUND

In September Fiji held its first election since the 2006 military coup. New electoral laws expanded restrictions on freedom of expression. A climate of fear and self-censorship prevailed. Abuses by security forces continued to occur, including one death in police custody in August.

FREEDOMS OF EXPRESSION, ASSEMBLY AND ASSOCIATION

Rights to freedoms of expression, peaceful assembly and association were criminalized, with people facing heavy fines and possible imprisonment under a number of decrees.

The Electoral Decree 2014 prohibited civil society organizations from "campaigning", including providing human rights education, on any issue relevant to elections. Breaching this Decree carried a penalty of FJ$50,000 (approx. US$27,000) and up to 10 years' imprisonment.

In August a human rights organization, Citizens' Constitutional Forum, was put under criminal investigation for breaching the Electoral Decree for organizing a series of public lectures on democracy and human rights.

In June the Media Industry Development Authority called for a criminal investigation against two university academics after they had called on police to stop the harassment and intimidation of journalists.

WORKERS' RIGHTS

The Essential National Industries (Employment) Decree 2011 continued to violate key workers' rights, including by limiting collective bargaining rights, curtailing the right to strike, banning overtime payments, and voiding existing collective agreements for workers in the sugar, aviation and tourism industries. Under electoral laws, trade union officials were not permitted to hold office in a political party or to engage in other political activities.

In January Daniel Urai, a trade union leader, was arrested and charged with participating in an unlawful strike, following a strike at a hotel in Nadi. The charges were dropped after two months.

TORTURE AND OTHER ILL-TREATMENT

Extensive immunities under the Constitution made it impossible to hold state perpetrators accountable for serious human rights violations such as torture and other ill-treatment. Members of the military and the police, as well as government officials, operated with civil and criminal immunity for violations of human rights. Many cases of torture and other ill-treatment, including several relating to recaptured prisoners, remained unaddressed.

In August Vilikesa Soko, who had been arrested on suspicion of robbery, died in police custody. The autopsy report showed that he suffered serious injuries consistent with assault, leading to multiple organ failure. While the new Police Commissioner promptly ordered an investigation into the death and suspended four police officers, no criminal charges had been brought against the alleged perpetrators at the end of the year.

FINLAND

Republic of Finland
Head of state: **Sauli Niinistö**
Head of government: **Alexander Stubb (replaced Jyrki Katainen in June)**

Asylum-seekers and migrants faced detention in unsuitable facilities. An investigation into Finland's involvement in the US-led rendition programme failed to find evidence. Support for victims of sexual and gender-based violence remained insufficient. Transgender people faced obstacles to legal gender recognition.

REFUGEES' AND MIGRANTS' RIGHTS

Finland continued to detain asylum-seekers and migrants, including children. During 2013, approximately 1,500 migrants were detained under the Aliens Act, of whom the majority were held in police detention facilities. Ten unaccompanied children were held together with adults in the Metsälä detention centre. In September 2014, a new detention centre intended to hold families with children and other vulnerable individuals, connected with the Joutseno reception facility, was opened.

In January, the Ombudsman for Minorities began monitoring forced removals of refused asylum-seekers and migrants.

COUNTER-TERROR AND SECURITY

In April, the Parliamentary Ombudsman published the results of his investigation into Finland's alleged role in the US-led programme of rendition and secret detention. The Ombudsman found no evidence that Finnish officials had any knowledge of rendition flights by the CIA in Finland, but "could not give any guarantees" as some flight information was not included in the probe because it was no longer available.[1]

VIOLENCE AGAINST WOMEN AND GIRLS

Rape is still defined by the degree of violence or threats of violence used by the perpetrator, rather than the violation of sexual autonomy and physical and mental integrity.

Support for victims of gender-based and sexual violence remains insufficient and at risk of deterioration. Two women's shelters were closed down in 2013, and only two crisis centres offered support to rape victims. Finland does not meet the shelter requirements set by the Council of Europe Istanbul Convention. Despite the government's stated intention to ratify the Convention, its proposal published in September included neither a dedicated budget nor an action plan for extending the required services to victims of violence.

A survey published in March by the European Union Agency for Fundamental Rights found that 47% of women had experienced physical or sexual violence since the age of 15 by a partner and/or non-partner. Only 10% of women contacted the police as a result of the most serious incident of violence by their partner.

In March, the CEDAW Committee recommended allocating adequate resources to a National Action Plan to prevent violence against women, establishing an institutional mechanism to co-ordinate and monitor any measures, ensuring sufficient and adequately resourced shelters, opening rape crisis centres and walk-in centres, and establishing a 24-hour helpline.

DISCRIMINATION – TRANSGENDER PEOPLE

Widespread prejudices and discriminatory legislation negatively affected the enjoyment of human rights by transgender individuals.[2] Transgender people can obtain legal gender recognition only if they agree to be sterilized, are diagnosed with a mental disorder, are of age and can prove that they are single. The Ministry of Social Affairs and Health finalized a draft law in November proposing the removal of the requirements regarding sterilization and single status; the bill had not been presented to Parliament by the end of the year.

PRISONERS OF CONSCIENCE

Conscientious objectors to military service continued to be imprisoned for refusing to undertake alternative civilian service, which remained punitive and discriminatory in length. Since February 2013, the duration of alternative civilian service has been 347 days, more than double the shortest military service period of 165 days.

---

1. Finland: CIA rendition probe findings 'disappointing' (Press release) www.amnesty.org/en/news/finland-cia-rendition-probe-findings-disappointing-2014-04-29

2. The state decides who I am: Lack of legal gender recognition for transgender people in Europe (EUR 01/001/2014) www.amnesty.org/en/library/info/EUR01/001/2014/en

FRANCE

French Republic
Head of state: **François Hollande**
Head of government: **Manuel Valls (replaced Jean-Marc Ayrault in March)**

Migrant Roma continued to be forcibly evicted from informal settlements; individuals and communities were often not consulted or offered adequate alternative accommodation. Concerns remained about the impartiality and thoroughness of investigations into allegations of ill-treatment by the police. Same-sex couples could enter into civil marriage following a change in the law in 2013.

DISCRIMINATION – ROMA

Officially, more than 19,000 people lived in 429 informal settlements at the beginning of the year. Most of them were migrant Roma from Romania, Bulgaria and the former Yugoslavia. The French authorities continued to forcibly evict them throughout the year. According to the League of Human Rights and the European Roma Rights Centre, more than 11,000 individuals were forcibly evicted in the first nine months of the year.

On 31 January, the Minister of Housing announced a plan to provide long-term housing solutions to the inhabitants of informal settlements. On 28 February, an agreement was signed between the government and Adoma, a publicly funded accommodation provider, and some communities evicted from informal settlements were offered alternative housing.

In spite of these developments, most of the evicted individuals and families reportedly did not receive any alternative housing. For instance, on 18 June, some 400 individuals were forcibly evicted from La Parette, the largest informal settlement in Marseille. Only 18 families (150 people) were offered some form of alternative accommodation.

On 21 October, more than 300 individuals were forcibly evicted from the informal settlement Les Coquetiers in Bobigny, a Paris suburb, following an eviction order issued by the municipality. According to the authorities, 134 individuals were offered some rehousing solutions. More than 100 reportedly left the settlement before the eviction took place as they had not been offered any alternative accommodation. About 60 individuals were forcibly evicted and subsequently offered short-term accommodation in Paris.[1]

While the authorities did not collect official data on hate crimes against Roma, civil society organizations reported several violent attacks against Roma. Concerns remained that the authorities often did not take into account any alleged discriminatory motive in the investigation of these cases. The criminal investigation against four police officers who had injured a Roma man in November 2011, while carrying out a forced eviction in Marseille, was still ongoing at the end of the year.[2]

RIGHTS OF LESBIAN, GAY, BISEXUAL, TRANSGENDER AND INTERSEX PEOPLE

On 18 May 2013, civil marriage was made available to all couples irrespective of gender. Adoption rights were extended to married same-gender couples.

Despite repeated commitments by the government to reform abusive practices, transgender people continued to be subjected to psychiatric diagnosis and unnecessary medical treatments such as surgery and sterilization in order to obtain legal recognition of their gender.[3]

DISCRIMINATION – MUSLIMS

Two judgments issued during the year failed to uphold Muslim women's right to freedoms of expression, religion and belief, and non-discrimination. On 25 June, the Court of Cassation found that the management of a private kindergarten did not discriminate against a Muslim employee in 2008 when she was dismissed for wearing a headscarf in the workplace. On 1 July, in the case of *SAS v. France*, the European Court of Human Rights found that the 2011 law prohibiting the complete covering of the face in public did not constitute a disproportionate restriction of the right to freedom of religion.[4]

POLICE AND SECURITY FORCES

In 2013, the Defender of Rights, an independent public authority, dealt with almost 1,000 allegations of acts of violence perpetrated by police. However, concerns remained about the impartiality and thoroughness of investigations into these allegations by judicial authorities.

In February 2014, the Court of Cassation reopened the case of Ali Ziri, an Algerian man who died in custody in 2009, which had been dismissed in 2012. On 19 November, the prosecuting authorities requested before the Rennes Appeal Court that further investigation be conducted into the case. However, on 12 December the Investigative Chamber of the Rennes Appeal Court confirmed the 2012 dismissal.

On 23 September, Raymond Gurême, an 89-year-old French Traveller, suffered several injuries allegedly as a result of excessive force during a police operation at the site where he lived. An investigation was ongoing at the end of the year.

On 26 October, 21-year-old Rémi Fraisse was fatally injured by an explosive anti-riot grenade thrown by National Gendarmerie officers during a demonstration against the Sivens dam project in the Tarn region. About 20 other complaints of police ill-treatment were reportedly filed by people protesting against the project. On 2 December, an internal investigation found that the National Gendarmerie officers abided by the law. Concerns remained about the impartiality and thoroughness of this investigation.

TORTURE AND OTHER ILL-TREATMENT

On 24 October the Lyon Court of Appeal authorized the extradition of Mukhtar Ablyazov, a Kazakhstani banker and opposition leader, to Russia, from where he could be forcibly returned to Kazakhstan. At the end of the year, an appeal was pending before the Court of Cassation. If extradited, he risked facing unfair trial in Russia and torture or other ill-treatment in Kazakhstan.[5]

REFUGEES' AND MIGRANTS' RIGHTS

On 16 October 2013, President Hollande announced that 500 Syrian refugees would be resettled in France during 2014. Between 300 and 350 were resettled by the end of the year. On 27 March, 85 Syrian nationals were reportedly stopped by police on arrival at Paris Gare de Lyon railway station. They were not given the opportunity to claim asylum and were given one month to leave France.

Also in March, a circular by the Minister of the Interior concerning undocumented migrants instructed authorities to deport foreign nationals whose asylum claims had been rejected by OFPRA, the French Office for Refugees and Stateless People, through the priority asylum procedure. While these decisions could be appealed against before the National Court of the Right to Asylum, the appeal did not have the effect of suspending the deportation. A bill aimed at reforming asylum procedures was adopted by the National Assembly and was pending before the Senate.

On 10 July, the European Court of Human Rights found that the refusal of French authorities to issue visas for the purpose of family reunification to the children of two refugees and three migrants residing in France violated the applicants' right to family life.

In October, more than 2,500 migrants and asylum-seekers, mainly from Afghanistan, Ethiopia, Eritrea and Syria, were living in harsh conditions in the Calais region. Most were attempting to reach the UK. In May, the authorities forcibly evicted 700 migrants and asylum-seekers from informal settlements in the area following a reported outbreak of scabies.[6] Discussions concerning the opening of a new reception centre were ongoing at the end of the year.

INTERNATIONAL JUSTICE

On 14 March, Rwandan national and former head of the Rwandan intelligence services Pascal Simbikangwa, was sentenced by the Paris Assize Court to 25 years' imprisonment for genocide and complicity in crimes against humanity perpetrated in the context of the 1994 Rwandan genocide. This was the first case to come to trial on the basis of extraterritorial jurisdiction since the establishment in 2012 of a specialized investigative unit tasked to deal with cases concerning genocide, war crimes and crimes against humanity. At the end of the year, the unit was investigating more than 30 alleged crimes perpetrated abroad.

FREEDOM OF ASSEMBLY

Several demonstrations concerning the situation in Gaza, including two demonstrations scheduled to take place in Paris on 19 and 26 July, were prohibited on grounds of security. The demonstrations took place despite the ban. Although some incidents of violence occurred, concerns remained as to whether the decisions to ban them were necessary and proportionate.

1. France: Bobigny forced eviction set to leave Roma families homeless (News story)
   www.amnesty.org/en/news/france-bobigny-forced-eviction-set-leave-roma-families-homeless-2014-10-20
2. "We ask for justice": Europe's failure to protect Roma from racist violence (EUR 01/007/2014)
   www.amnesty.org/en/library/info/EUR01/007/2014/en
3. The state decides who I am: Lack of legal gender recognition for transgender people in Europe (EUR 01/001/2014)
   www.amnesty.org/en/library/info/EUR01/001/2014/en
4. European Court ruling on full-face veils punishes women for expressing their beliefs (News story)
   www.amnesty.org/en/news/european-court-ruling-full-face-veils-punishes-women-expressing-their-religion-2014-07-01
5. France: Stop extradition of Kazakhstani opposition activist at risk of torture (News story)
   www.amnesty.org/en/news/france-stop-extradition-kazakhstani-opposition-activist-risk-torture-2014-10-24
6. France: Forced evictions add to climate of fear amid alleged hate crimes (EUR 21/003/2014)
   www.amnesty.org/en/library/info/EUR21/003/2014/en

GAMBIA

Republic of the Gambia
Head of state and government: **Yahya Jammeh**

2014 marked 20 years since President Yahya Jammeh came to power.[1] The authorities continued to repress dissent. The government continued its policy of non-co-operation with UN human rights mechanisms. Successive legislation was passed further restricting freedom of expression and increasing punitive measures against journalists. Human rights defenders and journalists continued to face imprisonment and harassment. The rights of lesbian, gay bisexual, transgender and intersex (LGBTI) people were further threatened. The year ended with an attempted coup on 30 December, leading to dozens of arrests and widespread crackdowns on media outlets.

BACKGROUND

Gambia's human rights record was assessed under the UN Universal Periodic Review (UPR) in October.[2] Concerns by UN member states included Gambia's restrictions on the right to freedom of expression, its renewed use of the death penalty, and discrimination and attacks on people on the basis of their sexual orientation and gender identity.

During their visit to Gambia in November, the UN Special Rapporteur on extrajudicial, summary or arbitrary executions and the Special Rapporteur on torture were denied access to detention centres where prisoners were believed to be at risk of torture. They described torture as a "consistent practice" in Gambia and expressed concerns about the 2012 executions and the climate of impunity.[3] In August, the authorities had unilaterally postponed the visit of the Special Rapporteurs, without adequate explanation.

In January 2013, President Jammeh suspended political dialogue with the EU following the inclusion of human rights on the agenda. Although discussions resumed in July 2013, little progress was made on implementing human rights commitments. In October 2013, President Jammeh announced Gambia's withdrawal from the Commonwealth, which was collaborating with the Gambian authorities on capacity-building initiatives for the judiciary and establishing a national human rights commission.

FREEDOM OF EXPRESSION

Successive legislation was passed in recent years restricting the right to freedom of expression.

In August 2014, the National Assembly passed the Criminal Code (Amendment) Act that introduced the charge "absconding state officials". This could be used to target individuals who expressed dissent and chose to remain outside the country.

In July 2013, the National Assembly passed the Information and Communication (Amendment) Act, allowing for penalties of up to 15 years' imprisonment and hefty fines for offences including: criticizing government officials online; spreading "false news" about the government or public officials; making derogatory statements against public officials; and inciting dissatisfaction or instigating violence against the government.

In May 2013, the National Assembly passed the Criminal Code (Amendment) Act, broadening the definition of various offences and imposing harsher punishments for acts of public disorder, such as "hurling abusive insults" or "singing abusive songs", and for giving false information to a public

servant. For example, the Act increased the punishment for providing false information to a public servant from six months' to five years' imprisonment and/or a larger fine.

Journalists

Journalists faced harassment, intimidation, arbitrary arrest and detention for carrying out their legitimate work.[4]

Sanna Camara was arrested on 27 June and charged with publishing false information after writing an article on human trafficking in Gambia for the *Standard* newspaper. He was denied access to a lawyer or his relatives. He was released on bail the next day and ordered to report to the police headquarters several times per week over several months.

HUMAN RIGHTS DEFENDERS

Human rights defenders faced harassment, intimidation, arbitrary arrest and detention, torture and enforced disappearance. There were risks of reprisals against Gambians who sought to engage in relation to the UPR examination on Gambia and ahead of the visit of the UN Special Rapporteurs.

By the end of the year no investigation had been instigated into the unlawful arrest and torture of Imam Baba Leigh, a prominent human rights defender and Muslim cleric. He had been arrested by National Intelligence Agency (NIA) officers in December 2012 and placed in incommunicado detention. He was repeatedly tortured for publicly condemning the government's use of the death penalty. He was released following a presidential pardon in May 2013 and subsequently left the country in fear for his safety.

TORTURE AND OTHER ILL-TREATMENT

Detainees were routinely tortured by law enforcement personnel as punishment and in order to force "confessions".

Abdou Jeli Keita, an officer with the National Drug Enforcement Agency and a former journalist, was pushed into a car outside his home in Wellingara on 1 August by five men wearing civilian clothes, believed to be members of the security services. He was blindfolded and driven to an undisclosed location where he said he was detained and beaten. Abdou Jeli Keita was not charged, nor allowed access to a lawyer or his relatives. He was told by his captors that he was detained because he was suspected of publicizing information on poor prison conditions. He was released the following day.

On 18 December 2013, Amadou Sanneh, national treasurer of the opposition United Democratic Party (UDP), and two other UDP members, Alhagie Sambou Fatty and Malang Fatty, were convicted of sedition and sentenced to up to five years' imprisonment. They were held incommunicado at the NIA headquarters for nearly a month prior to their trial in October 2013. All three alleged they were tortured to confess on national television. Alhagie Sambou Fatty and Malang Fatty had no legal representation throughout their detention and trial. The three men are prisoners of conscience.

DEATH PENALTY

In November, the Supreme Court commuted the death sentences of Lang Tombong Tamba and six others to life imprisonment. The seven men – Chief of Defence Staff Lieutenant General Lang Tombong Tamba, Brigadier General Omar Bun Mbye, Major Lamin Bo Badgie, Lieutenant Colonel Kawsu Camara, former Deputy Inspector General of Police Momodou B. Gaye, Gibril Ngorr Secka and Abdoulie Joof – were convicted of treason and sentenced to death in 2010. They had been sentenced to death for treason, contrary to the Constitution which permits the death penalty only for crimes "resulting in the death of another person".

In a media interview in August 2013, President Jammeh justified the retention of the death penalty as being "divine law" and stated that he would not pardon anybody condemned to death. This would deny defendants' right under international law to seek clemency.

RIGHTS OF LESBIAN, GAY, BISEXUAL, TRANSGENDER AND INTERSEX PEOPLE

At least eight people, including three women and a 17-year-old youth, were arrested by men identifying themselves as agents of the NIA and Presidential Guards between 7 and 13 November and threatened with torture because of their presumed sexual orientation. They were told that if they did not "confess" their homosexuality, including by providing the names of others, a device would be forced into their anus or vagina to "test" their sexual orientation. Such treatment would violate international law prohibiting torture and other ill-treatment. A further six women were reportedly arrested on 18 and 19 November on the same grounds.[5]

In August, the National Assembly passed the Criminal Code (Amendment) Act 2014 which created the crime of "aggravated homosexuality", carrying a life sentence. The wording of the Amendment was vague, making it open to wide-ranging abuse by the authorities. Among those who could be charged with "aggravated homosexuality" were "repeat offenders" and people living with HIV who were suspected of being gay or lesbian.[6]

In a speech on national television in February, President Jammeh attacked LGBTI rights, stating, "We will fight these vermin called homosexuals or gays the same way we are fighting malaria-causing mosquitoes – if not more aggressively." In May, President Jammeh threatened Gambians seeking asylum as a result of discrimination on the basis of their sexual orientation.

IMPUNITY

The government made no progress towards implementing the judgments of the ECOWAS Court of Justice in the enforced disappearance of journalist Ebrima Manneh, the torture of journalist Musa Saidykhan and the unlawful killing of Deyda Hydara.[7]

1. Gambia: President Jammeh must put an end to 20 years of repression and impunity for human rights violations (AFR 27/009/2014)
www.amnesty.org/en/library/info/AFR27/009/2014/en

2. Gambia: Deteriorating human rights situation: Amnesty International submission to the UN Universal Periodic Review, October-November 2014 (AFR 27/006/2014)
www.amnesty.org/en/library/info/AFR27/006/2014/en

3. Gambia: UN monitors denied prison access as they condemn "consistent practice" of torture (Press release)
www.amnesty.org.uk/press-releases/gambia-un-inspectors-denied-prison-access-after-they-condemn-consistent-practice

4. Gambia: Further information: journalists acquitted and discharged (AFR 27/014/2014)
www.amnesty.org/en/library/info/AFR27/014/2014/en

5. Gambia must stop wave of homophobic arrests and torture (News story)
www.amnesty.org/en/news/gambia-must-stop-wave-homophobic-arrests-and-torture-2014-11-18

6. Gambia: "Aggravated homosexuality" offence carries life sentence (News story)
www.amnesty.org/en/news/gambia-aggravated-homosexuality-offence-carries-life-sentence-2014-11-21

7. Gambia: President Jammeh must put an end to 20 years of repression and impunity for human rights violations (AFR 27/009/2014)
www.amnesty.org/en/library/info/AFR27/009/2014/en

GEORGIA

Georgia
Head of state: **Giorgi Margvelashvili**
Head of government: **Irakli Garibashvili**

Religious and sexual minorities continued to face discrimination and violence and in several instances were unable to exercise their right to freedom of assembly. Opposition politicians were subject to violent attacks. Allegations of ill-treatment by police and penitentiary officials continued to be reported and were often inadequately investigated. Domestic violence against women remained widespread.

BACKGROUND

On 27 June, the European Union signed the Association Agreement with Georgia.

Allegations of the selective prosecution of figures associated with the opposition party United National Movement (UNM) persisted. On 13 August, the Chief Prosecutor's Office charged former President Mikheil Saakashvili in his absence with embezzlement and abuse of office. On 9 December, the OSCE trial monitoring, which focused on criminal cases against senior officials in President Saakashvili's government, identified concerns related to a number of fair trial rights, including equality of arms between parties and the presumption of innocence.

Defence minister Irakli Alasania was sacked on 4 November following the arrests of five senior defence officials on 28 October, which he had dismissed as politically motivated. The officials were accused of misspending GEL 4.1 million (US$2.1 million) in what the prosecution claimed was a sham tender. Several ministerial resignations followed resulting in the breakdown of the parliamentary coalition.

In November, three detainees from the US detention facility at Guantánamo Bay were transferred to Georgia for resettlement.

On 24 November, the de facto authorities in Georgia's Abkhazia region signed the Agreement on Alliance and Strategic Partnership with the Russian Federation making the breakaway territory even more dependent on Russia in defence, external relations and economic matters.

DISCRIMINATION

On 2 May, an anti-discrimination law was adopted but without provisions which had been included in an earlier draft. These would have introduced an independent oversight mechanism and financial penalties for violations.

Reported incidents of violent religious intolerance increased. The authorities failed to protect the rights of religious minorities, address recurring violence and effectively investigate attacks.

On 1 June, local Orthodox Christians in the town of Terjola, western Georgia, gathered to protest against the construction of a place of worship for Jehovah's Witnesses. They threatened to use physical violence and destroy property. Several Jehovah's Witnesses reported being harassed and intimidated by local residents, including receiving death threats and having stones thrown at their houses. Police issued written warnings to the alleged offenders but did not conduct any formal investigation.

In September, residents of the town of Kobuleti, western Georgia, repeatedly blocked an entry to the local Muslim boarding school and physically prevented staff and schoolchildren from entering the building. On the first day of the new school year, a pig was slaughtered at the building entrance and its head was nailed to the door. A criminal investigation was opened.

FREEDOM OF ASSEMBLY

On 22 October, clashes between the police and the local Muslim community broke out in the village of Mokhe, western Georgia, after the local authorities began to construct a library on the site of a derelict building which, the Muslim community claimed, was once a mosque. Police reportedly insulted and used disproportionate force against protesters, arresting 14. Several detainees were reportedly beaten, among them a woman who received serious injuries to her face. Three detainees were released the next day without charges while the others were fined 250 lari (US$140) each by the court in the town of Akhaltsikhe.

In May, lesbian, gay, bisexual, transgender and intersex activists abandoned plans to organize a public action to mark the International Day Against Homophobia and Transphobia (IDAHO) due to the lack of security guarantees by the authorities. In 2013, the IDAHO street event was thwarted by a violent attack by thousands of counter-demonstrators while the police failed to ensure people's safety.

POLICE AND SECURITY FORCES

A number of violent attacks against opposition politicians were reported in which the police failed to prevent violence.

On 9 June, Gigi Ugulava and Giga Bokeria, leaders of the opposition party United National Movement (UNM), were assaulted by members of the Georgian Dream Coalition (GDC) during a pre-election meeting with voters in the town of Tsageri. According to eyewitnesses, police officers standing nearby did not intervene to stop the violence.

On 30 September, the office of the NGO Free Zone, which was associated with the UNM, was attacked by about 50 people. Several staff members were injured as the police failed to arrive promptly despite the warnings of possible violence.

TORTURE AND OTHER ILL-TREATMENT

There were several reports of torture and other ill-treatment of detainees in prison and in police custody. Official investigations were often slow and ineffective. Of the 18 cases of alleged ill-treatment in prison documented by the Public Defender (Ombudsman), in just one case an investigation was opened for charges of ill-treatment. No prosecutions were reported at the end of the year.

On 15 March, Irakli Kelbakiani reported being forced into a police car, beaten with hands and iron bats on his head, face and body, and asphyxiated by police officers. According to the initial incident report, bruises and other injuries were evident on his arrival at the police station.

Amiran Dzebisashvili reported that on 31 October he was forced inside a police car and threatened after he had testified in court that Vasil Lomsadze was beaten by police officers during his arrest on 27 October 2013. Vasil Lomsadze was standing trial for resisting arrest and allegedly attacking police officers during this incident. There had been no effective investigation into Vasil Lomsadze's allegations of being beaten by police at the end of the year, despite several eyewitness accounts and his recorded injuries.

VIOLENCE AGAINST WOMEN AND GIRLS
At least 25 women and girls were reported to have been killed as a result of domestic violence. In several cases the victims had previously asked police for protection but had not received adequate support.

RIGHT TO PRIVACY
The legislative amendments of 28 November allowed security agencies to retain direct access to communications surveillance amidst concerns that such an access can be misused by the agencies to bypass the judicial oversight for surveillance.

GERMANY

Federal Republic of Germany
Head of state: **Joachim Gauck**
Head of government: **Angela Merkel**

Humanitarian admission programmes for 20,000 Syrian refugees were approved. There were no improvements in the investigation of serious human rights violations by police. The National Agency for the Prevention of Torture remained under-resourced. Discriminatory attacks against asylum-seekers and minorities continued and concerns regarding the investigation and prosecution of these crimes remained. Human rights criteria for arms exports were implemented.

REFUGEES AND ASYLUM-SEEKERS
Between 2013 and 2014, Germany started three humanitarian admission programmes for 20,000 Syrian refugees from Syria's neighbouring countries and Egypt. The main aim was extended family reunification. Three

hundred refugees were offered resettlement through a UNHCR programme. In December, Germany also decided to offer resettlement to 500 refugees per year starting in 2015. In September, Serbia, Macedonia and Bosnia and Herzegovina were legally defined as safe countries of origin, which reduced opportunities for nationals of these countries to seek protection. A law was passed allowing asylum-seekers to move freely within the country after three months of residence and to have unhindered access to the job market after 15 months. The amended Asylum Seekers Benefit Act, due to enter into force in April 2015, fell short of human rights standards particularly regarding health care.

TORTURE AND OTHER ILL-TREATMENT
The authorities failed to address obstacles in the effective investigation of allegations of ill-treatment by police. None of the federal states established an independent complaints mechanism to investigate allegations of serious human rights violations by the police. Except for the federal states of Berlin, Brandenburg, Rhineland-Palatinate and Schleswig-Holstein, there was no obligation for police officers to wear identity badges.

The National Agency for the Prevention of Torture, Germany's preventive mechanism under the Optional Protocol to the UN Convention against Torture, remained severely under-resourced, even though there was an increase of funds and a doubling of members for the Joint Commission of the Federal States, one of the two constituent bodies of the Agency. Contrary to international standards, the appointment procedure of the National Agency's members lacked independence and transparency and excluded civil society.

Investigations and proceedings for excessive use of force by the Stuttgart Police in relation to the disproportionate use of water cannons during demonstrations in the city in September 2010 continued.

In September, the Federal Court of Justice upheld the December 2012 conviction of a police officer by the Magdeburg Regional Court, which convicted the officer for negligent homicide in connection with the death of Oury Jalloh, who died in a fire in a cell in a Dessau police station in 2005. The circumstances of Oury Jalloh's death remained unclear.

Also in September, media reports exposed the repeated ill-treatment of asylum-seekers by private security personnel in three reception facilities in North Rhine-Westphalia.

DISCRIMINATION

In August 2013, the ad-hoc federal Parliamentary Committee of Inquiry published ground-breaking conclusions regarding the authorities' failure to investigate a series of murders targeting minorities perpetrated by the far-right group National Socialist Underground (NSU). In particular, the authorities had failed to co-operate and to investigate the racist motive of the murders. The Committee recommended reforming the Criminal Code and the system used by police to collect data on "politically motivated crimes", which included information on hate crimes.

In August 2014, the government proposed amending Section 46 of the Criminal Code to require courts to take into account racist, xenophobic or any other "degrading" motive when deciding sentences. The proposal was pending before Parliament at the end of the year.

In the first half of 2014, according to civil society data, there were 155 protests against the establishment of reception facilities for asylum-seekers, mostly by far-right groups. Eighteen attacks against asylum-seekers were also reported.

RIGHTS OF LESBIAN, GAY, BISEXUAL, TRANSGENDER AND INTERSEX PEOPLE

The 1980 Law on Changing First Names and the Establishment of Sex Status in Special Cases remained in force, requiring transgender people to comply with mandatory criteria to legally change their gender and names. These included obtaining a psychiatric diagnosis and an expert assessment ordered by courts. These requirements violated transgender people's rights to private life and to the highest attainable standard of health.[1]

ARMS TRADE

In anticipation of more stringent EU regulations on surveillance technologies, the Minister of Economic Affairs and Energy ordered stricter controls on exports of surveillance technologies to countries which commit human rights violations. Germany ratified the UN Arms Trade Treaty in April and started implementing articles 6 and 7 on human rights criteria for arms exports and transfers before its entry into force, due on 24 December. However, data on arms exports licensed in 2014, including small arms components for Saudi Arabia, raised concern.

CORPORATE ACCOUNTABILITY

In November, the Foreign Office, in co-operation with other ministries, business representatives and civil society groups, took steps towards the introduction of a national action plan on business and human rights to implement relevant UN guiding principles.

INTERNATIONAL JUSTICE

The first trial based on the 2002 Code of Crimes under International Law against Rwandan citizens Ignace Murwanashyaka and Straton Musoni continued at Stuttgart Higher Regional Court.

On 18 February, the Frankfurt Higher Regional Court found Rwandan citizen Onesphore Rwabukombe guilty of abetting genocide. In this first German judgement regarding the Rwandan genocide of the Tutsi minority in 1994, Onesphore Rwabukombe was sentenced to 14 years' imprisonment for aiding the commission of a massacre at the Kiziguro church compound.

1. The state decides who I am: lack of legal gender recognition for transgender people in Europe (EUR 01/001/2014) www.amnesty.org/en/library/info/EUR01/001/2014/en

reported to the police-run Domestic Violence Support Unit in 2013. Although the law prohibits domestic violence, victims were not provided with adequate protection and legal assistance to lodge complaints with the Unit.

GHANA

Republic of Ghana
Head of state and government: **John Dramani Mahama**

Ghana continued to hand down death sentences although an ongoing constitutional review process could lead to abolition. Domestic violence against women remained widespread.

DEATH PENALTY

Courts continued to hand down death sentences. No executions have taken place since 1993.

In March the Constitutional Review Implementation Committee submitted a draft bill to the Attorney General and Minister of Justice to amend provisions of the 1992 Constitution; these included a proposal to abolish the death penalty. The bill was expected to be referred back to Parliament for approval before a referendum is conducted.

In March, in the case of *Dexter Eddie Johnson v. Ghana*, the UN Human Rights Committee condemned the use of automatic and mandatory death sentences in Ghana. It called on the government to provide Dexter Eddie Johnson with an effective remedy, including the commutation of his death sentence, and to adjust its legislation to avoid similar violations in the future. The government had not responded by the end of the year.

VIOLENCE AGAINST WOMEN AND GIRLS

Violence against women and girls remained widespread. A total of 16,275 cases were

GREECE

Hellenic Republic
Head of state: **Karolos Papoulias**
Head of government: **Antonis Samaras**

Allegations of excessive use of force and ill-treatment by law enforcement officers persisted and continued to be inadequately investigated. Detention conditions remained very poor. The maximum length of administrative detention of irregular migrants was extended beyond 18 months. Unlawful push-backs of migrants across the Greece-Turkey border continued. New hate crime legislation was adopted in September amid growing concern at the levels of racist violence.

BACKGROUND

In October the Public Prosecutor proposed the indictment of 67 members and leaders of Golden Dawn, a far right-wing party, for forming, directing or participating in a criminal organization. Fifty-seven individuals, including six MPs, were accused of a series of additional offences, including the murder in September 2013 of anti-fascist singer Pavlos Fyssas, causing "unprovoked bodily harm to migrants" and the unlawful possession of weapons.

In November, anarchist Nikos Romanos, detained at Korydallos prison near the capital, Athens, began a prolonged hunger strike in protest at the refusal of the authorities to allow him educational leave to attend a university course. He had been imprisoned in October after being convicted along with three other men of armed robbery. In February 2013, Nikos Romanos and two of the other men reported that they were tortured while in detention following their arrest in the northern town of Veroia. On 10 December, Nikos Romanos ended his hunger strike after a legislative amendment was passed allowing prisoners to attend campus courses while wearing electronic tags.

REFUGEES' AND MIGRANTS' RIGHTS

Strengthened border controls and greater co-operation with Turkish border guards contributed to a sharp decline in the number of irregular migrants and asylum-seekers entering Greece across its land borders. As a result, the number attempting to reach Greece by sea increased markedly in the first eight months of the year. By the end of the year more than 103 refugees and migrants, including many children, drowned or were unaccounted for while attempting the crossing.[1]

There were documented cases of frequent unlawful push-backs of irregular migrants across the Greece-Turkey border.

On 20 January, three women and eight children died when a fishing boat carrying 27 refugees sank near the island of Farmakonisi. Survivors said that the boat sank as Greek coastguards were towing their vessel towards Turkey during a push-back operation. The survivors also reported that they were stripped and beaten after they arrived at Farmakonisi. The authorities denied that any push-back or ill-treatment had taken place. In August, the Prosecutors of the Pireus Naval Court closed the case following a preliminary investigation.

National NGOs continued to document very poor detention conditions in areas where migrants and asylum-seekers were held for immigration purposes. Detainees faced considerable obstacles in applying for asylum. In March, the Minister of Public Order authorized the detention of irregular migrants pending deportation beyond the 18 months period allowed under EU law.

In September, the National Commission on Human Rights criticized the Ministry of Public Order and Citizen Protection for compromising the independence of the Asylum Appeals Board by failing to appoint any of the candidates it had proposed.

Reception conditions for refugees remained of serious concern. At the end of November, between 200 and 250 Syrian refugees, including many women and children, started a protest and subsequently a hunger strike at the Parliament square in Athens requesting the authorities to provide them with shelter and travel documents.

In July, a court in Patras found two foremen guilty of causing serious bodily harm by shooting at Bangladeshi migrant workers on a strawberry farm in Nea Manolada, in April 2013, following a dispute over pay and working conditions. The owner of the farm and another foreman were acquitted. At the end of October, the Supreme Court Prosecutor rejected a request made by two NGOs, the Hellenic League for Human Rights and the Greek Council for Refugees, to annul the verdict because of procedural flaws during the investigation and trial.

DISCRIMINATION
Hate crimes
Between October 2011 and January 2014, the Racist Violence Recording Network recorded more than 350 incidents of racist violence. The Network noted a decrease in organized racist attacks against migrants and an increase in hate crimes against lesbian, gay, bisexual, transgender and intersex people in 2014. Between January and June, the Police Departments and Offices tackling racist violence recorded 31 incidents with a possible racist motive.

The response of the criminal justice system to hate crimes remained inadequate. Investigators continued to fail to investigate possible hate motives, prosecutors failed to present such evidence in court, and judges failed to consider racist or other hate motives an aggravating circumstance when sentencing offenders.

In a unanimous ruling in April, a court in Athens sentenced two Greek nationals to life imprisonment after convicting them of stabbing to death S. Luqman, a Pakistani national, in January 2013. Despite the trial prosecutor underlining the racist motive behind the attack, the court did not take it into account as an aggravating circumstance during sentencing.

A Joint Ministerial Decision, adopted in June, provided for the suspension of administrative detention and deportation orders issued against victims and witnesses of hate crimes. It also granted special residence permits to cover the time required for the prosecution and conviction of perpetrators.

In September, amendments to hate crime legislation were adopted that increased penalties for committing and inciting racist violence, criminalized Holocaust denial and included sexual orientation, gender identity and disability among the prohibited grounds for discrimination. A proposal that would have legally recognized same-sex unions was rejected.

Roma

Roma families continued to face forced evictions. Many Roma children were excluded from or segregated in education. Discriminatory police raids on Roma settlements continued.

By the end of the year, 74 Roma families living in a settlement in Halandri, Athens, continued to be at risk of forced eviction. Initial plans to evict the families in February were postponed following an injunction by the UN Human Rights Committee. In September, the Halandri municipal authorities sought to demolish 12 homes despite a renewal of the injunction. Following protests by the Roma residents, only five homes, which at the time were uninhabited, were demolished. The Decentralized Administration of Attika committed to finding an adequate alternative location to resettle the families.

In November, a court in the town of Messolonghi sentenced three men to eight months' imprisonment with suspension for causing serious bodily harm to Paraskevi Kokoni, a Romani woman, and her nephew in October 2012. It was not clear whether the court took the hate motive into account during sentencing.[2]

TORTURE AND OTHER ILL-TREATMENT

In October, the European Committee for the Prevention of Torture issued its report on its 2013 visit to Greece. It highlighted the large number of allegations of ill-treatment of people detained in police and border guard stations by law enforcement officials and a number of allegations of verbal abuse, including of a racist nature. The report criticized overcrowding, unhygienic conditions and inadequate health care in Greek prisons.

Allegations of torture and other ill-treatment against prisoners, migrants and refugees continued. In March, guards at Nigrita prison in northern Greece reportedly tortured to death Ilia Kareli, an inmate of Albanian nationality. In October, 13 prison guards were charged with "aggravated torture that caused death".

Police used excessive force and misused chemical irritants against protesters and journalists on several occasions throughout the year. A large number of the reported abuses took place during two student protests, one against a university lock-out on 13 November, and another during a protest for the anniversary of the 1973 students' uprising on 17 November. Sporadic convictions of offending law enforcement officers failed to dent the longstanding culture of impunity for police abuses.[3]

Despite legislative changes introduced in March extending the mandate of the Office for Incidents of Arbitrary Conduct to cover racist incidents and allowing for the Ombudsman to attend hearings, concerns remained over its effectiveness and independence.

CONSCIENTIOUS OBJECTORS

The arrests and convictions of conscientious objectors continued during the year. At least four conscientious objectors were convicted for insubordination and received suspended prison sentences. Six individuals refusing to serve both the military and the punitive alternative service were also arrested and detained for short periods.

FREEDOM OF EXPRESSION

In January, an Athens court convicted a blogger of "religious insult". His 10-month prison sentence was suspended on appeal. The blogger had set up a Facebook page on which he satirized an orthodox monk who had died.

---

1. Greece: Frontier of hope and fear – migrants and refugees pushed back at Europe's border (EUR 25/004/2014)
   www.amnesty.org/en/library/info/EUR25/004/2014/en

2. We ask for justice: Europe's failure to protect Roma from Racist Violence (EUR 01/007/2014)
   www.amnesty.org/en/library/info/EUR01/007/2014/en

3. A law unto themselves: A culture of abuse and impunity in the Greek police (EUR 25/005/2014)
   www.amnesty.org/en/library/info/EUR25/005/2014/en

GUATEMALA

Republic of Guatemala
Head of state and government: **Otto Pérez Molina**

Impunity continued for genocide, war crimes and crimes against humanity carried out during the internal armed conflict between 1960 and 1996. Violence against women and girls remained a concern. People protesting over hydroelectric and mining projects were subject to forced evictions and excessive use of force by the security forces. Guatemala retained the death penalty in law for ordinary crimes. However, no prisoners were on death row and no death sentences were handed down during the year.

BACKGROUND

Street gangs and drug trafficking cartels contributed to a precarious public security situation. The authorities reported over 5,000 homicides committed during the year.

In June, the former National Director of Police, Erwin Sperisen, was convicted in Switzerland for his role in the extrajudicial execution of seven unarmed prisoners during a police operation in the El Pavón prison in 2006.

VIOLENCE AGAINST WOMEN AND GIRLS

Local human rights organizations reported over 500 killings of women during the year.

In May the Inter-American Court of Human Rights ruled against Guatemala in the case of María Isabel Franco, who was sexually assaulted, tortured and murdered in 2001, at the age of 15. The Court concluded that Guatemala had acted in a discriminatory manner due to María Isabel's gender, and that in the context of pervasive violence against women, the authorities had not acted promptly when María Isabel's mother alerted the police of her daughter's disappearance.

IMPUNITY

The right to truth, justice and reparation for victims of crimes against humanity during the internal armed conflict (1960 to 1996) remained a concern. Former President Efraín Ríos Montt was convicted in May 2013 of committing genocide and crimes against humanity against members of Maya-Ixil Indigenous community during his presidency. The Constitutional Court overturned his conviction 10 days later on a technicality. He had yet to be retried by the end of 2014.

In February, the Attorney General's term was cut short by the Constitutional Court. There were concerns that her removal was the result of her role in ensuring that former President Ríos Montt was brought to trial, and her commitment to investigate human rights violations that occurred during the internal armed conflict.

In May, Congress passed a non-binding resolution stating that genocide had not occurred during the internal armed conflict. The resolution directly contradicted a 1999 UN investigation which concluded that genocide, war crimes and crimes against humanity had occurred during the internal armed conflict, in which 200,000 people were killed and 45,000 people were forcibly disappeared. Over 80% of those killed and disappeared were of Indigenous Maya ethnicity.

In July, Fermín Solano Barrillas, a former member of the armed opposition during the internal armed conflict, was sentenced to 90 years in prison for directing the massacre of 22 people in 1988, in El Aguacate, Chimaltenango department.

LAND DISPUTES

Fearing impacts on their livelihoods, communities continued to oppose existing and proposed hydroelectric and mining projects, and protested against the lack of consultation around these projects.

In May 2013, in response to this opposition, the government proposed a moratorium on the issuing of new mining licences. Yet concerns remained that the proposed legislation to approve mining licences fell short of international standards and did not address Indigenous and rural communities' concerns around lack of consultation and free, prior and informed consent.

In May, local activists occupying a mining site in San José del Golfo, Guatemala department, were forcibly removed by the police. The Office of UN High Commissioner for Human Rights expressed concern at the use of excessive force by the security forces during their removal.

In June, local communities protested against the proposed construction of the Xalalá hydroelectric dam in Alta Verapaz and Quiché departments. In August, three people

from the community of Monte Olivo, Alta Verapaz department were killed. They were reportedly shot by police officers during the forced eviction of a community opposed to the construction of a hydroelectric project in the area. By the end of the year nobody had been held to account for their deaths.

HUMAN RIGHTS DEFENDERS

Attacks, threats and intimidation against human rights defenders and journalists continued during the year.

In August, Gustavo Illescas, a journalist with the Independent Media Centre in Guatemala, was threatened after he reported on police violence during the forced eviction in Monte Olivo (see above). A colleague was detained by masked men and told to convey a threatening message to Gustavo Illescas. The colleague was also beaten and sexually assaulted. By the end of the year nobody had been held to account for his ill-treatment or for the threats against Gustavo Illescas.

GUINEA

Republic of Guinea
Head of state: **Alpha Condé**
Head of government: **Mohamed Said Fofana**

One of the largest Ebola Virus Disease outbreaks since the virus was discovered in 1976 hit the country; many essential provisions remained lacking. Security forces regularly used excessive force against civilians. Journalists were subjected to intimidation. Concerns about poor and inhumane conditions of detention, and torture and other ill-treatment of detainees, were highlighted by the UN Committee against Torture and the UN Office of the High Commissioner for Human Rights (OHCHR). At the end of the year, a preliminary examination by the Prosecutor

of the International Criminal Court (ICC) remained open from 2009.

BACKGROUND

One of the worst Ebola outbreaks emerged in Guinea, quickly spreading to neighbouring countries. By the end of the year, more than 1,700 people had died, including at least 70 health workers.

Legislative elections took place in September 2013 after repeated delays. Violence between members of opposing political parties erupted both before and after the elections. International observers reported voting irregularities. The Supreme Court validated the results nearly two months later, resulting in protests and allegations of fraud. Prime Minister Fofana was reappointed in January 2014 and a new government was installed. The National Assembly convened for the first time in 2014 under President Kory Kondiano.

INTERNATIONAL SCRUTINY

The UN Committee against Torture and the OHCHR reviewed Guinea's human rights record. The OHCHR reported that detainees and prisoners were held in squalid and overcrowded facilities that fell far short of international standards. In some cases minors were detained with adults and there were no prisons specifically for women. The OHCHR also documented 11 cases of death in detention due to lack of medical care. The Committee raised concerns about recent cases of torture, as well as detention conditions, confessions extracted under torture, and impunity for perpetrators of torture.

EXCESSIVE USE OF FORCE

Security forces (police and the gendarmerie) continued to use excessive force against civilians in the capital, Conakry, and other towns, as well as in the southeastern forest region of Guinée Forestière.

In March, security forces in Guinée Forestière dispersed a peaceful

demonstration of women with tear gas, batons and gunshots. The women were protesting against the hiring policy of a palm oil and rubber production company.

Four people were reportedly shot dead in March during a demonstration in Diécké. They included a student, Mathieu Maomy. No investigation had been opened by the end of the year.

TORTURE AND OTHER ILL-TREATMENT

Torture and other ill-treatment were widespread in detention centres throughout 2013 and 2014, resulting in at least one death in custody. Security forces continued to act with impunity.

The UN Committee against Torture recommended in its Concluding Observations that Guinea should conduct thorough, independent and impartial investigations without delay into all allegations of torture and ill-treatment. In addition the Committee urged Guinea to eliminate the practice of female genital mutilation. The OHCHR documented cases of torture in the regions of Haute Guinée and Guinée Forestière, and urged the government to adopt a law prohibiting torture and to investigate torture in detention facilities.

DEATHS IN CUSTODY

In February, Tafsir Sylla died in hospital from his injuries after being beaten by police while resisting arrest in Fria. He had been arrested along with three others for consuming Indian hemp. The following day, hundreds of people protested by attacking the police station, the mayor's office and the local prison, resulting in the escape of at least 20 prisoners.

FREEDOM OF EXPRESSION

There were continued restrictions on press freedom and journalists were targeted.

In September, police in Guinée Forestière confiscated the cameras of journalists and human rights defenders who were investigating the killings of eight men who had been attacked by the local population during an Ebola awareness campaign. The cameras were returned the following day with all the material deleted.

IMPUNITY

Investigations continued into the massacre in the Grand Stade de Conakry on 28 September 2009, when security forces killed more than 100 peaceful demonstrators and injured at least 1,500 others. Dozens of women were raped and others disappeared. Moussa Dadis Camara, then head of the military junta, was questioned in Burkina Faso in July.

No progress was made towards bringing to trial gendarmes and police officers suspected of criminal responsibility for torturing detainees in 2011 and 2012. Between 2011 and the end of 2014, in Conakry and Fria, only seven officers were summoned to court by an investigating judge. They all failed to appear at their hearing, despite the legal obligation to do so.

INTERNATIONAL JUSTICE

Since 2009 Guinea has remained under preliminary investigation by the Prosecutor of the ICC for crimes committed on 28 September 2009 and in the aftermath of the massacre. The Office of the Prosecutor concluded that there were reasonable grounds to believe that these amounted to crimes against humanity, including murder, torture, rape and other forms of sexual violence, persecution and enforced disappearances. A delegation from the Office of the Prosecutor visited Guinea in February 2014 and noted that investigations had advanced, but not sufficiently. In June, Sékouba Konaté, then Minister of Defence, submitted a list of suspects to the ICC Prosecutor.

RIGHT TO HEALTH – EBOLA OUTBREAK

Delayed responses by the government and the international community reportedly contributed to the rapid spread of the epidemic. Although Ebola response

committees were eventually organized to co-ordinate provision of care and communication, many essential resources remained lacking.

In September, during an awareness-raising campaign by humanitarian workers in Womey, N'Zérékoré region, eight members of the delegation, including health workers, a journalist and members of a local radio station, were killed by villagers who suspected them of carrying the virus. Also in September, two members of the Guinean Red Cross were forced to flee the town of Forécariah when people threw rocks at their vehicle after the corpse of a woman which the health workers were carrying fell from a body bag.

GUINEA-BISSAU

Republic of Guinea-Bissau
Head of state: José Mário Vaz (replaced Manuel Serifo Nhamadjo in June)
Head of government: Domingos Simões Pereira (replaced Rui Duarte de Barros in July)

Persistent political tensions and human rights violations eased following elections in April and the setting up of a new government in July. Impunity for past human rights violations, including political killings in 2009, persisted. Social tension decreased following the resumption of international aid and the payment of arrears on some public sector salaries.

BACKGROUND

After several postponements, parliamentary and presidential elections were finally held in April. The African Party for the Independence of Guinea-Bissau and Cape Verde (PAIGC) won the parliamentary election. Presidential elections were won by José Mário Vaz of the PAIGC, with 61% of the vote.

Sanctions imposed by the international community following a coup in April 2012 were lifted in July and international aid resumed. The new government began paying salary arrears to public servants, which reduced social tension and the threat of strikes.

In September, the UN Security Council extended the mandate of the UN Integrated Peace-Building Office in Guinea-Bissau until November.

Also in September, President Vaz dismissed the Chief-of-Staff of the Armed Forces, General António Indjai, who led the April 2012 coup.

POLICE AND SECURITY FORCES

Although the election campaign was largely peaceful, there were some reports of threats, beatings and abduction of politicians by security forces in the pre-election period, apparently intended to coerce support for certain presidential candidates. In February, the president and another leading member of the political party People's Manifest publicly stated that they had received death threats, which they attributed to the security services.

In March, security personnel abducted Mário Fambé, a leading member of the Social Renewal Party, in the capital, Bissau, and took him to the Navy Headquarters where they beat him to persuade him to support their favoured candidate. He sustained serious injuries. The following day, soldiers took him to the Military Hospital for treatment and released him.

The day before the second round of presidential elections in May, some 12 members of the PAIGC were beaten by security officers in two separate incidents in Bissau and in the northern town of Bafata. They included some newly elected parliamentarians and at least two women. There were no investigations into these incidents.

IMPUNITY

By the end of the year, no one had been held accountable for human rights violations committed in the context of the 2012 coup, nor for the political killings that had occurred since 2009.

JUSTICE SYSTEM

A law against domestic violence which was promulgated in January, had not come into effect by the end of the year.

Nine people accused of an attack on a military base in Bissau in October 2012 and convicted in March 2013 after an unfair trial by a military court were released in September 2014. Three were released following an appeal to the High Military Court, which accepted that there was no evidence of their participation in the attack. The remaining six were released two weeks later following a presidential pardon.

WOMEN'S RIGHTS

In February, the UN Special Rapporteur on extreme poverty and human rights visited Guinea-Bissau and found that gender inequality and discrimination were the main factors underlying poverty. She attributed the high maternal mortality rate to the fact that 60% of pregnant women did not receive adequate ante-natal care. In August the new government introduced free medical care for children under five years of age, pregnant women and the elderly.

GUYANA

Co-operative Republic of Guyana
Head of state and government: **Donald Ramotar**

Police ill-treatment remained a concern. Violence against women and girls was also a concern, and conviction rates for sexual offences remained low.

BACKGROUND

Following commitments made during Guyana's UN Universal Periodic Review (UPR) in 2010, the government finally began public consultations on corporal punishment in schools. However, consultations into the abolition of the death penalty, the repeal of legislation criminalizing consensual same-sex relations, and discrimination against LGBTI people, to which the government also committed in 2010, had yet to begin by the end of the year.

Following a vote of no confidence by the opposition in August, in November the President announced a suspension of the National Assembly for up to six months, citing among other things the urgent need to address "issues relating to economic growth".

TORTURE AND OTHER ILL-TREATMENT

Colwyn Harding alleged that he was sodomized with a police baton during his arrest by police on 15 November 2013 in Timehri. On 2 June 2014, two police officers were charged with causing actual bodily harm, and one of them was also charged with common assault.

On 30 April, 15-year-old Alex Griffith was allegedly shot in the mouth by a police officer playing "Russian roulette" with his firearm. The police officer was investigating an armed robbery allegedly committed against a member of the officer's family. The officer was charged in June with unlawful assault and discharging a firearm with intent to maim. Both cases were still before the courts at the end of the year.

VIOLENCE AGAINST WOMEN AND GIRLS

Physical and sexual violence against women and girls remained a concern. According to reports, more than 140 cases of rape had been reported to the police by early September. Conviction rates for sexual offences remained low. The Ministry of Legal Affairs stated in April that there had been no conviction for sexual offences in any of the 22 cases heard in 2012 and 2013.

Implementation of the Sexual Offences Act, enacted in February 2013, and the National Domestic Violence Policy, launched in June 2008, remained very slow. Concerns were raised by women's rights advocates that there was no political will to fully implement either act. For example, judicial, law enforcement and health officials had not received sufficient training on the new acts, and the public had not been sufficiently made aware of the important changes to protect the lives of women and girls that came into force with the enactment of these laws. A National Plan for the Prevention of Sexual Violence had yet to be drafted, despite the new legislation stipulating its creation.

FREEDOM OF EXPRESSION

In November, the Inter-American Commission on Human Rights requested precautionary measures on behalf of staff at the newspaper *Kaieteur News* after they received threats.

RIGHTS OF LESBIAN, GAY, BISEXUAL, TRANSGENDER AND INTERSEX PEOPLE

Consensual sex between men remained criminalized. There were continuing reports of discrimination against LGBTI persons, particularly transgender persons.

Four transgender individuals were fired upon from a passing vehicle on the night of 7 April in central Georgetown. According to reports, the police refused to take their complaint, and Georgetown Public Hospital refused to treat them.

DEATH PENALTY

In December, Guyana voted for the fifth time against a UN resolution to establish a moratorium on executions, despite the promise to hold a national consultation on the issue.

HAITI

Republic of Haiti
Head of state: **Michel Joseph Martelly**
Head of government: **Laurent Salvador Lamothe**
(resigned on 14 December)

More than 80,000 people made homeless by the January 2010 earthquake remained displaced. The authorities failed to establish durable measures to prevent forced evictions. Concerns remained over the overall lack of independence of the justice system. Several human rights defenders were threatened and attacked.

BACKGROUND

Long-overdue local and legislative elections for a third of seats in the Senate had not taken place by the end of 2014. This was largely due to disagreements between the government and parliament over the electoral council, as a result of which six senators refused to vote for the proposed reform of the electoral law. On 14 December, the Prime Minister resigned after a consultative commission appointed by the President had recommended his resignation among a number of measures to be taken to appease tensions. Concerns remained at the end of the year over the country's political stability, as the terms of another third of the Senate and all members of the House of Deputies were due to expire in mid-January 2015.

In October, the UN Security Council renewed the mandate of the UN Stabilization Mission in Haiti (MINUSTAH) for an 11th year and recommended a radical reduction of its military component.

Although a significant reduction in the number of cases was reported in the first half of 2014, the cholera epidemic persisted. At least 8,573 people died of cholera between October 2010 and July 2014. A lawsuit filed in October 2013 by Haitian and US human rights groups against the UN for its alleged responsibility for introducing the disease into Haiti in 2010 was pending before a US court at the end of 2014.

Following the establishment of the Inter-Ministerial Committee on human rights, a number of international and regional human rights conventions were signed or ratified. In October, the UN Human Rights Committee examined Haiti's initial report.[1]

INTERNALLY DISPLACED PEOPLE

At the end of September, more than 80,000 people made homeless by the January 2010 earthquake were still living in 123 makeshift camps. Most of the displaced people who left the camps did so either spontaneously or after being allocated one-year rental subsidies. Following his visit to Haiti in July, the UN Special Rapporteur on the human rights of internally displaced persons highlighted the fact that, although there had been a significant reduction in the number of displaced people living in camps since July 2010, the majority of people who left the camps did not benefit from durable solutions.

HOUSING RIGHTS – FORCED EVICTIONS

There were fewer forced evictions from displacement camps and other informal settlements in 2014 compared with previous years. However, the authorities failed to provide remedies to victims of forced eviction[2] and did not put in place sustainable measures to avoid forced evictions in the future.[3]

At the end of May, hundreds of families were made homeless after the government ordered the demolition of buildings in the centre of the capital, Port-au-Prince. The vast majority of affected people did not receive adequate notice of the demolition and only a tiny minority of house owners had received compensation at the time of the demolition.

VIOLENCE AGAINST WOMEN AND GIRLS

According to women's rights organizations, violence against women and girls remained widespread. The government failed to publish consolidated statistics on gender-based violence. A bill on the prevention, prosecution and eradication of violence against women drafted in 2011 in collaboration with women's rights groups had still not been introduced in parliament by the end of 2014. Haitian human rights organizations reported that, although the number of trials and convictions in cases of sexual violence had increased, these represented a tiny fraction of the reported cases.

IMPUNITY

In February, the Port-au-Prince Court of Appeal reversed a 2012 decision by an investigative judge that former President Jean-Claude Duvalier could not be prosecuted for crimes against humanity. The Court appointed one of its sitting judges to investigate the allegations of crimes against humanity involving Jean-Claude Duvalier among others. However, the failure to provide additional resources to the judge or to disclose official documents which could be useful in the proceedings fuelled concerns about the capacity of the Haitian justice system to provide effective remedies to the victims of past human rights violations. Following the death of Jean-Claude Duvalier in October, national and international human rights organizations called on the authorities to continue the legal proceedings against his former collaborators.[4]

JUSTICE SYSTEM

Concerns remained about the overall lack of independence of the justice system. The High Council of the Judiciary, an institution considered key for the reform of the justice system, only started the process of vetting existing judges towards the end of the year. The failure to fill several judicial vacancies exacerbated the problem of prolonged pre-trial detention. At the end of June, pre-trial detainees accounted for more than 70% of the prison population.

In August, a judge investigating corruption charges against former President Jean-

Bertrand Aristide issued an arrest warrant against him after he failed to appear to answer a summons issued the previous day. In September, the same judge ordered that Jean-Bertrand Aristide be put under house arrest. The Port-au-Prince Bar Association and several Haitian human rights organizations challenged the legality of these decisions, which were widely considered to be politically motivated.

HUMAN RIGHTS DEFENDERS

Several human rights defenders were attacked, threatened and harassed because of their legitimate human rights work.[5] In the vast majority of cases, the authorities failed to carry out thorough and prompt investigations or to provide effective protection measures.

RIGHTS OF LESBIAN, GAY, BISEXUAL, TRANSGENDER AND INTERSEX PEOPLE

A number of verbal and physical attacks against LGBTI people were reported during the year, most of which were not thoroughly investigated. According to LGBTI rights organizations, police officers were often reluctant to intervene in these cases and their responses to victims revealed deeply discriminatory attitudes towards LGBTI people.

Nobody was brought to justice for attacks against LGBTI people during and after country-wide marches against LGBTI rights in mid-2013.

---

1. Haiti: Submission to the UN Human Rights Committee: 112th Session of the UN Human Rights Committee , 7-31 October 2014 (AMR 36/012/2014)

   www.amnesty.org/en/library/info/AMR36/012/2014/en

2. Haiti: Families at imminent risk of forced eviction (AMR 36/007/2014)

   www.amnesty.org/en/library/info/AMR36/007/2014/en

3. Haiti must take immediate action to prevent forced evictions and relocate internally displaced persons: Amnesty International oral statement to the 25th Session of the UN Human Rights Council (AMR 36/008/2014)

   www.amnesty.org/en/library/info/AMR36/008/2014/en

4. Haiti: The truth must not die with Jean-Claude Duvalier (Press release)

www.amnesty.org/press-releases/2014/10/haiti-truth-must-not-die-jean-claude-duvalier/

5. Haiti: Activists fighting for justice threatened (AMR 36/011/2014)

www.amnesty.org/en/library/info/AMR36/011/2014/en

Haiti: Women's human rights defenders threatened (AMR 36/010/2014)

www.amnesty.org/en/library/info/AMR36/010/2014/en

Haiti: Fear for safety of human rights defender: Pierre Espérance (AMR 36/009/2014)

www.amnesty.org/en/library/info/AMR36/009/2014/en

HONDURAS

Republic of Honduras
Head of state and government: **Juan Orlando Hernández Alvarado (Replaced Porfirio Lobo Sosa in January)**

Human rights violations and abuses against human rights defenders, journalists, women and girls, LGBTI people, Indigenous, Afro-descendant and *campesino* (peasant farmer) communities continued to be a serious concern. These violations took place in a context where impunity for human rights violations and abuses was endemic and where levels of organized and common crime were high.

BACKGROUND

President Juan Orlando Hernández was sworn in on 27 January with a four-year mandate. His commitment to the implementation of the Public Policy and National Plan of Action on Human Rights, adopted in 2013, had yet to be reflected in specific policies, measures and actions at the end of the year.

According to UN figures, Honduras had the world's highest homicide rate. Poverty and extreme poverty continued to undermine the realization of human rights for large sectors of society; more than 60% of the population were living in poverty and more than 40% in extreme poverty.

POLICE AND SECURITY FORCES

In response to the high levels of crime and to the weakness, lack of credibility and widespread corruption of the National Police Force, some policing functions continued to be undertaken by the military and special groups including the Inter-institutional Security Force (Fuerza de Seguridad Interinstitucional – Fusina) created in 2014, and the TIGRES Unit (Investigation Troop and Security Special Response Group) and Public Order Military Police (Policía Militar de Orden Público), both created in 2013. Concerns were raised that these groups were not adequately trained in the respect and protection of human rights, following a number of cases of human rights violations committed during the exercise of policing functions in previous years.

Honduras also experienced a proliferation of firearms and of private security companies. It was legally permitted to possess and carry up to five firearms, and given the high levels of insecurity, many people carried firearms to protect themselves. Following a visit in 2013, the UN Working Group on the use of mercenaries stated that private security companies were committing abuses with the permission or participation of the police and the military, and with impunity.

JUSTICE SYSTEM

The Attorney General's Office continued to be overwhelmed by the high levels of violence and crime in the country. In April 2013, the then Attorney General stated that the Public Prosecution Service only had the capacity to investigate 20% of the country's homicides. The Attorney General and his deputy were subsequently suspended and then removed from their posts. New officials were elected to these posts; however, human rights organizations described the election as unconstitutional, biased and lacking in transparency.

HUMAN RIGHTS DEFENDERS

Scores of human rights defenders, including Indigenous and *campesino* leaders, LGBTI activists, justice officials and journalists were victims of human rights violations. They suffered killings, physical violence, kidnapping, threats, harassment and verbal attacks.

On 24 February, Mario Argeñal became the target of intimidation and harassment for demanding justice from the authorities for the death of his brother, journalist Carlos Argeñal, who was shot dead at his home in Danlí, department of El Paraíso on 7 December 2013.[1]

On 4 June, a member of the Committee of the Families of the Detained and Disappeared in Honduras (COFADEH) was kidnapped in Tegucigalpa for two hours; she was physically attacked, almost strangled with a cable and robbed before being released.[2]

On 27 August, prominent *campesino* leader Margarita Murillo was shot dead in the community of El Planón, north western Honduras.[3]

In June, Congress discussed the first draft of the Law to Protect Journalists, Human Rights Defenders and Justice System Workers. In August, following national and international pressure, the draft law was finally shared with civil society. The law was yet to be approved at the end of the year, as was a mechanism for the effective protection of those at risk.

INDIGENOUS PEOPLES AND AFRO-DESCENDANT COMMUNITIES

Indigenous Peoples and Garífuna (Afro-descendant) communities continued to face discrimination and inequality, including in relation to their rights to land, housing, water, health and education. Large-scale projects continued to be carried out on their lands without their consultation or their free, prior and informed consent. Indigenous and

Garífuna leaders faced fabricated criminal charges and were the target of attacks and intimidation in reprisal for their work in defence of human rights. On 17 July, members of a Garífuna community in north-eastern Honduras, including human rights defender Miriam Miranda, were temporarily abducted by armed men after discovering an illegal runway used by drug traffickers on the community's territory.[4]

LAND DISPUTES

Longstanding land disputes between peasant communities and powerful landowners were one of the underlying causes of the high levels of violence faced by *campesino* communities, such as in the region of Bajo Aguán. In August, the Inter-American Commission on Human Rights expressed serious concerns about the situation in Bajo Aguán following a series of violent evictions as well as threats against and arrests of various *campesino* leaders, who had been beneficiaries of precautionary measures granted by the Commission in May.

VIOLENCE AGAINST WOMEN

Violence against women and girls was rife. Civil society groups reported 636 femicides in 2013, the highest number since 2005. Since 2013, the Honduran Criminal Code has recognized the crime of femicide. Between December 2013 and January 2014 there was a wave of killings of women sex workers in San Pedro Sula city, northern Honduras.[5]

Abortion continued to be banned in all circumstances. The government had yet to re-establish the legality of the emergency contraceptive pill, which had been prohibited in 2009 by decree (Acuerdo Ministerial) under the then de facto authorities.

1. Honduras: Further information - brother of killed journalist at risk (AMR 37/004/2014)
www.amnesty.org/en/library/info/AMR37/004/2014/en

2. Honduras: Surveillance and attacks on human rights NGO (AMR 37/007/2014)
www.amnesty.org/en/library/info/AMR37/007/2014/en
3. Campesino leader shot dead in Honduras (AMR 37/010/2014)
www.amnesty.org/es/library/info/AMR37/010/2014/es
4. Afro-descendant community at risk in Honduras (AMR 37/009/2014)
www.amnesty.org/en/library/info/AMR37/009/2014/en
5. Sex workers targeted and killed in Honduras (AMR 37/001/2014)
www.amnesty.org/en/library/info/AMR37/001/2014/en

HUNGARY

Hungary
Head of state: **János Áder**
Head of government: **Viktor Orbán**

The government launched smear campaigns against several NGOs for alleged funding irregularities and ordered audits of their accounts. Roma continued to face discrimination in access to health care, housing, and by law enforcement agencies. The European Court of Human Rights ruled that the obligatory re-registration of religious organizations violated the right to freedom of religion.

BACKGROUND

In general elections in April, the ruling Fidesz party secured a two-thirds parliamentary majority with 45% of the vote. The OSCE criticized the government for amending electoral legislation and noted that this and other legislation, including the Constitution, had been amended using procedures that circumvented the requirement for public consultation and debate.

FREEDOM OF ASSOCIATION – NGOS

The government adopted an increasingly hostile attitude towards critical civil society groups and NGOs, which they accused of acting in the pay and interests of foreign governments.[1] In April 2014, the Chief of the Prime Minister's cabinet alleged that Norway Grants – a government-backed funding vehicle for social cohesion projects in 16 EU member states – was financing groups linked to opposition parties. The Norwegian government and the NGOs in question dismissed the allegations.

In June, the Prime Minister's Office ordered the Hungarian Government Control Office (KEHI) to carry out an audit of NGOs involved in distributing and receiving the European Economic Area (EEA)/Norway Grants. The Norwegian government and the NGOs in question strongly contested the legality of the audit, as the funds were not part of the Hungarian state budget and the authority to conduct or order audits of the grants resided with a Financial Mechanism Office in Brussels under bilateral agreements between Hungary and Norway.

In July, the Council of Europe Commissioner for Human Rights denounced the government's "stigmatizing rhetoric… questioning the legitimacy of NGOs". The Hungarian authorities continued with their allegations against NGOs. In a speech in July the Prime Minister referred to the NGOs involved with the Norway Grants as "paid political activists who are attempting to enforce foreign interests here in Hungary".

On 8 September, police raided the offices of Ökotárs and Demnet, two of the NGOs responsible for the distribution of the Norway Grants. Their files and computer servers were confiscated. The basis of the police investigation was reportedly allegations of mismanagement of the funds.[2]

Also in September, the KEHI initiated procedures to suspend the tax numbers of the four NGOs involved in the distribution of Norway Grants, alleging non-co-operation with the government-imposed audit. The NGOs denied the allegations.

In October, the KEHI released a report based on its audit, and announced it would seek criminal sanctions against several NGOs. In December, the suspension of the tax numbers entered into force in the case of at least one of the NGOs in question. The NGOs aimed to challenge the suspension in a court of law.

In July, the first instance court held that the spokesperson of the Fidesz party damaged the reputation of an NGO, the Hungarian Helsinki Committee, when he claimed that it was paid by "American speculators… to attack the Hungarian government". The spokesperson appealed against the decision.

DISCRIMINATION – ROMA

Roma were subjected to ethnic profiling and disproportionately targeted by the police for minor administrative offences. In September, the UN Committee on the Rights of the Child noted that Roma continued to be denied health services, including emergency aid services, and were discriminated against by health practitioners.

About 450 residents of the predominantly Roma neighbourhood known as Numbered Streets, in the city of Miskolc, were put at risk of forced eviction and possible homelessness.[3] In May, the local government adopted a decree declaring the houses in the neighbourhood "old and inadequate" and announced that the tenancy agreements would be terminated. The municipality stated that "there was no place for slums" in the city and that its plans to demolish the buildings were supported by 35,000 individuals who signed the petition calling for an eviction. In August, the municipality evicted two families; approximately 50 other families were expecting eviction notices at the end of the year.

FREEDOM OF RELIGION

In September, the Grand Chamber of the European Court of Human Rights upheld a decision that Hungary violated the right to freedom of religion when it adopted a law in 2011 that required all recognized churches and religious organizations to re-register. The law only allowed them to do so if they could prove that they had existed in Hungary for at least 20 years and had at least 1,000 members. The European Court ruled that the government should reach an agreement with the churches on the restoration of their registration and on just compensation for any damages.

REFUGEES AND ASYLUM-SEEKERS

Asylum-seekers were frequently detained pending the determination of their claims. In a report published in May, the Hungarian Helsinki Committee (HHC) stated that 40% of male first-time asylum-seekers were detained and that the judicial review of asylum detention was ineffective. In September, the HHC reported that in 2013 it observed 262 cases of expelled or returned individuals trying to enter Hungary through the Serbian-Hungarian border.

In September, the UN Committee on the Rights of the Child criticized Hungary for holding children seeking asylum and unaccompanied migrant children in administrative detention.

TORTURE AND OTHER ILL-TREATMENT

In May, the European Court of Human Rights ruled that the possibility of life imprisonment without parole – a provision included in the Constitution of Hungary adopted in 2011 – amounted to an inhuman and degrading punishment.

---

1. Hungary: Stop targeting NGOs (EUR 27/002/2014)
   www.amnesty.org/download/Documents/8000/eur270022014en.pdf
2. Hungarian government must end its intimidation of NGOs (EUR 27/004/2014)
   www.amnesty.eu/content/assets/Doc2014/eur270042014en.pdf
3. Hungary: Mayor of Miskolc must halt evictions of Roma (Press Release) (EUR 27/003/2014)
   www.amnesty.eu/en/news/press-releases/eu/hungary-mayor-of-miskolc-must-halt-evictions-of-roma-0771/#.VGowKvmsXu0

INDIA

Republic of India
Head of state: **Pranab Mukherjee**
Head of government: **Narendra Modi (replaced Manmohan Singh in May)**

Impunity was widespread for human rights abuses by state and non-state actors. Despite progressive legal reform and court rulings, state authorities often failed to prevent and at times committed crimes against Indian citizens, including children, women, Dalits and Adivasi (Indigenous) people. Arbitrary arrest and detention, torture and extrajudicial executions often went unpunished. The overburdened and underfunded criminal justice system contributed to justice being denied to those who suffered abuses, and to violations of the fair trial rights of the accused. Violence by armed groups in Jammu and Kashmir, northeastern states and areas where Maoist forces operated continued to put civilians at risk.

BACKGROUND

National elections in May saw a government led by the Bharatiya Janata Party come to power with a landslide victory. Prime Minister Narendra Modi, who campaigned on promises of good governance and development for all, made commitments to improve access to financial services and sanitation for people living in poverty. However, the government took steps towards reducing requirements to consult with communities affected by corporate-led projects. The authorities continued to violate people's rights to privacy and freedom of expression. There was a rise in communal violence in Uttar Pradesh and some other states, and corruption, caste-based discrimination and caste violence remained pervasive.

ARBITRARY ARRESTS AND DETENTIONS

Arbitrary arrests and detentions of protesters, journalists and human rights defenders persisted. National Human Rights Commission data indicated that 123 illegal arrests and 203 cases of unlawful detention were reported from April to July. The authorities used laws authorizing administrative detention to detain journalists and human rights defenders in custody under executive orders without charge or trial. Adivasi villagers in Maoist-affected areas in central India also remained at risk of being arbitrarily arrested and detained.

"Anti-terror" laws such as the Unlawful Activities (Prevention) Act, which did not meet international human rights standards, were also used. In May, the Supreme Court acquitted six men convicted under anti-terror laws for attacking the Akshardham temple in Gujarat in 2002, ruling that there was no evidence against them and the investigation had been incompetent.

ABUSES BY ARMED GROUPS

Human rights abuses by armed groups were reported in various regions, including Jammu and Kashmir, north-eastern states and central India. Armed groups killed and injured civilians and destroyed property in indiscriminate and at times targeted attacks. Their actions also displaced people. Clashes between security forces and armed Maoist groups led to several civilian deaths.

In the lead-up to national elections in May, armed groups allegedly killed local government officials and electoral officials in Jammu and Kashmir, Jharkhand and Chhattisgarh states, in order to intimidate voters and disrupt elections.

In January and May, armed groups in Assam were accused of killing dozens of Muslims, and in December, they were accused of killing scores of Adivasis. Armed groups in other north-eastern states were also accused of targeting civilians, instigating violence and causing large-scale displacement.

CHILDREN'S RIGHTS

In August, the government introduced a bill to Parliament seeking to amend juvenile justice laws to allow for children aged between 16 and 18 to be prosecuted and punished as adults in cases of serious crimes. India's official child rights and mental health institutions opposed the move.

Protests over the rape of a six-year-old girl in a school in Bangalore in July drew attention to the inadequate enforcement of laws on child sexual abuse.

Incidents of corporal punishment were reported from several states, despite its prohibition under law. Laws requiring private schools to reserve 25% of places at the entry level for children from disadvantaged families were poorly implemented. Dalit and Adivasi children continued to face discrimination in school.

In June, the UN Committee on the Rights of the Child expressed concern about the disparity in access to education, health care, safe water and sanitation among different groups of children. Child labour and child trafficking remained serious issues. In October, Kailash Satyarthi, a children's rights campaigner who works on these issues, was awarded the Nobel Peace Prize.

COMMUNAL VIOLENCE

A string of communally charged incidents in Uttar Pradesh prior to elections led to an increase in tensions between Hindu and Muslim communities. Three people were killed in clashes in Saharanpur, Uttar Pradesh state, in July. Politicians were accused of, and in some cases criminally charged with, making provocative speeches. Communal clashes also occurred in some other states. In December, Hindu groups were accused of forcibly converting several Muslims and Christians to Hinduism.

In January, survivors of violence between Hindus and Muslims in Muzzafarnagar, Uttar Pradesh, in late 2013 were forcibly evicted from relief camps. Investigations into the violence were incomplete. Thousands of people, mainly Muslims, remained displaced at the end of the year.

November marked the 30th anniversary of violence in Delhi in 1984 which led to the massacre of thousands of Sikhs. Hundreds of criminal cases closed by the police citing lack of evidence were not reopened, despite large public demonstrations seeking an end to impunity.

Progress in investigations and trials in cases related to the 2002 violence in Gujarat, which killed at least 2,000 people, mostly Muslims, continued to be slow. In November, the Nanavati-Mehta Commission, appointed in 2002 to investigate the violence, submitted its final report to the Gujarat state government. The report was not made public.

Ethnic clashes over the disputed Nagaland-Assam border in August resulted in the deaths of 10 people and the displacement of over 10,000. Caste-based violence was also reported in several states including Uttar Pradesh, Bihar, Karnataka and Tamil Nadu.

CORPORATE ACCOUNTABILITY

In September, the Supreme Court cancelled over 200 coal mining licences which it said were granted arbitrarily. The Environment Ministry weakened existing mechanisms for consultation with communities affected by industrial projects, particularly coal mining. The Ministry also lifted moratoriums on new industries in critically polluted areas.

The authorities and businesses failed to meaningfully consult local communities in several instances. In August, a subsidiary of UK-based Vedanta Resources conducted a public hearing towards expanding its alumina refinery in Lanjigarh, Odisha state, without addressing existing impacts or adequately informing and consulting affected communities.

In December, the government passed a temporary law which removed requirements related to seeking the consent of affected communities and assessing social impact when state authorities acquired land for certain projects.

Thousands of people remained at risk of being forcibly evicted from their homes and lands for large infrastructure projects. Particularly vulnerable were Adivasi communities living near new and expanding mines and dams.

December marked the 30th anniversary of the 1984 Bhopal gas leak disaster. Survivors continued to experience serious health problems linked to the leak and to continuing pollution from the factory site. In November, a Bhopal court asked for its criminal summons against the Dow Chemical Company to be re-issued, after the company failed to comply with an earlier summons. Also in November, the Indian government agreed to use medical and scientific data to increase a multi-million US dollar compensation claim against Union Carbide. The Indian government had yet to clean up the contaminated factory site.

DEATH PENALTY

In January, the Supreme Court ruled that undue delay in the carrying out of death sentences amounted to torture, and that the execution of people suffering from mental illness would be unconstitutional. The Court also laid down guidelines for safeguarding the rights of people under a sentence of death.

In April, three men were sentenced to death by a Mumbai court under a new law enacted in 2013 which introduced the death penalty for those convicted in multiple cases of rape. In December, the government introduced to Parliament an anti-hijacking bill which seeks to impose the death penalty for hijacking that results in the death of a hostage or security personnel.

EXTRAJUDICIAL EXECUTIONS

Proceedings continued before the Supreme Court relating to a petition seeking investigations into over 1,500 alleged "fake encounters" – a term referring to staged extrajudicial executions – in Manipur state. Courts in Delhi, Bihar and Punjab convicted police personnel of being involved in fake encounter killings. The National Human

Rights Commission ordered compensation for the families of people killed in a number of fake encounters. It also expressed concern about fake encounter killings in Uttar Pradesh by the state police.

In February, the country's top investigative agency charged former officers of India's internal intelligence agency with murder and kidnapping in an investigation into a fake encounter case in Gujarat in 2004. The Gujarat and Rajasthan state governments reinstated into service police officers on trial for their alleged involvement in fake encounter cases after they were released on bail from pre-trial detention.

In September, the Supreme Court laid down new requirements for investigations into deaths in encounters with the police, including that the deaths be investigated by a team from a different police station or a separate investigative wing.

FREEDOM OF EXPRESSION

Laws on criminal defamation and sedition which fell short of international standards were used to harass and persecute journalists, human rights defenders and others for peacefully exercising their right to free expression. The government also used broad and imprecise laws to curb free expression on the internet. Around the general election in May, a number of people were arrested for statements made about Prime Minister Narendra Modi, which police said amounted to criminal offences.

The authorities also implemented and expanded large-scale surveillance of telephone and internet communications, without disclosing details of these projects or safeguards to prevent their misuse.

IMPUNITY – SECURITY FORCES

Despite some signs of progress, almost absolute impunity for violations by Indian security forces continued. Legislation providing virtual immunity from prosecution such as the Armed Forces Special Powers Act and Disturbed Areas Act were still in force in

Jammu and Kashmir and parts of north-east India, despite ongoing protests.

In January, the army dismissed without trial charges of murder and conspiracy filed against five of its personnel by the Central Bureau of Investigation. The Supreme Court had ruled in 2012 that the army should try its personnel by court-martial for the extrajudicial executions of five villagers from Pathribal, Jammu and Kashmir, in 2000. In September, an army court-martial convicted five soldiers of killing three men in an extrajudicial execution in Machil, Jammu and Kashmir state, in 2010. In November, an army investigation charged nine soldiers in a case involving the killing of two Kashmiri teenagers in Budgam district.

Perpetrators of past violations in Jammu and Kashmir, Nagaland, Manipur, Punjab and Assam continued to evade justice.

RIGHTS OF LESBIAN, GAY, BISEXUAL, TRANSGENDER AND INTERSEX PEOPLE

The Supreme Court agreed to hear a petition seeking a review of its ruling in December 2013 which effectively recriminalized consensual same-sex sexual activity by upholding Section 377 of the Indian Penal Code. In the run-up to the 2014 parliamentary elections, prominent political parties committed to decriminalizing homosexuality.

In April, the Supreme Court granted legal recognition to transgender people in a landmark judgment. It directed authorities to recognize transgender persons' self-identification as male, female or a "third gender" and put in place social welfare policies and quotas in education and employment. However, cases of harassment and violence against transgender people continued to be reported.

WORKERS' RIGHTS

The lack of effective regulation of visa brokers and rogue recruiting agents continued to put Indian migrant workers travelling to Middle East countries at risk of human rights

abuses including forced labour and human trafficking.

Hundreds of Indian migrants including 46 nurses were stranded in Iraq as fighting between armed groups and the Iraqi government intensified. In June, 39 Indian migrants in Iraq were abducted and were believed to be still held by armed groups at the end of the year.

Bonded labour remained widespread. Millions of people were forced to work as bonded labourers in industries including brick-making, mining, silk and cotton production, and agriculture. A number of cases were reported of domestic workers, mostly women, suffering abuses by their employers.

PRISONERS OF CONSCIENCE

Adivasi activists and prisoners of conscience Soni Sori and Lingaram Kodopi were granted bail by the Supreme Court in February. Soni Sori stood for parliamentary elections in May.

Manipuri activist Irom Sharmila continued her 14-year hunger strike, demanding the repeal of the draconian Armed Forces Special Powers Act. She was detained on charges of attempted suicide and was released on 20 August by a court which ruled that the charges were baseless. However, she was rearrested two days later for the same alleged offence.

PROLONGED PRE-TRIAL DETENTION

Prolonged pre-trial detention and overcrowding in prisons persisted. As of December 2013, over 278,000 prisoners – more than two-thirds of the country's prison population – were pre-trial detainees. Dalits, Adivasis and Muslims continued to be disproportionately represented in the pre-trial prison population. Indiscriminate arrests, slow investigations and prosecutions, weak legal aid systems and inadequate safeguards against lengthy detention periods contributed to the problem.

In September, the Supreme Court directed district judges to immediately identify and release all pre-trial detainees who had been in prison for over half of the term they would have faced if convicted. Following advocacy by Amnesty International India, the government of Karnataka state directed state authorities to set up review committees to monitor lengthy pre-trial detention.

FREEDOM OF ASSOCIATION

Authorities used the Foreign Contribution (Regulation) Act to harass NGOs and civil society organizations that received funding from abroad. In particular, groups critical of large infrastructure, mining and nuclear power projects faced repeated queries, threats of investigations and blocking of foreign funding by the government.

In June, media organizations reported on a classified document prepared by India's internal intelligence agency, which described a number of foreign-funded NGOs as "negatively impacting economic development".

TORTURE AND OTHER ILL-TREATMENT

Torture and other ill-treatment continued to be used in state detention, particularly against women, Dalits and Adivasis. A deeply flawed anti-torture bill lapsed with the end of the central government's term in May.

In August, the Bombay High Court directed the installation of closed-circuit television cameras in all police stations in Maharashtra to curb the use of torture.

WOMEN'S RIGHTS

Violence against women remained widespread. The authorities did not effectively implement new laws on crimes against women that were enacted in 2013, or undertake important police and judicial reforms to ensure that they were enforced. Rape within marriage was still not recognized as a crime if the wife was over 15 years of age. A number of public officials and political leaders made statements that appeared to justify crimes against women, contributing to a culture of impunity.

Reports of crimes against women rose, but under-reporting was still considered to be widespread. Dalit women and girls continued to face multiple levels of caste-based discrimination and violence. Self-appointed village councils issued illegal decrees ordering punishments against women for perceived social transgressions.

In April, the UN Special Rapporteur on violence against women drew attention to the inability of the authorities to ensure accountability and redress for survivors of violence. In July, the CEDAW Committee recommended the government allocate resources to set up special courts, complaints procedures and support services to better enforce laws.

In November, 16 women died after participating in a botched mass sterilization drive in Chhattisgarh. The government's target-driven approach to family planning continued to allow for compromises on the quality of health care and curtailed women's right to choose appropriate family planning methods.

INDONESIA

Republic of Indonesia
Head of state and government: **Joko Widodo**
(replaced Susilo Bambang Yudhoyono in October)

Security forces faced persistent allegations of human rights violations, including torture and other ill-treatment. Political activists from the Papua region and Maluku province continued to be arrested and imprisoned for their peaceful political expression and at least 60 prisoners of conscience remained imprisoned. Intimidation and attacks against religious minorities continued. A new Islamic Criminal Code by-law in Aceh province, passed in September, increased offences punishable by caning. There was a lack of progress in ensuring truth, justice and reparations for victims of past human rights violations. No executions were reported.

BACKGROUND

Joko Widodo was inaugurated in October as the new President; he had made pledges during his election campaign to address serious past human rights abuses, protect freedom of religion, reform the police and open up access to the Papua region.[1] On 30 April and 1 May, the UN Committee on Economic, Social and Cultural Rights reviewed Indonesia's initial report. In June the UN Committee on the Rights of the Child reviewed Indonesia's third and fourth periodic reports.

POLICE AND SECURITY FORCES

Reports continued of serious human rights violations by the police and military, including unlawful killings, unnecessary or excessive use of force, torture and other cruel, inhuman or degrading treatment or punishment, and enforced disappearance.

In February, seven people were tortured or otherwise ill-treated during arrest and interrogation after police and military personnel raided a gathering organized by the armed Papuan pro-independence National Liberation Army in Sasawa village, Yapen Islands district, Papua province. Security officers chained the men's hands together and beat and kicked them. They were forced to crawl around the village as the beatings continued and at least two men alleged that they were given electric shocks by the police. According to their lawyers, none of the men were involved or had links with the armed pro-independence struggle. They were each charged with rebellion, convicted and sentenced to three and a half years' imprisonment in November by the Sorong District Court. No independent investigation into the incident had begun by the end of the year.

In March, eight men from the Suku Anak Dalam Indigenous community of Bungku village, Batanghari district, Jambi province, were tortured or otherwise ill-treated after protesting against the operation of a palm oil company near their village. Puji Hartono died from his injuries after his hands were tied behind his back with a rope and he was beaten by military personnel and company security guards. Titus Simanjuntak was stripped and beaten by military personnel and forced to lick his blood stains on the floor while being stepped on. Police officers watched as the abuses took place. In August, the Palembang military court convicted six military personnel of ill-treatment and sentenced them to three months' imprisonment. At the end of the year, no one was known to have been held accountable for the killing of Puji Hartono.

In October, six military personnel were convicted by a military court in Medan of the abduction and ill-treatment of Dedek Khairudin and sentenced to between 14 and 17 months' imprisonment. Dedek Khairudin was subjected to enforced disappearance in November 2013 after being detained by a military intelligence officer from the Army Resort Military Command (Korem 011/LW) and at least eight marines from Pangkalan Brandan region in North Sumatra province. His whereabouts remained unclarified at the end of the year.

In December, at least four men were killed and over a dozen injured when security forces, both police and military, allegedly opened fire on a crowd that was protesting at the Karel Gobai field near the Paniai District Military Command in Papua province. The crowd was protesting against soldiers from the Special Team Battalion 753 who had allegedly beaten a child from Ipakije village. No one had been held accountable for the attack by the end of the year.

FREEDOM OF EXPRESSION

Cases continued to be documented of the arrest and detention of peaceful political activists, particularly in areas with a history of pro-independence movements such as Papua and Maluku.

On 25 April, 10 political activists from Maluku province were arrested by police for planning to commemorate the anniversary of the Republic of South Maluku (RMS) movement's declaration of independence and carrying "Benang Raja" flags – a prohibited symbol of the movement. Nine of them were subsequently charged with "rebellion" under Articles 106 and 110 of the Criminal Code (crimes against the security of the state). Their trial began in September and had not been completed by the end of the year.

Two French journalists were arrested on 6 August in Wamena, Papua province, after making a documentary on the separatist movement in the Papuan region. In October, they were convicted by the Jayapura District Court of immigration violations and sentenced to four months' imprisonment. Areki Wanimbo, Head of the Lani Besar Tribal Council (Dewan Adat) who had met the two journalists, was also arrested by police on the same day and accused of supporting separatist activities. He was later charged with "rebellion" and was awaiting trial at the end of the year.

At least nine people remained detained or imprisoned under blasphemy laws solely for their religious views or the manifestation of their beliefs, or for the lawful exercise of their right to freedom of expression.[2]

In June, Abraham Sujoko was convicted by the Dompu District Court in West Nusa Tenggara province for "defamation of religion" under Article 27(3) of the Information and Electronic Transaction Law. He was sentenced to two years' imprisonment and a fine of 3,500,000 rupiah (US$288). Abraham Sujoko had posted a video of himself on YouTube saying that the Ka'bah (an Islamic holy shrine in Mecca) was a "mere stone idol", and had urged Muslims not to face it while praying.

FREEDOM OF RELIGION

Harassment, intimidation and attacks against religious minorities persisted, fuelled by discriminatory laws and regulations at both national and local levels.

In May, the Bekasi city authority issued a decree to close the Al-Misbah Ahmadiyya mosque in Bekasi, West Java province, referring to a 2008 Joint Ministerial Decree forbidding the Ahmadiyya community from promoting their activities and spreading their religious teachings. The Bekasi local government police then locked and sealed the mosque. On 26 June, the local government in Ciamis district, West Java province, closed down the Nur Khilafat Ahmadiyya mosque, citing the need to "maintain religious harmony" and to stop the spread of a "deviant interpretation of Islamic teaching". Days before, hundreds of supporters of hardline Islamist groups had protested outside the office of the local district chief demanding the closure of the mosque. In October, the local government in Depok district, West Java, closed down the Al-Hidayah Ahmadiyya mosque to prevent "social disharmony".

By the end of the year, a displaced Shi'a community from Sampang, East Java, who were attacked and evicted by an anti-Shi'a mob in 2012, remained in temporary accommodation in Sidoarjo and prevented from returning to their homes. The authorities failed to provide remedies for a displaced Ahmadiyya community in Lombok, West Nusa Tenggara, forcibly evicted by a mob from their homes in 2006.

Concerns about the "forced relocation of religious minorities, particularly Shi'a and Ahmadiyya communities, which were instigated by mobs and based on religious incitement" were raised by the UN Special Rapporteur on adequate housing in March. In May, the UN Committee on Economic, Social and Cultural Rights raised concerns about the situation of several groups, including displaced religious communities, which suffered "multiple discriminations".

In November, the newly elected Minister of Religious Affairs and the Minister of Home Affairs both stated that the government would make the protection of minority rights one of its priorities.

IMPUNITY

Victims of past human rights violations and abuses continued to demand justice, truth and reparation for crimes under international law which occurred under the rule of former President Suharto (1965-1998) and during the subsequent *reformasi* period. These included unlawful killings, rape and other crimes of sexual violence, enforced disappearances, and torture and other ill-treatment. No progress was reported on numerous cases of alleged gross violations of human rights that were submitted by the National Human Rights Commission (Komnas HAM) to the Attorney General's office after a preliminary pro-justicia inquiry was conducted by the Commission.

Former President Yudhoyono failed to act on certain recommendations by Parliament from 2009: to bring to justice those involved in the enforced disappearance of 13 pro-democracy activists in 1997 and 1998, to conduct an immediate search for activists who had disappeared, and to provide rehabilitation and compensation to their families.

By the end of the year, Komnas HAM had completed only two out of five pro-justicia inquiries into "gross human rights violations" during the Aceh conflict (1989-2005). These included the 1999 Simpang KKA incident in North Aceh when the military shot dead 21 protesters, and the Jamboe Keupok case in South Aceh where four people were shot dead and 12 burned alive by soldiers in May 2003.

An Aceh Truth and Reconciliation by-law (*qanun*) passed in December 2013 was not implemented. No progress was reported on a new law on a national Truth and Reconciliation Commission.

More than 10 years after the murder of prominent human rights defender Munir Said Thalib, the authorities had failed to bring all the perpetrators to justice.

The government failed to implement recommendations made by the bilateral Indonesia-Timor-Leste Commission of Truth and Friendship, in particular to establish a commission for disappeared persons tasked with identifying the whereabouts of all children from Timor-Leste who were separated from their parents around the 1999 independence referendum.

CRUEL, INHUMAN OR DEGRADING PUNISHMENT

At least 76 people were caned in Aceh for Shari'a offences including gambling, drinking alcohol and adultery during the year. In September, the Aceh parliament passed a new by-law, the Islamic Criminal Code, which expanded the use of caning as punishment to other "crimes", including same-sex sexual relations and intimacy between unmarried couples. There were concerns that the definition and evidentiary procedures related to the offence of rape and sexual abuse in the by-law did not meet international human rights standards. The Aceh Islamic Criminal Code applied to Muslims in Aceh province. Non-Muslims could also be convicted under the by-law of offences not currently covered by the Indonesian Criminal Code.

WOMEN'S RIGHTS

By the end of the year, the House of Representatives had yet to pass a Domestic Worker Protection Bill, leaving millions of domestic workers, the majority of them women and girls, vulnerable to economic exploitation and human rights abuses.

SEXUAL AND REPRODUCTIVE RIGHTS

In February the Ministry of Health issued a new regulation withdrawing a 2010 regulation authorizing certain medical practitioners, such as doctors, midwives and nurses, to conduct "female circumcision". By the end of the year, the government had yet to pass specific legislation prohibiting female genital mutilation.

Government Regulation No. 61/2014 on Reproductive Health, an implementing regulation to the 2009 Health Law, was issued in July 2014, restricting to 40 days the time period for rape survivors to access legal abortion. It was feared that this shortened timeframe would prevent many rape survivors from being able to access safe legal abortion.

DEATH PENALTY

No executions were reported. At least two death sentences were handed down during the year and at least 140 people remained under sentence of death.

1. Indonesia: Setting the agenda – human rights priorities for the new government (ASA 21/011/2014)
   www.amnesty.org/en/library/info/ASA21/011/2014/en

2. Prosecuting beliefs: Indonesia's blasphemy laws (ASA 21/018/2014)
   www.amnesty.org/en/library/info/ASA21/018/2014/en

IRAN

Islamic Republic of Iran
Head of state: **Ayatollah Sayed 'Ali Khamenei (Leader of the Islamic Republic of Iran)**
Head of government: **Hassan Rouhani (President)**

The authorities restricted freedoms of expression, association and assembly, arresting, detaining and prosecuting in unfair trials minority and women's rights activists, journalists, human rights defenders and others who voiced dissent. Torture and other ill-treatment remained prevalent and were committed with impunity. Women and ethnic and religious minorities faced pervasive discrimination in law and practice. Flogging and amputation sentences were reportedly carried out, some
in public. Executions continued at a high rate; juvenile offenders were among those executed. Judges continued to impose sentences of execution by stoning, although none were reported to have been carried out.

BACKGROUND

The June 2013 election of Hassan Rouhani as President raised hopes that his administration would introduce much needed human rights reforms, but little had been achieved by the end of 2014. Attempts by the administration to relax official controls on academic freedom, for example, prompted a backlash from conservatives within parliament.

Negotiations continued between Iran and the USA and other states amid persistent tensions over Iran's nuclear development programme and the impact on Iran of international financial and other sanctions. In November 2013, an interim agreement had brought Iran some relief from these sanctions in return for concessions on nuclear enrichment.

A Charter of Citizens' Rights proposed by the presidency and opened for consultation in 2013 remained in draft form throughout 2014. It failed to afford adequate protection of human rights, in particular the rights to life, non-discrimination, and protection from torture.

The UN Human Rights Council renewed the mandate of the UN Special Rapporteur on the situation of human rights in Iran in March but the Iranian authorities continued to block visits to Iran by him or other UN Human Rights Council experts.

In October, the UN Human Rights Council considered Iran's human rights record under the UN Universal Periodic Review (UPR) process. The Council noted Iran's dire human rights situation and the authorities' failure to implement the recommendations they had accepted following the 2010 UPR. Iran withheld its position on all the recommendations made until the next session of the UN Human Rights Council in March 2015.

FREEDOMS OF EXPRESSION, ASSOCIATION AND ASSEMBLY

The authorities maintained curbs on freedom of expression and the media, including by jamming foreign satellite broadcasting and closing media outlets. Authorities retained the mandatory dress code for women and the criminalization of dress code violations under the Islamic Penal Code. Opposition figures, Mir Hossein Mousavi, Mehdi Karoubi and Zahra Rahnavard remained under house arrest without charge or trial, despite their deteriorating health.[1] Scores of prisoners of conscience were serving prison terms for peacefully exercising their human rights. Among them were government critics, journalists, lawyers, trade unionists, student activists, and minority and women's rights activists.

The authorities continued to target journalists, who faced arrest, detention, imprisonment and flogging for critical reporting of the authorities.[2] In August, two photographers who criticized in writing a book of photographs published by a government official in the city of Qazvin, northwest Iran, were sentenced to floggings.

Online activists also faced prosecution. In May, a Revolutionary Court in Tehran convicted eight people on charges including "insulting religious sanctities" and "insulting the authorities" for posts on the website Facebook, and sentenced them to prison terms of between seven and 20 years.

Although the Supreme Leader, President Rouhani and other senior officials all used social media websites such as Facebook, Twitter and Instagram to communicate, the authorities continued to filter such websites. In September, a senior judiciary official instructed the Minister of Communications and Information Technology to take measures within a month to "block and effectively control the content" of social media websites after the circulation of jokes deemed offensive to the former Supreme Leader, Ayatollah Khomeini. The authorities said they had arrested 11 people in relation to the jokes.

In October, authorities in the cities of Tehran and Esfahan arrested protesters who were demanding an end to violence against women following a series of acid attacks against women in Esfahan. One of those arrested remained in detention at the end of the year. At least four journalists were also arrested in connection with their coverage of the acid attacks.

TORTURE AND OTHER ILL-TREATMENT

Torture and other ill-treatment, particularly during pre-trial detention, remained common, facilitated by routine denial of access to lawyers and the virtual impunity of perpetrators. Methods reported included prolonged solitary confinement, confinement in uncomfortably small spaces, severe beatings, and threats against detainees' family members. The authorities generally failed to investigate allegations of torture and prosecute and punish those responsible.

The authorities systematically denied detainees and prisoners access to adequate medical care, including for injuries resulting from torture or health problems exacerbated by harsh prison conditions.

A revised Code of Criminal Procedure passed in April failed to address the inadequacy of national laws to afford detainees effective protection against torture and other ill-treatment. It denied detainees access to lawyers for up to one week after arrest in cases concerning national security and some other offences, and provided no clear and comprehensive definition of torture conforming to international law.

State security and intelligence agencies operated their own detention facilities outside the control of the State Prison Organization, in breach of national law. Torture and other ill-treatment was common in these facilities. In some cases, the authorities subjected death row prisoners to enforced disappearance by moving them to such facilities prior to execution.

Sentences of flogging and amputations continued to be imposed for a wide range of offences, including alcohol consumption, eating in public during Ramadan, and theft. These sentences were increasingly implemented in public.

In April, security officials assaulted prisoners held in Section 350 of Tehran's Evin Prison during a search of their cells, beating and injuring many of them. The authorities reportedly failed to investigate the incident or prosecute and punish the perpetrators.[3] In August, authorities reportedly used excessive force against inmates of Ghezel Hesar Prison in the city of Karaj who protested against the transfer of 14 death row prisoners to solitary confinement prior to execution.

UNFAIR TRIALS

The judiciary continued to lack independence and remained subject to interference by the security authorities. Trials, particularly those before Revolutionary Courts, were largely unfair.

The new Code of Criminal Procedure enhanced detainees' access to lawyers but did not guarantee access from the time of arrest, required to help safeguard detainees against torture. The Code allowed prosecutors to prevent lawyers accessing some or all of the case documents against their clients if they determine that disclosure would impede "discovery of the truth", and in cases relating to national or external security, hindering the right to adequately prepare a defence. In August, Parliament's Judicial and Legal Commission submitted a bill proposing postponement of the Code's planned entry into force in October, due to the "existence of serious problems and barriers for [its] implementation". Additionally, the bill, in a regressive move, proposed amendments to 19 articles, which largely aimed to reverse the improvements made in the new Code including with regard to access to lawyers.

Courts continued to convict defendants in the absence of defence lawyers or on the basis of "confessions" or other evidence obtained through torture or other ill-treatment. In some cases, the authorities broadcast detainees' "confessions" on television before trial, breaching the presumption of innocence.

In September, the cabinet passed a Bill of Attorneyship, drafted by the judiciary, and submitted it to Parliament for approval. The draft bill discriminated against non-Muslims by disqualifying them from membership of the Board of Directors of the Iranian Bar Association, and threatened the independence of the Association.

DISCRIMINATION – ETHNIC AND RELIGIOUS MINORITIES

President Rouhani's appointment of a special adviser on ethnic and religious minorities did not result in a reduction in the pervasive discrimination against Iran's ethnic minority communities, including Ahwazi Arabs, Azerbaijanis, Baluchis, Kurds and Turkmen, or against religious minorities, including Ahl-e Haq, Baha'is, Christian converts, Sufis and Sunni Muslims.

Discrimination against ethnic minorities affected their access to basic services such as housing, water and sanitation, employment and education. Ethnic minorities were not permitted to use their minority language as a medium of instruction in education and were denied adequate opportunities to learn it.

Members of ethnic minority groups also faced a high risk of prosecution on vague charges such as "enmity against God" and "corruption on earth", which could carry the death penalty. The authorities secretly executed at least eight Ahwazi Arabs after they were convicted on charges that included "enmity against God" after grossly unfair trials, and refused to hand over their bodies to their families. By October, the authorities held at least 33 Sunni men, mostly members of the Kurdish minority, on death row on charges of "gathering and colluding against national security", "spreading propaganda against the system", "membership of Salafist groups", "corruption on Earth" and "enmity against God". Converts from Shi'a to Sunni Islam faced increased persecution.[4]

In December, the authorities used threats of immediate execution and other punitive measures against 24 Kurdish prisoners who were on hunger strike in protest against conditions in Ward 12 of Oroumieh Central Prison, West Azerbaijan Province, where they and other political prisoners were held.[5]

The authorities subjected Baha'is to further persecution by closing down their businesses and destroying their cemeteries. Dozens of Baha'is remained in prison.

In September, the authorities arrested over 800 Gonabadi Dervishes at a peaceful protest held in Tehran in solidarity with nine imprisoned Gonabadi Dervishes who were on hunger strike. The hunger strikers had demanded that the authorities respect the civil rights of Gonabadi Dervishes and treat them as equal members of society.[6]

Dissident Shi'a clerics and others who expressed alternatives to the official interpretation of Shi'a Islam, as well as atheists, remained at risk of persecution, including arrest, imprisonment and possible execution.

WOMEN'S RIGHTS

Women remained subject to widespread and systematic discrimination in law and practice. Personal status laws giving women subordinate status to men in matters such as marriage, divorce, child custody and inheritance remained in force.

Two population-related draft bills under parliamentary consideration threatened to reduce women's access to sexual and reproductive health services, thereby affecting their rights to life, privacy, gender equality and the freedom to decide the number and spacing of their children. One draft bill aimed to prevent surgical procedures aimed at permanently preventing pregnancies by imposing disciplinary measures on

health professionals who conducted such procedures. The other bill sought to reduce divorces and remove family disputes from judicial decision-making, hence prioritizing preservation of families over addressing domestic violence. Neither law had been enacted by the end of the year. A proposed law to afford women protection against violence made no progress and the authorities failed to take steps to address violence against women and girls, including early and forced marriages, marital rape and domestic violence.

Women also faced restrictions on employment. Official statistics from September showed that the number of women in employment had fallen by 100,000 annually over the previous eight years. In August, the Head of the Public Buildings Office of the Police said that no women should be employed in coffee shops or traditional Iranian restaurants except in their kitchens, out of public view. In July, the Tehran Municipality reportedly prohibited its managers from recruiting women to secretarial and other administrative posts. Official efforts to create gender-segregated workplaces intensified.

Authorities had also banned women musicians from appearing on stage in 13 of Iran's 31 provinces by the end of the year. In June, security authorities arrested women who participated in a peaceful protest outside Azadi Stadium, a Tehran sports venue, to demand equal access by women to sport stadiums.[7]

RIGHT TO PRIVACY

All sexual conduct between unmarried individuals remained criminalized.

The authorities continued to persecute individuals on account of their actual or perceived sexual orientation and gender identity. The revised Islamic Penal Code maintained provisions criminalizing all consensual same-sex sexual conduct between adults. The Code made such conduct subject to punishments ranging from 100 lashes to the death penalty.

Iranian authorities blocked and banned publication of any material discussing homosexuality or sexual conduct outside heterosexual marriages, using the Cyber Crimes Law's provisions on "crimes against chastity" and "sexual perversion".

Individuals who did not conform to stereotypical norms of femininity and masculinity continued to face discrimination and violence. Transgender individuals were denied legal gender recognition and were denied their rights, including to education and employment, unless they underwent gender reassignment surgeries. In February, Iran's official Football Federation barred seven women footballers from competition on grounds of their "gender ambiguity".

RIGHT TO EDUCATION

The authorities continued to restrict the right to education, maintaining the exclusion of hundreds of students from Iran's universities because of their peaceful exercise of the right to freedom of expression or other human rights, and systematically denying Baha'is access to higher education. Dozens of other students and academics, including some associated with the Baha'i Institute for Higher Education suppressed by the government in 2011, remained in prison. Efforts by the Ministry of Science, Research and Technology to allow some banned students and academic staff to return to universities did not result in concrete measures to end arbitrary exclusions of students from higher education.[8] Such attempts were opposed by conservatives within Parliament.

The gender quota system used by the authorities to reverse the trend towards greater participation by women in higher education remained in place, but saw some relaxation in the 2013-2014 academic year. Official policies aimed at keeping women at home pursuing "traditional" roles as wives and mothers continued.

DEATH PENALTY

Iran retained the death penalty for a wide range of offences, including vaguely defined crimes such as "enmity against God", and 2014 saw the authorities maintain a high rate of execution. Some executions were carried out in public.

Under the revised Islamic Penal Code, courts continued to impose death sentences for offences that did not meet the threshold of "most serious crimes" under international law, and others such as "insulting the Prophet of Islam", that should not be considered crimes.[9]

In many cases, courts imposed death sentences after proceedings that failed to respect international fair trial standards, including by accepting as evidence "confessions" elicited under torture or other ill-treatment. Detainees were frequently denied access to lawyers during pre-trial investigations.[10]

Scores of juvenile offenders, including some sentenced in previous years for crimes committed under the age of 18, remained on death row, and others were executed. Courts sentenced further juvenile offenders to death.[11] The revised Islamic Penal Code allowed the execution of juvenile offenders for qesas (retribution-in-kind) and hodoud (offences carrying fixed penalties prescribed by Islamic law) unless it is determined that the offender did not understand the nature of the crime or its consequences, or the offender's mental capacity is in doubt. International law prohibits the death penalty for children under 18.

The revised Islamic Penal Code also retained the penalty of stoning to death for the offence of "adultery while married". At least one stoning sentence was reported to have been imposed in Ghaemshahr, Mazandaran province; no executions by stoning were reported.

1. Iran: Release opposition leaders under house arrest three years on (MDE 13/009/2014)
   www.amnesty.org/en/library/info/MDE13/009/2014/en
2. Jailed for being a journalist (MDE 13/044/2014)
   www.amnesty.org/en/library/info/MDE13/044/2014/en Iran: Iranian-American detained for journalism (MDE 13/065/2014)
   www.amnesty.org/en/library/info/MDE13/065/2014/en
3. Justice is an alien word: Ill-treatment of political prisoners in Evin Prison (MDE 13/023/2014)
   www.amnesty.org/en/library/info/MDE13/023/2014/en
4. Iran: No progress on human rights: Amnesty International Submission to the UN Universal Periodic Review, October-November 2014 (MDE 13/034/2014)
   www.amnesty.org/en/library/info/MDE13/034/2014/en
5. Iran: Alleged juvenile offender among 10 hunger strikers threatened with immediate execution (News story)
   www.amnestyusa.org/news/news-item/iran-alleged-juvenile-offender-among-10-hunger-strikers-threatened-with-immediate-execution
6. Iran: Hunger striking Dervishes critically ill (MDE 13/051/2014)
   www.amnesty.org/en/library/info/MDE13/051/2014/en
7. Iran: Jailed for women's right to watch sports (MDE 13/048/2014)
   www.amnesty.org/en/library/info/MDE13/048/2014/en
8. Silenced, expelled, imprisoned: Repression of students and academics in Iran (/015/2014)
   www.amnesty.org/en/library/info/MDE13/015/2014/en
9. Iran: Facing death for "insulting the Prophet": Rouhollah Tavana (MDE 13/012/2014)
   www.amnesty.org/en/library/info/MDE13/012/2014/en
   Iran: Death sentence for "insulting the Prophet": Soheil Arabi (MDE 13/064/2014)
   www.amnesty.org/en/library/info/MDE13/064/2014/en
10. Execution of young woman a bloody stain on Iran's human rights record
    www.amnesty.org.uk/press-releases/iran-execution-young-woman-another-bloody-stain-human-rights-record
11. Iran: Juvenile offender at risk of execution in Iran: Rasoul Holoumi (MDE 13/040/2014)
    www.amnesty.org/en/library/info/MDE13/040/2014/en; Iran: Juvenile offender nearing execution (MDE 13/0037/2014)
    www.amnesty.org/en/library/info/MDE13/037/2014/en; Iran: Kurdish juvenile offender facing execution: Saman Naseem (MDE 13/049/2014)
    www.amnesty.org/en/library/info/MDE13/049/2014/en

IRAQ

Republic of Iraq
Head of state: **Fuad Masum (replaced Jalal Talabani in July)**
Head of government: **Haider al-Abadi (replaced Nuri al-Maliki in September)**

There was a marked deterioration in human rights as armed conflict intensified between government security forces and fighters of the Islamic State (IS, formerly ISIS) armed group, which gained control of large parts of central and northern Iraq. IS fighters committed widespread war crimes, including ethnic cleansing of religious and ethnic minorities through a campaign of mass killings of men and abduction and sexual and other abuse of women and girls. Government forces carried out indiscriminate bombing and shelling in IS-controlled areas, and government-backed Shi'a militias abducted and executed scores of Sunni men in areas under government control. The conflict caused the deaths of some 10,000 civilians between January and October, forcibly displaced almost 2 million people and created a humanitarian crisis. This was exacerbated by the continuing influx of thousands of refugees from Syria, mostly to Iraq's semi-autonomous Kurdistan Region. The government continued to hold thousands of detainees without charge or trial, many of them in secret detention with no access to the outside world. Torture and other ill-treatment in detention remained rife, and many trials were unfair. Courts passed many death sentences, mostly on terrorism charges; more than 1,000 prisoners were on death row, and executions continued at a high rate.

BACKGROUND

Armed conflict flared in January between government security forces and the Islamic State in Iraq and al-Sham (ISIS) armed group, a month after the authorities forcibly dispersed a year-long protest camp set up by members of the Sunni community in Ramadi, Anbar province. Government forces used indiscriminate shelling to regain control over Fallujah and parts of Ramadi from ISIS, killing civilians and causing damage to civilian infrastructure. Anbar province remained in conflict throughout the year amid allegations that Prime Minister Nuri al-Maliki had undermined efforts by tribal leaders to broker a solution.

The government's failure to resolve the crisis, among other factors, left Anbar unable to stem the rapid military advance of ISIS, whose fighters seized control of Mosul, Iraq's second largest city, in June and then much of Anbar, Diyala, Kirkuk, Ninevah and Salah al-Din provinces. This sparked a dramatic resurgence in sectarian tensions and massive displacement of communities at risk from armed attacks by ISIS or government air strikes. Ethnic and religious minorities were particularly targeted by ISIS, which forced all non-Sunni and non-Muslims out of the areas under its control.

On 30 June, ISIS declared a "caliphate", renamed itself Islamic State (IS) under the leadership of Iraqi-born Abu Baker al-Baghdadi, and called on Muslims around the world to declare allegiance to him.

In August, IS fighters seized control of the Sinjar region, killing and abducting large numbers of its Yezidi inhabitants who were unable to flee. Following IS advances and the public beheading of UK and US nationals in IS captivity, a US-led international coalition of 40 countries began air strikes against IS in August, and increased military support and training to Iraqi government forces and Kurdish Peshmerga forces fighting against IS.

Parliamentary elections took place in April amid violence that saw two members of the Independent High Electoral Commission and at least three candidates killed, and attacks by gunmen on polling stations in Anbar, Diyala and other predominantly Sunni areas. Nuri al-Maliki's State of Law Coalition, mostly

Shi'a, won the largest bloc of seats but he did not secure a third term as Prime Minister and was replaced in September, following domestic and foreign demands for a more inclusive government.

The proposed Ja'fari Law, intended as a personal status law for Shi'a communities in Iraq, was withdrawn after widespread criticism that it could undermine the rights of women and girls, including by legalizing marriage for girls as young as nine.

Tension between the Baghdad authorities and the semi-autonomous Kurdistan Regional Government (KRG) in the north eased following an interim agreement in November over oil revenues and KRG contributions to the federal budget.

INTERNAL ARMED CONFLICT

Government forces and Shi'a militias armed and backed by the government committed war crimes and human rights violations, predominantly targeting Sunni communities. In Anbar, Mosul and other areas under IS control, government forces carried out indiscriminate air strikes in civilian areas, including with barrel bombs, that killed and injured civilians. In September, Prime Minister al-Abadi called on the security forces to cease all shelling of civilian areas, but air strikes in IS-controlled areas continued, with ensuing civilian casualties.

Security forces and Shi'a militias abducted or detained Sunnis and carried out scores of extrajudicial executions with impunity. In areas where they regained control from IS, they also destroyed homes and businesses of Sunni residents, in reprisal for the alleged support for IS by members of those communities. KRG Peshmerga forces also carried out reprisal destruction of homes of Sunni Arab residents in areas they recaptured from IS.

ABUSES BY ARMED GROUPS

Armed groups carried out indiscriminate suicide and car bomb attacks throughout Iraq, killing and injuring thousands of civilians. As they gained control of much of northwestern Iraq, IS fighters embarked on a systematic campaign of ethnic cleansing in which they committed war crimes, including mass summary killings and abductions that targeted religious and ethnic minorities, including Christians, Yezidis, Shi'a Turkmen and Shi'a Shabaks.

Hundreds of detainees, mainly Shi'a, were killed by IS fighters who seized Badush Central Prison, west of Mosul, in June. In July, IS fighters forced thousands of Christians from their homes and communities, threatening them with death unless they converted to Islam, and in August carried out deadly mass attacks against the Yezidi minority. IS fighters who attacked the Sinjar region abducted thousands of Yezidi civilians, summarily killing hundreds of men and boys as young as 12 in Qiniyeh, Kocho and other villages. Hundreds, possibly thousands, including entire families remained missing. Hundreds of women and girls were subjected to sexual abuse.

IS fighters also killed members of the Sunni community they suspected of opposing them or of working for the government, its security forces or previously for US forces in Iraq. In October, IS killed over 320 members of the Sunni Albu Nimr tribe in Anbar as the government sought to mobilize and arm Sunni tribes to fight against IS.

IS fighters carried out summary killings of hundreds of people they captured, including government soldiers. In June, they summarily executed more than 1,000 soldiers and army volunteers taken prisoner as they fled unarmed from Camp Speicher, a major military base in Tikrit. IS posted video footage of some of the killings on the internet.

IS forces destroyed or desecrated historical sites and places of worship across all ethnic and religious communities, established Shari'a courts in areas they controlled and called for those who had worked for the government or US forces to repent. They issued strict rules on individual behaviour, requiring women and girls to wear face veils and to be with a male relative outside the home, segregating males and females at schools and workplaces, and banning smoking and "western-style" activities and lifestyles.

VIOLENCE AGAINST WOMEN AND GIRLS

Women and girls, mainly from the Yezidi community, were abducted by IS fighters and subjected to forced marriage, rape and other sexual abuses. They were also reportedly sold as slaves and sexually exploited, both within Iraq and in IS-controlled areas of neighbouring Syria. By November, more than 200 women and chidren, some only a few months old, had managed to escape from IS captivity. Among them was an 18-year-old woman who was abducted with other relatives when IS fighters raided the Sinjar area in August and forcibly "married" to an IS fighter who repeatedly raped her and beat her after she tried to escape. She escaped together with a girl aged 15 who had also been abducted and given to an IS fighter as a "wife". Other women were victims of unlawful execution-style killings for criticizing the IS or disobeying its orders. In October, IS killed a former parliamentarian, Iman Muhammad Younes, after holding her in captivity for weeks.

ARBITRARY ARRESTS AND DETENTIONS

The authorities held thousands of detainees without charge or trial under provisions of the anti-terrorism law. In February, the head of the Parliament's Human Rights Committee alleged that around 40,000 detainees remained in prison awaiting investigations. Many were held in prisons and detention centres run by various government ministries.

A letter sent by the Central Investigation Court to the Head of the Supreme Judicial Council in 2013, published in April 2014, reported that authorities continued to carry out unlawful arrests using a list containing partial names of thousands of suspects that the Anti-terrorism General Directorate had sent to police stations in connection with sectarian violence in 2006 and 2007. This was believed to have led to the detention of the wrong people on the basis that part of their names corresponded to partial names on the list.

TORTURE AND OTHER ILL-TREATMENT

Torture and other ill-treatment remained common and widespread in prisons and detention centres, particularly those controlled by the Ministries of the Interior and Defence, and were committed with impunity. These centres were blocked to inspection by the Independent High Commission for Human Rights. Interrogators tortured detainees to extract information and "confessions" for use against them at trial; sometimes detainees were tortured to death. Government representatives attending the Universal Periodic Review of Iraq at the UN Human Rights Council said the authorities had investigated 516 torture cases between 2008 and 2014, with many resulting in prosecutions, but provided no details and did not identify the security agencies responsible.

'Uday Taha Kurdi, a lawyer and father of two, died in June after 15 days of detention by Anti-terrorism General Directorate officials in Baghdad. In a letter to the Iraqi Lawyers' Union in July, the Ministry of the Interior said that 'Uday Taha Kurdi had suffered a "health problem" in detention and had been taken to hospital, where he died. The Ministry also said that a judge had concluded that 'Uday Taha Kurdi, whose brother was held on terrorism charges, was "from the IS leadership" and belonged to "a terrorist family", and that he had told the judge, when asked, that he had not been tortured. The Supreme Judicial Council said his death resulted from kidney failure, not torture as alleged. However, photographs of 'Uday Taha Kurdi's body taken at the morgue and obtained by Amnesty International showed that he had sustained bruises, open wounds and burns – consistent with allegations of torture – prior to his death.

UNFAIR TRIALS

The criminal justice system remained deeply flawed. The judiciary lacked independence. Judges and lawyers involved in trials of members of armed groups continued to be targets for killings, abductions and assaults by armed groups. Trials, particularly of defendants facing terrorism charges, were frequently unfair; courts returned guilty verdicts on the basis of torture-tainted "confessions", which were often broadcast on the government-controlled al-Iraqiya TV channel. Other guilty verdicts were based on evidence from secret, unidentified informants, including in cases that resulted in death sentences.

In November, a Baghdad court sentenced former leading Sunni parliamentarian Ahmed al-'Alwani to death on terrorism-related charges after a grossly unfair trial. Security forces had arrested him in December 2013 after they forcibly dispersed a year-long protest in Anbar.

FREEDOM OF EXPRESSION

Journalists worked in extremely hazardous conditions and faced threats from both state and non-state actors. Some were victims of targeted killings or assassination attempts; others were physically assaulted.

In March, Mohammad Bdaiwi al-Shammari, a university professor and Baghdad Bureau Chief for Radio Free Iraq, was shot dead at a checkpoint in Baghdad by a Presidential Guards officer during an argument over access to the presidential complex. In August, a court sentenced the officer to life imprisonment.

In June, the government-controlled Communications and Media Commission issued "mandatory" guidelines regulating media activities "during the war on terror", demanding that media outlets not make public information about insurgent forces, and requiring them to not criticize government forces and to report on government forces only in favourable terms.

Journalists were abducted and executed by IS in areas under their control. In October, Ra'ad Mohammed Al-'Azawi, cameraman for Sama Salah al-Din TV Channel, was beheaded in Samarra, after a month in captivity, reportedly for refusing to co-operate with IS.

INTERNALLY DISPLACED PEOPLE

Almost 2 million people were forced from their homes due to the fighting in the Anbar, Diyala, Kirkuk, Ninevah and Salah al-Din provinces, with half of them fleeing to Iraq's Kurdistan Region, which by November was also hosting some 225,000 refugees from Syria. Thousands of Iraqi refugees returned to Iraq from Syria and elsewhere but could not return to their homes, swelling the number of internally displaced persons.

The unprecedented scale of the humanitarian crisis in Iraq led the UN to categorize it at the highest level of emergency and advised governments to afford international protection to Iraqi asylum-seekers and safeguard them from forcible return.

KURDISTAN REGION OF IRAQ

Although Kurdish Peshmerga forces battled against IS in several areas of northern Iraq, the three provinces that comprise the semi-autonomous Kurdistan Region remained largely immune from the violence engulfing much of the rest of Iraq until November, when a car bomb exploded outside an Erbil governorate building killing at least four and injuring 22 others.

The KRG authorities continued to target those who openly criticized official corruption or expressed dissent. The executive authorities continued to interfere in the judiciary, influencing trials. Incidents of torture and other ill-treatment continued to be reported. People arrested on terrorism charges were held incommunicado without access to family or lawyers for prolonged periods.

KRG authorities continued to detain journalist Niaz Aziz Saleh, held since January 2012 for allegedly disclosing details of election rigging, without charge or trial. General Security (Asayish Gishti) in Erbil reportedly refused repeatedly to take him to court to stand trial.

DEATH PENALTY

Courts continued to impose death sentences for a range of crimes. Most of the defendants had been convicted on terrorism-related charges, often after unfair trials. In April, the Justice Ministry said 600 prisoners were on death row at al-Nassiriya Prison alone, where new execution facilities were installed. In August, the Justice Minister said that a total of 1,724 prisoners were awaiting execution, including some whose sentences had still to be finally confirmed.

The authorities continued to carry out large numbers of executions, including multiple executions. On 21 January, the authorities executed 26 prisoners less than a week after UN Secretary-General Ban Ki-moon urged the Iraqi authorities to impose a moratorium on executions. Rebuffing this call during a joint press conference with Ban Ki-moon, Prime Minister Nuri al-Maliki said that his government did "not believe that the rights of someone who kills people must be respected".

IRELAND

Republic of Ireland
Head of state: **Michael D. Higgins**
Head of government: **Enda Kenny**

Abortion legislation and guidance failed to comply with Ireland's human rights obligations. Transgender individuals faced barriers to legal gender recognition. Responses to victims of past institutional

abuse fell below adequate standards of truth, justice and reparations.

SEXUAL AND REPRODUCTIVE RIGHTS

The Protection of Life during Pregnancy Act (the Act) was enacted in 2013 to respond to the 2010 European Court of Human Rights decision in *A, B and C v. Ireland*, with the stated aim of ensuring pregnant women's or girls' access to abortion when there is a "real and substantial risk" to their life as permitted under the Constitution. Neither the Act nor related guidance published in September 2014 provided sufficient assistance to medical professionals in assessing when a pregnancy posed such a risk to life, or adequately protected the rights of the pregnant woman or girl. In December, the Council of Europe's Committee of Ministers closed its examination of the implementation of the *A, B and C v. Ireland* decision.[1]

The Act recriminalized abortion in all other circumstances, with a potential penalty of 14 years' imprisonment.

In July, the UN Human Rights Committee criticized the criminalization of abortion, and the Act's requirements of excessive scrutiny of pregnant and suicidal women or girls which could lead to further mental distress. The Committee called on Ireland to revise its laws, including its Constitution, to provide for access to abortion in cases of rape, incest, serious risks to the health of the woman or girl, and fatal foetal impairment.

DISCRIMINATION

Transgender people

In December the government published a bill proposing legislative provision for legal gender recognition.[2] The bill's proposals fell short of human rights standards, including by requiring transgender individuals to dissolve their marriages or civil partnerships before applying for legal gender recognition.[3]

People with disabilities

Independent registration and inspections of residential care centres for people with disabilities began in November 2013. In December 2014, a current affairs television programme revealed secretly recorded evidence of abusive treatment, and denial of basic rights and autonomy, of three people in one centre, raising wider concerns about other centres.

REFUGEES AND ASYLUM-SEEKERS

There were continuing delays in the determination of individuals' asylum or other protection needs, with many people remaining for years in "direct provision" accommodation unsuitable for long-stay residence, especially for families, children and victims of torture.

VIOLENCE AGAINST WOMEN AND CHILDREN

In February 2013, the government published a report purporting to clarify the state's interaction with the religious-run "Magdalene Laundries". The report and the ex gratia compensation scheme announced thereafter fell below adequate standards of truth, justice and reparations.[4]

In June, following international outcry at allegations of past abuses of women and children in so-called "mother and baby homes", operated by religious orders with state funding between the 1920s and 1990s, the government committed to establishing an independent Commission of Investigation.[5]

LEGAL, CONSTITUTIONAL OR INSTITUTIONAL DEVELOPMENTS

In July legislation was enacted creating the Irish Human Rights and Equality Commission as the new National Human Rights Institution (NHRI), the result of a merger between the Irish Human Rights Commission (the former NHRI) and Ireland's equality body. The legislation contained two definitions of human rights, limiting the new NHRI's enforcement and powers to a narrow definition which excluded the majority of economic, social and cultural rights.

The government-appointed Constitutional Convention recommended several amendments to the Constitution, including providing for equal access to civil marriage for same-sex couples and removing the offence of blasphemy; the government accepted both recommendations and committed to putting them to referendum in 2015. In February, the Convention recommended constitutional incorporation of economic, social and cultural rights.

Ireland ratified the Optional Protocol to the UN Convention on the Rights of the Child on a communications procedure in September.

In December, the government requested that the European Court of Human Rights review its 1978 judgment in *Ireland v. United Kingdom*, a landmark case concerning the torture and ill-treatment of 14 Irish nationals held by UK authorities under internment powers in Northern Ireland during 1971-72 (see UK entry).[6]

1. Ireland: Submission to the UN Committee on Economic, Social and Cultural Rights: Pre-sessional working group (EUR 29/003/2014) www. amnesty.org/en/library/info/EUR29/003/2014/en

2. The state decides who I am: Lack of legal gender recognition for transgender people in Europe (EUR 01/001/2014) www. amnesty.org/en/library/info/EUR01/001/2014/en

3. The state decides who I am: Lack of legal gender recognition for transgender people in Europe (EUR 01/001/2014) www.amnesty.org/en/library/info/EUR01/001/2014/en Ireland: Transgender people 'short-changed' by new bill (Press release) www.amnesty.org/en/articles/news/2014/12/ireland-transgender-people-short-changed-new-bill/

4. Ireland: Submission to the UN Human Rights Committee (EUR 29/001/2014) www.amnesty.org/en/library/info/EUR29/001/2014/en

5. Ireland: 'Tuam babies' mass grave allegations must spark urgent investigation (Press release) www.amnesty.org/en/articles/news/2014/06/ireland-tuam-babies-mass-grave-allegations-must-spark-urgent-investigation/

6. Ireland: Decision to reopen "Hooded Men" court case triumph of justice after four decades of waiting (Press release) www.amnesty.org/press-releases/2014/12/ireland-decision-reopen-hooded-men-court-case-triumph-justice-after-four-de/

ISRAEL AND THE OCCUPIED PALESTINIAN TERRITORIES

State of Israel
Head of state: **Reuven Rivlin (replaced Shimon Peres in July)**
Head of government: **Benjamin Netanyahu**

Israeli forces committed war crimes and human rights violations during a 50-day military offensive in the Gaza Strip that killed over 1,500 civilians, including 539 children, wounded thousands more civilians, and caused massive civilian displacement and destruction of property and vital services. Israel maintained its air, sea and land blockade of Gaza, imposing collective punishment on its approximately 1.8 million inhabitants and stoking the humanitarian crisis. In the West Bank, Israeli forces carried out unlawful killings of Palestinian protesters, including children, and maintained an array of oppressive restrictions on Palestinians' freedom of movement while continuing to promote illegal settlements and allow Israeli settlers to attack Palestinians and destroy their property with near total impunity. Israeli forces detained thousands of Palestinians, some of whom reported being tortured, and held around 500 administrative detainees without trial. Within Israel, the authorities continued to demolish homes of Palestinian Bedouin in "unrecognized villages" in the Negev/Naqab region and commit forcible evictions. They also detained and summarily expelled thousands of foreign migrants, including asylum-seekers, and imprisoned Israeli conscientious objectors.

BACKGROUND

Tensions between Israelis and Palestinians mounted rapidly amid the collapse of US-sponsored negotiations in April, a Fatah-Hamas reconciliation agreement, and Israel's continuing illegal settlement expansion in the West Bank and blockade of Gaza. The tensions flared into renewed armed conflict in July following the killing of at least 15 Palestinians by Israeli forces since the beginning of the year, the abduction and killing of three Israeli teenagers in the West Bank by Palestinian men affiliated to Hamas, the reprisal killing of a Palestinian youth by Israelis, and rocket-firing from Gaza into Israel. The Israeli military launched an offensive, Operation Protective Edge, on 8 July against the Gaza Strip while Hamas and other Palestinian armed groups increased rocket firing into southern Israel. After 10 days of air strikes, Israel launched a ground invasion in Gaza, withdrawing shortly before a US and Egypt-brokered ceasefire took effect after 50 days of hostilities.

The ceasefire brought an end to open conflict but tension remained acute, particularly in the West Bank. Community relations were inflamed by a series of attacks by Palestinians targeting Israeli civilians, including one on worshippers in a synagogue; new killings of Palestinians, including protesters, by Israeli forces; the government's announcement of new land expropriations and plans to build additional housing units for settlers in East Jerusalem; and the Israeli authorities' decision in November to temporarily close access to Jerusalem's Temple Mount, preventing worshippers from reaching the Al-Aqsa mosque, one of Islam's holiest sites. Growing international recognition of Palestine as a state also contributed to tensions.

In December , Prime Minister Netanyahu dismissed two ministers for reasons including disagreements on a proposed "Nation-State Bill" defining Israel as a state for the Jewish people. The Knesset voted for dissolution and the holding of new elections in March 2015, upon the Prime Minister's initiative.

ARMED CONFLICT

Israel's Protective Edge military offensive, which Israel said it launched in response to an upsurge in rocket firing into Israel by Palestinian armed groups in Gaza, killed more than 2,000 inhabitants of Gaza, including more than 1,500 civilians, among them some 539 children. Israeli air and ground attacks damaged or destroyed thousands of civilian homes and internally displaced around 110,000 Palestinians, as well as severing power generation and water supplies, and damaging other civil infrastructure. In Israel, indiscriminate rockets and other weapons fired by Palestinian armed groups from Gaza in breach of the laws of war killed six civilians, including one child, injured dozens and damaged civilian property.

During the 50 days of conflict before a ceasefire took effect on 26 August, Israeli forces committed war crimes, including disproportionate and indiscriminate attacks on Gaza's densely populated civilian areas as well as targeted attacks on schools sheltering civilians and other civilian buildings that the Israeli forces claimed were used by Hamas as command centres or to store or fire rockets. On the night of 30 July, Israeli artillery fire hit the Jabaliya elementary school where more than 3,000 civilians had taken refuge, killing at least 20 and injuring others. It was the sixth time a school being used by the UN to shelter civilians had been attacked since the conflict began three weeks earlier.

Israeli forces also attacked hospitals and medical workers, including ambulance staff seeking to assist the wounded or retrieve the bodies of those killed. Dozens of homes were destroyed or damaged by missiles or aerial bombs with families still inside. For example, in eight cases documented by Amnesty International, Israeli strikes on inhabited houses killed at least 104 civilians, including 62 children. Often the Israeli military gave no reason for specific attacks.

In the days immediately leading up to the ceasefire, Israeli forces launched attacks that destroyed three multistorey residential buildings in Gaza City and a modern commercial centre in Rafah, amid vague assertions that the residential buildings housed a Hamas command centre and "facilities linked to Palestinian militants" but without providing any compelling evidence or explanation why, if there were legitimate military reasons to justify the attacks, less destructive means were not selected.

Israeli authorities sought publicly to shift the blame for the large loss of life and wholesale destruction caused by the Israeli offensive in Gaza onto Hamas and Palestinian armed groups on the grounds that they fired rockets and other weapons from within or near civilian residential areas and concealed munitions in civilian buildings.

FREEDOM OF MOVEMENT – GAZA BLOCKADE AND WEST BANK RESTRICTIONS

Israeli forces maintained their land, sea and air blockade of Gaza throughout the year, effectively imposing collective punishment on the territory's approximately 1.8 million, predominantly civilian, inhabitants, with all imports and exports, and any movements of people into or out of Gaza, subject to Israeli approval; Egypt's continued closure of its Rafah border crossing kept Gaza effectively sealed. The already severe humanitarian consequences of the blockade, in force continuously since June 2007, were evidenced by the sizeable proportion of Gaza's population that depended on international humanitarian aid for their survival, and were greatly exacerbated by the devastation and population displacement caused during Israel's Operation Protective Edge.

Israeli forces policed the blockade using live fire against Palestinians who entered or approached a 500m-wide buffer zone that they imposed inside Gaza's land border with Israel, and against fishermen who entered or approached the "exclusion zone" that Israel maintains along the full length of Gaza's coast. Israeli forces shot dead seven Palestinian civilians in or near the buffer zone before Operation Protective Edge, and another after the ceasefire, when the buffer zone was to be reduced and the permitted fishing zone extended. Shooting incidents remained frequent; some fishermen were also shot and wounded by Israeli navy forces.

In the West Bank, Israel continued its construction of the wall/fence with attached guard towers, mostly on Palestinian land, routing it to afford protection to illegal settlements while cutting off Palestinian villagers from their lands. Palestinian farmers were required to obtain special permits to access their lands between the wall and the Green Line demarcating the West Bank's border with Israel. Throughout the West Bank, Israeli forces maintained other restrictions on the free movement of Palestinians by using military checkpoints and restricting access to certain areas by preventing Palestinians using bypass roads constructed for the use of Israeli settlers. These restrictions hindered Palestinians' access to hospitals, schools and workplaces. Furthermore, Israel forcibly transferred Palestinians out of occupied East Jerusalem to other areas in the West Bank.

Restrictions were tightened further during Operation Brother's Keeper, the Israeli authorities' crackdown following the abduction of three Israeli teenage hitchhikers in the West Bank in June. Operation Brother's Keeper saw a heightened Israeli military presence in Palestinian towns and villages, the killing of at least five Palestinians, mass arrests and detentions, the imposition of arbitrary travel restrictions and raids on Palestinian homes.

EXCESSIVE USE OF FORCE

Israeli soldiers and border guards unlawfully killed at least 50 Palestinian civilians in the West Bank and continued to use excessive force, including live fire, during protests against Israel's continued military occupation, when arresting political activists and during Israel's 50-day military offensive against Gaza. Some killings may have amounted to extrajudicial executions. In September, the UN Office for the Coordination of Humanitarian Affairs reported that the number of Palestinians wounded by Israeli forces in the West Bank – more than 4,200 since the start of 2014 – already exceeded the 2013 total, and that many of those wounded, including children, had been hit by rubber-coated metal bullets fired by Israeli forces. As in previous years, soldiers and border guards used live fire against protesters, including those who threw stones and other projectiles, who posed no serious threat to their lives.

IMPUNITY

The authorities failed to conduct independent investigations into alleged war crimes and human rights violations committed by Israeli forces during Operation Protective Edge and refused to co-operate with an international investigation appointed by the UN Human Rights Council. However, they apparently co-operated with the UN Secretary-General's Board of Inquiry, established to look into incidents relating to UN buildings in Gaza.

In August, the military's Chief of General Staff ordered an inquiry into more than 90 "exceptional incidents" during Operation Protective Edge where there was "reasonable ground for suspicion of a violation of the law". In September, it was announced that the Military Advocate General had closed investigations into nine cases and ordered criminal investigations into 10 others.

Authorities also failed to carry out adequate investigations into shootings of Palestinians during protests in the West Bank despite compelling evidence that Israeli forces repeatedly used excessive force and resorted to live fire in circumstances where such lethal means were unwarranted.

DETENTION WITHOUT TRIAL

Hundreds of Palestinians from the Occupied Palestinian Territories were held without charge or trial under administrative detention orders issued against them on the basis of secret information to which they and their lawyers had no access, and were unable to effectively challenge. The number of administrative detainees more than doubled following the security forces' round-up of Palestinians after the abduction and killing of three Israeli teenagers in June, rising from nearly 200 in May to 468 in September.

TORTURE AND OTHER ILL-TREATMENT

Palestinian detainees continued to be tortured and otherwise ill-treated by Israeli security officials, particularly Internal Security Agency officials, who frequently held detainees incommunicado during interrogation for days and sometimes weeks. Methods used included physical assault such as slapping and throttling, prolonged shackling and stress positions, sleep deprivation, and threats against the detainee and their family. Reports of torture increased amid the wave of arrests that followed the abduction of Israeli teenagers in June.

The authorities failed to take adequate steps either to prevent torture or to conduct independent investigations when detainees alleged torture, fuelling a climate of impunity.

HOUSING RIGHTS – FORCED EVICTIONS AND DEMOLITIONS

In the West Bank, Israeli forces continued to demolish Palestinian homes and other structures, forcibly evicting hundreds from their homes often without warning or prior consultation. Families of Palestinians who had carried out attacks on Israelis also faced demolition of their homes as a punitive measure.

Palestinian Bedouin citizens of Israel living in "unrecognized" and newly recognized villages also faced destruction of homes and structures because the authorities said that they had been built without permission.

Israeli authorities prohibited all construction without official permits, which were denied to Arab inhabitants of the villages, while also denying them access to basic services such as electricity and piped water supplies. Under the 2011 Prawer Plan, the authorities proposed to demolish 35 "unrecognized" villages and forcibly displace up to 70,000 Bedouin inhabitants from their current lands and homes, and relocate them to officially designated sites. Implementation of the plan, which was adopted without consultation with the affected Bedouin communities, remained stalled following the resignation in December 2013 of the government minister overseeing it. Official statements announced its cancellation, but the army continued to demolish homes and other structures.

CONSCIENTIOUS OBJECTORS

Military tribunals continued to impose prison sentences on Israeli citizens who refused to undertake compulsory military service on grounds of conscience. At least six conscientious objectors were imprisoned during the year. Omar Sa'ad was released in June after serving 150 days in a military prison and then declared unsuitable and exempted from military service.

REFUGEES AND ASYLUM-SEEKERS

Asylum-seekers in need of international protection were denied access to a fair determination process. Authorities held more than 2,000 African asylum-seekers in indefinite detention in a facility in the Negev/Naqab desert.

The authorities held more than 2,200 Eritrean and Sudanese asylum-seekers at Holot, a desert detention facility opened after the government rushed through Amendment 4 of the Prevention of Infiltration Law in 2013. In September, the High Court of Justice struck down Amendment 4, under which the authorities had taken powers to automatically detain all newly arrived asylum-seekers for one year, ruling that it infringed the right to human dignity. The Court ordered the government to close the Holot facility or establish an alternative legislative arrangement within 90 days. In December, the Knesset passed new amendments to the law that would allow the authorities to continue automatic detention of asylum-seekers.

Eritrean and Sudanese nationals, who made up more than 90% of an estimated 47,000 African asylum-seekers in Israel, continued in practice to be denied access to fair refugee determination procedures. By the end of the year, Israeli authorities had extended refugee status to just two Eritreans and no Sudanese, dismissing many other claims without due consideration. Asylum-seekers were prohibited by law from taking paid work and had little or no access to health care and welfare services. Meanwhile, the authorities pressured many to leave Israel "voluntarily" under a process that paid them to withdraw their asylum claims and return to their home countries or travel to third countries. More than 5,000 Eritrean and Sudanese nationals were reported to have accepted "voluntary return" in the first 10 months of the year, some leaving after facing imminent risk of detention, despite fears that they faced persecution or torture in the countries from which they had fled. Some were reported to have been detained when they returned to Sudan and accused of spying for Israel.

Israel allegedly maintained secret agreements with certain African countries allowing for the transfer of asylum-seekers under conditions which denied them access to a fair refugee determination process in Israel or any protection from possible subsequent transfers to their home countries, including in cases where such returns amounted to *refoulement*.

ITALY

Republic of Italy
Head of state: **Giorgio Napolitano**
Head of government: **Matteo Renzi**

Over 170,000 refugees and migrants trying to reach Italy from North Africa on unseaworthy vessels were rescued at sea by Italian authorities. The government's decision to stop a dedicated operation to save lives at sea, Mare Nostrum, at the end of October raised concerns that the death toll could increase significantly. The authorities failed to ensure adequate reception conditions for the high number of seaborne refugees and migrants. Discrimination against Roma continued, with thousands segregated in camps. Italy failed to introduce the crime of torture into domestic legislation and to establish an independent national human rights institution.

REFUGEES' AND MIGRANTS' RIGHTS

Over 170,000 refugees and migrants arrived in Italy by sea, including more than 10,000 unaccompanied children, the vast majority having departed from Libya. 156,362 had been rescued through Operation Mare Nostrum (OMN) by the end of October. A further 13,668 people were rescued by Italian authorities in November and December. Despite these unilateral efforts, over 3,400 refugees and migrants were believed to have drowned attempting to cross the Mediterranean. On 31 October, the government announced OMN's end, to coincide with the start on 1 November of the smaller, border control-focused Operation Triton by Frontex, the EU border management agency. NGOs expressed concern that this would place people's lives at risk.[1]

The authorities struggled to ensure adequate reception conditions for the tens of thousands of refugees and migrants who disembarked in Sicily and other southern ports, including traumatized shipwreck survivors, and to adequately protect thousands of unaccompanied children.

There was no progress in investigating the circumstances of the deaths of some 200 people who drowned when a trawler carrying over 400 mostly Syrian refugees and migrants sank on 11 October 2013. There was concern that failures by Maltese and Italian authorities might have delayed their rescue.

In October, in the case of *Sharifi and Others v. Italy and Greece*, the European Court of Human Rights found that Italy had violated the prohibition of collective expulsions and exposed four Afghan nationals, who had arrived irregularly, to the risk of ill-treatment and other violations by returning them to Greece, as well as to the further risk of torture and death in case of deportation to Afghanistan.

Refugees and asylum-seekers, including children, remained at risk of destitution.

In April, the Parliament passed legislation requiring the government to abolish the crime of "irregular entry and stay" within 18 months. Irregular migrants re-entering the country following an expulsion would still face criminal sanctions. However, "irregular entry and stay" remained a crime at the end of the year.

In September, the Ministry of the Interior authorized police to use force to ensure the collection of fingerprints during the identification of refugees and migrants. This was immediately followed by reports of excessive use of force in the course of identification procedures.

In October, legislation was adopted reducing the maximum period of detention for irregular migrants pending deportation from 18 months to 90 days. Conditions in detention centres for irregular migrants remained inadequate.

Migrant workers continued to be exploited and remained vulnerable to abuse and were often unable to access justice.

DISCRIMINATION – ROMA

Thousands of Roma families continued to live in poor conditions in segregated camps and centres, including more than 4,000 in Rome alone. The government failed to implement the National Strategy for the Inclusion of Roma, especially with regard to adequate housing. Several forced evictions of Roma were reported across the country.

A European Commission inquiry into possible breaches by Italy of the EU Race Equality Directive in relation to access by Roma to adequate housing was ongoing.

Roma families transferred from the authorized camp of Cesarina in Rome in December 2013, to allow for its refurbishment, continued to live in inadequate conditions in a Roma-only reception facility. Rome municipal authorities stated they would return the families to the camp once works were completed. No alternative adequate housing options were made available.

Roma remained excluded from accessing social housing. Rome housing authorities did not withdraw a January 2013 circular discriminating against Roma families living in authorized camps in the allocation of social housing. However, in June, in the context of the inquiry regarding the EU Race Equality Directive, they stated that they intended to apply the circular in a non-discriminatory manner.

COUNTER-TERROR AND SECURITY

The Italian Constitutional Court ruled in February that the government enjoyed absolute discretion to invoke the "state secrets" doctrine in national security-related cases. The Court of Cassation, Italy's highest court, affirmed the Constitutional Court ruling and annulled the convictions of high-level Italian intelligence officials, convicted in relation to the abduction of Usama Mostafa Hassan Nasr (known as Abu Omar) from a Milan street in 2003. Following his abduction, Abu Omar had been handed over to the US Central Intelligence Agency (CIA) and rendered to Egypt, where he was tortured.

In March, the Court of Cassation upheld the convictions of three CIA officials, including former Rome CIA chief Jeff Castelli and former Milan CIA chief Robert Seldon Lady, for the abduction of Abu Omar. The Court ruled that the CIA operatives were not covered by diplomatic immunity. In total, 26 US nationals had been convicted in their absence in the Abu Omar case.

TORTURE AND OTHER ILL-TREATMENT

Attempts to incorporate the crime of torture into national legislation failed again, a 25-year breach of Italy's obligations under the UN Convention against Torture.

In November, the Court of Cassation annulled the conviction for perjury against Francesco Colucci, who was head of police in Genoa when scores of protesters were tortured and otherwise ill-treated during the 2001 G8 summit meeting. Francesco Colucci had been convicted of perjury for trying to shelter from accountability the then national head of police, Gianni De Gennaro, and a senior official of the police special operations branch of Genoa. The statute of limitation for the offence expired in December rendering a retrial impossible.

Overcrowding and poor conditions remained common throughout the prison system. Legislation to reduce the length of prison sentences for certain offences and to increase the use of non-custodial sentences was adopted in August 2013 and February 2014 to ease overcrowding. A national ombudsperson for the rights of detainees was also created. The measures followed a 2013 European Court ruling that Italy had violated the prohibition of torture and inhuman or degrading treatment by subjecting detainees to excessively harsh conditions due to overcrowded cells and insufficient living space.

DEATHS IN CUSTODY

Despite progress in a few cases, concerns remained about the lack of accountability for deaths in custody as a result of flawed investigations and shortcomings in judicial proceedings.

In April, the Perugia court of appeal upheld the conviction of a prison officer for falsifying documents and failing to assist Aldo Bianzino, who died in a Perugia prison two days after his arrest in 2007. The ruling confirmed that there were failings in the initial investigation.

In July, in the case of Giuseppe Uva, who died at a hospital in Varese shortly after being stopped by police in 2008, a trial started against seven police officers for manslaughter, unlawful arrest and abuse of authority. In October 2013, a judge had refused the prosecutor's request to close the case and had ordered a fresh investigation. Forensic examinations in December 2011 revealed that Giuseppe Uva may have been raped and otherwise ill-treated.

In October, the Rome court of appeal acquitted the doctors, nurses and police officers charged with manslaughter in the case of Stefano Cucchi, who died a week after his arrest in the prison wing of a Rome hospital in 2009. Forensic evidence was inconclusive. Stefano Cucchi's family was concerned that signs of ill-treatment had been downplayed.

LEGAL, CONSTITUTIONAL OR INSTITUTIONAL DEVELOPMENTS

Italy failed again to establish a national human rights institution in accordance with the Principles relating to the Status of National Institutions (Paris Principles), despite having repeatedly committed to doing so.

---

1. Lives adrift: Refugees and migrants in peril in the central Mediterranean (EUR 05/006/2014)
www.amnesty.org/en/library/info/EUR05/006/2014/en

JAMAICA

Jamaica
Head of state: Queen Elizabeth II, represented by Patrick Linton Allen
Head of government: Portia Simpson Miller

Police brutality remained a concern. Attacks and harassment of lesbian, gay, bisexual, transgender and intersex (LGBTI) people continued. Steps were taken to deal with the issue of impunity. Jamaica retained the death penalty.

BACKGROUND

Levels of homicide remained high, mainly in marginalized inner-city communities, although there was a decrease on 2013 figures. The Jamaica Constabulary Force reported that 699 people had been killed up to 14 September, 15% fewer than in the corresponding period for 2013.

POLICE AND SECURITY FORCES

Following rising numbers in police killings in recent years (210 in 2011, 219 in 2012 and 258 in 2013), 2014 saw a reduction in the number of police killings according to the Independent Commission of Investigations (INDECOM), an independent police oversight agency. By the end of October, 103 civilians had been killed by police, compared with 220 for the same period in 2013. A number of people were killed in circumstances suggesting that they may have been extrajudicially executed.

Following the death of Mario Deane in suspicious circumstances in police custody in August, in September the Ministers of Justice and National Security announced a review of the detention system in order to "develop a strategic response to the issue of the treatment of persons in lock-ups and correctional facilities".

The Criminal Justice (Suppression of Criminal Organizations) Act, which is aimed at "disruption and suppression of criminal organizations" became law in April. Concerns were raised that this law could be used to criminalize whole communities by association.

In February a Commission of Enquiry was finally established into the state of emergency of May 2010, when 76 civilians were killed during an operation by the security forces. The three-person Commission began its work on 1 December. In April the Office of the Public Defender handed over all files pertaining to its investigations into the state of emergency to INDECOM. The files include the cases of 44 people alleged to have been unlawfully killed by the security forces.

Eleven police officers from Clarendon suspected of being part of a "death squad" were arrested and charged in April by INDECOM. They were alleged to have been involved in the murder of nine civilians since 2009. Investigations were ongoing at the end of the year.

JUSTICE SYSTEM

Overburdened courts led to continued delays in the justice system. In February, the National Security Minister stated there was a backlog of approximately 40,000 cases. In June, the Chief Justice said that the unavailability of forensic evidence, outstanding statements and ballistic reports, as well as an absence of adequate court infrastructure, human and financial resources, were seriously hampering the justice system.

VIOLENCE AGAINST WOMEN AND GIRLS

Sexual violence against women and girls remained a concern. Police statistics from the 2013 Economic and Social Survey published in April 2014 by the Planning Institute of Jamaica showed that 814 cases of rape were recorded in 2013, and that 128 women were murdered in 2013.

A review of the draft National Strategic Action Plan to Eliminate Gender-Based Violence, announced in September 2013, was still ongoing at the end of 2014.

Following a Senate motion in October 2013 calling for greater legislative protection for women and girls, a joint select committee of Parliament was finally established in July 2014 to review the Sexual Offences Act, Offences against the Person Act, Domestic Violence Act, and the Child Care and Protection Act, with the objective of improving protection for women, children, persons living with disabilities and the elderly from violence and abuse.

CHILDREN'S RIGHTS

Children continued to be kept in police cells alongside adults, in some cases for several days, in contravention of the Child Care and Protection Act and international law.

RIGHTS OF LESBIAN, GAY, BISEXUAL, TRANSGENDER AND INTERSEX PEOPLE

Consensual sex between men remained criminalized. LGBTI organizations continued to report attacks, harassment and threats against individuals based on their real or perceived sexual orientation, which were not fully and promptly investigated.

On 14 June a mob attacked a young man at a shopping mall in the town of May Pen because he was allegedly seen putting on lipstick. There was no police investigation into the incident.

In August, Javed Jaghai, a member of the Jamaica Forum of Lesbians, All-Sexuals and Gays, discontinued the constitutional challenge he had filed in February 2013 against laws criminalizing sex between men, following the receipt of threats against him and his family.

A "conscience vote" by MPs on legislation criminalizing consensual same-sex relations, which the government announced would be held before April, did not take place.

JAPAN

Japan
Head of government: **Shinzo Abe**

Japan continued to move away from international human rights standards. The government failed to effectively address discrimination against foreign nationals and their descendants living in Japan, such as ethnic Koreans. It also failed to refute and combat attempts to deny Japan's military sexual slavery system during World War II. The number of recognized refugees remained very small. It was feared that the Act on the Protection of Specially Designated Secrets which came into force in December could negatively impact transparency.

DISCRIMINATION

The government failed to speak out against discriminatory rhetoric, or curb the use of racially pejorative terms and harassments against ethnic Koreans and their descendants, who are commonly referred to as *Zainichi* (literally "residing in Japan"). Public demonstrations were held in towns with a high proportion of Korean residents. In December, the Supreme Court ruled to ban the high-profile group "Zainichi Tokken wo Yurusanai Shimin no Kai" from using discriminatory and intimidating language while demonstrating near an ethnic Korean elementary school located in Kyoto. This decision marked the first time that the issue was treated as one of racial discrimination, based on the definition in the International Convention on the Elimination of All Forms of Racial Discrimination, rather than coming under other criminal offences such as defamation or damage of property. However, by the end of the year the government had still not passed legislation prohibiting advocacy of hatred that constitutes incitement to discrimination, hostility or violence, in line with international standards.[1]

JUSTICE SYSTEM

The *daiyo kangoku* system, which allows police to detain suspects for up to 23 days prior to charge, continued to facilitate torture and other ill-treatment to extract confessions during interrogation. Despite recommendations from international bodies, no steps were taken to abolish or reform the system in line with international standards.

VIOLENCE AGAINST WOMEN AND GIRLS

The government attempted to back away from the landmark apology – known as the Kono Statement – it had made two decades earlier to the survivors of the military sexual slavery system, in which it had acknowledged responsibility and apologized to the survivors. In June the results were made public of a government-appointed study group which re-examined the drafting process of the Kono Statement. Although previous discussions and decisions were respected, the review itself increased tensions with neighbouring countries such as the Republic of Korea, as it was seen as an attempt to deny governmental responsibility. Several high-profile public figures made statements to deny or justify the system. The government continued to refuse to officially use the term "sexual slavery", and to deny full and effective reparation to survivors.

DEATH PENALTY

Executions continued to be carried out. In March a district court ordered a retrial and the immediate release of Hakamada Iwao. Hakamada had been sentenced to death in 1968 after an unfair trial on the basis of a forced confession, and was the longest-serving death row inmate in the world. He suffers from mental illness due to more than four decades of detention mainly in solitary confinement. The Prosecutor's appeal against a retrial was being examined at the Tokyo High Court.

REFUGEES AND ASYLUM-SEEKERS

An estimated 4,500 individuals applied for asylum in Japan but the numbers of refugees recognized under the UN Refugee Convention remained very small. A steady increase in the number of applications has occurred since 2006. Applicants from Myanmar decreased and there was an increase in applicants from countries such as Ghana and Cameroon.

FREEDOM OF EXPRESSION

The Act on the Protection of Specially Designated Secrets came into force in December 2014. This would allow the government to classify information as "Specially Designated Secrets (SDS)" when a "leak can cause a serious obstacle to national security" in the categories of defence, diplomacy and so-called "harmful activities" and "terrorism". The law could restrict transparency by limiting access to information held by public authorities, as the definition of SDS was vague and the monitoring body lacked binding powers.

---

1. Japan: Submission to the UN Human Rights Committee: 111th session
   of the Human Rights Committee (7-25th July 2014)
   www.amnesty.org/en/library/info/ASA22/002/2014/en

JORDAN

Hashemite Kingdom of Jordan
Head of state: **King Abdullah II bin al-Hussein**
Head of government: **Abdullah Ensour**

The authorities maintained strict controls on the rights to freedom of expression, association and assembly. Government critics faced arbitrary arrest and detention; some were prosecuted and jailed. The government amended the 2006 Anti-Terrorism law to encompass acts deemed disruptive to Jordan's foreign relations

and the dissemination of ideas deemed supportive of terrorism. The State Security Court (SSC) continued to try people accused under anti-terrorism legislation; some of the accused alleged torture or other ill-treatment. Jordan continued to receive and host thousands of refugees from Syria and, increasingly, Iraq, but barred entry to Palestinians from Syria. Women faced discrimination in law and in practice; at least 14 people were victims of so-called "honour killings". Eleven prisoners were executed in December, the first executions since 2006.

BACKGROUND

Jordan felt the impact of events beyond its borders, notably the armed conflicts in Syria and Iraq, and Israel's military offensive in Gaza. The Syrian conflict generated further refugee flows into Jordan. Jordan hosted over 600,000 refugees from Syria, according to UNHCR, the UN refugee agency, and 30,000 refugees from Iraq. Demonstrations in March over the killing of a Jordanian judge by Israeli forces at the Allenby Bridge crossing between Jordan and the West Bank were followed by mass protests in July and August against Israel's bombing campaign in Gaza.

Conditions were tense along the border with Syria and the government tightened controls there and along the border with Iraq. In April, the government said Jordanian warplanes had fired on members of Syrian armed groups seeking to cross into Jordan. In June, the USA agreed to send missiles and military aircraft to Jordan, and in September, Jordan joined the US-led international alliance against the Islamic State armed group.

The government made little progress in implementing promised political reforms but the King gained sole authority to appoint the heads of the armed forces and the General Intelligence Department (GID) under a constitutional amendment.

FREEDOMS OF EXPRESSION, ASSOCIATION AND ASSEMBLY

The government maintained strict controls on freedom of expression, using provisions criminalizing defamation of the monarchy and other institutions and religion, the Press and Publications Law, and the 2010 Law on Information System Crimes, which gave the authorities wide powers to censor print, broadcast and online media. The authorities blocked some news websites.

In early 2014, the jurisdiction of the State Security Court (SSC) was restricted to five crimes: treason, espionage, terrorism, drugs offences, and money counterfeiting. However, amendments to the Anti-Terrorism Law enacted in May imposed new curbs on freedom of expression by equating acts deemed to disrupt Jordan's foreign relations, including criticism of foreign leaders, and the dissemination of certain ideas, with terrorism.

The authorities continued to detain and prosecute political opposition activists, online critics and journalists, including members of the banned Hizb ut-Tahrir party, at least 18 of whom faced trial before the SSC, despite its poor record of upholding international fair trial standards. In March, Nayef Lafi and Ibrahim al-Kharabsheh were arrested as they lobbied parliament against amendments to the Anti-Terrorism Law, and faced up to seven years' imprisonment on charges of "illegal actions" threatening the government, and membership of a banned organization. Wassim Abu Ayesh was tried by the SSC on terrorism charges. He was accused of posting an Islamic State group video on Facebook, which he claimed was in fact a film about the abuse of detainees in Iraq, and said that his interrogators made him sign a statement without allowing him to read it.

In July, security forces attacked and assaulted journalists at an anti-Israel protest in Amman. In August, they arrested Abdulhadi Raji Majali, an *Al Ra'i* newspaper journalist, by order of Amman prosecutors for an online post to which the authorities took offence. He was released on bail one week later awaiting trial.

Also in July, the SSC imposed three-month prison terms on three peaceful pro-reform activists, Mahdi al-Saafin, Ayham Mohamed Alseem and Fadi Masamra, on charges of "undermining" the state and "insulting" the King.

Mohamed Said Bakr and Adel Awad, senior Muslim Brotherhood members, were brought to trial before the SSC following their arrest in September, accused of threatening state security in public statements that criticized Jordan's leaders and links with the USA. In December, the case against Adel Awad was thrown out due to lack of evidence.

TORTURE AND OTHER ILL-TREATMENT

Torture and other ill-treatment remained a significant concern. Among those alleging such abuses were detainees arrested on suspicion of supporting or fighting for armed groups, such as Jabhat al-Nusra, in Syria.

In June, the SSC acquitted Abu Qatada of terrorism charges. UK authorities had deported him to Jordan in 2013 after negotiating diplomatic assurances allegedly to ensure that "confessions" gained from others through torture would be inadmissible in a new criminal trial. In reaching its verdict the SSC did not disregard the "confession" evidence, considering it a matter of record, but concluded that it was not supported by other evidence. In September, the SCC acquitted Abu Qatada on separate charges and ordered his release.

ADMINISTRATIVE DETENTION

Provincial authorities held hundreds, possibly thousands, of criminal suspects in administrative detention without charge or trial using the Law on Crime Prevention, in force since 1954. The law empowers provincial governors to authorize the arrests and indefinite detention of those they deem a "danger to society" and affords those detained no means of appeal or legal remedy.

REFUGEES' AND MIGRANTS' RIGHTS

Jordan hosted over 600,000 refugees from Syria, about one third of whom were accommodated in six camps, the largest of which had a population of over 100,000. The majority of refugees lived in towns and cities throughout Jordan. While in principle maintaining an open-border policy to refugees from Syria, the authorities closed the border to Syrian refugees on a number of occasions and prevented the entry into Jordan of Palestinians and Iraqis fleeing the Syrian conflict. The presence of so many refugees was a huge economic strain and placed a burden on Jordan's resources, including water, education and health care. Insecurity increased due to the potential for the conflict to spread into Jordan.

WOMEN'S RIGHTS

Women remained subject to discrimination in law and practice, and were inadequately protected from sexual and other violence, including so-called honour crimes. Tens of thousands of women married to foreigners continued to be denied the right to pass on their nationality to their spouses and children. In November, the government afforded them greater access to education and medical care, but failed to end discrimination. The Ministry of Justice was also reportedly considering Penal Code changes to protect women against sexual harassment.

At least 12 women and two children, a girl and a boy, were victims of so-called honour killings. In at least two cases courts immediately commuted the death sentences imposed on perpetrators of such killings to 10-year prison terms, apparently under a provision allowing courts to commute or reduce sentences if the victim's family requests leniency.

In July, UNICEF, the UN children's agency, reported an increase in early marriage among Syrian refugees, noting the associated risks this posed to girls. The legal age of marriage for women in Jordan was 18 unless special dispensation for an earlier marriage was

obtained from a judge. Jordanian NGO Sisterhood is Global reported that 13.2% of registered marriages in 2013 took place before the bride's 18th birthday.

DEATH PENALTY

Eleven men were executed on 21 December, the first executions in Jordan since 2006. This followed the establishment in November of a special committee of the cabinet to look into the resumption of executions.

KAZAKHSTAN

Republic of Kazakhstan
Head of state: **Nursultan Nazarbayev**
Head of government: **Karim Massimov (replaced Serik Akhmetov in April)**

There was no improvement in investigating reports of human rights violations by law enforcement and security services and holding alleged perpetrators to account. Bureaucratic obstacles and opaque internal ministerial regulations prevented victims of torture and their relatives from obtaining justice. Similar obstacles continued to hinder effective independent monitoring of places of detention. The right to freedom of assembly continued to be restricted. Civil society activists feared that new legislative proposals would restrict their freedoms of expression and association.

TORTURE AND OTHER ILL-TREATMENT

The authorities repeatedly asserted their commitment to eliminating torture and other ill-treatment. In September 2013, the Prosecutor General instructed national prosecutors to "open a criminal investigation into every incident of torture". However, in practice investigations into allegations of torture and other ill-treatment fell far short of international standards and failed to deliver justice.

In November the UN Committee against Torture expressed concern at "the gap between legislation and protection from torture", noting that the use of torture and other ill-treatment to obtain confessions "went beyond isolated incidents", and that less than 2% of complaints of torture led to prosecution. In October, at Kazakhstan's second round Universal Periodic Review, the UN Human Rights Council recommended that Kazakhstan establish an independent investigations mechanism.

The Criminal Procedural Code provides that an official body should not investigate complaints against its own officials. However, complaints of torture and other ill-treatment made against law enforcement and national security officials were routinely referred to the internal investigations departments of the Ministry of Internal Affairs, Financial Police or the Committee for National Security (KNB). These internal investigation departments are governed by internal regulations, which have not been made public. In practice this meant that instead of an impartial investigation by a separate authority, torture complaints were put through an internal screening process, which usually failed to check them objectively. In most cases, screening procedures concluded that complaints were unfounded or that the perpetrators could not be identified.

Independent NGOs registered between 350 and 400 complaints of torture and other ill-treatment in Kazakhstan annually in 2013 and 2014. However, they estimated that since 2010 the authorities had succeeded in bringing only some 50 officials to justice. According to the website of the Office of the Prosecutor General, only 43 crimes of torture were registered from January to September, with 47 individuals identified as alleged victims, including 11 prisoners, three minors and one elderly person. During the same period, 17 torture-related cases went on trial and 30 cases were closed because of the "absence of elements of a crime", official language typically used after inadequate internal investigations. The website also stated that in 2013 and the first half of 2014, 31 police officers were convicted of torture-related crimes, but did not specify the nature of the crimes committed, nor the number of incidents these related to.

In November 2013, Kostanai Regional Court awarded 2 million Kazakhstani Tenge (US$13,000) in compensation to Aleksandr Gerasimov following a decision by the UN Committee against Torture in May 2012, which found Kazakhstan responsible for his torture. However, the authorities had yet to carry out a full and independent investigation into Aleksandr Gerasimov's torture complaint.

In November, Roza Tuletaeva, a labour rights activist, was released from prison on parole. She had been serving a five-year sentence for "inciting social discord" during the 2011 oil workers' strike in Zhanaozen. At her trial in 2012 she told the court that she had been tortured during interrogations. There was no information of any impartial investigations into her allegations of torture.

COUNTER-TERROR AND SECURITY

The authorities continued to invoke countering terrorism and other threats to national security as crucial to securing national and regional stability. There were frequent reports of KNB officers violating human rights, including using torture and other ill-treatment to obtain confessions.

Among those particularly targeted by the KNB were members or presumed members of banned or unregistered Islamic groups and Islamist parties; members of religious minorities; and asylum-seekers from neighbouring countries, particularly China and Uzbekistan.

Relatives of some of those convicted of terrorism-related offences claimed that prisoners in Shymkent and Arkalyk high security prisons were serving their sentences in cruel, inhuman and degrading conditions.

Only limited independent monitoring access was allowed at these facilities.

In January 2013, legislation was introduced which provided for broader measures in countering terrorism and extremism, and the newly adopted Criminal Code, signed by President Nazarbayev on 3 July 2014 and expected to come into force in January 2015, lowered the age of criminal liability for terrorism-related offences to 14 years. The crime of "terrorism with loss of life", in Article 49.1 of the Criminal Code, was the only crime still punishable by death although Kazakhstan remained abolitionist in practice.

PRISON CONDITIONS

In 2013 Kazakhstan adopted legislation to set up a National Preventive Mechanism (NPM). Its civil society members were elected on 19 February 2014 at the first session of the NPM Coordination Council, after which they began monitoring detention facilities across Kazakhstan. However, the NPM mandate did not extend to all places of deprivation of liberty. For example, the monitoring group was not permitted to inspect offices of police departments and had no access to other closed state institutions such as orphanages, nursing homes and military barracks. The NPM also faced bureaucratic obstacles: in order to undertake an urgent and unplanned visit, NPM members had to obtain written permission from the Ombudsman, which could only be obtained during working hours, thus restricting the NPM's ability to respond rapidly to reports of torture. The NPM was also not allowed to publish the results of its findings until the Ombudsman had approved its annual report.

FREEDOM OF ASSEMBLY

Freedom of assembly was restricted and peaceful protesters continued to be detained and fined. Activists were required to obtain prior permission from the local authorities for any public gathering or single-person picket. Distributing leaflets, joining spontaneous protests or wearing clothing displaying political slogans without prior permission were often regarded as violations of legislation on public protests. In several incidents law enforcement officials used force to break up unauthorized peaceful meetings. In dozens of cases, organizers and participants were fined or sentenced to administrative detention for up to 15 days.

FREEDOM OF ASSOCIATION

NGO registration was compulsory. Authorities enjoyed wide discretion to deny such status and to close down groups for alleged, often minor, violations of the law. The new Criminal Code and other related laws contained provisions that human rights groups believed could be used to harass NGOs and their members, and to restrict their legitimate activities.

The new Criminal Code classified "leading, participating in or financing unregistered or banned associations" as criminal offences. It also criminalized "unlawful interference" in the activities of state agencies by members of public associations and defined leaders of public associations as a separate category of offenders, providing for stiffer penalties for them for a number of crimes.

A working group set up by the Ministry of Culture was drafting a law regulating NGO activities that would establish legal grounds for channelling all state and non-state funding for NGOs through a special NGO set up by the government. NGOs were concerned this might limit their opportunities for independent fundraising.

FREEDOM OF EXPRESSION – MEDIA

Freedom of expression significantly deteriorated for independent media. In February, *Pravdivaya Gazeta* newspaper was closed down under a court ruling for minor transgressions. Social media and blogs were often restricted and internet-based resources were blocked by court decisions taken in closed proceedings, due to their supposedly extremist or otherwise illegal content.

KENYA

Republic of Kenya
Head of state and government: **Uhuru Muigai Kenyatta**

Attacks attributed to the Somali-based armed group, Al-Shabaab, increased. Police counter-terror operations resulted in several deaths and the arrest of hundreds of people. The authorities intensified measures to restrict and control the activities of civil society organizations. There were incidents of unlawful killing, rape, torture or other ill-treatment by the police. Violence against women and girls persisted.

BACKGROUND

Kenya's economy and security were affected by a number of violent attacks in north-eastern Kenya, in the capital, Nairobi, and the coastal towns of Mombasa and Lamu, which triggered the adoption of new security laws with wide-reaching human rights implications. Implementation of the devolved system of government continued although challenges remained including inconsistent policy, legal and institutional frameworks. County authorities demanded constitutional amendments to increase their share of national treasury resources. The trial of Deputy President William Samoei Ruto and journalist Joshua Arap Sang continued at the International Criminal Court while the Prosecutor withdrew charges against President Kenyatta.

COUNTER-TERROR AND SECURITY

Violent attacks increased, mostly attributed to Al-Shabaab, an armed group operating in Somalia. Al-Shabaab claimed the attacks were in retaliation for the continued presence of Kenya's armed forces in Somalia, as part of the African Union Mission to Somalia (AMISOM). Grenade and bomb attacks resulting in fatalities and serious injuries

occurred in various places including in a restaurant, a densely populated market and on commuter buses. The majority of the attacks took place in northeastern Kenya, Nairobi, Mombasa and Lamu.

On 23 March, gunmen opened fire in a Mombasa church during a service, killing six and injuring at least 15 people.

On 15 June, gunmen attacked the town of Mpeketoni in Lamu County, killing at least 48 people. The gunmen also burned 44 vehicles and about 26 buildings. At least 14 other people were killed in two separate attacks in nearby villages on 16 and 24 June. Al-Shabaab claimed responsibility for the attacks but the authorities blamed local politicians. The Governor of Lamu County was arrested and released on bail on suspicion of being involved in the killings, but investigations failed to gather sufficient evidence against him. An investigation by the Independent Policing Oversight Authority (IPOA) into police action around the attacks found that the police response was slow and disjointed. A dusk-to-dawn curfew imposed in Lamu town in the aftermath of the killings was lifted on 24 December.

On 22 November, gunmen attacked a bus in Mandera, northeastern Kenya, killing 28 passengers. The gunmen reportedly separated Muslims from non-Muslims before killing the latter. On 2 December, 36 miners were killed in another attack at a quarry in Koromei, Mandera County. Following the attacks, the Inspector General of Police resigned; the Cabinet Secretary of Interior and Co-ordination of National Government was sacked. Also in December, the government hastily and without meaningful public participation enacted a new security law, amending numerous provisions in 22 existing laws with far-reaching human rights implications. Among other things, it creates new criminal offences with harsh penalties, limits the rights of arrested and accused people, expands the powers of intelligence officers to arrest suspects and monitor communications, and caps the number of refugees in Kenya at 150,000. The law was enacted despite a chaotic and disorderly parliamentary sitting.

The police conducted a number of counter-terror operations during the year including in mosques believed to be recruiting and training young attendees to become jihadists. In February, seven people were reportedly shot dead while 129 were arrested when the police conducted an operation in a mosque in Mombasa. Most of those arrested were later released without charge. One man who was arrested during the operation has not been seen since.

In April, thousands of Somali refugees and asylum-seekers were arbitrarily arrested, harassed, extorted and ill-treated as part of a counter-terror operation known as "Usalama Watch" (see Somalia entry). Over five thousand individuals were forcibly relocated to refugee camps in northern Kenya and at least 359 others were expelled back to Somalia. In June, the High Court ruled that the forced relocation of refugees to camps was constitutional, contradicting a previous decision on the same matter. In July, the IPOA issued a report which concluded that, in addition to violating human rights, the operation was counter-productive as it engendered perceptions of ethnic profiling and discrimination among Somalis.

In November, the police conducted operations in four mosques in Mombasa. One person was shot dead during the operations while more than 300 were arrested. The police reported that they recovered grenades and other crude weapons from the mosques. The operations provoked violent clashes in Mombasa.

The Anti-Terror Police Unit continued to be accused by both local and international civil society organizations of human rights violations including extrajudicial killings and enforced disappearances. A number of Mombasa-based Muslim clerics were shot dead by unidentified assailants during the year; both radical and moderate clerics were targeted. On 1 April, a Muslim cleric accused by the police of recruiting youths into Al-Shabaab was gunned down in a Mombasa street. In June, an anti-jihad cleric and chairperson of the Council of Imams and Preachers of Kenya was shot dead at a mosque. In November a Muslim cleric supportive of government efforts against radicalization was shot dead.

INTERNATIONAL JUSTICE

The International Criminal Court (ICC) trial of Deputy President William Samoei Ruto and journalist Joshua Arap Sang for alleged crimes against humanity committed during the 2007/2008 post-election violence continued throughout the year. The trial was undermined by alleged witness intimidation and bribery, and the withdrawal of other witnesses. The Trial Chamber issued summonses to nine prosecution witnesses who no longer wished to appear voluntarily. By the end of the year, three of the nine witnesses had testified via video-link from an undisclosed location in Nairobi.

On 5 December, the ICC Prosecutor withdrew charges against President Kenyatta. He had been charged with crimes against humanity committed during the post-election violence. The Prosecutor explained that the evidence at her disposal was insufficient to prove President Kenyatta's alleged criminal responsibility beyond reasonable doubt. She stated that efforts by her office to gather relevant evidence had been hampered by the death of several key witnesses, intimidation of prosecution witnesses leading to the withdrawal of at least seven testimonies, and non-co-operation by the Kenyan government. On 3 December, while rejecting the Prosecutor's request for a further adjournment of the case, the ICC Trial Chamber ruled that the Kenyan government's conduct in the case fell short of the standard of good faith co-operation but declined to refer a formal finding of non-co-operation to the Assembly of States Parties.

The ICC arrest warrant issued for Walter Osapiri Barasa had not been executed at the end of the year.

The government continued its efforts to discredit and weaken the ICC. In March, Kenya submitted to the UN Secretary-General five proposed amendments to the Rome Statute of the ICC, including that Article 27 be amended to preclude the ICC from prosecuting heads of state and government while in office. In November, the Kenyan government requested the inclusion of a supplementary agenda item titled "Special session to discuss the conduct of the Court and the Office of the Prosecutor", to the provisional agenda of the 13th session of the Assembly of State Parties in December. The request was denied.

IMPUNITY – POST-ELECTION VIOLENCE

Perpetrators of crimes committed during the post-election violence remained unpunished at the national level. In February, the Director of Public Prosecutions announced that a review of more than 4,000 post-election investigation files had failed to identify any prosecutable cases due to lack of evidence. In March a group of internally displaced people protested outside State House against the government's failure to provide them with assistance. No concrete steps were taken to establish the International Crimes Division of the High Court or to implement the recommendations of the Truth, Justice and Reconciliation Commission.

Three civil cases filed by victims and civil society organizations challenging the failure of the government to address various violations committed during the post-election violence were still pending at the end of the year.

In October, an opposition political party submitted to Parliament a draft bill titled "The Post Election Violence Tribunal Bill – 2014". The draft bill proposed the establishment of a tribunal to try perpetrators of crimes against humanity committed during the post-election violence. Provisions in the draft bill included trials in the absence of the accused, the death penalty and posthumous convictions. The draft bill was pending at the end of the year.

POLICE AND SECURITY FORCES
Police reforms

In April, the National Police Service Commission Act was amended, subjecting the human resources functions of the National Police Service Commission (NPSC) to the authority of the Inspector General of Police. In June, the National Police Service Act was amended to make the Inspector General of Police responsible for all matters relating to the command and discipline of the police. The police operated without adequate resources and equipment. On 31 October, at least 19 police officers were ambushed and killed by armed bandits in Kapedo, Baringo County.

The vetting of police officers continued. At the end of November, the NPSC had vetted 198 police officers, 16 of whom were deemed unfit to serve in the force mainly for reasons related to corruption. The process was hampered by lack of finances, limited public participation, and the resignation of four key members of the vetting board. Local NGOs and the IPOA expressed concern that the process had failed to clean up the force and that it had not seriously taken into account the human rights record of police officers.

Human rights violations by police

There were incidents of unlawful killing, rape and torture or other ill-treatment by police.

In August, a 14-year-old girl was shot dead when eight police officers stormed her family's home ostensibly to arrest her uncle. Two police officers were subsequently charged with her murder.

In October, a woman who had gone to a police post to report an assault was reportedly raped by a police officer. The IPOA launched investigations into the incident.

During the year, at least two separate police county commanders issued public statements instructing police officers under their command to use lethal force against suspected terrorists. The Kenya National Commission on Human Rights and the IPOA condemned the instructions as unlawful.

CRACKDOWN ON CIVIL SOCIETY ORGANIZATIONS

The authorities intensified measures to restrict and control the activities of civil society organizations. In May, Parliament published a bill proposing amendments to the Public Benefits Organizations (PBO) Act. In October, an earlier proposal to limit foreign funding of NGOs to 15% was retabled in Parliament. In December, the government deregistered and froze the financial accounts of 510 NGOs that it said had not complied with the NGO law. Among these were 15 unnamed NGOs accused of financing terrorism. The government also issued a 21 days' notice to 10 international NGOs and two other local NGOs to submit audited financial accounts.

HOUSING RIGHTS – FORCED EVICTIONS

In February, a taskforce established in 2012 to develop an evictions and resettlement law presented a proposed bill to the Cabinet Secretary for Land, Housing and Urban Development. In March, the Cabinet Secretary issued a public statement pledging to expedite the enactment of an evictions law. By the end of the year, the draft bill had not been submitted to Parliament for debate.

In October, the High Court ordered the government to pay compensation of 33.6 million shillings (US$390,000) to residents of City Carton informal settlement in Nairobi, who were forcefully evicted from their homes in May 2013. The High Court ruled that the government was under an obligation to protect slum dwellers from forced eviction by third parties. By the end of the year, the government had not complied with a number of orders emanating from previous court decisions on the right to housing.

VIOLENCE AGAINST WOMEN AND GIRLS

Violence against women and girls, including rape and other forms of sexual violence,

persisted. Despite a 2011 law prohibiting female genital mutilation (FGM), the practice continued in several parts of the country including in northern Kenya and among the Maasai, Kisii and Kuria ethnic communities. In June, hundreds of women and men from the Maasai community held two separate demonstrations protesting against the prohibition of FGM. The police took action against government local administrators who were alleged accomplices in acts of FGM. In April, a chief was charged in court after his two daughters underwent FGM, while another was charged with failing to report acts of FGM carried out within his administrative area.

In November in Nairobi, there were at least five incidents of public stripping and groping of women deemed by mobs of men to be indecently dressed. In one incident a police officer was part of a group of men on a commuter bus who groped and threatened a woman with rape. The perpetrators of the incident were charged in court with a number of offences. Following a public demonstration on 17 November calling on the authorities to take swift action to prevent and punish acts of violence against women, the police formed an Anti-stripping Squad to monitor and investigate incidents of public stripping of women.

KOREA (DEMOCRATIC PEOPLE'S REPUBLIC OF)

Democratic People's Republic of Korea
Head of state: Kim Jong-un
Head of government: Pak Pong-ju

The UN released a comprehensive report on the human rights situation in the Democratic People's Republic of Korea (North Korea, DPRK), which gave details on the systematic violation of almost the entire range of human rights. Hundreds of thousands of people continued to be detained in prison camps and other detention facilities, many of them without being charged or tried for any internationally recognizable crime. Freedoms of expression, religion and movement, both within and outside the country, remained severely restricted. The fate of people forcibly disappeared was still unknown, despite the government admitting the involvement of state agents in the abduction of some individuals.

BACKGROUND

The third year of Kim Jong-un's rule started in December 2013 with the high-profile trial and execution of Jang Song-taek, vice-chairman of the National Defence Commission and uncle of Kim Jong-un. This was believed to be the beginning of a series of political purges in order to further consolidate Kim Jong-un's power, although there were no other confirmed executions of political opponents linked with Jang during 2014.

An officially illegal, but government-tolerated, private economy continued to expand, including privately operated food and clothing stalls. It was feared by observers that the apparent economic opening could create greater income disparities. It was not accompanied by an improvement in the general human rights situation.

The government attempted to bring in foreign exchange currency, including through tourism. Despite such efforts, the state remained highly sensitive to any actions by foreign visitors that were perceived to be spreading political or religious ideas not compatible with those promoted by the state. Freedom of information was limited and the internet was not publicly accessible. A national "intranet" was set up instead.

A rare display of accountability from the government was seen in May, when state media reported promptly the collapse of an apartment building in the capital, Pyongyang, that killed more than 300 people. Foreign media in Pyongyang reported that citizens had expressed their anger over the incident and the government issued an apology over faulty construction methods.

INTERNATIONAL SCRUTINY

The UN Commission of Inquiry on Human Rights in the Democratic People's Republic of Korea released its report in February.[1] The 372-page document presented a comprehensive review of "systematic, widespread and gross human rights violations" and concluded that many of these amounted to crimes against humanity.

The report was presented to the UN Human Rights Council in March, where a strong resolution was passed welcoming the report, which garnered support from a majority of Council member states.[2]

The DPRK underwent a second Universal Periodic Review (UPR) process in May. The government was more engaged than during its first UPR in 2010, and this time gave responses on which recommendations it supported, including those relating to the effective operation of humanitarian aid. However, the government refused to accept more than half of the recommendations, in particular those directed at co-operation with the Commission of Inquiry and the Special Rapporteur on the situation of human rights in the DPRK. It also rejected outright recommendations to close its political prison camps, or to allow foreign victims of enforced disappearance to return freely to their countries of origin.[3]

In December, the UN General Assembly passed a strong resolution recommending the referral of the human rights situation in the DPRK to the International Criminal Court.

ARBITRARY ARRESTS AND DETENTIONS

Hundreds of thousands of people remained detained in political prison camps and other detention facilities, where they were subject to systematic, widespread and gross human rights violations such as extrajudicial executions and torture and other ill-treatment, including beatings, long periods of forced hard labour without rest and deprivation of food.

Many of those held in political prison camps had not been convicted of any internationally recognizable crime, but were relatives of those deemed threatening to the administration. They were detained without a fair trial, through "guilt-by-association".

The government continued to deny the existence of political prison camps, even though satellite images showed not only their presence, but also ongoing expansion at some of the camps as of the end of 2013.

North Koreans as well as foreign citizens were subject to arbitrary detention after unfair trials. Kenneth Bae and Matthew Todd Miller, both US nationals, were convicted of "hostile acts" against the regime in 2013 and 2014 respectively. Before their release in November, they had begun serving terms of forced hard labour of 15 and six years respectively. In an interview with foreign media in August, Kenneth Bae spoke about the unfair trial he received as well as his deteriorating health while working in a labour camp.

FREEDOM OF RELIGION

The practice of any religion continued to be severely restricted. Both DPRK and foreign nationals reportedly received heavy punishments for exercising their freedom of religion, including detention in prison camps.[4]

John Short, an Australian missionary, was arrested for promoting his religious beliefs and was deported in March only after apologizing publicly. Kim Jung-wook, a missionary from South Korea, was detained for more than six months without access to a lawyer, before being convicted of setting up an underground church and spying. He was sentenced to forced hard labour for life.

Jeffrey Fowle, a tourist from the USA, was arrested in May for leaving a bible at a club in Chongjin. He was detained for more than five months without trial before being released in October.

FREEDOM OF EXPRESSION

Authorities continued to impose severe restrictions on the exercise of the right to freedoms of expression, opinion and peaceful assembly. There appeared to be no independent civil society organizations, newspapers or political parties. North Koreans were liable to be searched by authorities for the possession of foreign media materials, and could be punished for listening to, watching or reading such materials.

FREEDOM OF MOVEMENT

Border controls remained tight. The number of people arriving in South Korea after fleeing from the north remained low in 2012 and 2013 compared with previous years.

The difficulty of crossing the border was increased through enhanced surveillance technology according to media in South Korea, including the use of jamming equipment designed to stop citizens using Chinese cellular phones along the border. The use of mobile phones for citizens remained confined to a closed local network within North Korea.

A group of approximately 29 people, including a one-year-old baby, were forcibly returned to North Korea in early August after being detained in China. While it was not known whether they were charged for crossing the border illegally, they would face possible imprisonment and torture and other ill-treatment, including forced labour, if such charges were brought against them.[5]

ENFORCED DISAPPEARANCES

The UN Working Group on Enforced or Involuntary Disappearances asked the DPRK in August for confirmation regarding the fate of 47 people who were known to have been abducted on foreign soil by North Korean security agents and who subsequently disappeared. A majority of these were citizens of South Korea.

The government engaged in meetings with Japan in May to address the issue of abductions, and launched a special committee to reinvestigate cases of Japanese nationals abducted during the 1970s and 1980s. The initial report of the reinvestigation was, however, rejected by Japan as it contained no new information about the 12 Japanese nationals already officially admitted by North Korea as having been abducted from Japan by North Korean security agents.

RIGHT TO FOOD

The World Food Programme reported in September that the situation of food availability in North Korea was "severe". Despite improved harvests in the two previous years, a dry spell in 2014 brought food ration levels down from 410 to only 250 grams per person per day in August, which was widely seen as an indication of imminent shortage in food availability. Latest statistics revealed that rates of chronic malnutrition remained relatively high in 2013, affecting one in four children aged under five.

While North Korea received humanitarian assistance from the World Food Programme and other relief agencies, the government did not allow the agencies to extend assistance to some of the most vulnerable communities. Restrictions remained in place for those attempting to monitor delivery of food aid to targeted groups.

1. North Korea: UN Security Council must act on crimes against humanity (Press Release)
www.amnesty.org/en/articles/news/2014/02/north-korea-un-security-council-must-act-crimes-against-humanity/
2. North Korea: UN vote a positive step to end crimes against humanity (Press Release)
www.amnesty.org/en/articles/news/2014/03/north-korea-human-rights-council/
3. Urgent need for accountability and cooperation with the international community by North Korea (ASA 24/006/2014)
www.amnesty.org/en/library/info/ASA24/006/2014/en
4. North Korea: End persecution of Christians after reports US tourist detained (Press Release)
www.amnesty.org/en/articles/news/2014/06/north-korea-end-persecution-christians-after-reports-us-tourist-detained/
5. China: Further information: Families forcibly returned to North Korea (ASA 17/048/2014)
www.amnesty.org/en/library/info/ASA17/048/2014/en

KOREA (REPUBLIC OF)

Republic of Korea
Head of state: **Park Geun-hye**
Head of government: **Chung Hong-won**

The rights of workers were violated through the denial of freedom of association, the curtailment of legitimate collective action and, for migrant workers, exploitation under the Employment Permit System. The government increasingly restricted freedom of expression by using the National Security Law to intimidate and imprison people. Police blocked peaceful protests. At least 635 conscientious objectors remained in prison.

BACKGROUND

The second year of Park Geun-hye's term as president showed a regressive trend in the realization of human rights. Numerous concerns surfaced including barriers to freedoms of assembly and expression. Following the deaths of more than 300 people, many of them students, in the accidental sinking of the Sewol ferry in April, further concerns were raised on issues such as disaster response effectiveness and impartiality of investigations. Further concerns about government abuse of power were raised in two espionage cases when the National Intelligence Service was criticized for allegedly fabricating evidence.

MIGRANT WORKERS' RIGHTS

Migrant agricultural workers under the Employment Permit System (EPS) endured excessive working hours, underpayment, denial of their weekly paid rest day and annual leave, illegal subcontracting and poor living conditions. Many were also discriminated against at work due to their nationality. The exclusion of agricultural workers from the Labour Standards Act provisions on working hours, daily breaks and weekly paid rest days was discriminatory in effect as it disproportionately affected migrant workers. Many were unable to escape exploitative working conditions due to severe government restrictions on migrants' ability to change jobs as well as the exclusion by the Labour Standards Act of agricultural workers from legal protection.

Many migrants interviewed by Amnesty International had been coerced by their employers into working under harsh conditions amounting to forced labour, most commonly through threats and violence. Many had been recruited using deception for the purpose of exploitation, a situation that amounted to trafficking.

Migrant workers lodging complaints often had to continue working for their employers during investigations, thereby putting them at risk of further abuse. Those who left their workplace risked being reported to immigration authorities as "runaways" by their employers, and subjected to arrest and deportation.

The EPS discouraged migrant workers from making complaints and changing jobs for fear of losing the ability to extend their contract, and some officials actively dissuaded migrants from making formal complaints. Consequently, employers abusing migrant workers rarely faced legal sanctions.[1]

FREEDOM OF ASSOCIATION – TRADE UNIONS

Trade unions faced increasing restrictions. Several trade union leaders were criminally charged or even imprisoned for engaging in collective action and other legitimate trade union activities.

Kim Jung-woo, a former leader of the Ssangyong Motor branch of the Korean Metal Workers' Union, had been sentenced in 2013 to 10 months in prison for preventing municipal government officials from dismantling a protest site in the capital Seoul. He was released on bail in April 2014 after completing his original sentence, but faced an appeal by the prosecution seeking a heavier sentence.

The Ministry of Labour and Employment sought to deregister the Korean Teachers' and Education Workers' Union (KTU) in 2013, and this was affirmed through a ruling by the Seoul Administrative Court in June 2014. However, the Seoul High Court suspended execution of this ruling in September, pending an appeal.

FREEDOM OF EXPRESSION

The government continued its use of the National Security Law (NSL) to curtail freedom of expression. At least 32 people were charged for violations of the NSL in the first eight months of the year. This was less than in 2013, when 129 people were investigated or charged under the NSL, the highest number in a decade, but remained a matter of great concern.

Lee Seok-ki, a National Assembly member from the Unified Progressive Party (UPP), was imprisoned along with six other party members for "conspiracy to revolt", "inciting an insurrection", and activities deemed to violate the NSL. On appeal in August, the Seoul High Court dismissed the charges of "conspiracy to revolt", but upheld the other charges, and reduced the prison sentences to terms ranging from two to nine years.

The government also sought to disband the UPP before the Constitutional Court, which ruled in December that the party had violated the basic democratic order and disbanded the party. This was the first such request from the government since democratization in 1987 and the first time a party was disbanded since 1958.

FREEDOM OF ASSEMBLY

Since the ferry accident in April, more than 300 people were arrested in attempts by police to quell peaceful demonstrations expressing discontent over the government's response to the ferry sinking. Police blockades of street rallies continued for months following the accident.

In June, the police cracked down on a peaceful protest in the city of Miryang, injuring 14 protesters. Some 300 protesters, many of whom were elderly, were protesting against the construction of high-voltage electricity transmission towers, and demanding genuine consultation.

CONSCIENTIOUS OBJECTORS

At least 635 conscientious objectors remained in prison at the end of the year.

Members of the public voiced concerns about the system of compulsory military service following the deaths of two male conscripts, which revealed evidence of ongoing ill-treatment in the military.

Amnesty International, along with several other NGOs, submitted arguments in August in a case before the Constitutional Court addressing the right to conscientious objection to military service as derived from

the right to freedom of thought, conscience and religion.[2]

ARMS TRADE

South Korea exported substantial amounts of tear gas shells to countries where tear gas was used indiscriminately in riot control.[3] Following pressure from Amnesty International and other human rights groups, the government announced a halt to shipments of tear gas to Bahrain in January.[4]

South Korea signed the Arms Trade Treaty in 2013, but had yet to ratify the treaty and incorporate it into domestic legislation by the end of 2014.

1. Bitter Harvest: Exploitation and forced labour of migrant agricultural workers in South Korea (ASA 25/004/2014)
   www.amnesty.org/en/library/info/ASA25/004/2014/en
2. Korea: The right to conscientious objection to military service: amicus curiae opinion (POL 31/001/2014)
   www.amnesty.org/en/library/info/POL31/001/2014/en
3. South Korea: Open letter to the President on first anniversary of inauguration (ASA 25/001/2014)
   www.amnesty.org/en/library/info/ASA25/001/2014/en
4. South Korea suspends tear gas supplies to Bahrain (NWS 11/003/2014)
   www.amnesty.org/press-releases/2014/01/south-korea-suspends-tear-gas-supplies-bahrain/

KUWAIT

State of Kuwait
Head of state: al-Shaikh Sabah al-Ahmad al-Jaber al-Sabah
Head of government: al-Shaikh Jaber al-Mubarak al-Hamad al-Sabah

Peaceful criticism of the Amir, other state authorities or Islam remained criminalized. Those targeted for arrest, detention and prosecution included human rights and political reform activists. Authorities used a telecommunications law to prosecute and imprison critics who expressed dissent using social media, and curtailed the right to public assembly. The government continued to withhold nationality and citizenship rights from tens of thousands of Bidun people, and arbitrarily stripped several critics and members of their families of their Kuwaiti citizenship. Women faced discrimination in law and practice. Foreign migrant workers, who comprised over half of the population, lacked adequate protection under the law and were subject to discrimination, exploitation and abuse. The death penalty remained in force for a range of crimes; no executions were reported.

FREEDOM OF EXPRESSION

In April, the Public Prosecutor banned media discussion about a publicly available video recording that reportedly showed two former senior political figures discussing a plot to replace the Amir and take control of the government. The authorities stripped a media owner of his Kuwaiti nationality after his TV and radio station allegedly breached the media ban.

At least eight people were sentenced for comments they had made on social media, following prosecutions under Penal Code provisions that criminalized "insult" to the Amir and other state authorities and religion, and provisions of a 2001 law prohibiting the use of telecommunications facilities to disseminate criticism. Up to 10 others faced a cycle of prosecution, trial, conviction and appeal in connection with the expression of their views, mainly via the website Twitter. They included human rights activist and blogger Abdullah Fairouz, arrested in November 2013, who was sentenced in January to five years in prison for messages he posted on Twitter.[1] In July, an appeal court upheld a 10-year prison sentence imposed on blogger Hamad al-Naqi in 2012 for allegedly defaming religion and foreign leaders.

In July, the authorities arrested former parliamentarian Musallam al-Barrak, a vocal government critic, after he reportedly accused senior officials of bribery and corruption in a speech to a large crowd in June. He was detained for 10 days and then released to stand trial on charges of "insulting" the judiciary. His arrest prompted widespread protests and accusations that the police had used excessive force against protesters, which the government denied. He continued to face a number of expression-related prosecutions at the end of the year.

DEPRIVATION OF NATIONALITY

The government resorted to the new tactic of arbitrarily stripping some of its critics and their dependents of their Kuwaiti citizenship rights under provisions of the 1959 nationality law.[2] In July, the authorities stripped the nationality of Ahmed Jabr al-Shammari, owner of the *Al-Yawm* newspaper and TV channel, and four others, along with their dependents, rendering over 30 people stateless. The authorities revoked the citizenship of at least 10 others in August and a further 15 in September.

TORTURE AND OTHER ILL-TREATMENT

The authorities failed to independently investigate allegations of torture of detainees by security officials. In a letter to Amnesty International in September, the government denied that arbitrary arrests took place during demonstrations or that officials committed torture or ill-treatment.

Bidun human rights activist 'Abdulhakim al-Fadhli complained to an investigating prosecutor in February that police had beaten him in detention to force him to sign a "confession". The prosecutor failed to order a medical examination requested by 'Abdulhakim al-Fadhli or to take any other steps to investigate the alleged torture.

DISCRIMINATION – BIDUN

The government continued to deny Kuwaiti nationality – and the rights and benefits associated with it, including free education, free health care and the right to vote – to tens of thousands of Bidun, although a small number were officially recognized as Kuwaiti citizens.

In October 2012, the Prime Minister had assured Amnesty International that the government would resolve the issue of citizenship for Kuwait's Bidun residents within five years; at the end of 2014 that appeared unlikely.

Members of the Bidun community demonstrated to demand an end to discrimination, despite the ban on public gatherings by "non-citizens". Some demonstrations were dispersed by police, but the government denied using excessive force. Scores of Bidun continued to face trial on charges of illegal gathering or public order offences. Many trials were repeatedly postponed, but in September 67 were acquitted. The authorities also detained at least 15 Bidun activists, mostly on charges relating to public order offences or "illegal gathering".

WOMEN'S RIGHTS

Kuwaiti women enjoyed greater rights than women in most other Gulf region states, including rights to stand as candidates and vote in elections, but they were not accorded equality under the law with men. The law required that women have a male "guardian" in family matters, such as divorce, child custody and inheritance, and when receiving medical treatment.

MIGRANT WORKERS' RIGHTS

Migrant workers, who made up the majority of Kuwait's workforce, continued to face exploitation and abuse linked partly to the official *kafala* sponsorship system. Migrant domestic workers, mostly women from Asian countries, were especially vulnerable as they were excluded from forms of protection afforded to other workers by Kuwait's labour laws.

DEATH PENALTY

The death penalty remained in force for murder and other crimes. At least five people were sentenced to death; no executions were reported.

1. Urgent Action: Mother of activist at risk of deportation (MDE 17/007/2014) ua.amnesty.ch/urgent-actions/2014/09/224-14?ua_language=en
2. Kuwait: Halt the deplorable revocation of nationality of naturalized citizens (MDE 17/004/2014) www.amnesty.org/en/documents/MDE17/004/2014/en/

KYRGYZSTAN

Kyrgyz Republic
Head of state: **Almaz Atambaev**
Head of government: **Dzhoomart Otorbaev**
(replaced Zhantoro Satibaldiev in April)

The authorities failed to take effective measures to address allegations of torture and other ill-treatment and bring perpetrators to justice. No impartial and effective investigation took place into human rights violations, including crimes against humanity, committed during the June 2010 violence and its aftermath. MPs initiated draft laws that if adopted would have a negative impact on civil society. Prisoner of conscience Azimjan Askarov remained in detention.

TORTURE AND OTHER ILL-TREATMENT

Torture and other ill-treatment persisted despite a programme of independent monitoring of places of detention and the establishment of the National Centre for the Prevention of Torture and Other Cruel, Inhuman or Degrading Treatment.

On 20 December 2013, the UN Committee against Torture issued its concluding observations on the second periodic report on

Kyrgyzstan. The Committee expressed grave concern "about the ongoing and widespread practice of torture and ill-treatment of persons deprived of their liberty, in particular while in police custody to extract confessions". On 23 April 2014, the UN Human Rights Committee considered the second periodic report of the Kyrgyz Republic.

Both Committees highlighted the failure of the authorities to promptly, impartially and fully investigate allegations of torture and other ill-treatment and to prosecute perpetrators. They expressed concern about the lack of a full and effective investigation into the June 2010 violence.[1] The Committees also urged Kyrgyzstan to address these concerns by taking immediate and effective measures to prevent acts of torture and ill-treatment, by tackling impunity, prosecuting perpetrators and conducting investigations into all allegations of torture and other ill-treatment, including in cases related to the June 2010 violence.

On 16 June 2014, the Jalal-Abad regional human rights organization Spravedlivost (Justice) recorded two incidents of torture during a monitoring visit to the Jalal-Abad temporary detention centre. A medical practitioner, who was part of the monitoring group, documented the signs of torture. One detainee alleged that police officers had beaten him with hands and fists and a book, and put a plastic bag over his head. He was handcuffed to a radiator until the next day. He suffered concussion as a result of the ill-treatment. Another detainee alleged that police officers hit him in the larynx, kicked him in the stomach and beat his head with a book. Spravedlivost submitted complaints to the Jalal-Abad city prosecutor. After conducting an initial check and ordering two forensic medical examinations, the city prosecutor nevertheless refused to open criminal investigations into these allegations.

In 2014 the European Court of Human Rights issued three judgments against Russia, in which it stated that if ethnic Uzbek applicants were to be extradited to Kyrgyzstan, they would be at risk of torture or other ill-treatment.

IMPUNITY

Criminal investigations into allegations of torture were rare. In the first half of 2014, the Prosecutor General's Office registered 109 complaints, but only in nine cases were criminal investigations initiated; of these only three went to trial. Trials were ongoing at the end of the year.

The media reported that on 26 November 2013, the Sverdlovsk District Court of Bishkek handed down the first ever conviction for torture under Article 305-1 of the Criminal Code. Police officer Adilet Motuev was sentenced to six years' imprisonment. The Court found that he had illegally brought a man to a police station after accusing him of stealing a mobile phone. Adilet Motuev threatened the man and forced him to confess to the theft by squeezing the handcuffs and putting a plastic bag on his head and suffocating him. However, in 2014 the Court of Second Instance acquitted Adilet Motuev of all torture charges and changed the sentence to two years' imprisonment for unauthorized conduct of an investigation.

The authorities failed to take any steps to fairly and effectively investigate the June 2010 violence and its aftermath in the cities of Osh and Jalal-Abad. Lawyers defending ethnic Uzbeks detained in the context of the violence continued to be targeted for their work, threatened and physically attacked, even in the courtroom, with no accountability for the perpetrators.

PRISONERS OF CONSCIENCE

On 3 September 2014, the Supreme Court once again turned down an appeal lodged by Azimjan Askarov's lawyer to re-investigate the case against him. Earlier in the year, Bishkek City Court had annulled the ruling by Bishkek District Court that the case must be reviewed on the basis that the defence had presented new evidence.

FREEDOM OF EXPRESSION AND ASSOCIATION

Civil society activists dealing with human rights issues reported pressure from the authorities because of their work, resulting in a heightened sense of insecurity among them.

In May 2014, the Ministry of Justice proposed amendments to NGO legislation that would abolish the right to establish NGOs without legal status. If passed, the amendments would criminalize the activities of all unregistered NGOs. Some deputies called for Parliament to push through the adoption of a law similar to that passed in Russia requiring NGOs to adopt the stigmatizing label of "foreign agents" if they receive foreign funds and engage in "political" activities. In November, the parliamentary Committee on Human Rights, Constitutional Law and State Structure recommended that the proposed amendments be withdrawn.

DISCRIMINATION

The UN Human Rights Committee expressed concerns about the lack of comprehensive anti-discrimination legislation prohibiting discrimination on grounds such as race, language, disability and ethnic origin.

On 15 October, Parliament passed in its first reading a draft law prohibiting the promotion of so-called non-traditional sexual relations, thus increasing the vulnerability of groups defending the rights of sexual minorities. The proposed amendments would criminalize any action aimed at creating a positive attitude to non-traditional sexual relationships and would restrict freedom of expression and the right to peaceful assembly.

Ethnic Uzbeks in the south of Kyrgyzstan continued to be vulnerable to physical attacks based on their ethnic origin. However, the authorities qualified these attacks as "petty hooliganism", and did not fully and impartially investigate them as alleged hate crimes.

On 4 August 2014, ethnic Uzbek Kabulzhan Osmonov needed emergency medical treatment for injuries inflicted by a group of men, described by eyewitnesses as ethnic Kyrgyz, who assaulted and beat him unconscious in an unprovoked attack at his place of work in Osh. They had addressed him as "sart", a derogatory term indicating Uzbek ethnicity. Kabulzhan Osmonov reported the attack to his local police station but it was not until the case attracted media coverage that a criminal investigation was opened. Following this, local prosecutors and police pressured Kabulzhan Osmonov to withdraw his complaint.

---

1. Will there ever be justice? Kyrgyzstan's failure to investigate June 2010 violence and its aftermath (EUR 58/001/2013) www.amnesty.org/en/library/info/EUR58/001/2013/en.

LAOS

Lao People's Democratic Republic
Head of state: **Choummaly Sayasone**
Head of government: **Thongsing Thammavong**

State control over the media, judiciary and political and social institutions continued to severely restrict freedom of expression, association and peaceful assembly. Lack of openness and a scarcity of information made independent monitoring of the human rights situation difficult. The enforced disappearance of a prominent member of civil society was unresolved at the end of the year. At least two prisoners of conscience remained imprisoned. Although Laos is abolitionist in practice, the death penalty was retained as a mandatory punishment for some drug offences.

BACKGROUND

The controversy over the building of large hydropower dams continued. Dissatisfaction within the country by those forced to relocate was reported, with some communities challenging loss of land and inadequate or unpaid compensation. In August Laos announced a temporary suspension of construction and a six-month consultation on its second major dam on the River Mekong following concerns raised by neighbouring countries; the consultation process was reportedly flawed and work on the dam continued. Environmental groups claimed that the Xayaburi and Don Sahong hydropower dams would impact the food security of around 60 million people downstream. A further nine dams were planned.

In November Laos submitted its national report ahead of its review under the UN Universal Periodic Review in January/February 2015. The report failed to adequately address key human rights concerns raised during the first review in May 2010.

New proposed guidelines for the operation and activities of international NGOs working on development projects were widely criticized for their heavy approval and reporting procedures. Similarly, there was concern that proposed amendments to the 2009 law regulating local associations would place further restrictions on civil society groups.

FREEDOM OF EXPRESSION

Tight restrictions on freedoms of expression, association and peaceful assembly were maintained. Draft laws and a decree to control the use of the internet and social media were completed by the end of the year. They included the Cybercrime Law and a Prime Ministerial Decree on management of information through the internet. The Decree enacted aimed to prevent circulation of criticism of the government and its policies. Users of Facebook were warned not to post information that might "disrupt social order and undermine security".

Two prisoners of conscience held since October 1999 for exercising their rights to freedom of expression and peaceful assembly by attempting to hold a peaceful protest

continued to serve 20-year prison terms. The authorities stated that two ethnic Hmong imprisoned in 2003 after a grossly unfair trial for helping two foreign journalists gather information were released early: Thao Moua in 2013 and Pa Fue Khang in May 2014. This could not be independently confirmed.

ENFORCED DISAPPEARANCES

A prominent member of civil society, Sombath Somphone,[1] remained disappeared since he was abducted outside a police post in the capital, Vientiane, in December 2012. During the year, only one vague public statement was made by the police about their investigation and no information was provided to the family. This compounded fears that the failure to properly investigate Sombath Somphone's abduction or to attempt to locate him indicated state complicity in his disappearance, which undermined the development of an active and confident civil society.[2]

---

1. Laos: Caught on camera – the enforced disappearance of Sombath Somphone (ASA 26/002/2013)
   www.amnesty.org/en/library/info/ASA26/002/2013/en

2. Laos: Seeking justice for "disappearance" victim, Sombath Somphone (ASA 26/001/2014)
   www.amnesty.org/en/library/info/ASA26/001/2014/en

LATVIA

Republic of Latvia
Head of state: **Andris Berzins**
Head of government: **Laimdota Straujuma**

Lesbian, gay, bisexual, transgender and intersex (LGBTI) people were inadequately protected against hate crimes. While some positive legislative steps were taken in 2013, the number of stateless people living in the country and being excluded from political rights remained high.

RIGHTS OF LESBIAN, GAY, BISEXUAL, TRANSGENDER AND INTERSEX PEOPLE

In September, the Parliament adopted amendments to legislation on hate crime. However, sexual orientation and gender identity were not included among the explicitly protected grounds in the revised hate crime provisions in the Criminal Code. Criminal law punished incitement to hatred and violence based on race, ethnicity, nationality, religion, disability, age and sex. Only racist motives were regarded as aggravating circumstances.

In 2013, the police recorded 22 cases of violence and incitement to hatred that were motivated by racism or xenophobia. The Latvian NGO MOZAIKA reported four cases of physical attacks against LGBTI people and one case of assault against a gay man with a disability.

On 18 September, the Parliament voted to pass an amendment to the Children's Rights Protection law requiring sexuality education in schools to be based on "traditional family values" and the concept of "marriage" defined as being between a man and a woman only. At the end of the year, the final adoption of the amendment was pending.

DISCRIMINATION – STATELESS PERSONS

According to the UN refugee agency UNHCR, 267,789 people remained stateless within the country as of January 2014.

On 1 October 2013, amendments to the Citizenship Law – aimed at simplifying the procedure for granting citizenship to a child born after 21 August 1991 to a non-citizen or stateless person – were adopted. In April, the UN Human Rights Committee expressed concerns over the high number of stateless people who continued to live in the country without access to political rights, while acknowledging progress in this area.

TORTURE AND OTHER ILL-TREATMENT

In December 2013, the UN Committee against Torture highlighted that the definition of torture included in Article 24 did not contain all the elements set out in the Convention against Torture and created loopholes for impunity. The Committee expressed concern that torture was not defined as a specific criminal offence in the Criminal Code and that some acts of torture or complicity in perpetrating acts of torture were subject to a 10-year statute of limitations.

The Committee also pointed to allegations of violence and ill-treatment perpetrated by law enforcement agents and highlighted the absence of an independent mechanism to investigate such allegations.

WOMEN'S RIGHTS

Domestic violence was not defined as a specific crime. In December, the UN Committee against Torture expressed concern over the absence of protection measures and the inadequate provision of shelters for victims of domestic violence.

REFUGEES AND ASYLUM-SEEKERS

In April, the UN Human Rights Committee expressed concern that the detention of asylum-seekers, including those as young as 14, was not just used as a measure of last resort. The Committee noted that the non-suspensive effect of appeals of negative decisions under the accelerated asylum procedure increased the risk of individuals being returned to countries where they were at risk of serious human rights violations or abuses.

LEBANON

Lebanese Republic
Head of state: **vacant since May, when Michel Suleiman's term ended**
Head of government: **Tammam Salam**

Pressures generated by the armed conflict in neighbouring Syria continued. There were new reports of torture and other ill-treatment of detainees. Lebanon hosted more than 1.2 million refugees from Syria but took steps to restrict the entry of refugees from Syria including Palestinians. Palestinian refugees long resident in Lebanon continued to face discrimination. Women remained subject to discrimination in law and in practice, and were inadequately protected against sexual and other violence. Foreign migrant workers, particularly women domestic workers, faced exploitation and other abuse. More than two dozen men faced prosecution for alleged consensual same-sex conduct. Some progress was made in clarifying cases of enforced disappearance dating back decades. The death penalty remained in force; there were no executions. The trial in their absence of five people in connection with the assassination of former Prime Minister Rafic Hariri opened before the Special Tribunal for Lebanon. Syrian government forces and armed groups based in Syria carried out indiscriminate attacks along the border.

BACKGROUND

Political infighting resulted in failure to agree a new President to replace Michel Suleiman, whose term of office ended in May. In February, however, the rival alliances agreed to form a national unity government with Tammam Salam as Prime Minister.

Lebanon avoided being drawn fully into the armed conflict in Syria, despite political, religious and social divisions, the continuing influx of refugees from Syria, and the participation of some Lebanese persons, notably members of Hezbollah, in the Syrian conflict. However, the conflict remained an ever-present threat.

Political tension remained high throughout the year, exacerbated by the Syrian conflict. By the end of the year, Lebanon hosted more than 1.15 million Syrian refugees and around 50,000 Palestinian refugees from Syria, swelling the population by a quarter and straining the country's resources. Tensions related to the conflict sparked repeated bouts of violence, especially in Tripoli, causing scores of deaths. The Syrian army periodically shelled the Bekaa valley and other areas inside Lebanon's border, and armed groups fired rockets from Syria into Lebanon's eastern border region, where abductions were also rife. In August, members of the Islamic State (IS) armed group posted videos on the internet showing them beheading two Lebanese soldiers whom they had taken hostage in fighting around Arsal, a Lebanese border town briefly seized by IS and other armed groups including Jabhat al-Nusra, who reportedly executed two other hostages in September and December respectively. A series of bomb attacks in Beirut and elsewhere also appeared to be connected to the Syrian conflict.

TORTURE AND OTHER ILL-TREATMENT

There were reports of torture and other ill-treatment of detained suspects. One detainee held by General Security in May reported after his release that interrogators had beaten him on his hands and legs with electric cable, trodden on and verbally insulted him. The authorities failed to undertake credible investigations into allegations of torture, including those made by a boy aged 15 and other people detained after clashes between the Lebanese army and armed groups in June 2013 in the Sidon area.

REFUGEES AND ASYLUM-SEEKERS

Refugees faced restrictions on their right to seek asylum and other rights. Lebanon was not a party to the UN Refugee Convention or its 1967 Protocol.

At the end of the year, according to UNHCR, the UN refugee agency, and UNWRA, the UN agency for Palestinian refugees, Lebanon was hosting more than 1.2 million refugees from Syria. In May, the government effectively closed the border to most Palestinians entering from Syria, and announced in June that it would only allow the entry of Syrian refugees from areas bordering Lebanon. In October, the authorities brought in further restrictions and asked UNHCR to stop registering refugees except for humanitarian cases. New regulations announced on 31 December required Syrians to apply for one of six types of entry visa in order to enter Lebanon. Instances of Syrian refugees and Palestinian refugees from Syria being sent back to Syria, in violation of international law, were documented.

The high cost of renewing annual residency permits, combined with opaque policies for the renewal of permits for refugees from Syria, led many refugees to become irregular in status, placing them at risk of arrest, detention and deportation. Some municipalities subjected refugees to curfews that limited their freedom of movement, prevented refugees from establishing informal tented settlements, or imposed additional taxes on local landlords who rented property to them. The Lebanese army and the Internal Security Forces also dismantled some informal tented settlements, ostensibly on security grounds.

The presence of so many refugees put Lebanon's health, education and other resources under enormous strain. This was exacerbated by inadequate international funding, and left many refugees unable to access adequate health care, shelter, education and other services.

Thousands of Palestinian long-term refugees continued to live in camps and informal gatherings in Lebanon, often in deprived conditions. They faced discriminatory laws and regulations, for example denying them the right to inherit property, the right to work in around 20 professions, and other basic rights.

WOMEN'S RIGHTS

Women faced discrimination in law and in practice. Personal status laws regulating issues such as marriage prevented Lebanese women with foreign spouses passing their nationality to their children. In April, a new law specifically criminalized domestic violence for the first time. Among other deficiencies, it failed to criminalize marital rape, although it provided for the establishment of temporary shelters and measures to strengthen police and prosecutors' effectiveness in addressing domestic violence.

MIGRANT WORKERS' RIGHTS

Migrant workers faced exploitation and abuse, particularly women domestic workers whose rights at work – including to fixed days off, rest periods, wages and humane conditions – were not protected by law, leaving them vulnerable to physical, sexual and other abuse by employers. Domestic workers were employed under contracts tying them to employers acting as their "sponsors", under conditions that facilitated abuse.

Employers frequently retained possession of workers' passports to prevent them from leaving abusive working conditions. In June, for the first time, a judge ordered an employer to return a domestic worker's passport, ruling that its retention by the employer violated the worker's freedom of movement.

RIGHTS OF LESBIAN, GAY, BISEXUAL, TRANSGENDER AND INTERSEX PEOPLE

Article 534 of the Penal Code, which prohibited sexual intercourse "contrary to the order of nature" was used to prosecute various consensual sexual activities, including sex between men. In January a judge ruled that Article 534 was not applicable in the case of a transgender woman having sexual relations with men. In August, the authorities arrested 27 men at a Beirut bath house and charged them with offences under Article 534 and provisions relating to "public decency" and prostitution.

In January, five men arrested on suspicion of consensual same-sex sexual activity were reported to have been subjected to anal examinations by a doctor, despite the Lebanese Order of Physicians declaring in 2012 that it was impermissible for doctors to carry out such examinations, which violate the international prohibition of torture and other ill-treatment, and a circular from the Minister of Justice in the same year, that called on public prosecutors to cease this practice.

INTERNATIONAL JUSTICE
Special Tribunal for Lebanon

The trial of four defendants accused in connection with the assassination of former Lebanese Prime Minister Rafic Hariri in 2005 opened in January before the Special Tribunal for Lebanon (STL) in the Netherlands. The four defendants, and a fifth whose trial was joined to theirs by the STL in February, all remained at large and were tried in their absence. In April, the STL brought contempt charges against two Lebanese journalists and their respective media outlets for disclosing confidential information about witnesses in the trial of the five accused.

IMPUNITY – ENFORCED DISAPPEARANCES AND ABDUCTIONS

The fate of thousands who were forcibly disappeared, abducted or otherwise unlawfully deprived of their liberty during and after Lebanon's 1975-1990 civil war, mostly remained undisclosed. In March, however, the Shura Council ruled that the full, as yet unpublished, report of the 2000 Official Committee of Inquiry to Investigate the Fate of Kidnapped and Missing Persons in Lebanon should be made available to the families of those missing. After the dismissal of appeals against this decision, the full report was provided to a lawyer representing the families in September.

Lebanon signed the International Convention against enforced disappearánce in 2007 but had yet to ratify it.

DEATH PENALTY

Courts continued to impose death sentences for murder and terrorism-related crimes, including some in the absence of the defendants. No executions had been carried out since 2004.

LIBYA

State of Libya
Head of state: Disputed (Agila Saleh Essa Gweider, President of the House of Representatives, replaced Nuri Abu Sahmain, President of the General National Congress in August)
Head of government: Disputed (Abdallah al-Thinni replaced Ali Zeidan in March; Ahmad Matiq briefly replaced Abdallah al-Thinni in May in a disputed vote ruled unconstitutional; Abdallah al-Thinni replaced Ahmad Matiq in June)

Militias and other armed forces committed possible war crimes, other serious violations of international humanitarian law and human rights abuses. They killed or injured hundreds of civilians and destroyed and damaged civilian infrastructure and objects in indiscriminate shelling of civilian areas in Benghazi, Tripoli, Warshafana, Zawiya, the Nafusa Mountains and elsewhere. Libya Dawn forces, Zintan Brigades and Warshafana militias abducted civilians based on their origin or political affiliation, tortured and otherwise ill-treated detainees, and in some cases summarily killed captured fighters. Islamist forces affiliated with the Shura Council of Benghazi Revolutionaries also abducted civilians and summarily killed scores of captured soldiers. Operation Dignity forces, which gained support of the interim government based in

Tobruk, carried out air strikes in residential areas causing damage to civilian objects and resulting in civilian casualties, tortured or otherwise ill-treated some detained civilians and fighters, and were responsible for several summary killings. Political killings were common and carried out with impunity; hundreds of security officials, state employees, religious leaders, activists, judges, journalists and rights activists were assassinated. The trial of 37 officials from the rule of Mu'ammar al-Gaddafi began amid serious due process concerns; torture remained rampant; journalists were targeted for their reporting, and assaults against foreign nationals increased. Impunity, including for past human rights violations and abuses, remained entrenched.

BACKGROUND

Following months of deepening political polarization and crisis over the legitimacy and mandate of the General National Congress (GNC), Libya's first elected parliament, the country descended into chaos as Benghazi, Derna, Tripoli, Warshafana, the Nafusa Mountains and other areas became engulfed in armed conflicts along political, ideological, regional and tribal lines.

Tensions were high at the time of February elections for a Constitution Drafting Assembly (CDA), tasked with devising a new Constitution. The CDA elections were marred by violence, a boycott by some ethnic minorities, and a low allocation of seats for women. By the end of the year, the CDA had released its preliminary recommendations and opened them for public consultation.

In May, retired army General Khalifa Haftar launched Operation Dignity, a military offensive with the stated aim of fighting terrorism, in Benghazi, against a coalition formed of Ansar al-Sharia and other Islamist armed groups (later named the Shura Council of Benghazi Revolutionaries). Initially denounced by the authorities, Operation Dignity, which subsequently spread to Derna, gained support from the new government

that took office following elections in June for a House of Representatives (HOR) that replaced the GNC. These elections, also marred by violence and a low turnout, resulted in a defeat for Islamist parties.

In July, a coalition of predominantly Misratah, Zawiya and Tripoli-based militias launched a military offensive, Libya Dawn, in the name of protecting the "17 February Revolution" against rival militias from Zintan and Warshafana, affiliated to the liberal and federalist parties dominating the HOR, which they accused of carrying out a counter-revolution alongside Operation Dignity. In August, the HOR relocated due to insecurity in Tripoli, establishing its base at Tobruk, amid a boycott by 30 of its members. It recognized Operation Dignity as a legitimate military operation led by the Libyan army, declared Libya Dawn forces and Ansar al-Sharia terrorist groups, and called for foreign intervention to protect civilians and state institutions. Aircraft from the United Arab Emirates flying from Egyptian airbases reportedly carried out air strikes on Libya Dawn forces as they fought to win control of Tripoli International Airport, which they achieved on 23 August, forced the Zintan Brigades from the capital, and seized control of state institutions there. The fighting and associated insecurity, including attacks on foreign diplomats and staff of international organizations, led the UN Support Mission in Libya (UNSMIL), whose mandate the UN Security Council renewed in March, foreign embassies and international organizations to suspend their operations in Tripoli and evacuate staff. Bombings and other attacks targeted government buildings and public places throughout the year.

After capturing Tripoli, Libya Dawn forces reconvened the GNC, which appointed a new Prime Minister and National Salvation Government (NSG). The NSG claimed that it had taken charge of most state institutions in the west, in opposition to the HOR government in Tobruk.

On 6 November, the Supreme Court issued a ruling that invalidated the elections for the HOR. The Tobruk-based government, recognized by the UN and backed by most of the international community, rejected the ruling, alleging that judges had been threatened by Libya Dawn. Armed clashes between rival tribes continued in Sabha and Obari in southwest Libya leading to a worsening of the humanitarian situation. Derna, an eastern city, was controlled by Islamist armed groups which enforced a strict interpretation of Shari'a law (Islamic law) and committed serious human rights abuses. In October, one armed group based in Derna, the Shura Council of Islamic Youth, declared allegiance to the Islamic State armed group fighting in Syria and Iraq.

INTERNAL ARMED CONFLICT

Warring parties in the east and west of Libya carried out indiscriminate attacks resulting in hundreds of civilian casualties and damage to civilian buildings and infrastructure including hospitals, homes, mosques, businesses, farms, power stations, airports, roads and a large fuel storage facility. They fired artillery, mortars, GRAD rockets and anti-aircraft weapons from and into residential areas. Operation Dignity forces carried out air strikes in Benghazi, Derna, Tripoli, Zuara, Bir al-Ghanem and Misratah, at times in residential areas, reportedly killing and injuring civilians and damaging civilian buildings. Zintan Brigades allegedly used antipersonnel mines around Tripoli International Airport.

The Libya Dawn attack on Zintan Brigades protecting Tripoli International Airport damaged several buildings and aircraft, according to officials. In December, a rocket hit a large oil tank at al-Sider port resulting in a fire and destroying up to 1.8 million barrels of crude oil.

With some exceptions, militias, army units and armed groups showed disregard for civilian life, objects and infrastructure and failed to take the necessary precautions to avoid or minimize civilian casualties and damage. Heavy fighting in residential areas caused disruption to health care, notably in Warshafana and Benghazi, where patients had to be evacuated from hospitals. Shortages of fuel, electricity, food and medicine were reported across Libya.

In Warshafana and Tripoli, Libya Dawn forces looted and burned civilian homes and other property on the basis of the owner's origin or political affiliation. Armed groups denied access for humanitarian relief in Obari and obstructed the evacuation of the wounded in Kikla.

UNHCR, the UN refugee agency, estimated that almost 395,000 people were internally displaced by the conflict between mid-May and mid-November. The Tawargha community, displaced since 2011, suffered further displacement and militia attacks; many sought shelter in municipal parks and car parks.

Armed forces on all sides carried out reprisal abductions, holding civilians solely on account of their origin or perceived political affiliation, often as hostages to secure prisoner exchanges. Both Libya Dawn forces and armed groups affiliated with the Zintan-Warshafana coalition tortured and otherwise ill-treated captured fighters and civilians they abducted, using electric shocks, stress positions, and denial of food, water and adequate washing facilities. Captured fighters were subjected to summary killings by all warring parties. In Benghazi, forces affiliated with the Shura Council of Benghazi Revolutionaries abducted civilians and carried out summary killings, including beheadings of captured soldiers and purported supporters of Operation Dignity. Groups aligned with Operation Dignity forces burned and destroyed scores of homes and other property of perceived Islamists; detained civilians on account of their political affiliation; and carried out several acts of torture and other ill-treatment and several summary killings.

UNLAWFUL KILLINGS

Hundreds of individuals, including security officials, state employees, religious leaders, activists, journalists, judges and prosecutors were killed in politically motivated assassinations in Benghazi, Derna and Sirte allegedly by Islamist armed groups. None of those responsible were held to account. In May, gunmen shot dead an International Red Cross delegate in Sirte.

In June, human rights lawyer and activist Salwa Bughaighis was shot dead in her home after she gave a media interview in which she accused armed groups of undermining parliamentary elections. In July unidentified assailants killed former GNC member Fariha Barkawi in Derna. On 19 September, known as Black Friday, at least 10 individuals, including two youth activists, were killed by unidentified assailants.

Two public execution-style killings, as well as public floggings, were carried out by the Shura Council of Islamic Youth, an armed group controlling Derna which established an Islamic Court there. In August, an Egyptian man accused of theft and murder was shot dead at a stadium in Derna. In November, three activists were beheaded in Derna following their abduction, allegedly by an Islamist armed group. In December, the Islamic Court issued a warning to current and former employees of the Ministries of the Interior, Justice and Defence.

FREEDOMS OF EXPRESSION, ASSOCIATION AND ASSEMBLY

The GNC tightened restrictions on freedoms of expression, association and assembly. Decree 5/2014, adopted by the GNC in January, banned satellite television stations from broadcasting views deemed "hostile to the 17 February Revolution", while decree 13/2014 empowered authorities to suspend the scholarships of students and salaries of state employees abroad who engaged in "activities hostile to the 17 February Revolution". Law 5/2014 amended Article 195 of the Penal Code to criminalize insults to

officials, the state's emblem and flag, and any act perceived as "an attack against the 17 February Revolution".

In January, a court sentenced an engineer to a three-year prison term for participating in a June 2011 protest in London, UK, against NATO's involvement in the Libyan conflict and allegedly publishing false information about Libya.

In November, newspaper editor Amara al-Khattabi was sentenced to five years in prison for insulting public officials, barred from practising journalism and stripped of his civil rights for the duration of the sentence and ordered to pay heavy fines.[1]

Militias increased their attacks on the media, abducting scores of journalists and subjecting others to physical assaults or other ill-treatment, arbitrary detention, threats and assassination attempts. At least four journalists were unlawfully killed, including newspaper editor Muftah Abu Zeid, who was shot dead by unidentified armed men in Benghazi in May. In August, Libya Dawn forces in Tripoli destroyed and burned the premises of two TV stations, Al-Assema and Libya International.

Scores of journalists, human rights defenders and activists fled abroad because of the threat posed to them by militias. In September, Libya Dawn forces reportedly raided the offices of the National Commission for Human Rights and removed its archive of individual complaints, raising concerns of reprisals against victims of abuses.

. In November, the National Council for Human Rights and Civil Liberties was closed, reportedly by Libya Dawn forces, amid intimidation of its members.

JUSTICE SYSTEM

The justice system remained paralyzed by violence and lawlessness, hampering investigations into abuses. In March, courts suspended work in Derna, Benghazi and Sirte amid threats and attacks against judges and prosecutors. The Ministry of Justice exercised only nominal control over many detention facilities holding perceived Mu'ammar al-Gaddafi loyalists.

A deadline set by the Law on Transitional Justice and extended by the GNC, to charge or release all detainees held in relation to the 2011 conflict by 2 April, was not met. As of March, only 10% of the 6,200 detainees held in prisons under the Ministry of Justice had been tried, while hundreds continued to be held without charge or trial in poor conditions. Release orders remained unimplemented due to militia pressure.

Delays in the processing of cases of perceived al-Gaddafi loyalists held since 2011 were exacerbated by the renewed conflicts as shelling prevented the transfer of detainees for trial. Family visits to prisons were suspended in several cities, prompting concern for the detainees' safety.

The trial of 37 former officials from Mu'ammar al-Gaddafi's rule began in March amid serious due process concerns. Defence lawyers were denied access to some evidence, given insufficient time to prepare, and were intimidated. Saif al-Islam al-Gaddafi, one of Mu'ammar al-Gaddafi's sons and the main defendant, appeared in court only by video link as he remained in militia custody in Zintan, casting doubt on the court's authority over him. Authorities controlling al-Hadba Prison complex, which hosts the courtroom, denied access to some independent trial observers including Amnesty International.

A video of the "confessions" of another of Mu'ammar al-Gaddafi's sons, Saadi al-Gaddafi, was broadcast on Libyan television following his extradition from Niger and imprisonment at al-Hadba. Prison authorities interrogated him without access to a lawyer, and denied access to him by UNSMIL, Amnesty International and others, despite the prosecution authorizing these visits.

In Zawiya, west of Tripoli, scores of al-Gaddafi loyalists were detained for periods of up to 18 months beyond the date they should have been released, as sentencing did not take into account the period of arbitrary detention by militias. Torture and other ill-treatment remained widespread in both state and militia prisons, and deaths in custody caused by torture continued to be reported.

IMPUNITY

The authorities failed to carry out meaningful investigations into alleged war crimes and serious human rights abuses committed during the 2011 armed conflict or to address the legacy of past violations under Mu'ammar al-Gaddafi's rule, including the 1996 mass killing of over 1,200 detainees in Abu Salim Prison.

The authorities failed to surrender Saif al-Islam al-Gaddafi to the International Criminal Court (ICC) to face prosecution on charges of crimes against humanity. In May, the ICC Appeals Chamber confirmed Libya's legal obligation to transfer him to ICC custody.

In July, the ICC Appeals Chamber upheld a decision that Abdallah al-Senussi, a former military intelligence chief accused of crimes against humanity, could be tried domestically. Serious concerns remained, however, about violations of his due process rights, including restricted access to a lawyer of his choice.

The ICC Prosecutor initiated a second case and began compiling evidence against suspects residing abroad in accordance with a 2013 agreement with the Libyan government on prosecutions of former al-Gaddafi officials. Despite expressing concern in November that "crimes within the ICC jurisdiction are being committed", the ICC Prosecutor failed to begin investigations into crimes committed by militias.

In August, UN Security Council Resolution 2174 extended the scope for international sanctions to include those responsible for "planning, directing, or committing" violations of international human rights law or international humanitarian law, or human rights abuses, in Libya.

WOMEN'S RIGHTS

Women continued to face discrimination in law and practice, and were inadequately protected against gender-based violence;

reports of sexual harassment increased. A decree providing for reparations to victims of sexual violence by state agents under Mu'ammar al-Gaddafi's rule and during the 2011 conflict was adopted but remained largely unimplemented.

Women candidates to the CDA faced difficulties in campaigning and registering to vote.

Women's rights activists faced intimidation and in some cases assault by militias. Unveiled women were increasingly stopped, harassed and threatened at checkpoints. Several women were reported to have been killed by male relatives in so-called "honour killings" in the Sabha area.

REFUGEES' AND MIGRANTS' RIGHTS

Thousands of undocumented migrants, asylum-seekers and refugees were detained indefinitely for migration-related offences following their interception at sea or identity checks. They faced torture and other ill-treatment in detention centres run by the Ministry of the Interior and militias, including on account of their religion, and were subjected to forced labour. Women faced intrusive strip-searches by male guards.

Foreign nationals, in particular Egyptian Copts, were abducted, abused and unlawfully killed on account of their religious beliefs. In February, seven Egyptian Coptic migrant workers were abducted and shot dead in Benghazi, allegedly by members of Ansar al-Sharia.

The authorities continued to subject foreign nationals to compulsory medical tests as a prerequisite for issuing residency and work permits, and detained anyone diagnosed with infections such as hepatitis B or C and HIV in preparation for deportation.

Foreign nationals faced abductions and abuse for ransom. Many were victims of human trafficking by smugglers upon irregular entry into Libya.

The escalation of violence impelled some 130,000 refugees and migrants, including refugees from Syria, to travel to Italy via unseaworthy and overcrowded fishing boats. Many spent weeks locked in houses by smugglers prior to departure and were exploited, coerced and abused. Smugglers forced sub-Saharan Africans to travel below deck in overheated engine rooms without water or ventilation; some died of suffocation or intoxication with fumes.

UNHCR reported in mid-November that 14,000 registered refugees and asylum-seekers were trapped in conflict zones in Libya.

DISCRIMINATION – RELIGIOUS AND ETHNIC MINORITIES

Attacks on Sufi religious sites continued while the authorities failed to provide adequate protection or conduct investigations. Sufi tombs were destroyed in Tripoli, Brak al-Shatti, Derna and Awjila. In July, unidentified assailants In Tripoli abducted Tarek Abbas, a Sufi imam; he was released in December.

Libyan atheists and agnostics faced threats and intimidation from militias in relation to their writings on social networking websites.

Tabu and Tuareg ethnic minorities continued to face obstacles in acquiring family identity booklets, hindering their access to health care, education and political participation.

DEATH PENALTY

The death penalty remained in force for a wide range of crimes. No judicial executions were reported.

---

1. Libya: Jail sentence of Libyan editor a blow to free expression (MDE 19/010/2014)

www.amnesty.org/en/documents/mde19/0010/2014/en/

LITHUANIA

Republic of Lithuania
Head of state: **Dalia Grybauskaitė**
Head of government: **Algirdas Butkevičius**

In February, the Prosecutor General opened an investigation into allegations that a Saudi Arabian national had been subjected to illegal rendition to Lithuania by the US CIA with the help of Lithuanian intelligence officials. A law, which aimed at "protecting minors" against detrimental public information, resulted in violations of the right to freedom of expression of lesbian, gay, bisexual, transgender and intersex (LGBTI) people.

COUNTER-TERROR AND SECURITY

In January, the Vilnius Regional Court ruled that the Lithuanian Prosecutor General's refusal to launch a pre-trial investigation into allegations that Saudi Arabian national Mustafa al-Hawsawi had been illegally transferred to and detained in a CIA detention centre at Antaviliai, near Vilnius, had been "groundless". Legal representatives for Mustafa al-Hawsawi had complained that he was tortured and subjected to enforced disappearance in Lithuania between 2004 and September 2006. In February, the Prosecutor General opened a pre-trial investigation focusing on Mustafa al-Hawsawi's alleged illegal transfer to Lithuania.

The Prosecutor General had previously refused to investigate similar allegations by lawyers for Palestinian Zayn al- Abidin Muhammad Husayn (known as Abu Zubaydah) . Abu Zubaydah's case against Lithuania was pending before the European Court of Human Rights at the end of the year . Both Mustafa al- Hawsawi and Abu Zubaydah remained held at Guantánamo Bay.

In May, the UN Committee against Torture urged the government to complete the investigation into Mustafa al-Hawsawi's alleged rendition in a timely and transparent manner. In the aftermath of the release in December of a US Senate report on CIA secret detention that contained references to "detention site violet", widely believed to have been located in Lithuania, it was reported that the Lithuanian authorities were seeking additional information from the USA to determine whether detainees had been held and tortured in Lithuania. Information in the Senate report regarding "detention site violet" conformed with a 2009 Lithuanian parliamentary inquiry that had concluded that the CIA had established two secret sites in Lithuania.

RIGHTS OF LESBIAN, GAY, BISEXUAL, TRANSGENDER AND INTERSEX PEOPLE

In May, the Office of the Inspector of Journalist Ethics concluded a book of fairy tales, which included stories of same-sex relationships, opposed "traditional family values", as protected by the Law on the Protection of Minors against the Detrimental Effects of Public Information. The book's distribution was stopped.

In September, the Office of the Inspector of Journalist Ethics found a video promoting tolerance towards LGBTI people and portraying same-sex families violated the Law on the Protection of Minors.

Transgender people continued to be denied access to legal gender recognition because of legislative gaps. Two proposals were pending before the parliament: one aimed at banning legal gender recognition, the other at allowing transgender people to seek legal recognition of their gender under certain compulsory conditions, including reassignment surgery.

MACEDONIA

The former Yugoslav Republic of Macedonia
Head of state: **Gjorge Ivanov**
Head of government: **Nikola Gruevski**

Human rights were increasingly curtailed. Relations between the Macedonian and ethnic Albanian populations were marred by violent protests. New details emerged about the rendition of a CIA detainee with the complicity of Macedonia.

BACKGROUND

The ruling party, Internal Macedonian Revolutionary Organization – Democratic Party for Macedonian National Unity, remained in power following parliamentary elections in May, which were not recognized by the main opposition party. Freedom of expression was increasingly curtailed. The authorities exercised excessive influence over the police and judiciary. While the European Commission again recommended that talks on EU accession should start, in December the EU Council of Ministers for the sixth time deferred the decision.

Relations between Macedonians and ethnic Albanians remained precarious. In May, the arrest of an ethnic Albanian student, suspected of killing a Macedonian student, triggered two days of inter-ethnic rioting in the Gorce Petrov municipality of Skopje, the capital.

On 30 June, six ethnic Albanians were convicted – two in their absence – of murder defined as "terrorism" for the killing of five ethnic Macedonians near Lake Smilkovci in April 2012, and sentenced to life imprisonment; one defendant was acquitted.

On 4 July, thousands of Albanians marched into the centre of Skopje, saying "We are not terrorists". The peaceful demonstration escalated outside the High Court with riot police using excessive force against protesters, including rubber bullets,

tear gas, stun grenades and water cannons. On 6 July, further protests took place. In the predominantly Albanian cities of Tetovo and Gostivar, police used tear gas and stun grenades. Six men were sentenced to three years' imprisonment for "participation in a crowd to commit a crime".

CRIMES UNDER INTERNATIONAL LAW

Impunity continued for war crimes and crimes against humanity which occurred during the 2001 internal armed conflict. No measures were taken to locate the bodies of 13 persons still missing after the armed conflict.

COUNTER-TERROR AND SECURITY

The December release of a US Senate report on CIA secret detention operations included confirmation that former detainee Khaled el-Masri's 2003 apprehension by the Macedonian authorities was a case of mistaken identity and the CIA took measures to cover up the incident. The European Court of Human Rights ruled in a 2013 landmark judgment that Macedonia was liable for Khaled el-Masri's incommunicado detention, enforced disappearance, torture and other ill-treatment, for his transfer out of Macedonia to locations where the German national suffered other serious violations of his human rights, and for the failure to carry out an effective investigation.

At the end of the year, the authorities had failed to submit to the Committee of Ministers an action plan, overdue since October 2013, to implement the Court's judgment.

TORTURE AND OTHER ILL-TREATMENT

Allegations against police officials continued, including disproportionately against Roma. In May, two Roma minors, wrongly suspected of stealing a purse, were beaten by members of the Alfi Special Police unit. The older child was interrogated in a police station for two hours in the absence of a lawyer or his parents, and suffered bruising to his head, neck and chest.

FREEDOM OF EXPRESSION

In April, the UN Special Rapporteur on freedom of expression criticized the deterioration of freedom of expression, pluralism and media independence. The government reportedly spent 1% of its budget on placing advertisements in, or otherwise favouring, pro-government media. International organizations reported that state media election coverage was biased towards the ruling party.

During the May riots, police seized equipment from three media outlets and erased their video footage. Politicians continued to file defamation cases against journalists. International and domestic organizations called for the Nova Makedonija journalist Tomislav Kezharovski to be released from house arrest. He was originally imprisoned in 2013 for revealing the identity of an alleged protected witness, in what was considered to be a politically motivated prosecution. After international protests, he was released into house arrest.

DISCRIMINATION – ROMA

The authorities failed to prevent, and protect Roma from, multiple forms of discrimination. Action plans for the Decade of Roma Inclusion and recommendations on the rights of Roma women made in 2013 by the UN CEDAW Committee were not implemented.

In June, the Constitutional Court ruled that articles of the Law on Travel Documents, enabling the authorities to revoke the passports of Macedonian citizens who had been returned or deported from another country, were incompatible with the right to freedom of movement. This followed a complaint by the NGO European Roma Rights Centre on behalf of Roma who experienced disproportionate discrimination by border officials.

RIGHTS OF LESBIAN, GAY, BISEXUAL, TRANSGENDER AND INTERSEX PEOPLE

Anti-discrimination legislation was not amended to prohibit discrimination on the grounds of sexual orientation. LGBTI human rights defenders were subject to regular threats. In October, 30 young men attacked a celebration of the second anniversary of the LGBTI Centre in Skopje, seriously injuring two people; no one has yet been brought to justice. In July the government proposed a constitutional amendment defining marriage as solely between a man and a woman.

REFUGEES, ASYLUM-SEEKERS AND MIGRANTS

Around 850 Kosovo Roma and Ashkali refugees remained in Macedonia, without a durable solution. By the end of September, 7,105 Macedonian citizens had applied for asylum in the EU.

Around 440 of the 1,260 registered asylum-seekers applied for asylum in Macedonia, but only 10 Syrians were granted refugee status and one person was granted subsidiary protection. Migrants, including women and unaccompanied minors, and Syrian refugees were detained in appalling conditions. Border guards were complicit in push-backs from Serbia.

MALAWI

Republic of Malawi
Head of state and government: **Arthur Peter Mutharika (replaced Joyce Banda in May)**

Those responsible for the deaths of two students in 2011 and 2012 were not brought to justice. Homosexuality continued to be criminalized under the penal code, although commitments were made to decriminalize consensual same-sex sexual activity. Death sentences continued to be imposed; no executions were carried out.

BACKGROUND

Controversy surrounded the general elections held on 20 May, with the then President Joyce Banda attempting to have the elections nullified, alleging fraud. However, opposition candidate Arthur Peter Mutharika's Democratic Progressive Party was declared the winning party following a High Court ruling. The new government faced perennial problems of deepening poverty, poor service delivery, mass unemployment, limited access to justice, gender-based violence and child marriages.

During the "hunger season" prior to the 2014 harvest, more than 1.4 million people in rural areas were at risk of malnutrition.

INTERNATIONAL SCRUTINY

In July, Malawi appeared before the UN Human Rights Committee for consideration of the country's first periodic report under the ICCPR. Among other things, the Committee recommended the amendment of Malawi's Human Rights Commission Act to give the Commission full independence in line with the UN Paris Principles. The Committee also recommended that Malawi adopt the Prison Act in conformity with international standards; strengthen the capacity and independence of the Inspectorate of Prisons and establish mechanisms to consistently consider its recommendations and make them public; and facilitate complaints from detainees.

IMPUNITY

Three police officers facing charges of manslaughter following the death in custody of Edson Msiska on 29 January 2012 in Mzuzu were discharged in July after state prosecutors failed to appear in court; no reason was given for their failure to appear. The charges were reinstated in August. Edson Msiska, a college student, died in suspicious circumstances four days after his arrest for alleged possession of stolen property.

The case of Robert Chasowa, a student activist who was found dead in suspicious circumstances in September 2011, remained unresolved, despite the 2012 recommendations of the Chasowa Commission Report which named some suspects.

RIGHTS OF LESBIAN, GAY, BISEXUAL, TRANSGENDER AND INTERSEX PEOPLE

Despite commitments by the previous and current governments that arrests of adults engaged in consensual same-sex sexual activity would be suspended, two men faced charges under the country's anti-homosexuality laws. The two men, who were arrested in May, were on remand at the end of the year. If convicted, they would face up to 14 years' imprisonment with hard labour.

In July, Solicitor General and Secretary for Justice Dr Janet Banda told the Human Rights Committee that while homosexual acts remained criminalized, such acts were not prosecuted by law enforcement agencies. She also reported that a process for the Malawi Law Commission to review the penal laws criminalizing same-sex acts had stalled largely due to financial constraints. Specifically, the Law Commission had been asked to give an opinion on the constitutionality of Articles 137A, 153 and 156 of the Penal Code, criminalizing homosexuality.

DEATH PENALTY

Death sentences continued to be imposed; no executions had been carried out since 1994.

MALAYSIA

Malaysia
Head of state: **King Abdul Halim Mu'adzam Shah**
Head of government: **Najib Tun Razak**

Freedom of expression came under attack as the government increasingly used the Sedition Act to arrest and charge human rights defenders and opposition politicians.

Reports of human rights violations by the police persisted, including deaths in custody, torture and other ill-treatment, and unnecessary and excessive use of force and firearms. Religious minorities and LGBTI people faced harassment and intimidation. The death penalty continued to be imposed, with executions reportedly carried out in secret.

BACKGROUND

In September Malaysia was elected to serve a two-year term on the UN Security Council. Opposition leader Anwar Ibrahim faced five years in prison and a ban from political office after his acquittal on politically motivated criminal "sodomy" charges was overturned by the Court of Appeal in March.[1] Also in March, Malaysia rejected key recommendations aimed at strengthening respect for and protection of human rights at the adoption of its Universal Periodic Review by the UN Human Rights Council in Geneva.[2]

FREEDOM OF EXPRESSION

Freedom of expression was subject to severe restrictions under a range of repressive laws. In August, the authorities began a crackdown on freedom of expression, using the Sedition Act to investigate, charge and imprison human rights defenders, opposition politicians, a journalist, academics and students.[3] At least two people were convicted of sedition during the year and sentenced to 10 and 12 months' imprisonment respectively, while at least 16 others faced charges by the end of the year. Many more were investigated under the Act, creating a chilling effect on free speech. In November, the Prime Minister reneged on his 2012 promise to repeal the Sedition Act, and instead announced plans to expand its scope.[4]

Human rights defenders faced intimidation and harassment because of their work, while the government persisted in its attempts to undermine civil society. Lena Hendry, a human rights defender with the NGO Pusat KOMAS, continued to face politically motivated criminal charges under the 2002 Film Censorship Act for screening the film *No fire zone: The killing fields of Sri Lanka* in July 2013.

Media outlets and publishing houses faced sweeping restrictions under the Printing Presses and Publications Act. The Act required that licences be obtained for print publications, which could be arbitrarily revoked by the Home Minister. Independent media outlets in particular faced difficulty in obtaining licences under the Act. Civil defamation suits were used by government officials and politicians in attempts to suppress criticism by media.[5]

POLICE AND SECURITY FORCES

Police faced persistent allegations of human rights violations, including deaths in custody, torture and other ill-treatment,[6] and unnecessary and excessive use of force and firearms. In August the Court of Appeal found the Inspector General of Police and two police officers responsible under civil law for the death of A. Kugan, who died in police custody in 2009.[7] At least 13 people were known to have died in police custody during 2014.

Investigations into human rights violations by the police were rare, and suspected perpetrators were seldom held to account. The government continued to reject calls to establish an Independent Police Complaints and Misconduct Commission as recommended in the 2005 report of the Royal Commission.

ARBITRARY ARRESTS AND DETENTIONS

The authorities continued to use the Prevention of Crime Act (PCA) and the Security Offences (Special Measures) Act to arbitrarily arrest and detain scores of individuals suspected of criminal activities. The PCA, which was amended in 2013, allows for indefinite, preventive detention without charge or trial and undermines key fair trial rights.

DISCRIMINATION

Instances of religious intolerance, as well as restrictions on the right to freedom of thought, conscience and religion, increased during the year. The authorities increasingly used religion as a justification for discrimination against minority religious groups. In June the Federal Court rejected an appeal seeking to overturn a ban preventing a Christian newspaper from using the world "Allah" in its publications. The authorities had claimed that the use of the word in non-Muslim literature was confusing and could cause Muslims to convert. The ban led to intimidation and harassment of Christians, including raids on places of worship by government authorities, and the seizure of books, videos and other materials. Other religious minority groups, including the Shi'a, faced intimidation and threats of criminalization, while civil society groups and human rights organizations also faced harassment and intimidation from both authorities and certain religious groups.

In a landmark decision, in November the Court of Appeal ruled that a Negeri Sembilan Shari'a law making cross-dressing illegal was inconsistent with the Constitution. However, reports were received during the year about the arrest and imprisonment of lesbian, gay, bisexual, transgender and intersex people purely on the basis of their sexuality, and they continued to face discrimination, both in law and practice.

REFUGEES AND ASYLUM-SEEKERS

Malaysia violated the international prohibition against refoulement by forcibly returning refugees and asylum-seekers to countries where they faced serious human rights violations. In May, the authorities forcibly returned two refugees and one asylum-seeker – all of them under the protection of UNHCR, the UN refugee agency – to Sri Lanka where they faced possible torture and other-ill-treatment.

DEATH PENALTY

In February and March respectively, following national and international criticism, the executions of Chandran Paskaran and Osariakhi Ernest Obayangbon were postponed. They had not been executed by the end of the year.[8] However, death sentences continued to be imposed and reports indicated that executions were carried out in a secretive manner, without prior or posthumous announcements.

---

1. Malaysia: Anwar Ibrahim decision a "bleak day for justice" (7 March 2014)
   www.amnesty.org/en/news/malaysia-anwar-ibrahim-decision-bleak-day-justice-2014-03-07

2. Malaysia again reneges on human rights commitments (ASA 28/003/2014)
   www.amnesty.org/en/library/info/ASA28/003/2014/en

3. Malaysia: Increasing use of the Sedition Act fosters a climate of repression (ASA 28/008/2014)
   www.amnesty.org/en/library/info/ASA28/008/2014/en

4. Malaysia: Open Letter: Use of the Sedition Act to restrict freedom of expression in Malaysia (ASA 28/011/2014)
   www.amnesty.org/en/library/info/ASA28/011/2014/en

5. Malaysia: Drop defamation lawsuit against news website (ASA 28/004/2014)
   www.amnesty.org/en/library/info/ASA28/004/2014/en

6. Malaysia: Detained student activist at risk of torture: Ali Abdul Jalil (ASA 28/010/2014)
   www.amnesty.org/en/library/info/ASA28/010/2014/en

7. Malaysia: Amnesty International welcomes Court of Appeal ruling, calls for investigations into custodial deaths (ASA 28/007/2014)
   www.amnesty.org/en/library/info/ASA28/007/2014/en

8. Malaysia: Stayed execution positive but hundreds of others still at risk (7 February 2014)
   www.amnesty.org/en/news/malaysia-stayed-execution-positive-hundreds-others-still-risk-2014-02-07

MALDIVES

Republic of Maldives
Head of state and government: **Abdulla Yameen Abdul Gayoom**

Preparations to resume executions put at risk the lives of at least 20 people on death row. Judicial flogging continued and the majority of those flogged were women. The government failed to bring to justice vigilantes who used violence against people promoting religious tolerance. Impunity continued for police and army officers responsible for unnecessary or excessive use of force.

BACKGROUND

Parliamentary elections took place in March and parties allied to the President won a majority. In April, the parliament adopted a new Penal Code, due to come into force in 2015.

DEATH PENALTY

The country was preparing to resume executions after more than 60 years. In April, the government introduced "procedural regulations on investigating and penalizing the crime of murder" under the Police Act and Clemency Act, clearing the way for executions to be carried out. The regulations also contained new procedures relating to the execution of individuals who were below 18 years old when the crime was committed, allowing for them to be executed once they turned 18. Two people were sentenced to death by the Juvenile Court for crimes committed when the offenders were under 18.

CRUEL, INHUMAN OR DEGRADING PUNISHMENT

People continued to be sentenced to flogging following convictions for having had sex outside marriage. Media reports and human rights defenders said that in the majority of cases, only women were convicted and flogged. The Office of the Prosecutor General told Amnesty International that convictions were primarily based on confessions. If the accused denied the allegations, the charge of "fornication" was dropped. They said men usually denied the allegations and were not charged. This was also true for some women, unless they had become pregnant or were under pressure from their communities to admit to the allegations.

Amnesty International spoke with a woman in 2013 who had been convicted of "fornication". She had been sentenced to 20 lashes and four months in prison in June 2012, when she was 17 years old. She said someone witnessed her having sex with her boyfriend and reported it to the police, after which she was arrested and taken to the Juvenile Court where she confessed. The woman said that this was the second time she had been flogged – the first time she was just 14 years old. She said that flogging was always carried out by a man and she described her experience: "It was very painful when they flogged me. I was bruised and had marks on my body for some time." Following the flogging she was sent to prison.

FREEDOMS OF RELIGION AND EXPRESSION

No one was brought to justice for the stabbing and serious wounding of religious freedom advocate Ismail "Hilath" Rasheed in 2012. He had also been attacked in 2011.

In June, an Islamist vigilante group abducted several young men, held them for hours, ill-treated them and warned them not to promote "atheism". None of the perpetrators were brought to justice.

In August, Ahmed Rilwan Abdulla, a well-known journalist with *Minivan News*, disappeared, possibly by force. He was last seen in the early hours of 8 August on the Malé-Hulhumalé ferry. There were national and international calls on the authorities to do more to uncover his whereabouts.

He had been investigating, among other things, the activities of vigilante Islamist groups. His possible enforced disappearance was believed to be linked to his work as a journalist.

EXCESSIVE USE OF FORCE

The government did not confirm whether it was investigating police officers who had used unnecessary force against youths peacefully attending a private music festival in April. Police ransacked their belongings, held 79 youths in handcuffs overnight and ill-treated some of them. One participant said she was kicked hard in the back by a policeman and another was sprayed with pepper spray without any provocation.

IMPUNITY

No police or army officers were brought to justice for beating and injuring dozens of members and leaders of the Maldivian Democratic Party in February 2012.

MALI

Republic of Mali
Head of state: **Ibrahim Boubacar Keïta**
Head of government: **Moussa Mara (replaced Oumar Tatam Ly in April)**

Internal armed conflict continued to create a climate of persistent insecurity, particularly in the north of the country. Armed groups committed abuses including abductions and killings. The authorities were slow to take action against those who committed human rights violations during the 2012 conflict.

BACKGROUND

Although a peace agreement was signed between the Malian government and several armed groups in Ouagadougou, Burkina Faso, in June 2013, the north of the country remained unstable, with parts of it beyond the control of the Malian authorities.

Violent clashes continued to erupt between armed groups and the Malian army in Kidal in May, in which at least 41 people, including eight civilians, were killed. Peace discussions continued in Algeria between the Malian government and armed groups, but outbreaks of violence persisted. There were repeated incidents of rocket attacks, mines and explosive devices in the north injuring and killing Malian and international military personnel. Between May and September, the UN Multidimensional Integrated Stabilization Mission in Mali (MINUSMA) was repeatedly attacked by armed groups. In October, nine Nigerian UN peacekeepers were killed when their convoy was ambushed by an armed group between the towns of Menaka and Ansongo in the Gao region of northeastern Mali.

In March, the National Assembly approved a law creating a commission for truth, justice and reconciliation. It also created a high court of justice to try officials suspected of treason and crimes during their terms in office.

Issaka Sidibé was elected President of the National Assembly in January. In April, Prime Minister Oumar Tatam Ly resigned and President Keïta named Moussa Mara the new Prime Minister.

ABUSES BY ARMED GROUPS

Investigations continued into the killings of two Radio France Internationale journalists, Ghislaine Dupont and Claude Verlon, after they were abducted in Kidal in November 2013. Both the French and Malian authorities opened judicial inquiries.

Five Malian staff of the International Committee of the Red Cross (ICRC) were taken hostage in February and held until April. The armed group Movement for Oneness and Jihad in West Africa claimed responsibility for the abductions.

In May, members of armed groups deliberately killed eight male civilians, including six government officials, at the

Governor's office in Kidal, northern Mali. They also took 30 people hostage including government employees from the Governor's office, some of whom were beaten. The hostages were released on their third day of captivity after negotiations with UN peacekeeping forces.[1]

In September, five men from the Tuareg tribe were abducted by an armed group in the market in Zouéra, a town situated 80km north of the city of Timbuktu. Four were released a few days later but Hama Ag-Sidi Ahmed was beheaded. His head was found suspended at the marketplace in Zouéra; his decapitated body was found under a tree in the centre of the town.

Serge Lazarevic, a French hostage abducted in November 2011 in Hombori, Mopti region, was released in November.

Three people from the same family were reportedly abducted near the town of Menaka in December.

IMPUNITY

The government began to tackle the issue of impunity and made some progress, notably in the case of the enforced disappearance of more than 20 soldiers in April 2012. An investigation into these disappearances began in March. A total of 28 people were arrested during the year, including General Amadou Sanogo, leader of the military junta that ruled Mali for part of 2012, and General Ibrahim Dahirou Dembélé, former Chief of Staff. All were charged with murder and complicity in kidnapping.

Few prosecutions were brought in connection with other cases of enforced disappearances and there were long delays in bringing to justice those responsible for committing human rights violations in the context of the conflict. Some cases, notably the disappearance of 11 men in Timbuktu in February 2013, were yet to be investigated.

CHILDREN'S RIGHTS

Children accused of being members of armed groups in the conflict continued to be imprisoned alongside adults without access to family or legal counsel.[2] In mid-2014, at least seven children were detained in the capital, Bamako, alongside adults, without protection measures for children in custody. Most were charged with being members of armed groups and with the illegal possession of firearms and ammunitions. Four were released in August but other children remained in detention.

DEATHS IN CUSTODY

At least seven people arrested in connection with the conflict died in custody between January 2012 and the end of 2014. At least two such detainees died in custody in Bamako during 2014 due to lack of medical care; Mohamed Ag Sana died in March and Ismagel Ag Achkou in May.

DEATH PENALTY

No executions had been carried out in Mali for several decades, but death sentences continued to be imposed. In August, Bassidiki Touré, Souleymane Diarra, Soumaila Dembélé and Almamy Traoré were sentenced to death for robbery and complicity. Sounkodjan Diarra was sentenced to death for premeditated murder. His co-accused was sentenced to life imprisonment.

---

1. Mali: All parties to the conflict must put an end to ongoing human rights violations (AFR 37/001/2014)
   www.amnesty.org/en/library/info/AFR37/001/2014/en

2. Mali: Children still paying a high price in ongoing conflict (Press release)
   www.amnesty.org/en/articles/news/2014/08/mali-children-still-paying-high-price-ongoing-conflict/

MALTA

Republic of Malta
Head of state: **Marie-Louise Coleiro Preca**
Head of government: **Joseph Muscat**

Malta maintained a restrictive interpretation of search and rescue obligations at sea. The authorities continued to automatically detain asylum-seekers and migrants, in breach of international standards, and to deny them effective remedies to challenge their detention. Same-sex couples were granted the same rights as heterosexuals in a civil marriage. Constitutional protection was extended to cover discrimination on grounds of sexual orientation and gender identity. Abortion remained prohibited under all circumstances.

REFUGEES AND ASYLUM-SEEKERS

Malta experienced a drop in irregular boat arrivals of refugees and migrants due to Italy's Operation Mare Nostrum during which refugees and migrants were being rescued at sea and disembarked on Italian territory. By the end of September, 565 people had been rescued and brought to Malta (compared to 2,008 people in 2013). Malta continued to apply a restrictive interpretation of search and rescue obligations at sea, aimed at limiting disembarkation of refugees and migrants in its territory.[1]

The authorities continued to automatically detain undocumented migrants, often for up to 18 months, and asylum-seekers, for up to 12 months, in breach of Malta's international human rights obligations. On 30 March, the Prime Minister publicly pledged to end migrant children's detention. However, children and other vulnerable people continued to be routinely detained as well as unaccompanied minors detained alongside adults while awaiting the outcome of their age or vulnerability assessment.[2]

Appeal procedures to challenge the length and lawfulness of detention remained in breach of international human rights standards, leaving asylum-seekers and migrants exposed to the risk of arbitrary detention.

Conditions in detention cent res remained sub-standard, with many asylum-seekers and migrants experiencing lack of privacy and poor recreation and leisure facilities.

The government refused to disclose information about the search and rescue operation regarding a trawler carrying over 400 people, mostly Syrian families, which sank on 11 October 2013. Survivors' testimonies and available data indicated that rescue may have been delayed due to failures by Maltese and Italian authorities.

In December, after a two year delay, the government published , the findings of the inquiry into the death of Mamadou Kamara, a 32-year-old Malian national, who died in custody in June 2012 . He had attempted to escape from Safi Barracks detention centre and was allegedly severely ill-treated when recaptured. The inquiry report recommended a review of the asylum-seekers and migrants detention system.

RIGHTS OF LESBIAN, GAY, BISEXUAL, TRANSGENDER AND INTERSEX PEOPLE

On 14 April, the Parliament passed the Civil Unions Act, granting same-sex couples the same rights as heterosexual couples in a civil marriage. Partners in a civil union were also allowed to jointly adopt children, with the same rights and obligations as parents in a civil marriage.

On the same day, Parliament amended the Constitution to include protection from discrimination on grounds of sexual orientation and gender identity.

SEXUAL AND REPRODUCTIVE RIGHTS

Abortion remained prohibited under all circumstances, including to save the life of the woman. In October, the UN Human Rights Committee, considering Malta under the ICCPR, raised concern about the compatibility of the prohibition with the right to life.

---

1. Lives adrift: Refugees and migrants in peril in the central Mediterranean (EUR 05/006/2014)
www.amnesty.org/en/library/info/EUR05/006/2014/en
2. Lives adrift: Refugees and migrants in peril in the central Mediterranean: Executive summary (EUR 05/007/2014)
www.amnesty.org/en/library/info/EUR05/007/2014/en

MAURITANIA

Islamic Republic of Mauritania
Head of state: **General Mohamed Ould Abdel Aziz**
Head of government: **Yahya Ould Hademine (replaced Moulaye Ould Mohamed Laghdaf in August)**

Torture and other ill-treatment were routinely used to extract confessions from detainees and as punishment in prisons. Slavery persisted, with generations of families, particularly women and girls, being held in slavery. The authorities restricted freedoms of expression and assembly, and human rights defenders faced harassment and intimidation.

BACKGROUND

President Aziz was re-elected for a second five-year term in June, obtaining more than 80% of the vote. The Independent National Electoral Commission received complaints contesting this result from four other candidates. President Aziz was also elected to serve as President of the AU for one year in January.

TORTURE AND OTHER ILL-TREATMENT

Prisoners of all ages, status and gender were at risk of torture and other ill-treatment. Women, children, homosexual prisoners, political prisoners and prisoners convicted of common law offences told Amnesty International that they were subjected to torture and other ill-treatment by security forces. Although mainly used to extract "confessions" from detainees, torture and other ill-treatment were also used as punishment in prison. The use of torture was facilitated by laws which allowed detainees to be held in police custody for up to 45 days on suspicion of national security offences. This limit was regularly exceeded. No action was taken when complaints of torture were made to judges or the police.

Reported torture methods included regular beatings, including beatings with batons; beatings on the back with the hands and feet handcuffed behind the back; enforced squatting for long periods; and having an iron bar placed between the knees and being suspended from two water barrels. Detainees reported being made to sign statements under threat without being allowed to read them.

SLAVERY

Despite the adoption of laws criminalizing slavery and the creation in December 2013 of a special tribunal to hear slavery cases, implementation in practice remained poor.

Court cases were subject to long delays. Between 2010 and the end of 2014, at least six cases of slavery were submitted to the Public Prosecutor, but no ruling had been made by the end of 2014.

A strategy to eradicate slavery was adopted by the government in March. Its 29 recommendations included amending the 2007 law against slavery to include further forms of slavery such as hereditary slavery, debt bondage and early marriage. It also recommended that the 2007 law should include provisions for reintegration programmes for people freed from slavery, and called for initiatives to raise awareness that slavery is a criminal offence.

In May, a complaint was filed against a slaveholder in the Echemin region for the enslavement of a 15-year-old girl, MBeirika Mint M'Bareck. The slaveholder was charged with exploitation of a minor, but human rights organizations called for the charges to be changed to slavery. When MBeirika Mint M'Bareck was freed in June, the Public Prosecutor charged her with *Zina* (unlawful sexual intercourse) as she was pregnant. The charge was later dropped. At the end of the year, her mother and two sisters were still being held in slavery in the town of Azamat, near the border with Mali.

Also in May, a woman and her five children were reported to be held in slavery in Ould Ramy, near Wembou in southeastern Mauritania, by the anti-slavery organization Initiative for the Resurgence of the Abolitionist Movement in Mauritania (IRA). The case was transferred to the police, who questioned the representatives of IRA, claiming they were an unrecognized organization. Gendarmes were sent to investigate but no progress was reported by the end of the year.

FREEDOMS OF EXPRESSION AND ASSEMBLY

The rights to freedom of assembly and freedom of expression were repeatedly curtailed.

In March there were demonstrations in several cities including Nouakchott, Kiffa and Aioun against an act of desecration of the Qur'an by unidentified men. Security forces in Nouakchott used tear gas, resulting in numerous injuries and the death by suffocation of one student demonstrator.

The government closed several Islamic health and education charities and sealed their offices in March. No official explanation was offered but the government accused these organizations of working outside the bounds of their missions.

HUMAN RIGHTS DEFENDERS

Human rights defenders and other activists faced harassment and intimidation, including death threats. Police and judicial authorities failed to bring the perpetrators of these acts to justice.

IRA member Cheikh Ould Vall was arrested in February without a warrant. He was held for three days, released and rearrested a week later, reportedly for assisting his mother in a court case over a land dispute. He was sentenced to one year in prison in April, with six months suspended. He was due to be released in August, but remained in detention at the end of the year.

In June, Aminetou Mint El Moctar, President of the Women's Association of Heads of Household, faced a *fatwa* (religious decree) including death threats. No action was known to have been taken by the authorities to investigate these threats.[1] The threats came after Aminetou Mint El Moctar called for a fair trial for Cheikh Ould Mkheitir, who had been arrested in January for publishing an allegedly blasphemous article and was detained in Nouadhibou Prison in northern Mauritania. He was charged with apostasy and faced the death penalty if convicted.

In September and November, at least 10 anti-slavery activists, including Biram Ould Dah Ould Abeid, President of the IRA, were arrested in Nouakchott and Rosso. At the end of the year, the activists were detained in different detention centres around the country, facing charges including public disorder.[2]

ENFORCED DISAPPEARANCES

Of the 14 men convicted of terrorism-related offences who were victims of enforced disappearance in 2011, one died in detention in May, while the other 13 were transferred to Nouakchott central prison in May and July.

Maarouf Ould Haiba, sentenced to death in 2010 for the murder of French tourists and then held incommunicado, died in detention in the unofficial detention centre Salah Eddin in May. He was transferred to a military hospital several times before his death. The circumstances of his death remained unclear and no investigation was opened. Salah

Eddin, situated in the north of the country, was closed in July. The remaining prisoners were transferred to the central prison in Nouakchott.

---

1. Mauritania: Human rights defender threatened, life at risk: Aminetou Mint El Moctar (AFR 38/002/2014) www.amnesty.org/en/library/info/AFR38/002/2014/en
2. Mauritania must end clampdown on anti-slavery activists (Press release) www.amnesty.org/en/articles/news/2014/11/mauritania-must-end-clamp-down-anti-slavery-activists/

MEXICO

United Mexican States
Head of state and government: **Enrique Peña Nieto**

There were new reports of enforced disappearances, extrajudicial executions and torture in the context of violent crime and lack of accountability in the police and military. Impunity for human rights violations and ordinary crimes remained the norm. More than 22,000 people remained abducted, forcibly disappeared or missing, according to official records, including 43 students from Guerrero state. Search efforts for missing people were generally ineffective. Reports of torture and other ill-treatment continued to be widespread, as was the failure on the part of federal and state prosecutors to adequately investigate complaints. The Supreme Court strengthened legal obligations to exclude evidence obtained under torture. Many human rights violations continued to be attributed to soldiers and navy marines, who continued to be deployed widely to carry out law enforcement operations including combating organized crime. Military jurisdiction over human rights violations committed by military personnel against civilians was abolished after decades of campaigning by victims and civil society organizations. Human rights defenders and journalists were harassed, threatened or killed. Some faced politically motivated criminal charges. Irregular migrants in transit faced the threat of murder, abduction, extortion, sexual violence and human trafficking; perpetrators were rarely brought to justice. Despite laws to combat violence against women, gender-based violence was routine in many states. Development and resource exploitation projects in different parts of the country affecting Indigenous communities led to protests and demands for adequate consultation and consent.

BACKGROUND
The government continued its programme of legislative reforms affecting the energy sector, education, telecommunications and political organization. Despite publishing a National Human Rights Program, there was little evidence of substantive measures to address the human rights situation.

Several states including Puebla, Quintana Roo, Chiapas and the Federal District adopted or sought to adopt laws on the use of force by law enforcement officials during demonstrations. These changes were inconsistent with international human rights standards and posed a threat to freedoms of expression and association. In Puebla state, which had recently approved such a law, police officers were under investigation at the end of the year for the death of a 13-year-old boy who died in the context of a demonstration, possibly as a result of excessive use of force. The changes to the law were put under review after the incident.

In November the Senate appointed the new president of the National Human Rights Commission (CNDH) for the period 2014 to 2019. Human rights organizations requested full consultation and transparency, in compliance with international standards. However, Senators only allowed for one meeting with civil society in which a limited number of organizations had to present their views briefly, without any further discussion. Human rights defenders reiterated their concerns over the ineffectiveness of the CNDH in addressing the grave human rights situation and called for the CNDH to fulfil its key role in the protection of human rights and the fight against impunity.

In response to massive demonstrations to demand justice in the case of 43 forcibly disappeared students, President Peña Nieto announced on 27 November a series of legislative and policy measures, including a constitutional change that would give the state control over local police. The measures were to be implemented in stages, starting in the states of Guerrero, Jalisco, Michoacán and Tamaulipas. The President also proposed setting up a nationwide emergency number 911, as well as special economic zones in the country's impoverished south.

POLICE AND SECURITY FORCES

Despite official claims that incidents of organized crime-related violence fell, the situation remained grave. The overall number of homicides in the first nine months of the year was 24,746, compared to 26,001 in the first nine months of 2013. In September, an official national survey estimated that the number of abductions in 2013 had reached 131,946, compared to 105,682 in 2012. Army and navy marines continued to carry out law enforcement duties in many states, often operating without effective accountability, resulting in reports of arbitrary detentions, torture and other ill-treatment and extrajudicial executions.

In response to the high levels of violence from organized crime, frequently in collusion with local authorities, several armed civilian self-defence groups emerged in Michoacán state. In consequence, the federal government deployed the armed forces and Federal Police in large numbers along with a new federal commissioner to oversee security policy in the state. Negotiations with

several self-defence groups resulted in their incorporation as rural police into official public security forces.

Indigenous communities in Guerrero state denounced the arrest and prosecution of some of their members and leaders. These communities had previously reached agreements with the government regarding their own law enforcement activities in their areas, against a backdrop of long-lasting neglect and rising crime levels. The cases appeared to be politically motivated.

In July, soldiers killed 22 people allegedly belonging to an armed gang in Tlatlaya, Mexico state, in what military authorities claimed was a firefight with gunmen. The Federal Prosecutor failed to investigate further, despite evidence that some of the victims were killed at close range. In September, media disclosed witness evidence indicating that after a brief exchange of fire many of those killed had been extrajudicially executed after surrendering. On 8 November, seven military personnel were charged and continued to be under investigation for the executions, but it remained unclear whether officials who had sought to cover up the incident would also be prosecuted in the civilian justice system.

After some delays, in August the new National Gendarmerie began operations with 5,000 officers forming a division of the Federal Police. The Gendarmerie was a significantly smaller force than originally proposed. Its role and operating practices remained unclear. The government failed to take on board recommendations to ensure strong accountability mechanisms, operating protocols and effective supervision to prevent human rights violations. The force was temporarily deployed in Mexico state and Guerrero to assume policing functions.

ENFORCED DISAPPEARANCES

Abductions and enforced disappearances continued to occur widely. The whereabouts of most victims remained undisclosed. During the year, federal officials made a series of contradictory statements regarding the number of persons reported disappeared or missing and whose whereabouts remained undisclosed. In August, the government acknowledged some 22,611 missing persons, 9,790 of whom went missing during the present administration and 12,821 during the administration of President Felipe Calderón (2006 to 2012). The government failed to make public how it had arrived at this figure. Impunity remained the norm for cases of enforced disappearance. In April the government stated that only seven convictions had ever been achieved for the crime of enforced disappearance at the federal level, all between 2005 and 2010.

In September, municipal police in the town of Iguala in collusion with organized criminals were responsible for the enforced disappearance of 43 students from a teacher training college in Ayotzinapa, Guerrero state. Investigations uncovered several mass graves and a dump site containing human remains. In November, the Federal Attorney General announced that the main line of investigation, based on the testimonies of three gang members apparently involved in the case, indicated that the students were killed, burned and dumped in a river. His announcement failed to address the general levels of impunity, corruption and unresolved cases of disappearance in Mexico. More than 70 local public officials and gang members were arrested and charged in relation to the case. There was no information regarding the possible responsibility, by omission or commission, of public officials at the state or federal level. On 7 December, the Federal Attorney General announced that the remains of one of the students had been identified by independent forensic experts. By the end of the year, the whereabouts of the other 42 remained undisclosed.

TORTURE AND OTHER ILL-TREATMENT

Arbitrary detention and torture and other ill-treatment by members of the armed forces, as well as federal, state and municipal police

forces remained widespread throughout the country. These violations were frequently used to extract "confessions" and other information to pursue criminal investigations or for other purposes such as extortion. Despite scores of complaints at the federal and state levels, there were few prosecutions and almost no convictions of public officials responsible.

As in previous years, the special medical examination procedure of the Federal Attorney General's Office for cases of alleged torture was not applied in most cases. In the minority of cases where it was carried out, it usually produced results unfavourable to the complainant. Officials generally failed to apply the procedure in compliance with the principles of the Istanbul Protocol, including promptness and providing victims with full results. In two exceptional cases the Federal Attorney General's Office dropped charges against the victims of torture after finally accepting evidence that they had been tortured in order to falsely implicate themselves. The victims had spent between three and five years in pre-trial detention. Independent medical examinations, which were conducted in line with the Istanbul Protocol, were central to demonstrating that they had been tortured.

In May the National Supreme Court published its 2013 judgment on the case of Israel Arzate who was arbitrarily arrested and tortured by army officers in order to accuse him of involvement in the Villas de Salvárcar massacre in 2010. The judgment set out important criteria for the inadmissibility of evidence deriving from unlawful detention and the obligation to investigate allegations of torture. However, the judgment did not set a binding precedent for other courts.

JUSTICE SYSTEM

Public security and criminal justice officials frequently ignored human rights violations and remained ineffective at investigating and prosecuting common crime as well as human rights violations, reinforcing impunity and distrust in the legal system. In March, a new National Criminal Procedural Code for all 33 federal and state criminal justice jurisdictions came into force as part of a gradual reform. The government argued that the application of the Code would improve the protection of human rights by making evidence obtained from human rights violations, such as unlawful detentions and torture, inadmissible. However, the Code had yet to be applied or the criteria for excluding evidence worked out in detail.

In January the Executive Commission for the Attention of Victims was established under the National Victims Law to provide victims of crime, including human rights violations, improved access to justice and reparations. It replaced the Social Procurator for victims of crime, but it remained unclear if it would enjoy the resources and powers sufficient to meet the needs of victims. The regulatory code for the National Victims Law was not approved, limiting implementation of the law.

In June, reforms to the Code of Military Justice came into force. The reforms, secured after years of campaigning by victims and human rights organizations, excluded from the system of military justice crimes committed by members of the armed forces against civilians. The reforms failed to exclude from military jurisdiction human rights violations committed against members of the armed forces. Nevertheless they were a major advance in ending impunity for abuses committed by military personnel. At the end of the year, four military personnel remained in detention in the civilian justice system accused of involvement in the 2002 rape of two Indigenous women, Inés Fernández Ortega and Valentiná Rosendo Cantú.

HUMAN RIGHTS DEFENDERS AND JOURNALISTS

Many human rights defenders and journalists were threatened, attacked or killed in reprisal for their legitimate work. No perpetrators were known to have been identified or brought to justice. This was largely due to

flawed investigations frequently as a result of official disinterest, particularly by state-level authorities. The pervasive impunity increased the climate of insecurity within which defenders and journalists operated.

The federal Mechanism for the Protection of Human Rights Defenders and Journalists announced in November that it had received 72 cases in the first nine months of the year. In general, it continued to fail to provide timely and effective protection. The agreed protection measures were often reliant on the support of local authorities, even in those cases where local authorities were thought to be involved in the attacks. Several beneficiaries of protection measures were temporarily forced to leave their communities for security reasons. Other defenders and journalists continued to wait for the mechanism to review their cases.

Several human rights defenders and community activists faced prosecution on criminal charges that appeared politically motivated in reprisal for their legitimate activities, including participating in protests. Many faced lengthy legal battles in unfair judicial proceedings to prove their innocence.

VIOLENCE AGAINST WOMEN AND GIRLS

Violence against women and girls remained endemic throughout the country, including rape, abductions and killings. Many authorities continued to fail to implement legal and administrative measures to improve prevention, protection from and investigation of gender-based violence. The National System for the Prevention, Sanction and Eradication of Violence against Women refused to apply the "Gender Alert" mechanism, which is designed to mobilize authorities to combat widespread gender violence and elicit an effective, official response to cases of violence.

In January, the National Supreme Court ordered the release of Adriana Manzanares Cayetano, an Indigenous woman who spent six years of a 22-year sentence in prison after being convicted of killing her newborn baby. Evidence that the child was stillborn was ignored, and violations of her right to an effective defence and the presumption of innocence resulted in an unsafe conviction.

REFUGEES' AND MIGRANTS' RIGHTS

Insecurity and social deprivation in their home countries drove increasing numbers of Central American migrants to cross Mexico to reach the USA, particularly unaccompanied children. Migrants continued to be killed, abducted and subject to extortion by criminal gangs, often operating in collusion with public officials. Women and children were particularly vulnerable to sexual violence and people trafficking. There were continued reports of ill-treatment by police and migration officials carrying out detentions. Irregular migrants continued to be held in administrative detention pending deportation.

Migrants' rights defenders providing safe havens to migrants and denouncing abuses suffered by migrants continued to face threats and intimidation. Several received protection measures, but in some cases these were not applied effectively and failed to prevent new threats being made. Those responsible for the threats were not brought to justice.

INDIGENOUS PEOPLES' RIGHTS

Indigenous communities continued to suffer discrimination in the criminal justice system as well as limited access to basic services, such as water, housing and health care. The failure to effectively consult Indigenous communities in order to obtain free, prior and informed consent regarding economic development projects affecting their lands and traditional way of living resulted in protests and disputes. These in turn led to threats and attacks on community leaders and in some cases criminal prosecutions of activists, apparently based on politically motivated charges.

INTERNATIONAL SCRUTINY

In March, Mexico accepted 166 of 176 recommendations of the UN Human Rights Council Universal Periodic Review of Mexico. In May, the UN Special Rapporteur on torture visited Mexico and issued preliminary conclusions that torture and other ill-treatment remained widespread. In June, the UN Special Rapporteur on extrajudicial executions published his report of his mission to Mexico in early 2013, which highlighted high levels of killings and impunity. In August the Special Rapporteur on migrants' rights of the Inter-American Commission on Human Rights issued his report of his visit to Mexico. The report detailed pervasive violence against migrants, the denial of due process and judicial protections, and other human rights abuses.

FREEDOM OF EXPRESSION

A telecommunications bill threatened to establish potentially arbitrary executive powers over the internet and insufficient judicial control over the interception of electronic communications.

MOLDOVA

Republic of Moldova
Head of state: **Nicolae Timofti**
Head of government: **Iurie Leancă**

Despite Moldova sentencing perpetrators of torture to terms of imprisonment for the first time, long-term systemic failings meant that the widespread problem of impunity persisted. The authorities failed to amend discriminatory legislation, leaving marginalized groups vulnerable.

TORTURE AND OTHER ILL-TREATMENT

The General Prosecutor's Office said it received significantly fewer complaints of torture and other ill-treatment than for 2013. For the first time, in July, three police officers were each sentenced to three years' imprisonment for the torture of two men in 2011, under Article 166 of the Criminal Code, which came into effect in December 2012. In September, a further two police officers were sentenced to six years' imprisonment and one officer was given a five-year suspended sentence for the torture of two brothers in early 2012. These developments reflect legislative changes that have facilitated prosecution for torture and efforts to ensure that law enforcement officers were better informed of their human rights obligations and the rights of detainees. However, impunity for past police abuses remained a significant problem.

2014 marked the fifth anniversary of the April 2009 post-election demonstrations and the authorities failed to deliver justice to the vast majority of those who were tortured or otherwise ill-treated by law enforcement officers during those events. Of 102 official complaints received by the General Prosecutor's Office, criminal investigations were initiated in 58 cases, of which only 31 cases reached the courts. Suspended sentences were passed against 27 police officers, and at the end of 2013 an officer was acquitted of the murder of Valeriu Boboc, who died as a result of injuries sustained through torture.

The five-year statute of limitations for alleged abuses committed by law enforcement officers expired in April, leaving a significant number of those who were subjected to torture and other ill-treatment during the events of April 2009 without further recourse to domestic remedy. In May, the Chisinau Court of Appeal overturned an earlier decision by the Supreme Court of Moldova and sentenced police officer Radu Starinschi to two years' imprisonment for the torture of Sergiu Cretu but the sentence could not be enforced as it fell outside the period of the statute of limitations. In October, the police officer was promoted. Not a single police officer has been imprisoned in connection with the April 2009 events. By the end of the year the European Court of Human Rights had ruled in seven cases and found violations of Article 3 (prohibition of torture) in each. In all seven cases, the Court found that the investigations were heavily flawed because of repeated refusals to start criminal investigations, and the failure to take into account vital evidence.

Torture and other ill-treatment of those held in mental health institutions was increasingly recognized as a concern. Following a pilot project establishing an ombudsperson for psychiatry which was initiated in 2011 in a collaboration between the UN and the Moldovan authorities, a high number of complaints of torture were received and progress was achieved in addressing them. Plans were in place to formalize the position and integrate it into Moldova's official health system.

CRUEL, INHUMAN OR DEGRADING PUNISHMENT

The May 2012 law introducing compulsory chemical castration as a punishment for violent child abusers was abolished by Parliament in December 2013.

DISCRIMINATION

The LGBTI community in Moldova celebrated the first successful Pride march in May. While the 2013 Pride march marked an historical first, the 2014 event saw participants able to walk the entire planned route through the centre of the capital, Chisinau, for the first time, and overall they were adequately secured by the police against threats by counter-demonstrators.

Despite this positive development, the Law on Ensuring Equality, which came into effect in January 2013, fell short of international standards. The law does not explicitly list sexual orientation and gender identity as one of the prohibited grounds for discrimination, apart from in relation to discrimination in the workplace. Police failed to adequately investigate a number of assaults on LGBTI rights activists.

MONGOLIA

Mongolia
Head of state: Tsakhia Elbegdorj
Head of government: Chimediin Saikhanbileg

Torture and other ill-treatment in police custody remained widespread. Forced evictions occurred in urban areas. Discrimination based on gender, sexual orientation and disability went largely unchallenged. Asylum-seekers were deported in violation of the *non-refoulement* principle by being forcibly returned to a country where they risked serious human rights violations.

BACKGROUND

The International Convention against enforced disappearance was ratified in October by Mongolia. However, the Second Optional Protocol to the ICCPR, aiming at the abolition of the death penalty, which had been ratified in 2012, had not led to changes in national legislation.

TORTURE AND OTHER ILL-TREATMENT

The use of torture and other ill-treatment, particularly to obtain "confessions", remained a serious human rights concern. Police officers and prison guards suspected of torture and other ill-treatment of people held at police stations and detention centres were not effectively investigated, leading to lack of accountability.

The Special Investigation Unit (SIU) in the State General Prosecutor's Office was disbanded in January. The SIU was responsible for investigating complaints against prosecutors, judges and police officers who allegedly coerced statements during interrogation. Mongolia therefore lacked an independent mechanism to effectively investigate allegations of torture and other ill-treatment as the police themselves were in charge of reviewing such claims.

In February, three former detainees who had been held in the pre-trial detention centre of Arkhangai province lodged a complaint with the National Human Rights Commission of Mongolia claiming that they had been subjected to beatings and electric shocks to extract "confessions" while held there. One of them claimed that he had been deprived of food for six days to coerce him into pleading guilty. Because the SIU had been disbanded, the police department of Arkhangai province was in charge of investigating their own colleagues. The allegations of torture and other ill-treatment were subsequently dismissed.

HOUSING RIGHTS – FORCED EVICTIONS

Residents of ger (traditional wool felt dwellings) districts in Ulaanbaatar suffered from lack of access to adequate housing and essential services including water and sanitation. Promised adequate alternative housing still had to be provided to some of the residents of the 7th micro-district of Ulaanbaatar who had been forcibly evicted from their homes in 2007 without genuine consultation or other appropriate legal or procedural safeguards or protection.

DISCRIMINATION

Discrimination persisted on the basis of ethnicity, gender, sexual orientation, gender identity and disability. Gender discrimination in particular affected women from marginalized groups such as those living in rural areas and ethnic minority women. Hostility, discrimination and violence especially against lesbian, gay, bisexual, transgender and intersex individuals continued. The legal definition of rape did not include men and boys so male victims of rape had particular difficulty in seeking adequate treatment, justice, redress and compensation.

REFUGEES AND ASYLUM-SEEKERS

In May, two Chinese asylum-seekers from the Inner-Mongolia Autonomous Region were deported back to the People's Republic of

China. This occurred even though at least one of them was in the process of having his claim for refugee status determined by UNHCR, the UN refugee agency, violating the *non-refoulement* principle by carrying out deportations before the process of status determination was completed, and sending individuals to a country where they were at risk of serious human rights violations.

MONTENEGRO

Montenegro
Head of state: **Filip Vujanović**
Head of government: **Milo Djukanović**

Decisions in war crimes cases continued to be inconsistent with international law. Independent journalists were subject to threats and attacks. Impunity persisted for law enforcement officers suspected of torture and other ill-treatment.

CRIMES UNDER INTERNATIONAL LAW
In June, both the Committee against Torture and the UN Working Group on Enforced Disappearances found that the courts had failed to fully apply domestic law and had misinterpreted international humanitarian law in decisions in cases prosecuted since 2008.

On 31 December 2013, a former Yugoslav Army commander and seven reservists were acquitted of the murder in April 1999 of 18 refugees from Kosovo in the village of Kaluđerski Laz near Rozaje.

In February, the Appellate Court upheld the conviction of four former Yugoslav Army reservists for the torture and other ill-treatment of around 250 Croatian Prisoners of War at Morinj detention camp in 1991-1992. They were sentenced to periods of imprisonment that were less than the statutory minimum and failed to reflect the gravity of their crimes. In March, seven former prisoners held at Morinj camp were each awarded compensation of between €20,000 and €30,000 for their ill-treatment. A further 200 former prisoners were claiming reparation.

In March, former police officials acquitted of war crimes in 2013 opened a case for compensation against Montenegro for €1 million, on the grounds that they were unlawfully detained and deprived of their liberty.

In August, Montenegro signed a regional declaration on missing persons, and committed to establishing the fate and whereabouts of 61 missing people.

FREEDOM OF EXPRESSION
Following the establishment in 2013 of a Commission to monitor police investigations into attacks and threats against journalists and independent media, investigations were reopened into the 2004 murder of Duško Jovanović, editor of the *Dan* newspaper. Suspects in the 2007 attack on journalist Tufik Softić were arrested in July for attempted murder. Investigations continued into a series of attacks on the daily newspaper *Vijesti*. Arrests were made in the case of *Dan* journalist Lidija Nikčević, who was attacked by masked men outside her office in Niksić in January.

TORTURE AND OTHER ILL-TREATMENT
In May the European Committee for the Prevention of Torture reported that in 2013 people detained or invited for "informative talks" by the police ran an "appreciable risk" of ill-treatment. They urged that law enforcement officers be regularly informed that ill-treatment is illegal.

In October, three police officers were convicted and sentenced to the minimum of three months' imprisonment for assisting in the ill-treatment of Aleksandar Pejanović in the Betonjerka detention centre in 2008 by up to 10 masked members of the Special Intervention Police Unit, whose identities were not disclosed to the prosecution by senior police officials.

RIGHTS OF LESBIAN, GAY, BISEXUAL, TRANSGENDER AND INTERSEX PEOPLE

Discrimination against LGBTI people, including threats and physical attacks, continued. Perpetrators were rarely identified, and where prosecutions took place, attacks were generally classified as misdemeanors. Legislative provisions introduced in 2013 allowing for the hate motive to be considered in sentencing were not applied. The LGBTIQ social centre in Podgorica was attacked 26 times during 2014, despite being provided with police protection; the authorities failed to conduct effective investigations and bring perpetrators to justice. The Podgorica Pride, held in November, was adequately protected by police; 10 counter-protestors were arrested.

DISCRIMINATION – ROMA

Roma, Ashkali and Egyptians displaced from Kosovo in 1999 remained without adequate housing, including those living in containers at the Konik collective centre. In November, the foundation stone was laid for the construction of adequate housing at Konik. In May, Roma families who had been under threat of eviction in Zverinjak for three years were promised adequate housing in 2015.

REFUGEES' AND MIGRANTS' RIGHTS

In July, eight men were acquitted of the unlawful transportation to Italy of 70 Roma refugees from Kosovo in 1999. Thirty-five of the refugees drowned when the boat *Miss Pat* – registered to carry six passengers – capsized in Montenegrin waters.

Around a third of the 16,000 refugees in Montenegro, including most of the 4,000 Roma, Ashkali and Egyptians displaced from Kosovo, remain at risk of statelessness. While a few had acquired the status of "foreigner with permanent residence", the remainder had not yet applied or faced barriers to obtaining personal documents, including passports, required to apply for the status before the December 2014 deadline. Montenegro remained a transit country for migrants and asylum-seekers. Asylum procedures were not effective; between January and November only two people were granted asylum.

MOROCCO/ WESTERN SAHARA

Kingdom of Morocco
Head of state: **King Mohamed VI**
Head of government: **Abdelilah Benkirane**

The authorities continued to restrict rights to freedom of expression, association and assembly. They curtailed dissent, prosecuting journalists and imprisoning activists, restricted human rights groups and other associations, and forcibly dispersed peaceful and other protests. Torture and other ill-treatment in detention persisted due to inadequate safeguards and accountability, and courts' acceptance of torture-tainted confessions. A new law closed a loophole that had enabled rapists to evade justice, but women remained inadequately protected against sexual violence. Authorities collaborated in the unlawful expulsion of migrants and asylum-seekers to Morocco from Spain. The death penalty remained in force but the government maintained a longstanding moratorium on executions.

BACKGROUND

Following the introduction of a new Constitution in 2011, the government began implementing legal and judicial reforms. Legislators approved a law to end trials of civilians before military courts and amended the Penal Code to prevent rapists evading punishment by marrying the victim. Draft Codes of Criminal and Civil Procedure had yet to be debated at the end of 2014.

Political dissent receded compared to previous years but social unrest continued, marked by protests on employment, housing, and a fairer distribution of the wealth generated from the country's natural resources.

FREEDOM OF EXPRESSION

Authorities prosecuted journalists, activists, artists and others who criticized, or were deemed to have insulted, the King or state institutions, or to have advocated "terrorism", according to the broad meaning of this term under Morocco's anti-terrorism legislation.

Journalist Ali Anouzla remained on trial charged with advocating and assisting terrorism for publishing an article on the Lakome online news website about a video released by the armed group al-Qa'ida in the Islamic Maghreb (AQIM). Although he did not republish the video, entitled *Morocco: Kingdom of Corruption and Despotism*, and branded it "propaganda", if convicted Ali Anouzla could face up to 20 years' imprisonment.[1]

Authorities brought defamation and public insult charges against journalist Hamid El Mahdaoui, after the national director of police complained about articles he had published on the Badil news website about the death of Karim Lachqar in Al Hoceima following his arrest and detention by police. The police called for the journalist to be banned from his profession for 10 years, and that he pay them heavy damages. His trial was continuing at the end of the year. Rabie Lablak, who witnessed Karim Lachqar's arrest, was prosecuted for "false reporting" about the circumstances of the arrest.

In June and July, two members of the Moroccan Association for Human Rights (AMDH), Oussama Housne and Wafae Charaf, were convicted on charges of "falsely reporting" that unidentified individuals had previously abducted and tortured them. They were sentenced to prison terms of three and two years respectively and ordered to pay compensation for "slander" of the police although neither of them had accused the police.[2] Their prosecution and imprisonment could deter victims of police abuses from coming forward.

In October, a court sentenced 17-year-old rapper Othman Atiq, who uses the stage name "Mr Crazy", to three months in prison for "insulting" Morocco's police force, "harming public morality" and "incitement to drugs consumption" in his songs and music videos.

FREEDOM OF ASSOCIATION

Authorities blocked efforts by several human rights groups to obtain official registration that would allow them to operate legally. They included AMDH branches and Freedom Now, a press freedom organization founded by Ali Anouzla and other independent journalists, human rights defenders and intellectuals. During the second half of 2014, authorities banned public events by several human rights groups across the country. Restrictions continued unabated until the end of the year despite a landmark administrative court ruling deeming the ban of an AMDH public event in Rabat in September to be unlawful.[3]

In September, authorities also prevented Amnesty International from holding its annual youth camp.[4]

FREEDOM OF ASSEMBLY

Police and other security forces dispersed peaceful and other protests by unemployed graduates, workers, students, social justice activists, and supporters of the 20 February Movement, which advocates political reform. Unnecessary or excessive force was often used. Other protests were banned. Some protesters were arrested and detained for months, then sentenced to prison terms after trials that failed to satisfy international standards of fair trial. Courts often relied on shaky evidence to convict protesters on charges of assaulting security forces or damaging property.

In December, authorities imposed a fine of 1 million dirhams (approximately €90,000) on 52 members of the Al-Adl Wal Ihsane (Justice and Spirituality) organization in the area of Tinghir and Ouarzazate for "holding unauthorized meetings" in private homes in 2008.

In April, police arrested nine men after they participated in a peaceful demonstration by graduates seeking public sector employment in Rabat. Youssef Mahfoud, Ahmed El Nioua, Moufid El Khamis, Rachid Benhamou, Soulimane Benirou, Abdelhak El Har, Aziz El Zitouni, Mohamed El Allali and Mustapha Abouzir subsequently received prison sentences of 28 months, 12 months of which were suspended, after being convicted of charges including "obstructing trains" and "rebellion".

Eleven members of the 20 February Movement were also arrested in April when they attended a peaceful and officially authorized trade union demonstration in Casablanca. Two of them received suspended sentences of two months' imprisonment and were released, but the nine others were held in pre-trial detention until June, when they were convicted on charges of assaulting police officers. They were sentenced to prison terms of six months or a year, as well as fined and ordered to pay compensation to the police. Their sentences were suspended on appeal.

REPRESSION OF DISSENT – SAHRAWI ACTIVISTS

Moroccan authorities continued to clamp down on all advocacy of Sahrawi self-determination in Western Sahara, annexed by Morocco in 1975. Sahrawi political activists, protesters, human rights defenders and media workers faced an array of restrictions affecting their rights to freedom of expression, association and assembly, and were liable to arrest, torture and other ill-treatment and prosecution. The authorities did not permit protests and forcibly dispersed gatherings when they did occur, often using excessive force.

Abdelmoutaleb Sarir alleged that police officers subjected him to torture, including rape with a bottle, after his arrest in February in connection with a protest in Laayoune, and forced him to sign an interrogation report without permitting him to read it. Judicial authorities are not known to have investigated his allegations or ordered a medical examination to identify torture-related injuries. On 10 September, a court sentenced him to 10 months in prison on charges that included "forming a criminal gang" and "insulting and assaulting security officers", on the basis of the confession contained in the interrogation report that he said he had been forced to sign.[5]

Moroccan officials in Western Sahara frustrated attempts by human rights groups such as the Sahrawi Association of Victims of Grave Human Rights Violations Committed by the Moroccan State (ASVDH) to obtain official registration, which they require to operate legally, have official premises, hold public events, and apply for funding.

At least 39 foreign journalists and activists reported that Moroccan authorities barred them from entry or expelled them from Western Sahara in 2014.

In April, the UN Security Council again extended the mandate of the UN Mission for the Referendum in Western Sahara (MINURSO) for a year, but without adding a human rights monitoring component.

TORTURE AND OTHER ILL-TREATMENT

Torture and other ill-treatment, often in the immediate aftermath of arrest, continued to be reported. In a few cases, medical examinations were ordered but generally the authorities failed to conduct investigations. Courts continued to accept as evidence of guilt confessions that defendants alleged had been obtained through torture or other ill-treatment.

The Minister of Justice and Liberties issued letters to prosecutors and judges in May, calling for them to order forensic medical examinations and investigations when faced with allegations of torture or other ill-treatment in detention.

In May, authorities re-opened an investigation into the torture of prisoner Ali Aarrass following a decision by the UN Committee against Torture. Ali Aarrass, detained in Morocco since his forcible return from Spain in 2010, reported being tortured and otherwise ill-treated during his detention in Morocco in 2010 and subsequently. The investigation was ongoing at the end of the year.

In August, a court in Agadir overturned the conviction of a defendant on the ground that his confession was coerced after a forensic medical examination had confirmed his torture. A police officer remained under investigation for alleged torture or other ill-treatment at the end of the year.

Prison inmates, including untried detainees, launched hunger strikes to protest against harsh conditions, including poor hygiene and sanitation, inadequate nutrition and health care, severe overcrowding, and limited visiting rights and access to education.

UNFAIR TRIALS

Courts frequently ignored complaints by defence lawyers about violations of criminal procedure and relied on confessions allegedly obtained through torture or other ill-treatment while defendants were held in pre-trial detention. In some cases, courts refused to allow defence lawyers to cross-examine prosecution witnesses or to call defence witnesses.

Authorities prosecuted protesters and activists on charges such as rebellion, armed gathering, assault, theft and property damage, or on drugs charges.

Mbarek Daoudi, a former Moroccan army soldier and advocate of Sahrawi self-determination, remained in detention awaiting trial before the Permanent Military Court in Rabat. The victim of an apparently politically motivated prosecution, he faced charges of possessing ammunition without a licence and attempted manufacturing of weapons, based on his possession of an antique rifle that police found when they arrested him in September 2013. His trial, due to open in January 2014, was postponed indefinitely at the prosecution's request.

In March, gendarmes arrested Omar Moujane, Ibrahim Hamdaoui and Abdessamad Madri, activists who were participating in a peaceful protest against the use of natural resources at a silver mine near Imider, in the southern Atlas mountains. The three were ill-treated during interrogation, and then tried and convicted on charges that included obstructing traffic and the right to work, unauthorized protest and criminal damage and rebellion. They were sentenced after an unfair trial to three-year prison terms, fined, and ordered to pay compensation to the mining company. The court relied heavily on interrogation reports that the defendants said they were misled into signing and not allowed to read. At the end of the year, the cases were awaiting review by the Court of Cassation.

LACK OF ACCOUNTABILITY

Despite progress on judicial reforms, the authorities made no progress on other key recommendations of the Equity and Reconciliation Commission concerning security sector reform and a national strategy to combat impunity. Victims of the serious human rights violations perpetrated between 1956 and 1999 continued to be denied justice, and several cases of enforced disappearance remained unresolved.

WOMEN'S AND GIRLS' RIGHTS

In January, parliament agreed an amendment to Article 475 of the Penal Code that removed a provision that had formerly allowed men who raped girls under 18 to escape justice by marrying the victims. However, a draft law on violence against women and children, intended to remedy the lack of a comprehensive legal and policy framework to address such abuses, remained under consideration by the expert committee to which it was referred in December 2013.

Women were inadequately protected against sexual violence, and consensual sex outside marriage remained a crime.

RIGHT TO PRIVACY

In May, September and December, courts in Fqih Ben Salah, Marrakech and Al Hoceima convicted eight men on charges that included engaging in homosexual acts and imposed prison terms of up to three years. Consensual same-sex acts remained a crime.

REFUGEES, ASYLUM-SEEKERS AND MIGRANTS

Authorities continued to collaborate with Spanish officials in unlawfully expelling migrants, mostly from sub-Saharan Africa, who entered Spain irregularly by crossing the border fence between Morocco and the Spanish enclaves of Melilla and Ceuta. Moroccan authorities co-operated in the readmission to Morocco of some of these migrants, including possible asylum-seekers, amid reports that both Spanish and Moroccan border police used unnecessary and excessive force. The authorities failed to investigate these deaths and injuries, and other incidents of racial violence against sub-Saharan migrants in August and September in Tangiers and Nador.

DEATH PENALTY

Courts imposed at least nine death sentences; there were no executions. The government maintained a de facto moratorium on executions in place since 1993. No death row prisoners had their sentences commuted to prison terms.

In December, Morocco abstained on a UN General Assembly resolution calling for a worldwide moratorium on executions.

POLISARIO CAMPS

The Tindouf camps in Algeria's Mhiriz region that accommodate Sahrawis who fled Western Sahara at the time of its annexation by Morocco continued to lack regular independent human rights monitoring. The Polisario Front took no measures to end impunity for those accused of committing human rights abuses in the camps during the 1970s and 1980s.

---

1. Morocco: Stop using 'terrorism' as a pretext to imprison journalists (Press release)
   www.amnesty.org/en/articles/news/2014/05/morocco-stop-using-terrorism-pretext-imprison-journalists/

2. Morocco: Activists jailed for reporting torture must be released immediately (Press release)
   www.amnesty.org/en/articles/news/2014/08/morocco-activists-jailed-reporting-torture-must-be-released-immediately/

3. Morocco/Western Sahara: Lift restrictions on associations (Public statement)
   www.amnesty.org/download/Documents/212000/mde290102014en.pdf

4. Amnesty International deplores the Moroccan authorities' decision to ban youth camp (MDE 29/006/2014)
   www.amnesty.org/en/library/info/MDE29/006/2014/en

5. Morocco: Sahrawis on hunger strike against torture (MDE 29/007/2014)
   www.amnesty.org/en/library/info/MDE29/007/2014/en

MOZAMBIQUE

Republic of Mozambique
Head of state and government: Filipe Jacinto Nyussi (replaced Armando Guebuza in October)

Police used unlawful force and firearms resulting in some deaths. Criticism of President Guebuza on Facebook led to criminal charges against one person. Draft laws impacting on the rights of women and girls were approved by Parliament, but still had to be passed into law.

BACKGROUND

On 23 May, Afonso Dhlakama, leader of the Mozambique National Resistance, declared that he would stand for Presidential elections. In September he returned to the capital, Maputo, and publicly signed a peace deal with President Armando Guebuza. Afonso Dhlakama had been in hiding since October 2013 when Mozambique armed forces invaded his base in Satunjira, Sofala province. The peace deal signed in September ended the two year-long clashes between Renamo fighters and the ForçasArmadas de Defesa de Moçambique (FADM), as well as the attacks by Renamo fighters on buses and cars on the main highway. The clashes resulted in the deaths of scores of people, including civilians.

On 15 October Mozambique held its fifth Presidential elections since independence in 1975. The ruling party, Front for the Liberation of Mozambique, maintained power and the former Minister of Defence, Filipe Jacinto Nyussi, became Mozambique's third democratically elected President.

Mozambique's human rights record was assessed at the 55th Ordinary Session of the African Commission on Human and Peoples' Rights hosted by Angola in Luanda from 28 April to 12 May.[1]

UNLAWFUL KILLINGS

Police reportedly made unlawful use of firearms in Maputo, Gaza and Nampula provinces resulting in at least four deaths. No investigations appear to have been carried out into these cases to determine the lawfulness of the use of firearms by the police.

In January, police shot and killed 26-year-old Ribeiro João Nhassengo and another person. A police spokesperson claimed that police responded to an anonymous call regarding cars outside a shop in the Triunfo neighbourhood of Maputo in the early hours around 29 January and found men in two cars with an alleged kidnapping victim. The police spokesperson stated that the suspects let the victim go, but a shoot-out ensued. Ribeiro João Nhassengo and

another unnamed individual were reportedly shot in the crossfire. However, footage of the incident showed that Ribeiro João Nhassengo had been shot and killed while inside a car with closed windows. No investigation has been carried out into the circumstances surrounding the deaths to determine the lawfulness of the use of firearms by police.

EXCESSIVE USE OF FORCE

There were reports of police using excessive force against alleged criminal suspects, those they suspected of being Renamo fighters, as well as unarmed civilians.

On 21 June, an armed police officer in the central neighbourhood of Maputo shot at a vehicle after an altercation regarding an illegal traffic manoeuvre. The officer from the Mozambique Republic Police reportedly stopped the driver around 8pm and questioned him about the illegal manoeuvre. When the driver requested a traffic officer be called to provide him with a traffic fine, the police officer reportedly threatened to kill him. An altercation ensued and the police officer reportedly shot at the car three times.

FREEDOM OF EXPRESSION

In August, parliament provisionally approved the Access to Information Bill, which had been in discussion since 2005. It still required further approval by parliament and signing into law by the President at the end of the year. Despite this step forward, the right to freedom of expression was suppressed.

In May, economist Carlos Nuno Castelo-Branco was called before the Public Prosecutor's office in Maputo to answer questions related to charges against him for defamation against the Head of State, which constitutes a crime against the security of the state. The charges emanated from an open letter Carlos Nuno Castelo-Branco had posted on his Facebook page in November 2013, questioning the governance of the country by President Guebuza. The open letter was subsequently published by some newspapers in the country. No further proceedings were reported by the end of the year.

WOMEN'S AND GIRLS' RIGHTS

In July, parliament approved the draft Criminal Code without a controversial article that would have enabled rapists to escape prosecution by marrying their victim. Human rights activists had campaigned against this article.[2]

The draft approved by Parliament further did not require an official complaint from relevant individuals in the case of sexual offences against those under 16 years of age before starting a criminal proceeding. It still required an official complaint to be made by all other victims of sexual offences before a criminal proceeding could be instituted. However, an article remained on the rape of minors, which referred to minors as those under 12 years of age. The draft law was waiting to be signed by the President before becoming law at the end of the year.

---

1. Statement on prison conditions to the African Commission on Human and Peoples' Rights

   www.amnesty.org/en/library/info/AFR01/008/2014/en

   Mozambique: Submission to the African Commission on Human and Peoples' Rights: 54th Ordinary Session of the African Commission on Human and Peoples' Rights

   www.amnesty.org/en/library/info/AFR41/007/2013/en

2. Mozambique: New Criminal Code puts women's rights at risk (AFR 41/001/2014)

   www.amnesty.org/en/documents/AFR41/001/2014/en/

MYANMAR

Republic of the Union of Myanmar
Head of state and government: **Thein Sein**

Despite ongoing political, legal and economic reforms, progress on human rights stalled, with some backward steps

in key areas. The situation of the Rohingya deteriorated, with ongoing discrimination in law and practice exacerbated by a dire humanitarian situation. Anti-Muslim violence persisted, with the authorities failing to hold suspected perpetrators to account. Reports of abuses of international human rights and humanitarian law in areas of armed conflict persisted. Freedoms of expression and peaceful assembly remained severely restricted, with scores of human rights defenders, journalists and political activists arrested and imprisoned. Impunity persisted for past crimes.

BACKGROUND

Myanmar assumed the chair of the Association of Southeast Asian Nations (ASEAN) in January. In March, the government announced parliamentary by-elections for the end of the year, later cancelled, and general elections in 2015. Despite a national campaign to amend the 2008 Constitution, led by the opposition National League for Democracy (NLD) and its leader Aung San Suu Kyi, by the end of the year she was still constitutionally barred from running for the presidency, and the military still held a veto power on any future constitutional changes.

DISCRIMINATION

The situation of the Rohingya worsened during the year. Individuals suffered persistent discrimination in law and policy, exacerbated by a deepening humanitarian crisis, ongoing eruptions of religious and anti-Muslim violence, and government failures to investigate attacks on Rohingya and other Muslims. The authorities also failed to address incitement to violence based on national, racial and religious hatred.

In January, reports emerged of clashes between security forces, Buddhist Rakhine and Muslim Rohingya in Du Chee Yar Tan village, Rakhine state. Two investigations – one by the government and one by the Myanmar National Human Rights

Commission (MNHRC) – claimed to have found no evidence to substantiate allegations of any violence. In July, two people were killed and dozens injured when religious violence broke out in Mandalay, the second largest city. Again, no independent investigation was known to have been carried out.

An estimated 139,000 people – mostly Rohingya – remained displaced in Rakhine state for a third year after violent clashes erupted between Rakhine Buddhists, Rohingya and other Muslims in 2012. The dire humanitarian situation worsened after the expulsion of some humanitarian organizations and the withdrawal of others in February and March, following attacks against them by Rakhine people. The displaced population were left without access to emergency and life-sustaining assistance. By the end of the year, although most organizations had returned, assistance was still not back to levels prior to the withdrawals.

Violence between religious communities and restricted humanitarian access continued within a broader context of discriminatory laws and policies against the Rohingya, who remained deprived of nationality under the 1982 Citizenship Act. As a result they continued to face restrictions on their freedom of movement, with repercussions for their access to livelihoods. On 30 March, one day before the start of the first national census in Myanmar since 1983, the Ministry of Information announced that Rohingya would have to register as "Bengalis" – a term used to deny recognition to the Rohingya and to imply that they are all migrants from Bangladesh. In October, the government announced a new Rakhine State Action Plan which if implemented would further entrench discrimination and segregation of Rohingya. The announcement of the plan appeared to trigger a new wave of people fleeing the country in boats, adding to the more than 87,000 who, according to UNHCR, the UN refugee agency, had already fled by sea since the violence started in 2012.

INTERNAL ARMED CONFLICTS

The government and ethnic armed groups failed to agree to a nationwide ceasefire, despite the signing in 2012 of preliminary ceasefire agreements. The armed conflict in Kachin and Northern Shan states continued into its fourth year, with violations of international humanitarian and human rights law reported on both sides, including unlawful killings and torture and other ill-treatment, including rape and other crimes of sexual violence.[1] The conflict started in June 2011 after the Myanmar Army broke its ceasefire with the Kachin Independence Army (KIA), leading to widespread and continuous displacement of civilian populations. Around 98,000 people remained displaced at the end of the year. The government continued to deny full and sustained access for humanitarian workers to displaced communities in Kachin state, particularly those displaced in KIA-controlled areas.

In September, fighting erupted in Karen and Mon states between the Myanmar Army and armed opposition groups, causing civilians to flee.

The Myanmar Army was reported to have discharged 376 children and young adults from its forces as part of ongoing efforts to end the use of child soldiers and underage military recruitment.

FREEDOMS OF EXPRESSION AND PEACEFUL ASSEMBLY

Freedoms of expression and peaceful assembly remained severely restricted, with scores of human rights defenders, journalists, political activists and farmers arrested or imprisoned solely for the peaceful exercise of their rights.

Ko Htin Kyaw, leader of the Movement for Democracy Current Force (MDCF), a community-based organization, was convicted on 11 different counts of violating Section 505(b) of the Penal Code and three separate counts under Article 18 of the Peaceful Assembly and Peaceful Procession Law. He was sentenced to a total of 13 years and four months' imprisonment for delivering speeches, distributing leaflets and holding protests calling on the government to resign and against land evictions. Three other members of MDCF were also jailed for peaceful political activities.[2]

In June the President signed into law amendments to the Peaceful Assembly and Peaceful Procession Law, commonly used by authorities to imprison peaceful protesters since its adoption in 2011. However, despite the revisions the law retained severe restrictions on the right to freedom of peaceful assembly.[3]

Media reforms were undermined by the arrest and imprisonment of journalists and other media workers. In July, five media workers for the *Unity* newspaper were sentenced to 10 years in prison under the Official Secrets Act for the publication of an article about an alleged secret chemical weapons factory. Their sentence was reduced on appeal to seven years' imprisonment in October.[4] At least 10 media workers remained in prison by the end of the year.

PRISONERS OF CONSCIENCE

The President failed to keep his promise to release all prisoners of conscience by the end of 2013, despite a far-reaching Presidential Pardon announced on 30 December 2013. Muslim leader Dr Tun Aung was among those not released under the pardon. One prisoner amnesty was announced in 2014, just weeks ahead of major international meetings in the country. Only one prisoner of conscience was believed to be among those released.

The Committee for Scrutinizing the Remaining Prisoners of Conscience, established by the government in February 2013, did not function effectively and it was unclear whether it would continue to operate beyond 2014.

LAND DISPUTES

Protests against land confiscations and forced evictions were widespread. A parliamentary committee established to investigate land disputes in 2012 had reportedly received over 6,000 reports of land confiscations. However, failures to resolve or respond to land disputes led farmers and other affected people increasingly to resort to so-called "plough protests", with farmers ploughing the disputed land. Some protests were met with unnecessary or excessive use of force by security forces. Many farmers and human rights defenders supporting them were arrested and charged, often under provisions in the Penal Code relating to trespass and criminal damage.

In March, members of the Michaungkan community resumed a sit-in protest close to Yangon's City Hall after the authorities failed to resolve their land dispute case. They were calling for the return of land which they alleged was confiscated by the military in the 1990s and for compensation for their losses. Community leader U Sein Than was subsequently arrested for protesting without permission and obstruction, and sentenced to two years' imprisonment.[5]

In December, police opened fire on protesters demonstrating against their lands being taken over for the Letpadaung copper mine in Sagaing region. One person was killed and several injured, sparking a series of peaceful protests in major cities across the country. At least seven peaceful activists were subsequently charged with protesting without permission and offences under the Penal Code. Environmental and human rights concerns related to the mining project had not been addressed by the end of the year.

TORTURE AND OTHER ILL-TREATMENT

Torture was still not criminalized as a distinct offence and Myanmar failed to ratify the UN Convention against Torture as promised by the Deputy Minister of Foreign Affairs in January. Officers from the police and military faced persistent allegations of torture and other ill-treatment, both conflict-related and of criminal suspects. Investigations into complaints were rare and suspected perpetrators were seldom held to account.

Victims and their families did not have access to effective remedy.[6]

In October it was reported that freelance journalist Aung Kyaw Naing, also known as Par Gyi, was killed while in the custody of the Myanmar Army. He had been detained on 30 September in Mon state while reporting on the resumption of fighting between the Myanmar Army and armed groups in the area. The Myanmar Army claimed that he was a "communications captain" for an armed opposition group, and that he was shot while attempting to escape military custody. After national and international pressure, in November the police and the MNHRC opened an investigation. At the end of the year no one was known to have been held to account for his death.[7]

In August, Myanmar Army soldiers detained and beat seven farmers in Kone Pyin village, Chin State, whom they accused of having contact with the Chin National Army, an armed opposition group. The seven were ill-treated – some of them tortured – over a period of between four and nine days. By the end of the year there was no information about an independent investigation into the case, or of suspected direct perpetrators or their superiors being brought to justice.[8]

IMPUNITY

Immunity from prosecution for past violations by the security forces and other government officials remained codified in Article 445 of the 2008 Constitution. Victims of past human rights violations and their families continued to be denied truth, justice, compensation and any other form of reparation.

More than three years after Sumlut Roi Ja was detained by the military, her fate and whereabouts remained unknown. She disappeared in October 2011 in Kachin state after being detained by Myanmar Army soldiers along with her husband and father-in-law. Her husband, who managed to escape with her father-in-law, lodged a case with the Supreme Court in January 2012. The case

was dismissed in March 2012, with the Court citing lack of evidence.

The MNHRC remained largely ineffective in responding to complaints of human rights violations. In March, the law establishing the MNHRC was adopted by the national Parliament and a new Commission was formed in September. Most members were government-affiliated and the selection and appointment process lacked transparency, casting further doubts on the independence and effectiveness of the Commission.

DEATH PENALTY

On 2 January the President commuted all death sentences to terms of imprisonment. However, provisions allowing for the imposition of the death penalty remained part of the legal framework, and at least one new death sentence was imposed during the year.

INTERNATIONAL SCRUTINY

The new UN Special Rapporteur on the situation of human rights in Myanmar visited the country in July; she presented her report to the General Assembly in October, warning against potential backtracking on human rights. The authorities failed to sign an agreement for the establishment of an Office of the UN High Commissioner for Human Rights and to ratify core international human rights treaties. In November, Myanmar was under increased scrutiny when world leaders gathered in the capital, Nay Pyi Taw, for the ASEAN and East Asia Summits. US President Barack Obama visited the country for the second time.

---

1. Myanmar: Three years on, conflict continues in Kachin State (ASA 16/010/2014)

   www.amnesty.org/en/library/info/ASA16/010/2014/en

2. Myanmar: Further Information: Activist organization targeted again (ASA 16/029/2014)

   www.amnesty.org/en/library/info/ASA16/029/2014/en

3. Myanmar: Stop using repressive law against peaceful protesters (ASA 16/025/2014)

   www.amnesty.org/en/library/info/ASA16/025/2014/en

4. Myanmar: Further Information: Myanmar media workers imprisoned in Myanmar (ASA 16/013/2014)
   www.amnesty.org/en/library/info/ASA16/023/2014/en

5. Myanmar: Further sentences for protester in Myanmar: U Sein Than (ASA 16/021/2014)
   www.amnesty.org/en/library/info/ASA16/021/2014/en

6. Myanmar: Take immediate steps to safeguard against torture (ASA 16/011/2014)
   www.amnesty.org/en/library/info/ASA16/011/2014/en

7. Myanmar: Ensure independent and impartial investigation into the death of journalist (ASA 16/028/2014)
   www.amnesty.org/en/library/info/ASA16/028/2014/en

8. Myanmar: Farmers at risk after beating by soldiers (ASA 16/002/2014)
   www.amnesty.org/en/library/info/ASA16/002/2014/en

NAMIBIA

Republic of Namibia
Head of state: Hifikipunye Pohamba
Head of government: Hage Geingob

The long-running treason trial of Caprivi detainees continued, with most of the men having spent more than 14 years in custody. The policy of not offering protection to refugees persecuted for their sexual orientation was challenged by a gay asylum-seeker from Uganda. Gender-based violence remained a concern.

BACKGROUND

General elections were held on 28 November. The South West Africa People's Organization (SWAPO) secured 87% of the presidential vote, and 80% of the National Assembly vote.

CAPRIVI DETAINEES' TRIAL

Sixty-five men in the Caprivi treason case remained in detention facing 278 charges, including counts of high treason, sedition, murder and attempted murder. Forty-three Caprivi detainees had been acquitted on 11 February 2013. Some of the released prisoners of conscience sued the government for damages. Nine detainees who were tried separately and had been found guilty by the High Court had their convictions set aside and their cases referred back to the High Court for retrial. Eight of the accused claimed that they had been abducted by state agents in Botswana and unlawfully transferred to Namibia on various dates between September 2002 and December 2013.

Many of the Caprivi detainees were possible prisoners of conscience because they were arrested solely on the basis of their actual or perceived political views, ethnicity or membership of certain organizations. The group was being tried under what is known as the "common purpose" doctrine, which shifts the burden of proof from the prosecution to the defendants and undermines the right to presumption of innocence. Another accused man was on trial separately; his trial had not concluded by the end of the year.

REFUGEES AND ASYLUM-SEEKERS

In April, Namibia's Commissioner for Refugees, Nkrumah Mushelenga, reportedly said in the press that "[Namibia's] domestic refugee law does not have a provision granting refugee status for being gay". However, as a signatory to the UN Refugee Convention and its 1967 Protocol, Namibia is expressly forbidden from returning refugees who face persecution in their country of origin on the basis of belonging to a social group with a well-founded fear of persecution.

In August, a Ugandan asylum-seeker was granted an urgent halt to his deportation from Namibia. The man had sought asylum because of his fear of persecution in Uganda on the basis of his sexual orientation. The man, who identifies himself as being gay, was detained in Walvis Bay and was facing deportation back to Uganda where legislation had recently been adopted criminalizing homosexuality (although the law was later annulled by Uganda's Constitutional Court).

EXCESSIVE USE OF FORCE

On 27 August an unarmed protester, Frieda Ndatipo, was shot dead by police during a demonstration outside the headquarters of the ruling SWAPO party. She was taking part in a protest by Children of the Liberation Struggle, a pressure group formed to demand benefits and employment from the government for the children of SWAPO members who died in exile prior to the country's independence.

VIOLENCE AGAINST WOMEN AND GIRLS

Gender-based violence remained a serious concern. The government declared 6 March as the national day of prayer for action against gender-based violence. A report by UNAIDS and Namibian NGO Victim 2 Survivors recommended, among other things, that gender-based violence be declared a national emergency, that a national action plan on gender-based violence be implemented, and that support be mobilized from all sectors of society, including the government, legislature, judiciary, civil society, traditional authorities, faith organizations, media outlets, the private sector and community members.

NAURU

Republic of Nauru
Head of state and government: **Baron Waqa**

Asylum-seekers were arbitrarily detained in harsh conditions in accordance with an agreement with the Australian government. The arbitrary removal of judges and suspension of parliamentarians raised concerns about the rule of law and freedom of expression.

REFUGEES AND ASYLUM-SEEKERS

As a small island nation, Nauru had limited capacity to meet the needs of its own population, including the rights to adequate housing, access to clean drinking water, education, health care and employment. The presence of refugees placed a significant strain on already limited resources.

As at 30 June 2014, there were 1,169 asylum-seekers in the Australian-run immigration detention centre on Nauru, including 193 children and 289 women. A total of 168 people who had received positive refugee assessments were accommodated separately.

At least 61 asylum-seekers were awaiting trial on charges relating to a disturbance at the detention centre in July 2013. There were concerns over fair trial rights for these asylum-seekers, including around inadequate legal representation and delays in court proceedings.

Asylum-seeking children were particularly vulnerable to mental health issues due to arbitrary and prolonged detention, lack of meaningful activities and inadequate provision for education. Allegations of physical and sexual abuse were made by asylum-seekers, but it was not clear what measures, if any, were taken by Australian or Nauruan authorities to investigate. Intolerable conditions in detention created a risk of refoulement, in cases where detainees felt they had no option but to return to a place where their lives or human rights were at risk.

In April 2014, the UN Working Group on Arbitrary Detention and Amnesty International were both refused access to the immigration detention centre.[1]

JUSTICE SYSTEM

In January, Nauru's only Magistrate and Chief Justice were effectively dismissed by the government, raising concerns around the independence of the judiciary and the rule of law.

FREEDOM OF EXPRESSION

In June, five opposition MPs were suspended for being critical of the government and speaking to foreign media. The MPs remained suspended at the end of the year, reducing the number of sitting parliamentarians from 19 to 14.

Increased visa fees for journalists from US$183 to US$7,328 limited the ability of foreign media to visit and report on events in Nauru.

---

1. Nauru's refusal of access to detention centre another attempt to hide conditions (NWS 11/081/2014)

www.amnesty.org/en/for-media/press-releases/nauru-s-refusal-access-detention-centre-another-attempt-hide-conditions-201

NEPAL

Federal Democratic Republic of Nepal
Head of state: **Ram Baran Yadav**
Head of government: **Sushil Koirala**

Impunity was further entrenched as the Constituent Assembly passed an act to establish a transitional justice mechanism with the power to recommend amnesties for crimes under international law committed during the country's civil war (1996-2006), in defiance of a Supreme Court ruling. National institutions protecting human rights were weakened by a lack of political will, and impunity persisted for past and current human rights violations. Discrimination, including on the basis of gender, caste, class, ethnic origin and religion, remained rife. Arbitrary detention, torture and extrajudicial executions were reported throughout the year.

BACKGROUND

The second Constituent Assembly was formed on 21 January; the first was dissolved in May 2012 after failing to draft a new Constitution. Sushil Koirala of the Nepali Congress Party was appointed as Prime Minister on 11 February. The new Constituent Assembly pledged to promulgate a new Constitution by 22 January 2015, although it remained unclear whether this could be achieved as political parties debated the model of federalism and greater autonomy for ethnic minorities and Indigenous Peoples. In July, the government adopted its fourth Five Year Human Rights National Action Plan. In September, a year after the terms of previous Commissioners of the National Human Rights Commission (NHRC) had expired, the government elected former Chief Justice Anup Raj Sharma as Chair and nominated new commissioners in October.

TRANSITIONAL JUSTICE

On 25 April, the parliament passed the Truth and Reconciliation Commission (TRC) Act, establishing two commissions, a TRC and a Commission on Enforced Disappearances, with the power to recommend amnesties, including for serious human rights violations. This was despite a Supreme Court ruling in January that a similar 2013 TRC ordinance with the power to recommend amnesties contravened international human rights law and the spirit of the 2007 Interim Constitution. Victims' families filed a petition with the Supreme Court for the provisions on amnesties to be amended.

IMPUNITY

Accountability for human rights abuses and victims' rights to justice, truth and reparation continued to be seriously undermined by police failures to register First Information Reports (FIRs), conduct investigations and follow court orders, including in cases of alleged extrajudicial executions, human trafficking, gender-based violence, and torture and other ill-treatment.

In July, forensic evidence collected by the NHRC on the 2003 enforced disappearance and extrajudicial execution of five students in Dhanusha district confirmed the identities of the victims, who had been blindfolded and shot at close range with ammunition used only by the Nepalese Army at the time. The police had delayed their investigation for the four previous years citing a lack of evidence, and had not acted on the new findings by the end of the year.

ABUSES IN THE TERAI REGION

A longstanding culture of impunity meant that, although the activities of armed groups operating in the Terai (Madhes) region declined, violations by police continued to be reported, including arbitrary detention, torture and extrajudicial executions. Police failed to file FIRs, conduct investigations or prosecute those responsible for these crimes.

C.K. Raut, a vocal proponent of independence for the Terai, was arrested and charged with sedition on 8 October for his alleged involvement in "anti-national activities"; he had called for an "independent Madhes" at a public rally in Morang. He was later arrested several times while on bail for attempting to hold public rallies. Several of his supporters were also arrested and injured in police crackdowns at public meetings.

MIGRANT WORKERS' RIGHTS

At least half a million Nepalese migrated abroad through official channels for work, largely in low-skilled sectors such as construction, manufacturing and domestic work. Many continued to be trafficked for exploitation and forced labour by recruitment agencies and brokers. Recruiters deceived migrant workers about their pay and working conditions, and charged fees in excess of government-imposed limits, forcing many to take up loans at exorbitant rates. Women aged under 30 were still banned from migrating for work to Gulf states. While this was intended to protect women, it meant that many were forced to use informal channels, thus increasing their risk of exploitation and abuse. Concerns on health and safety were highlighted as deaths of workers abroad reached 880 between July 2013 and July 2014.

The government made some efforts to address trafficking and corruption in the recruitment process. However, in practice, unscrupulous recruitment agencies continued to operate with impunity while trafficked victims and their families faced enormous obstacles in accessing complaints and compensation mechanisms, such as the Foreign Employment Welfare Fund.

TORTURE AND OTHER ILL-TREATMENT

Torture and other ill-treatment of men, women and children continued to be perpetrated by police, particularly during pre-trial detention, to extract confessions and intimidate individuals. In April, the UN Human Rights Committee reminded Nepal of its obligation to enact a law defining and criminalizing torture, and to introduce effective sanctions and remedies for the crime of torture and other ill-treatment in line with international standards. At the end of 2014 no action had been taken to address these issues.

DISCRIMINATION

Discrimination, including on the basis of gender, caste, class, ethnic origin and religion, persisted. Victims were subject to exclusion and ill-treatment, and torture including rape and other sexual violence. Women from marginalized groups, including Dalits and impoverished women, continued to face particular hardship because of multiple forms of discrimination. The Caste-based Discrimination and Untouchability Act of 2011 was applied in only a handful of criminal cases due to a lack of awareness about the Act and victims' fears of reporting attacks. Rape laws continued to be inadequate and to reflect discriminatory attitudes towards women.

SEXUAL AND REPRODUCTIVE RIGHTS AND RIGHT TO HEALTH

Women and girls in Nepal continued to experience serious gender-based discrimination. This limited their ability to control their sexuality and make choices related to reproduction, including use of contraception; to challenge early marriages;

to ensure adequate antenatal and maternal health care; and to access sufficient nutritious food. It also put them at risk of domestic violence, including marital rape. One consequence of these factors was that women and girls continued to be at high risk of developing the reproductive health condition uterine prolapse, often at a very early age.

Government efforts to eradicate gender discrimination against women and girls continued to be ineffective in reducing women's risk of uterine prolapse. Despite progress in reducing maternal mortality, the unmet need for contraception remained high and significant numbers of women and girls were unable to access skilled birth attendants. Disparities across ethnic groups and geographical regions meant this was a particular problem for Dalit women, Muslim women and women living in the Terai. The government's Five Year Human Rights National Action Plan expressed, among other things, the intention of the Ministry of Health and Population to "adopt preventive measures to end uterine prolapse." This welcome step, however, did not contain details on the measures or on how the government planned to ensure their implementation.

NETHERLANDS

Kingdom of the Netherlands
Head of state: **King Willem-Alexander**
Head of government: **Mark Rutte**

Irregular migrants continued to face long periods of immigration detention under excessively strict conditions. Concerns were raised around ethnic profiling by law enforcement agencies.

REFUGEES' AND MIGRANTS' RIGHTS
Immigration detention
Although the number of people placed in immigration detention was declining, migrants without regular legal status continued to face disproportionately long periods of detention under excessively strict conditions. In December 2013 the Minister for Security and Justice made legislative proposals to reform immigration detention. However, in February 2014, Amnesty International and 10 other civil society organizations raised numerous concerns about the draft legislation. In October, the government opened a child-friendly closed location for families with children whose detention it deemed unavoidable, instead of holding them in a prison-like facility.
Refoulement
In June, the Council of State rejected requests for asylum from three men from the Democratic Republic of the Congo. The men had given testimony to the International Criminal Court in proceedings against a Congolese former militia leader accused of war crimes and crimes against humanity. The men, who themselves face allegations of having committed gross human rights abuses, were returned to the Democratic Republic of the Congo in July, despite the risk of torture and the death penalty that they would face there.[1]

The Netherlands continued to deport rejected asylum-seekers to Somalia, against guidelines issued by UNHCR, the UN refugee agency. In one case from November 2013, Ahmed Said was deported from the Netherlands to Mogadishu and injured three days later in a suicide bombing.
Economic, social and cultural rights
In October 2013, the European Committee of Social Rights recommended that the Netherlands introduce measures to meet the needs of persons at immediate risk of destitution in response to a complaint brought by the Conference of European Churches about the situation of migrants without

regular legal status. No steps were taken to implement the decision in 2014.

There were ongoing reports during the year of migrants without regular status setting up makeshift accommodation and facing threats of eviction. In June, a pilot project in Amsterdam to accommodate rejected asylum-seekers was closed.

DISCRIMINATION – ETHNIC PROFILING

NGOs and intergovernmental bodies continued to raise concerns about ethnic profiling by law enforcement agencies, in particular around the lack of clear guidelines to avoid racial profiling, and on data gathering in stop-and-search operations. In response to criticism by the European Commission against Racism and Intolerance and Amnesty International, among others, the Dutch government and the Dutch police both explicitly rejected ethnic profiling as discriminatory.

INTERNATIONAL JUSTICE

On 6 September 2013 the Netherlands Supreme Court found the Dutch state liable for the deaths of three men during the Srebrenica genocide.[2] Dutch troops serving as UN peacekeepers in Srebrenica sent three Bosniak Muslim men, part of a larger group of over 300 men, away from a "safe area" on 13 July 1995, effectively handing them over to Bosnian Serb forces, who killed the majority of those handed over. In July, the Hague District Court ruled that the Dutch state was liable for the loss suffered by the families of the more than 300 men and boys mentioned above, but not for the acts of the Dutch troops prior to the fall of Srebrenica, or the failure of those troops to hold the "safe area".

UNLAWFUL KILLINGS

In November, the European Court of Human Rights ruled that the Netherlands' investigation into the fatal shooting by army personnel of an Iraqi civilian in June 2004 in Iraq violated his right to life and awarded the victim's father compensation of €25,000.

1. Netherlands: Do not return ICC witnesses at risk of death penalty, ill-treatment and unfair trials to the Democratic Republic of Congo (EUR 35/001/2014)
www.amnesty.org/en/library/info/EUR35/001/2014/en

2. Netherlands: Supreme Court hands down historic judgment over Srebrenica genocide (PRE 01/449/2013)
www.amnesty.org.uk/press-releases/netherlands-supreme-court-hands-down-historic-judgment-over-srebrenica-genocide

NEW ZEALAND

New Zealand
Head of state: **Queen Elizabeth II, represented by Jerry Mateparae**
Head of government: **John Key**

Economic, social and cultural rights lacked equal legal protection to civil and political rights. Māori (Indigenous People) continued to be over-represented in the prison system. Family violence was widespread and levels of child poverty remained high.

LEGAL, CONSTITUTIONAL OR INSTITUTIONAL DEVELOPMENTS

The government did not respond formally to recommendations made in the 2013 Constitutional Advisory Panel report to improve the Bill of Rights Act.

New Zealand's second UN Universal Periodic Review took place in January 2014 where concerns included the lack of human rights oversight in parliamentary processes. New Zealand rejected many recommendations to strengthen domestic human rights protections.[1] Economic, social and cultural rights lacked full protection in domestic legislation, and remedies for breaches remained inadequate.

JUSTICE SYSTEM

The UN Working Group on Arbitrary Detention visited New Zealand in 2014 and expressed concern that Māori made up 50% of the total prison population and 65% of the female prison population, despite being only 15% of the general population.

The Working Group underlined the inadequacy of legal protections for 17-year-olds, considered adults under criminal law, and criticized New Zealand's reservation to Article 37(c) of the UN Convention on the Rights of the Child on the detention of youth and adult offenders in the same facilities.

WOMEN'S AND CHILDREN'S RIGHTS

The 2013 Technical Report on Child Poverty found that 27% of New Zealand children remained in poverty. Māori and Pacific Island children were disproportionately represented in child poverty statistics, highlighting systemic discrimination.

Violence against women and children remained high. Māori were over-represented as both victims and perpetrators of domestic violence. The Vulnerable Children Act 2014 aimed to protect children from violence but there was no national plan of action to combat domestic violence.

REFUGEES AND ASYLUM-SEEKERS

New Zealand retained the option to enact legislation to utilize offshore immigration detention centres. Disparities remained in the quality of services provided to refugees who arrived under the humanitarian intake of UNHCR, the UN refugee agency, and those arriving in the country spontaneously and whose refugee claims were accepted by the government.

RIGHTS TO PRIVACY AND FREEDOM OF MOVEMENT

A 2013 report found the Government Communication Security Bureau (GCSB) illegally spied on individuals within New Zealand. Domestic legislation was subsequently amended to allow the GCSB to target New Zealanders' communications.

In 2014 the government passed the Countering Terrorist Fighters Legislation Act

which significantly impacted rights to privacy and freedom of movement. The extremely limited time period for consideration of the bill restricted public consultation and prohibited a robust assessment of compliance with international human rights standards.[2]

---

1. New Zealand rejects international recommendations to address inequality (Press release)
   www.amnesty.org.nz/news/new-zealand-rejects-international-recommendations-address-inequality
2. Joint statement on the Countering Terrorist Fighters (Foreign Fighters) Bill 2014 (Public statement)
   www.amnesty.org.nz/files/NEW-ZEALAND_Joint-Statement-on-Countering-Terrorist-Fighters-Bill.pdf

NICARAGUA

Republic of Nicaragua
Head of state and government: **Daniel Ortega Saavedra**

Changes introduced by the government to the Comprehensive Law against Violence against Women raised serious concerns. The total ban on abortion remained in place.

BACKGROUND

Amendments to the Constitution entered into force in February, allowing the President to be elected with a simple majority. Restrictions on consecutive presidential re-election were also lifted.

In May, the UN Subcommittee on Prevention of Torture expressed deep concern at the situation of people deprived of liberty in the country. Nicaragua's human rights record was assessed under the UN Universal Periodic Review (UPR). The state accepted recommendations relating to discrimination against Indigenous Peoples and people of African descent but rejected calls for the decriminalization of abortion and to accede to additional international human rights instruments.

On 19 July, people travelling home after attending the Sandinista revolution anniversary celebrations were shot at in two separate incidents. Five people died and 19 were injured. In October, 12 men were tried and sentenced to between two and 30 years' imprisonment for the attack. Three of them testified in court that they were tortured and forced to give a confession, raising concerns about the investigation and the fairness of the trial.

WOMEN'S RIGHTS

Reforms passed in September 2013 weakened the effectiveness of the Comprehensive Law against Violence against Women (Law 779), introduced in 2012. As a result of the reforms, women who filed complaints about domestic violence may be offered mediation with their attackers in cases involving crimes punishable by less than five years' imprisonment, such as actual bodily harm, the abduction of children, and threats. This means that women may find themselves having to face their attackers in the mediation process, while those accused of committing abuses may avoid being held to account for their crimes. According to the NGO Women's Network against Violence, seven of the 47 women killed in the first six months of 2014 had been in mediation with their abusive partner. An executive decree issued in July further reinforced the mediation aspect of the law and reduced the definition of femicide to killings of women within relationships. The executive decree raised concerns around the use of mediation to redress violence against women. Numerous legal challenges against the decree were submitted to the Supreme Court of Justice.

The total ban on all forms of abortion remained in place. Since the total ban was introduced in 2006, dozens of appeals against it have been submitted to the Supreme Court of Justice. However, the Court had yet to rule on these appeals.

On 8 March, International Women's Day, a peaceful demonstration to highlight gender inequalities and violence against women was blocked by police. Women human rights defenders claimed they had obtained the necessary permission for the event and feared it marked a further limitation on independent civil society movements.

FREEDOM OF ASSEMBLY

No progress was made in investigating alleged beatings of students and senior citizen demonstrators in Managua in June 2013 by what appeared to be government supporters, while the police stood by. More than 100 students supported the protest by senior citizen groups to demand a minimum state pension.

INDIGENOUS PEOPLES' RIGHTS

In March, Indigenous, Afro-descendant and other groups expressed concern at the government's decision to grant a licence for the construction of a major infrastructure project known as the Gran Canal Interoceánico, a channel connecting the Atlantic Ocean and Pacific Ocean. Among other concerns, the groups claimed that the licence was granted without the free, prior or informed consent of the Indigenous groups whose territory the canal would cut across. Works started in December, amid protests that resulted in clashes with protesters and included reports of police beatings of detainees.

NIGER

Republic of Niger
Head of state: Mahamadou Issoufou
Head of government: Brigi Rafini

A new government was appointed in August 2013 incorporating members of the opposition; but some of them resigned later in protest at under-representation. The government implemented strict anti-terrorism security measures, including restricted movement in certain neighbourhoods of Niamey, the capital, where foreign embassies were located. Niger was hosting over 57,000 refugees at the end of the year, including 16,000 as a result of the 2013 Mali conflict and the ongoing violence in northeastern Nigeria.

LEGAL, CONSTITUTIONAL OR INSTITUTIONAL DEVELOPMENTS

In May, more than 30 members of the political opposition, the Nigerien Democratic Movement for an African Federation, were arrested. The arrests happened in connection with an investigation into shots fired at the home of a deputy of the party in power, the Nigerien Party for Democracy and Socialism, and a Molotov cocktail attack on the party's headquarters. They were detained for two weeks to three months and charged with undermining the authority of the State. A trial had not been held by the end of the year.

ARMED CONFLICT

Armed groups, including the Movement for Oneness and Jihad in West Africa and Boko Haram, perpetrated attacks in different locations around the country during 2013 and 2014, including attacks against civilians.

In October, armed groups launched simultaneous attacks on a security post of the Mangaïzé camp for Malian refugees, Ouallam prison, and a military patrol at Bani Bangou, all in the Tillabéry region near the border with Mali. At least nine members of the security forces were killed.

EXCESSIVE USE OF FORCE

In May, student demonstrations took place over the late payment of scholarships. The police used excessive force to repress the protest. At least 30 students were injured and 72 were arrested and released after 19 days of detention. There was a hunger strike to protest against the arrests. The students were charged with acts of vandalism and attacks on public property and were on provisional release at the end of the year.

FREEDOM OF EXPRESSION – HUMAN RIGHTS DEFENDERS AND JOURNALISTS

In January, two journalists, including Soumana Idrissa Maïga, director of the private daily L'Enquêteur, were held in police custody for 96 hours in Niamey and charged with plotting against state security after publishing an article which reported that certain persons were saying the days of the administration were numbered. No trial had been organized at the end of the year.

In July, Ali Idrissa, co-ordinator for the civil society network Publish What You Pay, was taken into police custody twice following a press conference during which he called on the French mining company AREVA to respect Niger's mining laws and denounced aspects of the France-Niger relationship as neo-colonial. A further 10 civil society leaders were also arrested in Niamey on 18 July and released the same evening.

INTERNATIONAL JUSTICE

In March, Colonel Mu'ammar al-Gaddafi's son, Saadi al-Gaddafi, was extradited to Libya. He had stayed in Niger on "humanitarian grounds" since September 2012. There were serious concerns over the Libyan authorities' ability to ensure a fair trial before an ordinary civilian court in this and other similar cases of al-Gaddafi loyalists, and that his trial may result in the death penalty.

NIGERIA

Federal Republic of Nigeria
Head of state and government: **Goodluck Ebele Jonathan**

Crimes under international law and serious human rights violations and abuses were committed by both sides in the conflict between the Nigerian military and the armed group Boko Haram, which escalated during the year. Torture and other ill-treatment by the police and security forces was widespread. A law criminalizing marriage or civil union and public displays of affection between same-sex couples came into force. Freedom of expression was restricted. The death penalty continued to be applied.

BACKGROUND

Preparations for general elections in February 2015, a five-month national conference of governmental, political and public figures, and the conflict between the government and Boko Haram dominated events during the year. The ruling People's Democratic Party (PDP) and the All Progressives Congress (APC), formed in February 2013 from several opposition parties, were the main parties campaigning for the 2015 election. Rivers State saw clashes in January and July between supporters and opponents of Governor Rotimi Amaechi, who defected to the APC in late 2013. The police were criticized for a perceived pro-PDP bias in their handling of the protests. Civil society organizations reported that politicians had begun to arm their supporters.

Between March and August, almost 500 prominent public figures gathered to discuss the state of Nigeria. The process, described as a "national conference", recommended over 600 constitutional, law and policy reforms, including the creation of new states and an increase in the portion of government revenue allocated to state governments.

A seven-member presidential panel is considering the conference's report and will advise the government on how to implement the recommendations.

Boko Haram increased its attacks on towns in the northeast of the country and captured major towns across three states. The state of emergency in Adamawa, Borno and Yobe, the states most affected by violence, was extended in May but not renewed in November.

ARMED CONFLICT
Boko Haram

Violent attacks by the armed group Boko Haram against government and civilian targets escalated. From July onwards Boko Haram captured and occupied more than 20 towns across Adamawa, Borno and Yobe states, targeting and killing several thousand civilians in towns across the northeast, in areas under the group's control, and in bomb attacks nationwide. In attacks on towns Boko Haram often abducted young women and girls, including 276 girls from Chibok town in April. Boko Haram forced abducted women and girls into marriage, forcibly recruited men, and tortured people living under its control who violated its rules. The group looted markets, shops and homes and deliberately targeted schools and other civilian facilities. Some of these acts amount to war crimes and crimes against humanity. The authorities failed to adequately investigate killings and abductions, bring suspected perpetrators to justice or prevent further attacks.

On 25 February, at least 43 people were shot dead by Boko Haram gunmen in an attack on a school in Buni Yadi, Yobe State. Many schoolchildren were among those killed in the attack.

On 14 April and 1 May, Boko Haram carried out car bomb attacks in Nyanya, a suburb of the capital Abuja, killing more than 70 people in the first attack and 19 people in the second, with more than 60 injured.

On 14 April, 276 girls were abducted by Boko Haram from the Government Girls Secondary School in Chibok, Borno State. Nigerian security forces had more than four hours' advance warning about the attack on Chibok, but failed to act.

On 5 May, Boko Haram killed at least 393 people in an attack in Gamborou Ngala, Borno State. The overwhelming majority of the casualties were civilians. Boko Haram burned market stalls, vehicles and nearby homes and shops.

On 6 August, Boko Haram captured the town of Gwoza and killed at least 600 civilians, although several sources suggested the figure was higher.

Boko Haram attacked and captured Bama town on 1 September, killing more than 50 civilians. According to eyewitnesses, the group imprisoned and later killed as many as 300 men and forced 30 women to marry its members.

On 28 November, three bombs exploded outside a mosque in Kano city and armed men, suspected to be Boko Haram fighters, fired into the crowd. At least 81 people died in the attack.

. Boko Haram killed 24 people and abducted more than 110 children and young men and women in two attacks on Gumsuri village on 12 and 14 December.

Security forces

In responding to Boko Haram, Nigerian security forces committed grave human rights violations and acts which constitute crimes under international law.

Arbitrary arrests by the military continued in northeast Nigeria. The military was known to enter communities, forcing the men to sit down outside in front of an informant in order to identify suspected Boko Haram members. Those singled out were detained by the military. In November the Nigerian military released at least 167 detainees from custody, a small portion of those arrested.

Detainees were denied access to the outside world, including lawyers, courts and families, and were held outside the protection of the law. Detainees were usually not informed of the reason for their arrest; their families were not given information about their fate or whereabouts. By the end of the year few, if any, of those detained by the military were brought before a court or permitted to challenge the lawfulness of their detention.

Many of those detained appeared to have been subjected to torture or other ill-treatment, as part of interrogations or as punishment. Detainees continued to die in military detention facilities as a result of torture or extremely harsh detention conditions.

The government failed to investigate deaths in custody and denied the National Human Rights Commission access to military detention facilities.

On 14 March, Boko Haram gunmen attacked the Giwa military barracks in the town of Maiduguri, freeing several hundred detainees. Witnesses said that as the military regained control of the barracks, more than 640 people, mostly unarmed recaptured detainees, were extrajudicially executed in various locations in and around Maiduguri. One of those executions, captured in footage, shows people who appear to be members of the Nigerian military and the Civilian Joint Task Force ("Civilian" JTF) using a blade to slit the throats of five detainees, before dumping them in an open mass grave. Nine people were killed this way and, according to witnesses, other detainees seen in the video were shot.

The government announced investigations into the 14 March events. However, the mandate, composition or timeline of the panels of inquiry had not been made public by the end of the year.

Nigerian security forces repeatedly carried out extrajudicial executions, often following the "screening" of suspects. For example, on 23 July 2013 the Nigerian armed forces and the "Civilian" JTF entered Bama central market and told all adult men in the vicinity to gather in one area and take off their clothes. The men were put into two groups – one group of around 35 men were designated, seemingly at random, as Boko Haram members and another group of up to 300 deemed to be innocent. A video showed the alleged Boko Haram members lying down side by side on the ground, being beaten with sticks and machetes by members of the military and "Civilian" JTF. Eyewitnesses confirmed that the 35 captives were loaded onto a single military vehicle and taken away to the local military barracks in Bama. On the afternoon of 29 July, military personnel took the men out of the barracks and brought them to their communities, where they shot them dead, several at a time, before dumping their bodies. All 35 captives were killed.

Refugees and internally displaced people

The humanitarian situation in the northeast deteriorated as a result of the violence. Since May 2013, at least 1.5 million people, mainly women, children and elderly people, were forced to flee to other parts of Nigeria or seek refuge in neighbouring countries. Families were separated, children were unable to attend school and many people were denied their source of livelihood. Host communities, government authorities and international organizations struggled to meet the humanitarian needs of displaced people. Two towns, Maiduguri and Biu, experienced cholera outbreaks in camps for the internally displaced, resulting in more than 100 deaths.

TORTURE AND OTHER ILL-TREATMENT

The use of torture remained widespread and routine within Nigeria's police and military. Countless people were subjected to physical and psychological torture and other ill-treatment. Suspects in police and military custody across the country were subjected to torture as punishment or to extract "confessions", particularly in cases involving armed robbery and murder, or related to Boko Haram.

Many police divisions in different states, including the Special Anti-Robbery Squad (SARS) and Criminal Investigation Division (CID), kept "torture chambers" for use during the interrogation of suspects. Arbitrary arrest and arbitrary and incommunicado detention were routine. Women detained for criminal offences, women relatives of criminal suspects, sex workers and women believed to be sex workers were often targeted for rape and other sexual violence by police officers. Children under the age of 18 were also detained and tortured or otherwise ill-treated in police stations.

HOUSING RIGHTS

In March, before the UN Human Rights Council, Nigeria reaffirmed its commitments to its international human rights obligations on the rights to adequate housing and effective remedy. Despite this, the Lagos state government violated the right to effective remedy of close to 9,000 people affected by a forced eviction in Badia East, Lagos State, in February 2013.[1] After mounting pressure and over a year after rendering thousands homeless, the Lagos state government provided some affected people with limited financial assistance instead of adequate compensation for their losses. Furthermore, in order to access the financial assistance the government required people to sign documents that effectively prevented them from accessing further remedy.

In June the Economic Community of West African States (ECOWAS) Court awarded almost US$70,000 in damages to members of the Bundu community in relation to an incident on 12 October 2009: armed security forces had opened fire on unarmed protesters in an informal settlement in Port Harcourt, killing one and seriously injuring 12 others. The protesters were demonstrating against plans to demolish their homes. The Court held that there was no justification for the shootings and the government had breached its obligation to protect and respect the right to peaceful association and assembly.

JUSTICE SYSTEM

The criminal justice system remained under-resourced, blighted by corruption and generally distrusted. Security forces often resorted to dragnet arrests instead of arresting individuals based on reasonable suspicion. Suspects were regularly subjected to inhuman and degrading treatment in detention.

In the past decade, at least five presidential committees and working groups on reforming the criminal justice system have been set up. However, the majority of their recommendations – including on combating torture – had not been implemented by the end of the year.

The Nigerian Police Force issued a Human Rights Practice Manual on 10 December, setting out standards expected of police officers and guidance on how to achieve these standards.

DEATH PENALTY

Nigeria continued to sentence people to death; no executions were carried out. During the adoption of the Universal Periodic Review outcomes of Nigeria at the UN Human Rights Council in March, Nigeria stated that it would continue with a national dialogue on the abolition of the death penalty.

In June 2014, the ECOWAS Court of Justice ordered Nigeria to remove from death row Thankgod Ebhos, who had not exhausted his right of appeal, and Maimuna Abdulmumini, who was a minor at the time of the alleged offence. In October 2014, after 19 years on death row and having narrowly escaped execution in June 2013, Thankgod Ebhos was released under an order issued by the Governor of Kaduna State. Four other men were executed in June 2013, the first known executions in the country since 2006.

Courts martial in September and December convicted a total of 70 soldiers of mutiny and sentenced them all to death.

FREEDOM OF EXPRESSION

Security forces curtailed freedom of expression during the year.

Over three days in June the military and the Department of State Security seized and destroyed several newspapers and searched newspaper delivery vans. The Defence Headquarters stated that the action had been in the interests of national security.

In August soldiers briefly detained two managers at the *Daily Trust* newspaper's Maiduguri offices, reportedly after the paper published a story claiming that soldiers had refused orders to fight Boko Haram.

In October police arrested Africa Independent Television journalist Amaechi Anakwe after he called an Assistant Inspector General of Police "controversial" on television. A court discharged him the following day.

COMMUNAL VIOLENCE

Communal violence occurred in many parts of the country, particularly in the Middle Belt area. The NGO International Crisis Group (ICG) estimated that, between January and July, more than 900 people were killed in intercommunal violence in the states of Kaduna, Katsina, Plateau, Zamfara, Taraba, Nasarawa and Benue.

On 14 and 15 March, gunmen thought to be Fulani herdsmen killed about 200 people in three villages in Kaduna State. Around 200 people were also killed in clashes between gunmen and local vigilante groups in Unguwar Galadima, Zamfara State, over two days in April. In August at least 60 people died in fighting between Fulani herdsmen and ethnic Eggon farmers in Nasarawa State. In another incident in the area in November, at least 40 people lost their lives in clashes between the Eggon and Gwadara ethnic groups over a piece of land. In April, 25 people died in Andoyaku in Taraba State when attackers burned down the entire village.

RIGHTS OF LESBIAN, GAY, BISEXUAL, TRANSGENDER AND INTERSEX PEOPLE

In January, President Jonathan signed into law the 2013 Same Sex Marriage (Prohibition) Act. The law criminalizes marriage or civil union for same-sex couples; the solemnization of same-sex marriage in places of worship; public displays of affection between same-sex couples; and the registration and support of gay clubs and societies in Nigeria. The law provides for sentences of between 10 to 14 years' imprisonment.

Days after the law came into force, lesbians, gay, bisexual, transgender and intersex (LGBTI) people and activists faced harassment, blackmail and threats to their lives. In Ibadan, Oyo State, police arrested five men on the basis of their perceived sexual orientation. They were later released on bail. In Awka, Anambra State, six people were reportedly arrested and detained by police under the new law. An Assistant Commissioner of Police in Bauchi said that police carried a list of suspected LGBTI people "under surveillance" as part of their "profiling of criminals".

CORPORATE ACCOUNTABILITY

Pollution from oil industry operations continued to cause environmental devastation and destroy livelihoods in the Niger Delta region. Hundreds of oil spills occurred in both 2013 and 2014, caused by the failure of oil company equipment, and by sabotage and oil theft. Oil companies continued to blame the vast majority of oil spills on sabotage and theft despite growing evidence of old and badly maintained pipelines and serious flaws in the oil spill investigation process which is led by the oil companies.

There were frequent delays in stopping and cleaning up oil spills. Clean-up processes continued to be inadequate.

NGOs continued to raise concerns over the failure of the government and the oil company Shell to implement the recommendations made by the 2011 UN Environment Programme (UNEP) scientific study on pollution in the Ogoniland region of the Niger Delta. Although the government continued to provide some drinking water to people whose water sources had been polluted by oil spills, the amount and quality of the water was widely reported to be inadequate. In September 2014, the Ministry of Petroleum initiated a multi-stakeholder process on the UNEP report, and established four working groups tasked with implementing different aspects of the recommendations.

A legal action against the oil company Shell, taken in the UK by people from the Bodo community where two massive oil spills from an old and leaking Shell pipeline devastated the area in 2008 and 2009, concluded in December with an out-of-court settlement. Shell paid £55 million (US$83 million) to the community. However, the damage caused by the two spills had not been properly cleaned up by the end of the year.

Court documents demonstrated that Shell had repeatedly made false claims about the size and impact of the two spills in the Bodo community in an attempt to minimize its compensation payments. The documents also showed that Shell had known for years that its Niger Delta pipelines were old and faulty. Using the same documents, the NGO Friends of the Earth Netherlands claimed that Shell had also lied to a Dutch court in a separate legal action over oil pollution in the Niger Delta.

Numerous oil spills occurred in the Ikarama area and other parts of Bayelsa State, from both Shell and ENI/Agip operations. A civil society group working with the local communities, Shareholders Alliance for Corporate Accountability (SACA), expressed concern about flawed clean-up and compensation processes in the area and the failure of oil companies to provide adequate security to protect their oil facilities from sabotage.

In November, the National Assembly's House of Representatives Committee on Environment recommended that Shell Nigerian Exploration and Production Company should pay damages of US$3.6 billion for losses incurred by coastal communities in Bayelsa State during the 2011 Bonga oil spill which reportedly affected 350 communities and satellite towns.

1. Nigeria: At the mercy of the government: Violation of the right to an effective remedy in Badia East, Lagos State (AFR 44/017/2014) www.amnesty.org/en/library/info/AFR44/017/2014/en

NORWAY

Kingdom of Norway
Head of state: **King Harald V**
Head of government: **Erna Solberg**

Transgender people continued to face significant obstacles to legal gender recognition. Impunity for rape and sexual violence continued to be the norm.

DISCRIMINATION – TRANSGENDER PEOPLE

Transgender people could only obtain legal recognition of their gender following a psychiatric diagnosis, compulsory hormone therapy and gender reassignment surgery including irreversible sterilization.[1] In December 2013, the Directorate of Health established an expert group composed of health professionals, legal experts and representatives of transgender organizations. It was tasked to develop recommendations on legal gender recognition and access to health care for transgender people by 25 February 2015.

In March, John Jeanette Solstad Remø applied to the Ministry of Health and Care Services to change her legal gender. The Ministry refused her request. In September, the Office of the Equality and Anti-Discrimination Ombud stated that the Ministry's requirement for diagnosis, hormone therapy and gender reassignment surgery including irreversible sterilization was discriminatory and breached the law against discrimination on the basis of sexual orientation, gender identity and gender expression.

VIOLENCE AGAINST WOMEN AND GIRLS

The first national study on the prevalence of rape and sexual violence, published in February, confirmed rape to be a widespread and gendered crime. Nearly one in 10 surveyed women reported having been raped. Half of the victims reported experiencing rape before the age of 18. The report documented that one in three victims had never told anyone about the abuse, and only one in 10 rapes had been reported to the police. Half of those who had reported being raped considered that the police had not investigated the crime. Police statistics indicated that eight out of 10 reported rape cases were dropped at various stages of the legal process, reinforcing longstanding concerns about attrition in rape prosecutions.

REFUGEES AND ASYLUM-SEEKERS

In October 2013, the government announced an amnesty for up to 578 minor children of asylum-seekers whose applications for asylum had been finally rejected and who had been in the country for over three years. NGOs criticized its restricted application to only children from countries with which Norway has a readmission agreement, arguing that such an arbitrary criterion was discriminatory and undermined the principle of best interests of the child. In April, the Minister of Justice stated publicly that only 130 out of the 578 children would be covered by the amnesty. In a new consultation paper issued in June, the Ministry of Justice proposed additional conditions on access to the scheme.

On 18 December, the Immigration Appeals Board announced that it was suspending all forced and voluntary returns to Uzbekistan of asylum-seekers whose applications had been finally rejected.

INTERNATIONAL JUSTICE

The appeal by a 47-year-old Rwandan national against his conviction for murder during the 1994 genocide in Rwanda remained outstanding at the end of the year.

On 14 February 2013, the Oslo District Court sentenced him to 21 years' imprisonment. He was convicted of premeditated murder under especially aggravating circumstances, but not of genocide, as the article defining the latter only entered into force in 2008 and does not have retrospective effect.

TORTURE AND OTHER ILL-TREATMENT

Following Norway's ratification of the Optional Protocol to the UN Convention against Torture in 2013, the National Preventive Mechanism, taken on by the Parliamentary Ombudsman, was fully operational by April 2014. The Mechanism was created with an advisory committee of members from the National Institution for Human Rights, the other Ombudspersons and civil society and NGO representatives.

---

1. The state decides who I am: Lack of legal gender recognition for transgender people in Europe (EUR 01/001/2014) www.amnesty.org/en/library/info/EUR01/001/2014/en

OMAN

Sultanate of Oman
Head of state and government: **Sultan Qaboos bin Said**

State authorities continued to restrict freedom of expression, including in the media and online. Freedom of assembly was not permitted. Several government critics were detained and held incommunicado for some weeks. Authorities forcibly returned a political activist to Bahrain despite a risk that he would face torture there. Women continued to face discrimination in law and practice. The death penalty remained in force; no executions were reported.

BACKGROUND

In January, Oman ratified the Gulf Cooperation Council (GCC) Security Agreement, the provisions of which jeopardized freedom of expression and other individual rights guaranteed in Oman's Constitution and in international treaties.

The government decreed a new citizenship law in August, to take effect in February 2015. It empowered the authorities to strip Omani nationals of their citizenship and associated rights if they are found to belong to a group deemed to uphold principles or beliefs that undermine Oman's "best interests", potentially allowing the government to arbitrarily withdraw the nationality of and expel its critics.

Also in August, Oman ratified the 1997 Anti-Personnel Mine Ban Convention.

FREEDOMS OF EXPRESSION AND ASSEMBLY

On 27 January, the Omani authorities arrested Bahraini actor and political activist Sadeq Ja'far Mansoor al-Sha'bani and forcibly returned him to Bahrain despite fears that he may be tortured there. He subsequently received a five-year prison sentence in Bahrain along with eight others on charges including "inciting hatred of the regime".

In May, police arrested and detained several men, who were subsequently released on 12 July after they reportedly signed pledges not to participate in advocacy activities or incite sectarianism. Two bloggers who criticized the authorities online were arrested in July and released without charge after several weeks.

In August, Dr Talib al-Ma'mari, a member of the Shura Council, and Saqr al-Balushi, a councillor in the city of Liwa, were sentenced to four years' and one year's imprisonment respectively, on charges including "public gathering with the aim of disturbing law and order" and "closing a road". The two men had participated in an anti-pollution demonstration in Liwa in August 2013.

Following a six-day visit to Oman in September, the UN Special Rapporteur on the rights to freedom of peaceful assembly and of association stated that limits on peaceful assembly in Oman were "quite restrictive, to the point where they often annul the essence of the right".

WOMEN'S RIGHTS

Women were not accorded equal rights with men under the criminal law, which attached less weight to the evidence of a woman than to the evidence of a man, and under personal status law, which accorded men greater rights in relation to divorce, child custody and inheritance.

MIGRANT WORKERS' RIGHTS

Migrant workers received inadequate protection under labour laws and faced exploitation and abuse. In May and November,, the government renewed for a further six months a bar on the entry of most foreign migrant workers for construction and other work sectors. In July, a new decree amended the labour law to prevent the employment of expatriates in professions reserved for Omani nationals. The government also stated that it would begin to strictly enforce a rule barring migrant workers who leave Oman from returning for two years, which was reported to facilitate labour exploitation.

DEATH PENALTY

Oman retained the death penalty for murder and other offences. In June, the State Council approved proposals to extend its use to drug trafficking offences. No executions were reported.

PAKISTAN

Islamic Republic of Pakistan
Head of state: **Mamnoon Hussain**
Head of government: **Muhammad Nawaz Sharif**

In December, the Pakistani Taliban-led attack on the Army Public School in Peshawar resulted in 149 deaths, including 132 children, marking the deadliest terrorist attack in Pakistan's history. In response, the government lifted the moratorium on carrying out death sentences and swiftly executed seven men previously convicted for other terror-related offences. The Prime Minister announced plans for allowing military courts to try terror suspects as part of the government's National Action Plan against terrorism, adding to concerns over fair trials. In October education rights activist Malala Yousafzai jointly won the Nobel Peace Prize in October along with Indian child rights activist Kailash Satyarthi. The National Assembly approved the Protection of Pakistan Act in July and other security laws during the year that enshrined sweeping powers for law enforcement and security forces, expanding the scope for arbitrary arrests, indefinite detention, the use of lethal force, and secret court proceedings which go well beyond international law enforcement and fair trial standards. Pakistan's media faced sustained harassment and other abuse, and the Pakistan Electronic Media Regulatory Authority briefly ordered the closure of the two largest private broadcasters because of content critical of the authorities. Religious minorities continued to face discrimination and persecution, especially due to the blasphemy laws.

BACKGROUND

Hearings in the treason trial of former military ruler General Pervez Musharraf continued to be delayed, creating tensions between the democratically elected government of Prime Minister Nawaz Sharif and the powerful military. The government and opposition political parties failed to secure a peace deal with the Pakistani Taliban, culminating in the latter carrying out an attack on Karachi International Airport that claimed at least 34 lives, mostly of security forces and Taliban fighters. That attack and continued pressure from the USA resulted in the Pakistan Army launching a major military operation against Taliban and al-Qa'ida sanctuaries in North Waziristan tribal agency in June, which was continuing as of the end of 2014.

Following their claims of rigging in the 2013 general elections, and disaffection with independent inquiries into these claims, demonstrators led by the opposition politician Imran Khan and the religious cleric Tahir ul Qadri held protests across the country calling on the government of Nawaz Sharif to step down and for fresh elections. After the killing of 12 political activists by police in Lahore's Model Town neighbourhood on 17 June, the protests became increasingly confrontational, peaking in August and September. Demonstrators briefly stormed the National Assembly and threatened to occupy the Prime Minister's official residence, creating a crisis that risked forcing the collapse of the government, until the military publicly backed the Prime Minister.

For the fourth year in a row major floods across Pakistan displaced hundreds of thousands, creating a major humanitarian crisis.

Attempts by the government to improve relations with India early in the year stalled as the armed forces of the two countries engaged in regular clashes across the Line of Control across Jammu and Kashmir.

ABUSES BY ARMED GROUPS

Armed groups were implicated in human rights abuses across the country. On 16 December, several men claimed by the Pakistani Taliban as its members attacked the Army Public School in the northwestern city of Peshawar, where 149 people were killed, 132 of them children, and dozens injured in shootings and suicide bombings. The Pakistani Taliban said the attack was in response to recent Pakistan Army operations in nearby North Waziristan in which hundreds of Taliban fighters had been killed.

Various factions of the Pakistani Taliban continued to carry out attacks, including against activists and journalists for promoting education and other rights, or for criticizing them. Ahrar ul Hind, a breakaway group from the Pakistani Taliban, claimed responsibility for the 3 March gun and suicide bomb attack on a court house in Islamabad that left 11 dead and several others injured, reportedly in response to the Pakistani Taliban's decision to enter peace talks with the government. Jamat ul Ahrar, another breakaway group from the Pakistani Taliban, claimed responsibility for the 2 November suicide bomb attack following the daily flag lowering parade at the Wagah Border Post between Pakistan and India, which left 61 dead and more than 100 injured.

Health workers involved in polio and other vaccination campaigns were killed in various parts of the country. Killings were particularly prevalent in parts of the northwest and the city of Karachi, areas with an active presence of Taliban and aligned groups which oppose vaccinations. Ethnic Baloch armed groups calling for a separate state of Balochistan were implicated in the killing and abduction of security forces and others on the basis of their ethnic or political affiliations, and carried out attacks on infrastructure. The anti-Shi'a armed group Lashkar-e-Jhangvi claimed responsibility for a series of assassinations and other attacks on the Shi'a Muslim population, particularly in the province of Balochistan and the cities of Karachi and Lahore. Rival armed groups frequently clashed, resulting in scores of fatalities.

ENFORCED DISAPPEARANCES

Despite clear rulings by the Supreme Court to the government in 2013 demanding the recovery of victims of enforced disappearances, the authorities did little to meet its obligations under international law and the Constitution to prevent these violations. The practices of state security forces, including actions within the scope of laws such as the Protection of Pakistan Act, resulted in men and boys being subjected to enforced disappearance across Pakistan and particularly in the provinces of Balochistan, Khyber Pakhtunkhwa and Sindh. Several victims were later found dead, bearing what appeared to be bullet wounds and torture marks. The government did not implement Supreme Court orders calling for security forces responsible for enforced disappearances to be brought to justice.

Zahid Baloch, Chairman of the Baloch Student Organisation-Azad, was abducted in Quetta, Balochistan, on 18 March. Witnesses claimed he was taken at gunpoint in the city's Satellite Town area by personnel of the Frontier Corps, a federal security force. The authorities denied knowledge of his arrest and failed to investigate his fate or whereabouts or to investigate the abduction adequately. No new information was known at the end of the year.[1]

The bodies of men and boys arbitrarily detained by the Pakistan armed forces in Khyber Pakhtunkhwa province and the Federally Administered Tribal Areas (FATA) continued to be recovered months or years later, while the authorities generally failed to abide by Peshawar High Court orders either to release those suspected of terrorism or charge them promptly and bring them to trial. Detainees continued to have limited access to families and lawyers. There were some rare instances of activists subjected to enforced disappearance being returned alive. On 5 February, Kareem Khan, an anti-drone activist and a relative of victims, was abducted by up to 20 armed men, some in police uniforms, from his home in the garrison city of Rawalpindi, days before he was due to travel to Europe to give testimony before the European Parliament on the impact of

US drone strikes on Pakistan's tribal areas. He was released nine days later following pressure from local and international rights groups and foreign governments. He claimed that he had been subjected to torture and repeatedly questioned about his activism and his investigation of drone strikes. The authorities failed to investigate the incident adequately and did not bring those responsible to justice.

Human rights groups criticized a judicial inquiry into mass graves discovered in Totak Balochistan on 25 January for failing to investigate state security forces adequately. Baloch activists claimed that the graves belonged to ethnic Baloch activists who had been subjected to enforced disappearance.[2]

INTERNAL ARMED CONFLICT

Parts of FATA in northwestern Pakistan continued to be affected by internal armed conflict, facing regular attacks by the Taliban and other armed groups, the Pakistan armed forces, and US drone aircraft that claimed hundreds of lives. In June the Pakistan Army launched a major military operation in North Waziristan tribal agency, and carried out sporadic operations in Khyber tribal agency and other parts of FATA. Affected communities routinely complained of the disproportionate use of force and indiscriminate attacks by all sides to the conflict, especially the Pakistan armed forces. The fighting displaced over a million residents, most of whom were forced to flee to the district of Bannu in neighbouring Khyber Pakhtunkhwa province during the hottest period of the year. US drone strikes continued sporadically from 11 June onwards after a hiatus of nearly six months, reigniting concerns of unlawful killings. On 5 June the Islamabad High Court ordered the arrest of a former CIA station chief for Pakistan over his alleged responsibility for unlawful killings due to pilotless drone aircraft in the tribal areas. On 12 September, security forces announced the arrest in North Waziristan of 10 men allegedly involved in the 2012 assassination attempt on education rights activist Malala Yousafzai. Questions remained as to how they were arrested, their treatment in detention and whether they would receive a fair trial.

FREEDOM OF EXPRESSION – JOURNALISTS

At least eight journalists were killed across Pakistan during the year in direct response to their work, marking the country out as one of the most dangerous in the world for the media profession.[3] High-profile television anchor Hamid Mir claimed that the Directorate for Inter-Services Intelligence, the most powerful intelligence service, was responsible for an attempt on his life which he narrowly escaped in Karachi on 19 April. Following the claims, which were broadcast nationally by Hamid Mir's television station Geo TV, the broadcaster was formally suspended for 15 days on 6 June. Several journalists associated with the outlet received daily threats and harassment by unidentified individuals by phone and in person. Many refused to enter their offices or identify themselves as belonging to Geo TV or associated media for fear of being attacked.

On 20 October, Geo TV's main rival, ARY News, was also suspended after the Lahore High Court held that the broadcaster and some of its journalists had been in contempt of court for airing the views of an individual facing trial before the court.

In March, the Prime Minister promised to appoint special public prosecutors to investigate attacks on journalists, and he personally visited Hamid Mir in hospital after the attempt on his life. No one had been brought to justice for this attempted killing or any other attack on journalists at the end of the year.[4]

DISCRIMINATION – RELIGIOUS MINORITIES

Religious minorities continued to face laws and practices that resulted in their discrimination and persecution. Dozens of ethnic Hazaras were killed in attacks in Quetta and other parts of Balochistan; the armed group Lashkar-e-Jhangvi claimed responsibility for many of these, saying they were because the Hazaras were Shi'a Muslims. Members of the Sikh religious community staged several protests throughout the year against killings, abductions and attacks on their places of worship in different parts of the country. They complained that the authorities consistently failed to provide adequate protection from such attacks or bring those responsible to justice.

The blasphemy laws remained in force, in violation of the rights to freedom of thought, conscience and religion and freedom of opinion and expression. Abuse connected with the blasphemy laws occurred regularly during the year as demonstrated in several high-profile cases. Renowned human rights lawyer Rashid Rehman was shot dead in front of colleagues in his office in the city of Multan, Punjab province, on 7 May. Prior to his killing, Rashid Rehman had received regular death threats because of his legal representation of a university teacher, Junaid Hafeez, who had been arrested on charges of blasphemy. On 18 September Professor Muhammad Shakil Auj, a noted religious scholar and dean of Islamic Studies at Karachi University, was gunned down by unidentified assailants while travelling to a meeting. He had faced death threats and charges of blasphemy from rival religious scholars in the months prior to his killing.

A mob burned down the homes of a small Ahmadiyya community in Punjab province on the evening of 27 July, after a resident was accused of blasphemy – two children and their grandmother died of smoke inhalation and several others were seriously injured. On 16 October the appeal bench of the Lahore High Court rejected an application by a Christian woman, Asia Bibi, to have her 2010 death sentence for blasphemy overturned.[5] In March, a Christian road sweeper, Savan Masih, was sentenced to death for blasphemy after a friend accused him of making blasphemous remarks during an argument.

The accusations provoked a two-day riot in his neighbourhood in Lahore, known as Joseph Colony, when a 3,000-strong mob burned around 200 homes of Christians. Police were warned of the impending attack but failed to take adequate measures to protect the community.

VIOLENCE AGAINST WOMEN AND GIRLS

A handful of high-profile so-called "honour" killing cases highlighted the risks to women from their own families for seeking to marry partners of their choice. On 27 May, Farzana Parveen was shot and beaten to death with a brick by members of her family, including her father and her ex-husband, outside the entrance to the Lahore High Court, after she had fled and married a man of her choosing. Several of her male relatives were arrested for the killing, as, separately, was her husband, Mohammad Iqbal, after he admitted to killing his first wife in order to be with Farzana Parveen.

Women also risked abuse while seeking to exercise their rights. For example, in September a *jirga* (traditional decision-making body) of male Uthmanzai tribal chiefs from North Waziristan tribal agency threatened women with violence for seeking access to humanitarian assistance in displaced persons camps in Bannu district of Khyber Pakhtunkhwa province, where the vast majority of people fleeing the conflict in the tribal agency were based.

DEATH PENALTY

The attack on the Army Public School in Peshawar on 16 December led to a resumption of executions after the six-year moratorium was lifted by Prime Minister Sharif. He announced plans for the execution of 500 people convicted for other terrorism-related offences. Seven men convicted previously were hanged in December in a swift series of executions, after President Hussain summarily rejected their appeals. The government also announced plans for early 2015 for the use of military courts in

trying terror suspects, as part of its National Action Plan against terrorism.

People continued to be sentenced to death. Shoaib Sarwar, a death row prisoner convicted of murder in 1998, was ordered to be executed in September after exhausting all his appeals. However, the execution was postponed several times by the authorities under pressure from anti-death penalty campaigners at home and abroad.[6]

1. Pakistan: Abducted political activist at risk of death (ASA 33/008/2014)
   www.amnesty.org/en/library/info/ASA33/008/2014/en
2. Pakistan: Mass graves a stark reminder of violations implicating the state in Balochistan (ASA 33/001/2014)
   www.amnesty.org/en/library/info/ASA33/001/2014/en
3. "A bullet has been chosen for you": Attacks on journalists in Pakistan (ASA 33/005/2014)
   www.amnesty.org/en/library/info/ASA33/005/2014/en
4. Pakistan: Open letter to the Prime Minister Nawaz Sharif: Joint statement of shared concerns about attacks on journalists in Pakistan (ASA 33/010/2014)
   www.amnesty.org/en/library/info/ASA33/010/2014/en
5. Pakistan: Woman sentenced to death for blasphemy - Asia Bibi (ASA 33/015/2014)
   www.amnesty.org/en/library/info/ASA33/015/2014/en
6. Pakistan: Stop first civilian execution in six years (Press release)
   www.amnesty.org/en/articles/news/2014/09/pakistan-stop-first-civilian-execution-six-years/

PALESTINE (STATE OF)

State of Palestine
Head of state: **Mahmoud Abbas**
Head of government: **Rami Hamdallah**

Authorities in the West Bank and Gaza restricted freedoms of expression and peaceful assembly, carried out arbitrary arrests and detentions, and tortured

and otherwise ill-treated detainees with impunity. Women and girls faced discrimination in law and practice, and were inadequately protected against gender-based violence. The death penalty remained in force; there were no executions in the West Bank, but the Hamas authorities in Gaza, who continued to try civilians before unfair military courts, carried out at least two executions. Hamas forces in Gaza carried out at least 22 extrajudicial executions of people they accused of "collaborating" with Israel. Israel's Protective Edge military offensive killed more than 1,500 civilians in Gaza, wounded thousands more, and caused huge devastation, exacerbating the hardship felt by Gaza's 1.8 million inhabitants due to Israel's continuing military blockade of the territory. During the 50-day conflict, Hamas and Palestinian armed groups fired thousands of indiscriminate rockets and mortar rounds into civilian areas of Israel, killing six civilians, including one child.

BACKGROUND

US-convened negotiations, which began in 2013 and aimed to resolve the decades-long Israeli-Palestinian conflict, concluded at the end of April without reaching any agreement.

The same month, Fatah, the ruling party of the Palestinian Authority, which administers the West Bank, and Hamas, the de facto administration in Gaza since 2007, announced a unity agreement. In June, Fatah, Hamas and other Palestinian factions agreed to a national reconciliation government of independent technocrats to run civilian affairs in both areas until parliamentary and presidential elections take place. No date for elections had been set by the end of the year.

There was growing international recognition of Palestinian statehood, despite opposition from Israel and the USA. In October, Sweden became the first EU member state to recognize the State of Palestine (although three other European states did so before joining the EU), and the UK's House of Commons and France's National Assembly

both passed non-binding votes in favour of recognition. In December, Jordan submitted a resolution to the UN Security Council that proposed setting a timetable for a negotiated settlement that would require Israel to end its occupation of Palestinian territories by the end of 2017.

In April, Palestine ratified the four Geneva Conventions and an array of international human rights and other treaties, including the ICCPR, ICESCR, CEDAW, the Convention on the Rights of the Child and its Optional Protocol on the involvement of children in armed conflict, and the UN Convention against Torture. On 31 December President Mahmoud Abbas signed 16 other international treaties as well as the Rome Statute recognizing the jurisdiction of the International Criminal Court in the Occupied Palestinian Territories including East Jerusalem from 13 June 2014.

Tensions were heightened by Israel's killing of at least 15 Palestinians by the end of June, the abduction and murder of three Israeli teenagers by Palestinians near Hebron and the revenge killing of a Palestinian youth by Israelis. The tensions spiralled into renewed armed conflict in July when Israel launched its Protective Edge military offensive, comprising aerial attacks and a ground invasion of Gaza. The offensive lasted for 50 days before the two sides agreed a ceasefire facilitated by the US and Egyptian governments. The offensive caused the deaths of more than 1,500 civilians in Gaza, including over 500 children, and the wounding of thousands more. It wrought huge devastation, damaging and destroying schools, hospitals, homes and other civilian infrastructure. Gaza remained under Israeli military blockade throughout the year.

ARMED CONFLICT

Hamas and Palestinian armed groups in Gaza repeatedly fired indiscriminate rockets and mortars into Israel. Firing greatly intensified in the period preceding and throughout Israel's Protective Edge military offensive in Gaza. By the time of the August ceasefire that ended the conflict, firing of indiscriminate weapons from Gaza by Palestinian armed groups had killed six civilians in Israel, including a child aged four, wounded other civilians and damaged a number of civilian homes. The firing also led directly to civilian deaths in Gaza, due to the premature explosion of some rockets; the killing of 10 Palestinian civilians including nine children in the al-Shati' refugee camp on 28 July was believed to have been caused by a rocket that fell short of its target. Palestinian armed groups also exposed civilians in Gaza to lethal harm from Israeli attacks by concealing and firing rockets and other projectiles from locations within or close to civilian residential areas. Firing was mostly halted after the ceasefire agreement.

ARBITRARY ARRESTS AND DETENTIONS
Security authorities in both the West Bank and Gaza arbitrarily arrested and detained their critics and supporters of rival political organizations.

TORTURE AND OTHER ILL-TREATMENT
Detainees were tortured and otherwise ill-treated with impunity. The Independent Commission for Human Rights (ICHR), a national body established to monitor human rights and receive complaints, said it received over 120 allegations of torture and other ill-treatment of detainees from the West Bank and over 440 allegations from Gaza during the year. Methods of torture included beatings and forcing detainees to stand or sit in stress positions (shabah) for long periods. In the West Bank, detainees alleged that they were tortured or otherwise ill-treated by police, Preventive Security, military intelligence and General Intelligence officials. In Gaza, at least three men died in custody allegedly from torture by Internal Security officials. Both authorities failed to protect detainees from torture and other ill-treatment, investigate allegations or hold those responsible to account.

UNFAIR TRIALS
Political and judicial authorities failed to ensure that detainees received prompt and fair trials. Authorities in the West Bank held detainees for indefinite periods without charge or trial. In Gaza, the Hamas authorities continued to subject civilians to unfair trials before military courts.

FREEDOMS OF EXPRESSION, ASSOCIATION AND ASSEMBLY
Authorities restricted freedoms of expression, association and assembly in the West Bank and Gaza. Security forces dispersed protests organized by opposition activists, frequently using excessive force. On many occasions, journalists reporting on protests complained that security forces assaulted them or damaged their equipment. Security officials also harassed and sought to intimidate journalists and social media activists, including by repeatedly summoning them for questioning and sometimes detaining them for their writings.

In March, police in the Gazan city of Khan Yunis used force to break up a commemorative event organized by Fatah supporters, reportedly firing in the air to disperse the gathering and arresting and briefly detaining many participants.

In the West Bank, security forces assaulted journalists from Palestinian broadcaster Wattan TV who were present to report on demonstrations. In one incident in October, security forces attacked a Wattan TV crew covering a demonstration in Hebron and seized their equipment.

EXTRAJUDICIAL EXECUTIONS
During the Israeli offensive Protective Edge, members of Hamas' military Izz ad-Din al-Qassam Brigades and the Internal Security Force committed at least 22 summary and extrajudicial executions of people whom they accused of "collaboration" with Israel. Those killed included a number of prisoners who were appealing against sentences of death or prison terms passed by military courts in

Gaza; others were detainees who had faced no formal charges or trial. On 5 August the de facto Ministry of Interior removed five inmates of Katiba Prison who were extrajudicially executed outside the prison. On 22 August Hamas forces removed 11 prisoners from Katiba Prison whose trials or appeals were pending, and extrajudicially executed them at the al-Jawazat Police Station. Later the same morning six men arrested during Operation Protective Edge were shot dead in public after Friday prayers. Izz ad-Din al-Qassam Brigades reportedly shot other suspected "collaborators" in the street during Operation Protective Edge.

IMPUNITY

Palestinian authorities failed to take any steps to investigate alleged war crimes and possible crimes against humanity committed by Hamas' military wing and other Palestinian armed groups in the run-up to and during the conflict in July and August or during previous conflicts with Israel in which Palestinian armed groups fired indiscriminate rockets and mortars into Israel. They also failed to hold to account officials who committed human rights violations, including excessive use of force against peaceful protesters and the torture of detainees.

VIOLENCE AGAINST WOMEN AND GIRLS

Women and girls continued to face discrimination in both law and practice, and remained inadequately protected against gender-based violence committed by male relatives, ostensibly for reasons of family "honour". At least 11 women and girls were murdered by male relatives in so-called "honour killings" during the year, according to reports of the ICHR. They included Islam Mohammad Al-Shami, 18, who died after she was stabbed in the neck on 20 October while praying inside her family home at Bani Suheila, Khan Yunis governorate.

DEATH PENALTY

The death penalty remained in force for murder and other crimes. There were no executions reported in the West Bank, but in Gaza, Hamas military and first instance courts sentenced at least eight people to death on murder charges. In May, Gaza authorities executed two men, both of whom had been sentenced to death on treason and murder charges.

PANAMA

Republic of Panama
Head of state and government: Juan Carlos Varela (replaced Ricardo Martinelli in July)

Former President Manuel Noriega faced new trials relating to human rights violations during his presidency and the killing of a soldier in 1969. A Special National Commission on victims of enforced disappearance had yet to be established. The rights of Indigenous Peoples were threatened by hydroelectricity projects. Local NGOs were prevented by the authorities from following up complaints of harsh prison conditions.

BACKGROUND

In July, Juan Carlos Varela was sworn in as President. In August, the UN Working Group of Experts on People of African Descent noted that, despite the adoption of anti-discrimination legislation, patterns of racial discrimination prevailed and persons of African descent – around 10% of the population – continued to suffer from political, social and economic marginalization.

IMPUNITY

In September the Supreme Court of Justice decided that Manuel Noriega, former de facto ruler of the country from 1983 to 1989, should face trial for his alleged role in the killing of a soldier in 1969. The decision came as Manuel Noriega was serving sentences related to the killing of two political opponents. He also faced new trials for enforced disappearances and killings during his presidency.

Despite previous pledges to search for people forcibly disappeared during the 1970s and 1980s, the government failed to make any progress. A Special National Commission to search for victims of enforced disappearance, which the government pledged to create in 2012, had still not been established by the end of the year.

INDIGENOUS PEOPLES' RIGHTS

There were protests in February, April and May in the area of Barro Blanco, resulting in clashes between members of the Ngöbe-Buglé Indigenous community and the police. The Ngöbe-Buglé opposed the construction of a large hydroelectric dam on their lands, claiming that future flooding resulting from it would render them homeless. They also alleged that their right to be consulted over the project prior to construction commencing was not met.

In May the UN Special Rapporteur on the rights of indigenous peoples noted that although the *comarca* system of Indigenous Peoples' administrative zones offered some protection, more needed to be done to protect Indigenous Peoples' land rights. The Special Rapporteur recommended that Panama ensure consultation of Indigenous Peoples and their free and informed consent, prior to proposing large construction projects on or near their lands. He also recommended that Panama increase its efforts to improve Indigenous Peoples' access to health, education and economic development. With regard to the Barro Blanco dam, he recommended that flooding of the local areas be halted until agreement with the Ngöbe-Buglé community had been reached.

PRISON CONDITIONS

In April, local human rights NGOs wrote to the UN Subcommittee on Prevention of Torture and other Cruel, Inhuman or Degrading Treatment or Punishment and the Inter-American Commission on Human Rights, raising concerns that they were being prevented by the authorities from accessing prisons, which was impeding their work in following up complaints of inhuman conditions in prisons.

PAPUA NEW GUINEA

Independent State of Papua New Guinea
Head of state: **Queen Elizabeth II, represented by Governor General Michael Ogio**
Head of government: **Peter Charles Paire O'Neill**

There were further reports of violence against women and children, including as a result of sorcery accusations. Reports of unnecessary and excessive use of force by police persisted. There were reports of violence and sexual assault by police during a forced eviction near Porgera mine. Violence and alleged inadequate medical treatment resulted in the deaths of two asylum-seekers at the Australian-run immigration detention centre on Manus Island.

BACKGROUND

The government took little action to address violence against women or sorcery-related violence, in spite of legal reforms in 2013 providing for harsher penalties.

As at 31 August there were 1,084 asylum-seekers at the Australian-run immigration detention centre on Manus Island, Papua New Guinea. Little progress had been made to improve conditions or to implement laws and policies required to process and settle asylum-seekers.[1]

According to government figures, at least 13 people have been sentenced to death since the death penalty was reintroduced in 1991. The government completed a global study tour in 2014 to research execution methods, even though none have taken place in the country since 1954.

VIOLENCE AGAINST WOMEN AND CHILDREN

A 2013 report by the UN Development Programme found that 80% of men in Bougainville admitted using physical or sexual violence against women.

There were further reports of women and children being subjected to violence, sometimes resulting in death, following accusations of sorcery. The UN Special Rapporteur on extrajudicial, summary or arbitrary executions highlighted sorcery-related killings as a major concern. He was the third Special Rapporteur to report on this issue in recent years.

EXCESSIVE USE OF FORCE

Unnecessary and excessive use of force, including lethal force, by police was highlighted as one of the key concerns by the UN Special Rapporteur on extrajudicial, summary or arbitrary executions following his visit to the country in March. Reports of physical and sexual assault of people in custody and extrajudicial killings by police continued.

In March a video surfaced of a man being attacked in the street by three police dogs. Police officers stood by and made no attempt to arrest or detain the man. While police authorities have attempted to investigate and address complaints against officers, reports of police brutality remained frequent.

HOUSING RIGHTS - FORCED EVICTIONS

Tensions escalated at the site of Porgera gold mine between the mining company and local residents. In June, around 200 homes were burned to the ground by police. Reports were received of physical and sexual violence by police during the forced eviction.

REFUGEES AND ASYLUM-SEEKERS

In February, violence erupted at the Australian-run immigration detention centre on Manus Island. After weeks of protests, asylum-seekers were attacked by private security guards and local police. In August, police charged two former employees of the Salvation Army and security contractor G4S in connection with the death of Iranian asylum-seeker Reza Berati, who died from severe head trauma during a riot at the detention centre on 17 February.[2] In September, human rights organizations lodged a complaint with the Organisation for Economic Co-operation and Development against G4S, alleging that it had failed to maintain basic human rights standards and protect asylum-seekers.

In September another Iranian asylum-seeker from Manus Island, Hamid Kehazaei, died in hospital in Australia after developing septicaemia from a cut on his foot. Reports claimed that inadequate or delayed medical treatment had led to his death.

Of the 1,084 asylum-seekers on Manus Island, a total of 79 applications for interim refugee status were processed, of which 41 were successful and 38 were rejected. Refugees and asylum-seekers remained detained at the facility at the end of the year.

Asylum-seekers continued to suffer lengthy delays, poor conditions and risk of harm.

---

1. This is breaking people: Human rights violations at Australia's asylum-seeker processing centre on Manus Island, Papua New Guinea (ASA 12/002/2013)
   www.amnesty.org/en/library/info/ASA12/002/2013/en

2. This is still breaking people: Update on human rights violations at Australia's asylum-seeker processing centre on Manus Island, Papua New Guinea (ASA 12/002/2014)
   www.amnesty.org/en/library/info/ASA12/002/2014/en

PARAGUAY

Republic of Paraguay
Head of state and government: **Horacio Manuel
Cartes Jara**

Despite some advances, Indigenous Peoples
continued to be denied access to their
traditional lands. Impunity for human rights
violations persisted. Abortion continued to
be criminalized in most cases.

INDIGENOUS PEOPLES' RIGHTS

Progress was made in resolving the land
claims of some Indigenous communities,
but others continued to be denied their
traditional lands.

In June, an expropriation law was passed
to return to the Sawhoyamaxa Indigenous
community their traditional land. The
community had lived in harsh conditions
by the side of a busy road for more than 20
years.[1] In September a constitutional action to
revoke the expropriation law was rejected by
the Supreme Court.

By the end of the year the Yakye Axa
community was still unable to resettle on their
land – despite an agreement between the
authorities and the landowner having been
finalized in January 2012 – because road
access to the land was not ready.

In May police officers raided the Y'apo Ava
Guaraní community in Canindeyú department
following a judicial eviction order. The
community fled before the raid. There were
reports of destruction of houses and sacred
temples. In June, the community reported
that private security guards further attempted
to forcibly evict them; many members of the
community were injured and one person
carrying out the eviction died. Investigations
into the event were ongoing at the end of
the year. The community claimed that the
area was part of their ancestral land. In
2001 a judicial decision had confirmed the
possession of the land by the community;

however, in April 2014 a judicial action was
filed by a company claiming ownership of the
land. A judicial decision was still pending at
the end of the year.

IMPUNITY

Judicial proceedings continued against 12
campesinos (peasant farmers) at the end of
the year for their alleged involvement in the
killings of six police officers and other related
crimes in the context of a 2012 land dispute
in Curuguaty district. Eleven peasant farmers
also died during the clashes; however, nobody
has been charged for their deaths, raising
concerns that the investigation was not
impartial.[2]

In April the Aché National Federation
filed in Argentina an additional criminal
complaint to the one already presented in
2013 by victims of human rights violations
committed during the regime of General
Alfredo Stroessner (1954-1989), in view of
the persistent reluctance of the Paraguayan
authorities to investigate those crimes.
The criminal complaint was subject to an
investigation under universal jurisdiction.

TORTURE AND OTHER ILL-TREATMENT

The newly established National Preventive
Mechanism against Torture issued its first
annual report in April. The report found that
the lack of sanctions and investigations into
allegations of torture and other ill-treatment
was one of the main causes of torture in the
country. The Mechanism was also seriously
concerned about poor prison conditions,
including overcrowding.

Investigations into allegations of torture
of *campesinos* during the 2012 clashes in
Curuguaty district were ongoing at the end of
the year.

Four prison officials were under
investigation in relation to the deaths of
two adolescents and the injury of at least
three other youths during riots in April and
August at Itauguá Educational Centre juvenile
detention facility.

WOMEN'S AND GIRLS' RIGHTS

A law submitted to Congress in 2012 to prevent, punish and eradicate sexual and gender violence was still pending.

In August the Senate passed legislation to reform an article in the Criminal Code which only sanctions domestic violence if the assault happens regularly. The reform proposes to sanction the crime even if committed only once. The reform also increases the penalties under this article and was pending final approval by the Deputy Chamber at the end of the year.

In August, Lucía Sandoval was acquitted of killing her husband in 2011 in the context of domestic violence. She spent three years in detention pending trial. The court found that there was insufficient evidence to prove her involvement in the killing and released her. The case raised concerns about the lack of appropriate measures to protect women survivors of domestic violence in Paraguay. An appeal against the decision was pending at the end of the year.

Abortion remained criminalized in most circumstances, including in cases where the pregnancy was the result of rape or incest or where the foetus would be unable to survive outside the womb. Abortion was only permitted when the life or health of the woman or girl was at risk.

DISCRIMINATION

In November, the Senate rejected legislation to prevent and combat discrimination on all grounds.

ARMS TRADE

Legislation to ratify the Arms Trade Treaty was passed.

---

1. Paraguay: Celebrations as law will return ancestral land to Indigenous community after two decades of destitution (NWS 11/109/2014)
   www.amnesty.org/press-releases/2014/06/paraguay-celebrations-law-will-return-ancestral-land-indigenous-community-a/

2. Paraguay: No justice for peasants in forced eviction killings (NWS 11/111/2014)
   www.amnesty.org/en/news/paraguay-no-justice-peasants-forced-eviction-killings-2014-06-15

PERU

Republic of Peru
Head of state and government: **Ollanta Moisés Humala Tasso**

Activists and government critics were attacked. Use of excessive force by security forces was reported. The rights of Indigenous Peoples to adequate consultation, and free, prior and informed consent were not fulfilled. Sexual and reproductive rights were not guaranteed. Impunity remained a concern.

BACKGROUND

Social conflict and protests in communities affected by extractive industries continued to be widespread. Some protests led to clashes with security forces.

At least four members of the security forces were killed and seven were injured in clashes with remnants of the armed opposition group, Shining Path.

A national mechanism for the prevention of torture and other ill-treatment was approved by the Congress in June. At the end of the year, it had not been implemented as the President had not ratified it.

Serious concerns were raised over the conditions in which over 100 prisoners were kept in Challapalca Prison situated over 4,600m above sea level in the Tacna region. The prison's inaccessibility to relatives, doctors and lawyers limits the prisoners' right to visits and constituted cruel, inhuman and degrading treatment.

In July, the second two-year National Plan for Human Rights was approved by Congress, amidst concerns that LGBTI rights were explicitly excluded, and that the Plan had not been fully resourced for its implementation.

A law which would grant equal rights to same-sex couples had not been discussed in Congress at the end of the year.

REPRESSION OF DISSENT

Activists and government critics, including human rights defenders, continued to be attacked, in particular those defending the rights of communities affected by extractive industries.

Security forces and private security personnel of the Yanacocha gold mining company intimidated and attacked Máxima Chaupe, her family and others from Indigenous and peasant communities in Cajamarca, Celendín and Hualgayoc-Bambamarca provinces, Cajamarca region. They opposed the mining on their lands claiming that they had not been consulted and that their right to water and means of subsistence were under attack. In May, the Inter-American Commission on Human Rights requested precautionary measures on their behalf. At the end of the year, no protection had been granted.

INDIGENOUS PEOPLES' RIGHTS

In September, Indigenous leaders Edwin Chota Valera, Jorge Ríos Pérez, Leoncio Quinticima Meléndez and Francisco Pinedo from the Asháninka Indigenous community of Alto Tamaya-Saweto, Ucayali region, were killed by suspected illegal loggers, in retaliation for their activism against illegal logging on their ancestral lands. Prior to the attack, the community had raised concerns about their safety and the authorities had failed to protect them. At the end of the year, an investigation had been opened. However, there were still concerns about the safety of the families of those killed.

In spite of some efforts to implement the 2011 law that guarantees the right to free, prior and informed consent of Indigenous Peoples, there were concerns over the lack of a clear methodology and consistency in its implementation prior to granting extractive industries' concessions. In January, the authorities granted a concession to expand the Camisea gas extraction project in the Cusco region, amid concerns that none of the Indigenous communities that could be affected had given their consent and that nearly a quarter of the territory could be occupied by Indigenous Peoples living in voluntary isolation.

In May, the trial of 53 people started, including Indigenous people and some of their leaders. They had been accused of the death of 12 police officers during a police and military operation to disperse a road blockade led by Indigenous people in Bagua, Amazon region, in 2009. A total of 33 people died, including 23 police officers, and over 200 people were injured. No police or military officers have been held accountable for the human rights violations committed against civilians.

IMPUNITY
Excessive use of force

At least nine people were killed and scores were injured amid concerns that the security forces had used excessive force during protests throughout the year. At the end of the year, no investigation was known to have been initiated into the deaths.

There were concerns that a new law passed in January could perpetuate impunity. The law exempted security forces of penal responsibility when killing or injuring people while on duty. In February, four police officers, who were being tried for their responsibility in the deaths of three protesters in Huancavelica in 2011, were acquitted when the judge applied the law retroactively. There were allegations of excessive use of force when scores of protesters were injured during the demonstrations.

Internal armed conflict

Eleven years after the publication of the Truth and Reconciliation Commission's report, progress to guarantee truth, justice and reparation to all the victims remained slow. There were concerns that the armed forces continued to fail to co-operate with the judiciary and that some cases were closed as the judges ruled that the crimes had prescribed.

SEXUAL AND REPRODUCTIVE RIGHTS

In January, the Public Prosecutor's Office in Lima, the capital, closed the cases of over 2,000 Indigenous and *campesino* women who were allegedly forcibly sterilized in the 1990s. After an investigation, which started in 2004 and lasted nearly 10 years, the Prosecutor only filed charges against some health professionals allegedly responsible in one of the cases. No charges were filed against any of the government authorities responsible for implementing the family planning programme, which resulted in these sterilizations.

In June, the Ministry of Health adopted technical guidelines for therapeutic abortion. There were concerns that the restrictive interpretation of therapeutic abortion in the protocol may lead women to seek unsafe and illegal terminations because the two access conditions required – presence and signature of a witness and approval of a board – were considered obstructive.

Abortion in cases of pregnancy resulting from rape or incest remained criminalized and the free distribution of emergency contraceptives, including in cases of sexual abuse, continued to be banned. At the end of the year, a draft law to legalize abortion for victims of rape, backed by 60,000 signatures, was waiting to be discussed in Congress.

PHILIPPINES

Republic of the Philippines
Head of state and government: **Benigno S. Aquino III**

Torture continued with impunity in the Philippines. Human rights defenders, local journalists and witnesses in the Maguindanao massacre trials, the world's largest single attack on journalists committed in 2009, remained at risk of unlawful killing. The Philippines acknowledged state accountability for human rights violations during the Martial Law under the Marcos regime and established a Human Rights Victims' Claims Board to determine the eligibility of claims for human rights violations and award reparations. The Supreme Court upheld the constitutionality of the Reproductive Health Law in April.

BACKGROUND

The Philippine government in March signed a comprehensive peace agreement with the armed group Moro Islamic Liberation Front, concluding 17 years of peace negotiations. The peace accord created the autonomous Bangsamoro region, providing greater political autonomy in southern Philippines in exchange for a commitment to end the insurgency and calls for a separate state. The Philippines continued its claim over the Spratly Islands against Brunei, China, Malaysia, Taiwan and Vietnam, submitting a memorandum before the International Tribunal on the Law of the Seas in March and protesting against China's actions in the Spratlys in May and November.

A visit by US President Barack Obama in April culminated in the signing of an Enhanced Defence Co-operation Agreement, further allowing US military troops to use Philippine military bases.

In early December, half a million people were evacuated in advance of Typhoon Hagupit and 27 casualties were reported.

TORTURE AND OTHER ILL-TREATMENT

Torture and other ill-treatment remained rife and appeared to be routine during interrogations in some police stations.[1] Torture methods included severe beating as well as electric shocks, mock executions, waterboarding, near-asphyxiation with plastic bags, and rape.

Among those most at risk were criminal suspects and repeat offenders, including juvenile offenders, informal police auxiliaries (known locally as "assets"), suspected members or sympathizers of armed groups and political activists. Most torture victims were from poor and marginalized backgrounds. In 2014, the Commission on Human Rights of the Philippines (CHR) reported that it recorded 75 cases of torture in 2013, and 28 cases from January to July 2014. The majority of reports of torture cited police officers as the alleged perpetrators. Despite its criminalization under the 2009 Anti-Torture Act, not one perpetrator has been convicted under the Act.

In January the CHR exposed a secret detention facility in Laguna province, in which police officers appeared to be torturing for entertainment by using a "roulette wheel" on which torture methods were described. Forty-three detainees were found inside the facility. In February the Philippine National Police (PNP) suspended 10 police officers. Investigations continued, but none were convicted at the end of the year. Twenty-three cases were filed for preliminary investigation and were pending resolution.

Alfreda Disbarro, a former police informant, was apprehended and tortured by police officers in October 2013. In April, the PNP Internal Affairs Service conducted an investigation into her case; the decision on the administrative case against the perpetrators was pending. The CHR concluded that human rights violations were committed and in July recommended the filing of a criminal complaint.

The Senate opened an enquiry into police torture the day after Amnesty International launched its report "Above the Law: Police torture in the Philippines" on 4 December.

ENFORCED DISAPPEARANCES

Concerns remained over the government's commitment to ending enforced disappearances following its failure to ratify the International Convention for the Protection of All Persons from Enforced Disappearance.

In February, the CHR announced that it would enter into a Memorandum of Agreement with the Department of Interior and Local Government, the Department of National Defense and the Department of Justice on the implementation of the Anti-Enforced or Involuntary Disappearance Act of 2012 which criminalized enforced disappearances. In August, the National Bureau of Investigation arrested retired General Jovito Palparan in Manila after three years in hiding. In 2011, he was charged with kidnapping, abduction and "serious illegal detention" of two women university students.

In February the Supreme Court upheld the finality of the Court of Appeals ruling identifying a military officer responsible for the abduction and disappearance of Jonas Burgos in 2007, and finding the military accountable for his abduction.

IMPUNITY

Trials in the civil and criminal cases relating to the 2009 Maguindanao massacre, in which state-armed militias led by government officials killed 58 people including 32 media workers, were ongoing. However, most of the proceedings were bail hearings only. By the end of the year, around 85 of the 197 suspects for whom arrest warrants had been issued remained at large and no convictions had been handed down.

Witnesses to the massacre and their families remained at risk of attacks, including killings, highlighting a lack of government protection. In November, Dennis Sakal and Butch Saudagal, both of whom were due to testify against primary suspects in the massacre, were shot by unidentified gunmen in Maguindanao province, killing Dennis Sakal. In December, Kagui Akmad Ampatuan, who reportedly convinced these witnesses to testify for the prosecution, survived a similar ambush in Maguindanao.

At least eight witnesses and their family members had been killed in similar attacks since November 2009. No one was held accountable for these killings.

FREEDOM OF EXPRESSION

At least three radio broadcasters and one newspaper reporter were killed by unidentified gunmen in 2014.

In February, the Supreme Court declared major provisions of the 2012 Cybercrime Prevention Act, including the online libel provision, as constitutional. The Court clarified that only original authors of libellous material were covered by the law, excluding those who reacted online to the libellous post.

ABUSES BY ARMED GROUPS

Attacks by hardline Islamist insurgents opposed to the peace accord between the government and the Moro Islamic Liberation Front continued. In July, an attack by Abu Sayyaf in Sulu province left 21 people dead. In December, 10 people were killed and more than 30 injured when a mortar bomb exploded on a public bus in Bukidnon province.

SEXUAL AND REPRODUCTIVE RIGHTS

Following a year-long suspension of its implementation, in April the Supreme Court upheld the Reproductive Health Law following a legal challenge by various faith-based groups. The law paves the way for government funding for modern contraceptive methods and seeks to introduce reproductive health and sexuality education in schools.

However, the Court's ruling found eight provisions to be unconstitutional. These included: prohibiting health practitioners from refusing to provide reproductive health services and penalizing them if they did; requiring all private health facilities, including those owned by religious groups, to provide family planning methods, including modern contraceptive supplies and procedures; allowing minors – including those who already have children or have had miscarriages – access to birth control without their parents' written consent; and allowing married individuals to undergo reproductive health procedures without their spouse's consent.

The Department of Justice failed to include exceptions to the total ban on abortion in the draft criminal code it sent to Congress. Due to the total ban on abortion, clandestine abortions remained widespread, resulting in unnecessary death and disability of women.

---

1. Above the law: Police torture in the Philippines (ASA 35/007/2014) www.amnesty.org/en/library/info/ASA35/007/2014/en

POLAND

Republic of Poland
Head of state: **Bronislaw Komorowski**
Head of government: **Ewa Kopacz (replaced Donald Tusk in September)**

Former Polish president has admitted that Poland hosted a secret CIA prison. The European Court of Human Rights ruled against Poland for complicity in CIA secret detention and torture. Concerns over protection and fulfilment of sexual and reproductive rights persisted. Poland has not ratified the Council of Europe Convention on preventing and combating violence against women and domestic violence.

COUNTER-TERROR AND SECURITY

Poland became the first EU member state to be found complicit in the USA's rendition and secret detention programmes, authorized by US President George W. Bush in the aftermath of the 11 September 2001 attacks in the USA. In July, the European Court of Human Rights ruled in two separate judgments that the Polish government colluded with the US Central Intelligence Agency (CIA) to establish a secret prison at Stare Kiejkuty, where detainees were held in secret, subjected to enforced disappearance, and tortured. The two claimants, Abd al-Rahim al-Nashiri and Zayn al-Abidin Muhammad Husayn (Abu Zubaydah), applied to the European Court in 2011 and 2013, respectively. Abd al-Rahim al-Nashiri, a Saudi Arabian national alleged to have masterminded the bombing of the USS Cole off the coast of Yemen in 2000, has claimed that he was questioned in a secret facility in Poland and subjected to "enhanced interrogation techniques" and other human rights violations, such as "mock execution" with a gun and threats of sexual assault against his family. Abu Zubaydah, a stateless Palestinian born in Saudi Arabia, also alleged that he was held in Poland, where he said he was subjected to extreme physical pain and psychological suffering, including "waterboarding". Abd al-Rahim Al-Nashiri faced a capital trial by military commission in Guantánamo Bay.

The European Court found Poland in violation of the European Convention on Human Rights for, among other things, the lack of an investigation into the men's claims, their torture and other ill-treatment, secret detention, and transfer to other places where they were at risk of further human rights violations. The Court also reaffirmed the victims' and the public's right to truth. In October, the government referred the cases to the Grand Chamber of the European Court for a review *de novo*. At the end of the year, the Chamber had not made a decision on the government's request.

A third man who had alleged that he was held at a secret detention site in 2003 was granted "injured person" status in October 2013 in Poland's national investigation into the CIA site. Walid bin Attash, a Yemeni national, is currently detained and awaiting trial by military commission at Guantánamo Bay. A fourth man, Mustafa al-Hawsawi, lodged an application with the prosecutors seeking injured person status in the ongoing investigation into allegations of the rendition and secret detention programmes. At the end of the year, the prosecutor was considering whether to reverse a prior negative decision on Mustafa al-Hawsawi's application.

After years of denials, former Polish president Aleksander Kwasniewski admitted in December that Poland had hosted a secret CIA prison where detainees were held between 2002 and 2003. The acknowledgment came in the aftermath of the release of a heavily redacted summary of a US Senate report on the CIA's secret detention programme. Although Poland was not named, the facts surrounding what was called "detention site blue" in the Senate report conformed to the dates of detention and accounts of torture described by Abu Zubaydah and Abd al-Rahim al-Nashiri in their European Court applications.

SEXUAL AND REPRODUCTIVE RIGHTS

Despite the judgment of the European Court of Human Rights in October 2012 in the case of *P. and S. v. Poland*, in which Poland was found to have violated the right to private life and to be free from inhuman and degrading treatment when a 14-year-old girl's right to a lawful abortion was denied, there has been little progress in ensuring access to legal abortion. The authorities failed to introduce measures to ensure effective implementation of the abortion law and to guarantee that the conscientious objection of health workers did not inhibit women's access to lawful services.

In June, a woman was denied access to an abortion despite prenatal tests indicating severe and irreversible damage of the fetus.

Although the law allows abortion in such cases, the Director of a public hospital in Warsaw refused to allow the abortion to be performed in the hospital, citing grounds of conscience, despite the fact that the conscientious objection exemption extends to individuals not institutions. The child died 10 days after the birth. In July, the Ministry of Health fined the hospital for violating the patient's rights and the Mayor of Warsaw dismissed the Director from his post. In response to the case, the Commissioner for Patients' Rights recommended that the government amend the regulations on conscientious objection.

DISCRIMINATION

In March, the UN Committee on the Elimination of Racial Discrimination noted an increase in hate crimes, including anti-Semitic attacks. It criticized the lack of a provision in the Criminal Code establishing racial motivation as an aggravating circumstance of a crime.

Anti-discrimination legislation failed to provide equal protection against discrimination in all areas on all grounds. Discrimination was not explicitly prohibited on the grounds of sexual identity, and was only prohibited in respect of sexual orientation in the sphere of employment.

JUSTICE SYSTEM

In January, the Act on Proceedings against Persons with Mental Disorders came into force. The new law allowed courts to impose preventive measures against convicted persons with mental disorders who threaten the life, health and sexual freedom of others. Possible measures included isolation in closed mental health units following a completed jail sentence. The President referred the law to the Constitutional Tribunal for review.

REFUGEES' AND MIGRANTS' RIGHTS

The new Law on Foreigners, which entered into force in May, extended the maximum period of detention for asylum-seekers to 24 months. According to the Polish NGOs Helsinki Foundation for Human Rights and the Association for Legal Intervention, nearly one in four people held in migration detention were children.

In October, the European Court of Human Rights asked the government to clarify the circumstances of the administrative detention of an ethnic Chechen asylum-seeker and her five children. The woman and children were deported to Chechnya in March, even though their asylum procedure was still pending.

PORTUGAL

Portuguese Republic
Head of state: **Aníbal António Cavaco Silva**
Head of government: **Pedro Manuel Mamede Passos Coelho**

Reports of excessive use of force by police and inadequate prison conditions continued. Roma continued to face discrimination. Austerity measures affected the enjoyment of economic and social rights and in some instances were found unconstitutional.

BACKGROUND

In May, the report of the Working Group on the UN Universal Periodic Review of Portugal highlighted the need for Portugal to protect the human rights of vulnerable groups from the negative impact of austerity measures adopted in 2013. Also in May, the Constitutional Court declared several austerity measures unconstitutional due to their disproportionate impact on economic and social rights. The measures adopted in 2013 were related to public servants' salaries, pensions and sickness and unemployment benefits. In the case of salaries, there was no retroactive reparation for the negative effects already created by such measures.

At the end of the year the government was planning to reintroduce similar measures in the new budget.

TORTURE AND OTHER ILL-TREATMENT

In July 2014, two prison officers were handed an eight-month suspended sentence by the court of Paços de Ferreira for using excessive force against a detainee in the Paços de Ferreira prison in 2010. The two officers had entered the prisoner's cell to force him to either clean it or leave in order for the cell to be cleaned. Even though the detainee obeyed orders to stand up, turn his back to the cell door and face the window, the officers used a Taser to immobilize him. The court considered that the Taser was used disproportionately, particularly as the man had not resorted to any violence against the prison officers.

Prison conditions

In December 2013, the UN Committee against Torture highlighted reports of ill-treatment and excessive use of force, as well as prison overcrowding and deplorable prison conditions, particularly in the Prison of Santa Cruz do Bispo and the Lisbon Central Prison.

DISCRIMINATION – ROMA

Forced evictions of Roma families continued to be reported.

In June, the homes of 67 members of the Vidigueira Roma Community, including 35 children and three pregnant women, were demolished by the municipality in their absence. According to reports, the eviction was implemented without prior notice and the families had no opportunity to collect their belongings before their homes were demolished. The families were made homeless as a result of the eviction. In September, a class consisting exclusively of Roma children, aged seven to 14, was created in a school in Tomar. No action was taken by relevant authorities to address the segregation of Roma children.

RIGHTS OF LESBIAN, GAY, BISEXUAL, TRANSGENDER AND INTERSEX PEOPLE

A proposed bill, amending current legislation to ensure the right of same-sex couples to co-adopt children, was rejected in March.

REFUGEES AND ASYLUM-SEEKERS

New asylum legislation adopted in January extended the criteria for detaining persons seeking international protection. Overcrowding remained in the Reception Centre for Refugees of the Portuguese Refugee Council in Lisbon, which accommodated asylum-seekers awaiting a decision on their status.

VIOLENCE AGAINST WOMEN AND GIRLS

According to data provided by the NGO UMAR (União de Mulheres Alternativa e Resposta), as of 30 November, 40 women were killed by partners, ex-partners and close family members. There were also 46 attempted murders. The number had risen since 2013, when 37 homicides were registered for the whole year.

PUERTO RICO

Commonwealth of Puerto Rico
Head of state: **Barack Obama**
Head of government: **Alejandro García Padilla**

The US Department of Justice continued to pursue death sentences on federal charges. Despite some advances in law, LGBTI people continued to be denied their right to non-discrimination. Laws restricting the rights to freedom of assembly and expression were repealed.

RIGHTS OF LESBIAN, GAY, BISEXUAL, TRANSGENDER AND INTERSEX PEOPLE

In October 2014, a US federal district judge in San Juan upheld Puerto Rico's ban on same-sex marriage. The judge stated: "Because no right to same-gender marriage emanates from the Constitution, the Commonwealth of Puerto Rico should not be compelled to recognize such unions." An appeal was pending before the US Federal Appeals Court at the end of the year.

In February 2013, the Supreme Court affirmed the ban on same-sex adoption. In a 5-4 vote, judges upheld the constitutionality of a law that states that a person cannot adopt a single-parent child if the would-be adopter is of the same sex as the child's mother or father without that parent losing their legal rights.

In 2013 there were advances in the creation of laws to protect the rights of LGBTI people, including a bill that prohibits employment discrimination based on gender identity or sexual orientation and a bill to extend domestic violence protections to same-sex couples. However, a proposed amendment to the Penal Code, which would have criminalized discrimination against LGBTI people, was removed. The revised Penal Code was before Governor Padilla awaiting endorsement at the end of the year.

SEXUAL AND REPRODUCTIVE RIGHTS

A civil society campaign to remove a 2011 amendment to the Penal Code limiting a woman's right to abortion to circumstances to protect life or health and making breaches of the law punishable with a fixed prison term of two years was unsuccessful. The 2011 statute violates the US Supreme Court ruling in *Roe v. Wade* and the Puerto Rico Supreme Court ruling in *Pueblo v. Duarte*.

POLICE AND SECURITY FORCES

In April 2013, Governor Padilla revoked provisions in the Penal Code that restricted the right to freedom of assembly and expression. These laws had criminalized protests in schools, universities and health institutions as well as those that interfered with local government.

In July 2013, the US Department of Justice and the government of Puerto Rico reached an agreement to reform the country's police force after a 2011 federal report found unconstitutional conduct by the police, including unlawful killings. Under the federally mandated reform programme, Puerto Rico has 10 years to carry out the reforms.

DEATH PENALTY

As a commonwealth of the USA, Puerto Rico is subject to some US federal laws. Although the death penalty on the island was abolished in 1929, the US Department of Justice has attempted over the years to obtain a death sentence on federal charges in a number of cases. During 2013, Puerto Rico juries voted for life imprisonment in three cases in which the US administration had been pursuing the death penalty. By the end of 2014, there were no authorized federal capital prosecutions pending trial in Puerto Rico.

QATAR

State of Qatar
Head of state: **Sheikh Tamim bin Hamad bin Khalifa Al Thani**
Head of government: **Sheikh Abdullah bin Nasser bin Khalifa Al Thani**

Migrant workers remained inadequately protected under the law and were exploited and abused. Women faced discrimination and violence. The authorities restricted freedom of expression and courts failed to uphold fair trial standards. At least two death sentences were passed; no executions were reported.

BACKGROUND

Elections for the advisory Shura Council, originally planned for 2013, did not take place. The term of the Shura Council had been extended until 2016 by the former

Emir prior to his abdication as head of state in 2013.

A rift between Qatar and other Gulf Cooperation Council states, reportedly over Qatar's support for the Muslim Brotherhood, among other things, saw Saudi Arabia, Bahrain and the United Arab Emirates withdraw their ambassadors from Qatar in March. In November, it was announced that they would be reinstated. In September, Qatar asked seven prominent Egyptian members of the Muslim Brotherhood to leave Qatar.

The government faced growing international pressure to address abuses of the rights of migrant workers. FIFA, football's world governing body, discussed the issue of migrant labour abuse at its March Executive Committee meeting, intensifying pressure on the authorities to address the abuse of workers ahead of the 2022 football World Cup in Qatar.

The UN Human Rights Council expressed concern about abuses of the rights of migrants, discrimination and violence against women, and restrictions on freedoms of expression and assembly during its Universal Periodic Review of Qatar in May.

MIGRANT WORKERS' RIGHTS

Employers continued to abuse and exploit foreign migrant workers, who comprised more than 90% of Qatar's total workforce. The authorities failed to adequately enforce the 2004 Labour Law and related decrees, which contained some protective provisions.

Workers' living conditions were often grossly inadequate and many workers said they were made to work excessive hours beyond the legal maximum or were paid far less than agreed when they were contracted. Some employers failed to pay workers their wages, and some did not issue residency permits to employees, leaving them undocumented and at risk of arrest and detention. Few workers possessed their own passports and some employers denied workers the exit permits they required to leave Qatar. Construction workers were exposed to

hazardous conditions. Under the Labour Law, migrant workers were prohibited from forming or joining trade unions.

The government announced that it had increased the number of labour inspectors; that it was subjecting more companies to punitive sanctions; and that it had planned measures to improve conditions for migrant workers, including new accommodation standards and an electronic wage protection system. However, these measures had not been made law by the end of the year.

Migrant domestic workers, mostly women, and certain other workers were specifically excluded from the Labour Law, exposing them to greater labour exploitation and abuse, including sexual abuse.[1] The government repeatedly stated its commitment to enact legislation to address this problem but it had not done so by the end of the year. Women domestic workers were liable to face prosecution and imprisonment for "illicit relations" if they reported sexual abuse by employers.

The 2009 Sponsorship Law, which requires foreign workers to obtain a sponsor's permission to leave Qatar or change employer, continued to be exploited by employers to prevent workers from complaining to the authorities or moving to a new job in the event of abuse. The sponsorship system increased the likelihood of workers being subjected to forced labour and human trafficking. In May, the government announced proposed reforms to the sponsorship system to amend the procedure for workers to leave Qatar and allow workers to change employers after the completion of their contract or after five years with the same employer. At the end of the year, no legislation had been passed and no drafts had been published.[2] In April the UN Special Rapporteur on the human rights of migrants urged the government to abolish the sponsorship system.

An international law firm commissioned by the government to review migrant labour in Qatar submitted its report in April. The authorities did not publish the report, although a leaked version containing more than 60 recommendations appeared on the internet. The government did not say whether it would implement the recommendations.

WOMEN'S RIGHTS

Women remained unable to fully exercise their human rights due to barriers in law, policy and practice. The absence of a law specifically criminalizing domestic violence exposed women to abuse within the family, while personal status laws discriminated against women in relation to marriage, divorce, nationality and freedom of movement.

FREEDOM OF EXPRESSION

Freedom of expression remained strictly controlled and the press routinely exercised self-censorship.

The poet Mohammed al-Ajami, also known as Mohammed Ibn al-Dheeb, remained in prison in solitary confinement after Qatar's highest court upheld his 15-year sentence on 20 October 2013. He had been convicted and sentenced to life imprisonment in November 2012 for writing and reciting poems deemed offensive to the state and the Emir, but his sentence was reduced on appeal. He was detained incommunicado for three months after his arrest and tried in secret. He was in solitary confinement throughout most of his imprisonment.

A new cybercrimes law was enacted in September. The law criminalized the dissemination of "false" news and the publication online of content deemed harmful to Qatar's "social values" or national interests. The law's vaguely worded provisions risked increasing self-censorship among journalists and further stifling online criticism of the authorities.

ARBITRARY ARRESTS AND DETENTIONS

On 31 August, security authorities in Doha detained two human rights workers, Krishna Prasad Upadhyaya and Ghimire Gundev, both UK nationals. They were subjected to enforced disappearance for one week, before officials acknowledged their detention and allowed them access to UK consular officials. They were held incommunicado and released without charge on 9 September. They were not able to leave Qatar until 19 September.[3]

JUSTICE SYSTEM

Following her visit to Qatar in January, the UN Special Rapporteur on the independence of judges and lawyers expressed concern at, among other things, the government's "interference" in judicial procedures, particularly in cases involving high-profile individuals or businesses, as well as violations of due process and the failure of the judiciary to meet international fair trial standards.

On 30 April, Doha Criminal Court convicted three Filipino nationals of espionage; one was sentenced to death, the other two to life imprisonment. The convictions were based largely on confessions reportedly extracted under torture. All three men lodged appeals.

DEATH PENALTY

At least two people were sentenced to death. No executions were reported.

1. 'My sleep is my break': Exploitation of migrant domestic workers in Qatar (MDE 22/004/2014)

www.amnesty.org/en/library/info/MDE22/004/2014/en

2. No extra time: How Qatar is still failing on workers' rights ahead of the World Cup (MDE 22/010/2014)

www.amnesty.org/en/library/info/MDE22/010/2014/en

3. Qatar: Further information – UK nationals released (MDE 22/008/2014)

www.a mnesty.org/en/library/info/MDE22/008/2014/en

ROMANIA

Romania
Head of state: **Klaus Iohannis (replaced Traian Băsescu in December)**
Head of government: **Victor Ponta**

A former senior intelligence official confirmed that Romania had co-operated with the CIA to establish a secret prison in the country. Roma continued to experience discrimination, forced evictions and other human rights violations. The parliamentary Commission for the Revision of the Constitution passed an amendment restricting protection against discrimination.

BACKGROUND

In January, the European Commission expressed concerns about the independence of the judicial system. International and Romanian NGOs expressed concerns over the failure of the authorities to seriously engage with the review process by the UN Committee on Economic, Social and Cultural Rights. In December, the Committee criticized the failure of the government to ensure the effective protection of a wide range of human rights enshrined in the ICESCR, including the right to adequate housing, water and sanitation, and sexual and reproductive rights, in the Committee's first review of the country for over 20 years.

DISCRIMINATION – ROMA

Roma continued to face systemic discrimination. Public officials used discriminatory and stigmatizing speech against Roma. In February, President Traian Băsescu was fined for the second time by the National Council for Combating Discrimination. During an official visit to Slovenia in November 2010, he stated that "among nomad Roma, very few want to work and many of them, traditionally, live off what they steal." In July, the Cluj-Napoca Court

of Appeal found that the government had failed to implement measures promised in the wake of attacks against Roma communities in Hădăreni, including community development projects to improve living conditions and inter-ethnic relations. The Hădăreni events were among some 30 incidents of mob violence directed at Romani communities throughout Romania in the early 1990s.

In September 2013, the High Court of Cassation and Justice upheld the 2011 decision of the National Council for Combating Discrimination that the concrete wall erected in Baia Mare to separate blocks of houses inhabited by Roma from the rest of the residential area amounted to discrimination.

HOUSING RIGHTS – FORCED EVICTIONS

The concluding observations of the UN Committee on Economic, Social and Cultural Rights called on the government to ensure access to adequate housing for disadvantaged and marginalized groups, including Roma, and to amend the legislation to prohibit forced evictions.[1]

Local authorities continued to forcibly evict Romani communities. Some were relocated to inadequate and segregated housing, while others were effectively made homeless.

Romani families living for over 40 years in an informal settlement in Eforie Sud, Constanța county, were repeatedly forcibly evicted from their homes. In September 2013, 101 people, including 55 children, were made homeless in severe weather conditions when their homes were demolished following a municipal order. Some of the families were subsequently offered temporary shelter in two abandoned school buildings in highly inadequate living conditions.[2] In July 2014, seven of the 10 families living in one of the former schools were relocated to segregated and inadequate containers on the outskirts of Eforie Sud, while the remaining three were left homeless. None of the families were provided with remedy or compensation for the violations suffered and for loss or damage to their possessions.

By the end of 2014, Romani families forcibly evicted in August 2013 from the Craica settlement in Baia Mare in connection with a waterworks project co-funded by the Romanian Ministry of Environment, the EU and the European Bank for Reconstruction and Development, had not been provided with adequate alternative housing.[3] The families continued to live in the improvised housing they built after the 2013 demolitions.

In December 2013, the Cluj-Napoca County Court ruled unlawful the Mayor's decision to forcibly evict around 300 Roma in December 2010 from the centre of the city and resettle them at a site adjacent to a waste dump. The court ordered the municipality to pay damages to the applicants and provide them with adequate housing. In October 2014, following the municipality's appeal, the Cluj Court of Appeal decided to remit the case to the Cluj District Court on the grounds that the case was a matter of private – rather than administrative – law, as the municipality had acted in its capacity of landlord/landowner rather than as a public authority. The case was still pending at the end of the year.

COUNTER-TERROR AND SECURITY

In December, a former chief of the intelligence service confirmed that Romania had co-operated with the CIA to establish a secret prison in the country in 2002. The admission followed the release of a US Senate report detailing the CIA's secret detention programme and the torture of detainees. In the report, "detention site black" was alleged to be a secret prison in Romania.

In 2012, Abd al-Rahim al-Nashiri, a Saudi Arabian national currently detained at Guantánamo Bay, lodged a complaint against Romania with the European Court of Human Rights alleging that he had been secretly detained in the capital, Bucharest, between 2004 and 2006.

TORTURE AND OTHER ILL-TREATMENT

In July, the European Court of Human Rights ruled that Romania had violated the right to life of Valentin Câmpeanu, an HIV-positive Romani man with a mental illness who died due to inappropriate care and living conditions at the Poiana Mare psychiatric hospital in 2004.

Also in July, the Council of Europe Commissioner for Human Rights criticized the inadequate living conditions and ongoing reports of ill-treatment in institutions for adults and children with mental and physical disabilities, despite the government's longstanding expressed objective to reduce the number of people with disabilities being held in institutions.

The Commissioner also expressed concern over reported cases of excessive use of force by police during searches carried out in Romani homes in Reghin, Mureş, in 2013 and recommended the establishment of an independent complaints mechanism for violations by law enforcement officials.

SEXUAL AND REPRODUCTIVE RIGHTS

According to several international and national NGOs, barriers inhibiting women's access to legal abortion services persisted. These included mandatory or biased counselling, conscientious objection by medical practitioners, and limited information about abortion services.

RIGHTS OF LESBIAN, GAY, BISEXUAL, TRANSGENDER AND INTERSEX PEOPLE

In June 2013, the parliamentary Commission for the Revision of the Constitution passed an amendment removing sexual orientation as a protected ground in the anti-discrimination provisions of the Constitution. The Commission rejected at second voting, after passing it initially, an amendment proposing a change in the definition of family to freely consented marriage between "a man and a woman" rather than between "spouses".

1. Romania falls short of its international human rights obligations on Economic, Social and Cultural Rights (EUR 39/004/2014) · www.amnesty.org/en/library/info/EUR39/004/2014/en

2. Romanian local authorities must provide housing for homeless families after forced eviction (EUR 39/018/2013) www. amnesty.org/en/library/info/EUR39/018/2013/enRomania: Families homeless after forced eviction (EUR 39/019/2013) www.amnesty.org/en/library/info/EUR39/019/2013/enRomanian government is failing homeless Roma in Eforie Sud (EUR 39/021/2013) www.amnesty.org/en/library/info/EUR39/021/2013/enRomania: Submission to the Pre-sessional Working Group of the UN Committee on Economic, Social and Cultural Rights, 53rd meeting (EUR 39/02/2014) www.amnesty.org/en/library/info/EUR39/002/2014/en

3. How the EBRD's funding contributed to forced evictions in Craica, Romania (EUR 39/001/2014) www.amnesty.org/en/library/info/EUR39/001/2014/en

RUSSIAN FEDERATION

Russian Federation
Head of state: **Vladimir Putin**
Head of government: **Dmitry Medvedev**

Media pluralism and the space for the expression of dissenting views shrank markedly. Restrictions on the rights to freedom of expression, assembly and association, introduced in 2012, were assiduously enforced and further added to. Some NGOs faced harassment, public smear campaigns and pressure to register as "foreign agents". Several protesters and civil society activists were convicted following unfair, politically motivated trials. Torture and other ill-treatment continued to be used with impunity. The situation in the North Caucasus remained volatile and marred by human rights violations, with no effective legal remedies for victims, and human rights defenders, independent journalists and lawyers continuing to face personal risks in their work.

BACKGROUND

In February, Russia hosted the well-attended Winter Olympic Games in Sochi. By the end of the year, following its annexation of Crimea from Ukraine in March and its continuing support for separatists in Ukraine's eastern region of Donbass, Russia was facing increasing international isolation.

The Russian authorities adopted an increasingly belligerent anti-Western and anti-Ukrainian rhetoric, which was widely echoed in the government-controlled mainstream media. Despite growing economic difficulties and projected cuts in social spending – caused in part by Western sanctions and falling oil prices (Russia's major export commodity), and corruption – the Russian leadership enjoyed a surge in popular support, fuelled in large measure by the widely hailed annexation of Crimea (which had been under Russian administration in the Soviet Union until 1954).

Fighting in Ukraine continued after a Russian-brokered truce in September, albeit on a reduced scale. The government consistently denied that Russia was supplying military hardware, personnel and other assistance to the separatists in Donbass, despite growing evidence to the contrary. In occupied Crimea, Russian laws took effect, and the rights to freedom of expression, assembly and association were significantly curtailed as a result.

FREEDOM OF EXPRESSION
Media and journalists

The government strengthened its control over mainstream media, which became noticeably less pluralistic. Most media not nominally under state control exercised an increasing degree of self-censorship, seldom if ever giving platform to views unwelcome by the authorities. Dissenting media outlets faced considerable pressure in the form of official warnings, the removal of editorial staff and the severing of business ties. Publicly owned and private media outlets with pro-government sympathies were used to smear political opponents and critical voices, including independent NGOs.

Dozhd TV was taken off air by satellite and cable broadcasters in late January after it initiated a controversial debate about the siege of Leningrad in World War II. It was also refused an extension on the lease of its studio space. Although commercial reasons were cited, the political influence on these business decisions was apparent. Dozhd TV was well known for its independent political broadcasting, giving the floor to opposing views and offering markedly different coverage of EuroMaydan events in Ukraine. It was forced to broadcast online only and resort to "crowdfunding" to survive.

In March, the owner of online news outlet Lenta.ru replaced its editor-in-chief after receiving an official warning for publishing an interview with a right-wing Ukrainian nationalist activist who had come to prominence during EuroMaydan. Many members of staff resigned in protest, and the previously independent editorial policy changed markedly.

Greater controls were imposed on the internet. In February a law was enacted giving the Prosecutor's Office the authority to order the media regulator, Roskomnadzor, to block websites without judicial authorization for purported violations, including publishing calls to participate in unauthorized public assemblies.

In March, popular online news outlets Ezhednevnyi Zhurnal (Daily Journal), Grani.ru and Kasparov.ru were blocked after reporting on the dispersal of several peaceful spontaneous street protests in Moscow. The Prosecutor's Office argued that their sympathetic reporting on these demonstrations amounted to calls for further "unlawful actions". Its decision was repeatedly upheld in subsequent legal challenges and the outlets remained blocked at the end of the year.[1]

Several independent media outlets received official warnings about "extremist" or other purportedly unlawful content. Independent radio station Echo Moskvy was forced to remove a transcript from its website of a studio discussion on 29 October with two journalists who had witnessed the fighting at Donetsk airport and expressed pro-Ukrainian views. Roskomnadzor alleged that the programme contained "information justifying the commission of war crimes". The host of the discussion, Aleksandr Pliuschev, was later suspended for two months in connection with an unrelated inappropriate personal tweet. His suspension was the result of a compromise reached between the editor-in-chief Aleksey Venediktov and the management of Gazprom Media, the station's principal shareholder, who had initially sought to dismiss Aleksandr Pliuschev and threatened to remove Aleksey Venediktov.

Physical attacks on journalists continued. In August, several were assaulted in separate incidents, as they attempted to report on secretive funerals of Russian military servicemen allegedly killed in Ukraine.

On 29 August, Lev Shlosberg, publisher of *Pskovskaya Guberniya,* the first newspaper to report on the secret funerals, was brutally beaten and hospitalized with head injuries. The investigation failed to identify his three assailants and was suspended at the end of the year.

Timur Kuashev, a journalist from Kabardino-Balkaria who worked closely with local human rights defenders, was found dead on 1 August. His unexplained death was reportedly caused by a lethal injection. The killings of other journalists in the North Caucasus in previous years, including Natalia Estemirova, Hajimurad Kamalov and Akhmednabi Akhmednabiev, were not effectively investigated and their killers remained unidentified. In June, five men were sentenced to imprisonment for the killing of investigative journalist Anna Politkovskaya in Moscow in October 2006, but those who ordered her killing remained unidentified.

ACTIVISTS

Individuals and groups with dissenting views also continued to be denied their right to freedom of expression. Sexual minorities were among those targeted, including under the 2013 federal law prohibiting "propaganda of non-traditional sexual relations among minors". LGBTI activists were consistently prevented from holding peaceful assemblies, including in locations specifically designated for public gatherings without prior permission, typically less frequented parks with low footfall. Courts upheld the right of LGBTI activists to peaceful assembly in relation to previously banned events on three occasions, but their rulings had no impact on future decisions.

In January, activist Elena Klimova, from Nizhniy Tagil, was accused of "propaganda" for her online project "Children 404" aimed at supporting LGBTI teenagers.[2] Charges were issued against her, then dropped, then issued again, threatening the closure of her project. In April, the screening of a film about "Children 404" in Moscow was disrupted by protesters who forced their way into the auditorium and shouted abusive slogans. They were accompanied by armed police who insisted on checking the identity documents of all those present in order to establish whether any minors were present.

FREEDOM OF ASSEMBLY

Street protest activity declined overall in comparison to previous years, but spiked briefly in February and March, and again in December, in response to the Bolotnaya trial and Russia's military involvement in Ukraine, and to the announced health care system reforms and the conviction of Aleksei and Oleg Navalny.

Onerous approval procedures for public assemblies remained in place. With few exceptions, most public protests were severely restricted, barred or dispersed.

In July, penalties were significantly increased and criminal liability punishable by imprisonment introduced for repeated violations of the law on public assemblies.[3]

The authorities proceeded with the prosecution of those accused in connection with the May 2012 Bolotnaya Square protest: 10 individuals were sentenced to between two and a half and four and a half years in prison for their participation in and alleged violence during the protest, which was qualified as "mass disorder". Sergei Udaltsov and Leonid Razvozzhaev were convicted of organizing the "mass disorder".

On 20 and 24 February, police violently dispersed hundreds of peaceful protesters assembled outside the court building in Moscow as it was delivering its verdict in the Bolotnaya trial and at subsequent gatherings in the city centre. Over 600 were arbitrarily arrested, most of whom received fines. At least six were sentenced to between five and 13 days' "administrative arrest".

In subsequent weeks, numerous peaceful protesters were arrested, fined and sometimes detained for their participation in protests against Russia's military involvement in Ukraine and the annexation of Crimea. At the same time, pro-government demonstrations on Ukraine were allowed to proceed in central locations that were regularly denied to opposition protesters.

In Samara, several activists received anonymous death threats after they held a series of single-person pickets (the only form of protest allowed without a prior authorization) on 2 March.[4]

In August, three women were briefly detained at a police station in Moscow for wearing clothes in blue and yellow, the colours of the Ukrainian flag. Similar incidents were reported across the country.

At the end of the year, small-scale protests took place, mostly unhindered, in a number of cities across Russia against planned health care cuts, but in Moscow, four protesters were sentenced to detention of between five and

15 days after demonstrators briefly blocked a road.

Over 200 people were detained in Moscow on 30 December when the verdict in a politically motivated criminal trial against political activist Aleksei Navalny and his brother Oleg was announced two weeks before it was scheduled, and spontaneous protests took place. Two detainees were sentenced to 15 days' detention and a further 67 held overnight and released pending trial in January.

FREEDOM OF ASSOCIATION

Civil society activists continued to face harassment, public attacks on their integrity and, in some instances, criminal prosecution.

Throughout the year, independent civil society organizations faced growing pressure under the so-called "foreign agents law". This was introduced in 2012 to force NGOs receiving foreign funding and undertaking loosely defined "political activities" to register as "organizations fulfilling the functions of a foreign agent" and mark their public materials accordingly. In 2013 and 2014, hundreds of NGOs were subjected to intrusive official "inspections" and dozens were embroiled in protracted court hearings to fend off this requirement. In May, the law was amended to give the Ministry of Justice the authority to register an NGO as a "foreign agent" without its consent. By the end of the year it had registered 29 NGOs including several leading human rights organizations as "foreign agents".[5] At least five NGOs chose to dissolve themselves as a direct result of harassment under the "foreign agents law".

Members of the NGO Environmental Watch for North Caucasus (Ekovakhta), who were highlighting environmental damage caused by the Sochi Olympics, were subjected to a sustained campaign of harassment by security officials ahead of the Games.[6] Two of them, Yevgeny Vitishko and Igor Kharchenko, were arrested on trumped-up administrative charges and detained during the Games' opening. While in detention, Yevgeny Vitishko lost an appeal in a criminal case on exaggerated charges brought to silence him and his NGO, and was transferred directly to a prison colony to serve his three-year sentence.[7] The work of Ekovakhta was suspended by a court decision in March, and the NGO was liquidated by another decision in November, for a minor formal transgression.

The Ministry of Justice applied to the courts to close the Russian Society Memorial for a purportedly incorrect form of registration. The hearing was postponed while the NGO took formal steps to rectify this.

TORTURE AND OTHER ILL-TREATMENT

Allegations of torture and other ill-treatment continued to be reported across the country, while many of those who sought redress faced pressure to withdraw their complaints. Investigations into such allegations were almost invariably ineffective. Confessions extracted under torture were used as evidence in court. In only a handful of cases, typically involving human rights NGOs, charges were brought against the implicated law enforcement officials.

Members of an independent public monitoring commission repeatedly documented instances of torture and other ill-treatment of detainees at the prison colony and pre-trial detention centre IK-5 in Sverdlovsk Region. In July, they requested the authorities to investigate allegations of the torture of E.G., held there on remand pending trial, and produced photographic evidence of his injuries. A member of the Prosecutor's Office responded in a letter that, based on staff questioning at IK-5 and the paperwork held by its administration, E.G. had not been subjected to violence at this institution and that his injuries predated his transfer there. No further investigation was undertaken.

NORTH CAUCASUS

The situation in the North Caucasus remained volatile, with armed groups engaging in sporadic attacks against security officials.

Over 200 people reportedly lost their lives in multiple incidents, including dozens of civilians. Security operations, conducted in Dagestan, Kabardino-Balkaria, Chechnya and elsewhere, were accompanied by serious human rights violations, including unlawful detention, torture and other ill-treatment, alleged enforced disappearances and extrajudicial executions.

On 4 December, armed fighters attacked government buildings in Grozny, Chechenya, killing at least one civilian and 14 police officers. The next day Ramzan Kadyrov, Head of the Republic, publicly promised to expel relatives of the armed group members from Chechnya and demolish their houses. At least 15 houses, homes to dozens of people including small children, were burnt down or demolished.[8] Human rights defenders who condemned this practice and demanded an investigation were pelted with eggs at a press conference in Moscow on 11 December. Ramzan Kadyrov used social media to accuse Igor Kalyapin, leader of the Joint Mobile Group for Chechnya, of supporting terrorists. The Group's office in Grozny was destroyed by fire on 14 December in an apparent arson attack, and its two members searched and detained for several hours by police without explanation, their phones, cameras and computers confiscated.

The near-total lack of legal remedies for victims of human rights violations prevailed, as the criminal justice system remained ineffective and subject – for the most part clandestinely – to high-level political pressure. However, in Chechnya judges and jury members were openly admonished by Ramzan Kadyrov for decisions in criminal cases that he considered lenient towards the defendants.

Reporting on human rights violations remained a difficult, and often dangerous, occupation, and many violations were believed to have gone unrecorded. Human rights defenders, independent journalists and lawyers who worked on cases involving human rights violations continued to face threats and harassment from law enforcement officials and unidentified individuals.

Civil society activist Ruslan Kutaev complained of torture, including beatings and electrocution, after his arrest in February on trumped-up charges of heroin possession. His injuries were well documented by independent monitors.[9] However, the investigative authorities accepted the alleged perpetrators' explanation that Ruslan Kutaev's injuries resulted from a fall, and refused to investigate his complaints further. He was convicted following an unfair trial in July in Urus-Martan, Chechnya, and sentenced to four years in prison, reduced by two months on appeal in October.

Dagestani lawyer Sapiyat Magomedova, who was seriously assaulted by police in 2010 at a police station when visiting a detained client, continued to receive anonymous death threats and threats from investigation officials, both veiled and open. None of her official complaints were effectively investigated. She remained concerned for her own, her colleagues' and her family's safety, but refused to give up her work.[10] The investigation into her beating by police in 2010 was formally reopened, but the authorities failed to demonstrate any progress or intention to prosecute her assailants.

1. Violation of the right to freedom of expression, association and assembly in Russia (EUR 46/048/2014) www.amnesty.org/en/library/info/EUR46/048/2014/en
2. Russian Federation: Journalist charged under "propaganda law": Elena Klimova (EUR 46/009/2014) www.amnesty.org/en/library/info/EUR46/009/2014/en
3. A right, not a crime: Violations of the right to freedom of assembly in Russia (EUR 46/028/2014) www.amnesty.org/en/library/info/EUR46/028/2014/en
4. Russian Federation: Peace activists receive death threats www.amnesty.org/en/library/asset/EUR46/022/2014/en/56bb391a-be6b-458f-8bca-05723a2eb17b/eur460222014en.html
5. Violations of the right to freedom of expression, association and assembly in Russia (EUR 46/048/2014) www.amnesty.org/en/library/info/EUR46/048/2014/en

6. Russian Federation: Serious human rights violations associated with the preparation for and staging of the Sochi Olympic Games, open letter to the Chair of the International Olympic Committee, 10 February 2014 (EUR 46/008/2014)
www.amnesty.org/en/library/info/EUR46/008/2014/en

7. "Russia: Legacy of Olympic games tarnished by arrests, 22 February 2014" (Press release)
www.amnesty.org/en/for-media/press-releases/russia-legacy-olympic-games-tarnished-arrests-2014-02-22

8. Russia: Burning down homes after Chechnya clashes appears to be collective punishment (News story)
www.amnesty.org/en/news/russia-burning-down-homes-after-chechnya-clashes-appears-be-collective-punishment-2014-12-09-0

9. Russian Federation: Imprisoned activist must be released immediately: Ruslan Kutaev (EUR 46/052/2014)
www.amnesty.org/en/library/info/EUR46/052/2014/en

10. Russian Federation: Further information: New death threats against Dagestan lawyers (EUR 46/034/2014)
www.amnesty.org/en/library/info/EUR46/034/2014/en

RWANDA

Republic of Rwanda
Head of state: **Paul Kagame**
Head of government: **Anastase Murekezi (replaced Pierre Damien Habumuremyi in July)**

Freedoms of expression and association in Rwanda continued to be unduly restricted by the authorities. Rwandans were unable to openly express critical views on issues perceived as sensitive by the authorities and the environment for journalists, human rights defenders and members of the opposition remained repressive. There were reports of unlawful detention by Rwandan military intelligence and past cases of torture were not investigated.

BACKGROUND

2014 marked the 20th anniversary of the 1994 genocide in which around 800,000 Rwandan Tutsi and Hutu opposed to the government were killed. Around the world, events held to remember the victims reiterated the need for the international community to continue to improve its response to emerging mass atrocities.[1]

Economic progress and development continued. However, the political landscape continued to be dominated by the ruling Rwandan Patriotic Front (RPF) without any meaningful opposition. The authorities continued to react harshly to any criticism, especially regarding its human rights record.

In late July, President Kagame reshuffled the cabinet and Prime Minister Habumuremyi was replaced. The President of the Senate, Jean-Damascène Ntawukuriryayo, resigned in September.

In June, a report by the UN Group of Experts noted that the fate of former combatants and political cadres of the March 23 Movement (M23) armed group remained unresolved, including escapes of individuals from camps in Rwanda. Many M23 members had fled to Rwanda following their defeat by the Democratic Republic of the Congo (DRC) troops in late 2013.

POLITICAL ASSASSINATIONS ABROAD

The Rwandan government denied allegations that they were linked to successful or attempted assassinations of political dissidents abroad.

On 1 January, Patrick Karegeya, a leading member of the opposition Rwandan National Congress (RNC) and former Head of External Intelligence (RDF), was found dead in a hotel room in Johannesburg, South Africa. Investigations into his killing were carried out; however, the perpetrators were not identified. Public statements following his death by the Rwandan authorities, including President Kagame, sought to justify the killing of people who were traitors to the country.

In August, a South African Court found four men guilty of the 2010 attempted assassination of Kayumba Nyamwasa, an exiled RNC dissident and former Chief of Staff of the RDF. The judge was cited in media reports as saying that the main culprits for the attempted assassination remained at large.

HUMAN RIGHTS DEFENDERS

Human rights defenders were subjected to personalized attacks and threats and faced intimidation and administrative obstacles. Space for criticism of the country's human rights record by civil society was almost non-existent. The human rights community remained weakened, with individuals taking a pro-government position in their work or employing self-censorship to avoid harassment by the authorities.

In August, Transparency International (TI) issued a statement reporting security risks experienced by its staff. According to TI, an armed man had attempted to enter its offices on 29 July and another staff member had reported security threats at his home. The killing in July 2013 of Gustave Makonene, who worked for TI, had a chilling effect on other activists working on potentially sensitive issues, such as corruption.

On 8 August, the High Court of Nyarugenge in Kigali ruled that the current executive committee of the Rwandan League for the Promotion and Defense of Human Rights (LIPRODHOR) should remain in place. The complaint had been brought by the former President of LIPRODHOR who had been ousted in July 2013 in a move supported by the Rwanda Governance Board, an official body charged with promoting and monitoring good governance in Rwanda. The complainant lodged an appeal against the judgment.

POLITICAL PRISONERS

Following the rejection of her appeal in December 2013, Victoire Ingabire, President of the United Democratic Forces party (FDU-Inkingi), remained in Kigali Central Prison serving a 15-year prison sentence for terrorism-related and freedom of expression offences. Some of the evidence used to convict her was linked to the legitimate expression of her ideas. Victoire Ingabire had returned to Rwanda in January 2010 after 16 years in exile in Europe.

Bernard Ntaganda, President of the Ideal Social Party (Parti Social-Imberakuri), was released from Mpanga prison after four years in detention. He had been found guilty in 2011 of "divisionism" for making public speeches criticizing government policies ahead of the 2010 elections, breaching state security and attempting to plan an "unauthorized demonstration".

FREEDOMS OF ASSOCIATION AND EXPRESSION

People continued to be imprisoned for the legitimate exercise of their rights to freedom of association or of expression.

Sylvain Sibomana and Anselme Mutuyimana, members of FDU-Inkingi, remained in prison. Both were sentenced in January following their conviction for inciting insurrection or trouble among the population after organizing a meeting in Rutsiro district in September 2012. An appeal was lodged against the convictions. Six members of FDU-Inkingi were released on 5 September after serving a two-year sentence for attending the same meeting in Rutsiro. Sylvain Sibomana was also convicted of participating in illegal gatherings for taking part in a demonstration outside the Supreme Court during Victoire Ingabire's appeal in March 2013.

Political parties

The few opposition parties permitted faced a repressive environment. Legal procedures for establishing political parties remained lengthy and time-consuming.

The Democratic Green Party of Rwanda (DGPR), which had been granted official registration in August 2013, called for an investigation to establish the whereabouts of a leading party member, Jean Damascène Munyeshyaka, who was last seen on 27 June 2014 in Nyamata, Bugesera District. The DGPR alleged that prior to his disappearance he had received a telephone call from an individual requesting that they meet immediately. The DGPR had previously reported administrative obstacles in registering and state surveillance, harassment and intimidation because of their political activities.

UNLAWFUL DETENTIONS BY THE MILITARY

Reports of unlawful detentions by the RDF continued. People were held in detention centres that were not part of the Rwanda Correctional Service, without access to lawyers or due process.

Past allegations of torture, including beatings, electric shocks and sensory deprivation, were not investigated.

The authorities rejected criticism of alleged unlawful detentions by military intelligence made by the US and UK governments. On 4 June 2014, President Kagame responded to recent reports by saying that those seeking to destabilize the country would be arrested or even killed.

UNFAIR TRIALS – STATE SECURITY TRIALS

High-ranking military officers were held on state security charges. The authorities failed to respect due process in their treatment of people suspected of terrorism-related offences.

The trial of Joel Mutabazi and 15 others ended in October. Joel Mutabazi, a former bodyguard to President Kagame, was convicted of plotting attacks against the government and sentenced to life imprisonment. He announced his intention to appeal the verdict. Many of his co-accused stated in court that they had been tortured and forced to make confessions. However, the court failed to investigate these allegations. Joel Mutabazi had been detained incommunicado by Rwanda's Department of Military Intelligence at Camp Kami for several months in 2010 and 2011 and tortured. He had fled to Uganda, where he was under the protection of the Ugandan authorities, but in October 2013 he was abducted and illegally returned to Rwanda.

Four people – Kizito Mihigo, a singer; Cassien Ntamuhanga, a journalist with Amazing Grace Radio; Jean Paul Dukuzumuremyi, a demobilized soldier; and Agnes Nyibizi, an accountant – were arrested in April and charged with state security offences. Official reports indicated they were accused of having been recruited by the RNC and the Democratic Forces for the Liberation of Rwanda, an armed group based in eastern Democratic Republic of the Congo, and of planning terrorist activities. It was reported that Kizito Mihigo may have held critical conversations by email with the opposition abroad; however, this remained unconfirmed. The four were detained pending trial at the end of the year.

In August, Rwandan military intelligence arrested four individuals linked to the RDF. They faced charges including tarnishing the image of the country or government, inciting insurrection or trouble among the population, concealing objects which were used or meant to commit an offence, and illegal possession of firearms. Three faced trials before a military court – Colonel Tom Byabagamba, retired General Frank Rusagara and Sergeant François Kabayiza. Captain David Kabuye was due to be tried before a civilian court. All four trials were pending at the end of 2014.

PRISONERS OF CONSCIENCE

In June, Agnès Nkusi Uwimana, editor of the private Kinyarwanda-language newspaper Umurabyo, was released after completing a four-year prison sentence. She had been imprisoned for threatening state security after writing opinion pieces critical of government policies and alleged corruption in the run-up to the 2010 presidential elections.

INTERNATIONAL JUSTICE

Trials of people suspected of involvement in the Rwandan genocide continued in national courts outside Rwanda.

On 18 February, former Mayor Onesphore Rwabukombe was found guilty of aiding and abetting genocide and was sentenced to 14 years' imprisonment by a German court.

On 14 March, a former Rwandan army captain, Pascal Simbikangwa, was found guilty by a French court of complicity in genocide and crimes against humanity. The court found that he played a key role in drawing up lists of Tutsi and moderate Hutu leaders to be targeted and contributed to the setting up of Radio Mille Collines, which broadcast messages inciting violence. He was sentenced to 25 years in prison. It was the first time a French court had tried a genocide suspect. Six other genocide suspects in France were awaiting trial or on trial at the end of the year.

On 7 May, the Quebec Superior Court upheld Désiré Munyaneza's conviction by a Canadian court for genocide, crimes against humanity and war crimes.

On 19 June, a Swedish court confirmed the sentence of life imprisonment for Stanislas Mbanenande for his role in five massacres in Kibuye during the genocide.

Extradition trials of four genocide suspects in the UK continued during the year.

In April, a Norwegian court sentenced Sadi Bugingo to 21 years' imprisonment for his role in the genocide. His appeal was pending at the end of the year. The request to the Norwegian authorities for the extradition of another genocide suspect was approved, but pending appeal at the end of the year.

In the Netherlands, the extraditions of two men were pending at the end of the year and in Denmark another genocide suspect was awaiting trial.

International Criminal Tribunal for Rwanda

The International Criminal Tribunal for Rwanda prepared to close down its operations. It had one case pending appeal at the end of 2014. The tribunal had completed 75 cases, 14 of which ended in acquittals and 10 were transferred to national jurisdictions.

1. Rwanda: Never again means never again (AFR 47/001/2014)
   www.amnesty.org/en/library/info/AFR47/001/2014/en

SAUDI ARABIA

Kingdom of Saudi Arabia
Head of state and government: **King Abdullah bin Abdul Aziz Al Saud**

The government severely restricted freedoms of expression, association and assembly, and cracked down on dissent, arresting and imprisoning critics, including human rights defenders. Many received unfair trials before courts that failed to respect due process, including a special anti-terrorism court that handed down death sentences. New legislation effectively equated criticism of the government and other peaceful activities with terrorism. The authorities clamped down on online activism and intimidated activists and family members who reported human rights violations. Discrimination against the Shi'a minority remained entrenched; some Shi'a activists were sentenced to death and scores received lengthy prison terms. Torture of detainees was reportedly common; courts convicted defendants on the basis of torture-tainted "confessions" and sentenced others to flogging. Women faced discrimination in law and practice, and were inadequately protected against sexual and other violence despite a new law criminalizing domestic violence. The authorities detained and summarily expelled thousands of foreign migrants, returning some to countries where they were at risk of serious human rights abuses. The authorities made extensive use of the death penalty and carried out dozens of public executions.

BACKGROUND

The government adopted increasingly tough measures against its critics and opponents, who ranged from peaceful dissidents to armed Islamist militants, reflected by its introduction and enforcement of sweeping new and severe anti-terrorism legislation. The authorities publicly deterred citizens from contributing funds, recruits or other support to militant Sunni armed groups in Syria and Iraq.

In September, Saudi Arabia joined the US-led military alliance formed to combat the Islamic State armed group and other armed groups in Syria and Iraq.

The UN Human Rights Council completed its Universal Periodic Review of Saudi Arabia in March. The government accepted the majority of the recommendations but rejected substantive calls, such as one urging Saudi Arabia to ratify the ICCPR. The government committed to dismantling or abolishing the male guardianship system and to allowing women greater freedom to travel, study, work and marry, but it had taken no discernible steps to implement these commitments by the end of the year.

FREEDOMS OF EXPRESSION, ASSOCIATION AND ASSEMBLY

The government remained intolerant of dissent and repressed its critics, including bloggers and other online commentators, political and women's rights activists, members of the Shi'a minority, and human rights activists and defenders. The government continued to ban judges from using social media for any purpose.

In May, a court in Jeddah sentenced blogger Raif Badawi to 10 years in prison and a flogging of 1,000 lashes after convicting him on charges that included "insulting Islam" for establishing the website Saudi Arabian Liberals, which promoted political and social debate, and for criticizing some religious leaders. He was initially charged with apostasy, which carries the death penalty. The court also ordered the closure of the website. His prison term and flogging sentence were confirmed by the Court of Appeal in September.

In October, the Specialized Criminal Court (SCC) in Riyadh sentenced three lawyers – Dr Abdulrahman al-Subaihi, Bander al-Nogaithan and Abdulrahman al-Rumaih

– to prison terms of up to eight years to be followed by bans on travel abroad after convicting them of "impinging public order" by using Twitter to criticize the Ministry of Justice. The court also banned them indefinitely from using any media outlets including social media.

The government did not permit the existence of political parties, trade unions and independent human rights groups, and it arrested, prosecuted and imprisoned those who set up or participated in unlicenced organizations.

The government continued to deny Amnesty International access to Saudi Arabia and took punitive action against activists and family members of victims who contacted Amnesty International.

All public gatherings, including demonstrations, remained prohibited under an order issued by the Interior Ministry in 2011. Those who sought to defy the ban faced arrest, prosecution and imprisonment on charges such as "inciting people against the authorities". In October, the government warned that it would arrest anyone who defied the ban by supporting the campaign for women drivers (see below).

HUMAN RIGHTS DEFENDERS

The authorities targeted the small but vocal community of human rights defenders, using anti-terrorism laws to suppress their peaceful actions to expose and address human rights violations. Those detained or serving sentences included founding members and activists of the Saudi Civil and Political Rights Association (ACPRA), an officially unrecognized group founded in 2009 which campaigns for the release or fair trial of long-term political detainees. At the end of the year, four ACPRA members were serving prison sentences of up to 15 years, three others were detained pending their trial outcomes, and two were detained without trial. The latter were Abdulrahman al-Hamid, arrested after he signed a statement in April calling for the Interior Minister to be put on trial, and Saleh al-Ashwan, held without charge since 2012. Two other ACPRA activists were at liberty awaiting the outcome of their trials. Those convicted were serving sentences imposed on vague, overly broad charges designed to stifle peaceful criticism. Other activists faced trial on similar charges.

In July, the SCC sentenced leading human rights lawyer Waleed Abu al-Khair to 15 years in prison, followed by a 15-year ban on travelling abroad, after convicting him on vague, overly broad charges arising from his peaceful and professional human rights activities.

In November, the Criminal Court in al-Khobar in the Eastern Province sentenced human rights defender Mikhlif bin Daham al-Shammari to two years in prison and a flogging of 200 lashes after convicting him on charges of "stirring public opinion by sitting with the Shi'a" and "violating the rulers' instructions by holding a private gathering and tweeting". He already faced a five-year prison term, followed by a 10-year travel ban, imposed on him by the SCC in June 2013. The SCC also banned him from writing in the press and on social media websites, and from appearing on television or radio. The SCC's appeal chamber confirmed this sentence in June 2014.

COUNTER-TERROR AND SECURITY

A new anti-terrorism law that took effect in February, following approval by the King, extended the authorities' already sweeping powers to combat "acts of terror". The new law failed to define terrorism but provided that words and actions deemed by the authorities to be directly or indirectly "disturbing" to public order, "destabilizing the security of society, or the stability of the state", "revoking the basic law of government", or "harming the reputation of the state or its standing" would be considered terrorist acts. In March, a series of decrees promulgated by the Interior Ministry extended Saudi Arabia's already wide definition of terrorism to include "calling for atheist thought" and "contacting any groups

or individuals opposed to the Kingdom", as well as "seeking to disrupt national unity" by calling for protests, and "harming other states and their leaders". In violation of international standards, the new decrees had retroactive effect, exposing those alleged to have committed acts in the past to prosecution on terrorism as well as other charges if they commit any new offence.

In July, the Ministry of Justice reaffirmed the exclusive jurisdiction of the SCC over cases involving alleged offences against state security.

ARBITRARY ARRESTS AND DETENTIONS

Security authorities carried out arbitrary arrests and continued to hold detainees without charge or trial for long periods, with scores of people held for more than six months without being referred to a competent court, in breach of the country's Code of Criminal Procedures. Detainees were frequently held incommunicado during interrogation and denied access to lawyers, in violation of international fair trial standards.

TORTURE AND OTHER ILL-TREATMENT

Torture and other ill-treatment remained common and widespread, according to former detainees, trial defendants and others, and were used with impunity. In a number of cases, courts convicted defendants solely on the basis of pre-trial "confessions" without investigating their claims that these confessions had been extracted under torture, in some cases sentencing the defendants to death.

Some prisoners sentenced on political grounds in previous years were reportedly ill-treated in prison, including the imprisoned ACPRA activists Dr Abdullah al-Hamid and Dr Mohammad al-Qahtani, who went on hunger strike in March to protest against their conditions. In August, Jeddah prison guards reportedly beat imprisoned human rights lawyer Waleed Abu al-Khair when forcibly removing him from his cell before transferring him to another prison.

DISCRIMINATION – SHI'A MINORITY

Members of the Shi'a minority, most of whom live in the oil-rich Eastern Province, continued to face entrenched discrimination that limited their access to government services and employment, and impacted them in many other ways. Members of the Shi'a community remained mostly excluded from senior posts. Shi'a leaders and activists faced arrest, imprisonment following unfair trials, and the death penalty.

In May, the SCC sentenced Ali Mohammed Baqir al-Nimr to death after convicting him on charges that included demonstrating against the government, possession of weapons and attacking the security forces. He denied the charges and told the court that he had been tortured and forced to confess in pre-trial detention. The court convicted him without investigating his torture allegations, and sentenced him to death although he was aged 17 at the time of the alleged offences. In October, his uncle, Sheikh Nimr Baqir al-Nimr, a Shi'a cleric from Qatif and vocal critic of the government's treatment of the Shi'a minority, was sentenced to death by the SCC. Security forces arrested Sheikh al-Nimr in July 2012 in disputed circumstances in which he was shot and paralyzed in one leg. In August, the SCC sentenced another prominent Shi'a cleric, Sheikh Tawfiq al-'Amr, to eight years in prison, to be followed by a 10-year ban on overseas travel and a ban on delivering religious sermons and public speeches.

In September, the SCC imposed a fine and a 14-year prison sentence followed by a 15-year foreign travel ban on Shi'a rights activist Fadhel al-Manasif after convicting him on charges that included "breaking allegiance with the ruler" and maintaining "contact with foreign news organizations". The sentence was upheld by the SCC's appeal division in December.

The SCC sentenced other Shi'a activists for their alleged participation in the protests of 2011 and 2012. At least five received death sentences; others received long prison terms.

WOMEN'S RIGHTS

Women and girls remained subject to discrimination in law and practice. Women had subordinate status to men under the law, particularly in relation to family matters such as marriage, divorce, child custody and inheritance, and they were inadequately protected against sexual and other violence. Domestic violence reportedly remained endemic, despite a government awareness-raising campaign launched in 2013. A 2013 law criminalizing domestic violence was not implemented in practice due to a lack of competent authorities to enforce it.

Women who supported the Women2Drive campaign, launched in 2011 to challenge the prohibition on women driving vehicles, faced harassment and intimidation by the authorities, who warned that women drivers would face arrest. Some were arrested but released after a short period. In early December, Loujain al-Hathloul and Mayssa al-Amoudi, two supporters of the campaign, were arrested at the border with the United Arab Emirates for driving their cars. The authorities later brought terrorism-related charges against both women, who remained in detention at the end of the year.

Women's rights activist Souad al-Shammari was detained in October after Bureau of Investigation and Prosecution officials in Jeddah summoned her for questioning. She was held without charge at Briman prison in Jeddah at the end of the year.

Women's rights activists Wajeha al-Huwaider and Fawzia al-Oyouni, whose 10-month prison sentences and two-year foreign travel bans were confirmed by an appeal court in 2013, remained at liberty. The authorities did not explain their failure to summon them to prison.

In April, two daughters of the King accused him of having held them and their two sisters captive within a royal compound for 13 years, and of denying them adequate food.

MIGRANT WORKERS' RIGHTS

After granting foreign workers several months to regularize their status, the government launched a crackdown on irregular foreign migrants in November 2013, arresting, detaining and deporting hundreds of thousands of foreign workers in order to open more jobs to Saudi Arabians. In March, the Interior Minister stated that the authorities had deported over 370,000 foreign migrants in the preceding five months and that 18,000 others were in detention. Thousands of workers were summarily returned to Somalia and other states where they were at risk of human rights abuses, with large numbers also returned to Yemen. Many migrants reported that prior to their deportation they had been packed into severely overcrowded makeshift detention facilities where they received little food and water and were abused by guards.

CRUEL, INHUMAN OR DEGRADING PUNISHMENT

The courts continued to impose sentences of flogging as punishment for many offences. Blogger Raif Badawi was sentenced to a flogging of 1,000 lashes in addition to a prison sentence. Human rights defender Mikhlif bin Daham al-Shammari was sentenced to 200 lashes as well as a prison term.

In September, the authorities released Ruth Cosrojas, a Filipino domestic worker sentenced to 18 months' imprisonment and 300 lashes after an unfair trial in October 2013 where she was convicted of organizing the sale of sex (*quwada*). She had received 150 lashes by the time of her release.

DEATH PENALTY

Courts continued to impose death sentences for a range of crimes, including some that did not involve violence, such as "sorcery", adultery and drug offences, frequently after unfair trials. Some defendants, including foreign nationals facing murder charges, alleged that they had been tortured or otherwise coerced or misled into making false confessions in pre-trial detention.

The authorities carried out dozens of executions, many by public beheading. Those executed included both Saudi nationals and foreign migrants.

SENEGAL

Republic of Senegal
Head of state: **Macky Sall**
Head of government: **Mohammed Dionne (replaced Aminata Touré in July)**

Police used excessive force to suppress demonstrations. Conditions in prison continued to be harsh. There was some progress in overcoming impunity for past human rights violations, although many cases remained unresolved. The long-running conflict in Casamance was less intense than in previous years.

BACKGROUND

In September 2013 the Minister of Justice committed to opening an official commission of inquiry into poor detention conditions in the Liberty 6 and Rebeuss prisons, but by the end of 2014 no progress had been made.

In March 2014, the UN Human Rights Council adopted the outcome of the Universal Periodic Review on Senegal. During the review process Amnesty International had raised concerns about excessive use of force by security forces to repress freedom of expression and assembly, torture and other ill-treatment, deaths in detention, and impunity for human rights violations, including some dating back 30 years. Senegal committed to protect the rights to freedom of expression, association and assembly; and to ensure that its security forces maintain public order without resorting to excessive use of force. However, it rejected recommendations to ratify the Second Optional Protocol to the ICCPR, aiming at the abolition of the death penalty, despite having committed to ratify it in a meeting with Amnesty International in December 2013. Senegal also rejected recommendations to amend national legislation to protect LGBTI people from discrimination, and claimed that there were no cases of enforced disappearance in Senegal despite repeated concerns raised by Amnesty International about the fate of dozens of disappeared Casamance people at the hands of government forces.

The corruption trial of Karim Wade, a former minister and son of former President Abdoulaye Wade, and other defendants, began in July. Karim Wade was charged with illicit acquisition of wealth and stood trial before the Court for the Repression of Illicit Acquisition of Wealth, which does not allow for appeals after the verdict.

EXCESSIVE USE OF FORCE

In January, in Oulampane, Casamance, high school students demonstrated to call for more teachers. Military forces intervened using live ammunition, injuring four students. The Army Command condemned these actions by military forces and announced that there would be accountability, although no concrete steps were taken and no investigation was opened during the year.

Throughout August, students protested against delays in paying scholarships at Cheikh-Anta-Diop University in Dakar and there were repeated confrontations with security forces. Student Bassirou Faye died after being shot in the head by police during a demonstration. A police officer was arrested in October and charged with his murder.

In September a convicted prisoner was shot dead in Sinthiou Roudji, near the town of Kédougou. His sentence allowed him to work out of prison during the day and return to the prison facility at night. Upon failure to return, security forces were sent for him, and he was shot by a security officer, reportedly while trying to flee. The Ministry of Justice committed to opening an investigation, and the officer was remanded in custody.

FREEDOM OF ASSEMBLY

Authorities prosecuted demonstrators who participated in or spoke out during demonstrations organized by political parties and NGOs.

Rapper Malal Talla, a leader of the Y'en a marre (We have had enough) movement, was arrested and detained for four days in June for denouncing police racketeering at a public gathering. He was charged with insulting the police, before being released after a judge determined that the charges were unfounded.

RIGHTS OF LESBIAN, GAY, BISEXUAL, TRANSGENDER AND INTERSEX PEOPLE

In February, police arrested four young men who had attacked five gay men in Rufisque, a town outside Dakar. Residents of the town marched in support of the accused, calling for their release.

IMPUNITY

The trial of police officers implicated in the death in custody of Dominique Lopy in 2007 was postponed from June to November 2014 at the request of the defendants' lawyers.

The trial of two gendarmerie commanders charged with killing demonstrators in two separate incidents in 2011 and 2012 was still pending. They were released from detention pending trial.

INTERNATIONAL JUSTICE

Former Chadian President Hissène Habré remained in custody awaiting trial before the Extraordinary African Chambers created by the AU in 2012 to try him in Senegal. On 30 June 2013 Hissène Habré was arrested, and was charged on 2 July 2013 with crimes against humanity, torture and war crimes committed in Chad between 1982 and 1990. In August the court rejected the Chadian government's request to be a civil party (*partie civile*) in the case. The court asked that Chad extradite certain key witnesses, but this request was refused. The court also asked the AU to intervene in the matter.

INTERNAL ARMED CONFLICT

The conflict between the army and the Democratic Forces of Casamance Movement (MFDC) became less intense, and one MFDC leader proclaimed a unilateral ceasefire in April.

Civilians continued to suffer from the impact of ongoing conflict, which rendered thousands unemployed or displaced from their villages. At least seven men were killed by landmines in August.

SERBIA

Republic of Serbia, including Kosovo
Head of state: **Tomislav Nikolić**
Head of government: **Aleksandar Vučić (replaced Ivica Dačić in April)**

Progress was made in investigations into the unsolved murders of prominent journalists. Slow progress was made in the prosecution of war crimes. The Belgrade Pride took place for the first time since being banned in 2010. In Kosovo, a special court was proposed to try former members of the Kosovo Liberation Army (KLA) for the abduction of Serbs in 1999. Violence in the north of Kosovo, inter-ethnic attacks and discrimination against minorities continued.

BACKGROUND

The Serbian Progressive Party took over the government in April. In May, severe flooding left 51 dead and tens of thousands homeless.

Before the opening of negotiations on accession to the EU, the European Commission called for action plans on the rule of law and fundamental rights, and commitment to the "normalization" of relations with Kosovo.

The government adopted austerity measures, as required by the International Monetary Fund, which included cuts to public sector salaries and state pensions and restrictions on trade unions.

INTERNATIONAL JUSTICE

In January, the Appeals Chamber at the International Criminal Tribunal for the former Yugoslavia (ICTY) upheld the conviction of Vlastimir Djordjević, former Serbian Assistant to the Minister of the Interior, for murder and persecution – including sexual assaults as crimes against humanity – and the forced deportation of 800,000 Kosovo Albanians. His sentence was reduced on appeal, along with those of three other senior officials, Nikola Šainović, Sreten Lukić and Vladimir Lazarević. Former military commander Nebojša Pavković's 22-year sentence was affirmed.

Vojislav Šešelj, leader of the Serb Radical Party, indicted in 2003 for war crimes and crimes against humanity, including the forced deportation and persecution of non-Serbs in Bosnia and Herzegovina, Croatia and Vojvodina, was granted provisional release in November to receive treatment for cancer and returned to Serbia after 12 years in detention.

Domestic prosecutions were hampered by insufficient resources in the Office of the War Crimes Prosecutor and inadequate police investigations.[1] Five indictments were published, and verdicts reached at first instance in only one case.

The Head of the Witness Protection Unit, which was alleged to have intimidated protected witnesses, was dismissed in June, allegedly for corruption. Prosecutors, police and witnesses received threats from war veterans while investigating the abduction of 19 civilians by Bosnian Serb paramilitaries in Štrpci in 1992. Fifteen suspects were subsequently arrested in December, in a joint operation with the Bosnian authorities.

An investigation started in August into Major General Dragan Živanović's command responsibility for war crimes in Kosovo, between 1 April and 15 May 1999, when he was commander of the 125th Motorized Brigade. He was suspected of failing to prevent "a campaign of terror against

Albanian civilians", including murder, the destruction of houses, plunder and forced expulsion.

A new law proposed in December failed to ensure adequate reparation for civilian victims of war, including relatives of the missing and victims of war crimes of sexual violence.

ENFORCED DISAPPEARANCES

Despite the exhumation of the bodies of 53 Kosovo Albanian civilians at Raška, where they had been reburied in 1999, and further investigations at Batajnica, where over 800 bodies were exhumed in 2000-2001, there was no progress in bringing to justice those who organized the transfer of the bodies from Kosovo.

FREEDOM OF EXPRESSION

The government tightened its hold on the media. Public comments critical of the government's response to the May floods, were removed from government websites, and critical individuals summoned for "informative talks" by police. The Pesčanik website was taken down by denial-of-service attacks, after publishing allegations of plagiarism by the Minister of the Interior.

Investigations continued into the murders of independent journalists, Dada Vujasinović, Slavko Ćuruvija and Milan Pantić, allegedly killed by state agents in 1994, 1999 and 2001 respectively. Four suspects were charged with the murder of Slavko Ćuruvija, including former national security chief, Radomir Marković, previously convicted for the 2000 assassination of former President Ivan Stambolić.

In December, 11 foreign nationals and supporters of the Falun Gong movement were unlawfully detained after their proposed protest against the Chinese government was banned, and subsequently deported.

DISCRIMINATION
Roma right to adequate housing
Roma organizations initiated a draft law on the legalization of informal Roma settlements.

Roma settlements were disproportionately affected by flooding in May, and 31 Roma (including 12 children), were denied access to an emergency reception centre in Belgrade and rehoused in a wartime shelter, without water or sanitation.

The EU-funded construction of social housing for Roma forcibly evicted from Belvil informal settlement in 2012 was delayed, even after resettlement sites were identified. Some 32 families chose instead to be resettled in village houses, but over 100 other families remained in inadequate metal containers. Another resettlement from Belvil, ahead of construction funded by the European Investment Bank, was delayed until December, when 24 of the 50 families were resettled. Roma and others remained at risk of forced eviction in advance of the planned demolition of their homes for the Belgrade Waterfront project.

Hate crimes
Threats and attacks against LGBTI rights defenders and organizations, including the Gay-Straight Alliance, were not effectively investigated, and the hate motive was seldom recognized and provisions for increased sentencing in cases of hate crime were rarely invoked.

In March, a police anti-terrorist spokesperson urged football fans online to attack a vigil by the NGO Women in Black, marking the anniversary of the Kosovo war. Prosecutors charged him with making threats to security, rather than with gender-based discrimination, so the hate motivation was not considered. In July, four members of the group were attacked and injured in Valjevo.

In October, after a drone bearing the symbol of Greater Albania was flown over a Serbia-Albania football match in Belgrade, at least 33 properties owned by Albanians were attacked, mainly in Vojvodina.

REFUGEES AND ASYLUM-SEEKERS
Between January and October, 18,955 Serbian citizens applied for asylum in the EU, the majority of them believed to be Roma.

Around 13,000 migrants and refugees, including 8,000 Syrians, registered their intent to claim asylum in Serbia, although most regarded Serbia as a transit country. Only five applicants had received asylum by mid-December in a refugee status determination process which failed to follow procedures set out in the Asylum Law. Border police reportedly pushed asylum-seekers and migrants back to Macedonia.

KOSOVO

Following parliamentary elections held in June, the Democratic Party of Kosovo, led by Hashim Thaçi, failed to gain a majority over a coalition of opposition parties, leading to a political impasse. In December, a coalition government with Isa Mustafa of the Democratic League of Kosovo as Prime Minister, was formed. Atifete Jahjaga continued as President. From June, EU-brokered talks on the normalization of relations with Serbia continued only at a technical level.

The mandate of the EU-led Police and Justice Mission (EULEX) was extended until June 2016. Under the new agreement, international judges no longer formed the majority on judicial panels in cases of serious crimes.

The EU High Representative in November announced an independent inquiry into allegations of corruption against a EULEX judge.

Inter-ethnic violence

Inter-ethnic tensions continued, particularly in the Serbian dominated north. Some Serbian politicians were prevented from entering Kosovo, and Kosovo Serbs, including returnees to Klina/Klinë in February and October, were subject to attacks – including arson – on their property, graveyards and religious buildings, which intensified after the Serbia-Albania football match in October.

In June, after clashes between Kosovo Police and Albanians demonstrating against the closure of the bridge over the river Ibar (which divides the Serbian and Albanian parts of Mitrovica), international EULEX police fired rubber bullets at demonstrators. The UN Mission in Kosovo (UNMIK) had banned their use after two men were killed in Pristina in 2007.

Crimes under international law

In July, a Special Investigative Task Force, established by EULEX to investigate allegations against senior KLA members, announced that unnamed individuals would be indicted for war crimes and crimes against humanity, including the unlawful killing, abduction, illegal detention, crimes of sexual violence against and forced displacement of Kosovo Serbs and Albanian civilians, unlawfully transferred to Albania in 1999. Suspects will be indicted and tried by a special court, yet to be established, outside of Kosovo in order to ensure effective witness protection.

In October, two protected witnesses contradicted their original testimonies during the retrial of seven members of the former KLA "Drenica" group, charged with war crimes against Albanians at Likovc/Likovac camp in 1998.

The retrial opened in September of Fatmir Limaj and nine others accused of the torture and ill-treatment of Albanian civilians at the Klečka/Klecke camp in 1999. They had been acquitted in September 2013, following the suicide of a protected witness on which the prosecution case relied.

Kosovo Serb political leader Oliver Ivanović, arrested in January, was indicted in August for incitement to commit war crimes in 1999, and incitement to aggravated murder in February 2000.

War crimes of sexual violence

In March, President Jahjaga launched a national council for the survivors of wartime sexual violence, to encourage them to come forward to claim reparation, including compensation, as set out in legal amendments adopted by the Assembly later in March.

In June, the Appeal Court overturned the acquittal of two Kosovo Serbs, and convicted them of war crimes for the rape of a 16-year-old Albanian girl in April 1999. They were sentenced to 12 and 10 years' imprisonment.

Enforced disappearances

Relatives of the disappeared protested against legal provisions ending their monthly compensation of €135 after the body of their family member was found. By November, 1,655 people remained missing after the armed conflict. The remains of 53 Kosovo Albanians exhumed at Raška were returned to their relatives by October.

UNMIK failed to provide reparation, including compensation, to the relatives of missing Kosovo Serbs, as recommended by the Human Rights Advisory Panel.

Freedom of expression

Government and state agencies unduly influenced the media through major contributions to their advertizing revenue. Attacks on investigative journalists continued. Visar Duriqi, a journalist for the newspaper Express, received serious death threats after reporting on Islamic extremist groups. The Association of Professional Journalists expressed concerns that EULEX had put pressure on Koha Ditore journalist, Vehbi Kajtazi, who had reported alleged corruption in EULEX.

In May, the first march celebrating the International Day against Homophobia and Transphobia took place without incident.

Discrimination – hate crimes

In March, three men were convicted and given suspended sentences for "Violating the Equal Status of Residents of Kosovo" for their part in an attack in 2012 on the launch of an issue of "Kosovo 2.0" online magazine, on sexual orientation and identity. No one was brought to justice for an attack on a Lesbian, Gay, Bisexual and Transgender centre the following day; or for threats made in 2013 against women human rights defenders for supporting the law on reparations for rape survivors.

Discrimination – Roma

Roma, Ashkali and Egyptians continued to face widespread and systematic discrimination, yet few measures for their integration were implemented. Around 360 families (1,700 individuals) had reportedly migrated from Kosovo by November, to seek asylum in Hungary. Plans to build housing for Roma in Hereq village, Gjakovë/Djakovica, were opposed by local residents.

Refugees and asylum-seekers

According to UNHCR, the UN refugee agency, 17,227 people – the majority of them Kosovo Serbs – remained displaced after the armed conflict. By 30 November, only 404 members of minority communities had voluntarily returned to Kosovo, where conditions for their reintegration remained grossly inadequate. By October, 11,000 people from Kosovo had applied for asylum in the EU.

---

1. Serbia: Ending impunity for crimes under international law (EUR 70/012/2014)

   www.amnesty.org/en/library/info/EUR70/012/2014/en

SIERRA LEONE

Republic of Sierra Leone
Head of state and government: **Ernest Bai Koroma**

An outbreak of the Ebola virus disease killed at least 2,758 people. A state of emergency was declared. Thousands suspected of committing crimes during the 11-year armed conflict in Sierra Leone have still not been investigated. At least two complaints of unlawful killings by the police occurred. The increased use of criminal defamation against journalists threatened freedom of expression.

BACKGROUND

In 2013, President Koroma launched a review of Sierra Leone's Constitution. Civil society groups began civic education programmes and engagement regarding the review. However, these were delayed by the Ebola outbreak. International assistance was inadequate, although there was some improvement later in the year.

EBOLA OUTBREAK

Sierra Leone was severely affected by the Ebola epidemic that spread across West Africa. By 31 December 2014 there were 9,446 confirmed cases and at least 2,758 people had died. The epidemic weakened fragile health care systems and more than 199 health workers were infected by 31 October. NGOs expressed concerns regarding food security, the disproportionate impact on women and the treatment of people in quarantine. In July 2014, the President declared a state of emergency and passed the Public Emergency Regulations 2014. By-laws for the Prevention of Ebola and Other Diseases were also passed by the Ministry of Local Government, including a ban on public gatherings.

INTERNATIONAL JUSTICE

In 2013, the Special Court for Sierra Leone upheld the 50-year prison sentence of former Liberian President Charles Taylor for his role in Sierra Leone's armed conflict, completing the court's mandate to try those bearing the greatest responsibility for crimes committed during the conflict. However, thousands suspected of committing crimes during the conflict have not been investigated and brought to justice. The issue of accountability for human rights violations was highlighted when the UN Panel of Experts on Liberia uncovered the presence of alleged arms dealer Ibrahim Bah, a Senegalese national, in Sierra Leone in 2013. A private prosecution was brought against him by victims of the conflict supported by a civil society organization, the Centre for Accountability and Rule of Law. Sierra Leone deported Ibrahim Bah to Senegal days before he was due to appear in court.

DEATH PENALTY

Sierra Leone retained the death penalty for treason and aggravated robbery, and it remained mandatory for murder. In May, the Attorney General and Minister of Justice told the UN Committee against Torture that Sierra Leone will shortly abolish the death penalty and later clarified that it would be done through a revision of the Criminal Procedure Act. No further action had been taken by the end of the year.

ARBITRARY DETENTIONS

People were regularly detained beyond constitutional time limits by the police. In August 2013, 18 members of the Republic of Sierra Leone Armed Forces were detained for allegedly plotting to mutiny at the Tekoh barracks in Makeni. They were held in incommunicado detention for eight months, in violation of constitutional detention time limits. Fourteen of them were indicted and brought to trial, which was ongoing at the end of the year.

POLICE AND SECURITY FORCES

The government took steps to strengthen accountability for the Sierra Leone Police (SLP). The police instituted a new performance management system in 2013 and parliament approved regulations to establish an Independent Police Complaints Board. However, the government failed to investigate and hold accountable police officers accused of using arbitrary or excessive force. The government has not prosecuted any police officers, despite the recommendation of independent inquiries conducted into incidents of alleged unlawful killings. There were at least two allegations of unlawful killings by the police in 2014, connected to police shootings in Kono in response to a riot relating to a suspected Ebola case.

JUSTICE SYSTEM

The justice system still suffers from a lack of resources with constant adjournments, indictment delays and a shortage of magistrates, contributing to lengthy pre-trial detention and prison overcrowding. Positive steps were taken to implement the Legal Aid Act, passed in 2013, but the Legal Aid Board is not yet operational. Steps were also taken to redraft the Criminal Procedure Act 1965. The Corrections Act was passed in 2014, reforming the 1960 Prison Rules, with a greater focus on prisoner rehabilitation.

In March 2014, the UN Human Rights Committee reviewed Sierra Leone's implementation of the ICCPR. It expressed concerns regarding several issues such as trial delays, prison conditions and police accountability.

WOMEN'S AND GIRLS' RIGHTS

Sexual and gender-based violence remained a disturbingly frequent occurrence. The Sexual Offences Act 2012 introduced improved definitions of, and stiffer penalties for, sexual violence. However, more work is needed to implement the provisions.

In September 2013 the Deputy Minister of Education, Science and Technology was fired following allegations of sexual assault and rape. During the trial, the media revealed the alleged victim's name, in contravention of both the 2012 Act and the Media Code of Practice. The presiding magistrate accepted an application for protective measures to be applied and subsequent witnesses were allowed to testify behind a screen. The Independent Media Commission publicly condemned specific media houses and is investigating complaints brought against them. The criminal case is still being heard.

The Gender Equality Bill, which provides for a minimum 30% representation of women in Parliament, local councils and ministries, departments and agencies, was not enacted. Sierra Leone has yet to ratify the Maputo Protocol (the Protocol to the African Charter on Human and Peoples' Rights on the Rights of Women in Africa). It is the only country in West Africa yet to do so. The Minister of Social Welfare, Gender and Children's Affairs made assurances in 2014 that steps would be taken towards ratification.

FREEDOM OF EXPRESSION

The increased use of criminal defamation against journalists threatened freedom of expression. In July 2013 Jonathan Leigh, managing editor of the *Independent Observer* newspaper, was charged with four counts of defamatory libel after publishing an article accusing a businessman of corrupt and fraudulent behaviour. The case was eventually resolved out of court.

In October 2013 Leigh and Bai Bai Sesay from the Independent Observer were charged with criminal defamation for publishing an article criticizing the President. The journalists pleaded guilty to conspiracy to publish a seditious article. They were cautioned and discharged in March 2014.

The Human Rights Commission of Sierra Leone, the Sierra Leone Association of Journalists and various civil society groups recommended the repeal of the country's criminal libel law.

In January 2014 David Tam Baryoh was arrested for seditious libel and released on bail. In May his radio programme *Monologue* was banned for two months following a government directive. He was arrested again in November for comments made on his programme regarding the government's response to the Ebola outbreak. He was detained for 11 days and released on bail.

In October 2013 the Right to Access Information Act was passed. It established a right to access government information and requires all parts of government to adopt and widely disseminate a plan for making records publicly available. The legislation also imposed a penalty for wilful obstruction of its provisions.

RIGHTS OF LESBIAN, GAY, BISEXUAL, TRANSGENDER AND INTERSEX PEOPLE

The UN Human Rights Committee expressed concern about reported violence against members of the LGBTI community and called on Sierra Leone to review its legislation to ensure that discrimination against the LGBTI community is prohibited.

Three LGBTI activists were assaulted, sent threatening messages and one of their homes was repeatedly broken into in 2013. Despite reporting these incidents to the police, no credible investigations were initiated. The harassment forced the activists to flee Sierra Leone and they were granted asylum in Europe.

SINGAPORE

Republic of Singapore
Head of state: **Tony Tan Keng Yam**
Head of government: **Lee Hsien Loong**

Human rights defenders and small opposition parties called for broader human rights change through public gatherings, online activities and constitutional challenges. The People's Action Party remained in power for a sixth decade.

DEATH PENALTY

The execution of one death row prisoner was stayed in March, but Singapore broke its three-year moratorium on executions in July when two men were hanged – a mandatory death sentence had been imposed under the Misuse of Drugs Act (MDA) prior to the November 2012 amendments abolishing some instances in which murder and drug trafficking carry a mandatory death penalty.

Commutations of death sentences to life imprisonment with 15 strokes of the cane continued, following the November 2012 legislative amendments. Some of those whose sentences were commuted had been judged as having "diminished responsibility" and others had aided anti-drug trafficking efforts and obtained "certificates of cooperation".

In July, parliament amended the Radiation Protection Act to allow for the imposition of the death penalty for nuclear-related offences with an intent to harm and that cause fatalities. There were no nuclear facilities in Singapore.

TORTURE AND OTHER ILL-TREATMENT

Caning remained a penalty for various offences, including immigration violations, vandalism and as an alternative (with life imprisonment) to the death penalty. In August, Yong Vui Kong, whose death sentence had been commuted to life imprisonment and caning, challenged his penalty of 15 strokes on the grounds that the Constitution prohibited torture. The Court of Appeal judgment was pending at the end of the year, but the Attorney-General took the position that caning did not amount to torture and that torture is not prohibited by the Constitution.

FREEDOM OF EXPRESSION

Opposition activists, former prisoners of conscience and human rights defenders expressed concerns about the shrinking space for public discussion of issues such as freedom of expression, the death penalty, lesbian, gay, bisexual, transgender and intersex rights, labour rights, poverty and inadequate living standards.

The government persisted in using defamation suits against critics. In May the Prime Minister sued blogger Roy Ngerng Yi Leng for defamation after Ngerng was alleged to have accused the Prime Minister of "criminal misappropriation" of public retirement funds in his blog. Despite a retraction and a public apology, as well as an offer of damages, the Prime Minister called for a summary judgment on the case in July. Ngerng was dismissed from his job with a public hospital in June. In view of financially ruinous outcomes from previous suits against critics, Ngerng turned to crowdfunding to finance his legal defence.

DETENTION WITHOUT TRIAL

Around 12 suspected Islamist militants remained held without trial under the Internal Security Act.

SLOVAKIA

Slovak Republic
Head of state: **Andrej Kiska (replaced Ivan Gašparovič in June)**
Head of government: **Robert Fico**

Roma children continued to face discrimination in the education system. The authorities extradited an asylum-seeker to the Russian Federation despite the risk of torture and other ill-treatment upon return. A referendum on proposals, which would block further rights for same-sex partnerships, was declared constitutional. In November, two detainees from the detention facility at Guantánamo Bay were transferred to Slovakia for resettlement. Slovakia had not ratified the Council of Europe Convention on preventing and combating violence against women and domestic violence.

DISCRIMINATION – ROMA

In June, during the UN Universal Periodic Review (UPR), Slovakia restated its commitment to tackling the issue of large numbers of Roma children in schools for children with mental disabilities. However, in July the Slovak Public Defender of Rights noted that Slovakia continued to violate Roma children's right to education through discriminatory diagnostic procedures.

The Ministry of Education persisted with plans developed together with the Office of the Plenipotentiary of the Government of the Slovak Republic for Roma communities to construct "modular schools" ostensibly with the aim of increasing access to education.

The Ministry planned to construct 15 such schools over the course of the year, several of them in Roma settlements. In May, however, the Plenipotentiary acknowledged that the project could result in increased segregation in education.

As part of the UPR, Slovakia acknowledged the need for measures to legalize informal Roma settlements. The Ministry of Transport and Construction developed proposals for a new Construction Act to address the issue of "illegal constructions", including informal Roma settlements. In July, the OSCE Office for Democratic Institutions and Human Rights expressed concern that the proposals lacked safeguards to protect residents of unauthorized buildings from forced evictions. It emphasized that eviction decisions should be subject to judicial review and that affected residents had to have access to remedies and compensation.

Police violence

In January, the Inspection of the Ministry of Interior initiated a criminal investigation into the excessive use of force during a police operation in the Roma settlement of Budulovská in the town of Moldava nad Bodvou on 19 June 2013. Earlier complaints by affected residents had been dismissed. The police operation was criticized by the Public Defender of Rights for having used excessive force, derogatory treatment and arbitrary searches.

At the end of the year, the trial of police officers, accused of the ill-treatment of six Roma boys at a police station in 2009 in the city of Košice, was still pending before the district court. In March, one of the police officers, who was dismissed following the allegations of ill-treatment, was reinstated.

RIGHTS OF LESBIAN, GAY, BISEXUAL, TRANSGENDER AND INTERSEX PEOPLE

On 4 June, the National Council (Parliament) adopted a constitutional amendment which defined marriage as "a unique union between a man and a woman". The amendment explicitly excluded same-sex couples from entering a marriage.[1] It came into force on 1 September.

In August, the organization "Alliance for Family" delivered a petition signed by 400,000 people to the President demanding a referendum that would ban any other form of partnership than a union between a man and a woman from being defined as "marriage". They also demanded to ban adoptions by same-sex couples, to deny legal recognition to any kind of partnership other than a "marriage between one man and one woman" and to prevent schools from providing mandatory sexuality education or information on ethical issues such as euthanasia, if the pupil or parent did not consent to such classes. In September, the President requested the Constitutional Court to review the constitutionality of a referendum on the issues raised by the petition. The Court ruled in October, that, with the exception of the question on the legal recognition of different forms of "partnership", all the other questions were constitutional. In November, the President set the date for the referendum for February 2015.

TORTURE AND OTHER ILL-TREATMENT

Slovakia continued to return individuals to countries where they would risk torture and other ill-treatment.

In July, Slovakia extradited Anzor Chentiev, an ethnic Chechen, to the Russian Federation where he was wanted in connection with various terrorism-related offences. Anzor Chentiev had been fighting against extradition for nine years. The Ministry of Justice approved the extradition despite the risk that he would be subjected to torture or other ill-treatment on his return and the fact that Anzor Chentiev had reapplied for asylum in Slovakia on 3 June.[2]

In August, the Supreme Court rejected Aslan Yandiev's appeal against the decision of the Regional Court in Trnava allowing his extradition to the Russian Federation, where he was accused of membership of an armed group. The Court was satisfied that

the assurances provided by the Prosecutor General of the Russian Federation in February 2011 were "specific and reliable". His extradition had previously been blocked by the European Court of Human Rights as well as the Slovak Constitutional Court on the grounds that it would expose Aslan Yandiev to the risk of torture and other ill-treatment and that his asylum application in Slovakia was pending.

---

1. Slovakia: The constitutional amendment defining marriage as the union between a man and a woman is discriminatory (EUR 72/001/2014)
   www.amnesty.org/en/library/info/EUR72/001/2014/en
2. Slovakia: Further information: Anzor Chentiev extradited to Russia (EUR 72/005/2014)
   www.amnesty.org/en/library/info/EUR72/005/2014/en

SLOVENIA

Republic of Slovenia
Head of state: **Borut Pahor**
Head of government: **Miro Cerar (replaced Alenka Bratušek in September)**

The authorities failed to restore the status of people whose permanent residency was unlawfully revoked in 1992 or provide them with adequate compensation, perpetuating the longstanding violation of their rights. Discrimination against Roma remained widespread.

DISCRIMINATION – THE "ERASED"

Despite some positive measures, the authorities failed to guarantee the rights of some former permanent residents of Slovenia originating from other former Yugoslav republics, known as the "erased", whose legal status was unlawfully revoked in 1992.

The 2010 Legal Status Act, which offered an avenue for the erased to restore their legal status, expired in July 2013. About 12,000 of the 25,671 "erased" had had their status restored by this date. In December 2013, legislation was adopted creating a compensation scheme for those whose status had been regulated. The scheme provided €50 for each month spent without legal status.

On 12 March 2014 the European Court of Human Rights, in *Kurić and Others v. Slovenia*, ordered Slovenia to pay the applicants between €30,000 and €70,000 for pecuniary damages. The judgment followed a ruling by the Grand Chamber in 2012, which established that the right to respect for private and family life, the right to effective legal remedy and the right to be free from discrimination had been violated, and ordered the payment of non-pecuniary damages also. These sums were far greater than the sums payable to recipients of compensation under the December 2013 scheme.

DISCRIMINATION – ROMA

Despite a number of initiatives in recent years to improve the situation of the approximately 10,000 Roma in Slovenia, the majority continued to face discrimination and social exclusion. Most lived in isolated, segregated settlements, lacking security of tenure and access to basic services such as water, electricity, sanitation and public transport. Widespread discrimination prevented Roma families from buying or renting housing outside of mainly Roma-populated areas, and they continued to face obstacles, including prejudice, in accessing social housing. Discrimination against Roma in the labour market remained commonplace and unemployment levels among Roma were extremely high.

State institutions created to combat and consider complaints of discrimination, such as the Human Rights Ombudsman and the Advocate of the Principle of Equality, had weak mandates and remained poorly resourced. The office of the Advocate of the

Principle of Equality had just one employee: the Advocate himself.

Throughout the year approximately 250 Roma living in the Škocjan-Dobruška vas settlement remained at risk of forced eviction. The settlement, part of which was designated for the development of an industrial zone in 2013, had been home to the Roma families for many years. Following public pressure and the intervention of the national authorities and Roma civil society, the municipality agreed in August 2014 to relocate two Roma families at imminent risk of forced eviction as development work commenced. However, no further plans were consulted with residents who remained at risk of losing their homes.

FREEDOM OF EXPRESSION

The trial of journalist Anuška Delić for publishing classified information began in October and was ongoing by the end of the year. The charges related to articles she published alleging links between members of the Slovenian Democratic Party and the far-right group Blood and Honour. The Slovenian Intelligence and Security Agency (SOVA) claimed subsequently that some of the information in her reports had been leaked from its files. The Slovenian criminal code does not provide for a public interest defence.

SOMALIA

Federal Republic of Somalia
Head of state: **Hassan Sheikh Mohamud**
Head of government: **Abdiweli Sheikh Ahmed**
Head of Somaliland Republic: **Ahmed Mohamed Mahamoud Silyano**

Armed conflict continued between pro-government forces, the African Union Mission in Somalia (AMISOM) and the Islamist armed group al-Shabaab in southern and central Somalia. Pro-government forces continued an offensive to take control of key towns. Over a hundred thousand civilians were killed, injured or displaced by armed conflict and generalized violence during the year. All parties to the conflict were responsible for serious violations of human rights and humanitarian law, including AMISOM. Armed groups continued to forcibly recruit people, including children, and to abduct, torture and unlawfully kill people; rape and other forms of sexual violence were widespread. Aid agencies' access remained constrained by fighting, insecurity and restrictions imposed by parties to the conflict. Journalists and media workers were attacked and harassed. One journalist was killed. Perpetrators of serious human rights abuses continued to enjoy impunity.

BACKGROUND

The Somali Federal Government (SFG) and AMISOM remained in control of the capital, Mogadishu. A joint offensive by the Somali National Armed Forces (SNAF) and AMISOM sought to flush out al-Shabaab operatives from areas of south and central Somalia with some success. However, al-Shabaab maintained control of much of south and central Somalia. Armed clashes and al-Shabaab attacks against civilians increased, particularly in contested areas. Increased abuses of international law were witnessed throughout the course of the offensive, allegedly caused by all parties to the conflict.

The partial lifting of the arms embargo on Somalia in 2013 appeared to contribute to abuses against civilians into 2014. In February, the UN Monitoring Group highlighted continuous violations of Somalia's arms embargoes, reporting the diversion of arms intended for use by non-government armed forces, including al-Shabaab. International support for government security forces, allied militias and AMISOM continued, despite lack of accountability for ongoing, serious human rights abuses.

Somalia's humanitarian situation deteriorated rapidly due to the ongoing conflict, drought and reduced humanitarian access with conditions as bad or worse than before the 2011 famine. A s of September, a bout 42% of the population were in crisis or needed assistance.

Somalia faced political crisis, too. Prime Minister Abdi Farah Shirdon Saaid resigned in December 2013 following a parliamentary vote of no confidence. In January a new, larger C abinet was appointed consisting of 25 ministers, with two council members retained from the previous administration. In May, MPs called for President Mohamud to resign. In November, following clashes between President Hassan and the incoming Prime Minister, a proposal for a second parliamentary vote of no confidence against the Prime Minister was put on hold due to the possibility of violence between opposing members of parliament. Plans for revising and implementing the constitution and the proposed federalization plan remained pending, leading to increases in clan-based conflict and abuses.

In June 2013, the UN Assistance Mission in Somalia (UNSOM) was established, which included a human rights monitoring and reporting mandate.

In September, a US drone strike killed Ahmed Abdi Godane, the leader of al-Shabaab. Internal divisions within al-Shabaab during 2013 had resulted in scores of deaths and the execution of key leaders of the movement, allowing Godane to consolidate his power. A new leader and known hardliner, 'Abu Ubaidah', was quickly announced. Retaliatory attacks took place, including a suicide attack a week after Godane's death, which killed at least 12 people, including four Americans.

ABUSES BY ARMED GROUPS
Indiscriminate attacks

Civilians continued to be killed and wounded indiscriminately in crossfire during armed clashes; in suicide attacks and in attacks involving improvised explosive devices (IEDs) and grenades. 2014 saw an increase in such attacks as well as on high profile targets. Al-Shabaab retained the ability to stage lethal attacks in the most heavily guarded parts of Mogadishu, killing or injuring hundreds of civilians. Two deadly attacks took place at Villa Somalia during the year, following a number of such attacks in 2013. In August, a complex attack was carried out on a national security detention facility, killing two civilians. At least 10 people were killed in an attack on parliament in May. Government and AMISOM offensives led to increases in abuses by all parties to the conflict. Air strikes continued to be carried out.

Direct targeting of civilians

Civilians remained at risk of targeted attacks and killings in Mogadishu. During Ramadan in July, recorded assassination attempts reached their highest level since al-Shabaab lost control of most parts of Mogadishu in 2010. On 27 July, a businessman was shot and killed by unknown armed men in his shop in Bakara market. On 23 September, a woman was shot and killed in Heliwa district. She had worked as a cook for SNAF forces in Mogadishu.

Al-Shabaab factions continued to torture and unlawfully kill people they accused of spying or not conforming to their strict interpretation of Islamic law. They killed people in public, including by stoning, and carried out amputations and floggings. They continued to impose restrictive behavioural codes on women and men. On 27 September, a woman was allegedly stoned to death in Barawe, a town in Lower Shabelle, on suspicion of marrying more than one husband. She was reportedly buried up to her neck and stoned to death by hooded men in front of a crowd. On 2 June, according to reports, al-Shabaab executed three men accused of being spies for the SFG and the Kenyan and US governments. The men were executed by firing squad in a park in Barawe in front of a gathering of several hundred people.[1]

Unlawful killings, extortion, arbitrary arrests and rape continued to be carried out by government forces and aligned militia, in part as a result of poor discipline and lack of command control. On 25 August, an SNAF soldier reportedly shot and killed a minibus driver in Afar-Irdood area, Xamar Weyne District, after the driver refused to pay extortion money.

CHILD SOLDIERS

Children continued to suffer grave abuses by all parties to the armed conflict. Al-Shabaab continued to target children for recruitment and forced marriage, and attacked schools. Government-affiliated militias were again accused of recruiting and using child soldiers. Implementation of the two action plans signed by the government in 2012 to end and prevent the recruitment and use of child soldiers, as well as the killing and maiming of children, was outstanding and children remained in the armed forces. The Minister of Defence and Minister of National Security signed standard operating procedures for handling children formerly associated with armed groups.

The SFG had not ratified the Convention on the Rights of the Child and its Optional Protocols by the end of the year, despite its commitments to ratify the conventions.

INTERNALLY DISPLACED PEOPLE, ASYLUM-SEEKERS AND REFUGEES

Over 1 million people in Somalia were in crisis and an additional 2.1 million people were in need of assistance. For the first time since the 2011 famine, food security began deteriorating rapidly. Insecurity and fighting reportedly caused over 60% of new displacement in 2014. Trade routes were heavily disrupted due to the SNAF and AMISOM military offensives; al-Shabaab blocked supply routes, causing major disruption to the work of humanitarian organizations trying to access towns. This led to sharp increases in food prices. These issues combined placed Somalia at significant risk of sliding back into a state of emergency.

In Mogadishu, tens of thousands of people were forcibly evicted from government and private property. Many of them moved to the outskirts of Mogadishu, including the Afgooye corridor, where there was little security provision or access to services. There were reports of increases in rape and other forms of sexual violence against women and girls in these areas. An IDP policy framework drafted in April was not adopted.

There were over 900,000 Somali refugees in the region, particularly in Ethiopia and Kenya. Plans by the Kenyan authorities to return Somalis continued despite serious human rights violations, including the forced return of 359 people and forcible encampment of thousands of others. Other states hosting Somali asylum-seekers and refugees, including some EU states, began attempts to return failed Somali asylum-seekers to Mogadishu on the grounds that they no longer needed protection due to an apparent improvement in security there.

FREEDOM OF EXPRESSION – JOURNALISTS

Somali journalists and media workers continued to be attacked, harassed and intimidated. On 21 June, Yusuf Ahmed Abukar was killed on his way to work when a bomb attached to his car exploded. Yusuf reported for the privately owned Mustaqbal radio station, in Mogadishu and a Nairobi-based radio station, Ergo. The Prime Minister stated that the attack was being investigated, however Amnesty International was not aware of any progress in the case by year's end.

Media freedom continued to be curtailed, journalists were arrested and media houses closed down. In August, broadcasters Radio Shabelle and Sky FM were closed down and 19 of their journalists and media workers arrested, including Abdimaalik Yusuf Mohamoud, the owner of Radio Shabelle, and Mohamud Mohamed Dahir, the director of Sky FM. On 21 October, Abdimaalik Yusuf

Mohamoud and Shabelle newscaster Ahmed Abdia Hassan were brought before the court on two charges relating to incitement to disturbance of public order and to commit offences. Both rejected the charges and were released on bail, while Shabelle's Editor Mohamed Bashir Hashi and Mohamud Mohamed Dahir were not brought to the hearing. In June, a restrictive media bill was submitted to Cabinet proposing to curtail media rights. In September, the National Intelligence and Security Agency (NISA) issued a ban on national media coverage of all al-Shabaab activities. Al-Shabaab imposed severe restrictions on media freedom and banned the internet in areas under its control. Little progress was made in addressing impunity for the murder of journalists, despite a government taskforce established for that purpose in 2012. People suspected of killing journalists continued to enjoy impunity. Of more than twenty journalists murdered since 2005, only two prosecutions had resulted in convictions by the end of the year. In March 2013, a military court convicted Adan Sheikh Abdi Sheikha Hussein for the murder of Hassan Yusuf Absuge in 2012, and sentenced him to death in a trial that did not meet due process standards. A firing squad executed Adan in August 2013.

DEATH PENALTY

Somalia continued to use the death penalty despite its support for the 2012 UN General Assembly resolution on the moratorium of the death penalty. Many executions were carried out by the military court, often involving members of Somali armed opposition groups such as al-Shabaab, government soldiers and people convicted of murder.

Executions were often carried out rapidly, after proceedings falling short of international fair trial standards, while there was an apparent spike in executions throughout the year. On 3 April, a man was executed by firing squad in Kismayo nine days after he allegedly murdered an elder. It was unclear which, if any, court found had him guilty. On

30 July, Somalia's military court sentenced three men to death for alleged membership of al-Shabaab. Four days later, pictures were circulated on twitter allegedly showing their bodies. On 30 August, Somalia's military court found alleged al-Shabaab members Ali Bashir Osman and Abdulahi Sharif Osman guilty of killing the journalist Timacade in 2013 and sentenced them to death. The two men were executed on 26 October by public firing squad.

---

1. Forced returns to south and central Somalia, including to al-Shabaab areas: A blatant violation of international law (AFR 52/005/2014) www.amnesty.org/en/library/info/AFR52/005/2014/en

SOUTH AFRICA

Republic of South Africa
Head of state and government: **Jacob G. Zuma**

Judicial commissions of inquiry highlighted police use of excessive force, including unlawful killings, and failures in delivery of services to poor communities. Incidents of property destruction and displacement of refugees and asylum-seekers continued to occur. Access to treatment for people living with HIV continued to expand and HIV treatment interventions for pregnant women contributed to a decline in maternal deaths. However, key discriminatory barriers continued to delay women and girls' access to antenatal care. Progress was made in addressing hate crimes based on the victims' sexual orientation or gender identity. Human rights defenders faced intimidation and threats.

BACKGROUND

Following the general elections in May the ruling African National Congress (ANC) party was returned to power in eight out of the nine provinces, but with a reduced national majority of 62.15%. A new political party, the Economic Freedom Fighters, gained 6.35% of the vote and with the established opposition Democratic Alliance increased pressure on the ANC government in the national parliament for greater transparency and accountability.

Access to anti-retroviral treatment for people living with HIV continued to expand, with 2.5 million South Africans on treatment according to official figures at July 2014. As a result, life expectancy in South Africa increased.

EXCESSIVE USE OF FORCE

The Marikana Commission of Inquiry into the fatal police shootings of 34 striking platinum mine workers at Marikana in August 2012 ended its public hearings on 14 November. Closing arguments were heard from legal parties representing the police, mining unions, LONMIN plc, the families of the 34 striking mine workers killed by police and the families of seven other people – three non-striking workers, two police officers and two LONMIN security guards – who were killed during the developing conflict. The Commissioners were due to report their conclusions and recommendations to President Zuma in 2015.

There were indications that the police attempted to conceal and destroy evidence and to fabricate a version of events intended to mislead the official inquiry from the start. A crucial meeting held by police officials on the evening of 15 August 2012 endorsed the decision to forcibly disarm, disperse and arrest the striking mine workers by the end of the following day. Senior police officials, most particularly the National Commissioner of Police, persistently failed to co-operate with the Commission's inquiries about the meeting. The decision to disarm the striking miners was taken despite the anticipation of loss of life and injury. It led to the deployment of "tactical units" armed with lethal force, the firing of over 600 rounds of live ammunition by police at two separate locations, and to 34 deaths. The fatal injuries were nearly all sustained to the head or upper body.[1]

Other evidence before the Commission indicated that those involved in the decision failed to plan for adequate emergency medical assistance to be available.

CORPORATE ACCOUNTABILITY

Evidence before the Marikana Commission on labour relations and socioeconomic conditions underlying the August 2012 strike was curtailed due to pressure to complete the Commission's work. However, LONMIN was scrutinized in the final months, in respect of its failures to take adequate measures to protect the lives of its security staff and employees, and its failure to fulfil the company's socioeconomic obligations linked to its mining lease in Marikana.

On 20 August, the state withdrew all charges, including possession of dangerous weapons and involvement in an illegal gathering, against 270 strikers arrested at the scene of the police shootings on 16 August 2012.

EXTRAJUDICIAL EXECUTIONS

The start of the trial of 27 police officers, the majority of whom are members of the Cato Manor Organized Crime Unit (CMU), on 28 counts of murder and other charges, was further delayed following their appearance in the Durban High Court on 23 June, and postponed until February 2015. The police officers faced criminal charges in connection with, among others, the death of Bongani Mkhize. In May, the Pietermaritzburg High Court ruled that the Minister of Police was liable to pay damages to the family of Bongani Mkhize, who had been killed by members of the CMU and the National Intervention Unit in February 2009.

In February 2014, the High Court had ruled that the decisions taken by the then National Director of Public Prosecutions (NDPP) to prosecute the former CMU commander Johan Booysen on seven charges of racketeering

under the Prevention of Organized Crime Act was arbitrary and offended the principle of legality. While ruling that the decisions to prosecute charges under the Act should be set aside, High Court judge Trevor Gorven emphasized that the ruling did not preclude the NDPP from reinstituting the charges on a proper basis in future.

TORTURE AND OTHER ILL-TREATMENT

Allegations of torture against members of the South African Police Service (SAPS) and the Department of Correctional Services were rife. Towards the end of the year the SAPS Legal Services issued a National Instruction to all SAPS members informing them of the absolute prohibition of torture and their obligations under the 2013 Prevention and Combating of Torture of Persons Act.

On 30 October, the Constitutional Court dismissed the appeal brought by the SAPS National Commissioner who had refused to investigate complaints of torture contained in a 2008 "dossier" by the Zimbabwe Exiles' Forum and the Southern African Human Rights Litigation Centre. The Constitutional Court concluded that the SAPS had both the power and the duty to investigate the alleged complaints, which amounted to crimes against humanity.

DEATH PENALTY

In September the North Gauteng High Court ruled that the deportation to Botswana of Edwin Samotse, a Botswana national, by Department of Home Affairs (DHA) officials was unlawful and unconstitutional. Edwin Samotse faced criminal charges in Botswana for which the death sentence was applicable. The South African authorities had not obtained the requisite undertaking from the Botswana authorities to ensure that the death sentence would not be imposed. The Court ordered the DHA to implement measures to prevent a recurrence of similar deportations.

REFUGEES AND ASYLUM-SEEKERS

During the year there were numerous incidents involving threats and violence against refugees, asylum-seekers and migrants, with looting or destruction of hundreds of their small businesses and homes. In the first four months of the year incidents in seven provinces led to the displacement of over 1,600 people. In June, sustained attacks in the Mamelodi area near Pretoria and the slow response of the police led to the looting or destruction of some 76 Somali-owned shops, large-scale displacements, the death of one refugee and injuries to 10 others.[2] There was continuing concern at the failure of the government to protect the life and physical integrity of refugees and others in need of international protection.

In September, the Supreme Court of Appeal (SCA) overturned a High Court ruling which had allowed in effect the forced closure of refugee-operated small businesses by police and municipal authorities under what was known as Operation Hard Stick. These closures had been accompanied by ill-treatment, abuses, displacement and destitution. The SCA ruled that both formally recognized refugees and asylum-seekers were entitled to apply for trading licences, particularly where the latter faced long delays in the final determination of their application for asylum.

In November, charges were withdrawn in the North Gauteng High Court against 15 of the 20 Congolese men who had been on trial on charges of contravening South Africa's Regulation of Foreign Military Assistance Act. They had also faced a second charge, conspiracy to commit murder, with the alleged targets including the President of the Democratic Republic of the Congo (DRC), Joseph Kabila, and military and other government officials. Five defendants, all originally from the DRC, remained on trial in the High Court on the same charges, with the trial due to resume in January 2015. All 20, when arrested in February

2013, were remanded in prison in Pretoria until the trial began 17 months later. The presiding judge ordered an investigation into allegations by the accused of ill-treatment, including prolonged periods of isolation in remand prison.

MATERNAL HEALTH AND HIV

HIV-infection continued to be the main cause of death of women and girls during pregnancy and shortly after birth, accounting for over 40% of deaths. Government data reported that 60% of all maternal deaths were potentially avoidable. HIV prevalence rates nationally for pregnant women of 29.5% remained a serious concern, with health districts in Mpumalanga and KwaZulu-Natal provinces showing rates of over 40%. New national figures published in 2014 reported that almost a quarter of all new HIV infections were occurring in girls and young women between 15 and 24 years.

In July, the Health Minister expressed concern that girls under 18 years of age accounted for 7.8% of all live births but 36% of maternal deaths. Department of Health figures indicated that the maternal mortality ratio had declined from 310 to 269 maternal deaths for every 100,000 live births.

In July, the government announced that access to free and lifelong anti-retroviral treatment would be available for all pregnant women living with HIV from January 2015. In August, the government launched a mobile phone messaging service, "Mom Connect", to provide pregnant women and girls with information during pregnancy.

However, barriers to accessing maternal health services continued. Pregnant women and girls accessed antenatal care late in their pregnancies and such delays were linked to nearly a quarter of avoidable maternal deaths in South Africa. Women and girls said that they delayed accessing antenatal care in part because of concerns that health facilities did not ensure confidentiality and informed consent, particularly in relation to implementation of HIV testing. They also cited a lack of access to information, negative attitudes by health care workers and unreliable or costly transport to health facilities as barriers to early access. Poverty was an exacerbating factor.[3]

RIGHTS OF LESBIAN, GAY, BISEXUAL, TRANSGENDER AND INTERSEX PEOPLE

Discriminatory violence against LGBTI people continued to cause concern and fear. In 2013 and 2014, at least five people, three of them lesbian women, were murdered in what appeared to be targeted violence related to their sexual orientation or gender identity.

There was some progress made in addressing hate crimes through the revival of the National Task Team process and establishment of a Rapid Response Team by Department of Justice and Constitutional Development officials, Constitutional Development officials, and others. In February, the Rapid Response Team reported progress in 19 out of 43 previously "unresolved" cases identified as suspected anti-LGBTI violence.

Civil society representatives and Department of Justice officials also held discussions on a draft hate crimes policy document, intended to assist the drafting of legislation on hate crimes. There was no further progress with the legislation by the end of the year.

In November, the Johannesburg High Court convicted a man of the rape and murder in 2013 of a lesbian woman, Duduzile Zozo. Judge Tshifhiwa Maumela issued a strong condemnation of the discriminatory attitudes which fuelled such crimes.[4]

At the end of the year, preliminary trial proceedings had begun against a suspect charged with the murder of 21-year-old David Olyn, who was beaten and burned to death in March, apparently because of his sexual orientation. However, civil society monitors expressed concern at limitations in the police investigation.

South Africa supported the adoption in May of Resolution 275 by the African Commission on Human and Peoples' Rights, urging states to end all acts of violence and abuse because of real or perceived sexual orientation or gender identity.

HUMAN RIGHTS DEFENDERS

Harassment of human rights defenders and organizations, and improper pressure on institutions, including oversight bodies, remained a major concern. The Office of the Public Protector and its Director, Thuli Madonsela, faced sustained pressure amounting to intimidation by members of the government in connection with the oversight body's investigation and report on the improper use of public funds by the President at his home in KwaZulu-Natal Province.

At the end of the year, criminal trial proceedings had not concluded against a Social Justice Coalition (SJC) founder member, Angy Peter, and three others. The SJC, including Angy Peter, had gathered evidence in 2012 to support a call for a commission of inquiry into police corruption and their failure to provide proper services to the poor community of Khayelitsha. The judicial Commission of Inquiry, which was established in August 2012, finally began its hearings in February 2014, and issued its report in August. The hearings had been delayed for over a year until the Constitutional Court ruled finally in 2013 against the then Minister of Police and the National Commissioner of Police who had opposed its establishment. The Commission's report confirmed many of the concerns documented by SJC.

Health rights activists came under increasing pressure, particularly in Free State province. Members of the Treatment Action Campaign (TAC) were reportedly threatened and intimidated by ANC ruling party provincial officials and anonymous callers because of their work for people living with HIV and against corruption. Sello Mokhalipi, then Free State Provincial Chairperson of TAC, temporarily went into hiding and later lodged criminal charges with the police in early 2014, following alleged death threats. TAC Free State Provincial Co-ordinator, Machobane Morake, was also allegedly subjected to threats and intimidation. In July, the two men and a third TAC colleague were alleged victims of an attempted night ambush on a remote road. At the time, they were supporting 127 Free State community health workers and TAC activists who had been arrested during a peaceful vigil at the offices of the Free State Department of Health. Those arrested were held in police stations in Bloemfontein for 36 hours before appearing in court where they were charged with participating in an illegal gathering. After two further remand hearings, their case was postponed to January 2015.

1. South Africa: Unlawful force and the pattern of concealment: Barriers to accountability for the killings at Marikana (AFR 53/004/2014) www.amnesty.org/en/library/info/AFR53/004/2014/en
2. South Africa: Government and police failing to protect Somali refugees from deadly attacks (News story) www.amnesty.org/en/news/south-africa-government-and-police-failing-protect-somali-refugees-deadly-attacks-2014-06-12
3. Struggle for maternal health: Access barriers to antenatal care in South Africa (AFR 53/006/2014) www.amnesty.org/en/library/info/AFR53/006/2014/en
4. South Africa: Court's judgment a positive step forward against hate crime (AFR 53/008/2014) www.amnesty.org/en/documents/AFR53/008/2014/en/

SOUTH SUDAN

Republic of South Sudan
Head of state and government: **Salva Kiir Mayardit**

The internal armed conflict that erupted in South Sudan in December 2013 resulted in tens of thousands of deaths and the destruction of entire towns. Approximately 1.4 million people were internally displaced and another 500,000 fled to neighbouring countries. An estimated 4 million people were at a high risk of food insecurity, with the UN repeatedly warning of a deepening humanitarian crisis and potential famine should fighting continue. Despite a cessation of hostilities agreement in January 2014 and continuous efforts by the Intergovernmental Authority on Development (IGAD) to negotiate a political solution to the conflict, fighting continued throughout 2014. The conflict was characterized by a total disregard for international human rights and humanitarian law and there was no accountability for abuses committed in the context of the conflict.

BACKGROUND

On 15 December 2013, a political dispute within South Sudan's ruling party, the Sudan People's Liberation Movement (SPLM), escalated into an armed confrontation in Juba between forces loyal to President Kiir and those loyal to former Vice-President Riek Machar. By the end of 2013, violence had spread to Jonglei, Unity and Upper Nile states.

IGAD, an eight-country East African regional organization, began mediating between the government of South Sudan and the Sudan People's Liberation Army/ Movement in Opposition (SPLA/M-IO) in January 2014. The parties signed a cessation of hostilities agreement on 23 January, but it was violated almost as soon as it was signed. The parties subsequently recommitted to the cessation of hostilities on 5 May and signed an agreement to resolve the crisis on 9 May, but fighting continued.

In June, participation in the IGAD negotiations was broadened to include other stakeholder groups. This included several SPLM leaders who were detained in December, accused of participating in an attempted coup. Seven were released at the end of January while four others stood trial for treason, but were released at the end of April after the government dropped charges against them. Delegates from civil society, political parties and faith-based groups also participated in the talks.

IGAD continued its efforts to reach a political settlement. On 8 November, IGAD heads of state issued a resolution granting the warring parties 15 days to consult with their constituencies on the structure of a transitional government. The resolution recommitted the parties to end all hostilities, and provided that further violations of the cessation of hostilities agreement would result in asset freezes, travel bans and an arms embargo. IGAD leaders further authorized the IGAD region to intervene directly in South Sudan to protect life and restore peace.

On 24 December 2013, the UN Security Council approved an increase in the military strength of the UN Mission in South Sudan (UNMISS) to 12,500 troops and an increase in the mission's police force to a maximum of 1,323 personnel. In May 2014, the Security Council revised the mandate of UNMISS to focus on protection of civilians, monitoring and investigating human rights, creating the conditions for the delivery of humanitarian assistance, and supporting the implementation of the cessation of hostilities agreement.

A Commission of Inquiry was established by the AU in March 2014, but its final report had not yet been publicly released by the end of the year. The AU Peace and Security Council (PSC) repeatedly condemned the killing of civilians and violations of the 23 January cessation of hostilities agreement by both parties to the conflict. The AU PSC also indicated its readiness, upon recommendation by IGAD, to take targeted sanctions and other measures against any party that undermined the search for a solution to the conflict.

INTERNAL ARMED CONFLICT

Both government and opposition forces demonstrated a disregard for international humanitarian law. Other armed groups, including the opposition-allied White Army and the Sudanese Justice and Equality Movement (JEM) fighting on behalf of the government, also committed violations of international humanitarian law.

In the days following the outbreak of violence in Juba, government soldiers targeted and killed people based on ethnicity and assumed political affiliation. Hundreds of Nuer civilians and government soldiers who had been captured and disarmed or otherwise placed *hors de combat* were executed, mainly by Dinka members of the armed forces. Many Nuer were killed in or near their homes. Some men were picked up at home or in the street, taken away and later killed in other locations. In one incident, over 300 people were killed in a police building in Gudele.

Parties to the conflict attacked civilians sheltering in hospitals and places of worship. For example, after government forces re-took control of Bor town on 18 January, the bodies of 18 women, all of them Dinka, were found in and around the compound of St Andrew's Cathedral. They were believed to have been victims of an attack by opposition forces. The remains of 15 men and women were found at Bor hospital. When opposition forces attacked Malakal for the third time in mid-February, they targeted Malakal Teaching Hospital, where civilians had previously found safe shelter. They shot dead a number of people.

Conflict-related sexual violence was widespread. This included cases of gang rape, of pregnant women being cut open and of women being raped using wooden sticks or plastic bottles.[1] At least four girls staying at Christ the King Church in Malakal were abducted by opposition forces on the night of 25 February and raped nearby.

Government and opposition forces burned down homes, damaged and destroyed medical facilities and looted public institutions and private property as well as food stores and humanitarian aid. Looting and destruction left Bor, Bentiu, Malakal and many other towns destroyed.

UNICEF estimated that parties to the conflict had recruited approximately 9,000 children to serve in armed forces and groups.

Civilians were injured, abducted and killed within or in the immediate vicinity of UN bases. On 19 December, approximately 2,000 armed youths surrounded the UNMISS base in Akobo, Jonglei state, and opened fire, killing two peacekeepers and an estimated 20 civilians who had sought refuge there. On 17 April, there was an armed assault on the UNMISS base in Bor during which more than 50 internally displaced people were killed.

Obstruction of humanitarian assistance significantly impeded civilians' access to life-saving assistance. Parties to the conflict also attacked UN and humanitarian workers. Members of the Mabanese Defense Force, a government-allied militia, killed five humanitarian workers of Nuer ethnicity in August. The whereabouts of two Nuer UN employees abducted in October by forces of the government-allied Shilluk militia leader Johnson Olony remained unknown. In September, a UNMISS helicopter was shot down, killing three of its crew members.

FREEDOM OF EXPRESSION

The authorities, especially the National Security Service (NSS), harassed and intimidated journalists and human rights defenders. The NSS summoned journalists for questioning, arbitrarily detained journalists and ordered a number of journalists to leave the country.

In March, the NSS ordered the *Almajhar Alsayasy* Arabic language newspaper to cease publication because of its description of the genesis of the conflict and for interviewing politicians critical of the government.

In June, NSS officers contacted the editors of several newspapers and instructed them to stop publishing articles discussing the federal system of government. On 2 July, NSS officers went to the offices of *Juba Monitor* and seized copies of the paper because it contained two opinion pieces about federalism. Around 15 armed NSS officers

confiscated all 3,000 copies of *The Citizen* newspaper on the morning of 7 July.

On 1 August, Deng Athuai Mawiir, acting chairperson of the South Sudan Civil Society Alliance and a member of the civil society delegation to the IGAD-brokered peace negotiations, was shot in the thigh by an unknown gunman. While the perpetrator and motive for the attack remained unknown, this incident contributed to a climate of fear among civil society activists, journalists and human rights defenders.[2]

JUSTICE SYSTEM

The criminal justice system routinely failed to ensure accountability for perpetrators of human rights abuses due to weaknesses in the criminal justice system. These included inadequate technical capacity in investigatory methods, a lack of forensic experts, interference or resistance by security services and the government and a lack of victim support and witness protection programmes.

The justice system also failed to guarantee due process and fair trials. Common human rights violations included arbitrary arrest and detention, prolonged pre-trial detention and the failure to ensure the right of an accused person to legal counsel.

Two UNMISS employees were arrested by the NSS in Wau in August and transported to Juba. They remained in detention at the NSS headquarters at the end of the year. They had not been charged or brought before a competent legal authority.

The internal armed conflict exacerbated pre-existing problems in the justice system, particularly in Jonglei, Unity and Upper Nile states. The capacity of the police and judiciary to enforce the law was undermined by militarization and the defection of many police officers. Representatives of the judiciary and the Ministry of Justice left these states following the outbreak of violence and had not returned to their posts by the end of 2014.

LACK OF ACCOUNTABILITY

The government did not conduct prompt, thorough, impartial and independent investigations with a view to prosecuting and holding accountable individuals suspected of crimes under international law and serious violations of human rights.

President Kiir established a committee to investigate human rights abuses allegedly committed during an attempted coup on 15 December 2013. The committee's eight members were selected by the President's Office, its activities were funded by the presidency and it was mandated to report directly to the President. No report, or update on its findings, was made public by the end of the year.

The SPLA set up two investigation committees at the end of December 2013. In February 2014, the SPLA announced that approximately 100 individuals had been arrested as a result of investigations. However, they all escaped on 5 March during a gunfight among soldiers at the Giyada military barracks in Juba, where they were detained. In November, the SPLA announced that two individuals had been rearrested for their role in violations committed in December. No information was made public about their identity or the charges against them.

On 30 December 2013, the AU PSC called for the establishment of an AU Commission of Inquiry into human rights violations and abuses committed during the armed conflict in South Sudan. Its mandate included recommending measures to ensure accountability and reconciliation. Members of the Commission, chaired by the former president of Nigeria, Olusegun Obasanjo, were sworn in by March 2014. In its June interim report, the Commission of Inquiry said it was not yet in a position to determine whether crimes under international law had been committed. The Commission of Inquiry submitted its final report to the AU Commission in October, but it had not been publicly released by the end of the year.

LEGAL DEVELOPMENTS

South Sudan was not party to any core international or regional human rights treaties. Although parliament voted to ratify several treaties and President Kiir signed their instruments of accession, the government failed to formally deposit instruments of accession with the AU or the UN. The treaties were: the African Charter on Human and Peoples' Rights; the AU Convention Governing the Specific Aspects of Refugee Problems in Africa; the UN Convention on the Rights of the Child; the UN Convention against Torture; and the UN Convention on the Elimination of All Forms of Discrimination against Women.

A National Security Service Bill was passed by Parliament on 8 October and was awaiting presidential assent in December 2014. The Bill grants the NSS broad powers, including the power to arrest and detain, without adequate provisions for independent oversight or safeguards against abuse. National and international human rights advocates as well as a number of members of Parliament called for President Kiir to refuse assent and to return the Bill to parliament for revisions.[3]

A draft Non-Governmental Organizations Bill was being considered by Parliament, which would restrict the right to freedom of association. The Bill would make registration compulsory, prohibit NGOs from operating without being registered, and criminalize voluntary activities carried out without a registration certificate.

The national legal framework failed to define and sanction crimes under international law, including crimes against humanity and genocide. It also failed to define or criminalize torture. In addition, it failed to provide for command or superior responsibility as a mode of liability for crimes under international law.

---

1. Nowhere safe: Civilians under attack in South Sudan (AFR 65/003/2014)

   www.amnesty.org/en/documents/afr65/003/2014/en/

2. South Sudan: Investigate shooting of civil society leader (AFR 65/008/2014)
   www.amnesty.org/en/documents/AFR65/008/2014/en/
3. Comments on the 8 October Draft Security Bill (AFR 65/013/2014)
   www.amnesty.org/en/documents/AFR65/013/2014/en/

SPAIN

Kingdom of Spain
Head of state: **King Felipe VI de Borbón (replaced King Juan Carlos I de Borbón in June)**
Prime Minister: **Mariano Rajoy**

Throughout the year thousands of demonstrations were organized to protest against austerity measures imposed by the government. Reports of abuses by police against demonstrators continued. Thousands of migrants, including asylum-seekers and refugees, some fleeing from Syria, attempted to irregularly enter the Spanish enclave cities of Ceuta and Melilla from Morocco. Reports of unlawful deportations and excessive use of force by Spanish border guards persisted.

BACKGROUND

Spain ratified the UN Arms Trade Treaty in April, and in August became the first country to update its regulations on arms transfers to include the "Golden Rule" prohibiting the transfer of arms where there was a real risk that they would contribute to human rights violations.

The teaching of human rights ceased to be obligatory in primary and secondary education following amendments to the Education Act adopted in December 2013.

On 9 November, the government of Catalonia held an informal consultation on the political future of Catalonia, in defiance of a Constitutional Court ruling ordering the consultation's suspension. 80% of those who participated declared their support for independence.

No violent attacks by the Basque Euskadi Ta Askatasuna (ETA) were reported during the year, after ETA announced the end of its armed struggle in 2011.

FREEDOM OF ASSEMBLY

Throughout the year, hundreds of individuals were detained and fined for participating in spontaneous and mostly peaceful demonstrations of more than 20 people. The law regulating the right to freedom of assembly failed to recognize the right to hold spontaneous demonstrations.

By the end of the year, bills to amend both the Criminal Code and the Law on the Protection of Public Safety were still under discussion in Parliament. If approved, they would further restrict the exercise of freedoms of assembly and expression. The draft Law on the Protection of Public Safety, if adopted, would introduce 21 additional offences, including the unauthorized dissemination of images that might put a police operation at risk. It would also allow for the imposition of fines on the organizers of peaceful spontaneous protests and those showing a lack of respect for law enforcement officers.

EXCESSIVE USE OF FORCE

Excessive force was frequently used by law enforcement officers to disperse and detain protesters.

In April, the Parliament of Catalonia banned the use of rubber balls by Catalan police. In previous years, several peaceful demonstrators were severely injured as a result of police firing rubber balls to disperse crowds.

In June, the Public Prosecutor requested the closure of the investigation into allegations of police abuses made by 26 participants in the "Surround Congress" rally in September 2012. A judicial decision on the closure of the case was still pending at the end of 2014. In the course of the rally, unidentified police officers beat peaceful demonstrators with batons, fired rubber bullets, and threatened journalists covering the events.

In September, the investigating judge in the case of Ester Quintana formally decided to prosecute two law enforcement officers for causing her serious bodily harm. She lost her left eye after being struck by a rubber ball fired by police officers at a demonstration in Barcelona in November 2012.

COUNTER-TERROR AND SECURITY

Spain continued to decline to implement recommendations of international human rights bodies to abolish the use of incommunicado detention for those suspected of terrorism-related offences.

By January at least 63 members of ETA had been released following a ruling by the European Court of Human Rights in 2013 in the case of *Del Rio Prada v. Spain* that the Spanish Supreme Court's "Parot Doctrine" on serious crimes violated the rights to liberty and to no punishment without law. In a reversal of earlier jurisprudence, a Supreme Court ruling in 2006 effectively excluded the possibility of early release for those sentenced to consecutive terms of imprisonment on multiple counts.

DISCRIMINATION

Law enforcement officers continued to carry out identity checks on the basis of racial or ethnic characteristics. The draft Law on the Protection of Public Safety contained a provision requiring identity checks to respect the principle of non-discrimination.

During the year, data on hate crimes was made public by the Ministry of Interior for the first time. According to the Ministry, 1,172 hate crimes were registered in 2013, most on the grounds of sexual orientation and identity and ethnicity. However, a protocol on the identification and registration of discriminatory incidents by law enforcement officers was not introduced. Not all regional security forces provided data on hate crimes.

Despite a 2013 Supreme Court ruling that the banning of full-face veils in municipal buildings in the city of Lleida was unlawful, similar legislation was introduced or proposed in several municipalities during 2014. In July, the Catalan government announced its intention to ban the wearing of full-face veils in public, but legislation to this effect had not been adopted by the end of the year.

VIOLENCE AGAINST WOMEN

According to the Ministry of Health, Social Policy and Equality, 45 women were killed by their partners or former partners during the year.

In August, the CEDAW Committee found that Spain had violated its obligations under the CEDAW Convention by failing to protect Angela González and her daughter Andrea from domestic violence. Andrea was murdered by her father in 2003. Despite more than 30 complaints, and repeated requests for protection, the courts had authorized unsupervised visits between Angela González' former partner and Andrea.

Statistics published during the year revealed a sharp decline in the rate of prosecutions of reported incidents of gender-based violence since the entry into force of the Law on Comprehensive Protection Measures against Gender-based Violence in 2005. The number of cases closed for lack of evidence by the specialized court for gender violence had increased by 158% between 2005 and 2013, prompting unheeded calls for a review of the effectiveness of both the Law and the specialized court .

REFUGEES' AND MIGRANTS' RIGHTS

Unlawful treatment of migrants, refugees and asylum-seekers, including their unlawful deportation to Morocco, and unnecessary or excessive use of force by law enforcement officials, were reported in the Spanish enclaves of Ceuta and Melilla throughout the year. By the end of the year, more than 1,500 Syrian refugees were waiting to be transferred to the mainland from the enclaves. In October, the Popular Party Parliamentary Group tabled an amendment to the draft

Law on Public Security that would legalize summary expulsions to Morocco from Ceuta and Melilla.

In February a group of around 250 migrants, refugees and asylum-seekers originating from Sub-Saharan Africa attempted to swim across the sea border between Morocco and Ceuta. Officials from the Civil Guard employed anti-riot equipment, including rubber balls, blanks and smoke, to stop them. Fifteen people drowned. A judicial investigation was ongoing at the end of the year.

Hundreds of thousands of irregular migrants continued to have their access to health care limited as a result of the implementation of Royal Decree Law 16/2012. With some exceptions, undocumented migrants had to pay to receive health care, including primary health care. In November, the Council of Europe European Committee of Social Rights highlighted that Royal Decree Law 16/2012 contravened the European Social Charter.

By the end of the year, the authorities granted international protection to 1,205 people. Only 255 were granted refugee status. Despite the government's announcement in December 2013 that it would resettle 130 Syrian refugees, by the end of 2014 none had been resettled.

CRIMES UNDER INTERNATIONAL LAW

The definitions of enforced disappearance and torture in Spanish legislation continued to fall short of international human rights standards.

Amendments to legislation governing universal jurisdiction in Spain that entered into force on 14 March limited the powers of Spanish authorities to investigate crimes under international law, including genocide, enforced disappearance, crimes against humanity and torture, committed outside Spain. The reforms were criticized by the UN Working Group on Enforced or Involuntary Disappearances and the UN Special Rapporteur on the promotion of truth, justice, reparation and guarantees of non-recurrence in July.

IMPUNITY

The rights to truth, justice and reparation for victims of crimes committed during the Civil War (1936 to 1939) and under Francisco Franco's rule (1939 to 1975) continued to be denied. Spanish authorities failed to adequately assist the Argentine judiciary, which has been exercising universal jurisdiction to investigate crimes under international law committed during the Franco era.

In July, the UN Working Group on Enforced or Involuntary Disappearances urged the Spanish authorities to strengthen efforts to establish the fate and whereabouts of persons disappeared during the Franco era.

SEXUAL AND REPRODUCTIVE RIGHTS

In September the government withdrew a draft bill, approved in December 2013, which would have introduced a series of obstacles to accessing a safe and legal abortion and possibly increased the number of women and girls resorting to dangerous, clandestine abortion procedures. However, the government reaffirmed its intention to reform existing legislation and require parental consent for girls between 16 and 18 years of age wishing to access a legal abortion.

SRI LANKA

Democratic Socialist Republic of Sri Lanka
Head of state and government: Mahinda Rajapaksa

Unlawful detentions and torture by security forces were carried out with impunity as the authorities continued to rely on the Prevention of Terrorism Act to arrest and detain suspects without charge or trial. Human rights defenders and family members of people subjected to enforced disappearance were threatened and arrested, and fatal attacks on religious minorities went unpunished. Systematic impunity for alleged war crimes and crimes against humanity led the UN Human Rights Council in March to pass a resolution calling for a comprehensive investigation to be undertaken by the UN Office of the High Commissioner for Human Rights – a move the government opposed and refused to co-operate with. Human rights defenders received threats of reprisals by government officials and supporters if they were suspected of contacting investigators or otherwise advocating human rights accountability. Political violence and intimidation – mainly against political opposition supporters and civil society activists – were reported in the run-up to the snap presidential election called for January 2015.

ARBITRARY ARRESTS AND DETENTIONS

Tamils suspected of links to the Liberation Tigers of Tamil Eelam (LTTE) continued to be arrested and detained under the Prevention of Terrorism Act (PTA) instead of ordinary criminal law. The PTA permits extended administrative detention, and shifts the burden of proof to a detainee alleging torture or other ill-treatment. It also restricts freedoms of expression and association and has been used to detain critics.

TORTURE AND OTHER ILL-TREATMENT

Torture and other ill-treatment of detainees – including sexual violence – remained widespread in Sri Lanka, especially at the moment of apprehension and during early stages of pre-trial detention. Victims reported torture of both adult and juvenile detainees; these included individuals arrested in the context of security operations as well as suspects in ordinary criminal cases.

EXCESSIVE USE OF FORCE

Unnecessary and excessive use of force, causing the deaths of demonstrators, continued to be reported and to go unpunished. In May, four army officers suspended in the wake of an internal inquiry into the shooting and killing of demonstrators in a 2013 protest against pollution of the water supply in Weliweriya were reinstated and assigned to new posts. One victim in this incident was reportedly beaten to death while sheltering in a church. The army's report on the shooting was not made public.

DEATHS IN CUSTODY

In June, the Friday Forum, an informal citizens' group, called on the Inspector General of Police to take action against the killings of criminal suspects while in police custody. Police often claimed that the suspects were killed in self-defence or while trying to escape. The Bar Association of Sri Lanka also condemned the killing of suspects in police custody. In late 2013, four men who had been arrested for the alleged murder of a police constable and his wife died under suspicious circumstances in custody within a two-week period. The Bar Association released a statement in December 2013 expressing concern that the police explanations were virtually identical to those of past cases and that the deaths appeared to be extrajudicial executions.

ENFORCED DISAPPEARANCES

The ad hoc Presidential Commission to Investigate into Complaints Regarding Missing Persons (the Disappearances Commission) was appointed in August 2013 to examine complaints between 10 June 1990 and 19 May 2009. It received some 15,000 civilian complaints as well as about 5,000 cases of missing armed forces personnel. By August 2014, the Commission had reportedly begun inquiries into less than 5% of these cases, or 462 complaints. Some complaints, which the Commission said were being analyzed for further investigation, were potentially over a decade old.

IMPUNITY

Serious violations of international law committed during the armed conflict, including enforced disappearances, extrajudicial executions and the intentional shelling of civilians and protected areas such as hospitals, remain unaddressed. The government continued to deny that such violations occurred until 15 July when it announced that it was expanding its Disappearances Commission to investigate other alleged crimes under international law. A panel of international lawyers was appointed to advise the government.

REFUGEES AND ASYLUM-SEEKERS

Sri Lanka detained and forcefully deported asylum-seekers without adequately assessing their asylum claims, including individuals who were registered with UNHCR, the UN refugee agency, and were awaiting interviews. Authorities arrested and detained 328 asylum-seekers between June and mid-September, and deported 183 of them to Pakistan and Afghanistan. UNHCR said in September that it believed there were still more than 100 people of concern to them in detention, including 38 Pakistani nationals and 64 Afghan nationals. Many belonged to minority religious groups which were subject to discrimination and violence in their home countries.

HUMAN RIGHTS DEFENDERS

Authorities continued to threaten, harass and arrest human rights defenders, including lawyers, family members of the disappeared and other activists. None of the incidents known to Amnesty International were effectively investigated, and no prosecutions were initiated. People calling for accountability for past and current human rights violations, including human rights defenders attempting to communicate concerns to the UN, were harassed and threatened. In some instances,

individuals suspected of "internationalizing" these issues through association with foreign colleagues were detained. Women activists in northern Sri Lanka were questioned and arrested: significantly, Balendran Jeyakumari, whose son was the victim of an alleged enforced disappearance, remained held since her arbitrary detention under the PTA in March. Prominent human rights defenders Ruki Fernando and Father Praveen Mahesan faced continued restrictions imposed by the courts after they were arrested for attempting to investigate her case.[1]

FREEDOMS OF EXPRESSION, PEACEFUL ASSEMBLY, ASSOCIATION AND MOVEMENT

There were continuing reports of intimidation and harassment of journalists by state officials, including physical attacks, death threats and politically motivated charges. Perpetrators acted with impunity in these cases; none of the incidents were adequately investigated, and those suspected of criminal conduct were not prosecuted. Impunity also persisted for older cases of violence against journalists, including for unlawful killings and enforced disappearances.

On 18 May, the fifth anniversary of the end of Sri Lanka's armed conflict, the military sealed the offices of *Uthayan*, a Jaffna-based newspaper. The newspaper and its employees had faced previous forced closures, threats and violent attacks.

Civil society organizations also came under pressure. On 1 July, the Ministry of Defence issued a memorandum to "all non-governmental organizations" warning them to stop holding press conferences, workshops and journalists' trainings, or disseminating press releases.

Students in many parts of the country were violently attacked, and there were repeated efforts by the authorities to prevent them from organizing, including by prohibiting student unions and suspending student activists.

In October, travel restrictions were reimposed requiring foreign travellers to the

Northern Province to obtain clearance from the Ministry of Defence.

In December, election monitors recorded dozens of reports of political violence, including attacks on political rallies, assaults and arson damage, most perpetrated by members of the ruling party.

JUSTICE SYSTEM

The independence of judicial institutions in Sri Lanka was compromised by the removal of checks and balances protecting the separation of powers. The 18th amendment to the Constitution, passed in 2010, gave the President the power to appoint and remove: the Chief Justice and judges of the Supreme Court; the President and judges of the Court of Appeal; the Attorney General and members of the Judicial Service Commission, which is the body responsible for appointments, transfers, dismissals and disciplinary control of judicial officers. In 2013, after the Supreme Court ruled against the government in several important cases, the Chief Justice was impeached by Parliament and then removed from office by the President, despite a Supreme Court decision that the impeachment was unconstitutional.

DISCRIMINATION – ATTACKS ON MINORITIES

Discrimination against ethnic, linguistic and religious minorities, including members of Tamil, Muslim and Christian communities, continued. Minorities were singled out for arbitrary restrictions on freedoms of expression and association. Tamils, particularly those from the north of the country, were harassed, threatened and arrested by security forces which suspected them of sympathy or links with the LTTE, based largely on their ethnicity and place of origin or residence.

The army and police actively suppressed the rights of northern Tamils to advocate for justice publicly or to commemorate or mourn those killed in the armed conflict. Hindu and Christian religious observance was restricted

in Tamil communities of northern Sri Lanka around key dates and the army's requirement that all public gatherings, including family events, be reported to local military authorities discouraged participation in these activities.

Police failed to protect religious minorities when they faced violence by communal forces, and did not arrest perpetrators of such violence, even when there was photographic evidence to identify them. Threats, harassment and violence against Muslims, Christians and their places of worship escalated in 2014 when large-scale violence in a Muslim neighbourhood in June in Aluthgama resulted in deaths and injuries among residents and the destruction of homes and businesses.

---

1. Activists in northern Sri Lanka at risk (ASA 37/006/2014) www.amnesty.org/en/library/info/ASA37/006/2014/en

SUDAN

Republic of the Sudan
Head of state and government: **Omar Hassan Ahmad al-Bashir**

Freedoms of expression, association and assembly were severely curtailed, with crackdowns on the media, public dialogue and demonstrations. The armed conflicts in Darfur, South Kordofan and Blue Nile states continued to cause mass displacement and civilian casualties; human rights abuses were perpetrated by all parties to the conflicts. The government armed forces were responsible for the destruction of civilian buildings including schools, hospitals and clinics in the conflict areas, and hindered humanitarian access to civilians displaced and otherwise affected by the ongoing hostilities.

BACKGROUND

In January, President Omar al-Bashir announced plans to achieve peace in Sudan and protect constitutional rights through a "national dialogue", open to participation by all parties and even armed movements. He followed this up in April with a promise to release all political detainees. Despite this announcement, restrictions on freedoms of expression, association and assembly prevailed, hindering meaningful attempts at a national dialogue. The national dialogue ceased following the arrest of Al-Sadiq Al-Mahdi, leader of the National Umma Party, over his statements about the Rapid Support Forces (RSF) pro-government militia, whom he accused of committing crimes against civilians.

In August, the National Umma Party and the Sudan Revolutionary Front signed the Paris Declaration, a joint statement calling for widespread reform in Sudan. The two parties declared that they would boycott future general elections unless a transitional government was first put in place to "provide public freedoms" and end the ongoing conflicts in Sudan's Darfur, Blue Nile and South Kordofan states. The ruling National Congress Party refused to recognize the Paris Declaration.

The conflicts in Darfur, Southern Kordofan and Blue Nile states continued unabated. Violations of human rights and international humanitarian law perpetrated by government forces and pro-government militias against civilians continued throughout the year in these three areas, and spread to Northern Kordofan. In Darfur, the government continued in its failure to protect civilians from abuses during a surge in fighting between predominantly ethnic Arab groups over land and other natural resources, in which pro-government militia participated.

The government was preparing for national elections in 2015.

FREEDOM OF EXPRESSION

The authorities increased restrictions on freedoms of expression, association and assembly throughout the country, in what appeared to be a concerted effort to shut down independent dialogue. The government continued to use the National Intelligence and Security Services (NISS) and other security forces to arbitrarily detain perceived opponents of the ruling National Congress Party, to censor media and to shut down public forums and protests. The arbitrary detention of activists, human rights defenders and political opposition figures continued unabated. These restrictions severely undermined the activities of civil society and prevented meaningful public consultation on Sudan's new Constitution, which the government declared would be based on Shari'a law.

Newspapers continued to be subject to closure and censorship for printing material perceived as being critical of the ruling National Congress Party. Journalists received threats from the NISS, which also seized entire print runs, causing large financial losses for newspapers. Eighteen newspapers repeatedly had their editions confiscated between January and September. By the end of the year, the authorities had confiscated newspapers 52 times. *Al Jareeda* newspaper, an independent daily publication, was arbitrarily confiscated by the NISS on 24 September. *Al Jareeda* had been suspended by the NISS 11 times by the end of the year. *Al Siha*, another newspaper, was suspended indefinitely by the NISS on 6 June.

The government also lifted the ban on three newspapers. On 29 January, the government lifted a two-year ban on *Ray al-Shaab* newspaper, affiliated to the Popular Congress Party. A two-year suspension against *Al Tayar* newspaper was lifted on 5 March. The suspension of *Al Midan* newspaper imposed on 3 May 2012 was lifted on 6 March. *Al Midan* is affiliated to the Sudanese Communist Party.

Taj Aldeen Arjaa, a 23-year-old Darfuri activist and blogger, was released from prison on 11 May. He was arrested by the NISS in Khartoum on 26 December 2013 after he verbally criticized President Omar al-Bashir and the President of Chad, Idriss Deby, at a joint press conference. He was reportedly tortured while in prison.

ARMED CONFLICT
Darfur
Widespread human rights abuses continued throughout Darfur. Civilians were displaced in large numbers as a result of violence between warring communities and attacks by government-allied militias and armed opposition groups.

In late February the government deployed the RSF in Darfur. The RSF drew many of its recruits from the former Janjaweed militias that in previous years were responsible for serious human rights violations, including unlawful killings and rape. The RSF destroyed scores of villages, causing a significant increase in displacement and civilian deaths.

Between January and July an estimated 388,000 people were displaced in Darfur, in addition to the 2 million displaced since the conflict in Darfur began in 2003. Many of those internally displaced were in remote areas where they received little or no humanitarian assistance and were vulnerable to attacks, abduction and sexual violence. On 22 March, the Khor Abeche camp for internally displaced persons in South Darfur was attacked by a group of armed men who looted and burned the camp to the ground.

The government continued to restrict access to areas of Darfur affected by conflict to the AU, the United Nations Mission in Darfur (UNAMID) and humanitarian organizations. In February, the International Committee of the Red Cross' main activities were suspended, while other organizations, such as the French development organization Agence d'Aide à la Coopération Technique et au Développement (ACTED), had their offices shut down.

On 2 July, UN Secretary-General Ban Ki-moon announced a review of investigations and reviews into UNAMID performance that had been carried out over the previous two years. This review, which was concluded in October, was announced in response to allegations that UNAMID staff had covered up human rights abuses in Darfur. The review did not find any evidence to support the allegations. However, it found that UNAMID had a tendency to under-report and maintained media silence in incidents involving human rights violations.

South Kordofan and Blue Nile
The armed conflict between government forces and the Sudan People's Liberation Army-North (SPLA-North) continued in South Kordofan and Blue Nile states, with indiscriminate attacks by both parties. Sudanese forces employed indiscriminate aerial bombardment and shelling on civilian villages. They also employed proxy forces in ground assaults, including the RSF. These proxy forces also perpetrated human rights abuses.

Many of the more than 1 million people displaced in the three-year conflict remained in Sudan. More than 200,000 were living in refugee camps in South Sudan or Ethiopia.

On 14 April, the government publicly launched its "Decisive Summer" military operation to "end all rebellion" in South Kordofan, Blue Nile and Darfur. From the onset of the operation, the Sudanese Armed Forces carried out sustained aerial bombardments in and around Kauda, a major town in Heiban County, as well as aerial bombardments and shelling in Um Dorein and Delami counties, destroying schools, clinics, hospitals and other civilian buildings and forcing people to flee their homes.

Sudan continued to obstruct humanitarian access to areas controlled by the SPLA-North. Both parties to the conflict failed to meet their obligation to facilitate humanitarian access.

FREEDOM OF ASSEMBLY

Amid the calls for national dialogue and political accommodation, Sudan continued to restrict the legitimate activities of opposition political parties and civil society. On 8 March, NISS prevented some 30 civil society organizations from celebrating International Women's Day in Khartoum.

On 11 March, economics student Ali Abakar Musa died from gunshot wounds sustained when security services opened fire during a demonstration at the University of Khartoum. The demonstration took place immediately after the conclusion of a public forum organized by the Darfur Students' Association concerning escalating violence in South Darfur. Students marched to the main university gate, where they were met by the police, NISS and student militias. The security services fired tear gas, rubber bullets and live ammunition at the students.

On 15 March, the authorities banned the National Consensus Forces – a coalition of 17 opposition political parties – from holding a public event in Khartoum North and deployed hundreds of security agents to cancel the event. On 1 May, the Political Parties Affairs Council – a government body – rejected the Republican Party application for registration; the Republican Party was considered heretical for its progressive views on Islam. The founder of the party, Mahmoud Mohammed Taha, was executed for apostasy in 1985.

On 29 May, 13 June and 17 August, the authorities refused to allow political and civil society activists to submit memorandums highlighting human rights violations by the government to the Sudan National Human Rights Commission office in Khartoum.

On 28 August, security forces forcibly prevented protesters from demanding the release of women political prisoners in front of Omdurman women's prison. The security services arrested 16 women activists and used tear gas and batons to disperse the protesters.

Three high-profile political leaders were arrested either for expressing their political opinion or for participating in peaceful political activities. On 17 May, Al Sadiq al-Mahdi, the former prime minister and leader of the opposition National Umma Party (NUP), was arrested after he accused the RSF of committing violations and abusing civilians. He was released without charge on 15 June. On 8 June, the leader of the Sudanese Congress Party, Ibrahim Al Sheikh Abdel Rahman, was arrested in Nuhud, North Kordofan following his criticism of the RSF. He was released without charge on 15 September. Mariam Al Sadiq al-Mahdi, deputy leader of NUP, was arrested in Khartoum on 11 August after attending talks in Paris, France, between the NUP and the Sudan Revolutionary Front; she was released without charge a month later.

In an attempt to stop a series of events organized to commemorate the deaths of protesters in September 2013, the NISS pre-emptively arrested over 70 political activists between 17 and 23 September, invoking its powers of "preventive detention". Those arrested were released without charge in early October.

Former detainees reported they were tortured and otherwise ill-treated while in detention.

FREEDOM OF ASSOCIATION

On 23 June, the Ministry of Justice cancelled the registration licence of the Salmmah Women's Resource Centre, a leading women's rights organization in Sudan, and confiscated their assets.

SURINAME

Republic of Suriname
Head of state and government: **Desiré Delano Bouterse**

The trial of President Bouterse and 24 others accused of the extrajudicial killing of 15 political opponents in 1982 failed to restart. Steps were taken towards the abolition of the death penalty.

IMPUNITY

Following a request by the accused, Edgar Ritfeld, in 2013 the Court of Justice ordered the resumption of Edgar Ritfeld's trial in a military court in January 2014. Edgar Ritfeld, who claims he is innocent, is one of 25 people accused of the extrajudicial executions of 15 opponents of the then military government in December 1982. The trial had been halted since 2012 following an amendment to the 1992 amnesty law granting immunity for the alleged torture and extrajudicial executions committed in December 1982. The 25 accused, including current President Desiré Delano "Dési" Bouterse, who was the country's military leader at the time of the killings, were put on trial before a military court in November 2007 for the killings.

Although the Court of Justice decided that the case of Edgar Ritfeld should resume, the military court decided in October not to resume the trial of the 24 others, including the trial of President Bouterse.

In August, families of the 15 people killed in December 1982 filed a case before the Inter-American Commission on Human Rights.

DEATH PENALTY

In May, the Minister for Justice and Police announced an amendment, yet to be presented to Parliament, to the ongoing reform of the Criminal Code aiming to abolish the death penalty and raise the maximum prison sentence from 20 to 30 years. Suriname had not carried out any executions since 1982.

SWAZILAND

Kingdom of Swaziland
Head of state: **King Mswati III**
Head of government: **Barnabas Sibusiso Dlamini**

The crisis in the rule of law and judicial independence deepened. The rights to freedom of expression, association and assembly continued to be violated. Unfair trials resulted in imprisonment for reasons of opinion and conscience.

BACKGROUND

In November Swaziland lost its preferential trade agreement under the African Growth and Opportunity Act (AGOA) with the USA after the government failed to take reform measures, which it had voluntarily undertaken to do in 2013, to address restrictions on freedoms of association, assembly and expression. The benchmarks included amending the Suppression of Terrorism Act, the Public Order Act and the Industrial Relations Act. The loss of preferential access to the US market for textiles led to almost immediate factory closures.

LEGAL DEVELOPMENTS

The rule of law, access to effective remedies and protection of human rights continued to deteriorate as a consequence of the further undermining of judicial independence.

FREEDOM OF ASSOCIATION

The Trade Union Congress of Swaziland (TUCOSWA) remained effectively banned for a third year, with arbitrary arrests conducted against activists for wearing TUCOSWA T-shirts or for attempting to hold meetings.

FREEDOM OF EXPRESSION

Journalists, lawyers, independent-minded judges, trade union officials and parliamentarians were threatened with violence, arrest, prosecution or other forms of pressure as a consequence of their advocacy for human rights, respect for the rule of law or for political reforms.

UNFAIR TRIALS

There was an upsurge in politically motivated trials and the use of laws which violate the principle of legality to suppress dissent.

On 25 July Bheki Makhubu, editor of the monthly news magazine *The Nation*, and human rights lawyer Thulani Maseko were sentenced by the High Court to two years in prison for contempt of court after a grossly unfair trial.[1] The two men were sentenced following their conviction on 17 July on two counts of contempt of court. In addition, *The Nation*, a small independent publication, and Swaziland Independent Publishers were fined 50,000 emalangeni (US$4,273) for each of the two counts, with the total payable within one month.

In March the two men were arrested after *The Nation* published their articles raising concerns about judicial independence and political accountability in Swaziland. The warrant used to arrest them, issued by Swaziland's Chief Justice Michael Ramodibedi, subverted the normal legal process. The police at Mbabane police station, where the men were initially detained prior to their appearance before the Chief Justice, also appeared to have been acting under instructions when they denied the men's lawyers access to them in the police cells. The two men were remanded into custody by the Chief Justice following a brief procedure behind closed doors in his office. In April, they were briefly released, following a ruling by High Court judge Mumcy Dlamini that the warrants used to

arrest them were defective. The Chief Justice immediately lodged an appeal against this ruling, the two men were rearrested and the trial against them began under High Court judge Mpendulo Simelane. The judge had a clear conflict of interest in the matter as he was named in one of the cited articles and intervened as a factual witness during the course of the trial. When sentencing the defendants, Judge Simelane criticized their "disgusting conduct", for running a "defiance campaign" against the administration of justice with "scurrilous" articles and, in respect of Thulani Maseko, for "pursuing regime change". An appeal was lodged by the two men and *The Nation* against the convictions and sentences.

In May, the Supreme Court overturned Bheki Makhubu's previous conviction in 2013 for one of two charges against him arising from an earlier article in *The Nation* on the importance of the judiciary in entrenching respect for the Constitution and improving the lives of the people. The Supreme Court upheld the conviction on the second charge arising from an article concerning the conduct of the country's powerful Chief Justice, but overturned the sentence of two years' imprisonment if the editor failed to pay a fine equivalent to nearly US$45,000 within three days. The Supreme Court judges substituted a fine equivalent of US$3,000 and a suspended sentence of three months' imprisonment conditional on not being convicted of a similar offence.

Activists were also detained and charged in several separate trials involving charges under the Suppression of Terrorism Act (STA) and the Sedition and Subversive Activities Act. The state revived a 2009 sedition charge against Thulani Maseko. His trial on this charge was scheduled to be heard in 2015. A challenge to the constitutionality of the Sedition and Subversive Activities Act, as well as the STA, was also pending in 2015. The challenge was brought by veteran activist and leader of the opposition People's United Democratic Movement (PUDEMO), Mario

Masuku, and eight others facing charges under both laws in three separate trials. The application was due to be heard in the High Court in March 2015.

The trial of Mario Masuku and youth leader Maxwell Dlamini was due to begin in February 2015. They were charged with sedition and remanded in custody in connection with slogans they allegedly shouted at a 2014 May Day rally. There was considerable concern at Mario Masuku's deteriorating health after he was remanded into custody. At the end of October there was a renewed attempt to secure his and Maxwell Dlamini's release on bail. On 31 October the High Court judge scheduled to hear the application was withdrawn. The application was heard and rejected in November by Judge Mpendulo Simelane.

Seven members of PUDEMO, which is banned under the STA, were also facing trial at the end of the year on charges under the STA following their arrest at the High Court during the trial of Thulani Maseko and Bheki Makhubu in April.

WOMEN'S RIGHTS
Despite high levels of gender-based violence, the Sexual Offences and Domestic Violence Bill had not been enacted by the end of the year. The Bill had been under discussion and consideration by parliament since 2006. Women's rights and service-providing organizations appealed for the enactment of the Bill in November.

1. Swaziland: Deplorable sentences against journalist and lawyer stifle
   free speech (News story)
   www.amnesty.org/en/news/swaziland-deplorable-sentences-against-
   journalist-and-lawyer-stifle-free-speech-2014-07-25

SWEDEN

Kingdom of Sweden
Head of state: **King Carl XVI Gustaf**
Head of government: **Stefan Löfven (replaced Fredrik Reinfeldt in October)**

An Egyptian national, who had been subjected to rendition from Sweden to Egypt in 2001, and subsequently tortured, was granted permission to return to Sweden. Investigations into an illegal Swedish police database of Romani people were ongoing. A governmental commission began to review shortcomings in rape investigations and prosecutions.

TORTURE AND OTHER ILL-TREATMENT
In November, the UN Committee against Torture recommended that Sweden adopt a definition of torture into its Criminal Code which was consistent with the UN Convention against Torture.[1] The Committee also called on Sweden to refrain from using diplomatic assurances as a means of returning a person to another country where the person would face a risk of torture.

In April, Egyptian national Mohammed al-Zari was granted a residence permit in Sweden. He was detained with Ahmed Agiza in Sweden in December 2001 and subjected to rendition from Sweden to Egypt on a CIA-leased plane. Both men were subsequently tortured and otherwise ill-treated while being held in Egypt. In 2008, the Chancellor of Justice awarded both men financial compensation for the human rights violations they suffered. Mohammed al-Zari was released from prison in October 2003 without having been charged with any crime. The award of a residence permit partially fulfilled his right to redress for the human rights violations he suffered. However, an effective, independent investigation into these violations remained outstanding.

DISCRIMINATION

In September 2013, the CERD Committee expressed concern about racially motivated hate speech against visible minorities, and called on Sweden to effectively investigate, prosecute and punish all hate crimes. The Committee also raised concerns about racist and extremist organizations continuing to function in Sweden.

On the same day that the CERD Committee raised concerns about discrimination against Roma, a Swedish newspaper revealed that the Skåne police department was operating an illegal database, named Travellers or Nomads (*Kringresande*), containing details of about 4,000 Romani people, for no apparent reason other than their ethnicity.[2] Local and national authorities apologized publicly following the revelations. The matter was subsequently investigated by Sweden's Commission on Security and Integrity Protection (*Säkerhets - och integritetsskyddsnämnden*) and the National Police-related Crimes Unit (*Riksenheten för polismål*), as well as internally by the National Police Board (*Rikspolisstyrelsen*), the latter of which found no illegality. The matter was under investigation by the Justice Ombudsman, whose findings were expected in November.

VIOLENCE AGAINST WOMEN AND GIRLS

In August, following an initiative by the parliamentary Committee on Justice, the government announced that it would set up a commission to examine how rape investigations are dealt with by the police and justice system. The aim was to analyze high rates of attrition in investigating and prosecuting reported rapes, and to recommend improvements to the legal process in rape cases. The commission is expected to review the penal provisions on the offence of rape and to consider a requirement for genuine consent.

1. Sweden: Submission to the United Nations Committee against Torture: 53rd Session (EUR 42/001/2014)
   www.amnesty.org/en/library/info/EUR42/001/2014/en
2. Sweden: Skåne police database violates human rights of Romanis (EUR 42/001/2013)
   www.amnesty.org/en/library/info/EUR42/001/2013/en

SWITZERLAND

Swiss Confederation
Head of state and government: **Didier Burkhalter**

The Swiss National Commission for the Prevention of Torture (NCPT) and NGOs continued to raise concern about the use of force during deportations. "Popular initiatives" that were incompatible with international law were left unimplemented.

DISCRIMINATION

In March, the UN CERD Committee recommended that the government introduce a clear and comprehensive definition of direct and indirect racial discrimination covering all fields of law. The Committee further called on the government to establish effective data collection on discrimination and to take measures to prevent targeting of individuals for identity checks, searches and other police operations on the grounds of race and ethnicity.

In November, the Administrative Court in the canton of St Gallen ruled that a school's ban on a Muslim student wearing a headscarf was disproportionate.

In September 2013, residents of the canton of Ticino had voted to ban the wearing of the full face veil. The ban cannot enter into force without the approval of the Federal Parliament.

REFUGEES AND ASYLUM-SEEKERS

The NCPT and domestic NGOs continued to raise concerns about the treatment of asylum-seekers, including violations of the *non-refoulement* principle and the use of force during removals.

The NCPT continued to observe and document disproportionate use of force and restraints during the transfer of people facing deportation from detention centres to the airport. To tackle varying practices by different police forces, the NCPT called for uniform practice and national regulation to be introduced by the Conference of Cantonal Directors of Justice and Police. The NCPT also called for greater respect for the principle of the best interests of the child, in response to the ongoing practice of temporarily separating children from their parents during forced returns.

In May, the Federal Office for Migration (FOM) made public the recommendations of internal and external reviews, following the arrests in Sri Lanka in July and August 2013 of two Tamil asylum-seekers forcibly returned from Switzerland. The two men were detained for several months by Sri Lankan authorities and transferred to a "rehabilitation" camp. In September 2013, following concerns raised by NGOs, the FOM had temporarily halted forced returns to Sri Lanka pending the outcome of the reviews. After a further fact-finding mission to Sri Lanka by Swiss authorities, the FOM announced in May that it would review the cases of Sri Lankan asylum-seekers whose applications had received a final rejection, and resume removals to Sri Lanka.

PRISON CONDITIONS

On 26 February, the Swiss Federal Court ruled that two prisoners being held in Champ-Dollon prison, in Geneva, were subject to inhumane conditions that breached Article 3 of the European Convention on Human Rights. The two prisoners were held consecutively for three months, confined for 23 hours per day with four other detainees in a cell measuring 23 square meters designed for three detainees, without access to any activities. The NCPT and Swiss NGOs repeatedly raised concerns about overcrowding in Champ-Dollon prison, which as of November held 811 persons in a space designed to accommodate 376. Disturbances at the prison in February resulted in injuries to eight guards and around 30 prisoners.

LEGISLATIVE, CONSTITUTIONAL OR INSTITUTIONAL DEVELOPMENTS

In March, the CERD Committee recommended establishing an independent mechanism to ensure that "popular initiatives" do not lead to laws that are incompatible with Switzerland's obligations under international human rights law. Several "popular initiatives" or referendums put forward by the Swiss People's Party were not implemented due to their incompatibility with international law, including the referendum known as the "Deportation initiative", passed in 2010. This referendum had called for a constitutional amendment to allow the automatic deportation of foreign nationals convicted of specified criminal offences. Similarly, the "Mass immigration initiative", which sought to introduce an arbitrary annual immigration quota, also remained unimplemented.

SYRIA

Syrian Arab Republic
Head of state: **Bashar al-Assad**
Head of government: **Wael Nader al-Halqi**

Syria's internal armed conflict continued relentlessly through the year and saw both government forces and non-state armed groups commit extensive war crimes and gross human rights abuses with impunity. Government forces deliberately targeted civilians, indiscriminately bombarding civilian residential areas and medical facilities with artillery, mortars, barrel bombs and chemical agents, unlawfully killing civilians. Government forces also enforced lengthy sieges, trapping civilians and depriving them of food, medical care and other necessitiès. Security forces arbitrarily arrested or continued to detain thousands, including peaceful activists, human rights defenders, media and humanitarian workers, and children, subjecting some to enforced disappearance and others to prolonged detention or unfair trials. Security forces systematically tortured and otherwise ill-treated detainees with impunity; thousands of detainees reportedly died due to torture or harsh conditions. Non-state armed groups, which controlled some areas and contested others, indiscriminately shelled and besieged areas containing civilians perceived to support the government. Some, particularly the Islamic State (IS, formerly known as ISIS) armed group, carried out indiscriminate suicide attacks and other bombings in civilian areas, and perpetrated numerous unlawful killings, including summary killings of captives and suspected opponents.

BACKGROUND

Fighting between government and disparate non-state armed groups continued to rage across Syria throughout the year, killing and injuring thousands and causing further mass population displacement and refugee outflows, particularly to Turkey, Lebanon, Jordan, Egypt and the Kurdistan Region of Iraq. By the end of the year, the conflict had caused a total of around 200,000 deaths, according to the UN. In addition, 7.6 million people were internally displaced and approximately 4 million had become refugees in other countries.

International efforts to resolve the armed conflict saw the UN, with support from the USA and Russia, convene the Geneva II conference in January. It was attended by representatives of the Syrian government and the opposition Syrian National Coalition, but not by armed groups outside the Syrian National Coalition's military command. The talks concluded in February without any agreement.

The UN Security Council remained divided on the issue, undermining efforts to pursue a peace agreement, but adopted a series of resolutions on the crisis. Resolution 2139 in February addressed the conduct of hostilities and arbitrary detentions, and demanded that all parties to the conflict allow humanitarian access across conflict lines and to besieged areas; however, they failed to do so. Resolution 2165 in July focused on the delivery of international humanitarian aid to besieged areas and across national borders. In August, resolution 2170 condemned unlawful killings, other gross abuses and recruitment of foreign fighters by the armed groups IS and Jabhat al-Nusra, and added six individuals affiliated with them to the UN al-Qa'ida Sanctions List. The UN Security Council failed to adopt other measures to address impunity in Syria. Russia and China vetoed a draft resolution to refer the situation in Syria to the Prosecutor of the International Criminal Court.

The independent international Commission of Inquiry on the Syrian Arab Republic, established by the UN Human Rights Council in 2011, continued to monitor and report on violations of international law committed by the parties to the conflict. However, it remained barred by the government from entering Syria.

In June, the Organization for the Prohibition of Chemical Weapons (OPCW) reported that the government had completed the handover of its chemical weapons stockpile for international destruction, in accordance with a September 2013 agreement with the US and Russian governments.

In September, a US-led international coalition began air strikes against IS and other armed groups in northern Syria. According to the UN Security Council, the air strikes killed some 50 civilians.

In June, President al-Assad won presidential elections held only in government-controlled areas, and returned to office for a third seven-year term. The following week, he announced an amnesty, which resulted in few prisoner releases; the vast majority of prisoners of conscience and other political prisoners held by the government continued to be detained.

INTERNAL ARMED CONFLICT – VIOLATIONS BY GOVERNMENT FORCES
Use of indiscriminate and prohibited weapons
Government forces mounted attacks on areas controlled or contested by armed opposition forces and committed unlawful killings of civilians; some attacks amounted to war crimes or crimes against humanity. Government forces repeatedly carried out both direct and indiscriminate attacks, including air strikes and artillery shelling of civilian residential areas, often using barrel bombs – high explosive unguided weapons dropped from helicopters – causing numerous civilian deaths and injuries, including of children. Despite the demand of UN Security Council resolution 2139 that all parties to the conflict end indiscriminate attacks, in the 10 months following the resolution's adoption, government forces killed almost 8,000 civilians in shelling and other indiscriminate attacks, according to the Violations Documentation Centre, a local monitoring NGO. In one incident on 29 October, government helicopters dropped four barrel bombs on a camp for displaced people in Idleb, killing at least 10 civilians and wounding dozens, according to the Syrian Observatory for Human Rights.

Government forces carried out several attacks using barrel bombs or other munitions containing chlorine, despite such munitions being prohibited under international law. Attacks using such munitions included those in April on the towns of Kafar Zeita, al-Tamana'a and Tal Minnis, according to the

UN's Commission of Inquiry. A fact-finding investigation by the OPCW confirmed in September that government forces had used chlorine "systematically and repeatedly" in these attacks. Government forces also used cluster munitions, indiscriminate weapons that deploy incendiary bomblets over a wide area exposing victims to serious, often fatal, burns.

Sieges and denial of humanitarian access
Government forces maintained long-running sieges of civilian areas in and around Damascus, including Yarmouk, Daraya and Eastern Ghouta, and elsewhere, including the Old City of Homs siege which ended in May. Armed opposition fighters were usually present in besieged areas and sometimes also posed a threat to civilians. Civilians trapped within the besieged areas faced starvation, lack of medical care and basic services, and were repeatedly exposed to artillery shelling, bombing from the air and sniper fire from government soldiers. In March, government soldiers fired on civilians who had sought to leave Eastern Ghouta under a white flag, killing women, men and children. Yarmouk, a Damascus suburb containing around 18,000 of the over 180,000 Palestinian refugees and Syrians who had lived there prior to the conflict, entered a third year of continuous siege in December. Despite a truce agreed in June, government forces continued to cut off food and water supplies and block some international humanitarian aid. When they allowed civilian evacuations from besieged areas, government forces detained men and boys among those evacuated, subjecting many to long-term detention for "screening".

Attacks on medical facilities and workers
Government forces continued to target health facilities and medical workers in areas controlled by armed groups. They bombed hospitals, barred the provision of medical supplies in humanitarian aid shipments to besieged areas, and arrested and detained medical workers and volunteers, apparently to disrupt and deny basic health care services in those areas. Physicians for Human Rights

accused government forces of systematically attacking the health care system in areas controlled by opposition groups and of having killed 569 health professionals between April 2011 and October 2014.

INTERNAL ARMED CONFLICT – ABUSES BY ARMED GROUPS

Non-state armed groups also committed war crimes and gross abuses of human rights. These included IS and Jabhat al-Nusra, both of which used foreign fighters, and groups that formed part of or were affiliated to the Free Syrian Army.

Use of indiscriminate weapons

Armed groups used indiscriminate weapons, including mortars, tank and artillery shells, during attacks on government-held civilian areas, causing many civilian casualties. In April and May, armed groups that attacked the Saif al-Dawla, al-Midan and al-Sulimaniya neighbourhoods in western Aleppo reportedly fired mortar shells and improvised gas-canister explosives into civilian areas. Jabhat al-Nusra carried out suicide car and lorry bombings in government-controlled areas, including Homs, killing and injuring civilians.

Unlawful killings

IS forces, in particular, committed unlawful killings of captured government soldiers, abducted civilians, including peaceful activists and media workers, foreigners and, reportedly, members of rival armed groups. In the al-Raqqa and eastern Aleppo areas, which IS controlled and subjected to its strict interpretation of Islamic law, IS members carried out frequent public executions; victims were first denounced, then shot or beheaded in front of crowds that often contained children. Most victims were men, but they also reportedly included boys as young as 15 and women.

IS forces publicized some of their crimes for propaganda purposes or to make demands, posting videos on the internet showing them beheading captives, including Syrian, Lebanese and Kurdish soldiers, and American and British journalists and aid workers who had been abducted by armed groups and transferred or "sold" to IS. In some cases, the beheading videos included threats to kill other captives.

Sieges, denial of humanitarian access and attacks on medical facilities and workers

IS, Jabhat al-Nusra and other armed groups jointly or separately laid siege to several government-held areas, including Zahraa and Nobel, northwest of Aleppo, as well as the area around Aleppo Central Prison until government forces broke that year-long siege in May. They shelled some areas indiscriminately, cut off food, water and other supplies to the civilian inhabitants, interfered with or prevented the distribution of humanitarian aid, and attacked and detained medical workers.

Abductions

Armed groups were responsible for numerous abductions and detentions of local activists, suspected government supporters, foreign journalists and aid workers, and others, subjecting many to torture or other ill-treatment and some to unlawful summary executions. Those held included children; in May, for example, IS forces abducted over 150 Kurdish boys from Manbej, between Aleppo and Kobani, subjecting some to torture. All had been released by October.

Kurdish areas

In northern Syria, the Democratic Union Party (PYD) largely controlled three predominantly Kurdish enclaves – 'Afrin, Kobani (also known as Ayn al-Arab) and Jazeera – following the withdrawal of government troops in 2012, until IS forces again attacked Kobani mid-year, causing massive forced displacement. In January, the PYD issued a new constitution for the three areas, where it had established a functioning justice system based on so-called Peoples' Courts. After visiting the area in February, Human Rights Watch urged the PYD authorities to stop arbitrary detentions, cease the use of children as soldiers and to man checkpoints, improve safeguards against detainee abuse, and investigate a spate of abductions and apparent political killings.

In July, the PYD demobilized 149 children from their armed ranks and committed to preventing children from taking part in hostilities.

REFUGEES AND INTERNALLY DISPLACED PEOPLE

Fighting across Syria continued to cause massive forced displacement of civilians. Approximately 4 million refugees fled from Syria between 2011 and the end of 2014, while the UN Office for the Coordination of Humanitarian Affairs reported that another 7.6 million people, half of them children, were internally displaced within Syria, an increase of more than 1 million since December 2013. In September, a renewed attack by IS forces on Kobani caused a massive refugee outflow, with tens of thousands of inhabitants crossing into Turkey in the space of a few days. In both Lebanon and Jordan, authorities limited the number of refugees entering from Syria, exposing those waiting in border areas to further attacks and deprivation, and continued to block the entry of Palestinian refugees from Syria, rendering them especially vulnerable.

ENFORCED DISAPPEARANCES

Government security forces continued to hold thousands of uncharged detainees in prolonged pre-trial detention, many in conditions that amounted to enforced disappearance.

Many prisoners arrested in previous years remained forcibly disappeared, amid concerns for their safety. The authorities rarely disclosed information about detainees and frequently denied them access to lawyers and their families.

Those who remained disappeared included entire families, among them married couple Abdulrahman Yasin and Rania Alabbasi, their six children aged between three and 15, and another woman who was present when security forces detained them at their home in March 2013. The authorities disclosed no information about them but a former detainee reported seeing Rania Alabbasi and her children in a Military Intelligence facility known as Branch 291.

Human rights lawyer Khalil Ma'touq and his friend Mohamed Thatha remained victims of enforced disappearance at the end of the year, after security forces detained them at a checkpoint near Damascus on 2 October 2013. The authorities did not confirm their arrest or disclose why or where they were being held, raising concerns for their safety.

Juwan Abd Rahman Khaled, a Kurdish rights activist, was also a victim of continued enforced disappearance. He was detained by State Security officials who raided the Wadi al-Mashari'a district of Damascus in the early hours of 3 September 2012. A former political detainee and victim of torture, his whereabouts and fate remained undisclosed at the end of 2014.

DEATHS IN CUSTODY

Torture and other ill-treatment of detainees being held by Political Security, Military Intelligence, Air Force Intelligence and other government security and intelligence branches remained systematic and widespread. Torture reportedly continued to result in a high incidence of detainee deaths.

In January, a group of forensic experts and former international war crimes prosecutors examined photographs taken at military hospitals of thousands of corpses of prisoners and reported that the Syrian authorities had engaged in systematic torture and unlawful killings of detainees. The government denied the experts' claim but failed to conduct an independent investigation amid continuing reports of torture and detainees' deaths during the year.

Many detainees were also reported to have died due to harsh conditions at various detention facilities. These included Military Intelligence Branch 235, also known as the "Palestine Branch". One released detainee reported that many detainees at Branch 235 had scabies or other skin ailments and digestive illnesses due to severe overcrowding, inadequate sanitation, and a lack of food, clean drinking water and medical care. Often, detainees' families were not officially informed of their deaths; in other cases, families were told that detainees had died of heart attacks, but were denied access to their bodies, which were not returned to them for burial.

In October, a UK inquest jury ruled that British medical doctor Abbas Khan was unlawfully killed in Syrian detention in December 2013, contradicting a Syrian government finding that he had committed suicide. Security forces had arrested Dr Khan in November 2012 within 48 hours of his arrival as a medical volunteer in Syria; he was reported to have been tortured and otherwise ill-treated during months in detention.

UNFAIR TRIALS

After often lengthy periods of pre-trial detention, scores of perceived government critics and peaceful opponents were prosecuted before the Anti-Terrorism Court, established in 2012, and Military Field Courts, where they did not receive fair trials. Some defendants tried by the Anti-Terrorism Court faced charges based on their legitimate exercise of freedom of expression or other rights. Defendants before Military Field Courts, many of whom were civilians, had no right to legal representation and faced judges who were serving military officers. They also had no opportunity to appeal their sentences.

Faten Rajab Fawaz, a physicist and peaceful pro-reform activist arrested by Air Force Intelligence officials in December 2011 in Damascus, was reported in September to be facing trial before a Military Field Court on undisclosed charges. Following her arrest, she was held at several detention facilities, sometimes in solitary confinement for months at a time, and reportedly tortured and otherwise ill-treated.

Mazen Darwish, Hani al-Zitani and Hussein Gharir, activists from the independent Syrian Center for Media and Freedom of Expression (SCM), faced charges of "publicizing terrorist acts" and possible 15-year prison terms. They were arrested when Air Force Intelligence officials raided the SCM's Damascus office in February 2012. Their trial before the Anti-Terrorism Court was adjourned continuously since February 2013; the outcome of their case remained unknown at the end of 2014.

Gebrail Moushe Kourie, president of the unauthorized political party Assyrian Democratic Organization, was arrested in December 2013 in Qamishly in northern Syria. After months of detention in facilities where torture was rife, he was charged with belonging to "an unlicensed secret political party" and "incitement of violence to topple the government" before a criminal court judge who referred him for trial by the Anti-Terrorism Court.

DEATH PENALTY

The death penalty remained in force for a wide range of offences. No information was available on death sentences handed down or executions carried out during the year.

TAIWAN

Taiwan
Head of state: **Ma Ying-jeou**
Head of government: **Ma Chi-kuo (replaced Jiang Yi-huah in December)**

While Taiwan took further steps to implement international human rights standards, serious concerns remained. Notable among these were the right to freedom of peaceful assembly, the death penalty, torture and other ill-treatment, housing and land rights, and gender discrimination.

INTERNATIONAL SCRUTINY

International groups of independent experts reviewed national reports on the implementation of the ICCPR and ICESCR in February 2013 and CEDAW in June 2014. In September the government pledged to amend 228 laws and regulations to comply with CEDAW. Laws were enacted to implement the Convention on the Rights of the Child and the Convention on the Rights of Persons with Disabilities by 2017.

FREEDOM OF ASSEMBLY

From 18 March to 10 April, hundreds of students and other activists occupied the Legislative Yuan (Parliament) to protest against a trade deal with China.[1] On 23 March, a group of protesters forced their way into the Executive Yuan (Cabinet) complex, and a crowd gathered in the surrounding areas. The police used excessive force while dispersing them. To date there has been no independent and impartial investigation into the police conduct.

Over several subsequent months, over 200 protesters were summoned for questioning under the Criminal Code and Assembly and Parade Act; they remained under threat of prosecution. At least 46 people who suffered injuries during the protests filed a series of private criminal lawsuits against the Premier and high-ranking police officers. By the end of the year, however, courts had declined to hear two of these cases on the grounds that they were too similar to one already under court review.

DEATH PENALTY

Little progress was made towards the abolition of the death penalty as Taiwan continued to impose death sentences and carry out executions.[2] In June the death sentence was abolished for two crimes related to kidnapping, but 55 offences remained punishable by death.

TORTURE AND OTHER ILL-TREATMENT

In January, Taiwan abolished its military court system during peacetime, including military prisons. This followed the death of Corporal Hung Chung-chiu in a military disciplinary

detention facility in July 2013.[3] In March, a civilian court of first instance convicted 13 military officers of Hung Chung-chiu's death, sentencing them to between three and eight months' imprisonment; five others were acquitted.

PRISON CONDITIONS

Overcrowding, unsanitary conditions and lack of adequate medical care remained serious problems in prisons and detention centres. An amendment to the Prison Camp Act, aimed at addressing prison overcrowding by expanding the use of minimum security prisons, was enacted in June.

HOUSING RIGHTS – FORCED EVICTIONS

Conflicts over housing and land rights continued to increase due to rising land prices and economic inequality. In July, the land expropriation for the Taoyuan Aerotropolis project, affecting an estimated 46,000 people, passed a key planning hurdle, despite concerns of inadequate consultation with residents as well as the indictment of a key official for related corruption.

Indigenous Peoples' rights

Concerns were raised about the use of traditional lands of Indigenous Peoples for tourism-related development.

RIGHTS OF LESBIAN, GAY, BISEXUAL, TRANSGENDER AND INTERSEX PEOPLE

Amendments to the Civil Code that would enshrine marriage equality stalled in the Legislative Yuan.

The Ministry of Interior failed to put into effect the Ministry of Health's recommendation that genital surgery and psychiatric evaluation should no longer be needed to change one's gender.

---

1. Taiwan: Restraint urged in protests over China trade deal (Press release)
www.amnesty.org.uk/press-releases/taiwan-restraint-urged-protests-over-china-trade-deal

2. Taiwan: Amnesty International condemns the execution of five people
   (ASA 38/002/2014)
   www.amnesty.org/en/library/info/ASA38/002/2014/en
3. Taiwan government must ensure the reform of military criminal
   procedure legislation lives up to its promise of greater accountability
   (ASA 38/001/2014)
   www.amnesty.org/en/library/info/ASA38/001/2014/en

TAJIKISTAN

Republic of Tajikistan
Head of state: **Emomali Rahmon**
Head of government: **Qokhir Rasulzoda**

Torture and other ill-treatment of detainees
remained pervasive and impunity for crimes
of torture continued. The government
imposed further restrictions on the rights
to freedom of expression, association
and assembly.

BACKGROUND

Emomali Rahmon was re-elected as President
for a fourth term in November 2013 with
84.32% of the vote.

In May, three people were killed and five
injured when a police operation in Khorog,
Gorno-Badakhshan Autonomous Region
(GBAO), led to clashes between security
forces and residents. An investigation into the
incident was reported to be ongoing at the
end of the year. There was still no effective
investigation into the clashes in Khorog in July
2012, in which dozens of people and at least
22 civilians were killed. Reliable information
about the number of victims was still lacking.

TORTURE AND OTHER ILL-TREATMENT

Torture and other ill-treatment remained
widespread despite the adoption of an Action
Plan to implement recommendations by the
UN Committee against Torture in 2013.

Tajikistani NGOs documented 24 cases
of torture between 1 December 2013 and 8

October 2014. However, most relatives and
victims declined to pursue complaints for fear
of reprisals. Many more cases of torture were
likely to have gone unreported.

Criminal prosecutions against law
enforcement officials suspected of torture
were rare, and frequently terminated or
suspended before completion. By the
end of the year, only four security officers
had been convicted of torture since its
criminalization in 2012. Two of them were
given suspended sentences.

In April, the investigation into allegations
involving two officials suspected of torturing
Ismonboy Boboev (who died in custody
in February 2010) was suspended again,
reportedly due to the poor health of one of
the suspects.

Tajikistan failed to implement decisions by
UN bodies on individual cases. In June 2013,
the UN Working Group on Arbitrary Detention
urged the release of Ilhom Ismonov, who
had been arbitrarily detained, tortured and
forced to sign a false confession in November
2010. He remained in detention at the end of
the year.

Lawyers were repeatedly denied access
to their clients in detention, often for days
at a time. This was particularly common
in facilities run by the State Committee for
National Security.

Individuals perceived to be threats to
national security, including members of
religious movements and Islamist groups
or parties, were at particular risk of
incommunicado detention, torture and other
ill-treatment.

Umed Tojiev, a member of the opposition
Islamic Renaissance Party (IRP), died
in hospital on 19 January. He had been
arrested by police on 30 October 2013 in
Sughd region, and charged on 4 November
2013 with organizing a criminal group, but
was denied access to his lawyer until 13
November 2013. His family claimed he was
subjected to suffocation, sleep and food
deprivation and electric shocks. He jumped
out of the Sughd police station window on 5

November 2013, breaking both his legs, but was not provided with adequate medical care until 4 January. His death, suspected to be due to criminal negligence, was still under investigation at the end of the year.

PRISON CONDITIONS

In February a monitoring group on detention facilities established by the Human Rights Ombudsman began its work. The group included civil society representatives. However, in some cases NGO representatives were arbitrarily denied access to detention facilities.

FREEDOM OF EXPRESSION

Politicians, civil society activists and journalists were harassed for criticizing the government.

In 2013-2014, some 15 lawsuits were brought against journalists and media outlets, including on charges of defamation and, in one case, criminal fraud.

In February, journalist Olga Tutubalina and newspaper *Asia Plus* were ordered by a court to pay TJS 30,000 (US$6,300) in damages to three plaintiffs for their "physical and mental suffering" in connection with an article published in 2013 which spoke unfavourably of the "intelligentsia" and in which none of the plaintiffs was mentioned.

Access to dozens of popular internet resources, including news websites and social media, was temporarily blocked on multiple occasions during the year. Reportedly, internet providers did so under direct orders from the state regulator Communications Service.

Reports abounded of politically motivated harassment of opposition political leaders. IRP members were particularly targeted. In July 2013 the UN Human Rights Committee expressed concern about the detention of Zayd Saidov, the leader of the opposition movement New Tajikistan. He was sentenced in December 2013 to 26 years in prison. In October 2014, the Supreme Court banned the Group 24 opposition movement, declaring it "extremist".

On 16 June, Alexander Sodiqov, a Tajikistani national studying for a PhD in Canada, was detained in Khorog while interviewing the deputy head of the opposition Social Democratic party of GBAO as part of his research on post-conflict. He was accused of spying and remained incommunicado for three days. On 19 June, the head of the State Committee for National Security, Saimumin Yatimov, stated in a thinly veiled reference to his case, that foreign spies were operating in Tajikistan under the guise of NGOs and trying to undermine national security. Alexander Sodiqov was a prisoner of conscience. He was released on bail on 22 July and allowed to travel to Canada on 10 September to continue his studies.

FREEDOM OF ASSOCIATION

Human rights and other NGOs continued to operate in an insecure environment and faced pressure from the authorities. Unscheduled inspections of NGOs increased, sometimes followed by legal actions for alleged infringements of the law.

On 24 June, the Constitutional Court considered a submission by the Association of Young Lawyers "Amparo" regarding discrepancies between the law "On Public Associations" and the Constitution. The Court concluded that the law lacked clarity on the grounds for closure of associations and recommended that it be amended by parliament. Amparo had been closed down by the authorities in October 2012 for a minor technical transgression. Its appeals against this decision were unsuccessful.

TANZANIA

United Republic of Tanzania
Head of state: **Jakaya Mrisho Kikwete**
Head of government: **Mizengo Peter Pinda**
Head of Zanzibar government: **Ali Mohamed Shein**

The constitutional review process continued, although challenges threatened to hinder the process. A Commission of Inquiry was established to investigate human rights abuses including at least 13 killings committed by security agencies during an anti-poaching operation conducted in October 2013. People with albinism remained at risk of being killed for their body parts and violence against women continued with impunity.

CONSTITUTIONAL DEVELOPMENTS

In February 2014, the Constituent Assembly was inaugurated to discuss the draft Constitution proposed by the Constitutional Review Committee. Proceedings suffered a setback in April when a coalition of opposition parties walked out in protest, accusing the ruling party of interfering with the process. In October, the Constituent Assembly adopted the draft Constitution amid claims by the opposition and civil society groups that the voting process was irregular. President Kikwete announced that the constitutional referendum would take place in April 2015 despite a September agreement by all political parties to postpone it until after the 2015 elections.

EXCESSIVE USE OF FORCE

In October 2013, security agencies including the armed forces used excessive force against civilians in an anti-poaching operation called Operation Tokomeza. At least 13 civilians were killed and many more suffered serious injuries. There were also reports of torture, including rape, destruction of property and killing of livestock by security agencies during the operation. In June 2014, President Kikwete, on the recommendation of Parliament, established a Commission of Inquiry with a three-month mandate to investigate human rights abuses committed during Operation Tokomeza. The Commission of Inquiry started its work in mid-August by visiting victims in affected regions. The Commission had not completed its investigations by the end of the year.

DISCRIMINATION – ATTACKS ON PEOPLE WITH ALBINISM

There was one report of an albino person who was killed for his body parts. At least five attempted killings were reported. In one such case, a man was killed as he defended his spouse. The government's efforts to prevent human rights abuses against people with albinism remained inadequate.

INTERNATIONAL SCRUTINY

In June 2014, the African Court on Human and Peoples' Rights found that Tanzania had violated the African Charter on Human and Peoples' Rights by prohibiting individuals from contesting presidential and parliamentary elections unless sponsored by a political party. The Court directed Tanzania to take constitutional and legislative measures to remedy the violation, publish a summary of the judgment within six months in both English and Kiswahili languages, and to publish the entire judgment on the government's website for one year. By the end of the year, Tanzania had not reported to the African Court on the measures taken to comply with the judgment.

VIOLENCE AGAINST WOMEN AND GIRLS

Sexual and other forms of gender-based violence, particularly domestic violence, remained widespread. In the towns of Mbeya and Geita alone, domestic violence resulted in the deaths of 26 and 27 women respectively during the first half of the year.

THAILAND

Kingdom of Thailand
Head of state: **King Bhumibol Adulyadej**
Head of government: **Prayuth Chan-ocha (replaced Niwattumrong Boonsongpaisan in May, who replaced Yingluck Shinawatra in May)**

Political tensions prevailed through the year and human rights protection weakened. Armed violence continued in the southern border provinces. Freedoms of expression, association and peaceful assembly were severely restricted, leading to the arbitrary arrest of many individuals, some of whom became prisoners of conscience.

BACKGROUND

Political deadlock between the government and demonstrators dominated the first five months of the year. The military staged a coup in May. Martial law remained in place at the end of the year.

The People's Democratic Reform Committee (PDRC), headed by the former Democrat Deputy Prime Minister, led mass demonstrations calling for the government to be replaced by a people's council to implement political reforms. In March the Constitutional Court ruled the February snap elections invalid. The Electoral Commission postponed polls scheduled for July on the basis of ongoing political violence. The opposition Democrat Party had boycotted polls in February and PDRC protesters impeded thousands of voters from casting votes by blockading polling stations. In May the Constitutional Court ordered Prime Minister Yingluck Shinawatra to step down, and the National Anti-Corruption Commission voted for her impeachment the following day.

On 20 May, the Commander-in-Chief of the armed forces invoked martial law and seized control of the country in a military coup on 22 May, suspending all but a few provisions in the 2007 Constitution. The coup leaders formed the National Council for Peace and Order (NCPO) and announced a reform process and road map, with no clear date for elections. After the promulgation of an interim Constitution in July, the NCPO selected a legislature, which elected NCPO leader General Prayuth Chan-ocha as Prime Minister in August.[1]

INTERNAL ARMED CONFLICT

Armed violence continued in the three southern provinces of Pattani, Yala, Narathiwat and parts of Songkhla.

Security forces were implicated in unlawful killings, and torture and other ill-treatment. In November the authorities announced the provision of 2,700 semi-automatic assault rifles to civilian paramilitary rangers.

Attacks targeting civilians were believed to have been carried out by armed groups through the year, including the bombing of public places. Forty-two members of the civilian administration and nine government teachers were among 162 civilians killed. In a number of instances assailants mutilated the corpses by burning and beheading them. Notes left at the scene in a number of attacks presented the killings as acts of retaliation for killings and arrests by government or paramilitary forces. In November banners were put up in all three provinces, criticizing official policies and threatening further killings of Buddhist civilians, bureaucrats and teachers. In October six schools in Pattani province were destroyed in arson attacks.

Two state-sponsored paramilitary rangers admitted killing three ethnic Malay-Muslim boys aged six, nine and 11, and wounding their father and pregnant mother, in an attack on the family's home in Bacho, Narathiwat, in February. One of the rangers said he carried out the attack because of the lack of progress on investigations into the murder of his brother and sister-in-law in August 2013, in which the children's father, a suspected insurgent, was implicated.

Between January and May, sporadic clashes between supporters of the government and the PDRC, and targeted attacks on demonstrations with weapons and explosive devices, led to the deaths of 28 people and injuries to 825 others.[2] Targeted attacks by unidentified individuals on prominent politicians and commentators from both sides were also carried out.

Suthin Tarathin, a prominent anti-government protester, was shot dead on 26 January while marching with anti-government protesters to prevent advance voting in the Bang Na district of the capital, Bangkok.

The house of Somsak Jeamteerasakul, a history professor and prominent commentator on Thailand's lese-majesty law, was attacked by unknown assailants who fired gunshots and threw homemade bombs at his home and car on 12 February.

TORTURE AND OTHER ILL-TREATMENT

Allegations of torture and other ill-treatment by police and armed forces continued throughout the year, including during incommunicado detention under martial law provisions and by PDRC guards at political demonstrations during the first half of the year.

A bill criminalizing torture and enforced disappearances remained in draft form at the end of the year.

The UN Committee against Torture expressed concern in May at the consistent and widespread allegations of torture and other ill-treatment in the country and inadequate provisions for redress.[3]

On 24 February, security guard Yuem Nillar said he was detained at a protest site for five days, tied up, denied food and beaten by two PDRC guards before being thrown into a river.

In February the relatives of a soldier beaten to death while attending a military training camp in 2011 agreed a compensation settlement of approximately 7 million baht (some US$215,000). Private Wichean Puaksom died as a result of torture after taking leave without authorization.

ENFORCED DISAPPEARANCES

In April, environmental activist Pholachi Rakchongcharoen was believed to have been subjected to enforced disappearance by officials in connection with his activities to seek redress for human rights violations in Kaengkrachan National Park, Petchaburi Province. He was last seen on 17 April after being detained and held in custody by the National Park Chief and three other park officials.

FREEDOMS OF EXPRESSION AND ASSEMBLY

Martial law orders imposed after the May coup remained in place at the end of the year. Freedoms of peaceful assembly and expression were heavily restricted, including a ban on "political" gatherings of more than five people. Following the coup, authorities blocked and shut down websites and community radio stations for weeks or months, and issued orders censoring media criticism of the NCPO.

Protesters were prosecuted in military courts for peaceful acts of protest in the weeks following the coup, including holding up a three-finger salute popularized in the *Hunger Games* films. Arrests of peaceful dissenters continued through the year. Officials continued to restrict and cancel private, public and academic meetings and seminars following the coup, including by arresting participants and requiring individuals and organizations to seek official approval in advance.

ARBITRARY ARRESTS AND DETENTIONS

Hundreds were subjected to arbitrary arrest and detention under martial law powers, including politicians, academics, journalists and activists. The majority were held for up to seven days without charge or trial after being publicly ordered to report to military authorities. Many were convicted of criminal offences for failing to report. The majority of those summoned were required to sign undertakings not to engage in political activities as a condition of release. At the end of the year officials continued to require individuals, including students, lawyers and civil society activists, to report to them privately and to sign such undertakings.

Arrests, prosecutions and imprisonment for acts of peaceful expression criminalized under Article 112 of the Penal Code – Thailand's abusive lese-majesty law – dramatically increased after the May coup; there were at least 28 new arrests and eight convictions. Lese-majesty detainees were consistently denied bail in pre-trial detention and during appeals after conviction.[4]

Pornthip Mankong and Patiwat Saraiyam were detained in August and charged with lese-majesty for organizing and acting in a play at Thammasat University in October 2013.

UNFAIR TRIALS

The NCPO expanded the jurisdiction of military courts to allow civilians to be prosecuted for disobeying the orders of the NCPO, offences against the monarchy, and internal security. No right of appeal was allowed.

IMPUNITY

No significant progress was made in addressing widespread official impunity for human rights violations.[5] The Interim Constitution proclaimed in July provided immunity to the NCPO and its agents from criminal responsibility for human rights violations.

On 28 August, the Criminal Court dismissed murder charges against former Prime Minister Abhisit Vejjajiva and his deputy, Suthep Thaugsuban, for the deaths of protesters during 2010. The Court ruled it had no jurisdiction over the case.

HUMAN RIGHTS DEFENDERS

Sweeping restrictions on freedom of expression and other human rights under martial law severely limited the work of human rights defenders. Many faced human rights violations as a result of their legitimate activities, including enforced disappearance, killings, attacks,[6] arbitrary arrests and prosecution.

In May the Royal Thai Army lodged a criminal complaint against Pornpen Khongkachonkiet and her organization Cross Cultural Foundation for "damaging the reputation" of Taharn Pran Paramilitary Unit 41, in Yala province, by requesting an investigation into an allegation of physical assault.

TRAFFICKING IN HUMAN BEINGS

In June, Thailand was downgraded in the US Department of State's annual report on Trafficking in Persons for failing to adequately address persistent and widespread trafficking of individuals for forced labour and the sex trade.

Throughout the year hundreds of people, including Rohingya from Myanmar, were rescued from camps where they had been held by smugglers in poor conditions for up to six months and subjected to severe violence.

REFUGEES AND ASYLUM-SEEKERS

In the absence of legal protection of the right to asylum, refugees and asylum-seekers remained at risk of arrest, arbitrary and indefinite detention, deportation as illegal immigrants and possible *refoulement*.

Immigration detainees, including refugees recognized by UNHCR, the UN refugee agency, continued to be held in poor conditions in facilities not built for long-term accommodation.

Fears of a crackdown on illegal labour led to some 220,000 migrant workers, mostly Cambodians, leaving the country in June; many later returned.

DEATH PENALTY

Death sentences were handed down during the year. There were no reported executions. A pilot project begun in 2013 to remove shackles from death row inmates in Bang Kwang high security prison in Bangkok was ongoing. The project had not been extended to other prisons by the end of the year.

1. Thailand: Attitude adjustment - 100 days under martial law (ASA 39/011/2014)
   www.amnesty.org/en/documents/ASA39/011/2014/en/
2. Thailand: Investigate grenade attack on anti-government protesters (News story)
   www.amnesty.org/en/news/thailand-investigate-grenade-attack-anti-government-protesters-2014-05-15
3. Thailand: Submission to the UN Committee against Torture (ASA 39/003/2014)
   www.amnesty.org/en/library/info/ASA39/003/2014/en
4. Thailand: Free speech crackdown creating 'spiral into silence' (Press release)
   www.amnesty.org/en/articles/news/2014/12/thailand-free-speech-crackdown-creating-spiral-silence/
   Thailand: Release activist imprisoned for allegedly insulting the monarchy (Press release)
   www.amnesty.org/en/articles/news/2014/09/thailand-release-activist-imprisoned-allegedly-insulting-monarchy/
   Thailand: Anniversary of activist's arrest a reminder of precarious state of freedom of expression (ASA 39/005/2014)
   www.amnesty.org/en/library/info/ASA39/005/2014/en
5. Thailand: Alleged torture victim denied redress (Press release)
   www.amnesty.org/en/documents/asa39/015/2014/en/
   Thailand: 10 years on, find truth and justice for family of Somchai Neelapaijit (ASA 39/001/2014)
   www.amnesty.org/en/library/info/ASA39/001/2014/en
6. Arbitrary detentions continue in Thailand (ASA 39/008/2014)
   www.amnesty.org/en/library/info/ASA39/008/2014/en
   Thailand: Threats to the lives of village leaders (ASA 39/009/2014)
   www.amnesty.org/en/library/info/ASA39/009/2014/en

TIMOR-LESTE

Democratic Republic of Timor-Leste
Head of state: **Taur Matan Ruak**
Head of government: **Kay Rala Xanana Gusmão**

Impunity persisted for gross human rights violations committed during the Indonesian occupation (1975-1999). Security forces were accused of ill-treatment and unnecessary or excessive use of force. Levels of domestic violence remained high. Parliament passed a restrictive media law before the Court of Appeal declared it unconstitutional.

BACKGROUND

In March, two groups, the Maubere Revolutionary Council (KRM) and the Popular Democratic Council of the Democratic Republic of Timor-Leste (CPD-RDTL), were declared illegal by a parliamentary resolution for "attempting to cause instability". Two of their leaders were charged and were awaiting trial.

IMPUNITY

Little progress was made in addressing crimes against humanity and other human rights violations committed by Indonesian security forces and their auxiliaries from 1975 to 1999. Many suspected perpetrators remained at large in Indonesia where they were safe from prosecution.[1]

In August, the Court of Appeal upheld the sentence of a former AHI (Aileu Hametin Integrasaun) militia member imprisoned for crimes against humanity committed in Aileu district around the 1999 independence referendum.

The Timorese government failed to implement recommendations from the Commission for Reception, Truth and Reconciliation (CAVR) and the bilateral Indonesia-Timor-Leste Commission of Truth and Friendship (CTF) relating to impunity. Parliament continued delaying consideration of two draft laws providing for a National Reparations Programme and establishment of a "Public Memory Institute", a body which would implement the recommendations of the CAVR and CTF, including the reparations programme. A commission to examine enforced disappearances, recommended by the CTF, had not been established by the end of the year. Initiatives undertaken with the Indonesian government to reunite children separated from their families in 1999 lacked transparency and adequate consultation with civil society.

JUSTICE SYSTEM

Reports continued of ill-treatment and unnecessary or excessive use of force by security forces. Accountability mechanisms remained weak.

Security forces reportedly arbitrarily arrested and ill-treated dozens of individuals in March allegedly linked to the two groups KRM and CPD-RDTL. Concerns were raised that the government may have violated the rights to freedom of association and expression by using parliament rather than the courts to declare the organizations illegal.

In October, the Timor-Leste parliament and government arbitrarily terminated the contracts of foreign judicial officers and advisors, raising serious concerns about judicial independence and impacting negatively on victims and their right to an effective remedy.[2]

WOMEN'S RIGHTS

The 2010 Law against Domestic Violence continued to be used to prosecute cases of domestic violence but many challenges remained for victims seeking to access justice. According to NGOs, courts tended to hand down suspended prison sentences or fines instead of imposing terms of imprisonment.

FREEDOM OF EXPRESSION – MEDIA

In May, parliament passed a Media Law which would impose severe restrictions on journalists and on freedom of expression. In August, the Court of Appeal found the law unconstitutional and returned it to parliament for review.[3] A revised law removing some restrictions was approved by the President in December.

1. Timor-Leste/Indonesia: Governments must expedite establishing fate of the disappeared (Public statement)
www.amnesty.org/download/Documents/8000/asa570012014en.pdf
2. Timor-Leste: Victims' rights and independence of judiciary threatened by arbitrary removal of judicial officers (ASA 57/003/2014)
www.amnesty.org/en/library/info/ASA57/003/2014/en
3. Timor-Leste: Unconstitutional media law threatens freedom of expression (ASA 57/002/2014)
www.amnesty.org/en/documents/asa57/002/2014/en/

TOGO

Togolese Republic
Head of state: **Faure Gnassingbé**
Head of government: **Kwesi Ahoomey-Zunu**

The security forces repeatedly used excessive force to disperse demonstrations. Torture and other ill-treatment were used to extract confessions from detainees, and prisoners were denied timely medical treatment. Threats to freedom of expression persisted, with journalists targeted for ill-treatment.

BACKGROUND

Elections which had been postponed at least twice from October 2012 finally took place in July 2013. President Faure Gnassingbé's party, Union for the Republic, won an absolute majority. Opposition parties protested at the results, which were confirmed by the Constitutional Court. Prime Minister Kwesi Ahoomey-Zunu was reappointed in September 2013.

In February 2013, the National Assembly passed a law granting the High Authority for Audiovisual and Communications discretionary powers to impose sanctions on the media without recourse to the courts, prompting protests by journalists' associations. The Constitutional Court ruled one month later that six articles of this law were unconstitutional.

In February 2014, the National Assembly rejected a government bill limiting the number of Presidential mandates.

In July 2014, the National Assembly approved the ratification of the International Convention against enforced disappearance without reservations.

Two major fires destroyed markets in Kara and the capital, Lomé, in January 2013. Later that month the National Assembly lifted the immunity of Agbéyomé Kodjo, formerly Prime Minister as well as President of the National Assembly, to allow his arrest in connection with the fires, along with other opposition members. Agbéyomé Kodjo was released in late February 2013 and Abass Kaboua, President of the Movement of Centrist Republicans, was released in September 2014. By the end of 2014, of 33 men originally charged, 20 remained in detention. A number of them were charged with conspiracy to associate with criminal intent.

EXCESSIVE USE OF FORCE

In April 2013, two students were killed when security forces shot live bullets at a crowd of protesters in the northern town of Dapaong.[1] One of the victims, Anselme Sindare Gouyano, was 12 years old. The government announced that those responsible would be brought to justice, but by the end of 2014 no investigations or prosecutions had been started.

In November 2014, security forces intervened near Aného, 45km from Lomé, against the selling of prohibited petrol. When the vendors resisted and threw stones, security forces fired into the crowd. Ayovi Koumako died after being shot and four other people were injured. The Minister of Justice issued a statement the same day stating that an investigation would be opened.

TORTURE AND OTHER ILL-TREATMENT

Torture and other ill-treatment was used by members of the security forces against detainees in pre-trial detention. Victims included Mohamed Loum, arrested in the market fires case, who was beaten and subjected to waterboarding in gendarmerie custody. He was also repeatedly subjected to prolonged restraint in handcuffs, often lasting 24 hours, and denied food or water.

A group of men convicted in September 2011 of participating in a 2009 coup plot took a complaint to the ECOWAS court, claiming they had been tortured during interrogations. In July 2013, the ECOWAS court found that the Togolese state was responsible for acts of torture and ordered reparations for the victims. The National Human Rights Commission of Togo had also found that these detainees had been subjected to inhuman and degrading acts of violence in February 2012. It recommended that the government impose exemplary punishments on all those who had participated, directly or indirectly. The government did not deny the torture allegations and reparations were paid to each of the plaintiffs in this case. Apart from transferring those responsible for the torture to other duties, no action was taken to investigate and prosecute the perpetrators.

Three members of this group – Adjinon Kossi Lambert, Towbeli Kouma and Pali Afeignindou – were pardoned in February 2013. Seven others, including Kpatcha Gnassingbé, brother of the President, Captain Kokou Tchaa Dontema and former Gendarmerie Lieutenant Efoé Sassouvi Sassou, remained in prison throughout 2014.

PRISON CONDITIONS

Denial of or delays in providing health care continued to put prisoners' lives at risk. Etienne Yakanou Kodjo, a member of the opposition National Alliance for Change, died in prison after being refused timely medical care in May 2013. No investigation had been opened into his death by the end of 2014.

FREEDOM OF EXPRESSION

Threats to freedom of expression continued. Journalists were injured by police officers while covering protests and were targeted with tear gas and bullets. In March 2013, journalist Zeus Aziadouvo, who had reported on the use of torture in the market fires case, was charged with complicity in the case. A radio station – Radio Légende FM – was closed down by police in July 2013.

Student associations were forbidden from demonstrating. The Association of Victims of Torture in Togo (ASVITTO) was also forbidden from holding sit-ins. A sit-in protest in March 2014 to claim reparations ordered by the ECOWAS court in the case of the men convicted of participating in a 2009 coup plot (see above) was dispersed with tear gas. Reparations were paid later that month.

Amah Olivier, President of the ASVITTO, was arrested in September 2013 and charged with incitement to rebellion for speaking about the political situation during a demonstration. He was conditionally released in February 2014 but was again summoned by the investigating judge in September. He reportedly received death threats in detention.

---

1. Togo: Excessive use of force and death in custody (AFR 57/002/2013)
www.amnesty.org/en/library/info/afr57/002/2013/en

TRINIDAD AND TOBAGO

Republic of Trinidad and Tobago
Head of state: **Anthony Thomas Aquinas Carmona**
Head of government: **Kamla Persad-Bissessar**

Killings by the security forces, and torture and other ill-treatment of detainees, including deaths in custody, remained a concern. People continued to be sentenced to death. The state failed to tackle violence against LGBTI people.

BACKGROUND

A second round of consultations on the reform of the Constitution was carried out in 2014, following a report by the Constitution Reform Commission and nationwide consultations in 2013.

The country continued to face a serious public security crisis: homicide rate remained at a high level with 403 murders reported by the police compared with 407 in 2013. In response, joint police and military patrols were deployed. In August 2014 the army's Defence Force Reserves were called to assist with street patrolling until 7 January 2015, despite serious concerns that the force was not trained to carry out these duties.

Prosecutor and senior attorney Dana Seetahal was assassinated by unidentified men in May 2014. She had been investigating high-profile cases including the kidnapping and murder of a businesswoman. An investigation into her killing was immediately opened by the authorities.

In August, pre-trial detainees in two prisons went on hunger strike to protest against the slow progress of their cases in the courts. According to the International Centre for Prison Studies, 43% of the prison population was in pre-trial detention.

EXCESSIVE USE OF FORCE

Reports of killings by the security forces suggested that they may have been unlawful and contradicted the official claims of "exchange of gunfire" with criminal elements.

Hakeem Alexander, 16, and his cousin Ievin Alexander, 15, were killed on 9 June 2014 in Morvant, Port of Spain, when police were called to intervene in a shoot-out. Eyewitnesses alleged that the two boys were executed by police officers while on their knees with their hands up. An investigation into the incident was ongoing at the end of the year.

TORTURE AND OTHER ILL-TREATMENT

In December 2013, Jameson John allegedly suffered burns to his torso, leg and genitals while in police custody. Six police officers were charged with misconduct and were awaiting trial at the end of the year.

DEATHS IN CUSTODY

On 24 June, Jahwi Ghany died in police custody in Chaguanas. A first autopsy stated he had died from heart failure. A second autopsy ordered by his family found that his death had been caused by trauma to the head. An investigation by the Police Complaint Authority was ongoing at the end of the year.

RIGHTS OF LESBIAN, GAY, BISEXUAL, TRANSGENDER AND INTERSEX PEOPLE

Although the Constitution Reform Commission recognized in 2013 the "high level of violence and abuse against LGBTI [people]", it failed to formulate recommendations towards achieving equality and ending discrimination. Laws criminalizing same-sex consensual acts and barring homosexuals from entering the country remained in place.

DEATH PENALTY

The death penalty continued to be mandatory for murder and death sentences were handed down. No executions have taken place since 1999. The 2013 report of the Constitution Reform Commission recommended the retention of the death penalty. In December, in response to the high homicide rate, Prime Minister Persad-Bissessar announced that she will seek to introduce new legislation to facilitate the resumption of executions.

TUNISIA

Republic of Tunisia
Head of state: **Beji Caid Essebsi (replaced Moncef Marzouki in December)**
Head of government: **Mehdi Jomaa**

A new Constitution adopted in January contained important human rights guarantees, but the authorities continued to restrict freedoms of expression and association. There were new reports of torture of detainees and at least two people were victims of apparently unlawful killings by police. The new Constitution contained improved safeguards for women's rights but failed to end legal and other discrimination against women or to address violence against women. A new process was established to address past human rights violations; however, a military appeals court significantly reduced the sentences of former senior officials convicted of responsibility for hundreds of unlawful killings during the 2010-2011 uprising. Tunisia kept its borders open to refugees fleeing fighting in Libya. Armed groups carried out attacks and killed members of the security forces. At least two people were sentenced to death; there were no executions.

BACKGROUND

Following the political crisis in 2013 sparked by the assassinations in February and July of two left-wing politicians, Chokri Belaid and Mohamed Brahmi, Tunisia's political parties reached an agreement that resulted in a new Constitution and the appointment of a new interim government in early 2014. The new government lifted the state of emergency, in force since 2011, on 5 March.

On 26 January, the National Constituent Assembly (NCA) adopted a new Constitution by a large majority after months of deadlock and an agreement by NCA members to reach a consensus on the most contentious issues. Three days later a new interim government took office pending legislative elections in October and presidential elections in November. The new Constitution guaranteed key human rights, including freedoms of expression and assembly; freedom of association, including the right to form political parties; freedom of movement; the right to citizenship; and the right to bodily integrity. It also guaranteed freedom from arbitrary detention, rights to fair trial and to political asylum, and prohibited torture and the use of any statute of limitations to prevent prosecutions for torture. Other articles, such as one prohibiting "attacks on the sacred", were more problematic, carrying a potential threat to free speech. The Constitution failed to abolish the death penalty.

COUNTER-TERROR AND SECURITY

The government submitted a new 163-article draft law to amend the 2003 Anti-terrorism Law to the NCA, which began discussing it in August. The new law aims to remove some of the most draconian features of the 2003 law.

In October, Prime Minister Jomaa said that the authorities had arrested over 1,500 suspected "terrorists" since the beginning of the year.

TORTURE AND OTHER ILL-TREATMENT

There were new reports of torture of detainees in police custody, mostly in the first few days after arrest and during interrogation. There was at least one suspicious death in custody. The law allowed police to hold detainees in pre-arraignment detention for up to six days without access to lawyers or relatives.

Following a visit to Tunisia in June, the UN Special Rapporteur on torture expressed concern that torture and other ill-treatment was continuing, and noted the low rate of successful prosecutions of perpetrators.

In 2013, the NCA adopted legislation to create a 16-member National Body for the Prevention of Torture, empowered to inspect detention facilities without first obtaining consent, except when urgent or compelling reasons prohibit it. By the end of the year, however, the National Body had yet to be established.

The death in hospital on 3 October of Mohamed Ali Snoussi, nine days after his arrest, drew renewed attention to police violence against suspects and the authorities' continuing failure to address it. Witnesses saw him being dragged from his house in handcuffs, beaten, stripped naked and taken away by masked police officers, who were heard to say that they belonged to the Brigade 17 police unit. Mohamed Ali Snoussi's wife said that she briefly saw him once in police detention, when he had visible marks of beatings but appeared too afraid to say how he had sustained them. When his family received his body it bore bruises and other injuries to the head, shoulders, back, testicles and feet. The Ministry of the Interior said that he had been arrested on drugs charges and that an autopsy concluded that his death was not caused by violence, but failed to give the autopsy report to the family despite their requests.

EXCESSIVE USE OF FORCE

Police officers shot and killed two women, Ahlem Dalhoumi and Ons Dalhoumi, on the night of 23 August as they drove home in the city of Kasserine with family members. The shooting occurred when police officers dressed in black, whom the car's occupants apparently assumed were armed robbers, signalled to them to stop, then opened fire as they drove on, killing the two women and injuring a third. The authorities said that police officers opened fire when the car ignored their order to stop and sped towards them. The surviving car occupants said the police did not identify themselves and opened fire without warning. The Ministry of the Interior stated in October that it had not suspended the police officers nor opened an administrative investigation, despite public announcements to the contrary.

TRANSITIONAL JUSTICE

Following the adoption of a Transitional Justice law in December 2013, a Truth and Dignity Commission was established in June to investigate human rights violations and arbitrate on cases of official corruption since 1 July 1955. An independent body, the Commission was also mandated to provide both material and symbolic reparations to victims and to draft recommendations to prevent the recurrence of human rights violations and the misuse of public funds and to promote democracy. The Commission, which has a four-year mandate extendable for up to one year, began its work in December after developing its rules and methods of operation.

The Transitional Justice law also provided for the establishment of Special Judicial Chambers to investigate and prosecute human rights violations committed by state agents between July 1955 and December 2013. In March, the Ministry of Justice appointed a technical committee to draft a decree on how these specialized chambers would function.

In April, the authorities released some of the former senior officials imprisoned in connection with the unlawful killings of protesters during the 2010-2011 uprising after the Military Court of Appeal amended the charges on which they had previously been convicted by military courts and reduced their sentences. Those released included former Minister of the Interior Rafiq Haj Kacem, whose 12-year sentence was reduced to a three-year term, including time spent in custody awaiting trial. Several family members of people killed or injured during the uprising went on hunger strike in protest.

FREEDOMS OF EXPRESSION AND ASSOCIATION

The authorities restricted freedoms of expression and association on counter-terrorism grounds following an armed group attack on 17 July that killed 15 government soldiers in Mount Chaambi, near the border with Algeria. The authorities ordered the immediate closure of all unauthorized radio and television stations, mosques and social media websites, suspended the activities of organizations deemed to have links with terrorism, and threatened to prosecute anyone who called Tunisia's military and security institutions into question. On 22 July, a government spokesperson said the authorities had suspended 157 organizations and two radio stations for alleged links to terrorist groups and for promoting violence. The executive authorities took this action despite Decree Law no. 2011-88 of 2011, which states that organizations may only be suspended pursuant to a judicial decision.

Jabeur Mejri, a blogger sentenced to a prison term in 2012 after being convicted of posting material online deemed insulting to Islam and the Prophet Mohamed, was released on 4 March. In April, he received a new eight-month prison sentence arising from an argument with a court official, but was released on 14 October under a presidential pardon.

WOMEN'S RIGHTS

Discrimination against women continued in law and practice. Tunisia officially lifted its reservations to CEDAW on 23 April; however, the government maintained a general declaration that it would take no organizational or legislative action required by CEDAW if it conflicted with Tunisia's Constitution.

The new Constitution adopted in January provided improved safeguards for women's rights, but women remained subject to discrimination under laws relating to family matters such as inheritance and child custody.

Article 46 of the Constitution afforded women greater protection against violence, but the Penal Code remained problematic, particularly its Article 227bis which allowed men who rape girls or women under the age of 20 to escape prosecution if they marry their victim. In June, the Secretary of State for

Women and Family said that the government planned to draft a framework law combating violence against women and girls with the assistance of an expert committee.

In March, a court sentenced two police officers to seven-year prison terms after convicting them of raping a woman in September 2012; a third police officer was sentenced to two years' imprisonment for taking her fiancé to a cash machine and trying to extort money from him. During the trial, defence lawyers accused the victim of indecency and offering sexual favours to the police after they found her alone with her fiancé. She lodged an appeal against the sentences on account of their relative leniency. In November the two officers convicted of rape had their sentences increased to 15-year prison terms on appeal; the third officer's sentence was confirmed on appeal.

REFUGEES' AND MIGRANTS' RIGHTS

Thousands of Libyans and other nationals reportedly crossed into Tunisia in July and August to escape fighting between rival armed militias in Libya. The authorities kept Tunisia's border with Libya open while warning that they would close it if the security or economic situation deteriorated. Properly documented Libyans were allowed to enter and remain in Tunisia but nationals of some other countries were allowed to enter Tunisia for transit only.

DEATH PENALTY

The death penalty remained in force for murder and other crimes; no executions have been carried out since 1991. At least two people were sentenced to death and at least three prisoners had their death sentences commuted during the year.

In November, Tunisia voted for a UN General Assembly resolution calling for a worldwide moratorium on the death penalty.

TURKEY

Republic of Turkey
Head of state: **Recep Tayyip Erdoğan (replaced Abdullah Gül in August)**
Head of government: **Ahmet Davutoğlu (replaced Recep Tayyip Erdoğan in August)**

Following the 2013 Gezi protests and the rupture with former ally Fethullah Gülen, the authorities became more authoritarian in responding to critics. They undermined the independence of the judiciary, introduced new restrictions on internet freedoms and handed unprecedented powers to the country's intelligence agency. The rights of peaceful demonstrators were violated and police officers enjoyed near-total impunity for the use of excessive force. Unfair trials continued, especially under anti-terrorism laws, but the excessive use and length of pre-trial detention declined. The authorities ignored the rights of conscientious objectors and of lesbian, gay, bisexual, transgender and intersex people and failed to take necessary steps to prevent violence against women. By the end of the year, 1.6 million Syrian refugees were living in Turkey, many of them destitute.

BACKGROUND

The authorities acted to crush a criminal investigation into alleged corruption within the inner circle of Prime Minister Erdoğan that became public on 17 December 2013. Police officers and prosecutors working on the case were transferred to other duties. The investigation was formally closed by prosecutors on 16 October 2014. The government branded the investigation a plot by supporters of influential cleric, Fethullah Gülen. The authorities vowed to take further action against Fethullah Gülen and his network of supporters in the police and judiciary.

In April, Parliament passed legislative amendments granting the National Intelligence Agency (MIT) unprecedented powers of surveillance and its officials near total immunity from prosecution.

In Soma, western Turkey, 301 miners died following an explosion at a coal mine in May. This latest disaster shone a spotlight on industrial safety in a country with one of the highest numbers of work-related deaths in the world.

The convictions of military officers for plotting to overthrow the AK Party government in the "Sledgehammer" case were overturned by the Constitutional Court on 18 June 2014, and sent for retrial. The "Ergenekon" prosecution against civilians accused of plotting to overthrow the government continued. Many of the defendants were released on the grounds that their detention had exceeded the maximum five-year term. Other defendants were released following rulings by the Constitutional Court. Prosecutions targeting Kurdish political activists for alleged membership of the PKK-linked Kurdistan Communities Union carried on across the country, but many of the defendants were released from pre-trial detention.

In August, the serving Prime Minister became Turkey's first directly elected President, bringing far greater power and influence to the role in practice, if not in law.

In October, 49 hostages taken from Turkey's consulate in Mosul, Iraq, were released after three months by the Islamic State armed group. The government refused to disclose what was provided to the armed group. It was alleged that 180 prisoners in Turkey were released in exchange for the hostages.

The two-year-old peace process between the authorities and the PKK continued but looked shakier than ever in the face of armed clashes, spillover from the conflicts in Syria and Iraq and lack of any concrete progress.

FREEDOM OF EXPRESSION

Criminal prosecutions threatening freedom of expression continued to be brought against journalists, activists and other dissenting voices, despite the adoption of legislative amendments intended to improve the law in 2013. Alongside anti-terrorism provisions, laws on defamation and provoking religious hatred were frequently used. The independence of the mainstream media continued to be undermined by its close business links with the government. More independent-minded journalists were forced out of their jobs by editors fearful of upsetting government and media owners. Press Law gagging orders were used to ban the reporting of several news stories, including the capture of 49 hostages from Turkey's Mosul consulate, on "national security grounds".

In March, the Parliament passed draconian amendments to the Internet Law increasing the authorities' powers to ban or block content and threatening users' privacy. Following the amendments, the authorities used administrative orders to block access to Twitter and YouTube after the social media sites were used to post items embarrassing to the government ahead of the local elections in March. Despite court orders requiring the lifting of the bans, the sites remained blocked for two weeks and two months respectively until the Constitutional Court ruled that the blocking order be lifted.

FREEDOM OF ASSEMBLY

The rights of peaceful demonstrators were denied by the authorities, with protests banned, prevented or dispersed with the use of excessive, unnecessary and often punitive force by police officers. People who attended demonstrations deemed unlawful by the authorities faced prosecution, often on trumped-up charges of violent conduct. The restrictive Law on Meetings and Demonstrations continued to be a barrier to freedom of peaceful assembly, despite superficial amendments in March. It unfairly restricted the time and location that assemblies could take place, while requiring overly burdensome notification from the organizers and discounted any possibility of spontaneous demonstrations.

On 1 May, 39,000 police and 50 water cannon vehicles were used to prevent trade unionists and others from marching on Taksim Square, the traditional location for May Day demonstrations. May Day demonstrations had taken place in Taksim Square for several years. In 2013 and 2014 they were banned and clashes ensued between police and demonstrators trying to reach the square. The authorities announced that Taksim would be permanently off-limits for all large demonstrations and instead offered two locations outside the centre of the city where demonstrations could take place. This policy was replicated in other cities across Turkey.

In June, the trial of members of Taksim Solidarity, an umbrella group of more than 100 organizations, set up to contest the redevelopment of Gezi Park and Taksim Square, started in Istanbul. Five prominent members stood accused of "founding a criminal organization", punishable by up to 15 years in prison, while all 26 defendants were charged with "refusing to disperse from an unauthorized demonstration" under the Law on Meetings and Demonstrations. The trial was continuing at the end of the year.[1]

TORTURE AND OTHER ILL-TREATMENT

Reported cases of torture in official places of detention remained far fewer than in previous years. More than two years after the ratification of the Optional Protocol to the UN Convention against Torture, the required domestic implementing mechanism had not been established. The National Human Rights Institution was earmarked by the authorities for this role but lacked the necessary skills, resources and guarantees of independence to fulfil it.

EXCESSIVE USE OF FORCE

Excessive and abusive force by police officers during demonstrations, including the firing of tear gas canisters directly at demonstrators from close range, and the use of water cannon and beatings of peaceful protesters, remained common. Ministry of Interior guidelines, introduced in June and July 2013 to combat excessive and unnecessary force, were mostly ignored.

In a number of cases, police used live ammunition during demonstrations, resulting in deaths and injury.

IMPUNITY

Investigations into abuses by public officials remained ineffective, and the chance of securing justice for the victims remote. In the absence of the long-promised but never-established independent police complaints mechanism, police units were effectively responsible for investigating their own alleged abuses under the instruction of under-resourced prosecutors. Police departments routinely failed to provide the most basic items of evidence to investigations.

No prosecution was opened against six police officers who were filmed with a camera phone beating Hakan Yaman and dragging him onto a fire, close to the scene of a Gezi Park demonstration in Istanbul in June 2013.[2] In the attack, Hakan Yaman lost his sight in one eye and suffered burns and broken bones for which he underwent six operations. At the end of the year, police departments had failed to provide the investigation with CCTV footage from the area and photographs of police officers on duty at the time. A parallel administrative investigation concluded without result on the grounds that the police officers could not be identified, despite the number of the water cannon vehicle that they were operating being clearly visible in mobile phone footage.

In October, more than 40 people were killed and scores injured in the predominately Kurdish area of southeastern Turkey, during clashes between rival groups and with the police, after protests erupted against the Islamic State armed group assault on the Kurdish city of Kobani in Syria. There were numerous reports of the failure to conduct prompt crime scene investigations or to question alleged perpetrators of attacks on rival groups.

In Siirt, Davut Naz died at the scene of a Kobani-related protest on 8 October. The provincial governor said in a statement that he had been killed by demonstrators and died of a neck injury while eyewitnesses reported that he was shot by police officers with live ammunition. His family reported that there were three gunshot wounds but no neck injury to the body. No crime scene investigation was conducted and the criminal investigation into the incident had not progressed by the end of the year.

UNFAIR TRIALS

Legislative amendments in July abolished the anti-terrorism and organized crime courts with special powers, but those accused of terrorism-related offences still risked conviction without substantive and convincing evidence in ordinary courts. Legislative amendments in 2013, imposing a maximum limit of five years for pre-trial detention and introducing greater protections against its unfair use, yielded results and resulted in fewer people being held and for less time.

The independence of the judiciary was undermined by changes to the top judicial body, the Higher Council of Judges and Prosecutors, that granted greater powers to the Minister of Justice, and allowed the transfer of hundreds of judges and prosecutors.

HOUSING RIGHTS

The central government and municipalities controlled by all the main political parties carried out urban transformation projects that failed to uphold the right of residents to adequate consultation, compensation or the provision of alternative housing.

Residents in Sarıgöl, a poor district of Istanbul with a significant Roma population, were forcibly evicted from their homes in a project to replace shanty houses with higher quality residential blocks. The cost of the new houses was vastly higher than the majority of residents could afford and the compensation for those who lost their houses was inadequate. Many of the families threatened with homelessness by the project did not have title deeds for the land despite living in the neighbourhood for generations.

VIOLENCE AGAINST WOMEN

The implementation of the 2012 Law on Protection of Family and Prevention of Violence against Women remained inadequate, under-resourced and ineffective in dealing with domestic violence. A number of women under judicial protection were reported to have been killed. The number of shelters for victims of domestic violence remained far below that required by law.

REFUGEES AND ASYLUM-SEEKERS

At the end of the year, the government estimated that there were 1.6 million Syrian refugees in the country, up from 700,000 in January.[3] The bulk of the financial burden was borne by the Turkish authorities with little assistance from the international community. More than 220,000 were accommodated in well-resourced, government-run refugee camps, but many of the more than 1.3 million refugees living outside camps were destitute and received little or no assistance. Despite Turkey's professed "open border policy", there were persistent reports of unlawful or abusive force by Turkish border guards at unofficial crossing points, including the use of live ammunition, beatings and pushing refugees back into war-torn Syria.

An estimated 30,000 Yezidi Kurdish refugees arrived from Iraq in August, but unlike the Syrians, they were not afforded a "temporary protection status", nor the rights and entitlements it brings. The Yezidi refugees joined an estimated 100,000 asylum-seekers from other countries residing in Turkey, almost all of whom faced severe delays in the processing of their asylum claims.

CONSCIENTIOUS OBJECTORS

Turkey did not recognize the right to conscientious objection to military service despite the explicit rulings from the European Court of Human Rights requiring it to do so. Instead, the authorities continued repeatedly to prosecute conscientious objectors for "desertion" and other similar offences.

In October, a military court convicted 56-year-old conscientious objector Ali Fikri Işık on three counts of desertion, sentencing him to 25 months in prison or a fine of 15,200 liras (US$6,725). His "desertion" related to his refusal, for reasons of conscience, to carry out military service during the 1980s. At 56 he was too old to serve and had already been considered "unfit for military service" by the military authorities. An appeal remained pending at the military Supreme Court of Appeals at the end of the year.

RIGHTS OF LESBIAN, GAY, BISEXUAL, TRANSGENDER AND INTERSEX PEOPLE

Lesbian, gay, bisexual, transgender and intersex people continued to face discrimination in employment and in interactions with the state authorities. No progress was made in bringing provisions to prohibit discrimination on grounds of sexual orientation and gender identity into the Constitution or into domestic law. A number of murders of transgender women were reported during the year.

The trial for the murder of Ahmet Yıldız, a gay man killed in a suspected honour killing in July 2008, failed to make any progress during 2014, with his father, the single suspect in the case, remaining at large. The authorities had failed to investigate death threats against Ahmet Yıldız ahead of the murder and to launch a prompt, effective investigation following the killing.

1. Gezi Park protests: Brutal denial of the right to peaceful assembly in Turkey (EUR 44/022/2013)
   www.amnesty.org/en/library/info/EUR44/022/2013/en

2. Gezi Park protests: Brutal denial of the right to peaceful assembly in Turkey (EUR 44/022/2013)
   www.amnesty.org/en/library/info/EUR44/022/2013/en

3. Struggling to survive: Refugees from Syria in Turkey (EUR 44/017/2014)
   www.amnesty.org/en/library/info/EUR44/017/2014/en

TURKMENISTAN

Turkmenistan
Head of state and government: **Gurbanguly Berdimuhamedov**

Despite improvements to laws on the media and political participation, opposition figures, journalists and human rights defenders continued to suffer harassment by the authorities. Judicial independence was limited; there were no meaningful appeals procedures, and acquittals in criminal trials were rare. Lawyers trying to work independently risked disbarment. Torture and other ill-treatment remained widespread.

BACKGROUND

In September 2013 Turkmenistan accepted recommendations from the UN Human Rights Council to co-operate with UN special procedures. However, the authorities severely restricted access to the country for international monitors. Turkmenistan did not respond to requests from Amnesty International to visit and there were 10 outstanding requests for visits from UN special procedures.

In the first multi-party elections in Turkmenistan, the opposition Party of Industrialists and Entrepreneurs won parliamentary seats in December 2013.

However, observers reported that this party did not represent a genuine challenge to the political leadership and that it proclaimed its loyalty to President Berdimuhamedov.

FREEDOM OF EXPRESSION

Since the passing of the Law on Mass Media on 4 January 2013, principles of media independence and the prohibition on state interference in media activities have been enshrined in law. Yet in practice, censorship remained extensive and newspapers were owned by ministries that answered to the President. No genuinely independent newspapers had been registered under the new law by the end of the year. In practice, people were barred from subscribing to foreign media outlets and access to the internet was monitored and restricted. Social networking websites were frequently blocked.

Human rights activists and journalists in Turkmenistan and in exile came under consistent pressure from the Turkmenistani authorities.

FREEDOM OF ASSOCIATION

Unreasonable state interference in public associations' activities continued. A Presidential decree in place since January 2013 required foreign grants to be registered with and approved by the government. Funding of activities deemed "political" was prohibited, as was membership of an unregistered association. The Law on Public Associations came into force in May, prohibiting state interference in associations, but also providing for substantial powers of official monitoring and oversight. Registration procedures for associations remained complicated. No organizations in Turkmenistan were openly engaged in independent human rights monitoring or social or political commentary.

TORTURE AND OTHER ILL-TREATMENT

Credible reports of torture and other ill-treatment by security forces against people suspected of criminal offences included methods such as pulling of the genitals with pliers, electric shocks, and beatings with chair legs and plastic bottles filled with water. Reports on prisons included a prisoner being forced to swallow pills and having threats made against his family; incidents of forced rape between prisoners; and shackling of prisoners serving life sentences.

In January, Geldy Kyarizov, his wife, sister-in-law and 12-year-old daughter were detained by security officers as they tried to travel to seek medical attention. They were held for questioning, subjected to ill-treatment and made to sign a paper saying that they would not lodge an official compliant.[1]

Activist Mansur Mingelov went on hunger strike in prison from 19 May until 8 June to demand a retrial.[2] He had been sentenced to 22 years' imprisonment after an unfair trial shortly after collating and passing to the Prosecutor General and foreign diplomats information about torture and ill-treatment of the Baloch ethnic community in Mary province in 2012.

ENFORCED DISAPPEARANCES

During the 2013 UN Universal Periodic Review on Turkmenistan, the state rejected recommendations from the UN Human Rights Council to provide information on the whereabouts of prisoners who were subjected to enforced disappearance after an alleged assassination attempt on then President Saparmurat Niyazov in November 2002. Non-governmental sources reported that at least eight of those convicted had died in detention. The families of the disappeared continued to be denied all contact with their loved ones and any official information about their fate or whereabouts for over a decade.

FREEDOM OF MOVEMENT

Although Turkmenistan ended the use of the exit visa system in 2006, in practice arbitrary restrictions on the right to travel abroad for those who have fallen out of favour with the authorities continued.

On 10 April, Ruslan Tukhbatullin was prevented from leaving Turkmenistan to meet his brother Farid Tukhbatullin and was told he and his nine-year-old son were blacklisted for travelling abroad. This was believed to be in retaliation for Farid Tukhbatullin's human rights work.[3]

FREEDOM OF RELIGION

Religious activity remained strictly controlled. Religious groups representing Shi'a Muslims, Catholics, Protestants and Jehovah's Witnesses faced difficulty in registering organizations. Six Jehovah's Witnesses imprisoned for conscientious objection were released in an amnesty in October. One remained in prison. Provisions in the Code of Administrative Offences, which came into force in January, punished the import, export and distribution of religious materials.

1. Further information: Former prisoner denied urgent medical care - Geldy Kyarizov (EUR 61/001/2014)
   www.amnesty.org/en/library/info/EUR61/001/2014/en
2. Urgent Action: Man to return to prison where he was beaten - Mansur Mingelov (EUR 61/002/2014)
   www.amnesty.org/en/library/info/EUR61/002/2014/en
3. Turkmenistan: Activist's family barred from travel abroad, brother of exiled rights defender halted at the airport (NWS 11/094/2014)
   www.amnesty.ca/news/news-releases/turkmenistan-activist%E2%80%99s-family-barred-from-travel-abroad-brother-of-exiled-rights

UGANDA

Republic of Uganda
Head of state and government: **Yoweri Kaguta Museveni**

Restrictions on freedoms of expression, peaceful assembly and association continued as the authorities used repressive and discriminatory legislation to stifle civil space. Discrimination, harassment and violence against lesbian, gay, bisexual, transgender and intersex (LGBTI) people increased. Violence against women remained widespread while state hostility increased towards civil society organizations and activists working on human rights, oil governance, corruption and land issues.

BACKGROUND

The succession of President Museveni as leader of the National Resistance Movement (NRM) and head of state dominated national discourse during 2014. In February the NRM passed a resolution urging party members to endorse President Museveni as sole candidate in the 2016 presidential elections. The resolution also discouraged leaders within the party from harbouring presidential ambitions. In September, Health Minister Ruhakana Rugunda replaced Amama Mbabazi as Prime Minister.

FREEDOMS OF EXPRESSION, ASSEMBLY AND ASSOCIATION

Restrictions on freedom of expression, peaceful assembly and association continued. The Public Order Management Act (POMA), which came into force in November 2013, was used to impose wide-ranging restrictions on public meetings. It gave the police powers to prohibit and disperse public gatherings of a political nature. A petition challenging the POMA's constitutionality filed with the Constitutional Court in December 2013 remained pending.

The POMA was used in the first quarter of 2014 to disperse peaceful assemblies organized as part of the Free and Fair Elections Now campaign and arrest political activists. Often, those arrested were not charged. In April, the Free and Fair Elections Now campaign steering team held a meeting with the Minister of Internal Affairs. The police did not interrupt subsequent rallies convened by the group.

On 26 February, police declared illegal and dispersed a peaceful protest organized by the

End Miniskirt Harassment Coalition outside the National Theatre in the capital, Kampala.

On 22 March in Mbale city, the police used tear gas and fired live ammunition into the air to disperse crowds of people who were marching to the venue of a rally organized by the Free and Fair Elections Now campaign team. Police said that the rally's organizers had not given the notification required under the POMA.

On 27 March, the police prevented Bishop Zac Niringiye, the retired Assistant Bishop of Kampala and anti-corruption activist, from speaking at Kabale University in western Uganda and participating in a scheduled broadcast on Kabale's Voice of Kigezi radio station. Police told Amnesty International that they acted because Bishop Zac had not received authorization from the university to hold a meeting on its premises and the scheduled radio show could incite violence.

During the year the police stopped peaceful demonstrations by a group of unemployed young people referring to themselves as the Jobless Brotherhood. On 17 June, two members of the Jobless Brotherhood, Norman Tumuhimbise and Robert Mayanja, were arrested after they entered Parliament with two piglets to protest against corruption and high youth unemployment. They were later charged with criminal trespass among other charges. On 4 August, nine members of the Jobless Brotherhood, carrying a coffin, were arrested as they demonstrated at the Independence Monument in Kampala. They were charged with participating in an unlawful assembly. In October, Norman Tumuhimbise and Robert Mayanja were arrested following another demonstration in Kampala involving piglets.

In June, the High Court issued its judgment in a case challenging the constitutionality of the February 2012 forced closure of an LGBTI activists' workshop in the town of Entebbe by the Minister of Ethics and Integrity. The applicants argued that the Minister's action violated their rights including freedom of expression, peaceful assembly and association. The High Court ruled that the applicants had not suffered any unlawful infringement of their rights and that they had participated in promoting "homosexual practices" which were offences against morality under the Penal Code.

RIGHTS OF LESBIAN, GAY, BISEXUAL, TRANSGENDER AND INTERSEX PEOPLE

In February, President Museveni signed the 2009 Anti-Homosexuality Bill into law. In August, the Constitutional Court declared the law null and void on the grounds that there was no quorum in Parliament when it was passed. Discrimination, arbitrary arrests, harassment and violence against LGBTI people increased during the five months that the Anti-Homosexuality Act (AHA) was in force. LGBTI support organizations observed a sharp increase in the number of arrests of LGBTI people under the AHA. Some LGBTI people were arrested by police when reporting a crime or when visiting a friend or colleague in detention. Many were held without charge for longer than the 48-hour maximum stipulated by the Constitution. Those arrested reported ill-treatment in detention, including being subjected to physical and sexual assaults, stripping, groping and forced anal examinations. A number of transgender individuals were stripped naked and paraded by the police in front of the media. Some HIV-positive detainees were denied access to anti-retroviral medication.

The authorities also targeted organizations providing services to LGBTI people.

In March, the authorities suspended the work of the Refugee Law Project (RLP) in refugee camps and settlements pending investigations into allegations that the organization was "promoting homosexuality", an offence under the AHA.

In May, the suspension was extended to cover all RLP work relating to refugees and asylum-seekers. The suspension continued to stand even after the Constitutional Court nullified the AHA.

On 3 April, police raided the Makerere University Walter Reed Project, an HIV research project run in partnership between Makerere University and the US Military HIV Research Program. One employee was taken into custody on suspicion of "recruiting homosexuals" but was subsequently released. The clinic was temporarily closed.

The AHA legitimized abuses and violence against LGBTI people by non-state actors whose actions went largely unpunished. One transgender woman was killed and another raped. Evictions, threats and blackmail were the most common abuses against LGBTI people. Increased threat levels for LGBTI people led some to flee Uganda. The AHA restricted the ability of LGBTI people to access health care, especially HIV/AIDS and sexual health care. In one positive move, the Ministry of Health issued a directive in June reaffirming the government's commitment to provide health services without discrimination, including on the basis of sexual orientation.

In October, the Chief Magistrates Court at Buganda Road, Kampala, dismissed charges against Mukisa Kim, a gay man, and Mukasa Jackson, a transgender woman, after the prosecution repeatedly failed to confirm they were ready to proceed with the trial. Mukisa Kim had been charged under the Penal Code with "having carnal knowledge of a person against the order of nature", while Mukasa Jackson had been charged with "permitting a male person to have carnal knowledge against the order of nature".

VIOLENCE AGAINST WOMEN AND GIRLS

President Museveni signed the Anti-Pornography Act (APA) into law on 6 February. Immediately after the signing, women whom the public deemed to be dressed indecently were attacked, stripped and beaten by mobs in the streets. The police confirmed four incidents in Kampala city centre but failed to record them or the victims' particulars in the official crime records, or to arrest the perpetrators of the attacks.

Police officers also used the APA to harass women.

In February, Patience Akumu, a journalist and women's rights activist, was briefly refused entry into Naguru police station because of the way she was dressed.

In February, Lilian Drabo, a lawyer based in Kampala, was threatened with arrest because of her clothing at the Nakawa Court in Kampala. The management of the Nakawa High Court Central Circuit had put up a notice warning that it would not tolerate indecent apparel on court premises.

A petition filed in May challenging the constitutionality of the APA remained pending. The then Prime Minister's commitment in February to review the APA had not been implemented by the end of the year.

RIGHT TO HEALTH – ACCESS TO HIV/AIDS HEALTH CARE SERVICES

In July, President Museveni signed into law the HIV/AIDS Prevention and Control Act. The Act criminalized HIV transmission and exposure and provided for mandatory HIV testing. The Act allowed unjustified breaches of the right to confidentiality. Local and international NGOs raised concerns that women in particular would be impacted adversely and disproportionately by the implementation of the Act.

HUMAN RIGHTS DEFENDERS

Civil society organizations and activists working on human rights, oil governance, corruption and land issues continued to face threats to their work. NGO offices and staff came under surveillance while several organizations reported receiving threats. The offices of a number of organizations including ActionAid Uganda, Foundation for Human Rights Initiative, Human Rights Network-Uganda (HURINET-U) and the Anti-corruption Coalition of Uganda were broken into by unidentified individuals. The break-ins appeared to be attempts to access information on the organizations' human rights and governance work. Police investigations into most of these break-ins remained pending.

On the night of 5 May, the offices of HURINET-U were broken into. A server, 29 computers, office cameras, safes, and security cameras were stolen.

On the night of 17 May, the offices of the Uganda Land Alliance were broken into. Documents, computers and cameras were stolen.

A petition challenging the constitutionality of the Non-Governmental Organizations Registration (Amendment) Act filed in 2006 remained pending. Proposals made in 2013 to further amend the NGO Law ostensibly to expand government control over NGO funding and activities remained pending before the Cabinet. Authorities also proposed a Civic Education Policy which if adopted would mean that any programmes to provide civic education – including on human rights – would need accreditation at the district level. Organizations deemed in breach of the policy could have their activities suspended for up to six months, have their accreditation revoked, or even blacklisted.

POLICE AND SECURITY FORCES

In July, groups of armed men staged violent attacks mainly on police posts in Bundibugyo, Kasese and Ntoroko. At least 65 people were killed in the attacks, including civilians, some of the attackers, and members of the police force and the army. Following the outbreak of conflict in South Sudan, Ugandan troops were deployed to Juba city in December 2013 in response to a request by the South Sudan government to help secure the capital. In January, Ugandan troops were present in Bor, Jonglei state, where they supported the South Sudan authorities to regain control of the city from opposition forces. Ugandan troops remained in South Sudan throughout 2014.

INTERNATIONAL JUSTICE

International Criminal Court arrest warrants issued in 2005 remained in force for Joseph Kony, the Lord's Resistance Army (LRA) leader, and three LRA commanders. The men were still at large at the end of the year.

Former LRA commander Thomas Kwoyelo, who in 2011 pleaded not guilty before the International Crimes Division of the High Court to charges of murder, wilful killing and other offences committed in the context of the conflict in northern Uganda, remained remanded in prison. The government appeal against the Constitutional Court's decision that Thomas Kwoyelo was entitled to amnesty under the Amnesty Act of 2000 remained pending before the Supreme Court. A complaint submitted by Thomas Kwoyelo to the African Commission on Human and Peoples' Rights challenging his continued detention by the Ugandan government remained pending.

UKRAINE

Ukraine
Head of state: **Petro Poroshenko (replaced Oleksandr Turchynov in June, who replaced Viktor Yanukovych in February)**
Head of government: **Arseniy Yatsenyuk (replaced Mykola Azarov in February)**

Violence resulting from the protests in the capital Kyiv and later in eastern Ukraine escalated into a civil conflict with Russian involvement. Violations by police, including torture and other ill-treatment as well as abusive use of force during demonstrations, continued with near-total impunity for the perpetrators, while investigations into such incidents remained ineffective. Abductions of individuals were carried out, particularly by pro-Russian paramilitaries in the occupied Autonomous Republic of Crimea and by both warring sides in eastern Ukraine affected by conflict. Both sides violated the laws of war. In Crimea, Russian restrictions

on the rights to freedom of expression, assembly and association were fully applied, and pro-Ukrainian activists and members of the Crimean Tatar community were targeted by paramilitaries and persecuted by the de facto authorities.

BACKGROUND

Pro-European demonstrations in Kyiv ("EuroMaydan") sparked in 2013 by the government's decision not to sign an Association Agreement with the EU, resulted in the ousting of President Yanukovych on 22 February. Following the violent dispersal by police of the initially peaceful demonstration on the night of 29 November 2013, the demonstrators became increasingly radicalized. Protesters erected tents on the central Independence Square and occupied several buildings. While most protesters remained peaceful, violence by both sides escalated. At least 85 demonstrators and 18 police officers died as a direct result of violence at EuroMaydan in Kyiv, and hundreds were injured.

After Viktor Yanukovych secretly left Ukraine and an interim government was formed, increasingly violent protests began in the predominantly Russian-speaking Donbass region in eastern Ukraine. In Crimea, buildings belonging to the local authorities were occupied by armed paramilitaries calling themselves "self-defence forces" on the night of 26 to 27 February. Jointly with members of regular Russian forces they blocked Ukrainian military installations across the peninsula, and on 27 February, in the presence of armed men, the Crimean parliament elected a new leadership. A "referendum" was called on 16 March on the status of Crimea. Participants overwhelmingly voted in favour of unification with Russia while opponents boycotted it. On 18 March, the de facto authorities of Crimea signed a "treaty" in Moscow resulting in its annexation by Russia.

By April, armed opponents of the new government in Kyiv had occupied government buildings, including police and security headquarters, in the cities of Donetsk and Luhansk and several smaller towns, effectively taking control over large parts of Donbass. On 15 April, the government announced the beginning of an "anti-terrorist operation". The situation rapidly escalated into an armed conflict between government forces and separatist armed groups supported by Russia. Pro-Kyiv forces were making steady advances until late August when Russia stepped up its covert military involvement in Ukraine.[1] A ceasefire between the warring sides was agreed at negotiations in Belarus in September, although fighting continued on a reduced scale, resulting in the deaths of more than 4,000 people by the end of the year. After the *de facto* authorities in Donetsk and Luhansk held "elections" on 2 November, Kyiv withdrew its offer of limited devolution for the region.

Early presidential and parliamentary elections were held on 25 May and 26 October respectively, returning pro-European parties and politicians to power. On 16 September the European Parliament and the Ukrainian parliament ratified the Association Agreement with the EU, but it had not been agreed by all EU member states by the end of the year.

IMPUNITY – EUROMAYDAN

The three months of EuroMaydan demonstrations shone a spotlight on the systemic problem of impunity for the abusive use of force, and for torture and other ill-treatment of individuals by law enforcement officers in Ukraine. Riot police first used force against entirely peaceful protesters on 30 November 2013, when they refused to disperse, resulting in dozens of injuries and the brief detention of 35 peaceful protesters on charges of hooliganism. In response to widespread condemnation, the authorities dismissed a senior Kyiv police official and reportedly initiated criminal proceedings against him and four others, but these were never brought to any conclusion. In the subsequent weeks and months, the police repeatedly resorted to the abusive use of force at EuroMaydan as well as making arbitrary arrests and attempting to initiate arbitrary criminal proceedings against demonstrators.[2] Eventually, firearms with live ammunition, including sniper rifles, were deployed at the demonstrations, although it remained unclear which forces had used them and under whose orders they had acted. The head of the Ukrainian Security Services (SBU) stated in November that 16 former riot police officers and five senior SBU officials had been arrested in connection with the killings of protesters in Kyiv.

After the downfall of Viktor Yanukovych, the new authorities publicly committed to effectively investigating and prosecuting those responsible for deaths during EuroMaydan and all the abuses against protesters. However, apart from indicting former senior political leadership, few if any concrete steps were taken in this direction.

Only two law enforcement officers stood trial for torture and other ill-treatment during EuroMaydan, both low-ranking conscripts from the Interior Ministry Troops. On 28 May, they were given suspended sentences of three and two years respectively for "exceeding authority or official powers" (Article 365 of the Criminal Code) for their ill-treatment of Mykhaylo Havryliuk on 22 January 2014. Video footage shows Mykhaylo Havryliuk being forced to stand naked in sub-zero temperatures in front of dozens of officers from both Interior Ministry Troops and riot police; many can be seen actively humiliating him by forcing him to pose for photographs before he is pushed into a bus.

Victims in 20 cases of abusive of use of force by police in EuroMaydan monitored by Amnesty International were frustrated by the slow speed or apparent lack of investigation into their allegations, the failure of the authorities to identify the perpetrators and poor communication from the Prosecutor's Office.[3]

An International Advisory Panel on Ukraine was established by the Council of Europe in April to review EuroMaydan-related investigations. It had not reported on the progress of the investigations by the end of the year.

ABDUCTIONS, DISAPPEARANCES AND KILLINGS

During the protests in Kyiv, several dozen EuroMaydan activists went missing. While the fate of over 20 remained unclarified at the end of the year, it transpired that some were abducted and ill-treated. In December, the Prosecutor General's Office reported that 11 men suspected of abducting EuroMaydan activists had been arrested and several others placed on a wanted list. None were law enforcement officials, although they allegedly acted under orders from former senior police officials.

Yury Verbytsky and Igor Lutsenko went missing on 21 January, from hospital. Igor Lutsenko reported that he was blindfolded and beaten by his captors, and then dumped in a forest in freezing temperatures. Yury Verbytsky was found dead in a forest, his ribs broken, with traces of duct tape around his head.

Abductions and ill-treatment of captives were common in Russian-occupied Crimea and the parts of eastern Ukraine controlled by separatists, affecting several hundred people. Among the first people targeted were members of local administrations, pro-Ukrainian political activists, journalists and international observers. In a press conference on 23 April, the then self-proclaimed "people's mayor" of Slovyansk, Vyacheslav Ponomarev, acknowledged that separatists were holding a number of people as "bargaining chips". Subsequently, several hundred captives were exchanged between the separatists and the Ukrainian authorities. Others were held for private ransom. Sasha, a 19-year-old pro-Kyiv activist, was abducted by members of an armed group in Luhansk on 12 June. Beaten continuously for 24 hours and tortured with electric shocks, he was released after his father reportedly paid a US$60,000 ransom.

Allegations of abductions were repeatedly made against members of pro-Kyiv forces, particularly so-called volunteer battalions deployed to fight alongside regular forces in Donbass. Several cases of abuses by Aidar battalion were documented between June and August in Luhansk Region. These included abductions of local men accused of collaborating with the separatists and holding them in makeshift detention facilities before either releasing them or handing them over to security services. In nearly all cases the captives were subjected to beatings, and had possessions, including cars and valuables, seized by the battalion members or had to pay a ransom for their release.[4]

MP Oleh Lyashko published several videos online of him leading a group of armed men in balaclavas apprehending, interrogating and ill-treating individuals he suspected of collaborating with separatists. No criminal investigation was initiated into his actions. He won a seat again at the parliamentary elections in October and his party entered the ruling coalition.

There was evidence of summary killings by each side in the conflict. Several separatist commanders boasted of having put captives to death for alleged crimes, and the de facto separatist authorities introduced the "death penalty" in their "criminal code".[5]

COMMUNAL VIOLENCE

With tensions affecting many regions of the country, demonstrators for and against the post-Yanukovych authorities clashed repeatedly in several cities, with police often failing to interfere or deal effectively with the resulting violence.

In Odessa, on 2 May, 48 anti-EuroMaydan protesters were killed, and over 200 injured, inside a burning building besieged by their opponents during violent clashes. Police failed to take effective action to prevent or contain the violence. Several criminal investigations into these events were opened.

In November, the first court hearings began in one of the related cases against 21 men, all of them pro-Russian activists, under charges relating to mass disorder and unlawful use of firearms and explosives. The secrecy surrounding the official investigations prompted concern about their effectiveness and impartiality.

ARMED CONFLICT

Over 4,000 people had died in the conflict in eastern Ukraine by the end of the year. Many civilian deaths resulted from the indiscriminate use of force by both sides, notably as a result of the use of unguided mortars and rockets in civilian areas.

Both sides failed to take reasonable precautions to protect civilians, in violation of the laws of war.[6] Both placed troops, weaponry and other military targets in residential areas. On numerous occasions, separatist forces used residential areas and buildings as firing positions, while pro-Kyiv forces returned fire to these positions. There was little indication that either side was seriously investigating alleged violations of international humanitarian law and possible war crimes by its own forces.

On 17 July, separatist forces reported the destruction of a Ukrainian military plane. When it transpired that a Malaysian Airlines civilian passenger jet had been shot down, killing nearly 300 people, the claim was retracted, with both sides since blaming the other for the act. An international investigation into the incident was ongoing by the end of the year.

DISPLACED PEOPLE

Those escaping the Russian occupation of Crimea – around 20,000 – received some state support for resettlement. Close to a million people were estimated to have been displaced as a result of the conflict in Donbass, around half of them internally and the rest mainly in Russia. In Ukraine, most received limited state support and relied on their own means, family networks and the assistance of volunteer organizations. The adoption of a law on internally displaced people, in October, had changed little on the ground by the end of the year.

CRIMEA

Following Russia's annexation of Crimea in March, its restrictive laws were used to suppress the rights to freedom of assembly, association and expression in the territory. Civil society organizations were effectively closed down for non-compliance with Russian legal requirements. Local residents were declared Russian citizens. Those wishing to retain Ukrainian citizenship were required to notify the authorities.

The self-styled "self-defence" paramilitary forces committed numerous grave abuses, including enforced disappearances, with impunity. De facto Prime Minister of Crimea, Sergei Aksionov, stated that although these paramilitaries had no official status or authority, his government relied on them and chose "sometimes to overlook" abuses committed by them.

There were numerous reports of abductions of pro-Ukrainian activists in Crimea.

EuroMaydan activists Oleksandra Ryazantseva and Kateryna Butko were abducted on 9 March after being stopped at a checkpoint, reportedly manned by riot police officers and Crimean "self-defence" paramilitaries armed with guns and knives. They were released on 12 March.[7]

Oleg Sentsov, a well known pro-Ukrainian activist and film director, was secretly arrested by Russian security officials in Crimea on 9 May and unlawfully transferred to Moscow, along with several other individuals. Criminal proceedings against him – under terrorism-related charges that appeared groundless – were conducted in secrecy, and his allegations of torture dismissed by the authorities.

Crimean Tatars, an ethnic group indigenous to the peninsula (deported to remote parts of the Soviet Union in 1944 and not allowed to

return until the late 1980s), were particularly targeted by the de facto authorities for the public expression of pro-Ukrainian views. Starting in March, there were a number of abductions and beatings of Crimean Tatars which the de facto authorities failed to investigate.

On 3 March Reshat Ametov, a Crimean Tatar, was led away by three men from the "self-defence" forces after staging a one-man protest in front of the Crimean Council of Ministers building in the region's capital Simferopol. His body was found almost two weeks later, showing signs of torture. His abductors were not identified.

The de facto authorities started a campaign to close the Mejlis, a body elected by the Crimean Tatar assembly (Kurultai) and recognized by the Ukrainian authorities as the representative organ of the Tatar community.

Mustafa Dzhemiliev, a veteran human rights defender and founder of the Mejlis, was banned from entering Crimea. He was repeatedly denied entry, including on 3 May when he tried to cross through a checkpoint at Armyansk. Hundreds of Crimean Tatars came to meet him. The de facto authorities claimed that this was an unlawful assembly, and dozens of participants were fined. The homes of several Crimean Tatar leaders were subsequently searched and at least four Crimean Tatars were arrested, charged with "extremism" and transferred to Russia for investigation.

On 5 July, Refat Chubarov, who succeeded Mustafa Dzhemiliev as the leader of the Mejlis, was also prevented from returning to Crimea and banned for five years. The newly appointed de facto Prosecutor of Crimea travelled to the border crossing to warn him that the activities of the Mejlis violated the Russian law on extremism. On 19 September, the Russian authorities confiscated the headquarters of the Mejlis on the grounds that its founder (Mustafa Dzhemiliev) was a foreign citizen, who had been banned from entering Russia.

On 16 May, just two days before the planned annual events to mark the 70th anniversary of the deportation of Crimean Tatars in 1944, the de facto Prime Minister of Crimea announced that all mass meetings in Crimea would be banned until 6 June, in order to "eliminate possible provocations by extremists" and to prevent "disruption of the summer holiday season". Just one commemorative Crimean Tatar event was allowed on the day, on the outskirts of Simferopol, with a heavy police presence.

RIGHTS OF LESBIAN, GAY, BISEXUAL, TRANSGENDER AND INTERSEX PEOPLE

An LGBTI Pride March planned for 5 July in Kyiv was cancelled after the police told the organizing committee that they could not secure the safety of participants in the face of expected counter-demonstrations. The newly elected Mayor of Kyiv, Vitaliy Klychko, stated on 27 June that this was not the time for such "entertainment events" in Ukraine.

1. Ukraine: Mounting evidence of war crimes and Russian involvement (News story)
www.amnesty.org/en/news/ukraine-mounting-evidence-war-crimes-and-russian-involvement-2014-09-05

2. Ukraine: Kyiv protest ban blatant attempt to "gag peaceful protesters" (News story)
www.amnesty.org.uk/press-releases/ukraine-kiev-protest-ban-blatant-attempt-gag-peaceful-protesters

3. Ukraine: a new country or business as usual? (EUR 50/028/2014)
www.amnesty.org/en/documents/EUR50/028/2014/en/

4. Ukraine: Abuses and war crimes by the AidarVolunteer Battalion in the north Luhansk region (EUR 50/040/2014)
www.amnesty.org/en/documents/EUR50/040/2014/en/

5. Summary: killings during the conflict in eastern Ukraine (EUR 50/042/2014)
www.amnesty.org/en/library/info/EUR50/042/2014/en

6. Eastern Ukraine: Both sides responsible for indiscriminate attacks (Press release)
www.amnesty.org/en/articles/news/2014/11/eastern-ukraine-both-sides-responsible-indiscriminate-attacks/

7. Ukraine: Journalists at risk of abduction in Crimea (EUR 50/015/2014)
www.amnesty.org/en/library/info/EUR50/015/2014/en

UNITED ARAB EMIRATES

United Arab Emirates
Head of state: **Sheikh Khalifa bin Zayed Al Nahyan**
Head of government: **Sheikh Mohammed bin Rashid Al Maktoum**

The government restricted the rights to freedom of expression and association, and prosecuted critics using provisions of the Penal Code and the 2012 cybercrimes law. Prisoners of conscience continued to be held after unfair trials in which courts accepted evidence allegedly obtained through torture and other violations of their rights. Women faced discrimination in law and practice. Migrants, especially women domestic workers, were inadequately protected by law and faced exploitation and abuse. The government declared a partial moratorium on executions after carrying out an execution in January.

BACKGROUND

The Federal National Council approved a draft child rights law. It was awaiting presidential approval at the end of the year. In April, a government minister announced that the authorities were preparing a law to regulate the activities of foreign NGOs. No draft had been published by the end of the year.

FREEDOMS OF EXPRESSION, ASSOCIATION AND ASSEMBLY

The authorities used provisions of the Penal Code and the cybercrimes law of 2012 to stifle dissent and to prosecute and imprison government critics on charges including "instigating hatred against the state", and "contacting foreign organizations", based on comments they had posted on social media. Those imprisoned included Osama al-Najjar, who was prosecuted on charges arising from his use of Twitter to campaign for the release of his father, Hussain Ali al-Najjar al-Hammadi.

Hussain Ali al-Najjar al-Hammadi and 60 others associated with al-Islah, the Reform and Social Guidance Association, remained in prison serving sentences of up to 10 years. They were convicted on national security charges in July 2013 after the unfair "UAE 94" trial before the State Security Chamber of the Federal Supreme Court (FSC). The Court failed to investigate allegations that some defendants were tortured during months of pre-trial incommunicado detention to obtain "confessions" that formed the basis of the prosecution case against them, and which the court accepted as evidence. The defendants were denied a right of appeal, in breach of international fair trial standards. They included prisoners of conscience Mohammed al-Roken, a prominent human rights lawyer, former judge Ahmed al-Zaabi, and bloggers Saleh Mohammed al-Dhufairi and Khalifa al-Nuaimi. The UN Working Group on Arbitrary Detention stated that the 61 defendants imprisoned were victims of arbitrary arrest and detention, and urged the government to release them and afford them appropriate reparation.

In February, after visiting the United Arab Emirates (UAE), the UN Special Rapporteur on the independence of judges and lawyers urged the government to conduct an independent investigation into allegations of torture of detainees and institute a right of appeal in cases heard in first instance by the FSC, among other reforms.

TORTURE AND OTHER ILL-TREATMENT

The authorities failed to conduct independent investigations into allegations of torture and other ill-treatment made by defendants in trials before the State Security Chamber of the FSC in 2013 and 2014 and by several British nationals detained by police on suspicion of drugs offences. Reported methods of torture and other ill-treatment included beating, electric shocks, exposure to extreme temperatures and continuous bright lights, sleep deprivation, and threats of rape and death.

In September, UAE authorities forcibly returned an Ethiopian national, despite fears that he would face torture in Ethiopia.

COUNTER-TERROR AND SECURITY

The authorities detained scores of people, including foreign nationals, as terrorism suspects and held them in undisclosed locations without access to their families or legal counsel, often for long periods.

In January, the State Security Chamber of the FSC imposed prison terms of up to five years on 10 Emiratis and 20 Egyptians after convicting them of secretly establishing an "international branch" of the Muslim Brotherhood in the UAE. The 10 Emiratis were already serving lengthy prison terms imposed at the end of the "UAE 94" trial in July 2013. Their trial did not meet international fair trial standards.

In March, the FSC convicted three men on charges including "financially and morally" supporting al-Islah, sentencing two Emiratis to five-year prison terms and a Qatari national to seven years' imprisonment. The defendants denied the charges but were convicted on the basis of "confessions" that they said security officials had obtained from them under torture or other duress.

In June, the FSC convicted seven foreign nationals on terrorism-related charges, imposing sentences of between seven years' and life imprisonment, and in September the Court began trying 15 defendants accused of involvement with armed groups participating in the Syrian conflict. In December, 11 of the defendants were convicted and sentenced to between three years' and life imprisonment; the others were acquitted.

A new anti-terrorism law enacted in August prescribed severe penalties, including death, for people convicted of terrorism, defined broadly to include any acts resulting in a "terrorist outcome," such as declaring by any public means "enmity to the state or regime" or "non-allegiance to its leadership".

In November, the government declared al-Islah and more than 80 other groups "terrorist" organizations; they included many armed groups active in other countries as well as several Muslim aid organizations.

WOMEN'S RIGHTS

Women faced discrimination in law and practice. The UN Special Rapporteur on the independence of judges and lawyers recorded "institutionalized gender discrimination within the administration of justice". She highlighted that women were not allowed to become federal court judges, in violation of CEDAW, to which the UAE is a party.

MIGRANT WORKER'S RIGHTS

Despite protective provisions in the 1980 Labour Law and subsequent decrees, foreign migrant workers were exploited and abused. Many workers, who had generally paid fees to recruiting agents, reported that they were deceived over the terms and conditions of their work. Construction workers often lived in poor and inadequate accommodation, while few held their own passports. Late payment or non-payment of wages was common. The *kafala* sponsorship system made workers vulnerable to abuse by employers, while those involved in collective action such as strikes or sit-ins were liable to arrest and deportation.

Domestic workers, mostly women from Asia, continued to be excluded from the protections afforded to other migrant workers, and faced physical violence, confinement to places of work and labour abuses. The authorities had been considering a draft law on domestic workers since at least 2012 but did not enact it in 2014.

DEATH PENALTY

Courts continued to impose death sentences, mostly for murder. In January, the authorities in Sharjah emirate executed a Sri Lankan man by firing squad. The following month, the President declared a stay on all pending executions for murder to enable the authorities to contact victims' families

and ascertain whether they would accept "blood money" for their relatives' deaths. In May, press reports indicated that a court in Abu Dhabi sentenced a woman to death by stoning for adultery.

UNITED KINGDOM

United Kingdom of Great Britain and Northern Ireland
Head of state: **Queen Elizabeth II**
Head of government: **David Cameron**

The Prime Minister confirmed that a Conservative Party government would repeal the Human Rights Act if elected in 2015. Allegations of torture in relation to counter-terrorism operations overseas remained unresolved. The government passed legislation extending communications data interception powers. Accountability mechanisms for historical human rights violations and abuses in Northern Ireland remained inadequate. Access to abortion remained extremely limited in Northern Ireland.

LEGAL, CONSTITUTIONAL OR INSTITUTIONAL DEVELOPMENTS

In a referendum held in Scotland in September, voters opted against independence.

Charities and civil society organizations expressed concerns about the Transparency of Lobbying, Non-Party Campaigning and Trade Union Administration Act 2014, which entered into force in September. The Act could significantly restrict their public-facing campaigning in a "regulated period" leading up to a national election.

The effects of cuts to legal aid made in 2012 and 2013, including under the Legal Aid, Sentencing and Punishment of Offenders Act, continued to restrict access to justice.

Legislation introduced to restrict judicial review raised similar concerns.

In October, Prime Minister Cameron confirmed that, if elected, a Conservative Party government would repeal the Human Rights Act and replace it with a British Bill of Rights, with a view to limiting the influence of the European Court of Human Rights. Draft proposals threatened significant restrictions on rights.

TORTURE AND OTHER ILL-TREATMENT
Detainee Inquiry

In December 2013, a report of the Detainee Inquiry's preparatory work was published, 23 months after the Justice Secretary's closure of an inquiry into allegations of UK involvement in torture and other violations against individuals detained abroad in counter-terrorism operations. The report set out lines of investigation for any future inquiry. The government announced that the matters raised by the Detainee Inquiry's report would be addressed by the parliamentary Intelligence and Security Committee, rather than by an independent, public inquiry.[1] The government deferred indefinitely the prospect of any new, independent, judge-led inquiry.

Libyan renditions

On 30 October, the Court of Appeal ruled that there were compelling reasons requiring it to exercise jurisdiction over a civil claim brought by married couple Abdul Hakim Belhaj and Fatima Boudchar, who alleged that they were victims of rendition, torture and other ill-treatment in 2004 by the US and Libyan governments, with the knowledge and co-operation of UK officials.[2] The government appealed against the decision.

Diplomatic assurances

The government continued to rely on unreliable and unenforceable diplomatic assurances when seeking to deport individuals allegedly posing a threat to national security to countries where they would be at risk of grave human rights violations, including torture.

In July 2013, the UK authorities deported Abu Qatada to Jordan where the State Security Court failed to disregard torture-tainted "confessions" in two criminal trials against him (see Jordan entry). In July 2014, the Court of Appeal heard an appeal by eight Algerian nationals against a January 2013 decision by the Special Immigration Appeals Commission to allow their deportation with assurances.

Armed forces in Iraq

In May 2013, the High Court ruled that the Iraq Historic Allegations Team (IHAT), a unit within the Ministry of Defence set up to investigate allegations of abuses of Iraqi civilians by UK armed forces between March 2003 and July 2009, was failing to meet its obligations to uphold the right to life. The judge ruled that small inquiries modelled on inquests were needed, but rejected the claimants' arguments that IHAT lacked independence and should be replaced by a single, public inquiry.

In May 2014, the Prosecutor of the International Criminal Court reopened a preliminary investigation into allegations that UK armed forces committed war crimes involving systematic detainee abuse in Iraq.

In November, a High Court judge ruled that two Pakistani men captured by UK forces in Iraq in 2004 and subsequently transferred to US custody in Afghanistan, had the right to sue the UK government in UK courts for damages.

In December, the Al-Sweady Inquiry, established in 2009 to examine allegations that British soldiers tortured or ill-treated nine Iraqi detainees after a battle near the town of Majar al-Kabir in southern Iraq in 2004, published its findings. The report found the most serious allegations to be "wholly without foundation", but acknowledged that detainee handling practices had been "less than satisfactory" and "developed on an ad hoc basis", and compounded by the lack of guidance for soldiers.

COUNTER-TERROR AND SECURITY

In October 2013, the Supreme Court stated its concern about the excessively broad statutory definition of terrorism in the case of *R v. Gul*, referring to reports by the Independent Reviewer of Terrorism Legislation. In February 2014, however, the High Court held that the decision to stop, question and detain David Miranda, the spouse of journalist Glenn Greenwald, in August 2013 under Schedule 7 of the Terrorism Act 2000 had been lawful and proportionate. The decision was appealed against. The Independent Reviewer reiterated his call for narrowing the definitions of "terrorism" and "terrorism-related activity" during the year.

In October, the prosecution of UK national Moazzam Begg collapsed. He was on trial for seven terrorism-related offences relating to Syria. The prosecution offered no evidence at trial after receiving new information, allegedly from the British security service MI5. The trial judge formally entered "not guilty" judgments on all seven charges.[3]

In November, the government introduced the Counter-Terrorism and Security Bill as fast-tracked legislation. The proposed powers included restricting the travel of people suspected of involvement in terrorism-related activity, including exclusion of certain UK residents who refuse to agree to government-imposed conditions on their return home. It also added powers under existing Terrorism Prevention and Investigation Measures, restricting the liberty, movement and activities of people believed to pose a threat to national security.

NORTHERN IRELAND

The mechanisms and institutions mandated to address "legacy" (conflict-related or historical) human rights violations in previous decades operated in a fragmented and incremental manner.

The Historical Enquiries Team (HET), mandated since 2006 to re-examine all deaths attributed to the conflict in Northern Ireland, was closed following wide criticism.

In July 2013, Her Majesty's Inspectorate of Constabulary had found that the HET reviewed cases involving the state with less rigour than non-state cases. The transfer, announced in December, of some of HET's work to a Legacy Investigative Branch within the Police Service of Northern Ireland (PSNI) prompted concerns over the independence of future case reviews.

Positive reforms to the Office of the Police Ombudsman for Northern Ireland (OPONI) continued throughout 2013 and 2014. A 30 September report by Criminal Justice Inspection Northern Ireland found that confidence in the OPONI's investigation of historical cases had been "fully restored". However, on the same day, cuts to the OPONI's budget led to a loss of 25% of staff working on legacy cases, and serious concerns about the OPONI's ability to complete "legacy" casework.

Under-resourcing and delays to Northern Ireland's coronial inquest system remained endemic. In a November judgment, the Lord Chief Justice of Northern Ireland noted that the legislative failure to remedy deficiencies in the inquest system were preventing coroners from exercising their role satisfactorily and expeditiously.

The government remained unwilling to establish public inquiries into legacy cases. In September 2013, the Northern Ireland Secretary refused to establish an inquiry into the August 1998 bombing by the Real IRA armed group in Omagh. The government continued to refuse to establish an independent inquiry into the 1989 killing of Belfast solicitor Patrick Finucane.[4]

In September 2013, inter-party talks chaired by former US diplomat Richard Haass began with the aim of reaching agreement on parades and protests; the use of flags, symbols and emblems; and how to deal with "the past". The talks ended without agreement on 31 December 2013. The draft Haass proposals detailed two mechanisms: an Historical Investigation Unit (HIU) and an Independent Commission for Information Retrieval (ICIR).[5] Further talks, which concluded in December 2014, agreed in principle to take forward the Haass proposals of an HIU and ICIR, although details of finance, resourcing, timeframes and legislation were not completely resolved at the end of the year.

In June, the Irish television channel RTÉ broadcast newly discovered archival material suggesting that the UK had misled the European Court of Human Rights in *Ireland v. UK*, over the use of five torture techniques used by British security forces in Northern Ireland in 1971-1972. In December, the Irish government sought a reopening of the case by the European Court. Lawyers for the victims also called for an independent, human rights-compliant investigation in the UK into the new evidence.[6]

SEXUAL AND REPRODUCTIVE RIGHTS

Access to abortion in Northern Ireland remained limited to exceptional cases where the life or health of the woman or girl was at risk. The Abortion Act 1967 did not apply to Northern Ireland. In October, the Department of Justice opened a consultation on legislating for access to abortion in cases of rape, incest and fatal foetal anomaly.

SURVEILLANCE

In July, the Data Retention and Investigatory Powers Act entered into force, extending the reach of the authorities' interception powers by providing potentially wide-ranging extraterritorial effects to UK interception warrants. Sufficient safeguards were not in place to ensure that such surveillance was authorized and carried out in conformity with the rights to privacy and freedom of expression.

In December, the Investigatory Powers Tribunal (IPT) made public its open judgment in the first part of a complaint brought by Amnesty International and other NGOs about the UK authorities' communications surveillance practices. The IPT found that the authorities' surveillance practices were in accordance with the law. Significant portions of the proceedings were held in secret.[7]

REFUGEES' AND MIGRANTS' RIGHTS

In January, the government announced that it would provide resettlement for 500 vulnerable Syrian refugees. The Vulnerable Persons Relocation scheme prioritizes assisting survivors of torture and violence, women and children at risk and those in need of medical care, as identified by UNHCR, the UN refugee agency.

In July 2013, an inquest jury returned a verdict of unlawful killing in the death in 2010 of Jimmy Mubenga, an Angolan national who died after being restrained by private security guards on board a plane deporting him to Angola. In December, the three guards involved in his removal were cleared of manslaughter.

In July, the High Court found that the long-term immigration detention of a Guinean woman constituted inhuman and degrading treatment. It was the sixth such court finding since 2011.

In December, the Court of Appeal found the policy underpinning the UK's "detained fast-track" asylum process to be unlawful and upheld the High Court's earlier July ruling that inadequate access to legal representation rendered the process unlawful.

TRAFFICKING IN HUMAN BEINGS

In June, the government published draft legislation to address slavery and human trafficking in England and Wales. The Modern Slavery Bill was amended to include UK-wide provisions, including the establishment of an anti-slavery commissioner.

Also in June, the anti-trafficking legislation was presented to the Northern Ireland Assembly. Similar legislation was presented to the Scottish Parliament in December.

---

1. United Kingdom: Joint NGO letter (EUR 45/005/2014)
   www.amnesty.org/en/library/info/EUR45/005/2014/en

2. UK: Court of Appeal allows lawsuit to proceed in case of illegal rendition to torture in Libya (EUR 45/010/2014)
www.amnesty.org/en/library/info/EUR45/010/2014/en

3. UK: Collapsed prosecution of Moazzam Begg (EUR 45/009/2014)
www.amnesty.org/en/library/info/EUR45/009/2014/en

4. United Kingdom/Northern Ireland: Still no public inquiry twenty-five years after the killing of Patrick Finucane (EUR 45/003/2014)
www.amnesty.org/en/library/info/EUR45/003/2014/en .

5. United Kingdom/Northern Ireland: Haass proposals on dealing with the past (EUR 45/001/2014)
www.amnesty.org/en/library/info/EUR45/001/2014/en

6. UK/Ireland: Landmark 'hooded men' torture case should be reopened (News story)
www.amnesty.org/en/news/ukireland-landmark-hooded-men-torture-case-should-be-re-opened-2014-11-24

7. UK court decision on government mass surveillance: 'Trust us' isn't enough (Press release)
www.amnesty.org/en/articles/news/2014/12/uk-court-decision-government-mass-surveillance-trust-us-isnt-enough/

UNITED STATES OF AMERICA

United States of America
Head of state and government: **Barack Obama**

President Obama acknowledged that torture had been carried out following the 11 September 2001 attacks (9/11) under a secret detention programme authorized by his predecessor and operated by the Central Intelligence Agency (CIA). However, accountability and remedy for the crimes under international law committed in that programme remained absent. The declassified summary of a Senate report into the programme was released in December. Scores of detainees remained in indefinite military detention at the US naval base at Guantánamo Bay in Cuba, while military commission trial proceedings continued in a handful of cases. Concern about the use of prolonged isolation in state and federal prisons and the excessive use of force by police continued. Thirty-three men and two women were executed during the year.

BACKGROUND

The USA appeared before three UN treaty bodies in 2014. In April, the Human Rights Committee criticized the USA on a range of issues – including the lack of accountability for abuses in the counter-terrorism context, solitary confinement in prisons, racial disparities in the criminal justice system, targeted killings by drones, excessive use of force by law enforcement officials, the treatment of migrants and the death penalty.[1] In August, the Committee on the Elimination of Racial Discrimination also made numerous recommendations to the USA. In November, the Committee against Torture's concluding observations similarly covered a range of issues.[2]

IMPUNITY

In August, President Obama acknowledged that the USA used torture in its response to the 9/11 attacks. He stated that torture was carried out under "some" of the "enhanced interrogation techniques" used in the programme, not just the one known as "waterboarding" (mock execution by interrupted drowning). Nevertheless, the President remained silent on accountability and redress, reflecting the USA's continuing refusal to meet its international obligations on these issues. Neither did he make any reference to enforced disappearance, a crime under international law to which most, if not all, of those held in the secret programme were subjected, some of them for years.[3]

In April, the Senate Select Committee on Intelligence (SSCI) voted to submit for declassification the summary of its report into the CIA's secret detention and interrogation programme operated between 2002 and 2008. Release of the summary came on 9 December and the 500-page document contained some new details on the programme and the torture and other human rights violations committed in it. The full 6,700 page report – containing "details of each detainee in CIA custody, the conditions under which they were detained, [and] how they were interrogated" – remained classified top secret.

COUNTER-TERROR – DETENTIONS

At the end of 2014, 127 men were held at Guantánamo, the majority without charge or trial. Almost half had been approved for transfer out of the base, most since January 2010 or earlier. Twenty-eight detainees were transferred out of the base during the year, following the 11 who had been transferred from there in 2013.

The transfer to Qatar in May of five Afghan men held in Guantánamo for more than a decade, in exchange for a US soldier held for five years in Taliban custody, sparked congressional opposition to President Obama's stated goal of closing the detention facility.[4]

Some detainees engaged in hunger strikes during the year, although not in the numbers seen during 2013.[5] Official transparency around hunger strikes remained at issue following the policy decision in late 2013 to stop making public the number of detainees engaging in such protests. In litigation in May 2014, the government disclosed that it possessed videotapes, classified as secret, of the forcible cell extractions and forced feeding of Abu Wa'el Dhiab, a Syrian man held at the base but approved for transfer since 2009. In October, over government opposition, a District Court judge ordered the videotape evidence to be unsealed and certain information redacted from the tapes. The administration appealed, and the case was pending in the US Court of Appeals at the end of the year.

In November, the US administration told the UN Committee against Torture that, in contrast to positions previously taken by the US government, the USA had now decided that the Convention against Torture applied at Guantánamo and on US-registered ships and aircraft.

In February, Ahmed Mohammed al Darbi, a Saudi Arabian national arrested by civilian authorities in Azerbaijan in June 2002 and transferred to US custody two months later, pleaded guilty at a hearing before a military commission judge at Guantánamo and agreed not to sue the USA over his treatment in custody. His conviction brought to eight the number of detainees convicted by military commission since detentions began at Guantánamo in January 2002. Six of these eight men were convicted under pre-trial plea bargains.

Pre-trial military commission proceedings continued against five Guantánamo detainees – Khalid Sheikh Mohammed, Walid bin Attash, Ramzi bin al-Shibh, 'Ali 'Abd al-'Aziz and Mustafa al Hawsawi – accused of involvement in the 9/11 attacks. The five and 'Abd al-Rahim al-Nashiri, who was arraigned for capital trial in 2011 on charges relating to the bombing of the USS Cole in Yemen in 2000, had been held incommunicado in secret US custody for up to four years prior to their transfer to Guantánamo in 2006. Their trials had not begun by the end of 2014.

Iraqi national 'Abd al Hadi al-Iraqi, who was reportedly arrested in Turkey in October 2006, transferred to US custody, held in secret by the CIA and transferred to Guantánamo in April 2007, was arraigned in June. His trial on charges under the Military Commissions Act (MCA) was pending at the end of 2014.

In May, the General Counsel for the US Department of Defense affirmed that the administration was continuing to use the 2001 Authorization for Use of Military Force (AUMF) as the underpinning of its detention operations in Afghanistan and Guantánamo and "capture or lethal operations" against individuals elsewhere. He pointed to the case of Libyan national Nazih Abdul-Hamed al-Ruqai, also known as Abu Anas al-Libi, as an example of an operation that relied on the AUMF. Abu al-Libi was abducted in Tripoli, Libya, by US forces on 5 October 2013 and interrogated aboard the *USS San Antonio* before being taken to the USA and charged in relation to the 1998 bombings of two US embassies in Kenya and Tanzania.

Abu al-Libi's lawyer alleged in court in 2014 that the abduction had been conducted "with the use of extreme physical and brutal force", and that after dragging the suspect from his car and "using tazer-like weapons" on him, the US forces had blindfolded him, and "bound, gagged and trussed [him] up". On the ship, he was held incommunicado and interrogated daily for the next week by CIA personnel and others. He alleged that he was subjected, effectively, to sleep deprivation, through the use of prolonged back-to-back interrogations. His incommunicado detention and interrogation were cut short due to a life-threatening illness. His trial was pending at the end of the year, but on 31 December, he was taken to hospital where he died on 2 January 2015.

US forces seized Ahmed Abu Khatallah near Benghazi, eastern Libya, on 15 June. On 17 June, the US administration informed the UN Security Council that the US operation to take Ahmed Khatallah into custody had been conducted under the USA's "inherent right to self-defense" on the grounds that he "continued to plan further armed attacks against US persons". The letter gave no information about this alleged planning, rendering an assessment of the USA's self-defence claim all but impossible. In October, Ahmed Khatallah was charged with offences punishable by the death penalty in relation to an attack on the US diplomatic mission in Benghazi in 2012 in which four US nationals were killed. He was being held in pre-trial solitary confinement in Virginia at the end of the year.[6]

During the year, the remaining non-Afghan detainees in US military detention at the Bagram airbase in Afghanistan were transferred to the custody of other governments. In August, two Yemeni nationals held in US custody in Afghanistan for more than a decade were transferred to Yemen.

In November, a Russian national who had been held in US military custody at Bagram since 2009 was transferred to the USA for prosecution in a federal court on terrorism charges. Ireq Ilgiz Hamidullin became the first detainee to be transferred from Bagram directly to the USA, almost 13 years after detentions began at the base.

Tunisian national Redha al Najar was transferred to Afghan custody on 10 December, the day after release of the SSCI summary report in which his case featured as one of those subjected to torture in a secret CIA facility in Afghanistan in 2002. On 11 December, the Department of Defense said that the Bagram detention facility was now closed.

In November, President Obama said that discussions between Congress and the administration were continuing on how to "right-size and update" the AUMF "to suit the current fight, rather than previous fights".

PRISON CONDITIONS

Tens of thousands of prisoners remained in isolation in state and federal prisons across the USA, confined to cells for between 22 and 24 hours a day in conditions of stark social and environmental deprivation.

In February, the Senate Judiciary Subcommittee held a second hearing on solitary confinement. Senator Durbin who chaired the hearing and urged reform of this practice, also pushed during the year for the opening of a new federal prison which would extend the number of federal isolation cells. Amnesty International's report into federal use of isolation concluded that conditions in the only current super-maximum security prison in Florence, Colorado, breached standards for the humane treatment of prisoners.[7]

In October, a settlement was reached in a class-action suit on behalf of more than 33,000 prisoners in Arizona's state prisons. Under this settlement, the Arizona Department of Corrections will allow prisoners in solitary confinement who have serious mental illnesses to have more mental health treatment and time outside their cells.

DEATH PENALTY

Thirty-three men and two women were put to death in 2014. Including the execution of 38 men and one woman in 2013, this brought to 1,394 the total number of people executed since the US Supreme Court approved new capital laws in 1976.

The number of executions in 2014 was the lowest since 1994. The continuing problems faced by states in obtaining drugs for lethal injections, and concerns over a number of "botched" executions, contributed to the slowdown. The 79 death sentences passed in 2013 and a similar number passed in 2014 represented a decline of about two thirds since the mid-1990s. A little under 3,000 men and about 55 women remained on death row at the end of the year.

Momentum against the death penalty continued with the announcement in February by the Governor of Washington State that he would not allow executions there while he held that office. This followed Maryland's abolition of the death penalty in 2013, bringing to 18 the number of abolitionist states, and strong indications that no executions would occur in Colorado under its current governor.

Executions in 2014 were carried out in seven states, two lower than in 2013. Just four states – Florida, Missouri, Oklahoma and Texas – accounted for 89% of the national judicial death toll in 2014. By the end of 2014, Texas accounted for 37% of all executions carried out in the USA since 1976. Texas has executed more people for crimes committed when they were 17, 18 or 19 years old than any other state has executed in total.[8]

On 27 May, the US Supreme Court clarified the protection for capital defendants with intellectual disability (formerly known in the USA as "mental retardation"). The Court ruled that Florida's law requiring a capital defendant to show an IQ score of 70 or below was unconstitutional as it blocked the presentation of evidence other than IQ that would demonstrate limitations in the defendant's mental faculties.[9]

Lawyers for Ramiro Hernandez Llanas, a Mexican national on death row in Texas, had sought a stay of execution until after the Supreme Court ruling to allow its impact on his case to be assessed. No stay was granted and he was executed on 9 April, despite a compelling claim that his intellectual disability rendered his execution unconstitutional. In January, Texas executed another Mexican national in violation of an order of the International Court of Justice and despite a finding by the Inter-American Commission on Human Rights that he had been denied a fair trial. Edgar Arias Tamayo had been denied his right to seek consular assistance after his arrest.

In January, Florida executed Askari Abdullah Muhammad (formerly Thomas Knight), who had been on death row for four decades and had a long history of serious mental illness. In September, Earl Ringo, an African American man, was executed in Missouri despite claims that race had tainted the prosecution; he was sentenced to death by an all-white jury at a trial in which the defence lawyer, the judge and the prosecutor were also white.[10]

During the year, seven previously condemned inmates were released on the grounds of innocence, bringing to 150 the number of such cases in the USA since 1973.

CHILDREN'S RIGHTS – LIFE IMPRISONMENT WITHOUT PAROLE

Defendants who were under 18 years old at the time of the crime continued to face life imprisonment without the possibility of parole (life without parole). States responded in various ways to the 2012 US Supreme Court decision, *Miller v. Alabama*, outlawing mandatory life without parole for this age group. By October 2014, eight state supreme courts had ruled that the *Miller* ruling was retroactive, compared to four that had ruled to the contrary. In December, the US Supreme Court agreed to review the appeal of a prisoner sentenced under Louisiana's mandatory sentencing scheme to life without parole for a crime committed when he was 17, to decide the *Miller* retroactivity question. The case was pending at the end of the year.

In August, the American Correctional Association adopted a resolution opposing life without parole against those who were under 18 at the time of the crime and supporting "sentencing policies that hold youthful offenders accountable in an age-appropriate way, while focusing on rehabilitation and reintegration into society".

EXCESSIVE USE OF FORCE

At least 35 people across 18 states died after being struck by police Tasers, bringing the total number of such deaths since 2001 to 602. Tasers have been listed as a cause or contributory factor in more than 60 deaths. Most of those who died after being struck with a Taser were not armed and did not appear to pose a serious threat when the Taser was deployed.

Michael Brown, an 18-year-old unarmed African American man, was fatally shot by police officer Darren Wilson in Ferguson, Missouri on 9 August. The shooting set off months of protests in and around Ferguson. The use of heavy-duty riot gear and military-grade weapons and equipment to police the demonstrations served to intimidate protesters who were exercising their right to peaceful assembly while the use of rubber bullets, tear gas and other aggressive dispersal tactics was not warranted, and protesters and journalists were injured as a result.

A number of other incidents demonstrated the need for a review of standards on the use of force in the USA. These included the deaths of Kajieme Powell, a 25-year-old black man, who was shot and killed by St Louis City Police on 19 August, with film footage of the incident appearing to contradict the initial official version of events; Ezell Ford, 25, an unarmed black man with a history of

mental illness, who was shot and killed by Los Angeles police officers on 11 August; and Eric Garner, a 43-year-old black man, who died on 17 July after being placed in a chokehold by New York Police Department officers while being arrested for selling loose, untaxed cigarettes. After a grand jury declined to return an indictment in the Garner case on 3 December, the US Attorney General announced a federal civil rights investigation into his death.

MIGRANTS' RIGHTS – UNACCOMPANIED CHILDREN

More than 50,000 unaccompanied migrant children were apprehended crossing the southern border of the USA in 2014, some as young as five. The US Border Patrol detained unaccompanied children for days or weeks in insanitary facilities and without access to legal counsel, translators or proper medical attention.

---

1. Loud and clear - UN Human Rights Committee makes wide-ranging recommendations to USA (AMR 51/022/2014)
   www.amnesty.org/en/library/info/AMR51/022/2014/en
2. USA should "put its money where its mouth is" and implement UN Committee against Torture findings (AMR 51/055/2014)
   www.amnesty.org/en/library/info/AMR51/055/2014/en
3. USA: "We tortured some folks" - The wait for truth, remedy and accountability continues as redaction issue delays release of senate report on CIA detentions (AMR 51/046/2014)
   www.amnesty.org/en/library/info/AMR51/046/2014/en
4. USA: "We have the ability to do things" - President and Congress should apply human rights principles and close Guantánamo (AMR 51/036/2014)
   www.amnesty.org/en/library/info/AMR51/036/2014/en
5. USA: "I have no reason to believe that I will ever leave this prison alive" - Indefinite detention at Guantánamo continues; 100 detainees on hunger strike (AMR 51/022/2013)
   www.amnesty.org/en/library/info/AMR51/022/2013/en
6. USA: Man seized in Libya faces death penalty in USA (AMR 51/037/2014)
   www.amnesty.org/en/library/info/AMR51/037/2014/en
7. Entombed: Isolation in the US federal prison system (AMR 51/040/2014)
   www.amnesty.org/en/library/info/AMR51/040/2014/en

8. USA: "He could have been a good kid" - Texas set to execute third young offender in two months (AMR 51/027/2014)
    www.amnesty.org/en/library/info/AMR51/027/2014/en
9. USA: "The nation we aspire to be" (AMR 51/034/2014)
    www.amnesty.org/en/library/info/AMR51/034/2014/en
10. USA: Call for race inquiry as execution nears - Earl Ringo (AMR 51/047/2014)
    www.amnesty.org/en/library/info/AMR51/047/2014/en

URUGUAY

Eastern Republic of Uruguay
Head of state and government: **José Alberto Mujica Cordano**

The fight for justice for human rights violations committed during the period of civil and military rule between 1973 and 1985 faced a possible step back following a Supreme Court decision in 2013. There were concerns over barriers to women's access to abortions.

BACKGROUND

Uruguay was reviewed under the UN Universal Periodic Review (UPR) process in January and accepted important recommendations, including to combat all forms of discrimination.

Uruguay ratified the UN Arms Trade Treaty in September.

Six detainees from the US detention centre in Guantánamo Bay, Cuba, were resettled in Uruguay in December.

General elections took place in October. Frente Amplio won following the second round in November.

IMPUNITY

In February 2013 the Supreme Court overturned two key articles of Law 18.831, adopted in 2011, which established that crimes committed during the period of civil and military rule between 1973 and 1985

were crimes against humanity and that no statute of limitations could be applied. The Supreme Court also concluded that no crimes against humanity were committed at the time because they were made criminal under national law only in 2006, and therefore they were subject to a statute of limitations.[1] During 2014 little progress was made to ensure that complaints for past human rights violations would be fully investigated.

The trial of a former police officer, charged in 2012 with complicity in the killing of teacher and journalist Julio Castro in 1977, continued at the end of the year.

SEXUAL AND REPRODUCTIVE RIGHTS

Compulsory requirements established by the 2012 law decriminalizing abortion remained a concern as they were a potential obstacle to accessing legal abortion. The 2012 law established a mandatory five-day reflection period and a review of cases by a panel of experts when an abortion is requested. Where pregnancy is a result of a rape, the law required that a judicial complaint be filed for the woman to access an abortion.

In April, in Salto, capital of Salto department, doctors refused to provide an abortion to a disabled pregnant girl who was a rape survivor, on grounds of conscientious objection. The girl had to travel to the capital Montevideo for the procedure.

PRISON CONDITIONS

In May, the UN Committee against Torture expressed concerns that two thirds of the prison population was awaiting trial, as well as concerns in relation to medical care, water supply, sanitation and ventilation in cells.

RIGHTS OF LESBIAN, GAY, BISEXUAL, TRANSGENDER AND INTERSEX PEOPLE

Investigations into the killings of five transsexual women between 2011 and 2012 showed little progress. In only one case, in the Department of Cerro Largo, three people were prosecuted.

1. Uruguay: Key human rights concerns - Amnesty International Submission to the UN Universal Periodic Review, January–February 2014 (AMR 52/001/2013) www.amnesty.org/en/library/info/AMR52/001/2013/en

UZBEKISTAN

Republic of Uzbekistan
Head of state: **Islam Karimov**
Head of government: **Shavkat Mirzioiev**

Torture and other ill-treatment in detention facilities remained routine and pervasive. The authorities continued to reject allegations of torture committed by law enforcement and National Security officers and failed to effectively investigate credible and persistent reports of such human rights violations. Prison sentences of individuals convicted of anti-state and terrorism offences were arbitrarily extended and many were denied necessary medical attention. Those forcibly returned from abroad were at real risk of torture and other ill-treatment.

TORTURE AND OTHER ILL-TREATMENT

Persistent and credible allegations continued to emerge of pervasive and routine torture and other ill-treatment by law enforcement and National Security (SNB) officers during arrest, transfer, in police custody and in pre-trial detention and by law enforcement and prison personnel in post-conviction detention facilities.[1]

The authorities continued to vigorously deny such reports, including during public examinations of Uzbekistan's human rights record at the EU-Uzbekistan Human Rights Dialogue in November. They instead pointed at the implementation of wide-ranging initiatives in the field of human rights education, such as numerous torture prevention training programmes for law enforcement officers and judicial and medical officials, and increased co-operation on human rights with the international community. However, as in previous years, these developments failed to lead to necessary, genuine and wide-reaching systemic reforms. Serious concerns remained about the authorities' failure to implement existing laws and safeguards and to adopt new effective measures towards the prevention of torture. The authorities also failed to effectively investigate reports of torture and other ill-treatment.

In November, the UN Human Rights Committee requested that Uzbekistan report on measures taken to implement the Committee's numerous previous recommendations to address torture from 1999, 2005 and 2010.

PRISON CONDITIONS

Certain categories of prisoners, such as human rights defenders, government critics and individuals convicted of membership in Islamist parties and groups or Islamic movements banned in Uzbekistan were often subjected to severe punishment regimes in prisons where they were serving their sentences. Some prisoners had their sentences extended for long periods – sometimes repeatedly – even for alleged minor infractions of the prison rules.

Murad Dzhuraev, a former parliamentarian who was sentenced to 12 years in prison on politically motivated charges in 1995, subsequently had his sentence extended four times under Article 221 of the Criminal Code for allegedly breaking prison rules.[2] One of the "violations" he had committed was failing to change out of slippers when entering the hall where prisoners slept.

Murad Dzhuraev's health seriously deteriorated during his extended time in prison. His wife was allowed to visit him for two days in July, and reported that he was almost blind and had lost all of his teeth. She alleged that he had not had access to adequate medical care since 1994. The prison authorities had also tried to isolate him from other prisoners by threatening to extend the sentences of every prisoner who dared to speak with him. He spent long periods of time in solitary confinement as a punishment allegedly for breaking prison rules.

At least two prisoners were reported to have died because they had not been provided with necessary medical care. Human rights defender Abdurasul Khudainazarov died of advanced terminal cancer on 26 June, three weeks after a court ordered his early release on humanitarian grounds. His family reported that over a period of eight years prison officials had repeatedly denied him necessary medical treatment for his cancer and other serious medical problems despite numerous requests and clear physical indications that his health was seriously deteriorating.

There were no independent monitoring mechanisms in place to inspect all places of detention and domestic or international NGOs did not carry out any form of regular, unannounced or unsupervised prison monitoring. Diplomats, while granted access to some detention facilities, were as a rule accompanied by prison or law enforcement officials during their visits. In January, the authorities granted a small number of independent human rights activists permission to visit four imprisoned colleagues. The human rights defenders were accompanied by law enforcement and prison officials and their visits were recorded on film. One of the prisoners reported that he had been allowed to have a hot shower before the meeting and was given new clothes ahead of the scheduled visit. In November, the NGO Human Rights Watch sent a delegation to Uzbekistan but all requests to visit prisoners and places of detention were denied by the authorities.

COUNTER-TERROR AND SECURITY

Individuals forcibly returned to Uzbekistan in the name of national security and the "fight against terrorism" were often held incommunicado, increasing their risk of torture or other ill-treatment. The authorities relentlessly pursued the return of individuals they suspected of involvement in bombings in the capital Tashkent in 1999 and 2004, protests in Andizhan in 2005 (during which hundreds of people were killed when the security forces fired on thousands of mostly peaceful protesters), and various other acts of violence. They accused some of being members of banned violent Islamist groups and also sought the extradition of political opponents, government critics, and wealthy individuals who had fallen out of favour with the authorities in Tashkent.

The European Court of Human Rights issued at least 15 judgments in 2013 and 2014 prohibiting the forcible transfer of individuals to Uzbekistan – especially those suspected of membership of an Islamist party or of a group banned in the country – due to the real risk of torture on return. The Court ruled in October, in the case of *Mamazhonov v Russia*, that the transfer of Ikromzhon Mamazhonov from Russia to Uzbekistan would violate Article 3 (prohibition of torture) of the European Convention on Human Rights. The Court noted "that there had been no improvement in the criminal justice system of Uzbekistan in recent years, in particular concerning prosecution for religiously and politically motivated crimes and that there was certain evidence that persons accused of such crimes were at risk of ill-treatment."

In November, Mirsobir Khamidkariev, a producer and businessman from Uzbekistan who had sought asylum in Moscow, Russian Federation, was sentenced to eight years in prison by a court in Tashkent.[3] He was convicted of membership of a banned Islamist organization, a charge he strongly denied. On 9 June he was reportedly abducted and ill-treated by officers of the Russian Federal Security Service (FSB) from a street in central Moscow, and handed over to Uzbekistani law enforcement officers at an airport in Moscow and illegally transferred to Tashkent the following day.

Mirsobir Khamidkariev's lawyer in Moscow did not know his whereabouts until he reappeared in the basement of a detention facility run by the Ministry of Internal Affairs in Tashkent two weeks later. According to his Russian lawyer, who was able to get access to him in Tashkent on 31 October, Mirsobir Khamidkariev was subjected to torture and other ill-treatment by law enforcement officers in Tashkent for two months to force him to confess to fabricated charges. He was tied head down to a bar attached to the wall, beaten repeatedly, and had seven of his teeth knocked out and two of his ribs broken.

1. Cases of torture and other ill-treatment in Uzbekistan (EUR 62/007/2014)
   www.amnesty.org/en/library/info/EUR62/007/2014/en
2. Uzbekistan: Jailed parliamentarian denied medical help - Murad Dzhuraev (EUR 62/003/2014)
   www.amnesty.org/en/library/info/EUR62/003/2014/en
3. Uzbekistan: Fear of unfair trial for extradited refugee - Mirsobir Khamidkariev (EUR 62/008/2014)
   www.amnesty.org/en/library/info/EUR62/008/2014/en

VENEZUELA

Bolivarian Republic of Venezuela
Head of state and government: **Nicolás Maduro Moros**

The security forces used excessive force to disperse protests. Scores of people were arbitrarily detained and denied access to lawyers and doctors. Torture and other ill-treatment of protesters and passers-by were reported. The judiciary continued to be used to silence government critics. Those defending human rights were intimidated and attacked. Prison conditions remained harsh.

BACKGROUND

President Maduro's first year in office was marked by growing discontent. Between February and July 2014, Venezuela was shaken by mass pro- and anti-government demonstrations in various parts of the country. Anti-government protesters and some opposition party leaders who called for the resignation of the President were accused of attempting to overthrow the government.

FREEDOM OF ASSEMBLY

At least 43 people were killed and more than 870 were injured – including protesters, security forces officials and passers-by – during mass pro- and anti-government protests between February and July. There were reports of human rights violations and of violent clashes between demonstrators and the security forces and armed pro-government groups.[1]

More than 3,000 people were detained in the context of the protests. Most were charged and released after a few days. At the end of the year over 70 people who took part in the demonstrations remained in pre-trial detention awaiting trial.

There were concerns that a ruling by the Supreme Court in March, which stated that any protest had to be pre-authorized, could jeopardize the rights to freedoms of peaceful assembly and association.

Excessive use of force

The security forces used excessive force to disperse protests. Among the measures deployed were the use of live ammunition at close range against unarmed people; the use of inappropriate firearms and riot equipment that had been tampered with; and the use of tear gas and rubber bullets in enclosed areas.

For example, in February, student Geraldín Moreno died three days after being shot in the eye with rubber bullets fired at close range during a protest in Valencia, Carabobo State. National Guard officers were charged in connection with her death and were awaiting trial at the end of the year. The same month, Marvinia Jiménez was beaten by police officers while she was filming a protest in Valencia and charged with, among other things, obstructing a public road and disturbing public order. At the end of the year, the arrest warrant against an officer responsible for her beating had yet to be served. In April, 16-year-old John Michael Ortiz Fernández was on the balcony of his house in San Cristobal, Táchira State, when a police officer fired a rubber bullet at the youth; the retina of his left eye was burned. At the end of the year, the case was under investigation.

Arbitrary arrests and detentions

Scores of people detained during the protests between February and July were arbitrarily detained. Many were denied access to a lawyer of their choice and to medical assistance during the first 48 hours of their detention before appearing before a judge.

Lawyer Marcelo Crovato and human rights defender Rosmit Mantilla were detained in April and May respectively, in relation to the protests. More than eight months after their arrest they remained in pre-trial detention, in spite of the lack of solid evidence to support the charges against them.

Torture and other ill-treatment

Torture and ill-treatment remained a concern despite some progress brought about by the 2013 Special Law to Prevent and Punish Torture and Other Cruel, Inhuman or Degrading Treatment.[2]

Student Daniel Quintero was beaten and threatened with being burned alive while in detention. He was arrested on his way from an anti-government demonstration in February in Maracaibo, Zulia State. An investigation into the allegations of torture was continuing at the end of the year.[3]

At least 23 people were detained during a joint National Guard and army operation in Rubio, Táchira State, on 19 March. While in detention they were kicked, beaten and threatened with death and sexual violence. All the detainees, both men and women, were held in the same room and kept blindfolded for several hours. They could hear those near them being beaten. At least one detainee was forced to watch while another detainee was beaten. Gloria Tobón was doused with water and then electric shocks were applied to her arms, breasts and genitals. She was threatened and told that she would be killed and buried in pieces. At the end of the year, the investigation into the allegations of torture had not concluded.

Wuaddy Moreno Duque was detained in February in La Grita, Táchira State, beaten and burned by National Guard officers who accused him of participating in the protests. He and his family were the target of intimidation after lodging a formal complaint.

HUMAN RIGHTS DEFENDERS

Human rights defenders continued to be attacked.

For example, two members of the Venezuelan Prisons Observatory were threatened and intimidated on a number of occasions. On 12 April 2013, Marianela Sánchez and her family received an anonymous death threat. She lodged a complaint, but by the end of the year the authorities had not initiated an effective investigation into the threat or provided the necessary security measures, consistent with the family's wishes.

The authorities repeatedly attempted to discredit Humberto Prado's human rights work and accused him of involvement in violence during the protests and of conspiracy to destabilize the government and the prison system.

JUSTICE SYSTEM

The justice system was subject to government interference, especially in cases involving government critics or those who were perceived to act in a way contrary to the authorities' interests.

For example, Judge María Lourdes Afiuni Mora – who had been detained in December 2010, hours after ordering the release of a banker charged with corruption, a decision publicly condemned by former President

Chávez – was awaiting trial at the end of the year. She was released on bail in June 2013 for humanitarian reasons.

Leopoldo López, leader of the opposition Voluntad Popular (Popular Will) party, remained in detention, despite the lack of evidence to support the charges against him, which appeared to be politically motivated. He faced charges of arson, damage to property, incitement to commit an offence and conspiracy to commit a crime, which carry sentences of up to 10 years' imprisonment.[4] In August, the UN Working Group on Arbitrary Detention stated that his detention was arbitrary and called for his release.

The UN Working Group also called for the immediate release of Daniel Ceballos, a Voluntad Popular member and Mayor of San Cristobal, Táchira State. He was arrested in March and was awaiting trial on charges of rebellion and conspiracy to commit a crime in connection with the February anti-government protests.[5]

INTERNATIONAL JUSTICE

In September 2013, following its denunciation of the American Convention on Human Rights a year earlier, Venezuela ceased to come under the jurisdiction of the Inter-American Court of Human Rights. As a result, victims of human rights violations and their relatives no longer have access to the Inter-American Court if the national judicial system fails to guarantee their rights.

IMPUNITY

Impunity remained a concern. Victims and their families were threatened and attacked.

For example, investigations and judicial proceedings relating to the killings of members of the Barrios family in Aragua State made little progress. The Barrios family has been the target of threats and intimidation for nearly two decades because of their demands for justice. Ten members of the family were killed between 1998 and May 2013 in circumstances suggesting the involvement of members of the police. In only one case, that

of Narciso Barrios, two police officers were convicted. Other family members have been subjected to intimidation and attacks by the police, in spite of the protection measures granted to the family since 2004 by the Inter-American Commission on Human Rights and more recently by the Inter-American Court of Human Rights.[6] At the end of the year, it was not known whether investigations had been initiated into any of the complaints of intimidation by police officers.

PRISON CONDITIONS

In spite of reforms to the prison system, prison conditions remained harsh. Lack of medical care, food and clean drinking water, unhygienic conditions, overcrowding and violence in prisons and police stations remained a concern. Firearms and other weapons continued to be routinely used in prison clashes.

In the first half of the year local human rights organizations reported 150 deaths in prisons and seven in police custody.

In November, two inmates were killed and at least eight were injured when security forces intervened to end a riot in the prison of San Francisco de Yare, Miranda State, in protest at the harsh prison conditions and ill-treatment of inmates.

In September, after three years and a number of delays in transferring him to a hospital where his medical needs could be assessed, a court granted former Police Commissioner Iván Simonovis permission to receive medical treatment at home under house arrest. He was reported to be suffering from a number of health problems caused by the conditions in which he had been held.

---

1. Venezuela: Human rights at risk amid protests (AMR 53/009/2014) www.amnesty.org/en/library/info/AMR53/009/2014/en
2. Venezuela: Briefing to the UN Committee against Torture, 53rd session, November 2014 (AMR 53/020/2014) www.amnesty.org/en/library/info/AMR53/020/2014/en

3. Protests in Venezuela: Human rights at risk, people in danger, case
    - Daniel Quintero (AMR 53/015/2014)
    www.amnesty.org/en/library/info/AMR53/015/2014/en

4. Venezuela: Opposition leader Leopoldo López should be released (AMR
    53/023/2014)
    www.amnesty.org/en/library/info/AMR53/023/2014/en

5. Venezuela: Further information - opposition member detained amid
    protests (AMR 53/010/2014)
    www.amnesty.org/en/library/info/AMR53/010/2014/en

6. Venezuela: Further information - police threaten and intimidate
    Barrios family (AMR 53/019/2014)
    www.amnesty.org/en/library/info/AMR53/019/2014/en

VIET NAM

Socialist Republic of Viet Nam
Head of state: **Truong Tan Sang**
Head of government: **Nguyen Tan Dung**

Severe restrictions on freedoms of expression, association and peaceful assembly continued. The state continued to control the media and the judiciary, as well as political and religious institutions. Scores of prisoners of conscience remained imprisoned in harsh conditions after unfair trials in previous years. They included bloggers, labour and land rights activists, political activists, religious followers, members of ethnic groups and advocates for human rights and social justice.[1] New arrests and trials of bloggers and human rights activists took place. The authorities attempted to curtail the activities of unauthorized civil society groups through harassment, surveillance and restrictions on freedom of movement. Security officers harassed and physically attacked peaceful activists, and held them in short-term detention. The death penalty was retained for a wide range of offences.

BACKGROUND

Viet Nam was elected to the UN Human Rights Council in January for a two-year term. In June Viet Nam rejected 45 of 227 recommendations made by the Working Group on the UN Universal Periodic Review in February. These included key recommendations on human rights defenders and dissidents, freedom of expression and the death penalty, among others.

The territorial conflict in the East China Sea escalated in May when China moved an exploration oil rig into disputed waters. The incident sparked anti-China riots by tens of thousands of workers at industrial parks in several provinces in southern and central Viet Nam. Chinese-owned factories were targeted, but Taiwanese, Korean and Japanese factories were also damaged and looted. An unconfirmed number of people were killed and injured, and around 700 people were arrested for their involvement.

An Amnesty International delegation visited Viet Nam for official meetings in February. During his visit in July, the UN Special Rapporteur on freedom of religion or belief found evidence of serious violations, including police raids, disruption of religious ceremonies, beatings and assaults of members of independent religious groups. Some individuals he was due to meet were subject to intimidation, harassment and surveillance by security officials.

LEGAL, CONSTITUTIONAL OR INSTITUTIONAL DEVELOPMENTS

The new Constitution, adopted in November 2013, came into force after an unprecedented but heavily controlled consultation process lasting around nine months. The Constitution provides a general protection of the rights to freedom of expression, association and peaceful assembly but limits them by vague and broad provisions in national legislation. Only a limited guarantee of fair trial rights is included.

Viet Nam signed the UN Convention against Torture in November 2013 and held several preparatory workshops during 2014; the National Assembly voted for ratification in November. Although torture is prohibited in the new Constitution, legislation contains no clear definition of what constitutes torture.

The National Assembly rejected a proposed amendment to the Law on Marriage and Family, which would have recognized same-sex cohabitation and joint custody. The government also announced that it would not legally recognize same-sex marriage.

The authorities stated that several laws relating to human rights were under preparation for approval by the National Assembly in 2016. They include an amended Penal Code, the Amended Law on the Press, the Law on Association, the Law on Demonstrations and the Law on Information Access.

REPRESSION OF DISSENT

Human rights activists and advocates for social and political change increased their peaceful activities despite the challenging environment and risk to their personal safety. Vaguely worded provisions of the 1999 Penal Code continued to be used to criminalize peaceful activism and those exercising their rights to freedom of expression, association and peaceful assembly.

Despite the early release of six dissidents in April and June,[2] at least 60 prisoners of conscience remained imprisoned. They were convicted after unfair trials and included peaceful bloggers, labour and land rights activists, political activists, religious followers and advocates for human rights and social justice. In addition, at least 18 bloggers and activists were tried and sentenced in six trials to between 15 months' and three years' imprisonment under Article 258 of the Penal Code for "abusing democratic freedoms to infringe on the interests of the state".

Blogger Nguyen Huu Vinh and his associate Nguyen Thi Minh Thuy were arrested in May and held under Article 258 of the Penal Code for "posting false information on the internet". Nguyen Huu Vinh, a former policeman, is well known for setting up the popular Ba Sam website in 2007, which included articles on a range of social and political issues. Three more prominent bloggers were arrested between 29 November and 27 December – Vietnamese-Japanese Professor Hong Le Tho, writer Nguyen Quang Lap and Nguyen Dinh Ngoc had written or posted articles criticizing government officials and policies.

Violent unprovoked physical attacks were carried out against activists by men suspected to be acting on the order of or in collusion with security forces. For example, in May human rights lawyer and former prisoner of conscience Nguyen Van Dai was attacked by a group of five men while he was in a café with friends. He sustained a head injury requiring stitches. The same month, blogger and human rights activist Tran Thi Nga was attacked by five assailants while on a motorcycle with her two young children. She suffered a broken arm and knee and other injuries. Activists attempting to observe the trial of three human rights defenders in August were harassed, beaten and arrested by security officials.[3] Three other activists were assaulted in October. In November independent journalist Truong Min Duc was attacked and beaten for the third time in two months, sustaining serious injuries.

FREEDOM OF MOVEMENT

Several peaceful activists were prevented from travelling to attend Viet Nam's consideration under the Universal Periodic Review in Geneva, Switzerland, in February. They were summoned for questioning by the police and their passports were confiscated. Others were detained for questioning on their return. Do Thi Minh Hanh, a labour rights activist and former prisoner of conscience released in June, was stopped at the airport and prevented from travelling to Austria to visit her seriously ill mother in August; she was subsequently allowed to go in October.

Activists attempting to attend informal civil society meetings, foreign embassy meetings and to observe dissident trials were harassed, intimidated and prevented from leaving their homes. Individuals reported being held under de facto house arrest.

PRISONERS OF CONSCIENCE
Conditions of detention for prisoners of conscience were harsh, including lack of adequate medical care and nutritious food. Some were subject to ill-treatment by other prisoners without intervention by prison guards, and to incommunicado detention. Family visits were conducted in the presence of guards who prohibited discussion of perceived sensitive subjects. Prisoners were sometimes moved without their families being informed, and some were held in prisons distant from their homes, making family visits difficult. Some prisoners were encouraged to "confess" to the offences for which they were convicted in order to be considered for release.

Environment activist and prisoner of conscience Dinh Dang Dinh died of stomach cancer in April following his temporary release from prison on medical grounds in February. Despite appeals from his family and the diplomatic community, the authorities failed to provide adequate access to medical treatment while he was serving his six-year prison sentence.[4]

DEATH PENALTY
The death penalty was retained for murder, drugs offences, treason and crimes against humanity. At least three executions by lethal injection were reported. The number of people on death row was estimated to be more than 650. The government did not provide accurate figures, and statistics on the death penalty remained classified as a state secret.

1. Silenced voices – Prisoners of conscience in Viet Nam (ASA/41/007/2013)
www.amnesty.org/en/library/info/ASA41/007/2013/en

2. Viet Nam: Release of woman labour rights activist positive but scores remain behind bars (Press release)
www.amnestyusa.org/news/news-item/vietnam-release-of-woman-labour-rights-activist-positive-but-scores-remain-behind-bars

3. Viet Nam: Police beatings outside court amid crackdown on activism (Press release)
www.amnestyusa.org/news/news-item/viet-nam-police-beatings-outside-court-amid-crackdown-on-activism

4. Death of activist Dinh Dang Dinh should be "wake-up call" for Viet Nam (Press release)
www.amnesty.org/en/for-media/press-releases/death-activist-dinh-dang-dinh-should-be-wake-call-viet-nam-2014-04-04

YEMEN

Republic of Yemen
Head of state: **Abd Rabbu Mansour Hadi**
Head of government: **Khaled Bahah (assumed office in October following dismissal of Mohammed Salim Basindwa in September)**

Government forces committed human rights violations, including unlawful killings and enforced disappearances, against supporters of secession in the south and amid renewed conflict with Huthi rebels in the north, who also committed abuses. Impunity prevailed and no progress was achieved in putting an end to political assassinations or addressing abuses committed in the past. Security forces dispersed peaceful protests in both Sana'a and southern cities using excessive force. Freedom of expression suffered as a result of ongoing attacks and other violations targeting journalists and media outlets. Women continued to face discrimination and high levels of domestic and other gender-based violence. Armed opposition groups carried out indiscriminate bombings and committed other abuses. US forces used drone strikes against suspected al-Qa'ida militants, resulting in deaths and injuries to civilians.

BACKGROUND

The process of political transition ignited by the popular uprising of 2011 continued but remained fragile. On 26 February, the UN Security Council passed Resolution 2140, creating sanctions targeting individuals and organizations seen as obstructing the transition.

The outbreak of renewed hostilities between the government and the Huthis, a Zaidi Shi'a armed group based in the Sa'ada and 'Amran governorates, posed a major threat to the transition process. In September, one day after signing a UN-brokered agreement to bring an end to the fighting, Huthi forces seized control of much of the capital Sana'a.

The 10 months-long National Dialogue Conference (NDC), which brought together 565 representatives of rival political parties and movements and civil society organizations, including women's and youth groups, concluded on 25 January. It generated over 1,800 recommendations, including some advocating greater protection for rights, and concluded that Yemen should become a federal state with a new Constitution.

In June, during the UN Universal Periodic Review of Yemen, government representatives confirmed that Yemen would become a party to the Rome Statute of the International Criminal Court and the International Convention against enforced disappearance. At the end of the year, parliament had still to adopt legislation to give effect to these ratifications.

The government failed to undertake significant reform of the army and two security agencies – National Security and Political Security – which were implicated in serious human rights violations and reported directly to the President.

ARMED CONFLICT

The year saw a continuing deterioration in security across the country, marked by killings of government and senior military officials, abductions of foreign nationals and other individuals, and resurgent armed conflict.

In the north, dozens were killed and hundreds wounded during armed clashes that began in 2013 between the Huthis and supporters of the Sunni Islamist al-Islah party and the Salafi al-Rashad party in the town of Dammaj in Sa'ada governorate. Thousands of al-Rashad supporters from Dammaj, mainly the families of students studying at the al-Rashad-affiliated Dar al-Hadith religious institute, were forcibly displaced after a ceasefire agreement in January 2014. Despite the ceasefire agreement, the fighting spread southward and by mid-2014 Huthi fighters had clashed with their opponents and the Yemeni army and taken over most of the 'Amran, Hajja and al-Jawf governorates. In September, Huthi forces attacked and took control of much of Sana'a after fighting in which over 270 people died and hundreds were wounded. Armed Huthi fighters in the capital looted army units, government buildings, political party headquarters, media outlets and the private homes of al-Islah party members. Later, despite agreeing to a ceasefire and joining a new government formed in November, Huthi forces moved south of Sana'a and clashed with local army units, tribesmen, and armed fighters affiliated with the armed group al-Qa'ida in the Arabian Peninsula (AQAP). In response, AQAP carried out attacks in Sana'a and other cities, which killed and injured many civilians, including children.

In the south, government forces clashed with AQAP fighters, who mounted suicide and other attacks targeting government installations, including an attack on 5 December 2013 that killed at least 57 people, including staff and patients, at a military hospital in Sana'a. In June, AQAP also attacked an army checkpoint in Shabwah, killing eight Yemeni army soldiers and six tribesmen assisting them. AQAP said the attacks were in response to US drone strikes on its forces, carried out with the support of the Yemeni government. The Yemeni army attacked AQAP positions in Abyan and Shabwa governorates in April; the ensuing fighting reportedly caused the forcible displacement of some 20,000 people. US military forces also attacked AQAP, carrying out drone strikes that targeted and killed AQAP militants, and also reportedly caused the death and injury of an unknown number of civilians. In December, an attempt by US military forces to free Luke Somers, a journalist held hostage by AQAP, resulted in his death and that of another hostage.

Both government forces and armed opposition groups recruited and used child soldiers, according to a report by the UN High Commissioner for Human Rights in August, despite efforts to ban the practice.

POLITICAL KILLINGS

Assassinations targeting political figures and security officials continued. On 21 January, one of the most prominent Huthi leaders, Ahmed Sharaf el-Din, was assassinated on his way to the National Dialogue Conference in Sana'a. In November, masked gunmen shot dead Dr Mohammad Abdul-Malik al-Mutawwakkil, a prominent political figure and university professor, in a Sana'a street. Between mid-2012 and the end of 2014, over 100 military officials and security officers were assassinated and dozens of others survived attempted assassinations. Those responsible for most of these killings were not identified and no report of any prosecutions of alleged perpetrators was received.

EXCESSIVE USE OF FORCE

On 9 September, army soldiers in Sana'a opened fire on a crowd of Huthi protesters demanding a change of government, killing at least seven and wounding others. Two days earlier, security forces had opened fire on Huthi demonstrators on the airport road in Sana'a, killing at least two peaceful protesters. Investigations were announced into some incidents of excessive force used to disperse demonstrations in the south (see below) and

also in Sana'a on 9 June 2013, which led to the deaths of at least 13 demonstrators and the wounding of over 50. The outcome of the investigations remained unclear at the end of the year.

REPRESSION OF DISSENT – SOUTHERN YEMEN

Serious unrest continued in Aden and surrounding areas. Some Southern Movement (al-Hirak al-Janoubi) factions participated in the NDC. Demonstrators in Aden and other cities continued to call for the south to secede and held strikes and other protests, some of which the army responded to with excessive and unlawful lethal force. On 21 February, security forces used excessive force to disperse demonstrations in al-Mukallah city and in Aden, causing two deaths and injuring over 20 protesters.

On 27 December 2013 the army's 33rd armoured brigade killed dozens of peaceful mourners at al-Sanah in al-Dale' governorate, prompting the President to announce an official investigation, the outcome of which had not been disclosed by the end of 2014. The same army brigade reportedly killed and injured more civilians in apparently indiscriminate shelling and other attacks in early 2014, including one on 16 January that killed 10 civilians, including two children, and wounded 20 other civilians in apparent reprisal for a Southern Movement attack on an army checkpoint in al-Dale'.

Government security forces arrested Southern Movement activists in Aden and other cities, subjecting some to enforced disappearance. On 31 August, Khaled al-Junaidi was beaten and then dragged into a car by unidentified gunmen, whom witnesses assumed were security officials. He then disappeared. The authorities did not acknowledge his detention and his family was unable to establish his fate or whereabouts. Security forces had previously detained him on at least four occasions, including for three weeks in November 2013 when he was kept in solitary confinement. He was released on 27 November, but was shot and killed, apparently by a member of the security forces, on 15 December.

LEGAL, CONSTITUTIONAL OR INSTITUTIONAL DEVELOPMENTS

In November 2013, amendments to the Judicial Authority Law handed powers previously exercised by the Ministry of Justice to the Supreme Judicial Council, enhancing judicial independence. New measures in 2014 included a draft law to create a National Human Rights Commission and a proposed Child Rights Law. The latter would, among other reforms, address the problem of early marriage by setting the minimum age of marriage at 18, prohibit the use of the death penalty on children under 18, and criminalize female genital mutilation. Both draft laws were awaiting enactment at the end of the year.

On 8 March, the President issued Presidential Decrees 26/2014 and 27/2014 establishing the Constitutional Drafting Commission and naming its 17 members. Under the Decrees, the Commission was granted a year to finish drafting the Constitution to be followed by public consultations and a referendum.

FREEDOM OF EXPRESSION

Journalists and other media workers were subject to threats and physical attacks by government forces and unidentified armed men. On 11 June, the Presidential Guard raided the Yemen Today satellite TV channel, forcing it to cease broadcasting, and closed down *Yemen Today* newspaper, apparently without authorization from the Public Prosecutor. Local media freedom organizations said they had recorded 146 incidents in the first half of 2014 of threats, attacks or other abuses against journalists. Armed Huthi fighters raided a number of media outlets in Sana'a in September and forcibly closed them down.

IMPUNITY

The authorities made little progress in addressing the widespread human rights abuses of previous years.

The government took no steps to clarify the fate of hundreds of political activists and others who were subjected to enforced disappearance under the former regime, headed for decades by former President Ali Abdullah Saleh, or to bring those responsible to justice, despite the reappearance of a number of people forcibly disappeared decades earlier.

Transitional justice

After numerous drafts that fell far short of safeguarding justice and accountability for past crimes, a draft Law on Transitional Justice and National Reconciliation, created at the NDC's behest, was submitted for cabinet approval in May but had not been made law by the end of the year. Similarly, at the end of the year, the President had still to appoint the members of a Commission of Inquiry to investigate human rights violations committed during the 2011 uprising, which he had announced in September 2012. Two other commissions that the President had announced in 2013 were inundated with claims. One, tasked with addressing the issue of land confiscation in southern Yemen in the 1990s, had received over 100,000 claims by May while the other, set up to review the forced dismissal of southerners from government employment, had registered 93,000 claims by the same time. Neither, however, appeared sufficiently resourced to address and resolve the claims they received.

WOMEN'S AND GIRLS' RIGHTS

Women and girls continued to face discrimination in both law and practice, notably in relation to marriage, divorce, child custody and inheritance. They also faced high levels of domestic and other gender-specific violence. Early marriage and forced marriages continued and in some areas female genital mutilation was widely practised.

The NDC recommended that universities and other higher education institutions should reserve 30% of places for the admission of women students, and that the new Constitution should require government agencies to operate a 30% quota for employing women.

REFUGEES' AND MIGRANTS' RIGHTS

Yemen dealt with a large flow of refugees, asylum-seekers and migrants seeking safety, protection or economic opportunities during the year. Many entered Yemen after crossing by boat from Ethiopia and Somalia. Transit and reception centres were fully managed by UNHCR, the UN refugee agency, and its implementing partners without the government taking an active role.

DEATH PENALTY

The death penalty remained in force for a wide range of crimes. Courts continued to impose death sentences and executions were carried out. Prisoners on death row reportedly included dozens of juvenile offenders sentenced for crimes committed while they were under 18 years of age.

ZAMBIA

Republic of Zambia
Head of state and government: Guy Scott (replaced Michael Chilufya Sata in October as acting President)

The human rights situation continued to decline under the late President Sata's government. Fundamental freedoms came under attack, with political opponents, civil society and sexual minorities being systematically targeted.

BACKGROUND

Guy Scott became acting President following the death of President Sata in October. Tensions within the ruling Patriotic Front to elect a presidential candidate for the presidential by-election set for 20 January 2015 resulted in some violent protests by rival party supporters.

FREEDOMS OF EXPRESSION, ASSOCIATION AND ASSEMBLY

In January, the leader of the opposition Alliance for Better Zambia party, Frank Bwalya, was arrested and charged with defamation for allegedly comparing President Sata to a sweet potato during a live radio broadcast. The authorities alleged that Frank Bwalya had used a Bemba (Bantu language) idiom used to describe a person who does not take advice. He was acquitted by the Kasama Principal Magistrate in July in a ruling that upheld his freedom of speech.

In February, a Lusaka court acquitted human rights activist Paul Kasonkomona. He had been charged in April 2013 with "soliciting for immoral purposes" after he urged the government to recognize the rights of lesbian, gay, bisexual, transgender and intersex people as part of a comprehensive fight against HIV/AIDS during a television debate. The court ruled that the state had failed to prove its case. The government indicated its intention to appeal against the ruling.

Also in February, 460 NGOs resolved not to register under the Non-Governmental Organizations Act of 2009, the provisions of which may be deemed unconstitutional due to restrictions on freedoms of association and movement. The government had announced in 2013 that NGOs failing to register under the Act would not be allowed to operate.

On 12 March, 49 young people were arrested by police during a march to commemorate Youth Day in the capital Lusaka. The young activists were arrested for wearing T-shirts and carrying placards bearing the message "Give us our constitution now". They were separated and detained for at least six hours, before being cautioned and released. Four of the youths were reportedly assaulted by police officers who beat them with their fists during their detention at Lusaka Central Police Station, resulting in one sustaining a serious ear injury. The activists were allegedly forced to remove their T-shirts, leaving some, including young women, partially undressed.

RIGHTS OF LESBIAN, GAY, BISEXUAL, TRANSGENDER AND INTERSEX PEOPLE

Individuals were harassed, intimidated and prosecuted for their real or perceived sexual orientation or gender identity. LGBTI individuals continued to live in fear as a result of homophobic attacks backed by the authorities. Following statements by senior government officials in 2013 urging people to report LGBTI people in their communities, individuals continued to suffer harassment and intimidation by their relatives, their communities and the police. Most suffered quietly with no support or protection from the state.

On 3 July 2014, a court in the town of Kapiri Mposhi acquitted two men charged under the country's anti-sodomy laws. James Mwape and Philip Mubiana were released after being held in custody for over a year. They denied the charge of "having sex against the order of nature". The judge found that the state had not proved its case beyond reasonable doubt. The two men, both aged 22, were first arrested on 25 April 2013, and detained until 2 May 2013, when they were released on bail. They were rearrested on 5 May 2013 and forced to undergo anal examinations – which violate the prohibition of torture and other ill-treatment – by government doctors.

ZIMBABWE

Republic of Zimbabwe
Head of state and government: **Robert Gabriel Mugabe**

The executive continued to enforce old unconstitutional laws including those limiting the rights to freedoms of expression, association and assembly. Violations of economic and social rights continued, including forced evictions in rural and urban areas. Mass job losses occurred as companies closed due to an unfavourable economic climate. Intra-party violence was recorded in the ruling ZANU-PF party and the main opposition party. There were reports of torture by the police.

BACKGROUND

Despite adopting a new Constitution in 2013 most laws that were rendered unconstitutional by the new Constitution remained in operation. The economy continued to lose the traction gained during the period of the Government of National Unity (February 2009 to August 2013). Intra-party jostling for positions within President Mugabe's ruling ZANU-PF party came to a head towards the party's sixth congress in December 2014. The intra-party tension, mainly fuelled by the uncertainty over the succession of the 91-year-old President, resulted in violent clashes during faction-sponsored demonstrations. Nine provincial chairpersons lost their positions, including party stalwarts Joice Mujuru (who was also the country's Vice-President), Rugare Gumbo, Nicholas Goche, Webster Shamu and Olivia Muchena, in an unprecedented purge of party structures fronted by President Mugabe's wife, Grace Mugabe. The purge created a sense of uncertainty and government ministers were split into two main factions.

REPRESSION OF DISSENT

The Zimbabwe Republic Police continued to use brutal force and torture against anti-Mugabe protesters and human rights defenders. Intra-party violence was recorded in both the ruling ZANU-PF party and the main opposition party, the Movement for Democratic Change (MDC-T) led by Morgan Tsvangirai.

State institutions' abuse against political opponents continued mainly in the context of factional rivalry within ZANU-PF. The police were used to arrest perceived opponents and prosecutions were brought on apparently politically motivated charges. For example, Jabulani Sibanda, a former war veterans' leader, was arrested on 27 November for refusing to attend Grace Mugabe's provincial rallies where other party leaders were denounced. He was charged under Section 33 of the Criminal Law (Reform and Codification) Act for "undermining the authority of the President", then released on bail. Jabulani Sibanda had reportedly accused President Mugabe of "attempting to stage a coup both in the boardroom and bedroom" in reference to his wife's appointment to the position of leader of ZANU-PF's women's league.

Deposed ZANU-PF party spokesperson Rugare Gumbo was questioned by police on allegations related to ongoing factional fights. It was reported that he had been interrogated on his links with a political online blogger known as Baba Jukwa on Facebook. Edmund Kudzayi, editor of a state-controlled newspaper, was arrested and faced several sedition charges which he denied. He was also accused of being linked to the same online blogger. The blogger had more than 400,000 followers and was involved in a naming and shaming campaign against ZANU-PF officials before the July 2013 elections. The trial continued at the end of the year.

On 6 November, journalist and pro-democracy activist Itai Dzamara was brutally attacked by anti-riot police in Harare and

left unconscious. He collapsed on admission to hospital and had to be resuscitated and admitted to the intensive care unit. As leader of the Occupy Africa Unity Square (OAUS) protest group, Itai Dzamara had submitted a petition to President Mugabe in October calling on him to resign. The group staged a sit-in protest in Harare's Africa Unity Square, a park adjacent to Parliament. Kennedy Masiye from the Zimbabwe Lawyers for Human Rights, who had responded to a call by the activists, was also beaten by anti-riot police despite identifying himself as a lawyer representing his client Itai Dzamara. Police threw away Kennedy Masiye's practising certificate and assaulted him; he suffered a broken arm and was hospitalized.

On 26 November, four members of OAUS, Tichaona Danho, Charles Nyoni, Terry Manzini and Shungu Mutize, were arrested and detained after submitting a petition to the Speaker of Parliament and staging a peaceful protest in the Speaker's gallery. They were severely beaten and released without charge after six hours. At the police station, the men were ordered to undress. Three officers whipped them, ordered them to beat each other, demanded to know their group's mission and implored them to stop protesting against President Mugabe. Efforts by human rights lawyers to represent them were frustrated by police officials who denied holding the men. Later they were ordered to dress, go home and not inform anyone about their detention.

Prominent MDC-T activist and former MP Job Sikhala was arrested on 27 November. He was released the following day and summoned to report back on 29 November. Job Sikhala reported with his lawyers, who were barred from accompanying him during interrogation, and was allegedly tortured. He was hospitalized soon after his release.

There was continued abuse of Section 121 of the Criminal Procedure and Evidence Act (CPEA), which allowed the authorities to veto bail granted by the courts to accused persons for seven days pending an appeal. On 22

August, the state prosecutor invoked Section 121 to delay the release of six MDC-T party activists and MP Ronia Bunjira, who had been arrested during protests demanding the fulfilment of ZANU-PF's pre-election pledge to create 2 million jobs. The opposition activists were accused of contravening the CPEA for allegedly obstructing or endangering free movement of persons or traffic. Angela Jimu, a journalist who was covering the opposition march, was beaten by police and had her cameras confiscated. She was detained by police. Section 121 was challenged in several cases before the Constitutional Court as it amounted to arbitrary denial of the right to liberty for accused persons, particularly in cases involving ZANU-PF opponents and human rights defenders.

Sixteen activists from the opposition Transform Zimbabwe party were detained in April for about five hours in Tsholotsho for distributing political material and were released without charge. The party's leader, Jacob Ngarivhume, continued to face charges under Section 24(6) of the draconian Public Order and Security Act (POSA). Police claimed that Jacob Ngarivhume addressed an unsanctioned political meeting when he delivered a sermon at a church in June, where he had been invited for a religious meeting.

On 14 July, 13 Transform Zimbabwe activists were arrested in the town of Gweru following a peaceful protest against the arrest of Jacob Ngarivhume, who had been arrested and detained on 12 July for convening a party executive meeting. Jacob Ngarivhume was charged with contravening Section 24(6) of POSA. The 13 activists were charged under Section 37(1)(a)(i) of the Criminal Law (Codification and Reform) Act for allegedly participating in a demonstration with the intention or realization that there was a risk or possibility of forcibly disturbing the peace, security and order of the public. The state alleged that the activists had gathered intending to promote public violence.

However, they were acquitted after the state failed to prove its case.

On 22 July, police using the POSA banned planned marches in Bulawayo, Gweru, Harare and Mutare by National Railways of Zimbabwe workers, who were members of the Zimbabwe Railway Artisans Union, to demand payment of outstanding salaries. However, on 6 August the High Court ruled that police had no powers to ban trade union demonstrations.

On 21 August, the Victoria Falls Magistrates' Court acquitted four officials from the civil society organization Bulawayo Agenda who were facing charges under POSA. Mmeli Dube, Butholezwe Kgosi Nyathi, Nthombiyezansi Mabunda Tozana and Thulani Moyo were arrested in June and charged with contravening Section 25(1) (b) of POSA for allegedly failing to notify the regulatory authority of a public meeting. The magistrate ruled that the state had failed to prove a case against the activists.

Abductions
In November, abductions were recorded for the first time since 2009.

On 12 November, former ZANU-PF Harare province chair, Jim Kunaka, was abducted by unknown people in Mbare township. He was reportedly forced into a car, blindfolded and driven to a bushy area where he was assaulted with iron bars before being dumped. The abduction was reported at Harare Central Police Station. Jim Kunaka's abduction took place at a time of intense jockeying for positions within ZANU-PF.

On 2 December, pro-democracy activists Allan Chinewaita, Jerry Mugweni and Itai Dzamara were abducted by men in three cars while engaging in a peaceful protest in Harare. They were reportedly taken to ZANU-PF headquarters and were robbed, slapped, beaten and spat at by party youths. They were then driven to Harare Central Police Station where they were handed to security agents who tortured them before releasing them without charge. They were hospitalized with severe injuries.

HOUSING RIGHTS – FORCED EVICTIONS

Despite provisions in Section 74 of the Constitution protecting people from arbitrary evictions, the government and local authorities carried out evictions without court orders.

On 25 September, Harare City Council served 324 "illegal settlers" with 48-hour eviction notices: a completely inadequate timeframe. In September, the Council demolished informal business structures in the city centre without a court order, threatening family livelihoods dependent on the informal sector, as the economy shrank with over 80% formal unemployment.

In August, the authorities forcibly shut down Chingwizi Holding Camp, established to accommodate an estimated 20,000 people displaced by the floods in Chivi district in early 2014, resulting from the construction of the Tokwe-Mukosi dam. The crisis at the camp was a result of the government's failure to plan for the relocation of the flood victims that saw them living in deplorable conditions lacking basic services including adequate access to clean water. The government restricted humanitarian access by barring NGOs from the settlement. The closure was carried out amid protests against attempts to close the camp clinic which turned violent. The authorities responded by using brutal force, beating villagers and indiscriminately arresting some 300 people, mainly men and community leaders, to facilitate the forcible relocation of women and children to one-hectare plots from which they had no possibility of deriving viable livelihoods. Thirty people were charged with committing public violence in contravention of Section 36 of the Criminal Law (Codification and Reform) Act. Twenty-six of the villagers were granted bail on 8 August. Another villager, Sophia Tagwireyi, was granted bail in September while two spent three months in custody before being granted bail. Patrick Chineunda Changwesha remained in detention at the end of the year. The detainees alleged they had been tortured by police while in custody.

Twenty-six of the villagers were acquitted in December.

In September, hundreds of family homes were demolished by the Epworth Local Board and Chitungwiza Town Council with police support, and without court orders. Evictions were carried out at night with no time provided for residents to remove belongings. Police used tear gas during the demolitions. At least 30 people were arrested and released without charge and 12 people were injured. The evictions in Epworth were stopped through a High Court order.